# THE QUARREL OF THE

Dr. A. C. Grayling is Reader in Philosophy at Birkbeck College, University of London, and a Supernumerary Fellow of St. Anne's College, Oxford. The author of numerous books on philosophy, he writes the 'Last Word' column in the *Guardian* and reviews regularly in the *Financial Times* and *Literary Review*. He is a member of the editorial board of *Prospect* magazine, writes frequently both for it and for London's leading broadsheet newspapers, and often appears on radio and television.

### ALSO BY A. C. GRAYLING

The Refutation of Scepticism, 1985, Duckworth

Berkeley: the Central Arguments, 1986, Duckworth

Wittgenstein, 1988, Oxford University Press
(Past Masters Series)

The Long March to the Fourth of June (as Li Xiao Jun
with Xu You Yu), 1991, Duckworth

China: A Literary Companion (with S. Whitfield),
1994, John Murray

Russell, 1996, Oxford University Press
(Past Masters Series)

Moral Values, 1997, Weidenfeld & Nicolson
(Predictions Series)

An Introduction to Philosophical Logic,
3rd edition, 1998, Blackwell

The Meaning of Things: The Last Word on Love,
Death and Life, 2001, Weidenfeld & Nicolson

*Edited Books*
Philosophy (Vol. 1), A Guide Through the Subject
(ed.), 1995, Oxford University Press

Philosophy (Vol. 2), Further Through the Subject
(ed.), 1998, Oxford University Press

# THE QUARREL
# OF THE AGE

The Life and Times of William Hazlitt

A. C. Grayling

PHOENIX
PRESS

5 UPPER SAINT MARTIN'S LANE
LONDON
WC2H 9EA

A PHOENIX PRESS PAPERBACK

First published in Great Britain
by Weidenfeld & Nicolson in 2000
This paperback edition published in 2001
by Phoenix Press,
a division of The Orion Publishing Group Ltd,
Orion House, 5 Upper St Martin's Lane,
London WC2H 9EA

A CIP catalogue record for this book is available from the
British Library.

Printed and bound in Great Britain by
Butler & Tanner Ltd, Frome and London

ISBN 1 84212 496 X

# CONTENTS

| | |
|---|---|
| List of illustrations | vii |
| Preface | ix |
| Introduction | 1 |
| | |
| ONE A Line of Blue Hills | 9 |
| TWO Hackney Radicalism | 31 |
| THREE The Reader and the Poets | 49 |
| FOUR Painting and Philosophy | 63 |
| FIVE Art and Metaphysics | 81 |
| SIX Towards Winterslow | 100 |
| SEVEN The Winterslow Years | 126 |
| EIGHT The Press of Drama | 146 |
| NINE Waterloo | 173 |
| TEN Fame and Infamy | 199 |
| ELEVEN Reputation and Calumny | 224 |
| TWELVE Love and Disaster | 252 |
| THIRTEEN The Traveller | 293 |
| FOURTEEN Napoleon and Twilight | 324 |
| FIFTEEN The Opinion of Death | 342 |
| | |
| APPENDIX ONE The Hazlitts in America | 350 |
| APPENDIX TWO The Essay | 359 |
| APPENDIX THREE Hazlitt's Philosophy: The Argument of the *Essay on the Principles of Human Action* | 362 |
| | |
| *Notes* | 366 |
| *Bibliography* | 386 |
| *Index* | 389 |

# ILLUSTRATIONS

William Hazlitt as a small boy, by John Hazlitt (Maidstone Museum and Art Gallery, Kent)

Hazlitt aged 13 years, by John Hazlitt (Maidstone Museum and Art Gallery, Kent)

Margaret Hazlitt, by John Hazlitt (Maidstone Museum and Art Gallery, Kent, UK/Bridgeman Art Library, London)

Reverend William Hazlitt, by John Hazlitt (Maidstone Museum and Art Gallery, Kent)

Reverend William Hazlitt, by his son (Maidstone Museum and Art Gallery, Kent)

Grace Loftus, by John Hazlitt (Maidstone Museum and Art Gallery, Kent)

William Hazlitt's house at 19 York Street, Westminster

William Hazlitt as a young man, by John Hazlitt (Maidstone Museum and Art Gallery, Kent)

John Hazlitt, a self-portrait (Maidstone Museum and Art Gallery, Kent)

Samuel Coleridge in 1796, by Peter Vandyke (National Portrait Gallery, London)

William Goodwin in 1802, by James Northcote (National Portrait Gallery, London)

William Wordsworth in 1798, by Robert Hancock (National Portrait Gallery, London)

Henry Crabb Robinson in 1855, by Henry Darvall (National Portrait Gallery, London)

Charles Lamb in 1804, by William Hazlitt (National Portrait Gallery, London)

Charles and Mary Lamb in 1834, by Francis Stephen Cary (National Portrait Gallery, London)

James Henry Leigh Hunt in 1837, by Samuel Laurence (National Portrait Gallery, London)

The Hazlitt home in Wem, Shropshire

John Keats in 1819, by Benjamin Robert Haydon (National Portrait Gallery, London)

The Fight: Tom Cribb, 'The Black Diamond', and Tom Molyneux of Virginia, 1812 (The Art Gallery and Museum, Brighton)

Francis Jeffrey in the 1820s, by Andrew Geddes (National Portrait Gallery, London)

Hazlitt drawn in 1825, by William Bewick (National Portrait Gallery, London)

Benjamin Robert Haydon in 1845, by Sir David Wilkie (National Portrait Gallery, London)

Napoleon Bonaparte in 1914, by Thomas Heaphy (National Portrait Gallery, London)

Hazlitt's death mask (Maidstone Museum and Art Gallery, Kent)

# PREFACE

WILLIAM HAZLITT is without question one of the greatest writers of prose in the English language, and equally without question the greatest exponent of the 'familiar essay', an art form which, because of its special riches of content and style, has always been celebrated by connoisseurs of literature. At the same time he is arguably the best and most important critic of the Romantic period, making original contributions to appreciation and understanding of art, theatre, literature and philosophy. And as if that were not enough, he was also a hard-hitting political polemicist and journalist who, at the expense of his own chances for advancement in worldly terms, defended a radical stance that was not just unpopular but actively persecuted in his day.

If the label 'Romantic' has any value in describing the character of Hazlitt's work, it is because he was an intensely personal writer, fully present in everything he wrote, taking responsibility for his opinions without appealing to the authority, or needing the protection, of any school or ideology. A good example is afforded by the new style of criticism he represented. Among his predecessors were critics who despised Shakespeare for failing to observe the theatrical 'unities' of time and place, as prescribed two thousand years before by Aristotle. Hazlitt was not interested in rules and formalities. He reacted to theatre – and to art, literature and ideas – as a man of deep feeling and independent mind, asking himself only whether he was being presented with truth, and in a manner that was well done of its kind. He demanded honesty, not a list of instructions, and he listened to his own responses, which were keen and searching, for the basis of all his judgements.

In this way he transmuted his life and thought into literature, leaving a body of work – twenty volumes' worth, in the standard collected edition – which continues to delight and instruct everyone who enjoys fine writing and vigorous thought. Many of his essays are classics of the English tongue. He has never been without admirers, and his reputation, great and controversial in his own day, though somewhat occluded by Victorian delicacy because of the frankness of his confessional style, has never ceased to grow.[1]

Hazlitt has been well served by posterity in at least this crucial respect: he has had outstanding commentators, biographers and editors. I am especially indebted to the work of Herschel Baker, David Bromwich, P. P. Howe, Stanley Jones, John Kinnaird, Roy Park, Tom Paulin and Ralph Wardle, and to the recent editorial labours of Duncan Wu, whose nine-volume selected edition of Hazlitt is valuable for its emendations and supplementations to the standard Howe edition of Hazlitt's *Complete Works*.[2]

It is likewise a pleasure to record more personal thanks – for discussion of Hazlitt, biography, his contemporaries, literature, life, philosophy, and much of more general relevance besides – to John Bayley, Carole Blake, William St Clair, Michael Foot, Katie Hickman, J. D. F. Jones, Jane O'Grady, Derek Parfitt, Miranda Seymour, Michael Symes, Susan Whitfield, Rebecca Wilson and Adam Zeman. Two of these add professional excellences to good friendship: Carole Blake, my redoubtable agent, and Rebecca Wilson, my editor at Weidenfeld & Nicolson. Michael Foot was always ready to help, and made a handsome gift to me of a tooled leather 1821 edition of Hazlitt's *Lectures on the Dramatic Literature of the Age of Elizabeth*. Elizabeth Cotton, Tanya Slater, Sarah Swinfield and Emma Walkers gave invaluable research assistance. I am grateful to Dr Michael Basinski and Dr Robert Bertholf of the Poetry and Rare Books Library at the State University of New York, Buffalo, for their help before and during the time I spent working on the Hazlitt archive there. I thank also Veronica Tonge, Curator of Fine and Applied Art at the Maidstone Museum and Art Gallery, and to her colleague for their kind help with the museum's collection of Hazlitt family paintings. Dr David Smith of the library at St Anne's College, Oxford, the staffs of the British Library, the London Library and the University of London Library at Senate House all have my gratitude too.

I dedicate this book to the memory of P. P. Howe, Hazlitt's principal editor and biographer. On my frequent crossings of Bedford Square (where Hazlitt used to visit Basil Montagu at No. 25) in Bloomsbury, London, to the offices of *Prospect* magazine at No. 4, or to Birkbeck College in nearby Gower Street, I think of the description Frank Swinnerton gives, in his affectionate essay on Howe, of that unassuming literatus taking the same route before the First World War – traversing Bedford Square to the offices of J. M. Dent & Co., where Swinnerton and Howe's elder brother worked; and later, after bitter war-time experiences in France, of his walks from the publishing house of Secker in John Street, where he was a partner, to the now sadly lost Bloomsbury Reading Room of the British Library. I did much of the early work for this book there too, harkening to the submarine echoes under Panizzi's beautiful dome, conscious that Howe had sat his hours there likewise, labouring peacefully among the ghosts of the great, searching for the sources of Hazlitt's many and frequent quotations. In the now standard manner, I use his edition of Hazlitt's *Complete Works* here. Duncan Wu has shown that Howe was fallible, scarcely surprising given the labour involved in compiling a twenty-one volume edition of the work of a writer so various, widely read and allusive as Hazlitt; but what Wu shows is that the worst of Howe's culpabilities was his over-reliance on the 1902–6 *Complete Works* edited by his predecessors, Waller and Glover, from whose text much of Howe's edition is a reprint. Nevertheless, as Wu generously allows, the Howe edition is a monument in its own right; the general reliability of its text and the richness of its apparatus of notes – despite the errors identified by Wu – are an achievement.

I profited much from the resources provided by Howe, Wu, Jones and the others named. Wherever I went among original manuscripts or in pursuit of solutions to puzzles in Howe's notes, I found myself well anticipated by Jones and Wu in particular; and when I wished to utilize the material available in Hazlitt's contemporaries' letters and diaries, I found that Jones and other biographers had done my homework for me. It was an enjoyment to follow the cleared path through the jungle of the past that Jones, especially, has made. If anyone wishes to know a matter of detail – as, say, when Hazlitt moved into such-and-such an address in London – he does well to rummage in rate-books and letters and the like; but he does even better to inspect Jones either in his biography or in the teeming pages of *Notes and Queries*. As this suggests, I have had the best helps a biographer could desire.

There was a quarrel between Sainte-Beuve and Proust over the question whether appreciation of literary works is deepened by a knowledge of their author's lives. Sainte-Beuve said Yes, Proust an emphatic No on the grounds that an author's work comes from a place too deep even for self-knowledge – from what Proust called *'le moi profond'*. Much might be said on either side of the question, but a short comment is that both are right, although in different ways. Whatever the critics say, readers know that some authors have to be placed in their historical and literary setting to be fully appreciated, while some works stand on their own without need of biographical props. In Hazlitt's case the former applies. Encountering him in person, so far as biography permits, illuminates his work and enriches the experience of reading it, and thereby explains his achievement and his tragedy. His achievement owed itself to his intellectual gifts and outstanding talents, while his tragedy owed itself to his untutorable sensibility and the unkindness of his times. These aspects of his character, and the facts of history, between them forged a brilliant writer and an extraordinary man. The following pages tell his story.

# INTRODUCTION

JOHN KEATS and his friend John Hamilton Reynolds were ardent admirers of Hazlitt. They attended his lectures, read aloud to each other from his essays, and formulated their theories of poetry in response to his views. Through their eyes Hazlitt appears at his best, because when he was with friends like them – ambitious young men of talent – he was relaxed and expansive, ready to talk endlessly about art and philosophy – not in monologue, as Coleridge did, but as a conversationalist in the same mould as his friend Charles Lamb.

In a letter of April 1817 Reynolds describes entertaining Hazlitt to dinner:

> On Thursday last Hazlitt was with me at home, and remained with us till 3 o'clock in the morning! – full of eloquence, – warm, lofty, and communicative on everything imaginative and intelligent, – breathing out with us the peculiar and favourite beauties of our best bards, – passing from grand and commanding argument to the gaieties and graces of wit and humour, – and the elegant and higher beauties of Poetry. He is indeed *great* company, and leaves a weight on the mind, which 'it can hardly bear'. He is full of what Dr Johnson terms 'good talk'. His countenance also is extremely fine: – a sunken and melancholy face, – a forehead lined with thought and bearing a full and strange pulsation on exciting subjects, – an eye, dashed in its light with sorrow, but kindling and *living* at intellectual moments, – and a stream of coal-black hair dropping around all. Such a face, so silent and so sensitive, is indeed the banner of the mind. 'It is a book, in which one may read strange things.' He would have become the pencil of Titian, and have done justice to the soul-fed colours of that bold and matchless Italian. I fear you will be tired of this long *personality*, but I remember having read a few papers of his to you, and therefore imagine you are not wholly uninterested in him.[1]

Reynolds's portrait has an air of hyperbole, but it exactly chimes with accounts given by others who enjoyed Hazlitt's friendship. Brilliant, earnest, and always well-judging, he forgot his own existence and its torments when absorbed in discussion. On those occasions he revealed the pure disinterested genius his contemporaries valued in him.

A very different picture is given by Thomas De Quincey, never a friend to

Hazlitt, and still less so after being detected in unacknowledged borrowings from Hazlitt's writings (for which he was uncomfortably obliged to apologize). 'His inveterate misanthropy was constitutional,' De Quincey wrote. 'Exasperated it certainly had been by accidents of life, by disappointments, by mortifications, by insults, and still more by having wilfully placed himself in collision from the first with all the interests that were in the sunshine of the world, and of all the persons that were then powerful in England ... A friend of his it was – a friend wishing to love him, and admiring him almost to extravagance – who told me, in illustration of the dark sinister gloom which sate for ever upon his countenance and gestures, that involuntarily, when Hazlitt put his hand within his waistcoat (as a mere unconscious trick of habit), he himself felt a sudden recoil of fear, as from one who was searching for a hidden dagger.'[2]

These two portraits – drawn from a number of either kind – could scarcely be more at variance. They mark the contradictory views taken of Hazlitt in his own day and afterwards. For two generations following his death it was the latter depiction that prevailed. Some thought him the greatest thinker and critical writer of his age; others, even those who acknowledged his genius, saw him as a gloomy pessimistic Jacobin motivated by party spleen and personal antipathies. Leaving aside the melodramatic reference to a dagger, chosen to allegorize Hazlitt's fearsome powers as a polemicist and debater in print, there is some truth in De Quincey's picture, for Hazlitt was indeed at loggerheads with the vested interests of his time, he indeed never courted favour with those 'in the sunshine of the world' because he suspected that most of them had got there by dishonest or despicable means, and he indeed suffered much from disappointments in his personal life and insults in his public life. The disappointments and insults were connected, for this was an age of violent polemic and party strife, in which Hazlitt was the subject of constant attack by the Tory press, of a kind we could not now tolerate and therefore do not now see. He returned their attacks with interest, but his enemies made ammunition out of his private sufferings, thereby doubling them.

Understanding this shows how to reconcile the two foregoing portraits. The painter James Smetham, commenting on De Quincey's pen-sketch, wrote: 'It is said in books we have read since then, that Hazlitt was a gloomy and rather dangerous-looking man, who seemed as if he were feeling for a dagger. We won't believe it. We will allow him to have been dark and solemn and quiet and Dantesque: but what was taken for sinister and malignant was only a knitting the sober brow of Il Penseroso frowning away "the brood of folly without father bred".'[3] Most who knew Hazlitt knew that this was so. Coleridge said he could be 'brow-hanging, shoe-contemplative, *strange*', others that he was 'lean, slouching, splenetic'; but Charles Lamb, Hazlitt's life-long friend, wrote in defending him against an attack by Southey: 'I should belie my own conscience, if I said less than that I think William Hazlitt to be, in his natural state, one of the wisest and finest spirits breathing. So far from being ashamed of that intimacy which was betwixt us, it is my boast that I was able for so many years to have preserved it entire; and I think I shall go to my grave without finding, or expecting to find, such another companion.'[4]

A man who could inspire such different responses, and who could think and write as Hazlitt did – 'we think we are very fine fellows nowadays,' Robert Louis Stevenson told his contemporaries, 'but none of us can write like Hazlitt' – deserves explanation. The explanation is his life, from which all that he felt and thought sprang, so to explain him is to tell his story.

According to Virginia Woolf, the aim of biography should be to connect hidden areas of its subject's personality – what she called the 'soul' – with external forces of society and history. A mere list of someone's doings would miss the point of our principal reason for reading biography, which is to gain insight into the motivations and meanings of a human life. In writing Hazlitt's biography the task of connecting inner and outer in this way is made easy by the fact that he is a completely autobiographical author, utterly himself in his writings. With Hazlitt, inner and outer are one. He lived a confessional existence, transposing his experience into literature, writing with stark honesty. He is among the very few who lived and wrote without a mask. This is not to say that he wrote without artistry and even artifice, but his material was his own thought and feeling, his own dealings with life's intractabilities, and he used that material unsparingly.

The autobiographical richness of Hazlitt's writings might itself seem a problem. Autobiography tends to be *apologia*, a self-serving exercise at best creative with truth and at worst – and too often – evasive, distorting, or dishonest. But Hazlitt was not a self-server, and he was incapable of lying. He did not care to conceal what he thought or felt about matters that stirred him. When he desired privacy for himself or others, he remained silent. To the mortification of his friends it was a desire he rarely felt.

In one good sense, then, to meet Hazlitt almost in the flesh, one need only open his works and read. 'Hazlitt was not one of those non-committal writers who shuffle off in a mist and die of their own insignificance,' Virginia Woolf wrote. 'His essays are emphatically himself ... So thin is the veil of the essay as Hazlitt wore it, his very look comes before us.'

Because Hazlitt is so autobiographical an author, his work has, for all its diversity and range, an intensely personal character, as if it constitutes a single long anecdote about a man responding to his world – to art, literature and drama, to politics and ideas – with nerves naked to their pressure. Some of the usual resources of biographers are in Hazlitt's case lacking: few letters to or from him survive, and he kept no diary. There are many contemporary records of him in the form of others' diaries and letters, and also in the great quarrel of the press, which involved him as a principal combatant; but the fact that he was a controversial figure, defended and attacked with equal violence by his peers, obliges a biographer to treat contemporary claims about him with caution.

Hazlitt was born in 1778, just two years after the American declaration of independence, and died in 1830, lingering long enough in his last illness to hear with pleasure that the Bourbons had again been driven from Paris. His life therefore spans a vivid epoch. Its core event is the French Revolution, which was Hazlitt's inspiration and guiding star. He witnessed the rise of Napoleon, whom he admired and whose biography he later wrote. He witnessed – literally so, reading the manuscript of the *Lyrical Ballads* before publication – the birth of a new world in poetry at the hands of Coleridge and Wordsworth, who were first his friends and later his enemies because they betrayed the cause of liberty – and in Coleridge's case, in Hazlitt's view, because he betrayed his talent too. He was an inspiration to Keats, whom he befriended. He influenced Stendhal long before the two of them met in person. Throughout his life Hazlitt opposed the repressive conservative politics of England, prompted by its fear of France's revolutionary example into quashing the reform movement that had been growing during the eighteenth century, and which briefly seemed about to catch fire from the conflagration in Paris.

Hazlitt thought and wrote always as an independent. He was trebly an alien in his own land and time: because of his inexorable personality, because he was of Dissenting stock, and because he was a radical in politics. It gives one pause to reflect that he was a contemporary of Jane Austen, whose delicately nuanced social world, with its pointillistic gradations of snobbery and rank in country house and vicarage settings, seems a world away from the middle-class intellectual community of London to which Hazlitt belonged, where professional writers chose their allegiances for themselves. But both their worlds are real parts of the history of their time, and Hazlitt's writings were read in both.

Mention of the 'middle-class intellectual community of London' reminds one that Hazlitt was, in fact, born into an aristocracy which, had the history of the late eighteenth century been different, even only a little different, might have inherited much of the world. It was not an aristocracy of title or land, but of intellect. In eighteenth-century England the best educated, most thoughtful and independent-minded people were to be found among the Dissenters, so called because they refused to subscribe to the Established church – the Church of England, headed by the currently reigning monarch – on the grounds that no secular authority is entitled to place itself higher than scripture, and that no test of faith and truth can be higher than an individual's own conscience. Dissenters were therefore disqualified from full participation in public life and the privileges of citizenship. In particular, they were disbarred from standing for Parliament or attending either of the ancient universities. Their response was to campaign with intelligence and persuasiveness for reform, and to found their own academies. These academies were the cutting edge of education in their day; while the old universities dozed on their rich endowments, sated on College feasts and soaked in port, at best and at most requiring their junior members to read a few classical texts, the new independent academies of Warrington, Hoxton and elsewhere taught science and mathematics, history and geography, philosophy, political economy and modern languages. Hazlitt was in no way a religious man – as a precocious boy he was given to sententious pronouncements of a religiose and moral sort, but as soon as he began to think seriously he turned agnostic – but the fiercely autonomous and intellectually questioning Dissenter upbringing he received explains much about his independence of mind and adherence to principle, traits which he shared with his father and which, in the usual way of the world, did no good to either of them in the material respects of life.

Hazlitt's father is a key figure in this regard. Square-jawed, square-shouldered, stubborn, uncompromising, sometimes unimaginative, but always kind, William Hazlitt senior was a paradigm – in the end, almost a caricature – of the Dissenting outlook. He was a fundamentalist, but a fundamentalist of reason, not of scripture or mysticism. He had the zeal and purity, the blindness and obtuseness of the typical fundamentalist, and the fact that the idols he worshipped were the Enlightenment values of rationality and autonomy did not save him from the marginalization that all fundamentalists ultimately suffer. After all, success even of the most ordinary kind in life requires compromises; like all true fundamentalists, William senior did not know the meaning of the word.

William senior's Unitarianism was an adult choice, and a disappointment to his own parents. He belonged to a branch of the Hazlitts which figured among the English Protestant colonists who flooded into Ireland after the conquests of the seventeenth century. His father sent him at the age of nineteen to prepare for the Presbyterian ministry at Glasgow University, where he was taught by Adam Smith among others. While an undergraduate there he concluded that he was a Unitarian. Unitarians were so independent in thought – at least, in William senior's day – that they scarcely agreed among themselves, and certainly did not accept dictation from one another on what to believe or say. Some Unitarians even rejected the label 'Christian' on the ground that Jesus, whom they regarded as a mere man, perhaps even a sinful and fallible one, is no more than a teacher and, at best, an exemplar. Scripture has to submit to reason and conscience, which form a higher tribunal. There is only one God; the term 'Unitarian' registers rejection of the Trinitarianism of orthodox forms of Christianity. There are, oddly, even atheist and agnostic sections of the Unitarian community.

Into this bulldog mould, fiercely rational, devoted to study, opposed to authority in any sphere but especially the religious, and apt to subject the most mundane matters to hard questioning, William Hazlitt senior fitted as if it had been tailored for him. The result was predictable: he lived thereafter a practically outcast life of penury and insignificance. But it might not have been so if the great reforming sweep of Dissent in the eighteenth century had been successful. If the Church of England had been disestablished, Parliament reformed, the universities opened to all, and religious and civil tests and disabilities abolished – if, in short, pigs had suddenly begun to fly – William senior might have found more appreciation of his virtues, at least in the form of a congregation both amenable to his stubbornly liberal views and rich enough to support him and his family in a decent manner of life. As it was, the French Revolution provoked strong political reaction in England, crushing hopes of reform. When the hopes revived decades later they were no longer of that ambitious, clear, hopeful vintage of the Age of Enlightenment; they had become the piecemeal and tip-toeing reform of compromise and pragmatism. Those who were leading lights in the Dissenting firmament, such as Richard Price and Joseph Priestley, suffered; much more so did their less celebrated colleagues like William senior.

As it happens, William senior's career began rather well. After adopting Unitarianism he took temporary charge of a congregation in Wisbech, Norfolk, and there met a mild-mannered, elfinly beautiful girl, Grace Loftus, daughter of a flourishing ironmonger and friend of another local family destined for fame and notoriety, the Godwins. Grace and her siblings were habitués of the Godwin household. She used to push the juvenile William Godwin in a go-cart round his family's garden, and the link thus established was inherited by her son the essayist, who maintained the acquaintance throughout his life, benefiting considerably from Godwin's help and friendship.

After William senior and Grace Loftus married they had a pleasant spell tending a small Unitarian flock at Marshfield in Gloucestershire, and then moved to the thriving and handsome town of Maidstone, county capital of Kent, which boasted a large well-built Unitarian chapel at its centre, whose well-heeled congregation provided a house in the next street for the preacher to accommodate his growing family. Today a plaque on the chapel's front commemorates William senior's ministry there, not for its own sake but because Hazlitt the essayist was born there on 10 April 1778, giving Maidstone its chief claim to literary fame.

William senior had good neighbours in Kent; he enjoyed the friendship of men who were leading names in Dissent and eighteenth-century reform, such as Dr Andrew Kippis, the celebrated Dr Price, and the even more celebrated Dr Priestley. At the house of his friend and fellow-preacher Mr Viny of nearby Tenterden he made the acquaintance of Benjamin Franklin. Under the pen names 'Rationalis' and 'Philalethes' he contributed articles to Priestley's *Theological Repository*, published two sermons on the subject of human authority in matters of faith (1774), and a book called *An Essay on the Justice of God* (1773).

These were promising beginnings among the Dissenting élite, and in other respects too (apart from suffering a common hazard of the time, the death of an infant son) the Hazlitts' time in Maidstone was happy – until a combination of the American War of Independence and William senior's dogged espousal of principle brought the idyll to an end.

After a decade of incompetent and increasingly provocative efforts by the British government to tax its American colonists, the latter had risen in rebellion in 1775. With much to occupy it at home and elsewhere in the world, the British government's endeavours to quash the revolt were half-hearted and badly organized. Nearly thirty thousand German mercenaries were hired to fight the Crown's war against its transatlantic subjects, whose skill and determination it badly underestimated. It was a civil war – apart from the mercenaries, a war of Briton against Briton – but the contempt of the home government so alienated the colonists that, through their experience of revolt, they forged a new and wholly independent identity.

Almost all liberal opinion at home in Britain was on the side of the colonists. William senior naturally supported them too. Some of the congregation sided with him, the rest did not. The dispute grew increasingly bitter as the years of war passed. Tensions eventually became such that one half of the congregation refused to attend chapel while the other half was present. By 1780 William senior's position had become untenable. He had no choice but to resign his ministry and quit Maidstone.

It was an unlucky move, the first of many such. Malign stars now seemed to take charge of William senior's affairs. He had to go where he could command a living, and the best he could find was in Ireland, at Bandon in County Cork. There was a camp for American prisoners-of-war at nearby Kinsale, and William senior befriended them, the more earnestly because of their ill-treatment by the soldiers of the 14th Dragoons who were guarding them. He visited the hapless Americans in prison, published letters in the local newspaper to protest at their treatment, and when three of them escaped he hid them from the authorities. His stance made him very unpopular with the troops' 'haughty officers'. He was barged into in the street, and threats were made. Undaunted, he wrote in complaint to the government in London, and through the medium of Dr Price had his representations heard at the highest level – by the Prime Minister himself, Lord Shelburne. An inquiry ensued; several officers were disciplined, and a new regiment was sent to Kinsale to relieve the 14th Dragoons of its duties.

This affair was the last straw for William senior. His championing of the American cause had cost him Maidstone and made him and his family wretched in Bandon. Perhaps, he thought, since his troubles stemmed from his friendship towards America, he would be welcomed there as a friend, and rewarded for his help by finding a home and opportunities among the erstwhile colonists. He resolved therefore – against the strenuous advice of his friends, including Dr Price – to emigrate to the New World with his family, and to embrace for his sake and theirs its promise of liberty and a fresh start.

But Dr Price and his other friends were right. William senior had three and a half thankless years of labour in America.[*] Despite Herculean efforts he could not find a satisfactory post, and was dismayed to discover that the puritanical Calvinists who dominated religious life in the new Republic were bitterly hostile to his brand of liberal Unitarianism. Defeated and dejected, and regretting the hardships to which he had fruitlessly subjected his family, he decided that he had no choice but to return to England. He sailed from Boston in November 1786, going alone so that he could find a job and a home for his wife and children to come back to. They followed him nine months later, reaching England in August 1787.

---

[*] The full story of the Hazlitts' experiences in America is told in Appendix 1.

# CHAPTER ONE

# A Line of Blue Hills

## 1786–1791

HAZLITT WAS five years of age when he went to America, nine when he returned to England. The record gives hardly any glimpses of him in these years. Five decades later his sister Peggy wrote an account of the family's American adventure, retrospectively filled with her own delight at the novelties of the New World. But although she did it for her nephew, Hazlitt's son, as part of a memoir of his famous father, there are few references to Hazlitt until England is regained. She gives tantalising vignettes: the boy Hazlitt marching beside William senior up the road to a neighbouring village, wailing at the prospect of death by drowning off New York's shore when their ship ran briefly aground there, disapproving of the birdless wastes of Cape Cod – and at the age of eight, not long before the return to England, beginning his study of Latin under his brother John's tutorship. Peggy says that he was an especially charming little boy, a favourite with their Boston neighbour Captain Abiah Whitman with whom he spent hours tramping the woods or following the plough, and he was 'doated upon' (sic) by another neighbour, 'old Mrs Derby', who 'would have indulged him in every whim.'

Hazlitt bursts into full notice in his own right at last in a letter written from Boston to his father on 12 November 1786, at just the time William senior was tossing in the Atlantic storms on his way back to England. 'My dear papa,' says the eight-year-old future essayist and polemicist, 'I shall never forget that we came to america. If we had not come to america we should not have been away from one another, though now it cannot be helped. I think for my part that it would have been a great deal better if the white people had not found it out. Let the [others? natives?] have it to themselves, for it was made for them. I have got a little of my grammar, sometimes I get three pages and sometimes but one. I do not sifer any at all. Mamma Peggy and Jacky are all very well, and I am to. I still remain Your most affectionate son William Hazlitt.'[1]

The letter is entirely characteristic; it displays, even at this early juncture,

9

traits distinctive of Hazlitt's adult personality. It manifests a precocity of intellect, and a preternatural philosophical bent, which are almost comical in one so young. 'For my part I think' might have been emblazoned as his motto.

For Hazlitt the American years were chiefly an experience of separation and restlessness. His father was often away, and the family were in transit everywhere, waiting to see whether a permanent settlement offered. It was a diasporic life. Peggy loved it, and loved America, and was never fully reconciled to life back home in England, but Hazlitt never mentioned America thereafter, except to make one remark on a single vivid childhood memory of the place: the taste of barberries found under snow, and eaten in the crisp early winter air.

William senior had been staying with friends in London, the Lewises, since returning to England, but because Mrs Hazlitt needed country air and rest after her sea-crossing with the children, he rented a house near Walworth, then a pleasantly healthful village in the Surrey countryside. Mrs Hazlitt's aged mother visited from Norfolk, not having expected to see her daughter or grandchildren again. To these latter she was a prodigy. Born at the beginning of Queen Anne's reign, she remembered how, as a girl aged eleven, she and her family had rejoiced, in not very Christian fashion, when news of the Queen's death reached their chapel on the first Sunday of August 1714; for Anne had been a vigorous persecutor of Dissent.

Reunited with his father, and home in England, Hazlitt's responses awoke. He was especially struck by the Montpelier Tea Gardens at Walworth, and remembered them in highly lyrical vein in an essay written long afterwards: 'the beds of larkspur with purple eyes; tall holy-oaks, red and yellow; the broad sun-flowers, caked in gold, with bees buzzing round them; wildernesses of pinks, and hot-glowing pionies; poppies run to seed; the sugared lily, and faint mignionette, all ranged in order, and as thick as they can grow; the box-tree borders; the gravel walks, the painted alcove, the confectionery, the clotted cream: – I think I see them now with sparkling looks; or have they vanished while I have been writing this description of them? No matter; they will return when I least think of them. All that I have observed since, of flowers and plants, and grass-plots, and of suburb delights, seems, to me, borrowed from "that first garden of my innocence" – to be slips and scions stolen from that bed of memory.'[2]

Whether or not Hazlitt knew it, the Montpelier Tea Gardens were the scene of an extraordinary event just a few years after his boyhood sojourn there, which in its curious way represents England at the eighteenth century's end. In July 1796 a Montpelier Cricket Club was formed, and that month played its first game at the Gardens. A few weeks later it hosted a unique cricket match, in which, as with all games of cricket at that time, the stakes were very high, in this case 1000 guineas. The bet was laid by two unnamed 'noble lords', who each personally selected a team of players from among the pensioners of the Greenwich Hospital, where disabled war veterans were housed if they had no other means of support. One team consisted of eleven one-legged men, the other of eleven one-armed men. The first ball was bowled at ten in the morning, but at three in the afternoon 'a riotous crowd broke in, demolished the gates and fences, and stopped the proceedings till six o'clock, when play was resumed.' On the second day the teams were brought back to the Tea Gardens in three Greenwich stage-coaches, accompanied by flags and music. The match was played to the finish, and the one-legged men beat the one-armed men by 103 runs.[3] Such was the England the Hazlitts had returned to; a world more accurately captured by a Rowlandson or Cruikshank caricature than an illustration to a Jane Austen novel – a sometimes bizarre world, of grotesque disparities between rich and poor, a world of disorder and repression, hypocritical conventionalities, corruption, and injustice. As Hazlitt grew up in it he increasingly felt alienated from its assumptions and values, an alienation which inspired some of his most brilliant political polemic.

The summer respite of 1787 brought pleasure to all the Hazlitt family. They moved back again into town, taking apartments in Percy Street off the Tottenham Court Road. This part of London was to have Hazlitt associations for many years, because John later took a studio round the corner in Rathbone Place, after living for a time in Long Acre, itself not far off in Covent Garden. Hazlitt was a frequent visitor at both places, and later, after completing his formal education, lodged with his brother in Rathbone Place. At the end of his life Hazlitt was resident in Frith Street in Soho, a mere hundred or so yards away.

Among the family's enjoyments was a visit to a Panorama of the Isle of Wight, which fascinated them because they had not long since seen the real thing from the rails of the *Nonpareil* which had brought them home from America. Peggy reports that 'While we remained in London, my chief business was to attend to William and see that he did not escape out of the front door and ramble about the streets by himself, which he was fond of doing. Yet he never lost his way.'[4]

William senior indulged Peggy in her artistic interests and helped John in his artistic ambitions. He took Peggy to gaze into the windows of print shops, and in Boydell's of Pall Mall purchased for her a print of *The Fish Stealers by Moonlight*. With the help of friends he brought John to the notice of Sir Joshua Reynolds, who accepted the young man as a pupil. For his third child he envisaged a longer-term opportunity: just then some of his old acquaintances were forming a committee to establish a 'New Academical Institution among the Protestant Dissenters for the education of Ministers and Youth', among them Dr Kippis, Dr Price and Dr Abraham Rees. They raised enough funds to buy a mansion in the parish of Hackney to house the 'New College', as it came to be called, and its doors opened to its first students on 29 September 1787. Just six years later Hazlitt was to be among Hackney New College's last students, and part of the reason for its demise.

William senior had high hopes of the Lewises, a family of rich merchants, who were busying themselves in his interest, trying to find him a comfortable post in or near London. A number of schemes were proposed, including the mastership of a school and a series of lectures. But his usual ill-luck held: the Lewises seem to have met a sudden problem, perhaps even bankruptcy or the threat of it, and in his accustomed position as the beggar who cannot choose, and desperate to find 'a resting place for the sole of his foot' (a Biblical phrase used so frequently by Peggy and Hazlitt in their writings that it was doubtless by then a family mantra), he accepted the poorly endowed security of a living at Wem, a small town in Shropshire about ten miles from Shrewsbury. It offered a mere £30 annual stipend, minutely supplemented by some schoolmastering if he would do it, and with small donations promised from a fund for the support of Unitarian ministers – about £5 a year.

In November 1787 the family left London and travelled north, arriving as rain coldly dripped from leafless trees in the purlieus of the little town which had once been an important part of the line of defence against the wild Welsh, with crenellated walls, but which had since shrunk into insignificance.

Peggy hated Wem. For one thing, it was the grave of her father's hopes. 'It was my father's ill-luck to settle and bury his talents [in Wem] until old age prevented his further usefulness … It was indeed a dismal place to sit down in after all that we had seen,' she wrote in her journal. But it was also a grave for her own hopes, and her pleasures; in this 'obscure inland town' where 'it was our lot to live for many years, the best years of our lives', they suffered 'dull monotony' and much that was disagreeable; for the neighbours were mainly unpleasant, unfriendly and provincial, and the house they were given was, although large, 'old and ugly … [and] had the appearance of a place ready to fall'.[5] She was then aged sixteen. Many years later, remembering the environs of Boston with deep affection, she wrote, 'How much pleasanter these [American] townships are, with a field or two between every house, than a little country town with its crooked, narrow, ill-paved streets.'⁶ She was remembering sleigh rides in winter, long visits in Boston, her girlfriends, perhaps even an unmentioned early attachment or two. She never married, but remained with, and cared for, her parents for the rest of their lives.

Although for a few years longer William senior continued to look for a more remunerative and interesting living, Hazlitt saw his father as one who had given up. 'After being tossed about from congregation to congregation in the heats of the Unitarian controversy, and squabbles about the American war, he had been relegated to an obscure village, where he was to spend the last thirty years of his life, far from the only converse that he loved, the talk about disputed texts of Scripture, and the cause of civil and religious liberty. Here he passed his days, repining but resigned, in the study of the Bible, and the perusal of the Commentators – huge folios, not easily got through, one of which would outlast a winter! Why did he pore on these from morn to night (with the exception of a walk in the fields or a turn in the garden to gather broccoli-plants of his own rearing, with no small degree of pride and pleasure)? Here were no "figures and fantasies" – neither poetry nor philosophy – nothing to dazzle, nothing to excite modern curiosity; but to his lack-lustre eyes there appeared, within the pages of the ponderous, unwieldy, neglected tomes, the sacred name of JEHOVAH in Hebrew capitals: pressed down by the weight of the style, worn to the last fading thinness of the understanding, there were glimpses, glimmering notions of the patriarchal wanderings, with palm-trees hovering in the horizon, and processions of camels at the distance of three thousand years; there was Moses with the Burning Bush, the number of the Twelve Tribes, types, shadows, glosses on the law and the prophets; there were discussions (dull enough) on the age of Methuselah, a mighty speculation! there were outlines, rude guesses at the shape of Noah's Ark and of the riches of Solomon's temple; questions as to the date of the creation, predictions of the end of all things; the great lapses of time, the strange mutations of the globe were unfolded with the voluminous leaf, as it turned over; and though the soul might slumber with an hieroglyphic veil of inscrutable mysteries drawn over it, yet it was in a slumber ill-exchanged for all the sharpened realities of sense, wit, fancy or reason. My father's life was comparatively a dream; but it was dream of infinity and eternity, of death, the resurrection, and a judgment to come!'⁷

Hazlitt himself delighted in Wem and its surrounding country. For the next six years, between the ages of nine and fifteen, he studied both under his father and at the local school, so hard that (as both Peggy reported and he himself later acknowledged) he 'injured' himself – psychologically, they meant. Writing of him in Wem Peggy said, 'He was at this time the most active, lively, and happiest of boys; his time, divided between his studies and childish sports, passed smoothly on. Beloved by all for his amiable temper and manners, pleasing above his years, the delight and pride of his own family, he felt not, like the rest, the sad change from the society of the most agreeable and worthy friends to the dullness, petty jealousies, and cabals of a little country town. Of the time passed here he always spoke with pleasure. The scenes of childhood are dear to all, and while safe under the parents' care, their years glide on, in innocence, without one anxious thought or fear of the storms that await them in after life. So it was with this dear boy.'

Allowing for the partiality of a sister, and the mildly saccharin character of the prose, this portrait of a pleasing and intelligent young boy seems, from other evidence, accurate enough. In America he had been liked by neighbours and was a decided favourite with some. In Wem the same thing happened. He so prompted the affection of a well-to-do widow of a West Indian merchant, one Mrs Tracey, that she invited him to stay with her in Liverpool so that he could study French with her daughters. Part of the charm must have been his precocious intelligence, and his sententiousness, manifested along with other auguries of his future character in the following letter to his brother John, written just before his tenth birthday:

Wem, Saturday morning (March 1788)
Dear Brother – I received your letter this morning. We were all glad to hear that you were well, and that you have so much business to do. We cannot be happy without being employed. I want you to tell me whether you go to the Academy or not, and what pictures you intend for the exhibition. Tell the exhibitioners to finish the exhibition soon, that you may come and see us. You must send your picture to us directly. You want to know what I do. I am a busybody, and do many silly things: I drew eyes and noses till about a fortnight ago. I have drawn a little boy since, a man's face, and a little boy's front face, taken from a bust. Next Monday I begin to read Ovid's Metamorphoses and Eutropius. I shall like to know all the Latin and Greek I can. I want to learn how to measure the stars. I shall not, I suppose, paint the worse for knowing everything else. I began to cypher a fortnight after Christmas, and shall go into the rule of three next week. I can teach a boy of sixteen already who was cyphering eight months before me; is he not a great dunce? I shall go through the whole cyphering book this summer, and then I am to learn Euclid. We go to school at nine every morning. Three boys begin with reading the Bible. Then I and two others show our exercises. We then read the Speaker. Then we all set about our lessons, and those who

are first ready say first. At eleven we write and cypher. In the afternoon we stand for places at spelling, and I am almost always first. We also read, and do a great deal of business besides. I can say no more about the boys here: some are so sulky they wont play; others are quarrelsome because they cannot learn, and are only fit for fighting like stupid dogs or cats. I can jump four yards at a running jump, and two at a standing jump. I intend to try you at this when you come down. We are not all well, because poor Peggy has a great cold ... Write again soon. I wish I could see all those paintings that you see, and that Peggy has a good prize. I dont want your old clothes. I shall go dancing this month. This is all I can say. I am your affectionate brother, William Hazlitt.

When not cyphering – doing arithmetic – learning Latin, and drawing, Hazlitt's recorded avocations included watering the vegetables in the kitchen-garden, gazing at the blue-topped Welsh hills as the setting sun slipped behind them, and flying his kite. 'I never see a child's kite in the air but it seems to pull at my heart,' he later wrote. 'It is to me "a thing of life". I feel the twinge at my elbow, the flutter and palpitation with which I used to let go the string of my own, as it rose in the air and towered among the clouds.'

Three months after Hazlitt's eleventh birthday there occurred a very great event: the beginning of the Revolution in France, in its symbolic commencement before the gates of the Bastille. It was an event that shaped much of the rest of his life. In common with many other turning points in history, it was its mythic character that counted, not the facts, which were as usual an admixture of the portentous and ugly.

On 12 July 1789 Louis XVI dismissed Jacques Necker, his reform-minded prime minister. The news enraged an already volatile Paris. A lawyer called Camille Desmoulins famously jumped onto a table in the Café-Royal and shouted 'Aux armes!', and led a mob around the city to gather support. The next day troops tried to quell the disorder, but succeeded only in worsening it. The rioters believed there were vast hidden supplies of grain somewhere in Paris, waiting to be broken open and distributed, so on 14 July they hurried to the Invalides to arm themselves. Thirty thousand muskets were taken; but there was no gunpowder for them, because the kegs had been moved for safety to the Bastille. To the Bastille, accordingly, the crowds went.

This notorious place was in reality an ancient crumbling medieval structure already due for demolition. Plans had been drawn up to replace it by a public open space, at its centre a statue of the king inscribed, with unconsciously magnificent irony, 'Louis XVI, Restorer of Public Freedom'. It had been a gaol since the seventeenth century, housing prisoners committed under *lettres de cachet* on the monarch's personal authority, without trial. It was used very infrequently; the occasional heretic, or seditious writer, or aristocratic no-good was held there, usually for short periods. When the mob arrived on 14 July it had just seven inmates: two madmen, four forgers found guilty after what had in fact been a proper trial, and the Comte de Solanges, locked up at the request of his own family because they were scandalized by his sexual misdemeanours and were trying to cool him down. *À propos*, the Marquis de Sade had just been there too; he had been transferred to the lunatic asylum at Charenton a bare ten days before.

Despite efforts by the Bastille's governor, the Marquis de Launay, to surrender the building to the crowd, they insisted on 'capturing' it. De Launay was arrested, marched to the Hôtel de Ville, and murdered. His head was hacked off and struck on a pike, to be carried around the city as a trophy.

The ugly farce of the event was, however, not the point. The Bastille's fall had immense symbolic power. All over Europe people were electrified by it. The French ambassador to St Petersburg, Louis Phillippe Comte de Ségur, was astonished by local reaction to the news in the Russian capital: 'I find it difficult to express the enthusiasm aroused among the shop-keepers, merchants, townsfolk and some young people of a higher class by the fall of this state prison and this first triumph of a stormy liberty. Frenchmen, Russians, Danes, Germans, Englishmen, Dutchmen, all were exchanging congratulations and embraces in the streets, as though they had been delivered from some excessively heavy chain that had been weighing down on them.'[8] Identical enthusiasm crackled all over Europe, not least in England. Wordsworth reported that 'the inert were roused, and lively natures rapt away!' and that it was bliss in that dawn to be alive. He was then an undergraduate at Cambridge, unsuccessfully attempting his examinations, and the news prompted him to go to France. Coleridge, a schoolboy at Christ's Hospital, wrote an enthusiastic ode entitled 'The Fall of the Bastille'. Southey described the events as the opening of a new visionary world. Dr Priestley hailed 'a totally new era in the history of mankind'. In the fastness of Wem, as everywhere else, the news flashed like fire: Peggy commented, in masterly understatement, that her father's thoughts were given 'full scope' not just by the fall of the Bastille but thereafter by everything connected with the 'rise and fall of the French revolution'.

To the boy Hazlitt it was unspeakably exciting, and felt like the beginning of the world all over again. Thirty-two years later he wrote, with fine understatement: 'For my part, I set out in life with the French Revolution, and that event had considerable influence on my early feelings, as on those of others. Youth was then doubly such. It was the dawn of a new era, a new impulse had been given to men's minds, and the sun of Liberty rose upon the sun of Life in the same day, and both were proud to run their race together. Little did I dream, while my first hopes and wishes went hand in hand with those of the human race, that long before my eyes should close, that dawn would be overcast, and set once more in the night of despotism – "total eclipse!" Happy that I did not. I felt for years, and during the best part of my existence, *heart-whole* in that cause, and triumphed in the triumphs over the enemies of man!'[9]

Despite the initial euphoria, the result for England of the events in France was disastrous, for it meant the death, within a very few years, of all the hopes for reform which many had been labouring to bring about since the days of Cromwell, chief among them the Dissenters. There were clear enough signs of this early on. Dr Price gave a warm welcome to the news from France with a lecture to the Revolutionary Society (so called in commemoration of the 'Glorious Revolution' of 1688), and the publication of a sermon entitled 'On the Love of our Country', in both of which he described what was happening in France as a vindication of the rights of the governed. The chief effect of his words was to rouse the magnificent crested rhetoric of Edmund Burke in defence of those traditional, conservative, monarchical values that the French Revolution opposed. Burke gave voice and cause to reaction, which, aided by the wings of his rhetoric, was swift in coming.

Although Hazlitt disagreed with Burke's *Reflections on the French Revolution* when he read it soon after its publication, he was immensely impressed by its style and power, and later described Burke as the greatest prose writer of the age – not knowing, or being too modest to see, that the appellation belongs to himself. Burke was his diametric opposite in politics, and yet Hazlitt understood and respected the springs of Burke's views, even if he was severe in his repugnance for their detail and application. The combination of his admiration and opposition are characteristic: he always gave merit its due, without letting his applause for it influence his own principles.

Despite the dazzling news that flowed from France in the months and years after the fateful 14 July 1789, life in the backwaters of Shropshire continued unchanged. Hazlitt and another promising Wem boy, George Dickin, were invited by Mrs Tracey to spend the summer of 1790 in

Liverpool, living in her house and sharing her daughters' French and geography lessons. Hazlitt gave the eldest daughter Latin lessons in return (the excellent practice of letting learners teach applied at home in Wem too: Hazlitt taught French to Peggy when he returned from Liverpool, reading Fénelon's *Télémaque* with her. 'To read it with him was a double pleasure,' she later wrote; 'The book is still a favourite with me, and perhaps for that reason.')[10] His stay is unusually well documented because a clutch of letters from him to his parents survives, again illuminating his extraordinary precocity – not to say sanctimony – at just twelve years of age.

To his father he wrote:

I now sit down to spend a little time in an employment, the productions of which I know will give you pleasure, though I know that every minute I am employed in doing anything that will be advantageous to me will give you pleasure. Happy indeed, unspeakably happy, are those people who, when at the point of death, are able to say, with a satisfaction none but themselves can have any idea of: 'I have done with this world, I shall now have no more of its temptations to struggle with, and praise be to God I have overcome them; now no more sorrow, now no more grief, but happiness for evermore!' But how unspeakably miserable is that man who, when his pleasures are going to end, when his lamp begins to grow dim, is compelled to say, – 'Oh that I had done my duty to God and man! oh that I had been wise, and spent my time which was kindly given me by Providence, for a purpose quite contrary to that which I employed it to, as I should have done; now it is gone; I cannot recall time, nor can I undo all my wicked actions. I cannot seek that mercy which I have so often despised. I have no hope remaining. I must do as well as I can – but who can endure everlasting fire?' Thus does the wicked man breathe his last, and without being able to rely upon his good, with his last breath, in the anguish of his soul, says, 'Have mercy upon me a sinner, O God!'

To these startlingly grave reflections, which seem to smack somewhat of the unforgiving Calvinism that Unitarians were supposed to repudiate, Hazlitt's father equally gravely replied:

The piety displayed in the first part [of your letter] was a great refreshment to me. Continue to cherish those thoughts which then occupied your mind, continue to be virtuous, and you will finally be that happy being whom you describe, and to this purpose you have nothing more to do than to pursue that conduct, which will always yield you the highest pleasures even in this present life. But he who once gives way to any known vice, in the very instant hazards his total depravity and ruin. You must, therefore, fixedly resolve never, through any possible motives, to do anything which you believe to be wrong. This will be only resolving never to be miserable, and this I rejoicingly expect will be the unwavering resolution of my William.

On this evidence it is not surprising that William senior cherished hopes for Hazlitt's future as a minister in the good cause. There had been no suggestion to that effect for John, whose future as an artist was always taken for granted. The preternaturally mature piety and intelligence of his younger son doubtless made William senior confident that his own work would be continued, only much more gloriously. He was destined for a sharp disappointment.

'After I sealed up my last letter to you,' Hazlitt continued the above, in sudden prosaic vein, 'George asked me if I were glad the Test Act was not repealed. I told him, No. Then he asked me why? and I told him because I thought that all the people who are the inhabitants of a country, of whatsoever sect or denomination, should have the same rights with others. – But, says he, then they would try to get their religion established, or something to that purpose. – Well, what if it should be so? – He said that the Church religion was an old one. – Well, said I, Popery is older than that. – But then, he said, the Church religion is better that Popery. – And the Presbyterian is better than that, said I. I told him I thought so for certain reasons, not because I went to chapel. But at last, when I had overpowered him with my arguments, he said he wished he understood it as well as I did, for I was too high learned for him. I then went to the concert.' To this William senior replied, 'Your conversation upon the Test Act did you honour. If we only think justly we shall always easily foil all the advocates of tyranny.'[11]

To his mother the twelve-year-old wrote admonishingly: 'I am concerned to hear that you have so little money, but I hope that your portion is not in this world, you have trouble for a few days, but have joy for many. The RICH take their fill in a few years, are cut short in the midst of their career, and fall into ruin; Never to rise again. But the good shall have joy for evermore. – Be sure to tell me if I may sell my old Buckles.'

Far from thinking that they were raising an alarming little prig, Hazlitt's parents were delighted by these performances. William senior wrote to say that he had received a letter from a Boston friend, Mr Booth, who wrote 'concerning you, "I read Billy's letter to Fanny, and she was delighted with it. She sends her love to him, but Fanny has lost the recollection of her little playfellow. The letter does Billy much credit. He has uncommon powers of mind, and if nothing happens to prevent his receiving a liberal education, he must make a great man." ' Then William senior added, 'This compliment, I know, will not make you proud or conceited, but more diligent. He, also, desires his and Mrs Booth's affectionate regards to Billy.'

Hazlitt enjoyed the concert referred to above; and reports that he had 'a very agreeable day yesterday, as I read 160 pages of Priestley, and heard two good sermons; the best of which, in my opinion, was Mr Lewin's.' According to Mrs Tracey his French was progressing well (although he spelled the name of his tutor, Monsieur de Lemprière, as 'Dolounghpryeé'; which however is a rather good rendition of the pronunciation). At the end of one letter, evidently brought to a close because he had run out of space, he remarked, 'I wish people made larger paper.'

As part of the social round in Liverpool Hazlitt dined with a Mr Fisher, 'a very rich man,' whose money came from plantations worked by slaves. 'The man who is a well-wisher to slavery,' the twelve-year-old moral politician accordingly wrote home, 'is always a slave himself. The King, who wishes to enslave all mankind, is a slave to ambition. The man who wishes to enslave all mankind for his King, is himself a slave to his King.' Hazlitt's opinions had formed early, and on this head never changed. 'The man who is a well-wisher to liberty,' he continued, 'wishes to have men good, and himself to be one of them, and knows that men are not good unless they are so willingly, and does not attempt to force them to it, but tries to put them in such a situation as will induce them to be good. Slavery is not a state for men to improve in, therefore he does not wish them to be in that condition. In a state of liberty men improve. He therefore wishes them to be in such a state.'[12]

In the same letter he shows that his precocious grasp was not restricted to matters of high principle; family practicality had its place too. 'The person who called on me last Tuesday was Isaac Kingston ... He said he attempted to get Papa to Cork, but found it was useless to attempt it ... He said he was sorry that Papa had not a better place, and wished he would set up a school, that is a boarding school; and that there was no man in the world to whom he would sooner send his children. He has 3 boys, the eldest of which is 5 years old, within a few months.' Navy press-gangs were looking for men and boys in Liverpool, in their usual brutal way. 'They were pressing on Saturday evening,' Hazlitt wrote at the end of this letter. 'The world is not quite perfect yet; nor will it ever be so whilst such practices are reckoned lawful.'

The sojourn in Liverpool was intended to be primarily educational, and Hazlitt, who was a willing scholar, reported good progress in French, Latin, geography and 'accompts'. But there were outings also, to Liverpool landmarks, and to his great relish, the theatre. 'On Friday I went to the play with Mr Corbett, at whose house I dined and drank tea. The play was *Love in many masks*, and the Farce, *No Song, No Supper*. It was very entertaining, and was performed by some of the best players in London, as for instance, Kemble, Suett, Dignum, the famous singer, Mrs Williams, Miss Hagley, Miss Romanzinin, and others. Suett, who acted in the character of Ned Blunt, was enough to make anyone laugh, though he stood still; and Kemble acted admirably as an officer. Mr Dignum sang beautifully, and Miss Hagley acted the country-girl with much exactness. Mr Corbett says he will take us to another play before we go.' This is the first of many theatre reviews by the great critic, and already shows an appreciation for the special quality which Hazlitt later dignified into his central concept of aesthetic evaluation, namely, 'gusto'.

A striking feature of Hazlitt's letters is the strong logical organization of the arguments they contain. It is evident that he relished a well-structured case. 'Yesterday I went to Meeting by myself in the morning, where we had a very good discourse on the 10th of the 2nd chapter of Thess. 2nd – "With all deceivableness of unrighteousness". From this he drew several CONCLUSIONS of the false pretences which are made by sin to her followers, to happiness; how people are drawn away, by imperceptible degrees, from one Degree of Sin to another, and so on to greater.' This contrasts with his contemptuous account of a visit to a Church of England service, for the first time ever: 'The Clergyman, after he had gabbled over half a dozen prayers, began his sermon, the text of which was as follows: 'Zachariah, 3rd chapter, 2nd verse, latter part – "Is not this a brand plucked out of the fire?" If a person had come in five minutes after he began, he would have thought that he had taken his text out of Joshua. In short, his sermon had neither head nor tail. I was sorry that so much time should be thrown away on such nonsense.'[13]

In the course of this letter Hazlitt had occasion to mention a delicate matter to his father: 'I shall have satis pecuniae, dum tu habeas opportunitatem mittendi aliquam partem mihi' ('I shall have enough money, if you have an opportunity to send some part to me'). He used Latin because, no doubt, he wished only his father to know that he needed extra cash; it bespeaks a complicity between them that fits well with the signs everywhere else in the letters of a warm mutual understanding. William senior's readiness to confide in the twelve-year-old, and to involve him in dealing with problems and plans, is touching. 'I have lately come to a resolution,' he wrote to his son, 'of taking half-a-dozen boys to educate, if such should offer, under ten years of age, at 25 guineas a year each. You may mention this where you are, as there are multitudes in the West Indies who want a good education.'

When Hazlitt was ready to return from Liverpool in the autumn of 1790 his father gave him detailed instructions about the journey home; by horse, if he could bear it, in a 'great-coat and spatter-dashes to protect you from the weather'. Despite the shortage of family money, the boy could purchase two necessary books: 'Enquire which is the best of the cheap French dictionaries. Enquire at the bookseller's there for Watt's *Geography and Astronomy*, and if it be there and you can purchase it for about half-a-crown, bring it with you. Do not forget to thank Mr Nichols for his civilities. But what must you say to Mrs Tracy? I leave that entirely to yourself. But present her with your mamma's respects and mine, and our sincere thanks for all favours, and tell her that we wish to see her again and that we also hope for this pleasure with all the young ladies, and all of them quite happy. My sermons will soon be printed. I shall embrace the first opportunity of sending Mrs Tracy her copy.'

William senior reposed some hopes in the volume of sermons about to be printed, *Discourses for the use of Families, on the Advantages of Free Enquiry, and on the Study of the Scripture*. The sermons were plainly and simply written, didactic in tone and exhortatory in nature. He hoped – his perennial hope – that they might help to procure him a better living somewhere. He approached Dr Kippis and other influential friends, as he had done so often before, asking them to bring him to the attention of selection committees. Dr Kippis wrote back saying, 'I am truly concerned for your disadvantageous situation, but I have had no opportunity of recommending you to a better. All the vacancies go to young men.' Evidently William senior had said something about his gifted son also; Kippis added, 'What is it you design or wish with regard to your younger son?'[14] This was a hopeful sign. Three years later, when Hazlitt went to the New College at Hackney, the annual fee of sixty guineas (more than twice his father's annual income) was either waived or paid by a gift or scholarship, most likely by one of William senior's colleagues, the Reverend John Ralph, who was able to arrange 'exhibitions' (minor scholarships) for gifted youths wishing to study at one or other of the Dissenting academies at Daventry, Hoxton and elsewhere. Ralph wrote to offer just such help to Hazlitt in 1791.

The Liverpool visit, and the fall of the Bastille so near it in date, formed an epoch in Hazlitt's life. The pleasing boy who went to Liverpool returned to Wem an adolescent. His return was soon followed by his first publication, like his letters an entirely characteristic production. It was a letter to the editor of the Shrewsbury *Chronicle*, and it was occasioned by a notorious event: the burning down of Dr Priestley's house in Birmingham by a mob opposed to the French revolution. This political arson, together with Priestley's eventual permanent departure for the United States in 1794, marked the end of the English eighteenth-century Enlightenment, in which Priestley was the leading figure.

Joseph Priestley was an extraordinary man. Born in Yorkshire in 1733 to a devout family, he was educated at the Dissenting academy at Daventry whose wide curriculum of science, ancient and modern languages and philosophy he devoured with brilliance. Despite an uncertain start to his career as preacher and teacher – he had a bad stammer – he was appointed to a tutorship at the equally celebrated Dissenting academy at Warrington, and established his fame with publication of *The Rudiments of English Grammar* in 1761 and *The Theory of Language and Universal Grammar* in 1762. At the same time he was absorbed by scientific interests also, especially by experimental work in chemistry, with outstanding results: he shares with Carl Wilhelm Scheele the credit for first isolating oxygen, and did the same for many other gases including nitrous oxide, nitrogen dioxide, hydrogen chloride, sulphur dioxide and ammonia. He discovered photosynthesis in 1772, for which he can surely be excused his lifelong belief in phlogiston, and his refusal to accept the developments in quantiative chemistry led by Antoine Lavoisier. His immense talents were quickly recognized: Edinburgh University made him Doctor of Laws in 1764, and he was elected a Fellow of the Royal Society in 1766. For six years he was secretary and librarian to the Earl of Shelburne, later Prime Minister. As these honours accumulated his reputation as a radical both in politics and theology grew. He vocally supported the American and French revolutions, and published vigorous defences of intellectual, civil and religious liberties, emphasizing in particular the importance of freedom of speech and enquiry as the only way of combating prejudice and overcoming ignorance. He became involved in bitter theological controversy with the Church of England over his claim, set out in his *History of the Corruption of Christianity* (1782), that the early church was Unitarian. Because of this the Church regarded him as their principal enemy. His world-view was underpinned by faith in a divine superintendence of history and an equal faith that God wills that man should use his reason to create, by both scientific and political experimentation, a paradise on earth.

On the second anniversary of the fall of the Bastille, 14 July 1791, a riotous Crown and Church mob marched on Priestley's home in Birmingham and set it alight, destroying his laboratory and his library. Fortunately Priestley and his family were away at the time, but the event meant they could not return to Birmingham. Priestley took refuge in London, and was given a co-pastorship at Hackney and a lectureship at the New College where, shortly afterwards, Hazlitt became one of his pupils. His position in England was however by this time too insecure politically, so in 1794 he emigrated to America, spending the rest of his life in Pennsylvania where, as noted, he inherited the benefits of William senior's labours on behalf of Unitarianism, and the credit for establishing it in America.

Priestley's influence on both the elder and the younger Hazlitt was very great, but in the case of the latter it worked by way of reaction as well. Hazlitt later published his own grammar of the English language, aiming to improve on earlier endeavours including Priestley's, and his philosophical work was premised on opposition to the 'associationist' psychological theories of the eighteenth-century thinker David Hartley, whose ideas Priestley accepted.

At the time of the Birmingham outrage Hazlitt, then thirteen, was among those who leaped to Priestley's defence. He wrote to the editor of the Shrewsbury *Chronicle* in his best magisterial style, in tones of a peroration like some young Brutus come to bury Caesar:

Mr Wood, – 'Tis really surprising that men – men, too, that aspire to the character of Christians – should seem to take such pleasure in endeavouring to load with infamy one of the best, one of the wisest, and one of the greatest of men.

One of your late correspondents, under the signature of OGDEIS, seems desirous of having Dr Priestley in chains, and indeed would not perhaps (from the gentleman's seemingly charitable disposition) be greatly averse to seeing him in the flames also. This is the Christian! This the mild spirit its great Master taught. Ah! Christianity, how art thou debased! How I am grieved to see that universal benevolence, that love to all mankind, that love even to our enemies, and that compassion for the failings of our fellow-men that thou art contracted to promote, contracted and shrunk up within the narrow limits that prejudice and bigotry mark out. But to return; – supposing the gentleman's end to be intentionally good, supposing him indeed to desire all this, in order to extirpate the Doctor's supposedly impious and erroneous doctrines, and promote the cause of truth; yet the means he would use are certainly wrong. For may I be allowed to remind him of this (which prejudice has hitherto apparently prevented him from seeing), that violence and force can never promote the cause of truth, but reason and argument or love, and whenever these fail, all other means are vain and ineffectual. And as the Doctor himself has said, in his letter to the inhabitants of Birmingham, 'that if they destroyed him, ten others would arise, as able or abler than himself, and stand forth immediately to defend his principles; and that were these destroyed, an hundred would appear; for the God of truth will not suffer his cause to lie defenceless.'

This letter of the Doctor's also, though it throughout breathes the pure and genuine spirit of Christianity, is, by another of your correspondents, charged with sedition and heresy; but, indeed, if such sentiments as those which it contains be sedition and heresy, sedition and heresy would be an honour; for all their sedition is that fortitude that becomes the dignity of man and the character of a Christian; and their heresy, Christianity. The whole letter, indeed, far from being seditious, is peaceable and charitable; and far from being heretical, that is, in the usual acceptance of the word, furnishing proofs of that resignation so worthy of himself. And to be sensible of this, 'tis only necessary, that any one laying aside prejudice read the letter itself with candour. What, or who, then, is free from the calumniating pen of malice, malice concealed, perhaps, under the specious disguise of religion and a love of truth?

Much about this letter is not only typical of Hazlitt's lifelong cast of thought, but it is prophetic, for Hazlitt himself later faced exactly the kind of character assassination he defends Priestley from – only, in larger and more vitriolic quantities, and in a way that mattered materially because it put his livelihood at risk. The persecution Hazlitt faced was political and personal, not religious; but the same considerations apply, especially as regards calumny, which Hazlitt was to experience in the bitterest sense. His defence of Priestley continues on these very themes: 'Religious persecution is the bane of all religion; and the friends of persecution are the worst enemies religion has; and of all persecutions, that of calumny is the most intolerable. Any other kind of persecution can affect our outward circumstances only, our properties, our lives; but this may affect our characters for ever. And this great man has not only had his goods spoiled, his habitation burned, and his life endangered, but is also calumniated, aspersed with the most malicious reflections, and charged with everything bad, for which a misrepresentation of the truth and prejudice can give the least pretence. And why all this? To the shame of some one, let it be replied, merely on account of particular speculative opinions, and not anything scandalous, shameful, or criminal in his moral character. "Where I see," says the great and admirable Robinson, "a spirit of intolerance, I think I see the great Devil." And 'tis certainly the worst of devils.' Hazlitt concluded by saying that Priestley would be long remembered after his critics were forgotten, and that their attacks on him were not so much like those of the wren on the eagle, as of the owl's futile attempt to hurl Mount

Etna into the ocean by flapping her wings. He signed himself ELIASON ('have mercy').[15]

Some commentators think that Hazlitt's father must have had a hand in this composition, which, they say, is too polished in thought and style for a thirteen-year-old. But his letters show that Hazlitt was more than equal to the task, and anyway the themes of the essay had been so much discussed in the parlour at Wem that its author would have required no further help. The style fully anticipates Hazlitt's mature manner, and Tom Paulin has rightly relished the word-play in it, as witness the deliberately equivocating neighbouring uses of 'contracted'.[16] It is a potent effort, both in content and manner, and it represents a large straw in the wind.

Other such straws were blowing too. 'When I was about fourteen (as long ago as 1792),' Hazlitt tells us, in an unpublished piece written in 1828, two years before his death, 'in consequence of a dispute, one day after coming out of meeting, between my father and an old lady of the congregation, respecting the repeal of the Corporation and Test Acts and the limits of religious toleration, I set about forming in my head [a] system of political rights and general jurisprudence. It was this circumstance that decided the fate of my future life; or rather, I would say it was from an original bias or craving to be satisfied of the reason of things, that I seized hold of this accidental opportunity.'[17] He set to work immediately on a draft of what was eventually to become 'A Project for a New Theory of Civil and Criminal Legislation'.

These abstract researches were added to an already intense habit of reading. The household library at Wem was well-thumbed but limited in scope. It contained small duodecimo volumes of the *Tatler*, which were dwarfed by massive tomes of theology and ecclesiastical history in which William senior delighted, as he did in what Hazlitt retrospectively described as the 'learned lumber' of an eight-volume collection of Unitarian treatises called the *Biblioteca Fratrum Polonorum*. For his part Hazlitt 'took a particular satisfaction' in the six volumes of Thomas Chubb's *Tracts and Posthumous Works*. The effects of this heavy diet are obvious in the juvenile sermons contained in his letters. Poetry and prose were available at school; Mrs Barbauld's verses, and the selections in Enfield's *Speaker*, an anthology of prose and poetry arranged for use in schools, gave him early delight, and he reports that 'I was much divided in my opinion between [Mrs Barbauld's] Ode to Spring and Collins's Ode to Evening'.[18] The *Speaker* proved to be an important influence. Enfield was a tutor at Warrington Academy, and he designed his selection of poetry and prose to help form literary taste in the young. Throughout his life Hazlitt could quote extensively from the authors he was introduced to by the *Speaker*. His love of Milton and Shakespeare, in particular, was sparked by it; and in it he read examples of the periodical essays of the eighteenth century – Addison and Swift, Steele and Dr Johnson. The *Speaker* did not confine itself to English literature but included rousing orations from classical sources – Hannibal inspiring his soldiers, Junius Brutus's speech over the body of Lucretia – and juxtaposed them with speeches from Shakespeare and recent political discourses by Walpole and others. A decade and a half later Hazlitt edited and published a selection of British political oratory, *The Eloquence of the British Senate*, informed by what he had learned from Enfield.

In 1792 a yet more important educational resource appeared. William senior took out a subscription to John Cooke's *Select Editions of British Novels*, published in instalments, which he doubtless intended as entertainment – otherwise hard to come by in Wem – for his wife and daughter. The chief beneficiary was Hazlitt. The effect of the novels was to fling open new realms of imagination and delight for him. 'Tom Jones, I remember, was the first work that broke the spell,' he recalled with relish. 'It smacked of the world I lived in, and in which I was to live.'

Hazlitt read with rare passion; his later reminiscences of early reading were blissful. He could be transported back by something as ordinary as 'a little musty duodecimo, to the time when "ignorance was bliss", and when we first got a peep at the raree-show of the world, through the glass of fiction – gazing at mankind, as we do at wild beasts in a menagerie, through the bars of their cages – or at curiosities in a museum, that we must not touch!' Not only did the books' contents come back to mind in all their vividness, but with them 'the old associations of the faces and persons of those I then knew, as they were in their life-time – the places where I sat to read the volume, the day when I got it, the feeling of the air, the fields, the sky –.' Tom Jones was just the beginning. There followed Joseph Andrews, Major Bath and Commodore Trunnion, Trim and Uncle Toby, Don Quixote and Sancho and Dapple, Gil Blas and Dame Lorenza Sephora, Laura 'and the fair Lucretia, whose lips open and shut like the buds of roses'. Recalling these books rekindled the old thrill: 'To what nameless ideas did they give rise, – with what airy delights I filled up the outlines, as I hung in silence over the page! – Let me still recall them, that they may breathe fresh life into me, and that I may live that birthday of thought and romantic pleasure over again! Talk of the *ideal*! This is the only true ideal – the heavenly tints of Fancy reflected in the bubbles that float upon the spring-tide of human life.'[9]

But in the midst of this delightful and pleasurable first discovery of the romance of the world, a dark note enters. At the same time that he was reading Fielding and Cervantes, Hazlitt was beginning the philosophical studies that were to preoccupy him for the next two decades. His first efforts were devoted to his 'Project for a New Theory of Civil and Criminal Legislation'. He was still only a teenaged boy, and his precocious and decided intelligence was no defence against the less intellectual exigencies of growing up. The almost inevitable happened: over-application and puberty caused, in combination, a crisis or breakdown, the exact nature of which remains obscure. In retrospect Hazlitt laconically remarked, 'I applied too close to my studies … and hurt myself irreparably by it.' A reminiscence by a friend of the Hazlitts, the Reverend Joseph Hunter, partly illuminates the event. Hunter came to know the Hazlitts long after the events he describes, and his remarks contain factual inaccuracies (for example: Hazlitt was twelve at the time of his Liverpool visit, not nine as Hunter says; and he was, as noted above, accompanying his father to chapel at fourteen, in refutation of Hunter's assertions), so it probably represents a garbled account of what happened; but it is suggestive never-theless. Hazlitt was already famous when Hunter met his parents and Peggy, so he is writing with Hazlitt's equivocal adult reputation in mind. 'He was,' Hunter says, 'one of the most entertaining and prepossessing children ever seen; and so he continued till he was about nine years old. It happened that a lady from Liverpool came to spend some time at Wem. She was wonderfully taken with this child, and she invited him to spend some little time with her at Liverpool. To Liverpool he went. But he soon found that he was not made so much of there as he had been at Wem. The lady went out visiting, leaving him at home by himself; and in short, the child of nine years old thought himself slighted: he became sullen: this sullenness continued ever after, and formed the predominant feature in his character during his schoolboy days. He now showed his talent for satire, mimicry, and caricature. By the time he was twelve or thirteen, he would not attend the devotions of his family. He would not go to chapel. He would shut himself up from the rest of his family: be seen by no one during the day: but at night would ramble forth no one knew where: and in the moonlit nights he used to scamper about the fields, like, as my informant says, any wild thing.'[20]

It is likely that the 'informant' was Peggy. To Hunter she gave a fair description of a teenage boy who reads, dreams, wanders about by himself, is restless with sexual longings, likes to be alone, shuts himself in his room, moons about the country lanes at night, and is pregnant with big ideas, big hopes and big plans. One thing that can be inferred with confidence is that part of the introspective moodiness was the product of Hazlitt's ambitious philosophical interests, and part of it was sexual desire and frustration. He had strong sexual instincts, as later events showed, and as an adult he made no secret of them; what he never succeeded in doing, disastrously for his happiness, was integrating his romantic notion of women as ideal love objects, such as he read about in novels, and women as sexual partners. This formed one of the central conflicts in his life, and it all but wrecked him. No man who remembers his own teenage years before the arrival of relief in the form of girlfriends and romance could read Hazlitt's '... the fair Lucretia, whose lips open and shut like the buds of roses ... To what nameless ideas did they give rise' without recognizing exactly what he was thinking – and doing – in his solitude.

Howe primly states that 'What the young Hazlitt was doing with his days, of course, was making [his] first intensive efforts at reading.' As the foregoing suggests, this innocent remark only touches one aspect of the truth. Looking down the reverse telescope of time, Peggy undoubtedly placed Hazlitt's moonlight wanderings too early; they better fit the period of years after his return from the New College at Hackney – that is, his later teenage years – when he was absorbed in his philosophical studies and his commencing struggle to write his first book.

But Hazlitt's youthful reading and dreaming, and the concomitant change in his personality, had certainly begun to take hold before he went to Hackney, as shown by a letter he wrote home either while at the college or some time in the year or two after he left (it is inscribed from his brother's London lodgings): 'I wrote, not so much because I have anything to communicate, as because I know that you, and my mother, and Peggy will be glad to hear from me. I know well the pleasure with which you will recognise the characters of my hand, characters calling back to the mind with strong impression the idea of the person by whom they were traced, & in vivid & thick succession, all the ready associations clinging to that idea, & impatience with which you will receive any news which I can give you of myself. I know these things: & I feel them. Amidst that repeated disappointment, & that long dejection, which have served to overcast & to throw into deep obscurity some of the best years of my life, years which the idle and illusive dreams of boyish expectation had presented glittering, & gay, & prosperous, decked out in all the fairness and all the brightness of colouring, & crowded with fantastic forms of numerous hues of ever-varying pleasure – amidst much dissatisfaction and much sorrow, the reflection that there are one or two persons in the world who are [not] quite indifferent towards me, nor altogether unanxious for my welfare, is that which is, perhaps, the most "soothing to my wounded spirit".'[21]

The shadow that fell at this onset of adolescence and the burgeoning of his intellect remained with Hazlitt for the rest of his life. People who did not know him well saw him as capable of being froward, scowling, anti-social, caustic and harsh. Some even thought he was like that habitually. Undoubtedly one element in such moods, when he fell into them, was disaffection with the society he lived in and the fools and blackguards, as he viewed them, who ran it. But the refrain in his writings is regret over his unrequited desire for love. 'Wanting that,' he says, repeatedly, 'I have wanted everything.' He suffered, in natural combination, a spiritual lone-liness and a sexual hunger which nothing and no-one ever satisfied, and which explains the miseries he suffered over women – and especially the disaster of the mad passion he later came to record in his strange, unsettling and notorious book, the *Liber Amoris*.

Wem might have seemed remote and parochial to Peggy and her father, but to Hazlitt in these adolescent throes it was a vivid and stormy theatre in which the figures of his reading, thinking and yearning were the chief actors. But he was conscious of the world beyond Wem, where history was continuing to revolve its courses in other ways during the years 1790 and 1791. Mirabeau died, and all France mourned. Mirabeau had translated Dr Price's 'Observations on the Importance of the American Revolution' for the benefit of his countrymen; now Dr Price too died, and Dr Priestley gave the funeral oration on 1 May 1791 at the Hackney chapel. He reminded his hearers that Dr Price had uttered the 'nunc dimittis' on hearing of the Bastille's fall – 'Lord now lettest thou thy servant depart in peace, for mine eyes hath seen thy salvation' – and likened his death to that of a warrior in the moment of victory. For the cause of reform in England, however, it was a Pyrrhic victory; even as Priestley spoke, the power of reaction was growing – he gave this address just ten weeks before the burning of his Birmingham house.

# CHAPTER TWO

# Hackney Radicalism

WILLIAM SENIOR'S choice of the New College at Hackney for his son was, from his own point of view, either a bold or a foolish one. For one thing, from its inception the college had the reputation of being a hotbed of heresy and sedition. One critic described it as 'a slaughterhouse of Christianity' – not, as events proved, without justification. Thomas Paine had been fêted as a guest there just before slipping away to France under the very noses of the authorities who were trying to arrest him. Part of the blame for inciting the anger of Birmingham's citizens in 1791, and the ensuing ugly scenes which sent Dr Priestley's house, books and experiments up in flames, was laid at the door of some students from the college. A different cause of complaint was that the college's management had been too ambitious in their purchase of property, and too ambitious in its curriculum and staffing, so that the whole venture was financially unsound. In the summer of 1793, just as Hazlitt was preparing to enrol, there were rumours that the place was about to go bankrupt. The two problems were linked; some among the college's Dissenter financial backers were not happy with the extremity of the political and religious (or, more to the point, non-religious) views and activities there, and they intimated that the continuation of their support could not be taken for granted.

But William senior sent Hazlitt anyway, perhaps out of loyalty to the friends who had founded it, but certainly in confidence that Hazlitt would receive a first-class education there while the place lasted, an education scarcely bettered by any other institution in the country. And he still hoped that Hazlitt would, despite his recent changes of demeanour, continue to prepare for ordination in the Unitarian ministry.

The New College at Hackney was a handsome place, consisting of a large mansion in excellent repair, standing in eighteen acres of grounds, with pleasant environs and views.[1] It was five miles from London, which, in those walking days, was no distance. Hazlitt easily visited his brother when opportunity offered, which was frequently. At the founding of the college Dr Price described its planned curriculum as 'comprehensive and liberal', fitting youth for civil and commercial life as well as the learned professions and the Dissenting ministry. The subjects offered were Greek, Latin, Hebrew, Greek and Roman antiquities, ancient and modern geography, universal grammar, rhetoric and composition, chronology, civil and ecclesiastical history, the principles of law and government, mathematics, astronomy, natural and experimental physics and chemistry, logic, metaphysics, and ethics, the evidences of both natural and revealed religion, theology, Jewish antiquities, critical lectures on the scriptures, and elocution. Students wishing to take French, other modern languages, and drawing, had to pay extra. In his prospectus for the college Price wrote that the 'best education' is one which 'impresses the heart with the love of virtue, and communicates the most expanded and ardent benevolence; which gives the deepest consciousness of the fallibility of the human understanding, and preserves from that vile dogmatism so prevalent in the world; which makes men diffident and modest, attentive to evidence, capable of proportioning their assent to the degree of it, quick in discerning it, and determined to follow it; which, in short, instead of producing acute casuists, conceited pedants, or furious polemics, produces fair enquirers.'[2] The production of fair enquirers was accordingly the college's aim, and it succeeded so well that practically all of its students became agnostics, at last precipitating the feared withdrawal of financial support from its devout Dissenting backers, and therefore its closure.

Hazlitt was quick to discover that the attitude of the college's teaching staff accorded with its educational mission. Soon after he arrived his tutor, John Corrie, set him an essay theme. It did not, in Hazlitt's words, 'suit his genius', and he neither could nor would bring himself to write it. When the assignment fell due on the following Saturday Corrie asked for it, and Hazlitt replied that he had not done it. 'You should have a very good reason, indeed, sir, for neglecting it,' Corrie said. 'Why really, sir, says I, I could not write it. Did you never write anything, then? says he. Yes, sir, I said, I have written some things. Very well, then, go along and write your theme immediately, said he,' expecting Hazlitt to occupy the hour until the next lecture in commencing his essay. At the end of that time Hazlitt's page was blank, and he was in tears. 'My eyes were much swollen, and I assumed as sullen a countenance as I could, intimating that he had not treated me well. After the lecture, as I was going away, he called me back, and asked me very mildly if I had never written anything. I answered, I had written several things. On which he desired me to let him see one of my compositions, if I had no objection. I immediately took him my essay on laws, and gave it to him.' This was the essay occasioned by William senior's debate with the old lady of the congregation, on which Hazlitt had begun work a year before. It started with an attempt to define the concept of a 'right' and proceeded with an enquiry into the nature of law and the 'real and necessary ground of civil government'.

Corrie was impressed. He asked Hazlitt some questions about it, and then said, 'Well, sir, I wish you'd write some more things such as this. Why, sir, said I, I intended to write several things, which I have planned, but that I could not write any of them in a week, or two or three weeks. What did you intend to write? says he. Among other things I told him that I intended to inlarge and improve the essay he had been reading. Aye, says he, I wish you would. Well! I will do it then, sir, said I. Do so, said he; take your own time now; I shall not ask you for it; only write it as soon as you can, for I shall often be thinking of it, and very desirous of it. This he repeated once or twice. On this I wished him a good morning, and came away, very well pleased with the reception I had met.'[3]

As would be expected of a youth of Hazlitt's parts, he did very well in his studies. Corrie praised his Greek translation in front of the class, and gave such a good report of him that his yearly allowance was increased.[4] He studied history with Dr Priestley, and Greek and Latin (at the outset reading Sophocles and Quintilian respectively) with Corrie, who was also his tutor for antiquities and geography. The celebrated Dr Belsham taught him Hebrew, which he liked; and with Dr Rees he studied mathematics, which he also liked. He walked for an hour and a half every afternoon, and read philosophy in the evening – commencing with the work of David Hartley, whom he soon subjected to sustained attack when he settled to the hard and long-drawn task of writing his own chief philosophical treatise.

Corrie so liked the expanded introduction to Hazlitt's 'essay on the political state of man' that he urged him again to continue with it. In a letter home Hazlitt sketched the essay's contents, saying that it surveyed man's natural political relations, and from thence deduced both his natural and artificial political rights and duties. William senior replied approvingly. In the same letter Hazlitt gave an account of his schedule of classes, and told his parents that he walked into town once a fortnight to see his brother John and sister-in-law Mary, who returned the compliment by visiting him for tea at the College. 'Since I came here I have spent above eight guineas,' Hazlitt adds. 'You need not, however, be alarmed at this, as in future I shall not spend, or at least, shall not spend more than five shillings a week. About a shilling a week for washing; about two for fire; another shilling for tea and sugar; and now another for candles, letters,

& c. Books, furniture, and other necessaries have run away with a good deal, but these expenses are extraordinary.'[5]

When Hazlitt first went to Hackney he left behind him parents concerned about his state of mind and well-being, a result of the adolescent stresses described. Their concern is reflected in a letter he sent them early on: 'Dear father – I received your very kind letter yesterday evening. With respect to my past behaviour, I have often said, and I now assure you, that it did not proceed from any real disaffection, but merely from the nervous disorders to which, you well know, I was so much subject. This was really the case, however improbable it may appear.' The reassurances were either unconvincing, or something else occurred to make William senior anxious; he changed his mind about the wisdom of Hazlitt's writing a major treatise unrelated to his other studies at Hackney, part of his reason being that it threatened to plunge Hazlitt into the 'gloomy and low-spirited' state he had suffered at Wem. He wrote twice saying that he wished Hazlitt to lay the essay aside. It seemed that William senior also urged, à propos these thoughts, that Hazlitt should strive to acquire politeness – by which he meant social polish. Hazlitt replied forbearingly: 'Dear Father, – I was sorry to hear from your last two letters that you wish me to discontinue my essay, as I am very desirous of finishing it ... So far is my studying this subject from making me gloomy and low-spirited, that I am never so perfectly easy as when I am, or have been, studying it ...' To propitiate his father somewhat he added, 'I shall certainly make it my study to acquire as much politeness as I can. However, this is not the best place possible for acquiring it ... the behaviour which suits a set of young fellows, or boys, does not suit any other society.'[6]

There were good grounds for William senior's anxieties, apart from the fear of further nervous disorders. These were that if Hazlitt still had any residual ideas of ordination, which was unlikely, he was being drawn rapidly away from them, and becoming more involved in the political excitements of the time – not just by writing an essay on political themes, but through meeting some of London's leading radicals at his brother's home. Chief among them was William Godwin, Hazlitt's mother's friend from Norfolk. Hazlitt met him at John's studio on 17 September 1794, at the beginning of his second year at the New College. Godwin was already famous; his *Enquiry Concerning Political Justice* had been published in 1793, a few weeks after the execution of Louis XVI. It was one of the flurry of books written in reply to Burke's *Reflections on the French Revolution*, along with Paine's *Rights of Man*, Mackintosh's *Vindiciae Gallicae* – both published in 1791 – and *A Vindication of the Rights of Men* and *A Vindication of the Rights of Woman*, published respectively in

1790 and 1792, by the brilliant and scandalous woman who a few years later became Godwin's wife, Mary Wollstonecraft. Godwin's book had an immense effect, inspiring radicals and alarming conservatives. It proclaimed that the American and French revolutions together heralded a new age of peace, progress and prosperity, and it breathed an optimistic Enlightenment spirit in its vision of rationally autonomous people behaving towards one another in ways calculated to increase their mutual good. Each individual is the final arbiter of how he or she should act, said Godwin; the only constraint is the utilitarian one that actions should aim at maximizing benefit all round. He anticipated such later utilitarians as John Stuart Mill in arguing that the life of the mind and sentiments of benevolence are the chief sources of happiness. His views horrified many of his readers because of their anarchic, atheistical and utopian character, although he was in fact neither politically naïve nor blind to the realities of life – his essays and letters manifest a firm grasp of contemporary political circumstances, and his novels have a surprisingly pessimistic side, quite in contrast to the millennial optimism of *Political Justice*.

Hazlitt read *Political Justice* 'with great avidity, and hoped, from its title and vast reputation, to get entire satisfaction from it'; but the satisfaction proved less than entire, because he found that Godwin had failed to distinguish between political justice and moral justice, which, he said, differ in that the former has to involve considerations of force, whereas the latter implies only an appeal to reason. Moreover, Hazlitt complained, Godwin was completely unrealistic in thinking that the 'omnipotence of reason' would, if allowed free rein, render law and government unnecessary.[7] To add to this disappointment he found Godwin's conversation, when at last he met him in person, 'flat as a pancake'. Years later, in his celebrated book *The Spirit of the Age*, Hazlitt anatomized Godwin with perfect accuracy – but sympathetically, because Godwin proved to be a good friend, and Hazlitt always felt warmly towards him – despite an act of plagiarism in 1820 when Godwin, writing on Malthus, made direct but unacknowledged use of Hazlitt's own earlier attack on Malthus's arguments.

To dramatize the points addressed in his *Political Justice* Godwin wrote a novel, *Caleb Williams* (originally entitled 'Things As They Are'), which was published in 1794 and quickly became a bestseller. Hazlitt called it 'a new and startling event in literary history'. It was the inspiration for a group of radical novelists, the 'Jacobin novelists', which included Mary Wollstonecraft, Elizabeth Inchbald and Thomas Holcroft. Hazlitt admired all of them, and with the exception of Mrs Inchbald he also knew all of them personally. Their publisher was the radical Dissenter Joseph Johnson, who later became Hazlitt's publisher also. In the public view these writers were associated with the Comte de Mirabeau and the group responsible for the 1792 Reign of Terror, Robespierre's blood-stained Society of Friends of the Constitution. But they were in fact advocates of peaceful reform, and their writings promoted ideals of human rights, democracy, equality, and universal education. These ideas were the commonplaces of Hazlitt's political outlook, learned from his father and strengthened and enlarged by this youthful acquaintance with liberals and radicals who were the most articulate and outspoken representatives of their cause in their time.

Hazlitt therefore found himself entirely at home in company with these people and their ideas. Because of what was happening in France, England was in a ferment. Hopes for reform had never been so high or radical enthusiasm so great. It seemed that it could only be a matter of time before change came in England – peacefully, as these intellectuals hoped; but the chance that it might come violently could not be discounted. In fact the government need not have worried. Historians of the period, chief among them Eli Halevy and E. P. Thompson, convincingly argue that the power of Methodism, the form of Dissent most widespread among the working classes (and which the aristocrats of Dissent, such as the Unitarians, despised), was pro-government and anti-revolution, and its influence was too powerful for full-scale revolution to break out among them. Few people, if any, realized this at the time, which is why the government took unduly repressive measures.

Not all of these measures worked. One of the chief excitements of the time was the Treason Trials of 1794, the principal figures in which were John Horne Tooke the radical parson and reformer, John Thelwall the writer, and Thomas Hardy the bootmaker and secretary of the London Corresponding Society, one of the organizations (sometimes called 'radical societies' or 'Jacobin clubs') set up, on the model of the American Revolutionary societies, to propagate ideas of parliamentary reform and democracy. About forty such societies came into existence in the 1790s. Some, like the London Corresponding Society, enjoyed wide support among the more literate working people, which further alarmed the government. (In contrast, Pitt did not think it necessary to arrest Godwin, because his book was too expensive for the common man.) In the government's view matters could no longer be ignored, because not only did they believe that unrest in the country was growing, but from the spring of 1793 England was at war with France. Pitt and his fellow ministers thought hostilities would be short-lived; their plan was that while its continental allies quashed France, England would use its sea power to expropriate France's overseas possessions. Alas, matters did not work out so well. The hammering dealt out by the French to their continental foes gave England a serious fright; far from being advantageously involved on the sidelines, England found itself fighting a war of survival against a formidable enemy.

Fired by Burkean resolve, therefore, the government was determined to crack down on liberals, radicals and revolutionary societies, and found its excuse in the attempts by some of the latter to answer Paine's call for a democratic alternative to Parliament. The corresponding societies' idea was to establish a 'British Convention', which would have more authority than Parliament because it would be set up by the people and would therefore properly express its will. At the end of 1793 Scottish organizers of a would-be Convention were arrested, and in the following spring were tried and transported. Then the government moved in England. On 12 May Thomas Hardy and Daniel Adams, the secretary of a brother organization called the Society for Constitutional Information, were arrested for High Treason, on the same grounds as were invoked against the Scots. At the end of May habeas corpus was suspended and a large wave of arrests followed. At one point the government held 800 warrants for the detention of suspected revolutionaries. Tooke and Thelwall were among those imprisoned in the Tower along with Hardy, and they followed him into the dock at the Old Bailey. Eight days of trial followed; but then, to delirious public excitement, the jury took no time in throwing out the indictments against all three men, one after the other. As each man emerged from court he was greeted by jubilant crowds, which were controlled with difficulty by troops. The prosecution had no alternative but to drop the charges against the rest.

Godwin had a significant role in securing the collapse of the prosecution case. Just before the trial began he published an anonymous article in the *Morning Chronicle* under the title 'Cursory Strictures' which influenced the trial judge, Lord Chief Justice Eyre, to change his opening direction to the jury, paving the way to acquittal and establishing the event as a landmark in the history of liberty. The editor of the *Morning Chronicle* was a Scotsman called James Perry, who was himself not long afterwards jailed for believing too much in the freedom of the press, and who, later still, was Hazlitt's editor when he first began to work as a journalist.

It was a great victory; but though the radicals had won the battle they thereby lost the war. The trials marked the death of reform, at least for another generation. Had Hardy and the others been jailed or transported, they would have been martyrs for reform, and the government might have had a harder time containing public restiveness. As it was, the government's crackdown had its intended effect anyway, because the banning of radical societies, suspension of habeas corpus, and a succession of other infamous 'gagging Acts' emasculated radical political opposition. The Treasonable Practices Act of 1795 made outspoken criticism of the government a 'high misdemeanour'. In the same year laws were passed controlling public assemblies, and requiring the licensing of meeting houses and itinerant preachers. In 1799 and 1800 came the Combination Acts, which, although primarily aimed at preventing seditious assembly, stalled the growth of trades unions for nearly two generations. Most of these laws were further toughened by Acts of Parliament in 1812, 1817 and – in the form of the infamous Six Acts following the Peterloo massacre – 1819. One of the chief measures was the imposition of taxes on periodicals, which were the principal vehicle of reforming opinion.

Godwin and other radical friends of John Hazlitt sat in the public gallery during the treason trials, and in John's studio discussed them avidly. Hazlitt was there, and heard these discussions; an added interest was that one of the New College's former students was among those arrested and then discharged without trial after the acquittals. Then as later Hazlitt was filled by revulsion for acts of government repression. The contrast between the earliest revolutionary hopes in France and the reactionary behaviour of an establishment intent on preserving itself against what he saw as the legitimate aspirations of the people, was too sharp for him to stomach, and he neither forgot nor forgave it. That is one of the chief reasons why, when people he knew to be ardent reformers and radicals in the 1790s – with some of whom he had then been friends – later came to join the establishment in its self-preserving repressions, he could not forgive the apostasy. They included Coleridge, Southey and Wordsworth.

Over a decade later Hazlitt was commissioned to edit and complete the memoirs of Thomas Holcroft the playwright and novelist, friend of Godwin and John Hazlitt, who was one of those indicted for High Treason because of his membership of the Society for Constitutional Information. Those who knew Holcroft were as astonished by the indictment as he was himself, because he was well known to have consistently preached peace and non-violence to his colleagues in the Society, arguing that philosophy and reason were the best routes to reform of human error and social wrong, 'for Truth is powerful'. When Holcroft heard he had been included on the bill of indictment he promptly surrendered himself at the High Court, saying that he wished the opportunity to clear himself. He was placed into custody at Newgate, and only learned of the details of his supposed treasonable activities some days later. When charges were dropped against all defendants after Hardy, Tooke and Thelwall were acquitted, Holcroft was angered to find that he would not have an opportunity to speak against the outrage of his arrest, the mere fact of which, despite its being unjustified, left a stain. To hostile elements in the press he was thereafter 'the acquitted felon Holcroft', and the mere fact of having been indicted for High Treason prejudiced opinion against him outside his own circles.

Holcroft wrote of the trial, 'perhaps this country never witnessed a moment more portentous. The hearts and countenances of men seemed pregnant with doubt and terror. They waited, in something like a stupor of amazement, for the fearful sentence on which their deliverance, or their destruction, seemed to depend. Never surely was the public mind more profoundly agitated. The whole power of Government was directed against Thomas Hardy: in his fate seemed involved the fate of the nation, and the verdict of Not Guilty appeared to burst its bonds, and to have released it from inconceivable miseries, and ages of impending slavery. The acclamations of the Old Bailey reverberated from the farthest shores of Scotland, and a whole people felt the enthusiastic transport of recovered freedom.'[8]

Remembering these heady days as he wrote about Holcroft's life, Hazlitt eulogized the bright hopes for liberty and virtue that filled them, and the belief that a new world was being born. People behaved towards one another with comradeship and fellow-feeling, disinterestedness and altruism, sympathy and tolerance. It has often been observed how *agape*, brotherly love, breaks out in euphoric times – as when peace is announced after a long war, or an unpopular government is at last defeated and thrown out of power. Hazlitt's belief in the possibility of disinterested sympathy towards others had its empirical foundation in these glad days for liberal-minded people. 'Kind feelings and generous actions there always have been, and there always will be, while the intercourse of mankind shall endure: but the hope, that such feelings and such actions might become universal, rose and set with the French revolution,' he wrote. But by the time he wrote these words, 'That light seems to have been extinguished for ever in this respect. The French revolution was the only match that ever took place between philosophy and experience: and waking from the trance of theory to the sense of reality, we hear the words, *truth, reason, virtue, liberty*, with the same indifference or contempt, that the cynic who has married a jilt or a termagant, listens to the rhapsodies of lovers.'[9] Hazlitt might be right in thinking that kind feelings and generous actions will never become universal, but wrong in thinking that the French revolution was the only encounter between philosophy and experience. Some of the more dramatic recent revolutions in human history, for example the Russian and Chinese revolutions of 1917 and 1949 respectively, are such; but it might well be argued that all life is an encounter between philosophy and experience, and that it is rare for either to come out the winner.

Politics was not the only thing that distracted Hazlitt from his studies. He indulged his love of the theatre, weeping throughout Garrick's *Isabella* with Mrs Siddons in the title role, and enjoying *The School for Scandal* so much that years later, when he was an established drama critic, he was moved to write, 'What would we not give to see it once more, as it was then acted, and with the same feelings which we saw it then.' He not only saw plays but read them. The first he ever read apart from Shakespeare was Schiller's *The Robbers* which, he says, 'stunned him like a blow'. Alluding to this experience in his lectures on the 'Dramatic Literature of the Age of Elizabeth' in 1819, he told his audience that Schiller's effect on him was so great that 'I have not recovered enough from it to describe how it was.' He remembered in particular the sentiments roused in him by the scene where the Moor 'looks through his tears at the evening sun from the mountain's brow, and says in despair, "It was my wish like him to live, like him to die: it was an idle thought, a boy's conceit." ' The image took hold of Hazlitt's imagination. 'That sun,' he wrote, 'has to me never set!' He meant that the hopes which impassioned his early years, including those for the liberation of mankind, never tarnished or faded; which was precisely his misfortune, because whereas other people can, with more or less regret, give up their youthful dreams in the face of what they take to be life's realities, Hazlitt was constitutionally unable to, and suffered accordingly.

He was not alone in being stunned by *The Robbers*. At about the same time that Hazlitt was reading Schiller at the New College in Hackney, Coleridge picked up a copy in the rooms of an undergraduate friend at Cambridge one night after supper, and upon getting back to his own rooms began to read. He found himself 'trembling like an aspen leaf'; he might have been staring into the equivocalities of his own future life as he contemplated 'this picture of a great misguided soul, endowed with every gift of excellence, yet lost in spite of all its gifts' because of the corrupting influence of his vices. 'My God, Southey,' he wrote next morning to his friend in Oxford, 'Who is this Schiller, this convulser of the heart?'

Politics, theatre, and especially philosophy, between them killed the last vestiges of religious faith in Hazlitt. The diarist Henry Crabb Robinson, who first met Hazlitt a few years later, and wrote a reminiscence of him after decades of acquaintanceship, claimed that he was 'one of the first students who left that college an avowed infidel'.[10] In fact he was not alone, for the great majority of his fellow-students had arrived at the same point. Dr Belsham, who in addition to lecturing on Hebrew and divinity was the assistant resident tutor, plaintively wrote that 'the studious and virtuous part of our family have very generally given up Christianity. This is an evil to which no remedy can be applied. Actions may be restrained, but thoughts must be left free.' With this recognition that the college had been defeated by its own principles, Belsham resigned. By that time a number of the college's backers had already withdrawn their support. One of the earliest was Gilbert Wakefield, who strongly disapproved of the students' involvement in politics, and cited their near-riotous behaviour at the time of the Warren Hastings trial as evidence of their 'dissipation of ideas and unsettlement of mind'. Twenty years later, in an article on the revolutionary ardours of the 1790s, in which he had participated but since repudiated, Southey wrote: 'It is well known that the Socinian Academy at Hackney was given up notwithstanding the high character and learning of some of its conductors, because almost all the students pushed the principles in which they were educated farther than their tutors. The dry-rot was in the foundation and the walls, as well as in the beams and rafters, and the unfortunate pupils came away believers in blind necessity and gross materialism – and nothing else.'[11] In its short existence – it was founded in 1787, only six years before Hazlitt entered – it had not only disappointed its backers but attracted the special hostility of those opposed to its threatening combination of Dissent in religion and radicalism in politics. Burke called it an 'arsenal' for manufacturing revolutionary weapons, and a breeding-ground of revolutionary ideas; other epithets were 'a volcano of sedition', a 'nursery of riot', and as already noted, 'a slaughterhouse of Christianity'. Hazlitt had indeed been at an outstanding educational institution, exactly apt for his cast of mind and spirit.

During the summer vacation of 1795, at the end of his second year of study, and just a few months after he turned seventeen years of age, Hazlitt told his father that he did not wish to return to the College and that he had no intention of entering the ministry. His father was wretchedly disappointed. He wrote in despair to his friend and colleague the Reverend Dr Andrew Kippis – one of the arrangers of financial support for Hazlitt's study at Hackney – who tried to comfort him by letter: 'What can I say to you? I can only say that I sincerely sympathise with you in your affliction. I deeply feel for your distress and disappointment, and wish that I could impart to you any sufficient thoughts or words of consolation. At any rate, you have the consciousness of your own integrity to support you. You have done everything in your power to make your son a wise and useful man, and may we not hope that he will be a wise and useful man in some other sphere of life?'

The following year Hackney New College closed. Its fate, and that of the fathers of other sons who had been there, would have reminded William senior that he was not alone in his disappointment even if he had not, in a similar way, upset his own father years before, by abandoning Presbyterianism for the radical Unitarian cause. Still, a certain loss of the old intimacy between father and son ensued. Hazlitt was struck by the way such discordances arise between generations in a family. 'The greatest misfortune that can happen among relations is a different way of bringing up, so as to set one another's opinions and characters in an entirely new point of view. This often lets in an unwelcome day-light on the subject, and breeds schisms, coldness and incurable heart-burnings in families. I have sometimes thought whether the progress of society and march of knowledge does not do harm in this respect, by loosening the ties of domestic attachment, and preventing those who are most interested in, and anxious to think well of one another, from feeling a cordial sympathy and approbation of each other's sentiments, manners, views, etc., than it does good by any real advantage to the community at large. The son, for instance, is brought up to the church, and nothing can exceed the pride, and pleasure the father takes in him, while all goes on well in this favourite direction. His notions change, and he imbibes a taste for the Fine Arts. From this moment there is an end of anything like the same unreserved communication between them. The young man may talk with enthusiasm of his "Rembrandts, Correggios, and stuff": it is all Hebrew to the elder; and whatever satisfaction he may feel in hearing of his son's progress, or good wishes for his success, he is never reconciled to the new pursuit, he still hankers after the first object that he had set his mind upon. Again, the grandfather is a Calvinist, who never gets the better of his disappointment at his son's going over to the Unitarian side of the question. The matter rests here, till the grandson, some years after, in the fashion of the day and "infinite agitation of men's wit", comes to doubt certain points in the creed in which he has been brought up, and the affair is all abroad again. Here are three generations made uncomfortable and in a manner set at variance, by a veering point of theology, and the officious meddling of biblical critics!'[12] This is a characteristically direct autobiographical account. Hazlitt's work is almost all such.

Hazlitt's Hackney experience was not wasted. Apart from what he read there, and what he learned from his tutors, and apart also from the people and conversation encountered at his brother's home, a signal event occurred in Hazlitt's mental life at Hackney which remained a permanent possession, and governed the course of much of his thinking and writing thereafter. It was his 'metaphysical discovery' concerning the 'natural disinterestedness of the human mind'. His reading of Hartley and other 'modern' philosophers had troubled him deeply because they all premised the claim that humans are fundamentally self-interested. To Hazlitt it seemed that if this were true, hopes of progress and liberty were illusory, because the moral sphere could only be a battlefield of selfish interests, however they might sometimes be disguised in sentiments of altruism and charity. He did not accept that human nature is fundamentally selfish, and he cast about for an argument, a proof, that disinterested sympathies genuinely exist, and can be claimed as the basis of action in the moral sphere. While reading Baron d'Holbach's *Système de la Nature* in his room at Hackney one night the answer burst on him as blindingly as a light. 'There are moments in the life of a solitary thinker which are to him what the evening of some great victory is to the conqueror and hero – milder triumphs long remembered with truer and deeper delight,' he wrote, recounting this experience. 'And though the shouts of the multitudes do not hail his success, though gay trophies, though the sounds of music, the glittering of armour, and the neighing of steeds do not mingle with his joy, yet shall he not want monuments and witnesses of his glory, the deep forest, the willowy brook, the gathering clouds of winter, or the silent gloom of his own chamber, "faithful remembrancers of his high endeavour, and his glad success", that as time passes by him with unreturning wing, still awaken the consciousness of a spirit patient, indefatigable in the search of truth, and a hope of surviving in the thoughts and minds of men.'[13] Elsewhere he put the matter in more sober vein, relating it directly to himself: 'I owed something to truth, for she had done something for me. Early in life I had made (what I thought) a metaphysical discovery; and after that, it was too late to think of retracting. My pride forbade it: my understanding revolted at it. I could not do better than go on as I had before. I, too, worshipped at no unhallowed shrine, and served in no mean presence. I had laid my hand on the ark, and could not turn back.'[14] But the discovery was the starting point, not the end point, for the philosophical labours required to make out the case in detail. It proved very hard work. The resulting book – his first – took ten years to write. 'Oh! how little do they know, who have never done anything but repeat after others by rote, the pangs, the labour, the yearnings and misgivings of mind it costs, to get the germ of an original idea – to dig it out of the hidden recesses of thought and nature, and bring it half-ashamed, struggling, and deformed into the day – to give words and intelligible symbols to that which was never imagined nor expressed before! It is as if the dumb should speak for the first time, or as if things should stammer out their own meaning, through the imperfect organs of mere sense.'[15]

Hazlitt's 'metaphysical discovery' – and with it his claim to be a philosopher, a contributor to the quest for truth and understanding, a participant in mankind's great debate about ultimate things – was the one thing he prided himself on: 'the only pretension, of which I am tenacious, is that of being a metaphysician.'[16] The importance of his philosophical ideas to his art criticism, his literary criticism, and his political polemics – despite the fact that all of it exists in unsystematic essay form – is central; he said that he 'hardly ever set about a paragraph or a criticism, but that there was an undercurrent of thought, or some generic distinction on which the whole turned.'[17] Nor were his claims in these respects idle. Even his contemporaries recognized and acknowledged them. Coleridge wrote (and this was after they had become enemies) that there was no questioning the 'vigour and originality' of Hazlitt's mind or his 'particular acuteness in speculative reasoning'.[18] Hazlitt reports that when he was young and unknown, 'Coleridge used to say of me ... that "I had the most metaphysical head he ever met with." '[19] An anonymous and rather unfriendly reviewer of Hazlitt's *Dramatic Literature in the Age of Elizabeth*, writing in the *London Magazine* in 1820, described him in passing as 'a master of metaphysics'.[20] Hazlitt's metaphysical discovery is described in its due place below.

For the next three years Hazlitt divided his time between Wem and his brother's lodgings in London, reading ('the greatest pleasure in life, while we are young') and continuing his study of philosophy. Despite his struggles to articulate the discovery he had made – he was, he records, 'entangled in the briars and thorns of subtle distinctions, of "fate, free-will, foreknowledge absolute" ' – he did not in retrospect regret the effort one jot. The sentence just quoted continues: 'though I cannot add that "in their wandering mazes I found no end"; for I did arrive at some very satisfactory and potent conclusions; nor will I go so far, however ungrateful the subject might seem, as to exclaim with Marlowe's Faustus – "Would I had never seen Wittenberg, never read a book" – that is, never studied such authors as Hartley, Hume, Berkeley, &c. Locke's Essay on the Human Understanding is, however, a work from which I never derived either pleasure or profit; and Hobbes, dry and powerful as he is, I did not read until long afterwards.'

These books fed his mind; his heart found nourishment in 'French romances and philosophy', which he 'devoured tooth and nail. Many a dainty repast have I made of the New Eloise; – the description of the kiss; the excursion on the water; the letter of St Preux, recalling the time of their first loves; and the account of Julia's death; these I read over and over again with unspeakable delight and wonder.' Rousseau remained a permanent influence, although not – as usual with Hazlitt, except in the single case of Napoleon – without reservations. Even so, he kept faith with his first impressions, and did not attempt to alter them in retrospect. 'Nothing could exceed the gravity, the solemnity with which I carried home and read the Dedication to the Social Contract, with some other pieces of the same author, which I had picked up at a stall in a coarse leathern cover. Of the Confessions I have spoken elsewhere, and may repeat what I have said – "Sweet is the dew of their memory, and pleasant the balm of their recollection!" Their beauties are not "scattered like stray gifts o'er the face of the earth", but sown thick on every page, rich and rare.' He also continued his reading of Condorcet, D'Holbach, and Helvetius, and included among the 'very satisfactory and potent con-clusions' of his *Essay on the Principles of Human Action* his criticisms of Helvetius along with his attack on Hartley.

Hazlitt's immense reading in the years immediately after Hackney sowed the seeds of a prodigious literary knowledge that blossoms richly every-where in the pages of his essays. From memory he could quote, at length, an amazing variety of sources, although not always with perfect accuracy. He read Spenser 'with a sort of voluptuous indolence', relished Chaucer, became familiar with the Restoration dramatists and with Dryden, Pope, Goldsmith and Collins. His favourite authors at that time were, he says, 'Burke, Junius and Rousseau. I was never weary of admiring and won-dering at the felicities of style, the turns of expression, the refinements of thought and sentiment: I laid the book down to find out the secret of so much strength and beauty, and took it up again to read on and admire.'[21]

Hazlitt's first encounter with Burke's writings – an important event for him – took place in 1796, in the form of excerpts from the latter's 'Letters to a Noble Lord', which he found reprinted in a newspaper. Hazlitt was instantly struck by their quality, not just of style but of thought. 'I said to myself, "This is true eloquence: this is a man pouring out his mind on paper."' It set a standard for Hazlitt which he himself later took to new heights – perhaps to heights not often exceeded, or even equalled, by any other writer in the language. The phrase exactly sums up Hazlitt's own work, which is *par excellence* 'a man eloquently pouring out his mind on paper'.

In comparison to Burke all other styles seemed to Hazlitt pedantic and 'impertinent' – that is, insufficiently to the point. 'Dr Johnson's was walking on stilts; and even Junius's (who was at that time a favourite with me) with all his terseness, shrunk up into little antithetic points and well-trimmed sentences. But Burke's style was forked and playful as the lightning, crested like the serpent. He delivered plain things on a plain ground; but when he rose, there was no end to his flights and circumgyrations.' This adaptability of prose to its subject always counted for Hazlitt as a central virtue. His objection to Dr Johnson was precisely that the great panjandrum always plods like an elephant in a heavy monotony of Latinate periods, neither stooping when the subject is trivial nor rising when it is lofty.

It is easy to enter Hazlitt's feelings when he reports buying a copy of Milton's *Paradise Lost* and Burke's *Reflections on the French Revolution* in Shrewsbury, and carrying them home to Wem 'at one proud swoop'; with these works to hand, he comments with relish, 'I was set up for one while'.

But if Burke gave the first promptings to his reflections on prose style, and at the same time gave him a political opponent he could sink his teeth into, it was Rousseau who stimulated his romantic and sentimental imagination. Of the *Confessions* and *La Nouvelle Héloïse* he said: 'I spent two whole years in reading those two works … they were the happiest years of my life.' Almost every detail of the circumstances in which he read and wept and sighed over these books engraved itself like silverpoint on his memory. 'I once sat on a sunny bank in a field in which the green blades of corn waved in the fitful northern breeze, and read the letter in the New Eloise in which St Preux describes the Pays de Vaud. I never felt what Shakespear calls my "glassy essence", so much as then. My thoughts were pure and free. They took a tone from the objects before me, and from the simple manners of the inhabitants of the mountain-scenery, so well described in the letter. The style gave me the same sensation as the drops of the morning dew before they are scorched by the sun; and I thought Julia did well to praise it. I wished I could have written such a letter. That wish, enhanced by my admiration of genius and the feeling of the objects around me, was accompanied with more pleasure than if I had written fifty such letters, or had gained all the reputation of its immortal author!' Hazlitt believed – on no very good authority, he admits – that the roughly sketched pictures in the volume, showing a cottage, a line of trees, a rustic scene, were illustrations of Annecy and Vevey where Rousseau's tale is set. They reminded him of a line in one of William Collins's poems, 'And bade the lovely scenes at distance hail', which he applied to the blue Welsh hills visible from Wem. Although set in a 'paltry landscape' these hills seemed to him to have 'a tender vernal tone and a dewy freshness' just like the landscape in which his imagination couched the New Héloïse. The association moved him: he wrote that he could look at the Welsh hills 'until my eyes filled with tears, and my heart dissolved in faintness. Why do I recall the circumstance after a lapse of years with so much interest? Because I felt it then. Those feeble outlines were linked in my mind to the purest, fondest yearnings after good, that dim, airy space contained my little all of hope, buoyed up by charming fears; the delight with which I dwelt upon it, enhanced by my ignorance of what was in store for me, was free from mortal grossness, familiarity or disappointment, and I drank pleasure out of the bosom of the silent hills and gleaming vallies as from a cup filled to the brim with love-philtres and poisonous sweetness by the sorceress, Fancy!'[22] Whatever else Hazlitt was, he was a master of nostalgia, the most expressive and reminiscent of all the writers of his age – with the obvious single exception of Wordsworth, his equal – in his yearning for what retrospect fashioned into the utopia of his youth, whose hopes and dreams remained vivid throughout his life, becoming as time went by as much a burden as a pleasure.

Hazlitt made a valuable new friend at this period, the Reverend Joseph Fawcett, by then living in retirement at Edgegrove near Watford, where he farmed a small plot of land and indulged his literary tastes. He was a widely read, independent-minded scholar and poet, who had been present in France at some of the great early moments of the Revolution. Fawcett was an old school-fellow of Godwin's, and had served as the Unitarian minister at Walthamstow ever since entering the ministry. From 1785 he was also the Sunday evening lecturer at London's Old Jewry meeting house, to which, by the style and content of his oratory, he attracted 'the largest and most genteel audience that ever assembled in a dissenting place of worship', among them the famous actress Mrs Siddons. Wordsworth attended one of Fawcett's lectures when passing through London on his way to France, and thrilled at the revolutionary sentiments he heard.[23] Although Fawcett was a supporter of the Revolution he was determinedly fair-minded. He is said to have bound Burke's *Reflections* and Paine's *Rights of Man* into a single volume, saying that together they made a very good book.[24]

Hazlitt called on Fawcett in the country with an introduction from Godwin, and a friendship immediately ensued. Fawcett told Hazlitt an amusing story about Godwin. He had told Godwin of Chatham's remark that because, as the old saying has it, an Englishman's house is his castle, it follows that 'though the wind and the rain might enter in, the King cannot'. Godwin stored the anecdote away, later making use of it in his biography of Chatham. But in retelling it he modified the last line into 'All the winds of heaven may whistle round it, but the King cannot.' Fawcett said that this showed that Godwin suffered 'a defect of *natural imagination*'.[25]

Fawcett had no such defect. Hazlitt said that although he possessed a wonderfully discriminating literary taste, it was nevertheless a very wide one, capable of enjoying all forms of excellence from Milton to Shenstone and from Butler to Smollett. In conversation Fawcett showed that he knew and loved everyone's favourite authors, and could quote from them and put his finger on both their subtlest and their best virtues. ' "Do you like Sterne?" – "Yes, to be sure," he would say, "I should deserve to be hanged if I didn't." ' He and Hazlitt talked about the English authors, and about Cervantes, Rousseau and Goethe, and their conversation doubled Hazlitt's pleasure in reading the books discussed. 'Some of the pleasantest days of my life were spent in Fawcett's company,' he later wrote. 'He was the friend of my early youth. He was the first person of literary eminence, whom I had then known; and the conversations I had with him on subjects of taste and philosophy (for his taste was as refined as his powers of reasoning were profound and subtle) gave me a delight such as I can never feel again.' Fawcett died in 1804, his death hastened, in Hazlitt's opinion, by the disappointment of his hopes for the French Revolution.[26]

Fawcett's taste and intellectual powers were an influence on Hazlitt, but an even greater influence was just about to burst upon him, in the form of a philosopher-poet of dazzling eloquence and seemingly limitless knowledge, who took a liking to the then shy young man, and gave him his first real impulse towards self-expression. The prodigy in question was Samuel Taylor Coleridge, and the date was January 1798, a few months before Hazlitt's twentieth birthday. This event is the subject of one of Hazlitt's most brilliant essays, the powerful and beautiful 'On My First Acquaintance with Poets'.

# CHAPTER THREE

# The Reader and the Poets

FOR COLERIDGE 1797 was also an important year. It was a period of wonderful poetic fertility in which he wrote, among other things, 'Kubla Khan' and 'The Rime of the Ancient Mariner'. His friendship with Wordsworth was in its first flower; the two poets were neighbours in the West Country, seeing each other constantly and planning their celebrated joint venture, the *Lyrical Ballads*. Coleridge had already established a reputation by lecturing – he not infrequently dressed in black and called his lectures 'sermons' to disguise their revolutionary, reformist, pacifist, anti-slavery cast – and more especially with his early publications, which came perilously close to sedition. His reputation was enough to put him in demand with newspaper editors, and he was earning a guinea a week writing for the *Morning Post*.[1] But that income met only half his requirements. With a wife and infant son to support, he calculated that £100 a year was the least that would do. For several years previously, in the course of lecturing at Bristol and elsewhere, he had attracted a following by his spellbinding powers of oratory and the extraordinary intellectual gifts they manifested. Some of his richer admirers made him gifts of money, not infrequently handsome ones. But this source of supply was both uncertain and irregular. He considered his options in the light of the political and religious principles he espoused, and decided to become a preacher in the Unitarian cause. One good reason was that an attractive possibility had presented itself: the Unitarian congregation at Shrewsbury required a preacher, and the living there offered £120 a year and a house. (William senior at Wem, ten miles away, was still receiving his £30 a year, after decades in a cause that Coleridge had just taken up.) The wealthy Wedgwood family, who were fulsome admirers of Coleridge's gifts, had just sent him a present of £100, but he returned it saying that he needed a permanent settlement, and for that reason was going to preach at Shrewsbury to see whether he and its Unitarian congregation could agree. His letter in reply to the Wedgwoods is a masterpiece, for in returning their bank draft he in effect asked them to give him an annual income – which is what, to the tune of £150 a year, they immediately did.[2] But between his letter and their offer he went to Shrewsbury to preach, and there he met Hazlitt.

Coleridge arrived in Shrewsbury at the very last minute, on the night before the Sunday morning of his first sermon. The incumbent minister for whose post he was being considered, one Mr Rowe, had been anxiously haunting the coach office in expectation of him. The last coach arrived and Rowe could see no-one in it who looked like a Unitarian minister. But from it alighted a plump, round-faced man in a short, ill-fitting black coat, talking unstoppably to the other passengers as he did so. As Rowe was about to walk away this individual announced himself as his putative successor. He did so 'by beginning to talk. He did not cease while he staid; nor has he since, that I know of,' Hazlitt wrote. 'He held the good town of Shrewsbury in delightful suspense for the three weeks that he remained there, "fluttering the *proud Salopians* like an eagle in a dove-cote;" and the Welch mountains that skirt the horizon with their tempestuous confusion, agree to have heard no such mystic sounds since the days of "High-born Hoel's harp or soft Llewellyn's lay!" '

It was the practice among neighbouring Unitarian ministers to exchange visits, not just as a matter of courtesy but as a way of nurturing shared hopes for political progress and religious freedom. 'A line of communication is thus established,' Hazlitt explained, 'by which the flame of civil and religious liberty is kept alive, and nourishes its smouldering fire unquenchable, like the fires in the Agamemnon of Aeschylus, placed at different stations, that waited for ten long years to announce with their blazing pyramids the destruction of Troy.' Hazlitt therefore knew that he and Coleridge would meet when the latter called on William senior in Wem. But he was so intrigued by Coleridge's advance reputation that he resolved to hear the prodigy for himself beforehand. 'It was in January 1798 that I rose one morning before daylight, to walk ten miles in the mud, and went to hear this celebrated person preach. Never, the longest day I have to live, shall I have such another walk as this cold, raw, comfortless one, in the winter of the year 1798 ... When I got there, the organ was playing the 100th psalm, and, when it was done, Mr Coleridge rose and gave out his text, "And he went up into the mountain to pray, HIMSELF, ALONE." As he gave out his text, his voice "rose like a steam of rich distilled perfumes," and when he came to the two last words, which he pronounced loud, deep, and distinct, it seemed to me, who was then young, as if the sounds had echoed from the bottom of the human heart, and as if that prayer might have floated in solemn silence through the universe. The idea of St John came into mind, "of one crying in the wilderness, who had his loins girt about, and whose food was locusts and wild honey". The preacher then launched into his subject, like an eagle dallying with the wind. The sermon was on peace and war; upon church and state – not their alliance, but their separation – on the spirit of the world and the spirit of Christianity, not as the same, but as opposed to one another. He talked of those who had "inscribed the cross of Christ on banners dripping with human gore". He made a poetical and pastoral excursion, – and to shew the fatal effects of war, drew a striking contrast between the simple shepherd boy, driving his team afield, or sitting under the hawthorn, piping to his flock, "as though he should never be old", and the same poor country-lad, crimped, kidnapped, brought into town, made drunk at an alehouse, turned into a wretched drummer-boy, with his hair sticking on end with powder and pomatum, a long cue at his back, and tricked out in the loathsome finery of the profession of blood. "Such were the notes our once lov'd poet sung." As for myself, I could not have been more delighted if I had heard the music of the spheres. Poetry and Philosophy had met together. Truth and Genius had embraced, under the eye and with the sanction of Religion. This was even beyond my hopes. I returned home well satisfied. The sun that was still labouring pale and wan through sky, obscured by thick mists, seemed an emblem of the *good cause*; and the cold dank drops of dew that hung half melted on the beard of the thistle, had something genial and refreshing in them; for there was a spirit of hope and youth in all nature, that turned every thing into good.' Many reported Coleridge's gifts as a talker, his eloquent loquacity, the magical and unstoppable fountain of words that played and glittered the livelong day if nothing chanced to stop it; but very few report, as Hazlitt here does, what he talked about.

On the following Tuesday Coleridge arrived at the Hazlitt house in Wem and stayed overnight. 'I was called down from my room where he was, and went half-hoping, half-afraid. He received me very graciously, and I listened for a long time without uttering a word. I did not suffer in his opinion by my silence. "For those two hours," he afterwards was pleased to say, "he was conversing with W. H.'s forehead!"' Hazlitt found his appearance different from what he had been led to expect by seeing him at a distance in the dim light of the Shrewsbury chapel; there it had seemed that Coleridge possessed 'a strange wildness in his aspect, a dusky obscurity, and I thought him pitted with the smallpox.' Now Hazlitt could see that his complexion was 'clear, and even bright – "As are the children of yon azure sheen." His forehead was broad and high, light as if built of ivory, with large projecting brows, and his eyes rolling beneath them like a sea with darkened lustre. "A certain tender bloom his face o'erspread," a purple tinge as we see it in the pale thoughtful complexions of the Spanish portrait-painters, Murillo and Velasquez. His mouth was gross, voluptuous, open, eloquent; his chin good-humoured and round; but his nose, the rudder of the face, the index of the will, was small, feeble, nothing – like what he has done. It might seem that the genius of his face as from a height surveyed and projected him (with sufficient capacity and huge aspiration) into the world unknown of thought and imagination, with nothing to support or guide his veering purpose, as if Columbus had launched his adventurous course for the New World in a scallop, without oars or compass. So at least I comment on it after the event. Coleridge in his person was rather above the common size, inclining to the corpulent, or like Lord Hamlet, "somewhat fat and pursy". His hair (now, alas! grey) was then black and glossy as the raven's, and fell in smooth masses over his forehead. This long pendulous hair is peculiar to enthusiasts, to those whose minds tend heavenwards; and is traditionally inseparable (though of a different colour) from the pictures of Christ. It ought to belong, as a character, to all who preach *Christ crucified*, and Coleridge was at that time one of those!'[3]

Hazlitt was struck by the contrast between Coleridge and his father, 'a veteran of the cause, and then declining into the vale of years'. It seemed to him that no two people could be less alike than the host and his guest. William senior was benignly indifferent to the idea of poets and their vatic and artistic claims; he could not quite make them out, and was not especially interested in doing so. As Hazlitt puts it, 'a poet was to my father a sort of nondescript.' But Coleridge delighted William senior, for 'whatever added grace to the Unitarian cause was to him welcome. He could hardly have been more surprised or pleased, if our visitor had worn wings. Indeed, his thoughts had wings; and as the silken sounds rustled round our little wainscoted parlour, my father threw back his spectacles over his forehead, his white hairs mixing with its sanguine hue; and a smile of delight beamed across his rugged cordial face, to think that Truth had found a new ally in Fancy! Besides, Coleridge seemed to take considerable notice of me, and that of itself was enough.'[4]

Coleridge talked to the two Hazlitts agreeably and familiarly about many things, and his eloquence seemed to increase, if that were possible, when dinner was served, perhaps because they were then joined by Mrs Hazlitt and Peggy. During it he 'dilated in a very edifying manner' on Mary Wollstonecraft and James Mackintosh. William senior praised the latter's *Vindiciae Gallicae*, but although Coleridge conceded its merits he could not allow its author's work to occupy the same rank as Burke's, 'either in matter or style. Burke was a metaphysician, Mackintosh a mere logician. Burke was an orator (almost a poet) who reasoned in figures, because he had an eye for nature: Mackintosh, on the other hand, was a rhetorician, who had only an eye to common-places.' At this point Hazlitt, who had until then been silent, spoke. He said, 'I have always entertained a great opinion of Burke, and that (as far as I could find) the speaking of him with contempt might be made the test of a vulgar democratical mind. This was the first observation I ever made to Coleridge, and he said it was a very just and striking one. I remember the leg of Welsh mutton and the turnips on the table that day had the finest flavour imaginable.'

No-one seemed to mind Coleridge's dig at a Hazlitt family friend: 'Godwin had once boasted to him of having carried on an argument with Macintosh for three hours with dubious success; Coleridge told him – "If there had been a man of genius in the room, he would have settled the question in five minutes." ' One reason for Coleridge's equivocal view of Mackintosh was that he had 'a very indifferent opinion' of his good friend Mr Wordsworth, which had prompted Coleridge to tell him that Wordsworth 'strides on so far before you, that he dwindles in the distance'.

Coleridge then made an observation that agreed with a view Hazlitt had developed independently. Coleridge asked him if he had ever met Mary Wollstonecraft. Hazlitt said, 'I had once for a few moments, and that she seemed to me to turn off Godwin's objections to something she advanced with quite a playful, easy air.' Coleridge replied that this was an example of 'the ascendancy which people of imagination exercise over those of mere intellect'. This struck a deep chord with Hazlitt whose view, embryonic then but crucial to him always, was that imagination is essential to philosophical understanding and to the appreciation of art and literature. Either without the other – imagination without intellect, intellect without imagination – is severely diminished by the other's absence; but imagination is the key, because only by its means are moral sympathy and critical discernment possible. Sympathy and discernment were, for Hazlitt, the core of life, in their turn making possible love, creativity, and respect – the respect between people from which civil and religious liberties naturally flow. This insight served as a principle for Hazlitt, who iterated it in hundreds of different ways and places throughout his writings. Although Coleridge's remark touches only one aspect of it, Hazlitt never forgot what he said because, coming from a man whose intellect he always respected despite their later differences and enmities, its conformity with his own view was profoundly welcome.

They talked also about the playwright Holcroft. Coleridge said that someone asked him 'if he had not been much struck *with* him', to which he replied that 'he thought himself in more danger of being struck *by* him.'

Hazlitt complained that it was uphill work conversing with Holcroft, who demanded a definition of every word, even the commonest, thus preventing an interlocutor from stating views or arguing a case: 'What do you mean by a *sensation*, Sir? What do you mean by an *idea*?' Coleridge sympathized; he said 'This was barricadoing the road to truth: – it was setting up a turnpike gate at every step we took.'⁵

'I forget a great number of things, many more than I remember,' Hazlitt wrote, despite this extraordinary recall of conversations a quarter of a century later, 'but the day passed off pleasantly, and the next morning Mr Coleridge was to return to Shrewsbury. When I came down to breakfast, I found that he had just received a letter from his friend T. Wedgwood, making him an offer of £150 a year if he chose to waive his present pursuit, and devote himself entirely to the study of poetry and philosophy. Coleridge seemed to close with this proposal in the act of tying on one of his shoes.' According to Coleridge's biographer Richard Holmes, Hazlitt did not then know Coleridge well enough to see that the apparent indifference was a mark of deep emotion; that he bent to tie his shoe to hide what he felt. Back in Shrewsbury Coleridge wrote to Wedgwood accepting the generous offer, saying that such benevolence 'filled his eyes with tears'. There is no reason to doubt his sincerity; it was the answer to a dream.

Hazlitt was deeply disappointed that Coleridge was not going to live near by after all. Wedgwood's letter 'threw an additional damp on his departure. It took the wayward enthusiast quite from us to cast him into Deva's winding vales, or by the shores of old romance. Instead of living at ten miles distance, of being the pastor of a Dissenting congregation at Shrewsbury, he was henceforth to inhabit the Hill of Parnassus, to be a shepherd on the Delectable Mountains. Alas! I knew not the way thither, and felt very little gratitude for Mr Wedgwood's bounty.' But the disappointment was instantly tempered by Coleridge's asking, when his toilet was complete, for pen and ink, which he took to a table and there wrote something on a card. Advancing towards Hazlitt with 'undulating step' he gave him the card – 'the precious document' – which Hazlitt found to contain the words: 'Mr Coleridge, Nether Stowey, Somersetshire'. Coleridge said 'that he should be glad to see me there in a few weeks' time, and, if I chose, would come half-way to meet me. I was not less surprised than the shepherd-boy (this simile is to be found in Cassandra) when he sees the thunder-bolt fall close to his feet. I stammered out my acknowledgements and acceptance of this offer (I thought Mr Wedgwood's annuity a trifle to it) as well as I could.'

Hazlitt accompanied Coleridge six of the ten miles back to Shrewsbury. It was a sunny winter's morning, perfect for the journey. Coleridge talked the whole way. 'The scholar in Chaucer is described as going "Sounding on his way". So Coleridge went on his. In digressing, in dilating, in passing from subject to subject, he appeared to me to float on air, to slide on ice.' He told Hazlitt confidentially that he would not have been accepted in Shrewsbury, because he planned to say things in his next two sermons (on Infant Baptism and on the Lord's Supper) that would have shown him to be too heterodox for the congregation's liking. (In any case Coleridge's conversion to a form of Unitarianism, which had happened while he was at Cambridge, was not securely based. His visit to Italy in 1806 reconverted him to Trinitarianism.) 'I observed that he continually crossed me on the way by shifting from one side of the foot-path to the other. This struck me as an odd movement; but I did not at that time connect it with any instability of purpose or involuntary charge of principles, as I have done since. He seemed unable to keep on in a straight line.'[6] This observation, made with much hindsight, encapsulates Hazlitt's final judgement on Coleridge, whom he came to charge with betrayal: betrayal of his early political radicalism through apostasy, betrayal of his gifts through sloth and opium, and betrayal of reason and rigour because of his collapse into 'mystic humbug' (which prompted Hazlitt to nickname him 'the Cock-lane Ghost of midday').[7] These were later judgements, made two decades after this first meeting; but even as Coleridge wove his way along the footpath towards Shrewsbury he began to offer Hazlitt grounds for a tempering of adulation. 'He spoke slightingly of Hume (whose Essay on Miracles he said was stolen from an objection started in one of South's sermons – *Credat Judaeus Apella*!). I was not very much pleased at this account of Hume, for I had just been reading, with infinite relish, that completest of metaphysical *choke-pears*, his *Treatise on Human Nature*, to which the *Essays*, in point of scholastic subtlety and close reasoning, are mere elegant trifling, light summer-reading. Coleridge even denied the excellence of Hume's general style, which I think betrayed a want of taste and candour.' Hazlitt has Coleridge on the hip here, since all posterity agrees with his and not Coleridge's estimation of Hume, and on excellent grounds. 'He however made me amends by the manner in which he spoke of Berkeley. He dwelt particularly on his *Essay on Vision* as a masterpiece of analytical reasoning. So it undoubtedly is.' As the conversation proceeded, with a comparison between the intellects of Berkeley and Paine (the former had a subtle mind, the latter an acute one, said Coleridge; and he added that 'the former is a philosopher's quality, the latter a shop-boy's'), and praise from Coleridge for Bishop Butler's profundity and conscientiousness, Hazlitt noticed an interesting fact about Coleridge's judgements: as with his choice of Berkeley's work on vision, rather than his chief philosophical works the *Principles of Human Knowledge* and *Three Dialogues Between Hylas and Philonous*, so in the case of Butler he chose to praise not the famous *Analogy* but a work Hazlitt had not then heard of, the *Sermons at the Rolls' Chapel*. Hazlitt cannily remarked: 'Coleridge somehow always contrived to prefer the *unknown* to the *known*.' At the same time as giving the appearance of wide reading and deep scholarship, this resource might protect a superficial knowledge from being found out in a test of the chief texts. But Hazlitt, writing twenty-five years later, adds, 'In this instance he was right. The *Analogy* is a tissue of sophistry, of wire-drawn, theological special-pleading; the *Sermons* (with the Preface to them) are in a fine vein of deep, matured reflection, a candid appeal to our observation of human nature, without pedantry and without bias.' And Hazlitt also noticed that Coleridge liked writers who defended religion, and despised those who were equivocal, or worse, towards it; and that whereas he spoke discerningly and insightfully about writers he liked, he could be crude and prejudiced in his attacks on those he disliked. Thus, although he had agreed with Hazlitt's first-ever remark to him about appreciating Burke's powers as a writer and reasoner while disagreeing vehemently with his politics, he did not always apply that standard in his own judgements.

Encouraged by the turn of the conversation towards philosophy in these observations on Hume and Butler, Hazlitt decided to tell Coleridge of his 'metaphysical discovery'. Coleridge listened with great willingness, but could not understand it. This failure to express his point clearly galvanized Hazlitt into trying yet again to get a statement of it written, returning to the task the moment he reached home later that day. He had attempted it any number of times already, preparing new pens and paper and sitting down to the task with determination, and always beginning with a list of the propositions to be argued. But as before, 'after trying in vain to pump up any words, images, notions, apprehensions, facts, or observations, from the gulph of abstraction in which I had plunged myself for four or five years preceding, [I] gave up the attempt as labour in vain, and shed tears of helpless despondency on the blank unfinished paper.' Hazlitt looked back on that struggle, as always, without a single regret. 'I can write fast enough now. Am I better than I was then? Oh no! One truth discovered, one pang of regret at not being able to express it, is better than all the fluency and flippancy in the world.'[8]

Hazlitt's failure to get his idea across to Coleridge did nothing to spoil their walk together along the road between Wem and Shrewsbury. Coleridge spoke at length about the famous theologian Dr Paley, praising his style, damning his mental powers, and stating that it was a national scandal that his writings on moral and political philosophy should be textbooks in the Universities. On this note they parted at the six-mile stone, and Hazlitt turned homewards, 'pensive but much pleased'. Coleridge had been kind and interested; he was the first real poet Hazlitt had met, and he lived up to that inspired name; and his powers of conversation, about which Hazlitt had heard much beforehand, had delighted and instructed him. 'On my way back, I had a sound in my ears, it was the voice of Fancy; I had a light before my eyes, it was the face of Poetry.' They had found much to agree about in philosophy, politics, literature and life. Hazlitt looked forward eagerly to visiting Coleridge in the spring, and his anticipation warmed and expedited what was left of winter.

Before the promised day came (and it had to be postponed for a fortnight beyond its original date, because of Coleridge's commitments) Hazlitt made a walking tour of the Vale of Llangollen, 'by way of initiating myself into the mysteries of natural scenery'. Before going on this Romantic excursion he read Coleridge's 'Ode on the Departing Year', and applied it 'con amore to the objects before me' as he walked. He had his twentieth birthday at an inn in the Vale (10 April 1798), solitarily reading Rousseau over a bottle of sherry and a cold chicken. He chose the passage in the New Eloise in which Saint-Preux describes his feelings on first glimpsing the Pays de Vaud. Hazlitt had been struck by the sudden beauty of the Vale of Llangollen as it appears, all at once, when the traveller reaches a certain point on the road from Wrexham: the valley 'opens like an amphitheatre' with the river Dee hurrying over its stone bed down the middle, the scene answering to the description in Coleridge's 'Faithful Shepherdess' of green woods, cool streams and wells, which Hazlitt had been quoting to himself while he walked.[9] 'That valley was to me (in a manner) the cradle of a new existence,' he wrote, enjoying the memory; 'in the river that winds through it, my spirit was baptized in the waters of Helicon!'[10]

In this exalted state of mind Hazlitt returned briefly home to Wem before setting out for Somerset, on foot, a journey of about one hundred and fifty miles. His route took him through Worcester and Gloucester, and as he walked by Upton he thought of Tom Jones 'and the adventure of the muff'. One day he was completely soaked in a downpour, and stopped at an inn, only to sit up the whole night reading Paul and Virginia, the romantic and heart-wrenching novel by Bernardin de Saint-Pierre about two French children growing up in Mauritius and learning about love, loss and tragedy. When it was published in 1788 it became an immediate bestseller and inspired songs, poems, plays, ballets, paintings and operas far into the nineteenth century. 'Sweet were the showers in my early youth that drenched my body, and sweet the drops of pity that fell upon the books I read!' wrote Hazlitt, remembering this sentimental tale. He had made such good progress in his journey that he was in danger of arriving at Nether Stowey two days early, so he paused at Bridgwater. When he was tired of sauntering on the banks of its muddy river – where he made another philosophical discovery, about 'likeness' and the association of ideas, which he soon afterwards reported to Coleridge – he returned to the inn and read *Camilla* by Fanny Burney, recently published.

He arrived at Nether Stowey to a warm welcome. The Coleridges' cottage stood near the sea in beautiful green hill country, not far from Alfoxden, a 'romantic old family mansion' which an acquaintance had lent Wordsworth and his sister. On that first afternoon Coleridge took Hazlitt to meet Wordsworth, but they found that he was away in Bristol. Dorothy Wordsworth entertained them by giving them a light meal and the manuscript of her brother's *Lyrical Ballads* to read. Hazlitt 'dipped into a few of these with great satisfaction'. The two stayed overnight, Hazlitt in an old room with blue hangings, full of family portraits from the time of the first Hanoverian kings. The next morning he was woken by the baying of a stag from a wood near the house. After breakfast he and Coleridge strolled in the park and sat on the fallen trunk of an ancient ash-tree, where Coleridge read aloud to him the ballad of 'Betty Foy'. Hazlitt was not at that early juncture inclined to be sceptical or critical; he saw 'touches of truth and nature, and took the rest for granted'. But then Coleridge recited 'The Thorn', 'The Mad Mother', and the 'Complaint of a Poor Indian Woman', and Hazlitt was stirred. 'I felt that deeper power and pathos which have been since acknowledged, "In spite of pride, in erring reason's spite", as the characteristics of this author; and the sense of a new style and a new spirit in poetry came over me.' He was, indeed, the first witness, and an alert one, of something original and important in literature, for the notion of the *Lyrical Ballads* had only just been devised by Coleridge and Wordsworth – literally, in the two or three weeks before Hazlitt's arrival. Their collaborative venture in seeing if the public would appreciate an innovative style and feeling in poetry was suddenly decided upon in mid-March 1798, and the manuscript was with their publisher Joseph Cottle in June. Most of Wordsworth's contribution was new material, whereas most of Coleridge's had already been written. The collection was daring in conception. It combined themes from low-life with fantasy and madness, and it employed provocatively plain styles and forms. These novelties were enhanced by Cottle's beautiful and adventurous design for the book – twenty lines to a page, with extravagantly wide margins.[11]

Hazlitt and Coleridge returned to Nether Stowey that evening, the latter talking in the summer moonlight of philosophy and poetry, lamenting

Wordsworth's matter-of-factness in his descriptive pieces, but praising the intuitive grasp of truth in his philosophical poetry. Wordsworth himself called the next day at Nether Stowey on his way home from Bristol. He seemed to Hazlitt rather like Don Quixote, gaunt and oddly dressed in a brown fustian jacket and striped pantaloons, and walking with a roll in his gait. Hazlitt observed him carefully. 'There was a severe, worn pressure of thought about the temples, a fire in his eyes (as if he saw something in objects more than the outward appearance), an intense high narrow forehead, a Roman nose, cheeks furrowed by strong purpose and feeling, and a convulsive inclination to laughter about the mouth, a good deal at variance with the solemn, stately expression of the rest of his face.' Wordsworth talked 'very naturally and freely, with a mixture of clear gushing accents in his voice, a deep guttural intonation, and a strong tincture of the Northern *burr*, like the crust on wine.' He was hungry and demolished half a Cheshire cheese on the table, telling them about the play he had seen at Bristol, which was Monk Lewis's 'Castle Spectre'. The audience had greatly enjoyed it – a fault, both poets quickly pointed out to Hazlitt, because popular approbation must be disdained. At one point Wordsworth looked out of the window and said, 'How beautifully the sun sets on that yellow bank!' and Hazlitt – enough in awe to interpret commonplaces as profundities – murmured to himself, 'With what eyes these poets see nature!' (As a wry comment on his early infatuation, he adds in his reminiscence of the occasion, 'and ever after, when I saw the sunset stream upon the objects facing it, I conceived I had made a discovery, or thanked Mr Wordsworth for having made one for me!')[12]

So began a close intimacy between Hazlitt and the poets. On the next morning he and Coleridge walked back to Alfoxden with Wordsworth, who there read them 'Peter Bell' in the open air, taking (Hazlitt remarked) great satisfaction in his performance. Hazlitt was intrigued by the 'chaunt' with which both poets read their work; it acted, he said, like a spell on the listener, and disarmed judgement. It made him wonder whether they deceived themselves by making habitual use of this 'ambiguous accompaniment'. Coleridge was the more dramatic of the two in this respect, Wordsworth the more lyrical, and Hazlitt put the difference down to what Coleridge told him of their different manners of composition: Coleridge liked to compose while walking over uneven ground, or breaking through the straggling branches of a wood, whereas Wordsworth liked to compose while strolling equably up and down a straight gravel path.

That evening, Hazlitt reports, he got into a metaphysical argument with Wordsworth 'while Coleridge was explaining the different notes of the nightingale to his sister'. He ruefully adds, 'Neither of us succeeded in making ourselves perfectly clear and intelligible.'[13] Wordsworth was not much given to metaphysical discussion of a technical, discursive kind, preferring intuitive and previously unspoken philosophical insights to make their appearance on their own terms in his poetry. He accordingly addressed Hazlitt in his poem 'The Tables Turned', giving him the name Matthew and describing him as 'the friend who was somewhat unreasonably attached to modern books of moral philosophy':

> Up! up! my Friend, and quit your books;
> Or surely you'll grow double;
> Up! up! my Friend, and clear your looks;
> Why all this toil and trouble?
>
> The sun, above the mountain's head,
> A freshening lustre mellow
> Through all the long green fields has spread,
> Her first sweet evening yellow...
>
> Enough of Science and of Art;
> Close up those barren leaves;
> Come forth, and bring with you a heart
> That watches and receives.[14]

Three weeks passed in this delightful manner at Nether Stowey and its neighbourhood. Hazlitt reports that they spent their afternoons sitting in an arbour, under two elm trees, sipping a drink called 'flip' and listening to the bees humming round them. Towards the end of his stay it was agreed that Coleridge, an admiring young friend of his called John Chester, and Hazlitt should make a walking tour down the Bristol Channel as far as Linton. John Chester trotted beside Coleridge 'like a footman beside a state coach' in order to lose nothing of the poet's *obiter dicta*. He scarcely spoke, except to tell Hazlitt that he thought Coleridge a 'wonderful man'. Hazlitt dryly adds, 'He afterwards followed Coleridge into Germany, where the Kantian philosophers were puzzled how to bring him under any of their categories.' They enjoyed the constantly changing views, which included seascapes – Hazlitt pointed out to Coleridge the bare masts of a ship framed in the red orb of the setting sun, just as in his *Ancient Mariner* – brown heathlands overlooking the channel, and villages nestling in the sheltered creases of hills close to the shore. When they reached the rugged environs of Linton a thunderstorm threatened; Coleridge rushed out into it to greet the elements, but as if in spite only a few drops fell.[15]

The party stayed at an inn in Linton for two nights, on the morning of the second day eating a breakfast Hazlitt remembered with relish: 'We breakfasted luxuriously in an old-fashioned parlour, on tea, toast, eggs, and honey, in the very sight of the bee-hives from which it had been taken, and a garden full of thyme and wild flowers that had produced it.' Coleridge told Hazlitt that he and Wordsworth had planned to make the Valley of Stones at Linton the scene of a jointly written novel inspired by the story in Genesis of Cain's murder of Abel, but had given up the idea. He also talked at length about Virgil's *Georgics*, but not to Hazlitt's satisfaction: 'I do not think he had much feeling for the classical or elegant.' Hazlitt remembered the conversation in the breakfast-parlour as vividly as the breakfast they ate while they talked. 'It was in this room that we found a little worn-out copy of the *Seasons* lying in a window-seat, on which Coleridge exclaimed, "*That* is true fame!" He said Thomson was a great poet, rather than a good one; his style was as meretricious as his thoughts were natural. He spoke of Cowper as the best modern poet. He said the *Lyrical Ballads* were an experiment about to be tried by him and Wordsworth, to see how far the public taste would endure poetry written in a more natural and simple style than had hitherto been attempted; totally discarding the artifices of poetical diction, and making use only of such words as had probably been common in the most ordinary language since the days of Henry II. Some comparison was introduced between Shakespear and Milton. He said "he hardly knew which to prefer. Shakespear appeared to him a mere stripling in the art; he was as tall and as strong, with infinitely more activity than Milton, but had never appeared to have come to man's estate; or if he had, he would not have been a man, but a monster." He spoke with contempt of Gray, and with intolerance of Pope. He did not like the versification of the latter. He observed that "the ears of these couplet-writers might be charged with having short memories, that could not retain the harmony of whole passages". He thought little of Junius as a writer; he had a dislike of Dr Johnson; and a much higher opinion of Burke as an orator and politician, than of Fox or Pitt. He however thought him very inferior in richness of style and imagery to some of our elder prose-writers, particularly Jeremy Taylor. He liked Richardson, but not Fielding; nor could I get him to enter into the merits of *Caleb Williams*. In short,' concluded Hazlitt, confirming his judgement of Coleridge's attitudes, 'he was profound and discriminating with respect to those authors whom he liked, and where he gave his judgment fair play; capricious, perverse, and prejudiced in his antipathies and distastes.' Hazlitt also found that he had little idea of painting. Not many of Coleridge's critical judgements proved stable; he certainly came to take a different view of Shakespeare, and the relative merits of Shakespeare and Milton, in his maturer critical work. But it is also clear that although the young Hazlitt listened as intently as John Chester listened avidly in the parlour at Linton, he did not agree with everything Coleridge said, and to Chester's surprise debated with him – and on one point at least taught him something: 'I broached to him an argument of mine to prove that *likeness* was not mere association of ideas. I said that the mark in the sand put one in mind of a man's foot, not because it was part of a former impression of a man's foot (for it was quite new) but because it was like the shape of a man's foot. He assented to the justness of this distinction ... John Chester listened, not from any interest in the subject, but because he was astonished that I should be able to suggest any thing to Coleridge that he did not already know.'[16] By this time they were strolling on the beach – hence the allusion to the footprints in the sand – and they met a fisherman who told them that a boy had drowned there on the previous day, and that the villagers had tried to save him at peril of their own lives. In answer to the question why they had taken the risk he said 'he did not know how it was that they ventured, but, Sir, we have a *nature* towards one another.' Coleridge turned to Hazlitt and remarked that this was a fine illustration of Hazlitt's theory of disinterestedness, which evidently Hazlitt had at last had some success in explaining to Coleridge while at Nether Stowey.

After three days they returned to Nether Stowey preparatory to going their different ways, Hazlitt home to Wem and Coleridge to Germany. They did not meet again for two years, which were spent by Coleridge 'wandering in the Hartz Forest' as Hazlitt significantly puts it, the pun subtly intentional and truer than the facts of the poet's actual itinerary in Germany during that time, which was more prosaic.

Hazlitt returned home enlarged and thoughtful. The interest shown in him by Coleridge was a great encouragement. 'He used to say of me,' he wrote in 1818, 'that I had the most metaphysical head he ever met with ... that if ever I got language for my ideas, the world would hear of it, for that I had guts in my brains.'[17] The encouragement made him more than ever intent on writing out his philosophical views, but he had at the same time to consider the practical matter of earning a living, for he was now aged twenty, and could not rely upon the family at home in Wem indefinitely. There had always been the thought that he might follow his brother's career as a portrait painter, and indeed he, like his sister Peggy, had enough skill with a drawing-pencil to make the idea more than feasible. Its attraction was that it offered an income along with some degree of independence, which for Hazlitt was a necessity.

At this juncture Hazlitt's idea of becoming a painter was simply a pragmatic one. But then he saw something in London that turned art into as much a passion as philosophy already was.

# CHAPTER FOUR

# Painting and Philosophy

## 1798–1803

B Y HIS OWN admission, until the age of twenty Hazlitt thought that nothing existed in the world to compare in importance with books.[1] He remembered sitting one afternoon with a volume of John Vanbrugh in his hand, reading *The Provoked Husband* with great enjoyment, and occasionally glancing up at a print of a Flemish landscape that happened to hang near by – a Ruysdael or Hobbema. He 'wondered what there could be in that sort of work to satisfy or delight the mind,' and asked himself 'whether I should ever feel an interest in it like what I took in reading Vanbrugh or Cibber?'[2] The question was soon and emphatically answered. In December 1798 a large number of Italian old master paintings, mainly from the collection of the Duc d'Orléans in Paris and therefore known as the Orleans Gallery, went on sale in Pall Mall in London. Hazlitt was in London too, staying with his brother at 12 Rathbone Place. He went to see the pictures, and was 'staggered' by them. He gazed at them with 'wondering and with longing eyes'. He could not keep away, returning day after day to inspect with mounting astonishment what artists of genius could do with paint on canvas or wood. 'A mist passed away from my sight; the scales fell off. A new sense came upon me, a new heaven and a new earth stood before me.' He had heard the names Titian, Raphael, Guido, Domenichino, the Caracci brothers; 'but to see them face to face, to be in the same room with their deathless productions, was like breaking some mighty spell – was almost an effect of necromancy! From that time I lived in a world of pictures. Battles, sieges, speeches in parliament seemed mere idle noise and fury, "signifying nothing", compared with these mighty works and dreaded names that spoke to me in the eternal silence of thought.'[3] He was ravished by the 'bewitching grace and modesty' of Susannah in Lodovico Carracci's *Susannah and the Elders*. He could scarcely take his eyes from Annibale Carracci's *Danae*, onto whose upwardly gazing and expectant body, 'desirable, ample, and worthy of a god', cascaded the shower of gold. He was astonished at how Sebastiano

63

del Piombo had captured the deathliness of Lazarus's flesh as the res-
urrected figure begins to emerge from the tomb. But if these painters
staggered him, how much more so did Titian, whose *Diana and Callisto*
was equalled only by his *Diana and Actaeon*. Hazlitt was overwhelmed
by the power, truth, *gusto*, and miracles of colouring in these pictures.
Years later he saw them again in the Marquis of Stafford's Gallery, and
wrote about them in his book *Sketches of the Principal Picture Galleries
in England*, concluding the peroration on Titian by adapting what Ari-
stophanes of Byzantium had said of Menander: 'Oh Titian and Nature!
which of you copied the other?'[4]

The idea of becoming a painter now had a new meaning. He began to
try his hand in his brother's studio, under his brother's instruction. It
proved enthralling. 'Finding the difficulties and beauties it unfolded,
opened a new field to me, and I began to conclude that there might be a
number of "other things between heaven and earth that were never dreamt
of in my philosophy".'[5]

John taught Hazlitt in the approved manner by making him copy. Hazlitt
recalled sitting on a wintry day in the little back room which served as a
studio in Rathbone Place, carefully trying to imitate a Rembrandt or a
landscape by Van Goyen, and afterwards placing his canvas where it might
catch a gleam of light from the embers in the fireplace, so that he could
gaze at it: 'As to that landscape, methinks I see it now ... how delighted I
was when I had made the tremulous, undulating reflection in the water,
and saw the dull canvas become a lucid mirror of the commonest features
of nature! Certainly, painting gives one a strong interest in nature and
humanity.'[6]

It was not enough merely to copy; he wished also to see as many first-
rate pictures as he could, and thereafter, when he travelled, he took every
opportunity to visit places known for their picture collections. That mainly
meant great country houses. It was the practice of the day for most such
places to admit visitors on request, though there were sometimes 'surly
porters and impertinent footmen' who did not wish to oblige. Hazlitt
prided himself on scarcely ever being defeated by such obstacles. His visits
to Lord Radnor's park to see the two magnificent canvases by Claude, to
Wilton to see the Van Dyke portrait of the Pembroke family, to Blenheim
for its magnificent collection of Rubens ('the greatest such collection in
the world'), to Knowsley for Rembrandt's depiction of *The Writing on the
Wall*, to Burleigh House to see Guido's angelic heads, were all first made
when he was a young aspiring artist, in the years on either side of 1800.
On each occasion he came away 'richer than the possessor' because the
treasure he had come to see was 'stamped on his brain, and lives there

thenceforward, a clue to nature, and a test of art. He furnishes out the chambers of his mind from the spoils of time, picks and chooses which shall have the best places – nearest his heart. He goes away richer than he came, richer than the possessor; and thinks that he may one day return, when he perhaps shall have done something of the same kind, or even from failure shall have learned to admire truth and genius more.'[7]

He also came to know some of the leading painters of the day, and frequented their studios. One of his biographers suggests that the knowledge he displays of technique could only have been learned at the Royal Academy School, but there is no evidence that he ever enrolled there.[8] It is more likely that he picked up all the standard artists' jargon and tricks from conversation and observation in these and his brother's studios. There were three big names in painting at that time, apart from Benjamin West who was the Academy's President but in Hazlitt's view 'a man of no mark or likelihood': they were John Opie, James Northcote and Henry Fuseli, who had been Mary Wollstonecraft's lover. Hazlitt met the latter two, both of them eccentric characters, and came to know Northcote well; towards the end of his life he published an extraordinary and entertaining book called *Conversations of James Northcote* in which, like Teucer firing his arrows from behind the shield of Ajax, Hazlitt gives free vent to his own opinions on almost everything. He was a frequent if not indeed daily visitor at Northcote's studio at 39 Argyle Street, passing hours in the artist's company, pottering about, picking out and looking at canvases painted before he was born, watching the diminutive figure of Northcote perch on its ladder to paint at the top of a canvas, or squat on the floor to rifle through prints. They talked all the time, agreeing on much. When Northcote spoke of Titian's powers as a colourist, tears came into his eyes, and Hazlitt felt the same way.

Hazlitt's first major effort in painting was a portrait of an old country-woman from the neighbourhood of Manchester. He attempted it in the style of Rembrandt, and worked exceedingly hard at it. 'I spared no pains to do my best. If art was long, I thought that life was so too at that moment.' On the first day he managed to capture the general effect, and was pleased with it – perhaps even more surprised than pleased to have achieved as much. Then he devoted weeks and months to finishing it in detail, for he disagreed with Sir Joshua Reynolds's view that artistic perfection consists in capturing overall effect. Hazlitt believed the opposite, as did the old masters: that perfection lies in detail. He was captivated by the 'gorgeous effect of light and shade' on the old woman's face, and sought to represent the delicacy and depth of this *chiaroscuro* in all its

65

'dim and scarce perceptible variety of tone and shadow'. He saw what was in nature, and tried to reproduce it in paint. He tried, but failed repeatedly: he tried harder, and at last 'succeeded, as I thought'. He saw that Rembrandt had been superbly faithful to nature in representing wrinkled skin as broken lines, and he 'strained every nerve' to get the same effect. 'If I could hit off this crumbling appearance, and insert the reflected light in the furrows of old age in half a morning, I did not think I had lost a day.' He noticed how, under the yellowed parchment-like skin of the old woman's face, the blood-colour still tingled, and with 'jealous, lynx-eyed watchfulness' attempted to catch it. He made endless revisions, endless attempts to get exactly the same position and expression as the day before; and he and his sitter waited for each day's light to adjust so that the shadows fell at the same angles and depths. He worked at portraying the puckering of the old woman's lips, the 'cautious introversion of the eye under the shadow of the bonnet, indicative of the feebleness and suspicion of old age' – which Hazlitt says he at last got 'to a tolerable nicety'.

Despite all this Herculean labour the picture was never finished. While painting it Hazlitt used to prop it up, after the day's work was over, to contemplate it, and 'saw revealed to me with swimming eyes the birth of new hopes, and of a new world of objects'. He kept it near him for decades, on a mantelpiece where he and others could see it, and only parted with it at last when desperate for money. It has not survived, but if it had it would be like others of Hazlitt's paintings, now practically invisible as a result of the decay wrought by time on the poor materials he used. Like his contemporaries he employed bitumen as an underpainting colour, to achieve the rich effects of the Old Masters' textures and tones. Neither he nor his contemporaries realized that bitumen is a self-destructive substance, and after a century or two begins to crack badly. This is the fate that has vanquished Hazlitt's remaining canvases. But his Old Woman gave him much quiet enjoyment in his lifetime. It was almost the only one of his paintings to please him. He was never satisfied with himself as a painter, despite the fact that he could be good, as is amply demonstrated by his self-portrait on the front cover of this book, and the portrait of Lamb included among the illustrations. But he was not nearly as good as he yearned to be, which is why he eventually gave up. Nevertheless he felt that he had earned an insider's view of the struggle that produces art – his Old Woman was his badge of proof – and his insider's view informs his art criticism profoundly.

Hazlitt's quiet pride in his Old Woman had something to do with the fact that in it he had managed, if very partially, to achieve a Rembrandt-esque effect after all. When the painter Benjamin Haydon first saw the picture he said in surprise, 'Hello! where did you get that Rembrandt? It looks like an early performance.'[9]

After these wrestlings he returned to London and began work on portraits of two young friends, the youthful poet James Sheridan Knowles and his sister Charlotte. Here too there were struggles to recover yesterday's expression – 'Hang your fat cheeks – frown, James!' Hazlitt once expostulated. He painted Charlotte in white muslin 'lamenting over a dead bird which she held in her lap'. Both were fond of Hazlitt, and he of them. Knowles later remembered Hazlitt's kindness and interest in his work: 'He taught me as a friend endearingly praising and condemning, as he saw cause, every little poem which I wrote. There was ore in him, but his mature friends were blind to it.'[10]

This last comment is a pertinent one. Hazlitt was then beginning to live an independent life, trying to earn his own keep, but he was venturing into the world with a handicap: he suffered from paralysing shyness in some circumstances, and when he was shy he was socially clumsy. Both are self-aggravating defects. Moreover, he was careless about his personal appearance, especially about the clothes he wore – something that later changed. Tongue-tied and unkempt, he appeared in society as an awkward, ill-at-ease young man, especially in new company, and even more especially in the company of young women. It was at this time – in 1799, during a visit to Bury St Edmunds in Suffolk – that the diarist Henry Crabb Robinson first met him, later recalling that he was 'struggling against a great difficulty of expression ... his bashfulness, want of words, slovenliness in dress, etc., made him the object of ridicule ... [he was] excessively shy, and in company the girls always made game of him ... he had a horror of the society of young ladies, especially of smart and handsome and modest young women. The prettiest girl of our parties about this time was Miss Kitchener. She used to drive him mad by teasing him.'[11] Robinson himself immediately recognized Hazlitt's true qualities, describing him as an 'extraordinary man'. They met frequently in London, breakfasting together and passing long mornings in talk. Hazlitt introduced Robinson to the work of Coleridge and Wordsworth, and when Robinson made a tour into Wales in the summer of 1799 he called at Wem to meet Hazlitt's family.

Hazlitt visited Bury St Edmunds because his brother had portrait commissions to fulfil there, including some among the Robinson family. John no doubt thought Hazlitt could benefit from meeting some of the Robinsons' circle of prosperous Bury friends, all merchants, Dissenters, and political reformers, who had made their town a centre of liberal thought. Hazlitt remained on good terms with several of them: with Anthony

Robinson, owner of a sugar refinery, who devoted his profits to phil-anthropy; with Capel Lofft, the constitutional lawyer and politician; and with Thomas Clarkson, the author and devoted warrior in the cause of abolishing slavery. Hazlitt called him 'a true apostle of human redemption' and retained a lifelong admiration for him. Among those John painted was the pretty Miss Kitchener, Hazlitt's tormentor.

The new endeavour of painting gave Hazlitt joy, but also misgiving. He saw 'old battered portraits' stacked outside the door of art dealers' shops, knocked down at second-hand prices, suffering yet more damage from the glare of the morning sun full on them. He shuddered to think what would happen to his own pictures, imperfect as they were. Then he saw a fine picture hanging in the shop's interior, and it made him hurry home to redouble his efforts.[12] But he had not ceased to think about philosophy, or to turn occasionally to the blank paper on which he hoped to write an account of his metaphysical discovery. Although the liberal cause in politics had been quashed by the Government and the war, its votaries still met to talk and repine together. Godwin's diary shows that he met Hazlitt thirteen times between January and November 1799, and in this year Hazlitt first met Southey, and attended James Mackintosh's lectures on 'Laws of Nature and Nations' at Lincoln's Inn Hall. The lectures were a disappointment, because Mackintosh was a follower of Hartley and – worse – had become an opponent of the French Revolution. He had been converted from the sentiments of his *Vindiciae Gallicae* by a single encounter with the man against whom that work is directed: Edmund Burke. Mackintosh began his lectures by giving a blunt statement of his change of mind: 'It is my intention to profess publicly and unequivocally that I abhor, abjure, and forever renounce the French Revolution, with its sanguinary history, its abominable principles, and for ever execrable leaders.' The lectures caused a stir. In the audience was a man who had been an enthusiast for the Revolution, and who now swung violently to the other extreme under Mackintosh's influence: he was John Stoddart, later to become editor of *The Times* – and fated also to become closely involved with Hazlitt in personal ways. Stoddart made careful notes of Mackintosh's lectures and thereafter treated Mackintosh's views as if they were holy writ.

Hazlitt himself made no comment on Mackintosh at the time of the lectures. He was keeping his powder dry until publication of his *Principles of Human Action* six years later, in 1805, where he pronounces that Mackintosh was 'no doubt a man of very clear understanding, of an imposing elocution, a very able disputant, and a very metaphysical lawyer, but by no means a profound metaphysician, not quite a Berkeley in subtlety of distinction'.[13] As for what Hazlitt saw as Mackintosh's political apostasy, it placed him in the same class as those others whom Hazlitt would never forgive for abandoning the hopes of the Revolution's blissful dawn.

The change of English opinion about the French Revolution had begun after the terrors and excesses of the years 1793–4. To begin with it was not merely liberals and reformists in England who had welcomed the Revolution, for many believed that the early events in France were a sign that the *ancien régime* prevailing there was being reformed in something like an English direction. But the Reign of Terror changed minds, and yet more minds were changed by the fact that the war started to go badly for England after 1796, when Spain formed an alliance with France and the British navy had to withdraw from the Mediterranean. French attempts to make a landing in Ireland, aided by Irish rebels, and the mutiny of the British fleets at Spithead and the Nore, made the English feel vulnerable and threatened. Anti-French opinion hardened further as a result. When Admiral Duncan beat the Dutch at Camperdown in October 1797, and Nelson destroyed the French fleet in the Nile in August 1798, there was belligerent rejoicing, and the government of William Pitt the Younger gathered widespread support for its war policy. This growth of war spirit, coupled with the government's repression of dissenting opinion, explains why Hazlitt, as a pro-Revolution diehard, was a member of a small and fast diminishing minority. When Napoleon seized power in November 1799 as First Consul, Hazlitt was one of very few to welcome the event.

Hazlitt's mixture of interests in painting and philosophy appears rather quaintly in a letter to his family, written on 16 December 1799 after he returned to London from a visit to Wem. He told his family that he had seen some enchanting views on the road, which he proposed to turn into little landscapes, from memory, when his painting equipment – left behind to be sent by the carrier – reached him in London. Then he added, 'When I looked back on the road to the Lea Hills, and saw how dim, and low they grew, and how small the objects upon them appeared, and recollected, that you were still further off, I wondered at the distinct Idea I had of you all: and yet I still recollect you as I saw you last in the parlour at breakfast.'[14] His letter also shows that he was having to live very economically. He made his return journey to London by walking part of the way, travelling on the freezing outside of a coach part of the way, and rationing the supplies of food he had brought from home. By this means he managed to limit the expense of the journey to forty-three shillings. (If it cost over two pounds to travel in this skimping way from Wem to London, one can imagine how little William senior's £30 a year was worth.) Hazlitt had been too cold to pause at Oxford to look at the colleges, and his seat on the outside of the coach was hideously uncomfortable – he had been 'very much shook on the coach box and wore out my gloves; and bruised my hands by the rubbing of the iron rail, which I was obliged to keep fast hold of, to prevent my being thrown from my seat.' Nevertheless he described himself as being in good spirits, satisfied with the scenery, and not without a philosophical reflection or two to report, as usual.

Hazlitt was in London for the first six months of 1800, as attested by references in Godwin's diary, living with John and working at his painting. In the summers of 1800 and 1801 he travelled in the provinces to find custom, chiefly in Liverpool and Manchester, using Wem as a base. As a way of establishing his professional credentials he decided to enter a picture for a Royal Academy exhibition, and to that end spent the closing months of 1801 in Wem painting a portrait of his father. During the work on this picture, which brought father and son together for long quiet hours, they recovered some of the intimacy they had lost after Hazlitt left Hackney New College. Hazlitt well knew that his father 'would rather I should have written a sermon than painted like Rembrandt or like Raphael'; but as the preacher sat in his chapel, reading Shaftesbury's *Characteristics* while his son painted him, he began to enjoy the process, and to take an interest in what Hazlitt was achieving by it. William senior 'was then in a green old age,' Hazlitt wrote, 'with strong-marked features, and scarred with the small-pox. I drew [him] with a broad light crossing the face, looking down, with spectacles on, reading. The book was Shaftesbury's Characteristics, in a fine old binding, with Gribelin's etchings. My father would as lieve it had been any other book; but for him to read was to be content, was "riches fineless". The sketch promised well; and I set to work to finish it, determined to spare no time or pains. My father was willing to sit as long as I pleased; for there is a natural desire in the mind of man to sit for one's picture, to be the object of continued attention, to have one's likeness multiplied; and besides his satisfaction in the picture, he had some pride in the artist ... Those winter days, with the gleams of sunshine coming through the chapel-windows, and cheered by the notes of the robin-redbreast in our garden (that "ever in the haunch of winter sings") – as my afternoon's work drew to a close, – were among the happiest of my life.' He was delighted if he managed to render the roughness of the skin, the 'pearly tone of a vein', a sense of the blood circulating under the shadows of one side of the face. When he succeeded in any of these ways, he records, 'I thought my fortune made; or rather it was already more than made, in my fancying that I might one day be able to say with

Correggio, "*I also am a painter!*" It was an idle thought, a boy's conceit; but it did not make me less happy at the time.'[15]

Hazlitt sent the picture 'with a throbbing heart' to compete for selection in the Exhibition, and was overjoyed when it was chosen. It pleased him to see it hanging beside a portrait of a gentleman called the Hon. Mr George Skeffington. The only thing that the two portrayed subjects had in common, Hazlitt observed, was that they both looked like very good-natured men.

Hazlitt wrote about painting his father's portrait twenty years after the event. It was not the only portrait he made of him, and in this reminiscence he conflates two different occasions; for he says that when he had at last finished the canvas, he propped it up to gaze at it in the dimming evening light in the chapel, and then went for a walk, where he saw 'the evening star set over a poor man's cottage'. It was, he says, the day that news of the Battle of Austerlitz came, and he looked at the star with 'other thoughts and feelings than I shall ever have again', for he then still had hopes that Napoleon would liberate Europe. But the Battle of Austerlitz took place in December 1805, and Hazlitt's portrait of his father reading Shaftesbury was exhibited in London in 1802. The point does not much matter; Hazlitt's nostalgic purpose never depended on accuracy of dates and places. In writing, although not in painting, he was of Reynolds's view about where perfection lies: namely, in impressions that capture a larger truth.

Acceptance by the Royal Academy gave Hazlitt a boost. He had himself carried the portrait of his father to town, and in the early months of the year lodged with John and visited the theatre, seeing Mrs Siddons in *The Winter's Tale* and Mrs Jordan in *The Wedding Day*. Mrs Siddons played Hermoine 'with true monumental dignity and noble passion', and Autolycus was played by Jack Bannister, whom Hazlitt had long admired for his 'life and laughter and joy' in comic parts. But necessity beckoned, so he resumed his provincial travels in quest of commissions, finding himself in Manchester in the spring of 1802 with scarcely any money. 'I once lived on coffee (as an experiment) for a fortnight together, while I was finishing the copy of a half-length portrait of a Manchester manufacturer, who had died worth a plum. I rather slurred over the coat, which was a reddish brown, "of formal cut", to receive my five guineas, with which I went to market myself, and dined on sausages and mashed potatoes, and while they were getting ready, and I could hear them hissing in the pan, read a volume of *Gil Blas*, containing the account of the fair Aurora. This was in the days of my youth. Gentle reader, do not smile! Neither Monsieur de Very, nor Louis XVIII, over an oyster-paté, nor Apicius himself, ever understood the meaning of the word *luxury*, better than I did at that moment!'[16] As was generally the case, Hazlitt wrote from experience; the essay in which these words occur is called 'On the Want of Money'. Equally characteristically, his recollections of this tour focus chiefly on what he read between commissions or – more frequently – as he vainly waited for commissions: in addition to the picaresque Spanish tale *Gil Blas* (an old favourite) he read for the first time Elizabeth Inchbald's *Simple Story*, which obliged him to go out for a walk to 'escape from one of the tenderest parts, in order to return to it again with double relish. An old crazy hand-organ was playing Robin Adair, a summer-shower dropped manna on my head, and slaked my feverish thirst of happiness. Her heroine, Miss Milner, was at my side.'[17] The passing reference to a summer-shower shows that he spent months in Manchester. That he records them as months of much enjoyed and fondly remembered reading is pure essence of Hazlitt, who took every opportunity to recall how he was – and therefore how the world seemed to him – when he was young: never happier than when reading, deeply in love with the heroines of books and moved to tears by their fate; full of youthful hopes for liberty and progress abroad, and success in painting and philosophy for himself; and full of longing for a woman like one of Mrs Inchbald's heroines, or perhaps like Mrs Inchbald herself, to love and be loved by. And of course it all seemed possible then, to the twenty-one year old painter-philosopher; it was fruit still waiting to be plucked from the bough. 'I have had more pleasure in reading the adventures of a novel (and perhaps in changing situations with the hero) than I ever had in my own. I do not think anyone can feel much happier – a greater degree of heart's ease – than I used to feel in reading Tristram Shandy, and Peregrine Pickle, and Tom Jones, and the Tatler, and Gil Blas of Santillane, and Werter, and Boccaccio. It was some years after that I read the last, but his tales "Dallied with the innocence of love,/Like the old Time" ... Mrs Inchbald was always a great favourite with me. There is the true soul of woman breathing from what she writes, as much as if you heard her voice. It is as if Venus had written books.'[18]

He moved on to Liverpool, and there painted a portrait of his father's friend, the Reverend Samuel Shepherd of Gateacre. He did not much enjoy revisiting the scene of his boyhood pleasures, for this time he found that Liverpudlians 'would persuade you that your merchant and manufacturer is your only gentleman and scholar'.[19] While there he called on an artist whose works he admired, Daniel Stringer, only to find to his dismay that Stringer had given up his interest in art in favour of drinking country ale with country squires.

*

The Liverpool visit proved, however, exceedingly fortunate, for while there Hazlitt met a wealthy industrialist called Joseph Railton, who wished to decorate his parlour with copies of Old Master paintings from the Louvre, and he commissioned Hazlitt to go to Paris to make them. This was a wonderful stroke of luck for Hazlitt. The Peace of Amiens had been concluded between England and France earlier in the year (at the end of March 1802), since when scores of English visitors had been flooding across the Channel, sending back excited reports of, among other things, the treasures at the Louvre. Napoleon's conquests had brought as booty an immense collection of Europe's finest works of art to Paris, providing an unequalled opportunity for the enthusiast.

Hazlitt was delighted. To prepare for his task he got hold of a catalogue of the newly gathered Louvre collection and pored over it. 'The pictures, the names of the painters, seemed to relish in the mouth,' he wrote seventeen years later. He read the descriptions of the paintings over and over again, 'with fond expectancy, and filled up the imaginary outline with whatever I could conceive of grace and dignity, and an antique *gusto* – all but equal to the original.'

This was not the only notable circumstance associated with Hazlitt's Liverpool visit, for it had romantic complications too. At some point Hazlitt might have nourished tender feelings for one of the daughters of the Reverend Mr Shepherd of Gateacre, but on this occasion he fell in love with Mr Railton's daughter.[20] His brother had painted a miniature of her on ivory some years before, capturing her delicate beauty. There is little direct allusion to the affair in Hazlitt's writings, but any number of indirect allusions denote it. When he set off for France in October 1802 he hoped that fulfilling Mr Railton's commission might bring other fulfilments in its wake. If so, he was disappointed – but the experience of Paris more than compensated.

Mr Railton had asked for five copies; Hazlitt brought back eleven, suggesting that once he had won the Railton commission he was able to get others. One of the copies was made as an act of kindness. Passing through London on his way to France he visited Northcote, and found the painter kneeling on the floor of his studio intently examining a print of Titian's *Ippolito de' Medici*, calling it 'one of the finest pictures in the whole world' – in agreement with Opie, who in similar vein described it as the best portrait ever painted. Since it was among the Louvre booty Hazlitt offered to bring Northcote a copy of it, and Northcote delightedly accepted.

Armed with letters of introduction from Thomas Holcroft and Robert Freebairn to the painter J. F. L. Mérimée – father of the writer Prosper Mérimée – Hazlitt set out in mid-October 1802, taking with him two of his own canvases for purposes of comparison and study. One of them was his Old Woman. Twenty years later he described his arrival on 'the laughing shores of France' in somewhat different terms from those used in the letters he wrote home at the time. In his retrospective account Calais was full of 'novelty and delight' and its busy murmur was 'like wine and oil poured into my ears'. He enjoyed walking among the French because they were free, 'not cast down and chained to the foot of arbitrary thrones'.[21] In the letter written at the time, dated 16 October, he said, 'Calais is a miserable place in itself, but the remains of the fortifications about it are very beautiful.' Coincidentally, Wordsworth had returned to France six weeks before Hazlitt, hoping to find a deterioration in the aspect of the French. In 1790 he had heard 'a homeless sound of joy in the sky', now he found the greeting 'good day, Citizen!' hollow to his ears. Possibly he was disappointed, as many English visitors were, to find France so prosperous and peaceful despite the war. He and Hazlitt did not meet in Paris, which was just as well, given the distance that had begun to grow between their attitudes to matters French.

Hazlitt met an Englishman in Calais called Lovelace. The literary association of the name – the male protagonist of Richardson's *Clarissa* is so called – immediately attracted him. Lovelace told him an anecdote that reinforced his admiration for Napoleon. This Lovelace had a nephew of the same name, an army officer, who was present at a reception in Paris shortly after the Treaty of Amiens was signed. Napoleon's standard question on being introduced to a military officer was, 'Where have you served, Sir?' but on meeting Lovelace he said, 'I perceive your name, Sir, is the same as that of the hero of Richardson's romance.' Hazlitt was delighted, and thought to himself: 'Here was a Consul!'[22]

Hazlitt travelled to Paris on foot. His tongue stuck to his palate as he tried out his French, and he told his family: 'I am so perplexed with French that I can hardly recollect a word of English.' His route took him through one of the least attractive parts of the country, and one of the least flourishing, so he saw beggars and noted the hard life of the peasantry. But closer to Paris prosperity increased. He was especially struck by the beauty of the vineyards. 'They have a most delightful appearance,' he wrote home, 'they look richer than any kind of agricultural production that we have in England, particularly the red vines.' Paris itself, however, was to begin with a disagreeable shock. London had wide streets, open squares, generously proportioned raised sidewalks, orderly though crowded and bustling traffic, and fairly hygienic arrangements for the emptying of slop-buckets and chamber-pots. Of course it also had its narrow slums and alleys, the 'rookeries', where these niceties were not observed; but they were avoidable regions for all but those who lived there, whereas the whole of Paris seemed like a London rookery. The narrow streets had no sidewalks, and were closed in by high buildings from any of whose windows at any moment the contents of chamber pots might shower down. The shops were greasy holes in the walls; butchers', fishmongers' and greengrocers' carts stood propped at the doorways of buildings, which latter were often enough either in a state of decay or had never been finished. The streets everywhere were claustrophobic, fetid, dark and cluttered. Pedestrians had to fight their way along the filthy gutters running down the middle of them, in peril of being bowled over by wagons and coaches, cabriolets and hackney-carriages, and small hand-carts pulled by mastiff dogs. Hazlitt had heard admiring things said of the way Parisian women walked, with their light tripping gait; he concluded that they stepped like that in order not to fall into the dirt of the round slippery cobblestones.

If Hazlitt thought that his room in the Hôtel Coq-Héron, in the Rue Coq-Héron near the Palais-Royal, would be a refuge from this tumult, he was disappointed. It was small, dark and cold. The only place he could find light and air, and an escape from the general squalor, was along the banks of the Seine, which – in the environs of the Louvre and Tuileries – he thought was 'much more splendid than any part of London'.[23]

On his first full day, after securing his 'card of security' from the police, he hastened to the Louvre, only to be baulked by the 'Republican doorkeepers, with their rough voices and affectation of equality', who would not let him into the gallery where the old masters hung, and of which he could only catch painfully tantalizing glimpses by peering through the door that barred his way. It was 'like looking out of purgatory into paradise – from Poussin's noble mellow-looking landscapes to where Rubens hung out his gaudy banner, and down the glimmering vista to the rich jewels of Titian and the Italian school'. After a while someone whispered that the only way to get in was to bribe the guards – which he duly did, and so entered paradise. 'It was *un beau jour* to me. I marched delighted through a quarter of a mile of the proudest efforts of the mind of man, a whole creation of genius, a universe of art! I ran the gauntlet of all the schools from the bottom to the top; and in the end got admitted into the inner room, where they had been repairing some of their greatest works. Here the Transfiguration, the St Peter Martyr, and the St Jerome of Domenichino stood on the floor, as if they had bent their knees, like camels stooping, to unlade their riches to the spectator. On one side, on an easel, stood Hippolito de Medici (a portrait by Titian) with a boar-spear in his hand, looking through those he saw, till you turned away from the keen glance; and thrown together in heaps were landscapes of the same hand, green pastoral hills and vales, and shepherds piping to their mild mistresses underneath the flowering shade.' It was the beginning of a deliriously happy sojourn. 'Here, for four months, I strolled and studied, and daily heard the warning sounds – "*Quatre heures passées, il faut fermer, Citoyens*" (ah! why did they ever change their style?) muttered in coarse provincial French; and brought away with me some loose draughts and fragments, which I have been forced to part with, like drops of life-blood, for "hard money". How often, thou tenantless mansion of godlike magnificence – how often has my heart since gone a pilgrimage to thee!'[24]

He called on Mérimée, who promised to accompany him the next day to get permission to copy anything he wished, and to help him buy paints and canvases. That night he wrote to his family telling them what he had seen and felt: his excitement at the historical paintings by Rubens, and his disappointment at finding that some of the best Titians were temporarily unavailable because they were 'put by to be copied'. Within a few days – as a result of Mérimée's help – he was at work copying one of those Titian portraits, starting with a complete sketch of the head, which took him three hours. On the basis of his preliminary survey he had decided to copy two other Titians, two Van Dycks, and a Raphael, all of them portraits. If he could not get them moved to the copying room, he wrote, he would, either by Mérimée's influence or bribery of the keepers, copy an alternative Titian, a Guercino, and some landscapes.

It turned out that only four days in the week were available for copying. On Fridays the Louvre was closed for cleaning, and the weekends were devoted to public viewing. So from Monday to Thursday Hazlitt went to the museum at about nine thirty or ten o'clock, and usually painted until half past three or four, sometimes longer. He resolved to employ the enforcedly long weekends in making copies of his copies for his own use, and in painting a self-portrait after the style of Titian's *Ippolito*. The result is reproduced on the front cover of this book. It is his only self-portrait, and because it is a study made in solitude at the central point of his efforts to be a painter, it is a striking piece of biographical evidence. It shows his twenty-five year old face with its dark, intense, single-minded gaze, expressive of vulnerability, intelligence, pride and loneliness. It is the face of a young man prone to shyness and romantic dreams, but at the same time strongly confident in his judgement. He later wrote that a Dissenter upbringing was apt to make people intellectually arrogant, a fault he had had to school out of himself. Something of that sense of superior mental power is discernible in the haunting broad-browed face with its luminously searching eyes.

In a letter to his family he wrote, 'There are great numbers of people in the rooms (most of them *English*) every day, and I was afraid at first that this would confuse and hinder me; but I found on beginning to copy that I was too occupied in my work to attend much to, or to care at all about what was passing around me; or if this had any effect upon me indirectly, it was to make me more attentive to what I was about.'

In a postscript to this letter he says, 'I saw Buonaparte.' It is a laconic report; he does not say where he saw him, or how. Napoleon, to whom he applied the phrase 'the god of my idolatry' and about whom, at the end of his own life, he wrote a large justificatory biography, was too big a subject to require any extended comment. In another letter soon afterwards he said he had not seen Napoleon close up. It was something of a compensation, however, that not long afterwards he met Napoleon's brother Lucien Buonaparte.

The crowds in the Louvre not only did not bother Hazlitt, they pleased him by providing admirers for his work. One afternoon, after finishing his main work for the day, he took a small canvas and began to sketch a head from a large historical picture. He was not sure he could manage it, but attempted it as an exercise none the less. It was a side-face that reminded him of his father. Within a couple of hours he had produced a good copy, which so pleased him that he decided to leave it in sketch form. He worked so swiftly and effectively that an Englishman, wandering the gallery with a group of family and friends, told him in French that he was doing very well. Hazlitt answered in English, to which the man, in surprise, responded, 'Upon my word, Sir, you get on with great spirit and boldness: you do us great credit, I am sure.' Later he returned to ask Hazlitt how long it had taken him to draw the head, and said he was the more pleased with his judgement for not having known him to be a fellow-countryman.

Another man asked him if he taught painting in oil. Hazlitt replied, 'I stood more in need of instruction myself; that that sort of rapid sketching was what I did better than anything else; and that, after the first hour or two, I generally made my pictures worse and worse, the more pains I took with them.' He then adds, 'However, seriously, I was much pleased with this kind of notice, as however confident I may be of the real merit of my work, it is not always so clear that it is done in a way to please most other people. This same sketch is certainly a very singular thing, as I do not believe there are ten people in the world who could do it in the same way.'[25]

Among the many English tourists who passed through the galleries was the celebrated Whig politician Charles James Fox, leader of the opposition to the Pitt government in the House of Commons. He came to the Louvre in company with John Opie among others. Hazlitt listened attentively to his comments, which he found unaffected and well-judged, and studied his appearance: 'hair grown grey in the service of the public, with a face pale and furrowed with thought, doing honour to the English character as its best representative'.[26] He also saw the hugely wealthy collector William Beckford of Fonthill Abbey, looking thin and wan in a loose greatcoat, who reputedly offered Napoleon a prince's ransom of two thousand guineas for Titian's *St Peter Martyr*, a painting Hazlitt passionately admired.

It was not only English compatriots who applauded him. The French copyists began to praise him too, after first being unfriendly. With a growing sense of satisfaction in his progress Hazlitt felt a growing assurance of taste. His admiration for the Italian masters began to outweigh his admiration for the Flemish masters. At the outset he looked at Reynolds's *Marquis of Granby* next to Van Dyck's *Charles I*, and saw that whereas the latter was beautifully rendered in its details and yet excellent as a whole, with 'all the lightness, distinctness and transparency of objects seen in the open air', the former 'looked heavy and muddled, from the mode of heaping on the colours, and the determination to produce effects alone, without attention to the subordinate details defeated itself'.[27] One of the canvases he proposed to copy was Van Dyck's portrait of Cardinal Bentivoglio. But he soon decided not to, because 'after Titian's portraits, there was a want of interest in Vandyke's which I could not get over.'[28] Before long 'Nothing would serve my turn but heads like Titian – Titian expression, Titian complexions, Titian dresses.'[29] Likewise Rubens's allegories had collapsed into 'wool or cotton' next to the gigantic Veronese canvas of *The Marriage at Cana*, whose texture 'was not wool or cotton, but stuff, jewels, flesh, marble, air, whatever composed the essence of the varied subjects, in endless relief and truth of handling'. This painting impressed Hazlitt by its size and power; it covered almost the whole of one side of a large room in the Louvre, 'and it seemed as if that side of the apartment was thrown open, and you looked out at the open sky, at buildings, marble pillars, galleries with people in them, emperors, female slaves, Turks, negroes, musicians, all the famous painters of the time, the tables loaded with viands, goblets, and dogs under them – a sparkling, overwhelming confusion, a bright, unexpected reality'.[30]

Hazlitt worked hard and consistently. He copied, among other things, Lana's *Death of Clorinda* for Railton, Titian's *Portrait of his Mistress* and *Ippolito de Medici* (twice), a *Holy Family*, which he described as 'one of the most beautiful things in the world', and a *Transfiguration*, which he worshipped, and the copy of which he thought his best – both by Raphael. But he did not work to the exclusion of all else. He walked all over Paris, attended the theatre, read Racine with a tutor (in French) and Shakespeare, and got to know some of the English residents, including his brother's friend John Rickman, the artist Richard Duppa, and the Italian artist Domenico Pellegrini, whom he had already met in England beforehand. Pellegrini introduced him to a most extraordinary man, the gifted but mad artist-collector Richard Cosway, whose home was more 'fairy palace' than house, filled with the oddest assortment of 'art, antiquarianism, and *virtu*, jumbled together in the richest disorder, dusty, shadowy, obscure ... with copies of Old Masters, cracked and damaged, that he touched and re-touched with his own hand, and yet swore they were the genuine, pure originals'. He claimed to have among his bric-à-brac mementoes of Abélard and Héloïse (the crucifix Abélard prayed to, a lock of Héloïse's hair), the dagger used to stab the Duke of Buckingham, Leonardo da Vinci's first sketch for La Gioconda, a Titian profile, a royal Egyptian mummy, a phoenix's feather, a piece of wood from Noah's Ark. But none of these exotica was as strange as Cosway himself. Despite the fact that he claimed to have conversed with at least one person of the Trinity, Hazlitt thought him delightful, and especially liked his wife Maria, also an artist, whom he considered 'the most lady-like of Englishwomen'.

Maria Cosway was the occasion of Hazlitt's meeting Lucien Buonaparte. He encountered them strolling arm-in-arm down the street, Lucien – a 'spirited, dashing-looking young man' – wearing a light drab-coloured greatcoat.[31] Hazlitt claimed to be the only person in England ever to read Lucien's two-volume poem *Charlemagne*, which Sir Walter Scott refused to translate on the grounds of its author's name and connections – 'Such was the petty spite of this understrapper of greatness,' remarked Hazlitt, who made a point of avoiding a meeting with Scott when in Scotland years later. Despite greatly admiring Scott's novels, he could not bear his politics, and chose to keep the man and his works separate.

Hazlitt was a scholar of human nature as well as of philosophy and art. He was intrigued by the French, whom he found lively and entertaining, but shallow; this seemed especially true of the French art students in the Louvre, who struck him as oblivious to the beauty, depth and power of the magnificent works around them. He was amazed to see a student copying Titian's *Mistress* by dividing his canvas into regular squares, and, starting at the top right-hand corner, filling in each square by turns. Another young man spent nearly three months sketching Leonardo's *Virgin of the Rocks* in pencil, very desultorily, wandering about the galleries, loitering in the sculpture room, fiddling with his drawing for a while to emend and correct, then drifting off again to stand over the fire 'for an hour together'. 'You see a solitary French artist in the Louvre copying a Raphael or Rubens, standing on one leg, not quite sure what he is about,' he remarked.[32] He did however think that with respect to certain subjects the French had more insight than the English. He overheard a conversation between an Englishman and a Frenchman in which, commenting on a story about a man who courted his wife for thirteen years before marrying her, the Englishman said, 'At least he would be acquainted with her character,' to which the Frenchman replied, 'No, not at all; for the very next day she might turn out the very reverse of the character that she had appeared in during all the preceding time.' Hazlitt remarked that he 'could not help admiring the superior sagacity' of the Frenchman.[33]

In the cold of early February 1803 Hazlitt took a seat in the diligence for Calais on the first stage of his journey home. In his pocket was a certificate signed by M. Derron, the Louvre's Director General, dated '12 Pluviose' (3 January 1803), listing the paintings he had copied. The experience had been a profound one; nearly two decades later he wrote: 'long after I returned, and even still, I sometimes dream of being there again – of asking for the old pictures – and not finding them, or finding them changed or faded from what they were, I cry myself awake.'[34]

Hazlitt probably delivered his commissions (necessary to collecting the remaining part of the fees for them) fairly promptly after returning to England, which meant going to Liverpool – and therefore of course making a detour to Wem to see his family. But by late March he was again in London, on the 22nd dining at Godwin's house where Coleridge and Holcroft were present, and with them an odd but fascinating couple, a man and his sister, friends of Coleridge since their schooldays. They were Charles and Mary Lamb, and this meeting marked the beginning of Hazlitt's longest and greatest friendship.

# CHAPTER FIVE

# Art and Metaphysics

## 1803–1806

CHARLES LAMB was thin and shy, with one blue eye and one brown eye. He had a stammer, and invariably wore plain dark old-fashioned clothing that made him look like a Quaker. He was twenty-eight years of age when Hazlitt met him, just three years older than Hazlitt himself. The two had already heard of one another from their mutual friend Coleridge. Coleridge and Lamb were once schoolfellows at Christ's Hospital, and their friendship had remained close ever since. Whenever Coleridge was in town he and Lamb met for cheerful tipsy evenings at a pub near Fleet Street called the Salutation & Cat.[1]

Hazlitt was immediately drawn to the charm of Lamb's conversation, and the richness of his literary knowledge, and he was amused by Lamb's whimsical, oblique way of thinking, and his always having, as Hazlitt put it, a *bon-mot* in his mouth. At one point during their first meeting at Godwin's dinner-table the guests began 'disputing fiercely which was the best – *Man as he was, or man as he is to be*'. Lamb said, 'Give me man as he is *not* to be.' Two decades later, in 1823, Hazlitt wrote, 'This saying was the beginning of a friendship between us, which I believe still continues.'[2]

Lamb lived with his older sister Mary, who was subject to periodic fits of madness. In one of her fits she killed her mother by stabbing her with a pair of scissors. Mary had in fact been trying to kill the family's maid, whom her mother, in turn, was trying to protect. Lamb was devoted to Mary, and dedicated himself to her care. Neither of them married, and they stayed together happily until his death. They had been brought up in the Inner Temple where their father was a barrister's clerk. On leaving Christ's Hospital Lamb took a clerkship in the East India Company, supporting the whole family after his father's retirement.

Lamb was well suited to a friendship with Hazlitt. He had a lively whimsical punning humour, and an enormous appetite for books. He is the other giant of the essay, but unlike his partner in that eminence – Hazlitt – his work is characteristically light, fay, amusing, private, enter-

taining, miniature, mannered, whereas Hazlitt's is powerful, bold, nostalgic, angry, ironic, heavy-punching, philosophical. Where one is a curricle
drawn by dapple greys, the other is an express train thundering through
the night. Or to vary the metaphor with equal anachronism: Lamb is the
Jane Austen of the essay, Hazlitt its Dostoevsky.

At that dinner, or on some date close to it, Coleridge and Hazlitt
discussed ways for the latter to make profitable use of his philosophical
interests. The idea came to them that he might abridge the vast and then
famous philosophical treatise by Abraham Tucker, *The Light of Nature
Pursued*, and that Coleridge would write an introduction to it. Coleridge
wrote a letter for Godwin to use in finding a publisher: 'A friend of mine,
every way calculated by his Taste and prior Studies for such a work is
willing to abridge & systematise that work from 8 to 2 volumes,' he wrote.
'I would prefix to it an Essay containing the whole substance of the first
Volume of Hartley, entirely defecated from all the corpuscular hypotheses –
with new illustrations – & give my name to the Essay. Likewise, I would
revise every sheet of the Abridgement.' Clearly the idea was to help Hazlitt
into print under Coleridge's aegis. 'You would essentially serve a young
man of profound Genius and original mind, who wishes to get his *Sabine*
Subsistence by some employment from the Booksellers, while he is employing the remainder of his Time in nursing up his Genius for the destiny,
which he believes appurtenant to it.'[3]

Nothing came of the idea immediately, but Hazlitt carried it into effect
four years later, in 1807, without Coleridge's participation. Coleridge's
next attempt to help involved persuading his rich friend Sir George Beaumont to commission portraits by Hazlitt of Coleridge and his son Hartley.
This gave Hazlitt the opportunity to travel to the Lake District, where the
poets now lived, and to spend the summer and part of the autumn of 1803
with them. He stayed first at Keswick with the Coleridges and while there
painted himself portraits of Hartley, Coleridge and Wordsworth. He then
moved to Grasmere as Wordsworth's guest, leaving the portraits at Keswick
to dry. They were on open exhibition to anyone who visited the house,
with the result that they received a flood of amateur reviews, all of them,
as Coleridge wrote to tell Wordsworth, negative. Sir George and Lady
Beaumont complained that Hazlitt pictured Wordsworth as a philosopher
rather than a poet. Mrs Wilkinson from Ormathwaite, wife of a painter,
swore that Hazlitt made Wordsworth look twenty years older than his
true age, and that Coleridge not only appeared equally old but 'lank' as
well. Coleridge reported that his children Hartley and Derwent recognized
Wordsworth in his portrait, but that they said that it was not as handsome
as he was in reality. Mary Stamper, the Coleridges' housekeeper, said it

was 'very *leek*, but it is not canny enough' – to which she then added, 'though Mr Wordsworth is not a *canny* man, to be sure.'

As to his own portrait Coleridge wrote: 'Every single person cries out! – What a likeness! – But the face is too long! you have a round face! – Hazlitt knows this: but he will not alter it. Why? – because the Likeness with him is a secondary Consideration – he wants it to be a fine Picture.'[4] To Southey, soon to join them at the Lakes, Coleridge wrote that 'young Hazlitt has taken masterly Portraits of me & Wordsworth, very much in the manner of Titian's Portraits – he wishes to take Lamb – & you'.[5] Southey arrived shortly afterwards and saw the pictures for himself, which prompted him to write an amusing account of them to Richard Duppa, Hazlitt's painter friend in Paris. Hazlitt had, he said, portrayed Wordsworth in such a dismal state of mind 'that one of his friends, on seeing it, exclaimed, "At the gallows – deeply affected by his deserved fate – yet determined to die like a man!" ' Writing to Coleridge he remarked that Hazlitt had likewise made '[you] look as if you were on your trial, and certainly had stolen the horse; but then you did it cleverly.'[6]

More than a decade later, in 1816, Wordsworth spoke to Lamb about Hazlitt's portrait of him, saying that one of his brothers had been 'literally *struck* with the strength of the signboard likeness; but never, until that moment, had he conceived that so much of the diabolical lurked under the innocent features of his quondam playmate, and respected Friend and dear Brother'. By that time Hazlitt and Wordsworth were enemies, and the latter made sport of the fact that Hazlitt had pictured him and Coleridge as devils: 'Devils may be divided into two large classes, first, the malignant and mischievous – those that are bent upon all of the evil-doing that is prayed against in the Litany; and secondly those which have so thorough a sense of their own damnation, and the misery consequent upon it, as to be incapable of harbouring a thought injurious to the tranquillity of others. The pencil of W. H. is potent in delineating both kinds of physiognomy. My portrait was an example of the one; and a Picture of Coleridge, now in existence at Keswick (mine has been burnt) is of the other. This piece of art is not producible for fear of fatal consequences to married Ladies, but is kept in a private room, as a special treat to those who may wish to sup upon horrors.'[7]

If Coleridge and Hazlitt hoped that Sir George Beaumont would become Hazlitt's patron, they were quickly and conclusively disappointed. The obstacle appeared when both were dining at Sir George's house in Keswick, and the conversation turned to the political essayist Junius. Coleridge attacked Junius with such venom that Hazlitt, after a time, felt obliged to defend him. Beaumont was annoyed with Hazlitt not only for defending

Junius, whose principles he thoroughly disliked, but for quarrelling with Coleridge, whom he thoroughly admired. The following morning Coleridge apologetically told Hazlitt that, actually, he was an admirer of Junius – he showed Hazlitt his copy of Junius's essays, heavily annotated – but that he had not wished to offend Sir George by revealing the fact – and he and Hazlitt ought not to quarrel about a writer whose virtues they both recognized: 'I am come to show you,' he said, 'how foolish it is for persons who respect each other to dispute warmly, for after all they will probably think the same.' Whether or not this was Hazlitt's first taste of Coleridge's capacity for trimming – for adjusting his views to the company (Sir George was a High Tory) – it was one reason why Hazlitt and he began to drift apart before long.

There was another occasion on which Hazlitt offended a prospective patron by speaking out when he would have gained more by holding his tongue. He records that he had once met 'a distinguished patron of art and rising merit at a little distance from Liverpool', from whom he received 'every mark of attention and politeness' until one day they disagreed over the merits of Pope's 'Ode on St Cecilia's Day'. The man was William Roscoe, banker and Whig, whose portrait Hazlitt was painting at the time. Roscoe remarked that nothing in English corresponded to the severity of the Italian ode, except perhaps Dryden's 'Alexander's Feast', and Pope's 'St Cecilia'. Hazlitt wryly records that 'I could no longer contain my desire to display my smattering in criticism, and began to maintain that Pope's ode was, as it appeared to me, far from an example of severity in writing. I soon perceived what I had done . . .'[8]

Hazlitt claimed in retrospect that Coleridge had lost him a patron, which is a not wholly fair, but neither an inaccurate, description of what happened. It is not wholly fair, because no doubt Sir George would have discovered Hazlitt's political views soon enough, by other means or in other conversations, and that would have ended their relationship anyway. Moreover, Coleridge – to his credit – had been trying to help Hazlitt; Sir George would not even have been on the cards as a patron for Hazlitt without Coleridge's efforts. But Hazlitt's claim is not strictly inaccurate, either, because Coleridge's pusillanimity was the immediate occasion for the breach.

When Hazlitt first went to meet Coleridge and Wordsworth in the West Country five years earlier, he had stopped at an inn to dry himself after a downpour, and had read Bernardin de Saint-Pierre's *Paul and Virginia* in one all-night sitting. This romance, an artful but saccharin and religiose exercise in primitive naturalism, is now scarcely readable, but it was so famous in Hazlitt's day that everyone read it – and inevitably it was discussed by the party at the Lakes. Coleridge said that he thought it demonstrated the 'gross indelicacy of French manners and the entire corruption of their imagination' because of a scene near the end where the heroine 'turns away from a person on board the sinking vessel, that offers to save her life, because he has thrown off his clothes to assist him in swimming'. Coleridge asked: 'Was this a time to think of such a circumstance?' A few days later, while sailing with Wordsworth in his boat on Grasmere, Hazlitt remarked that he thought Wordsworth must have borrowed the idea for his *Poems on the Naming of Places* from the local inscriptions of the same kind in *Paul and Virginia*. Wordsworth hotly denied this, and defended his own originality – which, Hazlitt later drily commented, was easy for him, because 'whatever *he* added or omitted would inevitably be worth all that any one else had done, and contain the marrow of the sentiment'.⁹ At the same time, Hazlitt saw in Wordsworth's home at Grasmere some drafts which became part of the *Excursion* and the *Prelude*, and their striking beauty lived in his mind; he quoted them (imperfectly, because he was doing so from memory) in his own writings long before Wordsworth published them.

Coleridge's attempts to help Hazlitt were not unqualified. His frank estimate of Hazlitt appears in a letter to his friend and patron Thomas Wedgwood, written in the course of discussing the latter's plans to travel on the Continent. Europe was still at peace after the Treaty of Amiens, despite increasingly militaristic rumblings in an England alarmed by what the French were doing – for they were re-arming, extending their control in Piedmont, Switzerland and elsewhere, and interfering with British trade on the Continent. Despite that, resumption of war did not seem especially imminent, and Britons were still travelling to Paris and beyond. Wedgwood asked Coleridge to accompany him there, but Coleridge declined, perhaps for family reasons, but more likely because he was now so seriously addicted to opium that he was unwilling to live too intimately with friends in case they observed the fact. A mutual acquaintance of Coleridge and the Wedgwoods, one Richard Sharp, had passed through the Lakes and met Hazlitt, whom he liked, and had mentioned Hazlitt to Wedgwood as a possible companion. Hazlitt spoke French, had not long returned from Paris, and was as versed in literature as art. Wedgwood accordingly wrote to ask whether Coleridge shared Sharp's opinion about Hazlitt's suitability. The letter Coleridge sent in reply is the first full pen-portrait of the adult Hazlitt.

Coleridge told Wedgwood that Hazlitt 'is a thinking, observant, original man, of great power as a Painter of Character Portraits, & far more in the manner of the old Painters, than any living Artist; [he] is disinterested, an enthusiastic Lover of the great men, who have been before us – he says things that are his own in a way of his own – & tho' from habitual Shyness & the Outside and bearskin at least of misanthropy, he is strangely confused & dark in his conversation & delivers himself of almost all of his conceptions with a Forceps, yet he says more than any man, I ever knew, yourself only excepted, that is his own in a way of his own – & oftentimes when he has warmed his mind & the synovial juice has come out & spread over his joints, he will gallop for half an hour together with real Eloquence. He sends well-headed and well-feathered Thoughts straight forwards to the mark with a Twang of the Bow-string.' Then Coleridge added his reservations. 'If you should recommend him, as a Portrait-painter, I should be glad;' but 'to be your travelling-companion he is utterly unfit. His manners are 99 in 100 singularly repulsive – : brow-hanging, shoe-contemplative, *strange*.' Note that 'repulsive' here has its literal meaning: pushing others away, keeping them at bay, not inviting them to friendship (not, as we now use the expression, 'nauseating' or 'disgusting'). 'He is, I verily believe, kindly-natured – is very fond of, attentive to, & patient with, children – but he is jealous, gloomy, & of irritable Pride.' Then Coleridge added a remark which doubtless sank his chances with the Wedgwoods altogether: '& [he is] addicted to women, as objects of sexual Indulgence.'[10]

This frank sketch is illuminating. It conveys Hazlitt's shyness, and his instinctive manner of keeping others at a distance. The 'jealous' (prickly, rebarbative, introspective) mien Coleridge mentions is a recognizable continuation of Hazlitt's difficult and awkward adolescent behaviour as described in the pen-sketch by the Reverend Joseph Hunter quoted earlier. Nor, as events proved, was Coleridge wrong about Hazlitt's 'addiction to women, as objects of sexual Indulgence'. Hazlitt never made a secret of his interest in sex, nor of his employing the services of prostitutes, and he was not – as events soon confirmed – hesitant about trying his luck with country girls. But he was painfully shy with girls of his own class – the middle class – and above. He idealized and romanticized them, and found it next to impossible to integrate the idea of women as the objects of such love with the idea of women as sexual partners. This is a common enough problem, a characteristic of Christian societies chiefly, and even more so of those where Protestantism has been influential – for Christianity is a religion deeply uneasy about sex and the body, and finds little ground between the extremes of Madonna and unreformed Magdalen. Whatever the cause, for the most part Hazlitt sharply separated the ideal and the sexual in his attitudes to women, which was the source of his difficulties, and ultimately of the devastating tragedy of the famous, or more accurately infamous, passion he suffered later in life, as recorded in his *Liber Amoris*.

These facts, together with Coleridge's comment, suggest that Hazlitt probably began his regular liaisons with prostitutes and country girls rather early, while he was at Hackney College or before. London swarmed with prostitutes, and the unmarried pregnancy rate among country girls shows that the age was not a notably prudish one. If Hazlitt had not begun his sexual career in Wem or London then he had ample opportunity in Paris, for the arcades of the Palais-Royal, just round the corner from his lodging in the Rue Coq-Héron, was where the 'business of Venus' was conducted, by crowds of girls in abundant ringlets and nipple-revealing décolletage, who accosted men sauntering along the colonnades by twining an arm into theirs. He wrote, no doubt with these girls partly in mind, 'If I were a law-giver, and chose to meddle in such matters, I would ordain that no woman should expose her shape publicly, unless she were a prostitute ... the thin muslin vest drawn tight round the slender waist, following with nice exactness the undulations of the shape downwards, disclosing each full swell, each coy recess, obtruding on the eye each opening charm, the play of the muscles, the working of the thighs, and by the help of a walk, of which every step seems a gird, and which keeps the limbs strained to the utmost point, displaying all those graceful involutions of person, and all those powers of fascinating motion, of which the female form is susceptible – these moving pictures of lust and nakedness, against which the greasy imaginations of grooms and porters may rub themselves ... are the very same, whose mothers and grandmothers buried themselves under a pile of clothes, whose timid steps hardly touched the ground, whose eyes were constantly averted from the rude gaze of the men, and who almost blushed at their own shadows. "Of such we in romances read." '[11]

Here is Hazlitt's dichotomous view: the tender virtuous heroines of romance, contrasted with the lust-engendering half-naked women who should only be so clad if available for sex. But he was not hostile to the latter. Years later his friend P. G. Patmore noted how kind and familiar he was with the prostitutes in Whitehall, along which he walked daily between his house in Westminster and the Fleet Street offices of the journals he wrote for.[12] In 1808 he had what might have been an attack of venereal disease, during which he ruefully joked that he would have to 'give up wenching'. He never did. He freely acknowledged that he preferred 'humble beauties, servant-maids and shepherd-girls, with their red elbows, hard hands, black stockings and mob-caps' to women of more decided pretensions, whether ladies, blue-stockings, opera singers or actresses. 'I admire the Clementinas and Clarissas at a distance; the Pamelas and Fannys of Richardson and Fielding make my blood tingle. I have written love-letters to such in my time, *d'un pathétique à faire fendre les rochers*, and with about as much effect as if they had been addressed to a stone. The simpletons only laughed, and said that "those were not the sort of things to gain the affections".'[13]

Hazlitt was however no different from most men in finding a diet of casual sex fundamentally unsatisfying, because it lacks the warmth and intimacy that comes with mutual attachment. So although he did not hesitate to scratch his itches, he always yearned for love – love of an ideal, exquisite, refined kind; an exalted state such as is described in literature and pictured in art. When he felt romantically towards a woman he immediately became tongue-tied and stumbling, thereby inviting the opposite of what he craved, which was affection, sympathy, understanding, and permission to love. In that same summer of 1803, just as Coleridge was writing to Wedgwood about Hazlitt's frank interest in sex, Hazlitt was writing the following words in the manuscript draft of his first book: 'There is but one instance in which appetite hangs about a man as a perpetual clog and dead-weight upon the reason, namely the sexual appetite'; and he added, 'the selfish habit produced by this constant state of animal sensibility seems to have a direct counterpoise given it by nature in the mutual sympathy of the sexes.'[14] Mutual sympathy was, however, precisely what eluded him.

Thomas De Quincey, who became friendly with the Wordsworths about four years later, and who was never on social terms with Hazlitt, claimed that Hazlitt proposed to Dorothy Wordsworth during this summer of 1803. She was seven years older than Hazlitt, and if the story is true she did well to turn him down, not least in light of the animosity that was later to arise between him and her brother.

What is most interesting in Coleridge's word-portrait, however, is its account of Hazlitt's powerful intellect, and the fact that at this early juncture his prodigious abilities were still in search of their voice. He was then still trying to put his 'metaphysical discovery' onto paper (but by this time with more success; publication was only two years away), and at the same time equally labouring to conquer his diffidence in conversation. Swift wrote that a man of many ideas, who has a wide choice of means to express them, is quite likely to stammer and pause because the abundance of his thoughts clogs their exit – just as, he said, a crowded church empties slowly owing to the press of people. By contrast, a man of few ideas and few alternative ways of putting them speaks glibly and quickly, like an almost empty church whose small congregation disperses with ease. Hazlitt was always a crowded church, but he soon enough learned how to open his doors wide.

After a spell with the Wordsworths at Grasmere Hazlitt returned to Keswick, and on 24 October 1803 he, Coleridge and Southey walked through Borrowdale into Watendlath and then 'home to a late dinner'.[15] On 26 October Coleridge records that he had 'a most unpleasant dispute' with Wordsworth and Hazlitt on the subject of the Divine Wisdom, which they spoke of so 'irreverently' and 'malignantly' that they upset him deeply. He confided to his notebook that he might expect as much from Hazlitt, but not from Wordsworth; indeed Coleridge was so hurt by Wordsworth's behaviour that he could only write, in sorrow, 'but *thou*, dearest Wordsworth'. On 27 October he reported a long metaphysical discussion with Hazlitt: '[I resolved] the whole business of the origin of Evil satisfactorily to my own mind, & forced H. to confess, that the metaphysical argument reduced itself to this: Why did not infinite Power *always* & exclusively produce such Beings as in each moment of their Duration were infinite – why in short did not the Almighty create an absolute infinite number of Almighties?'[16]

Hazlitt's departure from the Lakes very soon thereafter was abrupt, prompted by an incident which amused Coleridge and Wordsworth at the time, but which, more than ten years later, they both attempted to represent as a sinister scandal, perhaps in revenge for what Hazlitt was by then writing about them – especially in Wordsworth's case, because he deeply resented Hazlitt's review of *The Excursion*. It involved a dalliance with a local girl which ended badly. The girl for some reason – by teasing him, or leading him on and then denying him – enraged Hazlitt and he, it seems, lifted her skirts and spanked her '*more puerum*', as Henry Crabb Robinson expressed it after hearing the story from Wordsworth. The phrase implies a spanking on the bottom as given to misbehaving schoolboys. In another recounting of the incident Wordsworth put matters thus: 'Some girl called him a black-faced rascal, when Hazlitt enraged pushed her down, and because she refused to gratify his abominable and devilish propensities, he lifted up her petticoats and *smote* her on the *bottom*.'[17] The girl naturally complained, so her fellow-villagers set out to find Hazlitt in order to give him a ducking. Coleridge embroidered the account into a manhunt by two hundred mounted villagers, from which he had to rescue Hazlitt by lending him shoes and money and hustling him away from Keswick to Grasmere in the middle of the night. There, the dramatic version continues, Wordsworth lent him clothes and more money, and he quitted the Lakes hurriedly, abandoning his canvases and equipment to Coleridge's care.

Wordsworth's later versions of this incident are scarcely borne out by the continuing friendly relations between the three men in the months and years after it occurred. Hazlitt did indeed leave the Lakes without his equipment, but there is nothing surprising in that, because travellers often had luggage sent after them especially if, as was Hazlitt's case, they were walking at least some of their way. With canvases and boxes of paints and brushes to transport, Hazlitt would certainly have them sent on by carrier. A letter from Coleridge a few months later (in January 1804) records arrangements with his wife for forwarding Hazlitt's portraits and sketches. In March of that same year Wordsworth wrote to Hazlitt at Wem to discuss his portrait of Hartley Coleridge; Hazlitt had proposed to alter it by cutting away the lower part of the canvas, and Wordsworth sought to dissuade him. Wordsworth mentions Hazlitt's luggage, still at Keswick, and says he will hurry the Coleridges along in sending it. Then in the friendliest fashion he adds: 'I should have liked to shew you 200 yards or so of mountain Brook scenery which I found out yesterday above Rydale. They are some of the finest old stumpified staring trees I ever saw, with a small waterfall, rocks of all shapes &c &c. I pass'd also under Nab scar at Rydale which you sketched part of: it is infinitely finer in winter than summer time; and indeed is a noble place.' He sent Hazlitt 'best remembrances' from his family and signed himself 'very affectionately yours'.[18] This is not a letter from a morally outraged man to a scapegrace. Hazlitt's escapade of the Lakes, whatever its exact details, had not yet been inflated into the satyriasis of Wordsworth's later account.

But if proof were needed that the incident was a minor one, it is that Southey was present at the time – indeed Coleridge claimed that Southey helped him to save Hazlitt's skin. Southey was a gossip, a writer of chatty letters, who loved to pass on news of anything amusing or scandalous. But none of his letters from the Lakes, then or later (he wrote at length to Richard Duppa in December 1803, a few weeks after the supposed mayhem occurred) mention anything about it.[19]

On 10 April 1804 Hazlitt turned twenty-six years of age. He was back at Wem, working with some freedom at last on the manuscript of his first book. From now on he was rarely without a writing project in hand, and he was just a few years away from beginning the dazzling and controversial career in periodical journalism which was to provide him with a tailor-made platform for the best expression of his personality and views.

This fact, and the merely intermittent character of his subsequent application to painting, suggests two things. First, Hazlitt had by this time come to the conclusion that although he could paint well, and could sometimes produce striking and successful portraits, he could not paint as well as he wished. He had nourished great aspirations to be a Titian or Raphael, but he knew now that he would never compare with them, and he felt that to be less was to be nothing. It meant much to him that he understood their genius from the inside, because he too had *looked* at things, and had striven to catch in oils on a two-dimensional surface the effects of nature, light, colour, and feeling. He knew well enough that he was a more than competent artist, and would certainly have improved further if, like his brother, he had devoted himself to the task. But competence was not enough.

Hazlitt did not give up painting, at least for a number of years yet. He continued to make occasional small sums from portraiture. But he painted less and less, and the ability he had acquired in the intense years of application before and during Paris and the Lakes, palpably faded.

In the preface to his abridgement of Tucker's *Light of Nature* Hazlitt wrote, 'I have been told by painters [of what] sometimes happens in copying a fine picture. Your mind is full of the original, and you see the imitation through this borrowed medium; you transfuse its grace and spirit into the copy; you connect its glowing tints and delicate touches with a meagre outline, and a warm fancy sheds its lustre over that which is little better than a blank: but when the original impression is faded, and you have nothing left but the copy for the imagination to feed on, you find the spirit evaporated, the expression gone, and you wonder at your own mistake.' This is a description of Hazlitt's experience in looking at his copies in the cold light of London and Wem after his sojourn in Paris. The message they gave him could not have been clearer. He loved art, but he would rather be an admirer and enjoyer of it than a merely competent practitioner of it. He never regretted the effort he had devoted to its study, because the pleasure it gave him, and the insights he learned, were invaluable.

Second, Hazlitt's earliest ambition, and one that he had never given up – to write – was anyway insistent within him. Even his early letters manifest his writerly gifts, but when he came to make his first mature effort to write for publication he chose an especially difficult project, a metaphysical treatise on the wellsprings of human action. The difficulty of the task lay like a boulder in his path, and prevented his writing anything else until it was finished. Part of the difficulty stemmed from his intellectual isolation. He was not a member of a university faculty, surrounded by colleagues with whom he could discuss his ideas. Coleridge was almost the only other person in the country who shared anything like his philosophical interests or knowledge, but the two men disagreed over fundamentals, and in any case Coleridge was an imaginative rather than, as Hazlitt was, a rigorously critical thinker. Hazlitt therefore worked alone, his only resources being the texts of the 'modern philosophers' – chiefly Hartley and Helvetius – and his own painful and solitary cogitations. From these he constructed his *Essay on the Principles of Human Action*. The topic of this work falls into an area of philosophical discussion now called 'moral psychology', which involves debate about the nature of moral motivation and character.

The *Essay* was finished in July 1804. Hazlitt carried it to London, at the end of that month calling twice on Godwin to discuss its publication. On 31 July Godwin wrote in his diary 'Call on Johnson (Hazlitt)', an allusion to Joseph Johnson, who in addition to being publisher to the causes of Dissent and radicalism, had published the *Discourses* by Hazlitt's father in 1790. To Hazlitt's great delight Johnson agreed to publish his *Essay*, and it appeared exactly a year later, in July 1805.

Publication of the *Essay* was a personal epoch for Hazlitt. He always regarded this book as containing not just his chief contribution to thought, but a real contribution to thought. He felt he had given the world something, and was always thereafter able to take consolation from the fact that he had a solid achievement to his credit, something which, even if his contemporaries did not fully appreciate it, later generations would.

The thesis of the *Essay* is that the human mind is 'naturally disinterested', that is, that people are interested in the welfare of others in the same way as, and for the same reasons that, they are interested in their own welfare. Hazlitt urged this in opposition to the view, then prevailing in moral philosophy, and still widespread if not indeed standard in most people's minds today, that the basic motivation for people's actions is self-interest – that even their acts of benevolence towards others have a self-regarding inspiration. His argument refuting this view and urging its opposite is, although on the face of it implausible, an ingenious and, on closer examination, a persuasive one. For the interested, it is outlined in Appendix 2.

It was not only for political reasons that the concepts of 'sympathetic imagination' and the natural altruism and fairness of the human mind were fundamental notions for Hazlitt. These concepts informed all his responses: to art, theatre, books and life. They were the foundation of his aesthetic as well as his moral outlook – and of the intimate connection between the two. In setting them out definitively in his *Essay* he had laid an intellectual foundation for the rest of his life and thought.[20]

The *Essay* is a work of technical philosophy. It is full of hard argument and sharp distinctions, sparing the reader little. In order to give a rigorous account of his views Hazlitt expressed them without rhetorical flourishes or decoration. The style is 'dry and meagre' – and therefore it fell 'still-born from the press'. Nevertheless, said Hazlitt, and with some justice, 'that work contains an important metaphysical discovery, supported by a continuous and severe train of reasoning, nearly as subtle and original as anything in Hume or Berkeley'.[21] But he was not entirely right to say that it fell stillborn from the press, because a certain amount of notice was taken of it, and not always uncomprehendingly. The first and best notice appeared in the *Monthly Review* for March 1806, describing Hazlitt as 'undoubtedly a most profound and able writer' and saying that 'the apparent ease with which he penetrates into the most difficult subjects and conducts the most subtle discussions shows that his mind has been long habituated to those operations which form the talents of a great meta-physician'. The glow these remarks might have induced was dimmed for Hazlitt by the obvious fact that the reviewer did not fully grasp his argument. It was a full year and a half before the next review appeared, in the *British Critic* for November 1806. It complained of the obscurity of Hazlitt's language, accused him of threatening the basis of religion, and described him as 'raving'. Some commentators suggest that this review was written by Christopher Wordsworth, the poet's brother, and that Hazlitt knew this – and that this was part of the reason he came to resent Wordsworth, on the grounds that he believed Wordsworth had encouraged Christopher to attack his morals and lack of religious faith.[22] Whether or not it was indeed Christopher Wordsworth who wrote the unfriendly piece, the argument is implausible: for, first, Hazlitt's later hostility to Wordsworth is more than amply explained by the latter's swing to reactionary politics, and secondly, at that time he and Wordsworth were still on good terms, as the letter quoted above shows. Wordsworth's chief ground for coming to resent Hazlitt, namely the latter's searching review of *The Excursion*, lay nearly a decade in the future. Moreover Wordsworth did not share Coleridge's religious sensitivities, so it is also unlikely that he would have been hostile to Hazlitt's discreet agnosticism.

A month after the *British Critic* review appeared, another followed, this time in the *Critical Review*, and this time friendly. The reviewer described Hazlitt as a thinker 'of more than ordinary merit and promise', and counselled readers not to be put off by the difficulty of the *Essay*'s language. A fourth review appeared in *The Anti-Jacobin Review and Magazine* for January 1807. This one wondered whether the *Essay* was a spoof, and ended by describing it as 'a little innocent, absurd essay, which a philosopher may be induced to read from seeing its title, and which he will lay aside with a smile of contempt'. In April a fifth reviewer reported enjoying Hazlitt's attack on those who hold that self-interest is the source of action, but he claimed not be able to understand the theory Hazlitt offered in its stead. Four months later, in August, the *Eclectic Review* lectured Hazlitt on points of style, suggesting that he draw up and study a list of his faults as a writer so that if the *Essay* had any sequels, they would be simpler to read and their sentences would be logically connected to each other.

Hazlitt was no doubt disappointed not to have a unanimous chorus of approval and admiration from all reviewers, but at the same time of course he had not really expected it. He was more pleased by reactions that came to him from sources other than anonymous reviewers in the periodicals. The lawyer and politician James Scarlett, later Sir James Scarlett and later still the first Lord Abinger, was so impressed by the *Essay* that he approached Hazlitt with the offer of a job. According to Hazlitt's early biographers the chief reason why he declined the offer is that William senior persuaded him to be suspicious of Scarlett, a Tory who had once been a Whig and was therefore doubly damned – for his politics, and for the apostasy that led him to them.[23] This tale is certainly apocryphal, for Scarlett was not knighted until the late 1820s, after brief service as Attorney General, and he was raised to the peerage some years later still, so his tergiversations over party affiliation occurred about seven years after William senior's death, at a time when there was anyway considerable fluidity in political loyalties.[24] Whatever the case, Hazlitt had the satisfaction of knowing he had stirred interest and approval among educated men.

Another such was Sir James Mackintosh, whose lectures Hazlitt had disapproved of six years before and whom he attacked in the course of the *Essay*. Despite that fact, Mackintosh too was impressed by it. Hazlitt said that when Mackintosh was in India, serving as Chief Justice of Bombay from 1804 to 1811, he 'languished after the friends and society he had left behind; and wrote over incessantly for books from England. One that was sent to him at this time was an *Essay on the Principles of Human Action*; and the way that he spoke of that dry, tough, metaphysical *choke-pear*, showed the dearth of intellectual intercourse in which he lived, and the craving in his mind after those studies which had once been his pride and to which he still turned for consolation in his remote solitude.'[25] Mackintosh's second wife admired Hazlitt's writing, and without his knowledge promoted his reputation in influential circles. Thus, the *Essay* was neither without uses or consequences. But it sold hardly any copies and was read by very few people, which naturally disappointed him.

Hazlitt returned to Wem in the autumn of 1805, stopping in Oxford to look at the colleges and the pictures hanging in them. Lamb wrote on 10 November to say that he was glad to hear that Hazlitt's journey had been so 'picturesque'. Lamb's letter is full of gossip about friends and happenings, and it alludes to three matters of note: the death of Nelson at the Battle of Trafalgar on 21 October, the farce Lamb was then engaged in writing, and Hazlitt's current work, the abridging of Abraham Tucker's *Light of Nature* – to which Lamb refers by saying, 'Luck to Ned Search', because the early volumes of Tucker's monumental work had been published under the pseudonym 'Edward Search'. Hazlitt varied his labours on Tucker by painting another portrait of his father, which he finished on the day news of the Battle of Austerlitz came in early December 1805. In the evening of this day Hazlitt walked out into the Wem countryside and saw a star glimmering over a poor man's cottage, and he thought about Napoleon's crusade against the old European order, for Austerlitz brought the Holy Roman Empire to an end. There are deep resonances in Hazlitt's writing: the star over the poor man's cottage recalls the star over the stable in Bethlehem, both in the season of Advent. Hazlitt was not religious, although he respected people who were sincerely so; but the moral resonances of religious imagery mattered to him, and reflection on the layers of meaning in his writings makes one wonder whether the poor man in question was not William senior himself, and the 'poor man's cottage' Hazlitt's family home.

The work on Tucker was quite advanced by the time Hazlitt returned to Wem. He had completed the reduction of the first two volumes before leaving London, and sent them to Joseph Johnson in August. 'Dear Sir,' he wrote, 'I have sent you the abridgement I have made of the first two volumes. The proportion in quantity is, as near as I can guess, about 210 pages to 790, that is, considerably less than a third. I imagine the last 3 volumes, though much longer, will not take more than the 2 first, and that the 3d and 4th will be about 400 pages, or perhaps more. If you should think this too much in quantity, the sooner you let me know the better. I find that going on in the way I have done, I can insert almost everything that is worth remembering in the book. I give the amusing passages almost entire. In fact I have done little more than leave out the repetitions, and other things that might as well never have been in the book.' The letter was written from his brother's home, now at 109 Great Russell Street in Bloomsbury, on 30 August.[26] Clearly, he had heard nothing by the time he wrote to Godwin on 5 January 1806, enclosing the manuscript of the final three volumes of the *Search* and asking him to forward it to Johnson. 'I have done my job quicker, and with less trouble than I expected,' he reported. Then he asked Godwin to prompt Johnson for a definite indication whether he would publish the abridgement, and if so, whether he would let Hazlitt have half or even all the payment for it in advance. He promised to be back in London in time to deal with proofs as soon as they were printed. And he added, 'If you see Lamb, will you tell him I expected to have heard from him before this?'

Evidently Hazlitt's parcel to Godwin crossed with a letter from Lamb, dated 7 January 1806, commenting on the preparations for Nelson's funeral and other items of news. But on the 15th Lamb wrote again, reporting at Godwin's request that Johnson had promised to give his answer about Tucker in a month's time, and that he liked Hazlitt's suggestion for a biography of Joseph Fawcett, who had just died. This idea must have been communicated to Johnson via Godwin in a letter now lost. 'Godwin went to Johnson yesterday about your business,' Lamb said. 'Johnson would not come down, or give any answer, but has promised to open the manuscript, and to give you an answer in one month. Godwin will go punctually again (Wednesday is Johnson's open day) yesterday four weeks next: i.e. in one lunar month from this time. Till when Johnson positively declines giving any answer.'[27] Godwin was a sterling friend to Hazlitt, as this shows. Not many famous authors, as Godwin was, would wait downstairs on a publisher's 'open day', to give and receive messages through a servant because the master will not come downstairs to speak to him, in the interest of a young friend just beginning his career. This was kindness above and beyond the normal.

In this same letter Lamb complains about having too many visitors and making too many visits – 'I never have an hour for my head to work its own workings: which you know is as necessary to the human system as sleep' – but they had one visitor with them, who had already been there a fortnight and who would stay a week more, who was not that kind of visitor, but instead 'is one of the few people who are not in the way when they are with you'. This was Mary's good friend Sarah Stoddart, sister of the John Stoddart (future editor of *The Times*) already encountered taking notes in Sir James Mackintosh's lectures, and being converted by them from excessive Jacobinism to excessive Toryism. The reference to Sarah Stoddart is significant; she was soon to acquire importance in Hazlitt's life.

In February 1806 Lamb wrote again to tell Hazlitt that he had finished his farce and sent it to the management of Drury Lane Theatre. There was no word from Johnson, however, because there had been a fire in his house and his affairs were disordered, so he could not send an answer for at least another month. In March Lamb wrote twice to tell Hazlitt about the art exhibitions in London, asking 'What do you in Shropshire when so many fine pictures are a-going, a-going every day in London?' Either the prompting was unnecessary or it had its intended effect, for Hazlitt was soon back in London – to Lamb's relief, because he had just said farewell to another close friend, Thomas Manning, who was going to China. Mary Lamb wrote to Sarah Stoddart, 'William Hazlitt, the brother of him you know, is in town. I believe you have heard us say we like him? He came in good time, for the loss of Manning made Charles very dull, and he likes Hazlitt better than anybody, except Manning.'[28]

Mary's wording was deliberate. Over the years she had been party to Sarah's many and fruitless efforts to find a husband, so any bachelor was a subject of consideration.[29] Sarah Stoddart was an intelligent, somewhat eccentric, well-read thirty-two-year-old woman, and it occurred to Mary that she would be more suited to Hazlitt – an intelligent, somewhat eccentric, well-read man, then aged twenty-eight – than to some of the other men she had set her cap at. Sarah was the daughter of a Navy lieutenant whose career had been very undistinguished, the bulk of it spent languishing at home on half-pay. When war broke out in 1793 he was given the unpleasant and unpopular shore job of officering a press-gang, which did nothing to improve his humour or his prospects.

Sarah Stoddart was very unlike her brother John. A small but telling anecdote from their childhood illustrates the difference: whenever they were offered a sip of grog by their father John would say 'No thank you, Father' and Sarah would say, 'Yes please, Father.' She and Mary Lamb liked to take brisk walks together, and to drink brandy ('three parts brandy to one part water' was Mary's recipe) while enjoying vigorous conversations. In 1802 John Stoddart went to Malta to serve as King's Advocate, and Sarah went too, after elaborate preparations – helped by Mary – of a wardrobe designed to catch the eye of an officer, whether military or colonial it did not matter. The attempt came to nothing, and Sarah, now back in England, was still actively looking for a husband. In the letter just quoted, announcing Hazlitt's arrival in town, Mary asked, 'I am very sorry you still hear nothing from Mr White. I am afraid that is all at an end. What do you intend to do about Mr Turner?'

On the face of it, Hazlitt was scarcely a good marriage prospect. At twenty-eight he still had no regular profession, and was scrimping along by painting the occasional portrait here and there, and by borrowing from friends. His early publications were not making money, and he had a personality whose virtues were the reverse of apparent to those who did not know him well. In his relations with women of his own class he was incompetent. During this same summer of 1806 Lamb took him to visit friends where there were young girls, and afterwards wrote to Wordsworth, 'W. Hazlitt is in town. I took him to see a very pretty girl professedly, where there were two young girls – the very head and sum of Girlery was two young girls – they neither laughed nor sneered nor giggled nor whispered – but they were young girls – and he sat and frowned blacker and blacker, indignant that there should be such a thing as youth and beauty, till he tore me away before supper in perfect misery and owned he could not bear young girls. They drove him mad. So I took him home to my old Nurse, where he recover'd perfect tranquillity. Independent of all this, and as I am not a young girl myself, he is a great acquisition to us.'[31]

Apart from Hazlitt's general incapacity to manage his feelings about women, there is an added poignancy in this incident. Earlier it was noted that he felt a *tendre* for the beautiful daughter of Joseph Railton, the merchant who commissioned his Paris copies. It might be she of whom Hazlitt wrote in his essay on Malthus in 1807, 'I never fell in love but once, and then it was with a girl who always wore her handkerchief pinned tight round her neck, with a fair face, gentle eyes, a soft smile, and cool auburn locks.'[31] He offers this as evidence that when romantically in love he does not suffer from the heats and lusts which Malthus thought are endemic to the human male – Malthus described sexual appetites as especially ungovernable in men of the working classes – and which there-fore cause the increase in population that, Malthus claimed, must inev-itably follow every rise in living standards. Hazlitt thought it necessary to make the point about how he loved – 'It was not a raging heat, a fever in the veins: but it was like a vision, a dream, like thoughts of childhood, an everlasting hope, a distant joy, a heaven, a world that might be. The dream is still left, and sometimes comes confusedly over me in solitude and silence, and mingles with the softness of the sky, and veils my eyes from mortal grossness' – because in the immediately preceding two pages he had described the upper classes as having more inducements to heat and lust than the working classes, by means of their revealing clothes, their balls and waltzes, their attendance at romantic plays and operas, and their visits to art exhibitions full of nudes of both sexes.

But Hazlitt's inability to tolerate Girlery because it gave him such pangs of romantic yearning was, as Mary Lamb astutely recognized, no obstacle to an arrangement with a woman like Sarah Stoddart. Sarah was no girl; she had a little property in the country and a modest annual income; she was sensible, educated, and desperate for a husband. Hazlitt, in Mary's view, needed a wife with a little property, an annual income, good sense, education, and no rooted objection – within generous limits – to anything male. Although Hazlitt did not yet know it, the match was a live option in Mary's mind. But nothing happened immediately, for such plans take time to fructify, and in any case there were still certain other marital possibilities in the offing for Sarah, which Mary observed with sceptical interest.

# CHAPTER SIX

# Towards Winterslow

## 1806–1808

O N A SUMMER Friday in 1806, at the end of June or perhaps early in July, Lamb and Hazlitt went to the theatre at Sadler's Wells for the evening, leaving Mary at home reading a manuscript by Hazlitt. She took the opportunity to write to Sarah Stoddart, telling her that Lamb's farce 'Mr H—' had been accepted by Drury Lane, and was to be staged there before Christmas. She also told Sarah that she and Charles were working together on their *Tales from Shakespeare*. Among the items of latest gossip she passed on was news that Mrs Wordsworth was unwell. The letter concludes, 'Write directly, for I am uneasy about your *Lovers*. I wish something was settled.' A couple of days later she wrote again: 'I am cooking a shoulder of Lamb (Hazlitt dines with us); it will be ready at two o'clock, if you can pop in and eat a bit with us.'[1] This was a joke: Sarah was in Salisbury.

As these letters show, Hazlitt was much in the Lambs' company at their lodgings in Mitre Court just off Fleet Street. Mary had a motive for keeping that fact before Sarah's mind, which was that John Stoddart was also playing matchmaker on Sarah's behalf, the result being a letter from him to Mary in October saying that Sarah was about to marry a young farmer called William Dowling. John Stoddart wanted Mary to travel to Salisbury to cast a critical eye over the prospective husband and to help draw up a marriage settlement. Mary, for her part, wanted none of it. She had been told enough about Mr Dowling to judge conclusively that he was unsuitable. She wrote to Sarah: 'If you fancy a very young man, and he likes an elderly gentlewoman; if he likes a learned and accomplished lady, and you like a not very learned youth, who may need a little polishing, which probably he will never acquire; it is all very well, and God bless you both together and may you be both very long in the same mind.'[2]

Hazlitt had more to occupy him than thoughts of finding a wife. Either Joseph Johnson or Hazlitt himself had decided against a biography of Fawcett, so that project disappeared from view. Hazlitt was still waiting to hear whether Johnson would publish his Tucker abridgement. He hardly noticed the waiting, however, because political events were absorbing his attention.

Pitt the Younger had recently died – on 23 January 1806 – broken by Austerlitz. Napoleon's victory in that battle enabled him to force Austria to a treaty (the Treaty of Pressburg, signed on Boxing Day 1805) giving up all possessions and influence in southern Germany, the Tyrol, Dalmatia, and Italy. Not only was the Holy Roman Empire finished, so too was the Triple Alliance of Britain, Austria and Russia that Pitt had forged with much difficulty. The collapse of the alliance was a heavy blow to him. When he died he was aged forty-six, and had been Prime Minister for all but a few years since the age of twenty-four. His death, accordingly, was the result as much of sheer exhaustion as disease. He was succeeded as Prime Minister by Lord Grenville, who took office at the head of a ministry chiefly staffed by the followers of Charles James Fox. Fox, who became Secretary of State, and his fellow Whigs had been out of power for decades, so their return delighted Hazlitt and all other liberals in the country, and gave them hope – for reform in general, but most especially that the war with France might quickly be brought to an end. One of Fox's first endeavours was to attempt just that, but it was too late – Napoleon's victory at Austerlitz had put him in a position of great strength, and he had no need to listen to overtures of peace.

Hazlitt was desperately keen to see England make terms with Napoleon.[3] News that the new ministry was failing to do so prompted him to write a pamphlet entitled *Free Thoughts on Public Affairs; or, Advice to a Patriot, in a Letter Addressed to a Member of the Old Opposition*. Its aim was to argue Fox into making peace. In it Hazlitt attacked the war as futile, costly and unjustifiable, and said that it was not a war of defence as Pitt had claimed, but a self-serving endeavour to extend England's colonial possessions at France's expense. He put the blame squarely on Pitt, in an excoriating attack on his character and policies, for the resumption of hostilities after the failure of the Peace of Amiens in 1803.

There was no likelihood of finding a publisher for the pamphlet, so Hazlitt, despite his chronically empty purse, printed it at his own expense, much to the disapproval of Lamb, who could not understand political passion. He wrote to Wordsworth, '[Hazlitt] is, rather imprudently, I think, printing a political pamphlet on his own account, and will have to pay for paper, &c. The first duty of an author, I take it, is never to pay for anything.'[4] (Evidently Lamb was speaking from experience; he printed his play *John Woodvil* at his own expense in 1802, and thereby made a loss of £25 – a sum nearly equal to William senior's total annual income.) No-one took any notice of Hazlitt's pamphlet; it was neither reviewed nor answered. But it was not wholly a waste. It allowed him to vent his feelings on a great matter of the day, and in the end he was able to recycle part of it – its 'character' of Pitt – in three different later publications.[5] His analysis of Pitt owed much to an essay by Coleridge in the *Morning Post* in February 1800, and to discussions he and Coleridge had as a result. Hazlitt acknowledged the debt; in a footnote in his pamphlet he described Coleridge's essay as 'masterly and unanswerable'.[6]

There was another consequence, or more accurately an opportunity, for Hazlitt in the political conditions of the time. As Trevelyan puts it, 'The great French war – alike in its first phase in the time of Pitt and Nelson, and in its last in the time of Castlereagh and Wellington – was fought by the House of Commons. The comparison of the Roman Senate fighting Hannibal was in the mind of every educated man. The persons whom the House trusted could wield the national power and purse, on condition of explaining their plans to the benches of country gentlemen, and winning their approval. For this reason Parliamentary eloquence was at its zenith.'[7] Public interest in Parliamentary eloquence was at its zenith too, and the Press crammed the gallery of the House of Commons to report what was said there. Six years later Hazlitt became one of those reporters, thus launching his journalistic career. But before that, inspired by the period of the Foxite 'Ministry of all the Talents', he began to make a collection of celebrated speeches from Parliament's history. Its title, when he published it two years later in 1808, was *The Eloquence of the British Senate*, which deliberately registered the Roman sentiments and the ideal of Ciceronian oratory to which Trevelyan alludes.

In 1806 began the Lambs' famous literary salon, their 'Wednesdays' (they later became 'Thursdays'), attended by, among others, Hazlitt, William Ayrton the music impresario, Captain James Burney – who had sailed with Captain Cook to the Pacific, and was the brother of the celebrated authoress Fanny Burney – and his son Martin, Coleridge and Wordsworth when they were in town, John Rickman, Edward Phillips (whom they called 'Ned'), and Mrs Reynolds. There flourished among the regulars in this group what Hazlitt called the 'soul of conversation', namely, sympathy. 'Authors should converse chiefly with authors, and their talk should be of books. "When Greek meets Greek, then comes the tug of war." ... There is a Free-masonry in all things. You can only speak to be understood, but this you cannot be, except by those who are in the secret.'[8] The only person he knew who could talk to anyone 'without caring a farthing for their understanding one word of what he says' was Coleridge; 'and *he* talks only for admiration and to be listened to, and accordingly the least interruption puts him out.'[9] But talking to impress does not compare with the pleasure of conversation in a mutually sympathetic group. 'When a set of adepts, of *illuminati*, get about a question, it is worthwhile to hear them talk. They may snarl and quarrel over it, like dogs; but they pick it bare to the bone, they masticate it thoroughly. This was the case formerly at L[amb]'s – where we used to have many lively skirmishes at their Thursday evening parties.' The memory of these occasions was in particular a memory of Lamb, at that time and in those circumstances at his best. He was, wrote Hazlitt, 'the most delightful, the most provoking, the most witty and sensible of men. He always made the best pun, and the best remark in the course of the evening. His serious conversation, like his serious writing, is the best. No one ever stammered out such fine, piquant, eloquent things in half a dozen sentences as he does. His jests scald like tears: and he probes a question with a play upon words. What a keen, laughing, hair-brained vein of home-felt truth!' The evenings were feasts of talk. 'How often did we cut into the haunch of letters, while we discussed the haunch of mutton on the table! How we skimmed the cream of criticism! How we got into the heart of controversy! How we picked out the marrow of authors! "And in our flowing cups, many a good name and true was remembered." '[10]

Not all the parties were the same. In addition to the core members there were others who came and went, occasional visitors, 'honorary members, lay-brothers'. The motto that stood notionally over the door was 'Wit and good fellowship'. When someone new arrived he was not asked whether he had written anything; instead 'we waited to see what he could do.' And it was enough if he could take a hand at piquet – or even if he enjoyed his snuff, for 'he would understand, by analogy, the pungency of other things'. But there were certain types who were never welcome: 'We abhorred insipidity, affectation, and fine gentlemen.'[11]

Hazlitt left a record of an especially representative conversation whose topic, he says, was suggested by Lamb, but which, since it stems from a hint in Abraham Tucker's *Light of Nature*, most probably came from Hazlitt himself. The question was: who among historical characters would you most like to meet? 'On the question being started, Ayrton said, "I suppose the two first persons you would choose to see would be the two greatest names in English literature, Sir Isaac Newton and Mr Locke?" In this Ayrton, as usual, reckoned without his host. Every one burst out laughing at the expression of Lamb's face, in which impatience was restrained by courtesy. "Yes, the greatest names," he stammered out hastily, "but they were not persons – not persons." – "Not persons?" said Ayrton, looking wise and foolish at the same time, afraid his triumph might be premature. "That is," rejoined Lamb, "not characters, you know. By Mr Locke and Sir Isaac Newton, you mean the Essay on the Human Understanding, and the *Principia*, which we have to this day. Beyond their contents there is nothing personally interesting in the men. But what we want to see any one *bodily* for, is when there is something peculiar, striking in the individuals, more than we can learn from their writings, and yet are curious to know. I dare say Locke and Newton were very like Kneller's portraits of them. But who could paint Shakespear?" – "Ay," retorted Ayrton, "there it is; then I suppose you would prefer seeing him and Milton instead?" – "No," said Lamb, "neither. I have seen so much of Shakespear on the book-stalls, in frontispieces and on mantelpieces, that I am quite tired of the everlasting repetition: and as to Milton's face, the impressions that have come down to us of it I do not like; it is too starched and puritanical; and I should be afraid of losing some of the manna of his poetry in the leaven of his countenance and the precisian's band and gown." – "I shall guess no more," said Ayrton. "Who is it, then, you would like to see 'in his habit as he lived', if you had your choice of the whole range of English literature?" Lamb then named Sir Thomas Browne and Fulke Greville, the friend of Sir Philip Sydney, as the two worthies whom he should feel the greatest pleasure to encounter on the floor of his apartment in their nightgown and slippers, and to exchange friendly greetings with them. At this Ayrton laughed outright, and conceived Lamb was jesting with him; but as no one followed his example, he thought there might be something in it, and waited for an explanation in a state of whimsical surprise. Lamb then (as well as I can remember a conversation that passed twenty years ago – how time slips!) went on as follows. "The reason why I pitch upon these two authors is, that their writings are riddles, and they themselves the most mysterious of personages. They resemble the soothsayers of old, who dealt in dark hints and doubtful oracles; and I should like to ask them the meaning of what no mortal but themselves, I should suppose, can fathom. There is Dr Johnson, I have no curiosity, no strange uncertainty about him; he and Boswell together have pretty well let me into the secret of what passed through his mind. He and other writers like him are sufficiently explicit: my friends, whose repose I should be tempted to disturb (were it in my power), are implicit, inextricable, inscrutable.

> And call up him who left half-told
> The story of Cambuscan bold.

When I look at that obscure but gorgeous prose-composition (the *Urn-*

*burial*) I seem to myself to look into a deep abyss, at the bottom of which are hid pearls and rich treasure; or it is like a stately labyrinth of doubt and withering speculation, and I would invoke the spirit of the author to lead me through it. Besides, who would not be curious to see the lineaments of a man who, having been twice married, wished that mankind were propagated like trees! As to Fulke Greville, he is like nothing but one of his own 'Prologues spoken by the ghost of an old king of Ormus', a truly formidable and inviting personage: his style is apocalyptical, cabalistical, a knot worthy of such an apparition to untie; and for the unravelling a passage or two, I would stand the brunt of an encounter with so portentous a commentator!" '[12]

Such was an evening's literate conversation in the first decade of the nineteenth century. Talk moved on to Donne, a volume of whose poetry was produced and read from at length. Someone mentioned that from the window of Lamb's apartment could be seen the Temple-walk where Chaucer used to take his exercise, and the company agreed that they would like to meet him. Hazlitt reports himself vexed with Ayrton for not appreciating the metre of the Canterbury Tales, and says he would give much to have been present at Chaucer's meeting with Petrarch, and even more so at his meeting with Boccaccio, 'and heard them exchange their best stories together, the Squire's Tale against the Story of the Falcon, the Wife of Bath's Prologue against the Adventures of the White Friar'. Hazlitt remembers himself growing eloquent. 'How fine to see the high mysterious brow which learning then wore, relieved by the gay, familiar tone of men of the world, and by the courtesies of genius. Surely, the thought and feelings which passed through the minds of these great revivers of learning, these Cadmuses who sowed the teeth of letters, must have stamped an expression on their features, as different from the moderns as their books, and well worth the perusal.'[13] Dante and Ugolino passed under review in the same way. Hazlitt spoke of the fine portrait of Ariosto 'by no less a hand than Titian's', and of the same painter's portrait of Aretino. Lamb asked him if he would like to see Spenser as well as Chaucer, to which Hazlitt replied: 'No; for that his beauties were ideal, visionary, not palpable or personal, and therefore connected with less curiosity about the man. His poetry was the essence of romance, a very halo round the bright orb of fancy; and the bringing in the individual might dissolve the charm. No tones of voice could come up to the mellifluous cadence of his verse; no form but of a winged angel could vie with the airy shapes he has described.' Captain Burney wished to see Christopher Columbus, and someone else the Wandering Jew; 'but the last was set aside as spurious, and the first made over to the New World.' Mary Lamb then surprised the company by saying, ' "I should like to have seen Pope talking with Patty Blount; and I *have* seen Goldsmith." Every one turned round to look at Miss Lamb, as if by doing so they too could get a sight of Goldsmith.' Someone wondered where Dr Johnson was in 1745–6, since there is no mention of him in Boswell relating to the period, nor did he write anything in those years. Was he in Scotland with the Young Pretender? But Pope had not left the scene; Ayrton said to Lamb: 'I thought that you of the Lake School did not like Pope?', to which Lamb replied: ' "Not like Pope! My dear sir, you must be under a mistake – I can read him over and over for ever!" – "Why, certainly, the Essay on Man must be allowed to be a masterpiece." – "It may be so, but I seldom look into it." – "Oh! then it's his Satires you admire?" – "No, not his Satires, but his friendly Epistles and his compliments." – "Compliments! I did not know that he ever made any." – "The finest," said Lamb, "that were ever paid by the wit of man. Each of them is worth an estate for life – nay, it is an immortality. There is that superb one to Lord Cornbury: "Despise low joys, low gains;/Disdain whatever Cornbury disdains;/Be virtuous, and be happy for your pains".' Here Lamb took his volume of Pope and sought out the compliments paid to Mansfield, Bolingbroke, Granville, Garth, Congreve, and many others, embedded in the Prologue and Epilogue to the *Satires*, until his voice failed him and 'throwing down the book, he said, "Do you think I would not wish to have been friends with such a man as this?" '

Dryden, Junius, Cromwell, Bunyan, Fielding, Richardson, the Elizabethan dramatists, Garrick, and others all proved worthy candidates for resurrection. Another 'Mitre-courtier' asked which of the metaphysicians they might profit by meeting, to which Hazlitt replied, 'there were only six in modern times deserving the name – Hobbes, Berkeley, Butler, Hartley, Hume, Leibnitz; and perhaps Jonathan Edwards, a Massachusetts man.' (Elsewhere Hazlitt was at pains to show that Locke's ideas come straight out of Hobbes – he wrote an essay on this theme, 'Locke a Great Plagiarist', in which he makes a convincing case[14] – which is why that redoubtable name does not figure in his list. The exclusion of Descartes and Spinoza is however questionable.) Someone else then said that were Coleridge present, he would name Thomas Aquinas and Duns Scotus, 'those profound and worthy scholiasts', and Hazlitt replied: 'This might be fair enough in him who had read or fancied he had read the original works, but I did not see how we could have any right to call up these authors to give an account of themselves in person, till we had looked into their writings.'[15] From Gay and Gray to Leonardo, Titian and Giorgioni; from Cimabue and Ghirlandaio to Voltaire, Montaigne, Rousseau, Rabelais, and Racine; from Alexander and Caesar to Tamerlaine and Genghis Khan, the candidates followed one another in riotous assembly, until Lamb brought the conversation to a halt by proposing, to everyone's surprise, Guy Fawkes and Judas Iscariot. There was a clamour for him to explain himself. ' "Why, I cannot but think," retorted he of the wistful countenance, "that Guy Faux, that poor fluttering annual scare-crow of straw and rags, is an ill-used gentleman. I would give something to see him sitting pale and emaciated, surrounded by his matches and his barrels of gunpowder, and expecting the moment that was to transport him to Paradise for his heroic self-devotion; but if I say more there is that fellow Hazlitt will make something of it. And as to Judas Iscariot, my reason is different. I would fain see the face of him, who, having dipped his hand in the same dish as the Son of Man, could afterwards betray him. I have no conception of such a thing; nor have I ever seen any picture (not even Leonardo's very fine one) that gave me the least idea of it." '[16] The conversation having taken a serious turn, the party began to break up. It was already dawn. 'The morning broke with that dim, dubious light by which Giotto, Cimabue and Ghirlandaio must have seen to paint their earliest works; and we parted to meet again and renew similar topics at night, the next night, and the night after that, till the night overspread Europe which saw no dawn. The same event, in truth, broke up our little Congress that broke up the great one. But that was to meet again; our deliberations have never been resumed.'

Here Hazlitt was thinking ahead to the last days of the Lambs' at-homes. The event in question was the return of Napoleon from Elba in 1814; the Congress in question was the meeting of Napoleon's enemies at which work was begun on redistributing Europe among the kings he had put to flight, and who were now creeping back to reclaim their pomp and privileges. The 'night' Hazlitt alludes to is the night that followed the Hundred Days, a night of monarchy and reaction, of renewed repression of liberal hopes, and of return to old institutions that favoured the few at the expense of the many. Soon after Napoleon's banishment to St Helena, Hazlitt gave up political writing altogether in the belief that the radical cause was hopeless, at least for his generation. In any event, his allusion to these matters at the end of this famous essay shows that the Lambs' at-homes lasted for about eight years from 1806 to 1814.

It was at this time – in 1806 – that Henry Crabb Robinson first met the Lambs. He had heard of them from Hazlitt, and was introduced to them by a mutual friend, a Mrs Clarkson. Referring to the Lambs' 'humble apartment' in Mitre Court he says, 'I spent many happy hours there, and saw a greater number of excellent persons than I had ever seen collected together in one room.' Such were the 'Wednesdays' and 'Thursdays' between Austerlitz and Elba.

On 10 December 1806 Lamb's farce 'Mr H—' opened at the Drury Lane Theatre. There was great expectation among Lamb's friends, and even – according to Hazlitt's later report – expectation among the theatre-going public: 'Bright shone the morning on the play-bills that announced thy appearance, and the streets were filled with the buzz of persons asking one another if they would go to see Mr H—, and answering that they would certainly.' Hazlitt and Crabb Robinson sat together in the front row of the pit, among many others of Lamb's friends. Lamb himself and his brother were in the 'public offices' of the theatre. Evidently, Hazlitt was convinced that the play would be a success, and he was mortally disappointed, even more so than Lamb himself, when part of the audience hissed it, and their hisses could not be overwhelmed by the opposing applause. The whole point of the farce turns on the secret of the hero's name, which he tries to keep secret in case it jeopardizes his chances – not least with the woman he loves – because it is so hideous. The name is revealed in the denouement, through the device of a letter that falls into the wrong hands, as 'Hogsflesh'. Hazlitt wrote later that he dreamed about the play every night for a month after its failure – dreamed that it succeeded, or was revived at 'the other House' (Covent Garden) after some revisions; and he relates how there had been a 'full diapason of applause at the end of the Prologue', which seemed to augur well. He personally had enjoyed parts of the play exceedingly, and he wondered whether it was ruined by having to follow a long tedious opera called *The Travellers*, when its sallies of wit might have done better after a tragedy.

Lamb himself was far more stoical about the failure. The morning afterwards he wrote to Wordsworth that he had not really expected it to succeed: 'Mr H. came out last night and failed. I had many fears; the subject was not substantial enough. John Bull must have solider fare than a *Letter*. We are pretty stout about it, have had plenty of condoling friends, but after all, we had rather it should have succeeded. You will see the Prologue in most of the morning papers. It was received with such shouts as I never witness'd to a Prologue.' Lamb had not originally supplied a Prologue, but the management asked for one, so he scribbled it quickly, setting no store by it – and yet it was the only thing the audience liked. 'How hard!' he commented. He had many friends in the audience and they applauded and clapped loudly. But, said Lamb, a hundred hisses outweigh a thousand claps, and that was enough to damn his play. 'Well, 'tis withdrawn, and there is an end,' he wrote.[17] In fact, it was not withdrawn – not, at least, by the Drury Lane managers, who intended to advertise the play as a success and to continue with performances of it; but Lamb refused, and asked them to take it off immediately. By one of the quirks that fate delights in, 'Mr H—' was staged in America some years later, and met with repeated success.[18]

Hazlitt's reason for liking the play was the same reason it failed: it was literary, and clever. 'Gentleman' Lewis of the 'other House' was present, and said he could have made a huge success of it with a few judicious adjustments. But for audiences raised on farces of situation, a comedy of literary jests was too refined. Moreover, the supposedly horrible name 'Hogsflesh' would not have offended cricket lovers, among whom one of the heroes of the day was the fearsome bowler Hogsflesh of Hambledon; nor would it have seemed strange to anyone acquainted with the seaside resort of Worthing, the keeper of one of whose two inns was called Hogsflesh. By coincidence, the keeper of the other was called Bacon; there was a rhyme about them: 'Brighton is a pretty street,/Worthing is much taken,/If you can't get any other meat/There's Hogsflesh and Bacon.'[19]

Hazlitt's abridgement of Abraham Tucker was accepted by Johnson at last, in the autumn of 1806, and by January 1807 the Preface was in print. At the same time as Johnson accepted Tucker, Hazlitt signed a contract with the publisher Thomas Ostell for his anthology of parliamentary speeches, *The Eloquence of the British Senate*. By the beginning of 1807 he was writing the introductions to his selections, and was pleased with progress. In a letter home he said that his critical discussions of 'these four viz. Burke, Chatham, Fox, Pitt, with Sir R. Walpole's, will be the chief articles of the work, and if I am not mistaken confounded good ones. I am only afraid they will be too good, that is, that they will contain more good things, than are exactly proper for the occasion.'[20]

A degree of financial independence ensued on these publishing deals, so in that same month of January 1807 Hazlitt moved from his brother's house in Great Russell Street to a home of his own at 34 Southampton Buildings, an elbow-shaped street connecting High Holborn and Chancery Lane. The large houses in it were given over to lodgings for bachelors, lawyers and clerks who wished to live near the Inns of Court and places of business in the vicinity. Southampton Buildings was to play a frequent, and eventually a wretched, part in Hazlitt's life thereafter.

Hazlitt's cousin Tom Loftus arrived in London after a visit to Shropshire, bringing with him a gift of mutton, pickled pork, and chicken from the family at Wem. Hazlitt wrote to thank them, saying that he had dined excellently on the mutton after a walk round Hampstead and Highgate –

'I never made a better dinner in my life' – and that Tom came to help him finish the remains on Saturday, in two sessions either side of a visit to the opera. Hazlitt was in two minds about the opera, because although he liked music by itself and theatre by itself, he regarded their mixture as distracting and therefore a detraction from both. He was socializing energetically. On 1 January 1807 he 'supped at Godwin's' and a few days later at Holcroft's. He reports in another letter to his father that he is going again to dine with Joseph Hume, having spent Christmas day with him a couple of weeks before: 'It was much such a day as it was two years ago, when I was painting your picture. *Tempus preterlabitur.* I am afraid I shall never do such another.' That this did not mean he had yet given up painting appears in what follows: 'I have done what I wanted in writing [meaning his metaphysical *Essay*], and I hope I may in painting.'

The Tucker abridgement appeared in March. Hazlitt stood in little need of instruction in the art of writing, but he had found the work of reducing Tucker's superfluity of volumes an instructive one – no-one can fail to profit from the exercise of editing a text to a third or less of its length, not only as a way of practising economy of expression, although that is a desideratum, but in revealing the bones and sinews of prose and training the pen in the subtle art of adapting style to content.

The *Abridgement*'s reception was favourable. The *Critical Review* for November 1807 described Hazlitt's editing as 'judicious, and the manner in which he has executed it is entitled to considerable praise'. The *British Critic* ran an enormous review over three issues (March, May and June 1808), which concluded that 'on the whole he appears to have performed the task which he prescribed to himself with great fidelity'.

In July 1807 Thomas Ostell published Hazlitt's two-volume *Eloquence of the British Senate; or, Select Specimens from the Speeches of the Most Distinguished Parliamentary Speakers, From the Beginning of the reign of Charles I to the Present Time*. It is full of choice matter – not just the oratory quoted at length, but Hazlitt's own pen-portraits of celebrated parliamentarians. He later modified some of his judgements, especially about Fox and Burke. But the characteristic Hazlittian polemical thrust and insight are already present in full. 'Fox in his opinions was governed by facts – Chatham was more influenced by the feelings of others respecting those facts. Fox endeavoured to find out what the consequences of any measure would be; Chatham attended more to what people would think of it. Fox appealed to the practical reason of mankind; Chatham to popular prejudice. The one repelled the encroachments of power by supplying his hearers with arguments against it; the other by rousing their passions and arming their resentment against those who would rob them of their birthright. Their vehemence and impetuosity arose also from very different feelings. In Chatham it was pride, passion, self-will, impatience of control, a determination to have his own way, to carry every thing before him; in Fox it was pure good nature, a sincere love of truth, an ardent attachment to what he conceived to be right; and anxious concern for the welfare and liberties of mankind.'[21] Hazlitt had loyalties, as this encomium of Fox shows. It happens that Hazlitt's imputation to Fox of lofty disinterest is more right than not, for Fox was a true champion of liberal values. But of course no man is as rosy as such a picture paints him. By the same token the picture of Chatham could portray almost any politician one cared to name, but politicians sometimes have convictions and sincerities too, and Hazlitt elsewhere gives Chatham his due. Still, the contrast Hazlitt draws between these great statesmen of George III's time is a telling one – and equally so for what it reveals about the crispness and inclusiveness of Hazlitt's mind and his political bent.

That he was prepared to give their due even to those whose views he opposed is again well demonstrated by his views on Burke. 'The simple clue to all his reasonings is, I think, as follows. He did not agree with some writers, that that mode of government is necessarily the best which is the cheapest. He saw in the constitution of society other principles at work, and other capacities of fulfilling the desires, and perfecting the nature of man, besides those of securing the equal enjoyment of the means of animal life, and doing this at as little expense as possible. He thought that the wants and happiness of men were not to be provided for, as we provide for those of a herd of cattle, merely by attending to their physical necessities. He thought more nobly of his fellows. He knew that man had affections and passions and powers of imagination, as well as hunger and thirst and the sense of heat and cold.'[22]

There was little response to the book. It did not sell well, as evidenced by the fact that when a year later John Murray brought out a second edition, it was made up from the original sheets. This time, however, Hazlitt's name was on the title page. In June 1809 the *Monthly Review* said of it, 'The criticisms, indeed, are of the boldest kind; and it would seem that their author is more anxious that his observations should excite sensation, than that they should produce conviction. His daring has in some instances struck out felicities, but, as is usually the case, has more frequently induced extravagances. The essential requisites of a critic are not wanting in this writer; and he appears to offend more from a want of temper and of a strong or properly directed moral sense than from a deficiency of ability or judgment.'

While at work on *The Eloquence of the British Senate* Hazlitt contributed a series of three letters to William Cobbett's *Weekly Political Register*. This famous journal, under its robust, combative, eccentric and independent owner-editor, was influential in keeping the idea of parliamentary reform alive even in the dark oppressive days of war. Cobbett attacked what he called 'Old Corruption' – the Establishment network of pensions, sinecures, rotten and pocket boroughs, patronage, and everything that went with it – and unflaggingly argued for a 'change of system' rather than a mere change of ministry to cure the country's ills. He spent the years 1810–12 in Newgate prison for seditious libel, gaining a reputation as a martyr for radicalism. He was, however, also a stumbling-block to radicalism, because he was highly inconsistent in his loyalties and principles, disputatious with allies, and a fertile source of splits and quarrels among them. He thereby weakened the radical cause. Moreover, he had started as an opponent of reform, which meant that enemies could quote his earlier writings to embarrass him. Hazlitt met Cobbett once and liked him: 'The only time I ever saw him he seemed to me a very pleasant man – easy of access, affable, clear-headed, simple and mild in his manner, deliberate and unruffled in his speech, though some of his expressions were not very qualified. His figure is tall and portly. He has a good sensible face – rather full, with little grey eyes, a hard, square forehead, a ruddy complexion, with hair grey or powdered; and had on a scarlet broad-cloth waistcoat with the flaps of the pocket hanging down, as was the custom for gentlemen-farmers in the last century, or as we see it in the pictures of Members of Parliament in the reign of George I. I certainly did not think less favourably of him for seeing him.'[23] Hazlitt's remarkable capacity for observation preserves the flaps of Cobbett's waistcoat pockets to posterity along with his grey eyes and square forehead. True to form, Hazlitt's liking for the man did not blind him to his faults. In his essay 'Character of Cobbett' he gives the farmer-polemicist full due: – 'He is not only unquestionably the most powerful political writer of the present day, but one of the best writers of the language' – and mercilessly describes his inconsistency: 'Paine said on some occasion – "What I have written, I have written" – as rendering any farther declaration of his principles unnecessary. Not so Mr Cobbett. What he has written is no rule to him what he is to write. He learns something every day, and every week he takes the field to maintain the opinions of the last six days against friend or foe. I doubt whether this outrageous inconsistency, this headstrong fickleness, this understood want of all rule and method, does not enable him to go on with the spirit, vigour and variety that he does.'

Hazlitt's three letters are a reply to the Reverend Thomas Malthus's

*Essay on the Principle of Population*, first published a decade before (in 1798), which asserts the doctrine that unless its procreative activity is restrained in some way, a population will increase in geometrical ratio while food supplies will increase only in arithmetical ratio. Malthus regarded this as an ineluctable law of nature, and argued that this law, rather than social or political arrangements, is what causes poverty: for as soon as the poor get a little richer, they simply have more children, thereby returning themselves to subsistence level. His *Essay* had a great influence on the debate about poor relief. After the introduction of the 'Speenhamland' system in 1795 the level of pauper assistance was linked to the price of food and the number of children in a family. The system was devised by a humane group of magistrates in Speenhamland in Berkshire, and its virtues prompted its wider adoption. But Malthus argued that the system was a serious mistake, for such relief could in his view only be an incentive to the poor to have more children. He blamed the sexual passions of the poor for their imprisonment in the subsistence cycle. His recommendation was to abolish poor relief altogether, and said that if a man could not support his children, 'they must starve'. Unhappily for the poor, not just of England but her empire, Malthus's views became the basis for policy; they underlay the harsh workhouse system introduced in England soon afterwards, a system designed to act as a disincentive to poverty. And because Malthus became a lecturer at Haileybury College in Hertfordshire, which trained administrators for India, his prescriptions were exported abroad with his pupils.

The premises of Malthus's idea are three: population cannot increase without a means of subsistence; when such means are available populations inevitably increase; and 'the superior power of population cannot be checked without producing misery or vice'. His assumption was that humans double in number every twenty-five years (that is, every generation). He based this assumption on data from America, where the population has increased in just this way over the preceding century and a half. By contrast, Malthus pointed out, agricultural land cannot be increased nearly so quickly (and anyway its increase has an eventual absolute limit). It follows that population growth is 'indefinitely greater' than the power of land to sustain it. The difference can be expressed mathematically: population increases in a geometric progression (1, 2, 4, 8, 16, 32, 64, 128, ...) and the means of subsistence by an arithmetic progression (1, 2, 3, 4, 5, 6, 7, 8, ...). After one hundred years the ratio of population to means of subsistence will be 16/5, after 225 years, 512/10, after 300 years 4096/13. The depressing conclusion is that the majority of mankind is doomed to poverty for ever. Worse: most of the world's population will forever hover round the point at which they are close to starvation. This state of affairs is called, in economist-speak, the 'subsistence equilibrium'.

It was not just the introduction of the Speenhamland system that prompted Malthus to write his *Essay*, but his concern to refute Godwin's utopian and Perfectibilist views as expressed in *Political Justice*, published in 1793. Malthus wished to protect the principle of property and to show that the poor have no claim on society because their circumstances are purely a result of the action of natural laws. Later, in 1820, he added an argument to the effect that society positively needs a leisured class, because the surplus produced by the conjunction of capital and labour cannot be consumed by either alone or even together, so there has to be an unproductive class to consume the excess. All these ideas were music to the ears of the leisured unproductive classes themselves, who of course resented giving pence to the poor because it interfered with their occupation of consuming society's excess – or more accurately, their occupation with excessive consumption. Malthus might not have been an original thinker (all his ideas predate him) but he expressed them at a time in history which was very receptive to them. According to E. P. Thompson, Malthus helped to tip the balance away from the eighteenth century's 'moral economy' based on custom, culture and community – in short: people – towards the 'political economy' of the nineteenth century, which gave priority to profit. It remains there still.

Hazlitt's 'letters' opposing Malthus appeared above the signature 'AO'. Between the appearance of the third, on 23 May 1807, and August of that year, he had written two more and a series of critical comments on passages excerpted from Malthus's book. He gathered all this material into a single volume under the title *A Reply to the Essay on Population*, and it was published by Longman, Hurst, Rees and Orme. In the preface Hazlitt acknowledged that his scheme of arrangement made for both repetition and divagation, and that some of his reviewers might complain – as they had done of other works – that his style was 'too flowery'; so, in ironic reference to his 'metaphysical choke-pear', he said that he would, if they preferred it, 'undertake to produce a work as dry and formal as they please, if they will undertake to find it readers'.[24]

What prompted Hazlitt to reply to Malthus at this juncture, nearly a decade after the latter's book appeared, was the introduction of a Bill in Parliament on 19 February 1807 which, if passed, would have had the effect of substituting education for the dole. The Bill was brought forward by Samuel Whitbread – a good-hearted man who, Hazlitt said, nevertheless had too little real understanding of the poor – with the intention of

establishing a free national education system. Hazlitt had his doubts about
the value of such a thing in the then prevailing state of society (he had his
doubts too about the extension of Christian missions to the new industrial
proletarians of the northern cities, on the grounds that attempting to
moralize at them would have the reverse effect). But he was chiefly concerned to rebut the Malthusian ideas that underlay suggestions for reform
of poor laws in general. These ideas had been iterated by their author in
the form of a *Letter to Samuel Whitbread* after the failure of the Bill,
during whose attempted passage Malthus was to be seen in the precincts
of the House of Commons, lobbying MPs with a copy of his *Essay* in his
hand. Hazlitt felt he had to attack.

His attack was as full of *ad hominem* argument against Malthus as
analysis and refutation of his views – a fact which, Hazlitt said in his
Preface, he could not help and would not apologize for. He despised
Malthus's principles, which urged acceptance of the view that war, famine
and starvation are 'benevolent remedies by which nature has enabled
human beings to correct the disorders that would arise from a redundance
of population'. He despised Malthus's espousal of the principle of self-
interest – which Hazlitt so vigorously repudiated in his own *Essay* – and
rejected his call on the 'lower classes of society' to limit their numbers by
'moral restraint'. Malthus's imputation of enlarged sexual appetite among
the poor prompted Hazlitt's graphic attack on the upper classes' far greater
inducements to licentiousness – the undress fashions of the women, the
bawdy plays they attended, the provocations and opportunities of balls
and great parties. It was not that Hazlitt was against sex (to repeat: on the
contrary); rather, he was against the hypocrisy and condescension of
Malthus's view, and tore at the mask of pieties that covered it, as when
Malthus recommended that parsons should discourage the poor from
marrying, and if the poor insisted nevertheless, parsons should lecture
them not to have children they cannot support. If a poor man still pays no
heed then, said Malthus, let him marry and breed, but 'When nature will
govern and punish for us, it is a very miserable ambition to wish to snatch
the rod from her hand and draw upon ourselves the odium of executioner.
To the punishment of nature therefore he should be left, the punishment
of want. He has erred in the face of the most precise warning, and can
have no reason to complain of any person but himself when he feels the
consequences of his error.' The consequences are of course death by
starvation first of his children, then of himself. Malthus does not question
a system that tolerates the accumulation of so much economic resource in
the hands of a few that the many have to strive or starve for want of a
share. He simply argues that the latter must starve if they do not strive

and do not deprive themselves of the comforts of love. Hazlitt was disgusted and enraged by this, which explains the vehemence of his attack.

Hazlitt had two chief arguments against Malthus. First, when society finds itself inconvenienced by increase of population, it will adjust the size of families by a natural self-regulating feedback mechanism, namely the process of new families not having so many children as was standard in the previous generation. This idea seems not to have occurred to Malthus. Second, neither the poor nor anyone else are as sexually and procreatively incontinent as Malthus himself must be, said Hazlitt, for he seems to be generalizing from his own unrepresentatively hot-blooded case to all men. Of the two criticisms, the former tells.

The polemical character of Hazlitt's *Reply* and its frank discussion of sexual matters might have been one reason why all but one of the periodicals ignored it. Only the *Monthly Review* ran an article on it, in May 1808, and then only to hold its nose over Hazlitt's 'disgusting and preposterous' defiance of all 'modesty, breeding, and a sense of decency', to which they give this 'slight notice . . . as a warning to others'.

Even as he was doing battle with Malthus, Hazlitt was engaged in seeing another two-volume collection of his father's sermons through the press, and at the same time painting a portrait of his publisher Joseph Johnson.[25] And as if these activities together were insufficient to occupy him, he was also taking the first steps towards a major change in his personal life. Under Mary Lamb's careful supervision he had, in the course of the preceding couple of years, been introduced first to Sarah Stoddart's name, and then to the lady herself. Just as Mary steered Sarah in the direction of thinking about Hazlitt as a potential husband, so she steered Hazlitt in the complementary direction. By the summer of 1807 these matrimonial suggestions were, in Mary's estimation, progressing well. Her handling of the affair was briefly interrupted by a bout of her malady, requiring a spell in the lunatic asylum at Hoxton where she usually went when an attack came. In her first letter to Sarah after returning home she wrote in such a way as to suggest that matters were quite advanced between Sarah and Hazlitt: she was agog, she wrote, 'to see how your comical love affair would turn out'. It seems that Sarah had written to complain about not getting a letter from Hazlitt, to which Mary responded (with amusing frankness in the first sentence, given her meddling and matchmaking all along): 'You know, I make a pretence not to interfere; but like all old maids I feel a mighty solicitude about the event of love stories. I learn from the Lover that he has not been so remiss in his duty as you supposed. His Effusion, and your complaints of his inconstancy, crossed each other on

William Hazlitt
as a small boy,
by John Hazlitt

Hazlitt aged 13 years,
by John Hazlitt

Margaret Hazlitt, by John Hazlitt

Reverend William
Hazlitt, by John Hazlitt

Reverend William
Hazlitt, by William
Hazlitt the essayist

Grace Loftus, wife of Reverend William Hazlitt, by John Hazlitt

The house of William Hazlitt and Sarah Stoddart at 19 York Street, Westminster

William Hazlitt as a young
man, by John Hazlitt

When Goldsmith was talking one day to Sir Joshua of writing a fable in which little fishes were to be introduced, Dr. Johnson rolled about uneasily in his seat & began to laugh, on which Goldsmith said rather angrily — "Why do you laugh? If you were to write a fable for little fishes, you would make them speak like great whales!" The reproof was just. John

William Hazlitt's writing, from his manuscript of a 'Table-Talk'

John Hazlitt, a self-portrait

Samuel Coleridge in 1796,
by Peter Vandyke

William Godwin in 1802,
by James Northcote

William Wordsworth in 1798, by Robert Hancock

the road. He tells me his was a very strange letter, and that probably it has affronted you. That it was a strange letter I can readily believe; but that you were affronted by a strange letter is not so easy for me to conceive, that not being your way of taking things. But however it be, let some answer come, either to him, or else to me, showing cause why you do not answer him. And pray, by all means, preserve the said letter, that I may one day have the pleasure of seeing how Mr Hazlitt treats of love.'

She did one day see how Mr Hazlitt treats of love; if not in the strange letter to Sarah, which unluckily does not survive, then fifteen years later in Hazlitt's even stranger *Liber Amoris*, his notorious account of a desperately different and painful love. That Sarah Stoddart would not be affronted by a 'strange letter' from Hazlitt is certainly believable. She was a friend of the clever, unconventional Lambs: that says much. She was herself unconventional, a well-read, intelligent, independent woman who, to the distress of her stiff brother John – who had acquired a baronet's daughter for a wife, and therefore cared all the more anxiously about social niceties – enjoyed fun and paid little heed to etiquette. John once lectured her for being 'deficient in those minutiae of taste and conduct which constitute elegance of manners and mental refinement'.[26] Hazlitt by contrast was attracted to her affability and matter-of-factness. He proposed to her while she was putting a kettle on for tea, a speaking concomitance of events, for Hazlitt loved tea. She was four years older than Hazlitt, who in 1807 was aged twenty-nine to her thirty-three, and she was determined – by now, very likely, anxiously so – to marry. She had known Hazlitt for several years, knew the value that the Lambs placed on him, and had read his work – she always read and kept his publications. She was clear-eyed about Hazlitt, and no letter from him would have seemed especially strange to her.

From Hazlitt's point of view, Sarah Stoddart's personal qualities were a great recommendation, and so too no doubt was the fact that she had a little property, which at the least included an income of £80 a year, enough for a couple to live on very modestly, and two cottages in the village of Winterslow near Salisbury.[27] Whatever the vicissitudes of crossed letters in the post, Hazlitt and Sarah had Mary Lamb's blessing, bestowed with a characteristic touch of kindness, affection and black humour mixed: 'Farewell – determine as wisely as you can in regard to Hazlitt; and, if your determination is to have him, Heaven send you many happy years together. If I am not mistaken, I have concluded letters on [other of your prospective marriages] with this same wish. I hope it is not ominous of change; for if I were sure you would not be quite starved to death, nor beaten to a mummy, I should like to see you and Hazlitt come together, if (as Charles observes) it were only for the joke's sake.'[28]

By 21 December 1807 matters were concluded in principle between Hazlitt and Sarah themselves. Mary wrote on that day to urge Sarah to the final step, which was to tell her brother John, for he was the only one of their circle who did not yet know about the proposed nuptials. 'You ought to tell your brother as soon as possible,' she wrote, 'for at present he is on very friendly visiting terms with Hazlitt.' Indeed, John had lately dined (on 8 December 1807) with Hazlitt at the latter's lodgings, in company with Charles and Mary Lamb, Joseph Hume and Godwin – and John was the only possible source of the lump sum (Mary nominated £100) required for first setting up home together. The intending bride and groom planned to rent a flat in the suburbs of London, in Walworth near the gardens Hazlitt remembered so fondly from boyhood, and they had to think of furniture and other necessities. 'If you chuse that I should tell him, I will,' Mary continued, 'but I think it would come better from you. If you can persuade Hazlitt to mention it, that would be still better; for I know your brother would be unwilling to give credit to you because you deceived yourself in regard to [other recent suitors]. Hazlitt, I know, is shy of speaking first; but I think it of such great importance to you to have your brother friendly in the business, that, if you can overcome his reluctance, it would be a great point gained. For you must begin the world with ready money.' She told Sarah that Hazlitt's brother John was 'mightily pleased' with the news of the wedding, and promised to give them what furniture he could spare. To this encouragement Mary added her own: 'I most heartily congratulate you on having so well got over your first difficulties; and now that it is quite settled, let us have no more fears. I now mean not only to hope and wish, but to persuade myself, that you will be very happy together.' That was a reasonable hope; Charles Lamb himself, unromantic and mildly sceptical about most things, said there was 'love o' both sides'.[29]

Charles Lamb was always inclined to see the merriment in human affairs. As an extension of the 'joke' of a marriage between people who were respectively his own and his sister's best friends, he wrote to Joseph Hume on 29 December to announce the forthcoming wedding with his habitual touch of blackness in the humour: 'I suppose you know what has happen'd to our poor friend Hazlitt. If not, take it as I read it in the Morning Post or Fashionable World of this morning: – "Last night Mr H. a portrait painter in Southampton Buildings, Holborn, put an end to his existence by cutting his throat in a shocking manner. It is supposed that he must have committed his purpose with a pallet knife, as the edges of the cicatrice or wound were found besmeared with a yellow consistence, but the knife could not be found. The reasons of this rash act are not assigned; an unfortunate passion has been mentioned; but nothing certain is known. The deceased was subject to hypochondria, low spirits, but he had lately seemed better, having paid more than usual attention to his dress and person. Besides being a painter, he had written some pretty things in prose and verse." '[30] There is much that is of the nature of an in-joke here – the palette knife, Hazlitt's dress, the surprising reference to verse.

Hazlitt saw the letter and wrote a response in the form of a 'humble petition and remonstrance' which included a statement of proofs that he was still alive. Among the proofs was the fact that he had rung his bell at eleven each night for the last month, to call the maid to bring a warming-pan for his bed; and that he had thereupon 'slept soundly for the next twelve or fourteen hours'; that he had risen every day at noon or one o'clock, dressed, drank tea, eaten two platefuls of buttered toast (the crusts removed 'as hurtful to the mouth and gums'), and that he has then 'sat for some hours with his eyes steadfastly fixed upon the fire, like a person in a state of deep thought, but doing nothing'. Not a day has passed in which he has not had food and drink, he writes, just like other people: 'For instance, he has swallowed eight dozen of pills, nine boluses, & as many purgative draughts of a most unsavoury quality. What he has fed on with the most relish has been a mess of chicken-broth, and he has sent out twice for a paper of almonds & raisins. His general diet is soup-meagre with bread & milk for supper. That it is true that the petitioner has abstained both from gross feeding and from all kinds of intoxicating liquors; a circumstance, he conceives, so far from denoting a natural decay and loss of faculties, that on the contrary it shews more wisdom than he was always possessed of.' Whimsy aside, the 'petition' shows that Hazlitt was confined to his rooms by reason of illness, even though he 'walked out at least once a week to get himself shaved' for – as he put it – decency's sake. Perhaps he was suffering from a severe cold, or flu, since it was the time of year for it; but the illness lasted several months, and a remark later in his mock-deposition suggests that it might have been a venereal disease, for among the 'good resolutions to be put in practice as soon as he recovers' he ends with 'to leave off wenching as injurious both to health and morals'. The symptoms associated with a urethritis of gonorrhoea, very commonly caught from London prostitutes, as Boswell's staggering number of recurrent infections shows (at least nineteen well-recorded separate attacks; he eventually died from the ensuing complications), included fever and lassitude, sometimes nausea and vomiting, and treatment centred upon a course of sulphur and mercury taken in pill form.[31] It would be surprising if Hazlitt entirely escaped the problems that could arise from employing prostitutes' services as regularly as he did. This episode is a candidate for an occasion when he did not.

On the other hand, he is unlikely to have had sexual relations with Sarah Stoddart while recovering from a venereal disease. He had an opportunity to do so while still indisposed, for he spent a week or two with her in the country in February. According to Hazlitt's later testimony, Sarah was not sexually inexperienced when they met. They were adults, and engaged to be married, and it would have been natural for them to sleep together while alone and private in the country. In any case, immediately after they were married at the beginning of May Sarah became pregnant, which means either that he was confident that he had recovered from any untoward affliction, or had not been so afflicted in the first place. Either way, the question of the nature of Hazlitt's long illness in the winter of 1807–8 is an open one.

Lamb continued the joke by treating the 'petition' as if it were not from Hazlitt himself but from his spirit, returned to earth. This return could not, said Lamb, be for the purpose of revealing – as is usual in the case of visits from the dead – where hidden treasures lay, for Hazlitt had never had any to hoard; 'it is highly improbable that he should have accumulated any such vast treasures, for the revealing of which a miracle was needed, without some suspicion of the fact among his friends during his Lifetime. I for my part always looked upon our dear friend as a man rich rather in the gifts of his mind than in earthly treasures. He had few rents or comings in, that I was ever aware of, small (if any) landed property, and by all that I could witness he subsisted more upon the well-timed contributions of a few chosen friends who knew his worth, than upon any Estate which could properly be called his own. I myself have contributed my part. God knows, I speak this not in reproach. I have never taken, nor indeed did the deceased offer, any *written acknowledgements* of the various sums which he has had of me, by which I could make the fact manifest to the legal eye of an Executor or Administrator. He was not a Man to affect these niceties in his transactions with friends. He would often say, money was nothing between intimate acquaintances, that Golden Streams had no Ebb, that a Purse mouth never regorged, that God loved a chearful giver but the Devil hated a free taker, that a paid Loan made angels groan, with many such like sayings: he had always free and generous notions about money. His nearest friends know this best.' Evidently Hazlitt's chronic poverty and his reliance on the generosity of friends – not an uncommon expedient in those days, as witness the generosity of friends to Coleridge and Wordsworth – was worth a dig. Joseph Hume's contribution to the exchange alludes among other things to the wenching resolution: 'He was a man of spirit in his better days. He therefore would have been ashamed on his own account and much more so as an example for the well being of society, to cast out of human conduct the habit of wenching.'

The rare treasure of a letter from Hazlitt to Sarah Stoddart dates from the time of these exchanges, written some time in January 1808. 'My dear love, about a week has passed,' he writes, 'and I have received no letter – not one of those letters "in which I live, or have no life at all". What is become of you? Are you married, hearing that I was dead (for so it has been reported)? Or are you gone into a nunnery? Or are you fallen in love with some of the amorous heroes of Boccaccio? Which of them is it? Is it with Chynon, who was transformed from a clown into a lover, and learned to spell by the force of beauty? Or with Lorenzo, the lover of Isabella, whom her three bretheren hated (as your brother does me), who was a merchant's clerk? Or with Federigo Alberigi, an honest gentleman, who ran through his entire fortune, and won his mistress by cooking a fair falcon for her dinner, though it was the only means left he had of getting a dinner for himself? This last is the man; and I am more persuaded of it, because I think I won your good liking myself by giving you an entertainment – of sausages, when I had no money to buy them with. Nay now, never deny it! Did not I ask your consent that very night after, and did you not give it? Well, I should be confoundedly jealous of those fine gallants, if I did not know that a living dog is better than a dead lion: though, now I think of it, Boccaccio does not in general make much of his lovers: it is his women who are so delicious. I almost wish I had lived in those times, and had been a little *more amiable*. Now if a woman had written the book, it would not have had this effect upon me: the men would have been heroes and angels, and the women nothing at all. Isn't there some truth in that?' This thought put Hazlitt in mind of a matter which seems to have been, if more playfully than not, a minor source of tension between them, in the shape of a woman Hazlitt had recently liked, and about whom Sarah affected jealousy. 'Talking of departed lovers,' he continues, 'I met my old flame the other day in the street. I did dream of her *one* night since, and only one: every other night I had the same dream I have had for these two months past. Now, if you are at all reasonable, this will satisfy you.' The parenthetical remark about John Stoddart's negative attitude to Hazlitt is a puzzle in the light of their recent friendly dinners together. As matters transpired, when Stoddart learned of the proposed marriage he was not pleased, but did not stand in its way. He even insisted on Sarah's being married from his house in proper form. Before too long, however, the divergence between his principles and Hazlitt's caused a full breach, which was never healed.

'I liked your note,' Hazlitt resumed his letter, 'it is just such a note as such a nice rogue as you ought to write after the *provocation* you received. I would not give a pin for a girl "whose cheeks never tingle", nor for myself if I could not make them tingle sometimes. Now, though I am always writing to you about "lips and noses", and such sort of stuff, yet as I sit by my fireside (which I do generally eight or ten hours a day), I oftener think of you in a serious, sober light. For, indeed, I never love you so well as when I think of sitting down with you to dinner on a scrag-end of mutton, and hot potatoes. You please my fancy more then than when I think of you in – no, you would never forgive me if I were to finish the sentence. Now I think of it, what do you mean to be dressed in when we are married? But it does not much matter! I wish you would let your hair grow; though perhaps nothing will be better than "the same air and look with which at first my heart was took". But now to business. I mean to call upon your brother *in form*, namely, as soon as I get quite well, which I hope to do in about another *fortnight*; and then I hope you will come up by the coach as fast as the horses can carry you, for I long mightily to be in your ladyship's presence – to vindicate my character. I think you had better sell the small house, I mean that at 4.10, and I will borrow 100L. So that we shall set off merrily in spite of all the prudence of Edinburgh. Good-bye, little dear.'[32]

The prudence in question presumably belonged to John Stoddart's Scottish wife, whom they suspected would stand in the way of any help Stoddart might be disposed to offer. Hazlitt's suggestion for their financial provision on first being married includes the sale of a small house of Sarah's – perhaps the second of the two she owned in Winterslow, or a remaining property in Salisbury. Howe suggests that the large loan of £100 was designed to come from Richard Sharpe ('Conversation' Sharpe, whom Hazlitt first met in the Lakes with the poets, and who is the probable subject of his encomium in the essay 'On the Want of Money', as the man who 'would lend his money freely and fearlessly in spite of circumstances; if you were likely to pay him, he grew peevish, and would pick a quarrel with you'[33]).

A few weeks after he wrote this letter Hazlitt decided to go to Sarah at Winterslow, despite still being ill. He had not heard from her and was anxious because of it. He travelled down on Saturday 6 February 1808, saying nothing to anyone about his journey, not even the Lambs. Mary had received from Sarah a letter and drawing intended for him, and wrote back saying, 'He left town on Saturday afternoon without telling us where he was going. He seemed very impatient at not hearing from you. He was very ill and I suppose is gone home to his father's to be nursed.' She then adds that she has spoken to John Stoddart, who was emphatic in saying that if the wedding was really going to happen, Sarah must be married from his home. He was expecting his father-in-law, the baronet, to visit until mid-April, but thereafter Sarah could come and stay. Mary underlined his insistence: 'He wishes that you should be married with all the proper decorums, *from his house*.'[34] That effectively suggested a date for the wedding at the end of April or the beginning of May 1808.

On the assumption that Hazlitt had gone home to convalesce, Mary forwarded Sarah's letter and drawing to Wem. In response came a worried letter from William senior, saying that Hazlitt was not with them, so what had happened? But by this time the mystery was solved. Lamb discovered that Hazlitt's landlord in Southampton Buildings had received a note from the wanderer asking for some shirts to be sent to Winterslow. Lamb wrote accordingly to William senior, enclosing a card with a drawing of the Winterslow cottage: 'We shrewdly suspect that at the time of writing that Letter which has given you all this trouble, a certain son of yours (who is both Painter and Author) was [at Winterslow].'

Few of the houses extant in Hazlitt's time remain in any of the Winterslow villages, of which there are now three, labelled East, Middle and West Winterslow respectively, strung close together on the Clarendon Way as it runs east from Salisbury near the southern margin of Salisbury Plain. Nevertheless, those that remain are representative enough of Sarah Stoddart's home; they are substantial thatched houses, commodious and comfortable, set in their own gardens, which might then have been larger than they are now. There Hazlitt remained for a week or two, returning in time for Lamb to write to his old school-friend Thomas Manning in China, 'A treaty of marriage is on foot between William Hazlitt and Miss Stoddart. Something about settlements only retards it. She has somewhere about £80 a year, to be £120 when her mother dies. He has no settlement except what he can claim from the Parish. *Pauper est Cinna, sed tamen amat*. The thing is therefore in abeyance.'[35]

Matters did not remain in abeyance long. On 18 March Hazlitt gave a tea-party at his lodgings at which John Stoddart was present, in company with Godwin, Holcroft, Charles Lamb, Crabb Robinson, and Northcote the painter. By this time everything was resolved. Mary wrote to Sarah about details of her bridesmaid's dress, asking whether she should wear the gown that Sarah sprigged for her, or one that could be made up from the silk that Manning had sent from China, of 'a sort of dead-whitish-bloom colour'. In the same letter she expresses regret at not being able to give Sarah a wedding present (of money or furniture, presumably) other than 'a willing mind, bringing nothing with me but many wishes, and not a few hopes, and a very little of fears of happy years to come'.[36]

A month later Wordsworth came to town and visited Lamb with the manuscript of 'The White Doe of Rylstone' in his pocket. 'I took the MSS to Lamb's to read it, or part of it, one evening,' he wrote to Coleridge on 19 April. 'There unluckily I found Hazlitt and his Beloved; of course, though I had the poem in my hand I declined, nay absolutely refused, to read it. But as they were very earnest in entreating me, I at last consented to read one Book, and when it was done I simply said that there was a passage which probably must have struck Hazlitt as a *Painter* "Now doth a delicate shadow fall" etc.'[37] The delicate shadow was discussed, he reports, and 'nothing more took place'. Had this meeting happened at a later date, Wordsworth's dismay at finding Hazlitt at Lamb's might be explained by the animosity that eventually estranged them; at this stage the 'unluckily' remark is probably explained by the fact that Wordsworth wished to read to the Lambs alone, before venturing the poem on other ears. He had enough experience, from earlier encounters, of Hazlitt's disinterested critical powers to fear their frost on a new growth. It is, however, true that the two men were growing less warm to each other than they were at their first acquaintance at Nether Stowey and Alfoxden. Wordsworth was constitutionally opposed to Hazlitt's ferocious intellectual approach to criticism, which Wordsworth believed was not calculated to give his poetry its due. Much has been said about the question of Wordsworth's long life and vast output (neither of which helps a poetic reputation), including the anonymous squib: 'Two voices are there; one is of the deep/And one is of an old half-witted sheep/And both, oh Wordsworth! are thine'; which is something Hazlitt saw, although – despite later animosities and the cruel gossip Wordsworth tried to spread about him – Hazlitt always acknowledged Wordsworth's poetic genius. But at this point there is no reason to think that the words 'There unluckily I found Hazlitt and his Beloved' is an indication that active hostilities had begun. Wordsworth knew that Hazlitt and Lamb were bosom friends and always in each other's company. Still, it was no doubt gratifying to be entreated, and to condescend to read 'one Book' to genuinely discerning ears.

One fact that Wordsworth's letter to Coleridge establishes is that Sarah was back in London by mid-April, resident with her brother, and preparing for the wedding. Hazlitt had bought a special marriage licence which made the reading of banns unnecessary, and in accordance with the law that forced Dissenters to hold their weddings on Church of England premises,

Sarah and Hazlitt were married at St Andrew's Church, Holborn, on Sunday 1 May 1808. The register described the consenting parties in due form as 'William Hazlitt of the Parish of St Andrew, Holborn, in the County of Middlesex, a Bachelor, and Sarah Stoddart of the Parish of Winterslow, in the County of Wilts, a Spinster'. Hazlitt's lodgings in Southampton Buildings fell in the Parish of St Andrew, which explains why he figures as a bachelor of it, and also why they were married there. Lamb suffered from a common affliction: an almost ungovernable inclination to giggle during solemn moments in church, such as weddings and funerals. In a letter of 1815 to Southey he talks of the wedding and reports that he was 'like to have been turned out several times during the ceremony. Anything awful makes me laugh.' The wedding breakfast was held at John Stoddart's house, where Lamb was free to laugh as much as he liked. There is no record of where the couple went immediately after-wards for their honeymoon – it might have been Winterslow, and it might have been (alternatively or as well) a journey north so that Hazlitt's family at Wem could meet its new member. The latter is likely. In any event Sarah met Hazlitt's family soon after the wedding, and quickly established lifelong friendships with Mrs Hazlitt and Peggy.

The couple were soon back in London, living in lodgings in Camberwell Green, not far from the Tea Gardens at Walworth, Hazlitt's boyhood idyll. It had been so then because he had just returned from America, which had proved a wilderness to his family, and been reunited with his father. Now, with a wife who had some property and an income, he might have felt as if he had left a notional wilderness and made a different kind of home-coming at last.

# CHAPTER SEVEN

# The Winterslow Years

## 1808–1811

IF THE HAZLITTS had a honeymoon before moving into their Walworth lodgings, it was a short one, and the principal reason was that Hazlitt was in the midst of exploring possibilities for several new literary projects. One was a commission for William Godwin, now a publisher of children's books under the pseudonym 'Edwin Baldwin' – some say, because his own name had bad associations in the public mind, not for his political stance of the 1790s but because he had written a too-frank biography of his late wife Mary Wollstonecraft; others say that because the publishing business was formally in the name of his second wife, he wished to keep a certain distance from it in the public eye at least, and to run it from behind the scenes. Hazlitt signed a contract with Godwin to write a new grammar of the English language, their joint hope being that it would have large sales as a school textbook. Hazlitt also proposed a translation and abridgement of Baron de Bourgoing's *Tableau de l'Espagne Moderne*, a book he reasonably thought would have topical interest, for the conflict that came to be called the Peninsular War had just begun, precipitated on the very day of his marriage to Sarah – 1 May 1808 – by a Spanish peasant killing a French soldier in a street in Madrid. The Bourgoing project came to nothing, but not until after Hazlitt had expended shoe-leather taking the idea to a number of publishers.

In the middle of November 1808, when Hazlitt had done as much as he could to advance arrangements for these two projects, he and Sarah left their Camberwell Green lodgings and moved to Sarah's cottage in Winterslow.[1] This had been their plan all along in any case, for living in their own house, with garden vegetables and chickens (and perhaps some other livestock)[2] to furnish their table, made for greater economy of living. Moreover Sarah was pregnant, and was due to give birth in January.

It was no hardship to them to go. Sarah loved Winterslow and its surrounding country, and Hazlitt immediately felt likewise on coming to know it. 'Here I came fifteen years ago, a willing exile; and as I trod the lengthened greensward by the low wood-side, repeated the old line, "My mind to me a kingdom is"!' Hazlitt wrote reminiscingly in the autumn of 1823. The pleasures of walking and thinking which had been his in Shropshire were revived here, and he particularly liked the large skies above Salisbury Plain, which reminded him of the work of Claude Lorrain, one of his favourite painters. In the intervals of writing his 'Grammar' he resumed landscape painting, taking his equipment with him into the woods to try to copy nature. His sister Peggy, who visited Winterslow the following summer, describes him taking 'his canvas, paints, etc., an hammer, and a nail, which he used to drive into a tree which served him as an easel to hang his picture on. A couple of eggs, boiled hard, and some bread and cheese for his dinner, but never any liquor of any kind. Usually coming home at four (except when we went to meet him in that beautiful wood), bringing home with him some promising beginning of the beautiful views around, but fated, alas, never to be finished. Several of these I remember, one in particular, the view of Norman Court, the seat of [Charles] Wall Esq.'³ Inspired by the landscape, and wishing to try something ambitious, Hazlitt began a large painting on the theme of Jacob's Ladder. It occupied his non-writing moments for much of the next two years.

Walking, wandering in the countryside, and painting were Hazlitt's favourite avocations, and he found them ideal as prompts for thought. Winterslow and its environs proved the perfect setting in this regard. He liked to lie on a sunny bank on the Plain, dreaming and remembering. When he wrote there, he said, ideas came easily, and words likewise, and he could spread his wings. 'If the reader is not already apprised of it, he will please to take notice that I write this at Winterslow,' Hazlitt says in one of his essays, abruptly interrupting his argument. 'My style there is apt to be redundant and excursive. At other times it may be cramped, dry, abrupt; but here it flows like a river and overspreads its banks. I have not to seek for thoughts or hunt for images: they come out of themselves, I inhale them with the breeze, and the silent groves are vocal with a thousand recollections:

> And visions, as poetic eyes avow,
> Hang on each leaf and cling to every bough . . .

I look out of my window and see that a shower has just fallen: the fields look green after it, and a rosy cloud hangs over the brow of the hill; a lily expands its petals in the moisture, dressed in its lovely green and white; a shepherd boy has just brought some pieces of turf with daisies and grass for his mistress to make a bed for her sky-lark, not doomed to dip his wings in the dappled dawn ... Really, it is wonderful how little the worse I am for fifteen years' wear and tear, how I come upon my legs again on the grounds of truth and nature, and "look abroad into universality", forgetting that there is any such person as myself in the world.'[4]

An added virtue of Winterslow was the proximity of large country houses with fine works of art in them, and the great and mysterious monument of Stonehenge itself. There was Wilton House, with its portrait by Van Dyke of the Pembroke family, and Longford Castle, seat of Lord Radnor, with its two spectacular Claudes, the *Morning of the Roman Empire* and the *Evening of the Roman Empire*, and its affecting *Magdalen* by Guido, her upturned eyes and hair streaming. Stourhead and Fonthill Abbey were not far away either, but Hazlitt did not think the collections there especially notable. Stonehenge he thought magnificent and striking; he described it as 'that "huge, dumb heap", that stands on the blasted heath, and looks like a group of giants, bewildered, not knowing what to do, encumbering the earth, and turned to stone, while in the act of warring on Heaven'.[5]

The absence of Sarah and Hazlitt from London was quickly and keenly felt by the Lambs and others of Hazlitt's circle. Mary Lamb wrote on 10 December to say that she had news of them only through John Stoddart, and as she and Charles were anxious for news of Sarah's health, they earnestly wished that one of them would write. 'You cannot think how very much we miss you and H of a Wednesday evening,' she continues; 'All the glory of the night, I may say, is at an end.' This is because 'Hazlitt was most brilliant, most ornamental, as a Wednesday-man.' But he was of even more use to them 'on common days, when he dropt in after a quarrel or a fit of the glooms.' With him away, said Mary, 'when we are in the dismals, there is now no hope of relief from any quarter whatsoever.'[6]

Sarah gave birth to a son at a quarter past four in the afternoon of 15 January 1809, and they called him William.[7] It was a spectacularly wet winter; the city of Salisbury, on its marshy many-channelled two rivers, the Avon and the Nadder, had been flooded so badly that the stalls in the cathedral choir were under water, and acres of fields in the surrounding country were drowned, including those belonging to the village of Wilton next door to Winterslow.[8] Winterslow itself was safe on its ridge, but the weather benefited no-one. As sometimes happens the dire winter gave way, in seeming compensation, to beautiful summers both in that year and the next, in each of which the Lambs came to spend their summer holidays with the Hazlitts.

But the holidays were islands in an otherwise difficult time. Worst was the death in July 1809 of the Hazlitts' infant son. Hazlitt was in London that spring, meeting Godwin to discuss his draft of the 'Grammar' and exploring the possibility of publishing, by subscription, a history of modern philosophy. He was suddenly called home to Winterslow by the news that his little boy was ill. Mary Lamb wrote to her friend Louisa Martin on 28 March to say 'Hazlitt's child is expected to die.' In a footnote to the letter Lamb added one of those perverse and macabre touches that puzzle his biographers, in the form of an apparently heartless joke: 'Hazlitt's child died of swallowing a bag of white paint, which the poor little innocent thing mistook for sugar candy. It told its Mother just two hours before it died, that it did not like soft sugar candy, and so it came out, which was not before suspected. When it was opened several other things were found in it, particularly a small hearth brush, two golden pippins and a letter which I had written Hazlitt from Bath.'[9] One suggestion for these strange sallies – sometimes wholly unseasonable, as this proved to be, for the child was dangerously ill – is that they protected a highly vulnerable sensibility; Lamb had once suffered an attack of madness like his sister's, and for the rest of his life feared a recurrence.

Sarah's first alarm about the baby's health was quietened by a partial recovery. Hazlitt returned to London to complete his business. He was frequently at Godwin's house, and more frequently at the Lambs', helping them to plan their impending visit to Winterslow. They were to be joined by young Martin Burney, Mary's favourite, and Ned Phillips, who proposed to contribute to the common pot by scouring the Winterslow woods with his gun, a sport that had occupied his undergraduate days at Oxford. Mary wrote to Sarah reassuring her about expenses, since the party planned to stay a whole month. She told her that Martin and the Lambs would give five pounds each, and that Martin could sleep on the floor of the 'best kitchen'. She added, 'You are not to say this to Hazlitt, lest his delicacy should be alarmed.' Just as all was anticipation and readiness, misfortune struck: in June Mary was suddenly attacked by her illness, requiring a stay in the asylum at Hoxton as usual, this time for a month. The visit was not cancelled but postponed *sine die*.

Worse quickly followed. The respite in the Hazlitts' baby's illness did not last. He died on 5 July 1809, aged just six months. This was the reason for Peggy Hazlitt's visit. She arrived two days after the little boy died, and later wrote that she could never forget the look of anguish on her brother's face when she greeted her. But although he was stricken, he kept silent, and applied himself to his work on the 'Grammar', and on solitary painting trips into the surrounding woods. It was not until 1822 that he could mention it. He then wrote, 'I have never seen death but once, and that was in an infant. It is years ago. The look was calm and placid, and the face was fair and firm. It was as if a waxen image had been laid out in the coffin, and strewed with innocent flowers. It was not like death, but more like an image of life! No breath moved the lips, no pulse stirred, no sight or sound would enter those eyes or ears more. While I looked at it, I saw no pain was there; it seemed to smile at the short pang of life which was over: but I could not bear the coffin-lid to be closed – it almost stifled me; and still as the nettles wave in a corner of the churchyard over his little grave, the welcome breeze helps to refresh me and ease the tightness at my breast.'[10] The little coffin was taken to Salisbury to be buried alongside its occupant's grandfather, old Lieutenant Stoddart, in St Martin's church-yard.

Work assuages grief, or keeps it at bay until it can be better borne. The 'Grammar' was completed during the course of the summer, and Hazlitt took the manuscript to town. When he arrived he found another oppor-tunity waiting. Thomas Holcroft the playwright had died in March, leaving an incomplete autobiography. A committee of Holcroft's friends wished to see the work finished and made ready for publication, and they com-missioned Hazlitt to undertake the task. Hazlitt was willing, despite being promised payment only after publication, chiefly because of the friendship he felt towards the deceased, and because the publication was designed to help Holcroft's widow, who had been left destitute.

Hazlitt did not have an easy time with Godwin over his *New and Improved Grammar of the English Tongue*. They consulted extensively over the drafts, of which there were several before a version of the book emerged that satisfied both of them. By November it was in print, as Hazlitt reported to his father in a letter written on Guy Fawkes Day. Perhaps as a result of their discussions of the *Grammar* Godwin had suddenly had an inspiration about teaching English in schools, and had written a 'New Guide to the English Tongue' for inclusion with a revamped edition of Mylius's *School Dictionary*, which he published in September. He now also paired his 'Guide' with Hazlitt's *Grammar*, and the combined book appeared on 11 November 1809.

But Godwin's ambition to capture the school text-book market would not allow him to let matters rest. He had already asked Hazlitt to attack the main opposition grammar, a famous and widely used book by Lindley Murray, to which Hazlitt, with an air of tried patience, responded: 'As to the attack upon Murray, I have hit at him several times, and whenever there is a question of a blunder, "his name is not far off". Perhaps it would look like jealousy to make a formal set at him. Besides I am already noted by the reviewers for want of liberality, and an undisciplined moral sense.'[11] Now Godwin asked Hazlitt to let him abridge the *Grammar* to make it conform better to the notions (as Godwin put it) of 'Heads of Seminaries of Education'. To this second suggestion, which Godwin made in March 1810, Hazlitt replied, 'Dear Sir, I was not at all offended, but a good deal vexed at the contents of your former letter ... I thought [the grammar] would answer the purpose, and as you seemed to approve of what I had done, I was sorry to be dashed in pieces against the dulness of schoolmasters.'[12] But he agreed nevertheless, and in June the *Morning Chronicle* carried an advertisement briskly announcing the abridgement's appearance: 'Published This Day: Many of the most respectable Heads of our Seminaries of Education having expressed a desire that the improvements contained in Mr Hazlitt's *Grammar* should be brought out in a form better adapted for the use of the Junior Classes of their Pupils, the following is now given to the public in compliance with this suggestion.'

Godwin had abridged Hazlitt despite a favourable reception for the original version in the *Critical Review* of December 1809, which described it as 'a more rational, simple and intelligible English grammar, than most of those in common use; and we think that it may with great benefit to the scholar, be introduced into our elementary schools'. At the same time Godwin thought well enough of the original to send it to the awesome *Edinburgh Review* with a covering letter explaining that its author was 'one of my inward friends, Mr William Hazlitt. He is a man of singular acuteness and sound understanding, and I think he has brought some new materials to elucidate a most ancient subject.'[13] The awesome *Edinburgh Review* took no notice. But Hazlitt had indeed brought something new to thinking about English grammar. He anticipates both recent grammarians and philosophers of language in stressing that the grammar of English cannot simply be modelled on that of Latin, as previous grammarians assumed; and in observing that the grammatical distinctions of words do not conform to things spoken about, but to our manner of speaking about things – from which a long and curly tale hangs in philosophical debate.[14]

Another admirer of the *Grammar* was Lamb – or at least, in a celebratedly convoluted pun, he marked his preference for it over Godwin's 'Guide' to which it was joined like a Siamese twin. Writing to his friend Manning in China on 2 January 1810, he says 'Hazlitt has written a *grammar* for Godwin. Godwin sells it bound up with a treatise of his own on language, but the *grey mare is the better horse*. I don't allude to Mrs Godwin, but to the word *grammar*, which comes near to *grey mare*, if you observe, in sound. That figure is called paranomasia in Greek. I am sometimes happy in it.'[15]

Lamb seems to have infected Hazlitt with his happy skill in punning during the postponed visit to Winterslow, which took place at last in October 1809, after Mary's recovery from her attack. She and Charles went down to Winterslow at the end of September, and were joined there on 15 October by Ned Phillips. Martin Burney could not come because of an impending law examination. The punning mood caught by Hazlitt appears in the letter he wrote to his father describing the visitors' activities. He said that they enjoyed fine weather, and took many long walks to Stonehenge, Salisbury, Wilton, and the woods around Winterslow. Then he added, 'We are I find just on the borders of Hampshire, and that part of the country which lies on the Hampshire side is as woody and pleasant as the Wilts side is bleak and desert. I suppose this was the origin of the two names, Hants, i.e. Haunts, and Wilts, i.e. Wilds.' A month in the country had been restorative for both Mary and Charles, he reported; Mary's health and spirits were unfailingly good throughout, and Charles neither smoked nor drank anything but 'tea and small beer'. There is an allusion in this to Charles's tendency to alcohol. Hazlitt told his father also that Ned Phillips, 'an Oxonian of idle renown', had shot a hare and a pheasant for their cooking pot, and that the party gathered mushrooms on their evening walks to add to the pot too – on one evening sitting up until midnight discussing Fielding because of it.[16]

The beauty of that autumn lived long in Hazlitt's memory. 'I used to walk out at this time with Mr and Miss L— of an evening, to look at the Claude Lorrain skies over our heads, melting from azure into purple and gold, and to gather mushrooms, that sprung up at our feet, to throw into our hashed mutton at supper. I was at that time an enthusiastic admirer of Claude, and could dwell forever on one or two of the finest prints from him hung round my little room; the fleecy flocks, the bending trees, the winding streams, the groves, the nodding temples, the air-wove hills, and distant sunny vales; and tried to translate them into their lovely living hues.'

Hazlitt's report of the Lambs' enjoyment and the flourishing health they took home from Winterslow is confirmed by Mary's own account. Writing to thank Sarah she said, 'I continue very well, and return you very sincere thanks for my good health, and improved looks which have almost made Mrs Godwin die with envy; she longs to come to Winterslow as much as the spiteful elder sister did to go to the well for a gift to spit diamonds.' This allusion reminded her to add a post-script, describing a joke played by Lamb: 'Charles told Mrs Godwin, Hazlitt found a well in his garden, which, water being scarce in your country, would bring him in two hundred a year; and she came in great haste the next morning to ask me if it were true.' This was Mary Jane Godwin, the authoress of books for children and Godwin's second wife, who had a somewhat mysterious past, having escaped wartime Europe under the pseudonym 'Mrs Clairmont'. Her daughter was the famous and dramatic Claire, lover of Shelley and Byron, and mother of the latter's daughter Allegra (and perhaps of the former's daughter Elena too, though the child was officially credited to Claire's half-sister Mary Godwin Shelley, creator of *Frankenstein*).[17]

The body of Mary's letter is a description in miniature of the month at Winterslow. 'The dear, quiet, lazy, delicious month we spent with you is remembered by me with such regret, that I feel quite discontent and Winterslow-sick. I assure you, I never passed such a pleasant time in the country in my life, both in the house and out of it, the card playing quarrels, and a few gaspings for breath after your swift footsteps up the high hills excepted, and those drawbacks are not unpleasant in the recollection. We have got some salt butter to make our toast seem like yours, and we have tried to eat meat suppers, but that would not do, for we have left our appetites behind us; and the dry loaf, which offended you, now comes in at night unaccompanied; but, sorry I am to add, it is soon followed by the pipe and the gin bottle. We smoked the very first night of our arrival.'[18]

In the weeks immediately after their guests left, Hazlitt set hard to work on the Life of Holcroft. He wrote in the evenings after painting all day, and in a week produced thirty-five pages – about seven thousand words, as calculated from his large clear hand as it slopes evenly across a foolscap leaf. This is good average going for a writer, and anyway came in addition to nearly a hundred pages transcribed from Holcroft's draft, in which the writer told his life's story as far as his fifteenth year. Hazlitt was working up the remainder of the life from the memoranda and anecdotes he had collected or been given by Mrs Holcroft, and from Holcroft's other writings. He hoped to finish by Christmas 1809, an ambitious target.[19]

As the work on Holcroft proceeded Hazlitt received a letter from his friend Crabb Robinson, who had recently decided to take up the law as a profession, after an exciting career as a foreign and war correspondent for *The Times*, which included a sojourn in Corunna to cover events in the Peninsular War. After returning to England Robinson served for a while as *The Times*'s Foreign Editor, but now, while he 'ate his dinners' at his Inn of Court to make the transition between journalism and law, he was helping with the establishment of a new periodical called *The London Review*. He wrote to Hazlitt to enlist his services in writing for it. Hazlitt replied that he was indeed willing, and would call in to discuss matters when he was next in town. He suggested reviewing Opie's *Lectures on Painting*, which he regarded as largely plagiarized from Fuseli. (He added that, nevertheless, he thought well of Opie's work on canvas.)

Hazlitt was not far out in his estimate of when he would finish the Holcroft biography. In early January 1810 Lamb wrote to Manning to say that Hazlitt had 'finished his Life – I do not mean his own life, but he has finished a life of Holcroft, which is going to press,' and Godwin's diary for 15 January records that Hazlitt had given him the manuscript.

Then, however, two ominous entries appear in Godwin's diary for 23 and 26 January. They read 'H[olcrof]t. revise'. He had encountered a serious problem, in the form of scandalous and sometimes libellous references to himself and Mary Wollstonecraft, among others, in the transcriptions from Holcroft's diaries which Hazlitt had included as an Appendix. Godwin was aghast. He wrote to tell Mrs Holcroft that he refused to be 'part or party to such a publication'.[20] Mary Lamb reported that Godwin's decision set Mrs Holcroft and the committee of Holcroft's friends by the ears: 'Mrs Holcroft still goes about from Nicholson to Tuthil, and from Tuthil to Godwin, and from Godwin to Tuthil, and from Tuthil to Nicholson, to consult on the publication, or no publication, of the life of the good man, her husband. It is called the Life Everlasting.'[21] Hazlitt had foreseen the trouble; in his letter to Crabb Robinson he remarked that a possible problem with his writing for *The London Review* was that his biography of Holcroft included some 'excellent stories' about the new periodical's editor, Richard Cumberland, 'which Cumberland, without being the most irritable man in the world, might be disposed to complain of. Indeed I am afraid I shall get into more than one scrape of this kind, in consequence of the philosophical and philanthropical studies of my author on his acquaintance in the above-named Diary.'[22] The net result of the trouble was a five-year delay before the book appeared – to Hazlitt's cost, for his payment was wholly dependent on publication.

Another important consequence of the fracas over Holcroft's diary, but a far happier one, was that it prompted Crabb Robinson to think of keeping a diary himself. To the delight of subsequent historians and biographers he began to do so early in 1811. It is a gold-mine, because he knew practically all the principal literary figures of his day, and was assiduous in keeping up with their visits to London, their publications, lectures, quarrels and conversations. He is a Boswell not to an individual but to an age, and therefore a valuable window onto it.

Cumberland's *London Review*, setting itself up as its title suggests to be a rival (a commercial rather than political one) to the august *Edinburgh Review*, failed after just four issues, before Hazlitt could begin contributing. One reason for its failure, and a significant one, was that its launch coincided with the birth of a much better funded and better organized periodical, the *Quarterly Review* – an ominous name for Hazlitt, as matters later turned out. The *Quarterly* was set up with secret government money to provide an answer to the high-quality liberal periodicals – chief among them the *Edinburgh Review* – which were especially feared by the government because of their influence among intelligent sections of society. The government could not suppress liberal periodicals outright, and such existing conservative organs as the *Anti-Jacobin* and the *British Critic* (a Church paper) did not have the intellectual authority to match them. So it founded the *Quarterly* as a heavyweight journal capable of counter-attacking on equal terms. Within a decade, by which time Hazlitt had himself become a famous journalist and critic, its influence was great. It proved to be one of Hazlitt's bitterest enemies, mounting vicious attacks on him, and producing from him in response some of the best examples of polemic vituperation in the English language. This was an age of violent writing, of warfare by essay, fuelled by deep and virulent political animosities. With the advent of the *Quarterly Review*, followed a few years later by the even more notorious *Blackwood's Magazine*, the heat of controversy was racked up by thousands of degrees. Hazlitt's part in the quarrels of the press was a leading one.

All this, however, lay in the future. With problems besetting the Holcroft biography, and with the *London Review* defunct, Hazlitt had to think of other schemes. He wrote to Crabb Robinson asking whether Mr Tipper, lately publisher of the *London Review* but now looking for other ventures, might be interested in a translation of Chateaubriand's *Les Martyrs*. Nothing came of the suggestion. He was also and more ambitiously thinking about a 'History of English Philosophy' in some form – as essays, perhaps, to be published by subscription; or perhaps as lectures, since a vogue for these was gathering strength. He printed a Prospectus for the History and sent it to possible supporters, among them William Windham MP, whose Parliamentary eloquence he admired. Windham had been Secretary of War during the Pitt administration, which might seem to put him in the wrong political camp from Hazlitt's point of view, but Crabb Robinson's friend Thomas Amyot was Windham's private secretary, and the two persuaded Hazlitt to give Windham a try, for his name would be a valuable one to have at the head of a subscription list. Hazlitt wrote a pro forma letter to Windham, sending a copy of the Prospectus with it.

There is no record of a response. Hazlitt was not one to give up; he simply changed his plan. If his History of Philosophy was not to be published as essays by subscription, he decided, he would give them as lectures.

On 6 March 1810 Sarah suffered a miscarriage. Depressed and unwell, and needing a change of scene, she wrote a week later to invite herself to stay with the Lambs in town, and shortly afterwards did so. Hazlitt's method of coping with painful circumstances was to immerse himself in work. He remained in the country, from where he wrote to Sarah to say that he was busy with his painting of Jacob's Ladder, and dreaming about it too. 'I have got in a pretty good background, and a *conception* of the ladder which I learned from the upping stone on the down, only making the stone into gold, and a few other improvements. I have no doubt there was such another in the field of Luz, and that an upping stone is the genuine Jacob's Ladder. But where are the angels to come from? That's another question, which I am not yet able to solve.'[23] Sarah had sent him some prints from town – they completed a series of Raphael cartoons he was especially fond of, having seen the originals in Hampton Court – and he explained why he had not come up to town to join her, as planned, to see the pictures being sold by Walsh Porter at Christie's on 14 April.[24] The reason was that the weather was bad, and because he was snug at home he did not relish the idea of the journey; moreover, there were too many 'Metsus and Terbrughs and boors smoking and ladies at harpsichords' for his taste.

There is another reason why Hazlitt chose not to go up to town that spring. It was that he had become infatuated with a local girl called Sally Baugh. His passion for her – his 'frenzy', as his wife called it, reminiscing about it later – was not reciprocated, and in any case she was on the point of marrying a young labourer called William Shepherd.[25] Hazlitt did not conceal anything from Sarah, including his proneness to infatuations. (A friend of later years, P. G. Patmore, says he never knew Hazlitt out of love.[26]) In his letter to Sarah he ruefully says, 'You are a good girl, and I must be a good boy. I have not been very good lately.' But his affection for Sarah herself is unmistakable: 'I do not wish you to overstay your month, but rather to set off on the Friday ... It is supper time, my dear, and I have been painting all day, and all day yesterday, and all the day before, and I am very, very tired, and so I hope you will let me leave off here, and bid you good night.'[27]

He was painting hard in half-hopes, at least, of being able to make some money thereby. In the letter just quoted he mentions, *à propos* the Christie's event, that he had toyed with the idea of sending his 'little copy of

Rembrandt' to be put on sale, 'to try whether it might not fetch two or three guineas'. The disincentive was that doing so involved certain expense for an uncertain return.

Another fine summer – the summer of 1810 – saw the Lambs in Winterslow again, arriving in July after an overnight coach journey which made them both mortally tired and stricken with headaches. The pleasant airs and walks of Winterslow revived them. They stayed a fortnight and then together with the Hazlitts made a visit to Oxford. Before going Lamb ordered a pair of trousers from the local tailor – a hunchback with (Hazlitt makes a point of telling us) a handsome daughter – who lived at Pitton, a neighbouring village. Lamb wanted his trousers in brown or snuff-coloured cloth; the tailor, a pragmatical old gentleman with an opinion of his own, instead brought him a pair in 'lively Lincoln-green'. Lamb was so delighted with them that he wore them when the party travelled to Oxford in 'Johnny Tremain's cross-country caravan ... the jest of the thing prevailing in his mind (as it always does) over the sense of personal dignity'.[28]

Hazlitt knew Oxford's colleges because he had more than once visited the pictures they owned. 'I can myself do the honours indifferently well to works of art and curiosity,' Hazlitt wrote later. 'I once took a party to Oxford with no mean *éclat* – showed them the seat of the Muses at a distance, "With glistering spires and pinnacles adorn'd" – descanted on the learned air that breathes from the grassy triangles and stone walls of halls and colleges – was at home in the Bodleian; and at Blenheim quite superseded the powdered Ciceroni that attended us, and that pointed in vain with his wand to common-place beauties in matchless pictures.'[29] One matter of regret for Lamb later was that they did not ask to see the Titian Gallery, which was never opened to visitors unless particularly requested, the reason being that the pictures were all of nudes.

The travelling proved too much for the Lambs. They were neither of them very robust, and lurching about in carts and coaches for whole days at a time was exhausting enough for anyone. In Mary's case, moreover, an excess of psychological stimulation almost invariably proved harmful. She fell ill immediately on returning to London, and had to go to Hoxton. Lamb himself was unwell and dispirited, writing to Hazlitt to say that he never wished to travel again; 'I have lost all wish for sights,' he said. The journey had a sad effect on Sarah too; she suffered yet another miscarriage on 6 September. At that point it must have seemed to the Hazlitts that they were fated to be childless, and the thought made them wretched.

At just that moment there appeared a very belated notice in the August 1810 *Edinburgh Review* of Hazlitt's attack on Malthus, conjoined with a review of another book on the population controversy. The reviewer was not in the slightest interested in grappling with either of the two books under consideration, only with stating and defending Malthus's theories. 'We should scarcely have thought it worth while to take any notice of these disquisitions,' it magisterially began, 'which consist, in a great degree, of strange misapprehensions and misrepresentations of the doctrines they profess to discuss, if we had not observed, among many persons besides [these two authors], an ignorance of the principles of population, which seems to us nearly unaccountable, considering the careful and detailed manner in which the subject has been lately explained.' The author – whose prose style is representative of his time; the contrast with Hazlitt is striking – then proceeds to give a summary of Malthus, without further discussion of the books ostensibly under review.

The *Edinburgh Review* was too big a fish not to be answered. Hazlitt counter-attacked hard, in the form of a letter to Cobbett at the *Political Register*. The letter itself consists of a list of rhetorical queries, which between them comprehensively demolish Malthus's case, and which are particularly scathing in their exposure of the protection Malthus's theory gives to injustices in society. Hazlitt asks angrily and contemptuously: 'Whether the avowed basis for the author's system on the poor-laws, is not the following: – that by the laws of God and nature, the rich have a right to starve the poor whenever they (the poor) cannot maintain themselves; and whether the deliberate sophistry by which this right is attempted to be made out, is not as gross an insult on the understanding as on the feelings of the public? Or whether this reasoning does not consist in a trite truism and a wilful contradiction; the truism being, that whenever the earth cannot maintain all its inhabitants, that then, by the laws of God and nature, or the physical constitution of things, some of them must perish; and the contradiction being, that the right of the rich to withhold a morsel of bread from the poor, while they themselves roll in abundance, is a law of God and nature, founded on the same physical necessity or absolute deficiency in the means of subsistence? Whether the commentators on the Essay have not fallen into the same unwarrantable mode of rea-soning, by confounding the real funds for the maintenance of labour, i.e. the actual produce of the soil, with the scanty pittance allowed out of it for the maintenance of the labourer (after the demands of luxury and idleness are satisfied) by the positive, varying laws of every country, or by the caprice of individuals? Whether these two things are not fundamentally distinct in themselves, and ought not to be kept so, in a question of such importance, as the right of the rich to starve the poor by system?'[30]

The letter was dated 21 November 1810, and it appeared in the *Political*

*Register* three days later. Lamb sent Hazlitt a copy of the *Register* straight away, remarking that he was sure Hazlitt would be pleased by Cobbett's attention in printing it so swiftly. A few days later Lamb wrote at more length, a troubled letter reporting that Mary had fallen ill yet again, although not quite badly enough to go to Hoxton. He blamed too many visitors – citing especially Dorothy Wordsworth and 'that damn'd infernal bitch Mrs Godwin coming and staying so late'. The solution was to have no visitors to stay: 'and therefore I am sure you will take it in good part if I say that if Mrs Hazlitt comes to town at any time, however glad we shall be to see her in the daytime, I cannot ask her to spend a night under our roof.'[31]

The seemingly interminable war with France – the Peninsular campaigns in Spain were still continuing – had begun to produce serious economic difficulties in England, with price inflation the most important consequence for people on small incomes. At the beginning of 1811 Hazlitt decided that he would have to spend part of his time in London seeking portrait and literary commissions. In February he rented rooms in his former lodging-house at 34 Southampton Buildings, and began painting a portrait of Thomas Robinson, Crabb's brother – no doubt an act of kindness on the part of the Robinson family to help him out.

In that same month Sarah's mother died. She had been living in a lunatic asylum since 1805. When Sarah and Hazlitt married they had been given to believe that their income would rise from £80 to £120 a year when Mrs Stoddart died, but matters turned out otherwise. For reasons now difficult to unearth, the old lady's annuity ceased with her death. The Hazlitts had counted heavily on the hope of this money, for as soon as the facts were plain they saw that they would at some point have to sell a part of Sarah's property at Winterslow, turning the proceeds into the basis of an annuity. This was eventually done, arranged (on a rather generous basis[32]) by John Stoddart. As these difficulties pressed, Sarah found that she had fallen pregnant again, and was due to give birth in September. With her history of miscarriages she chose, or was advised, to remain quietly in the country. So Hazlitt went to town alone, and set himself to earn an income.

Crabb Robinson's diary gives some indication of Hazlitt's renewed bachelor existence in the winter and spring of 1811. He received guests, and had a party in his rooms on 29 March; was frequently at the Lambs', and dined with Crabb Robinson himself on 10 March, and earlier, on 4 March, when the diarist 'took tea with W. Hazlitt and had two hours pleasant chat with him', told him about the incident with Coleridge and Sir George Beaumont in the Lakes. The revival of ambivalent feelings towards Coleridge is explained by the fact that the poet, who was residing principally with his friends the Morgans in Hammersmith, had taken a *pied à terre* near Hazlitt in Southampton Buildings, so the two of them were again frequently in company together. Coleridge's proximity reminded Hazlitt of 'losing the expectation of gaining a patron', and Hazlitt also felt that Coleridge's remaining late into the night at the Lambs' home, pouring out to Mary his troubles over a late and severe breach with Wordsworth, were upsetting both Lambs but especially Mary. That Coleridge thought the same about Hazlitt shows that there was now a degree of tension in their relationship, at least partly occasioned by the dislike Hazlitt felt for Coleridge's increasingly pro-war and pro-government views, expressed in the paragraphs he was writing for *The Courier* newspaper, a hack task which Crabb Robinson thought a tragic waste of Coleridge's talents, and which the Lambs' friend Mrs Clarkson called 'a humiliation'. Hazlitt saw it as an unforgivable betrayal of the radical cause. He later wrote, 'Alas! Frailty, thy name is *Genius!* – What is become of all this mighty heap of hope, of thought, of learning and humanity? It has ended in swallowing doses of oblivion and in writing paragraphs in the *Courier.* Such and so little is the mind of man!'[33] But there was no open breach at this point. Coleridge and Hazlitt were too often in one another's company, and they too greatly respected one another's talents, for that to happen yet.[34]

At the party Hazlitt gave in his rooms he and Coleridge discussed philosophy. The latter 'said that all systems of philosophy might be reduced to two, the dynamical and the mechanical, the one converting all quantity into quality, the other vice versa,' reported Crabb Robinson. 'He and Hazlitt joined in an obscure statement concerning abstract ideas. Hazlitt said that he had learnt from painting that it was difficult to form an idea of an individual object, that we had first only a *general idea*, that is, vague broken and imperfect recollection of the individual object. This, I had observed, was what the mob generally meant by a general idea, and Hazlitt said he had no other.'

Hazlitt was commissioned by a number of sitters for portraits in addition to Thomas Robinson, among them the Quaker abolitionist Thomas Clarkson, a Mr Howel, and a young man described as 'handsome'. But the work did not go well and he knew it. The truth is that he had lost his knack for portraiture. He struggled with the pictures, especially with the one of Thomas Robinson, which he refused to let anyone see. Crabb Robinson described the picture of Mr Howel as 'a good caricature likeness but a coarse painting', and added, 'I fear poor Hazlitt will never succeed. With very great talents and uncommon powers of mind I fear he is doomed to pass a life of poverty and unavailing repinings against society and his evil destiny.'[35] Evidently Hazlitt was frustrated and anxious about the work, and matters came to a head when in mid-April he delivered the portrait of the handsome young man, and the handsome young man's mother angrily rejected it, writing Hazlitt a sharp letter to tell him as much. Hazlitt left town abruptly, in 'great agony'. He was distressed by the obstacle thus posed to getting a livelihood by portraiture, but even more so by what was in effect an iteration of proof that his dream of creating art was at an end. Twelve years later he wrote a thinly disguised account of the reason for his failure and the pain it caused him. Speaking of the unreflective energy and application of painters like Balthasar Denner and Sir Joshua Reynolds, he observed that confidence and a 'sense of power' – i.e., ability, competence – urged them on to their pleasurable tasks 'with a sort of vernal cheerfulness and vigour'. But if either man had felt doubt about his capacity, or regretted that he did not produce the works of art which he might wish to have rivalled in excellence, 'the feeling of weakness and incapacity would have made his hand soon falter, would have rebutted him from his object; or had the canvas mocked, and been insensible to his toil, instead of gradually turning to "A lucid mirror, in which nature saw/All her reflected features", he would, like so many others, have thrown down his pencil in despair, or proceeded reluctantly, without spirit and without success. Claude Lorrain, in like manner, spent whole mornings on the banks of the Tiber or in his study, eliciting beauty after beauty, luxuriating in endless felicity – not merely giving the salient points, but filling up the whole intermediate space with continuous grace and beauty! What farther motive was necessary to induce him to persevere, but the bounty of his fate? What greater pleasure could he seek for, than that of seeing the perfect image of his mind reflected in the work of his hand? But as is the pleasure and the confidence produced by consummate skill, so is the pain and the desponding effect of total failure. When for the fair face of nature, we only see an unsightly blot issuing from our best endeavours, then the nerves slacken, the tears fill the eyes, and the painter turns away from his art, as the lover from a mistress that scorns him. Alas! how many have, as the poet says, "Begun in gladness;/Whereof has come in the end despondency and madness" – not for the want of will to proceed, (oh! no,) but for lack of power!'[36] The obstacle – his inability to rise to the level of Claude or Titian – was now coupled with an immediate practical obstacle – his lack of practice in portraiture. He was so far from seeing 'the perfect image of his mind reflected in the work of his hand' that it was a torment; and to have it objectively confirmed by a client's disgust was agonizing.

Effectively, this was the end of Hazlitt's ambitions as a painter, and – a lesser thing, but not an inconsiderable one – the end of the thought that he could make occasional money, or even a living, from portraiture. He still did not give up painting entirely; every year he took up 'the pencil' and dabbled, and occasionally tried his hand at capturing an especially enchanting idea – Mrs Basil Montagu's daughter as Psyche, for example – but it was like a blinded man reaching out to touch his reading spectacles and a book, and thinking about what had been and what might have been. Some years later, in 1814, discussing whether 'the fine arts are promoted by academies', Hazlitt described his own career as a painter, to explain – chiefly to himself – what had happened to his aspiration. He describes the failed artist as one who 'from having his imagination habitually raised to an over-strained standard of refinement, by the sight of the most exquisite examples in art, he becomes impatient and dissatisfied with his own attempts, determines to reach the same perfection all at once, or throws down his pencil in despair. Thus the young enthusiast, whose genius and energy were to rival the great Masters of antiquity, or create a new aera in the art itself, baffled in his first sanguine expectations, reposes in indolence on what others have done: wonders how such perfection could have been achieved, – grows familiar with the minutest peculiarities of the different schools, – flutters between the splendour of Rubens and the grace of Raphael, finds it easier to copy pictures than to paint them, and easier to *see* than to copy them, takes infinite pains to gain admission to all the great collections, lounges from one auction room to another, and writes newspaper criticisms on the Fine Arts.'[37] In these words Hazlitt tells the unvarnished truth about his own case. It was also the case, as it happens, of most of those who, unlike him, had received a formal training in art – all but the part about writing newspaper criticisms, that is, for few had Hazlitt's powers of discernment and judgement, or his ability to write. Hazlitt put part of the blame for their and his failure on the fact that the basic mode of training for artists was copying other paintings, which he had come to see was a mistake. In painting, as in all else, he believed that the only master and model should be Nature itself.

Still, he had several remaining portrait commissions in hand, part paid for, and they had to be finished. In June, some weeks after his flight from town, Thomas Robinson wrote enquiring about his own portrait, which Hazlitt had taken to Winterslow with him. Hazlitt replied, 'Dear Sir – I was quite ashamed to receive your letter, and know not what to answer. I have the picture by me, and brought it down with a full intention to set about improving it immediately. I have however put it off from day to day and week to week first from an unfortunate habit that what I ought to do I seldom do, and secondly from a fear of doing away with what likeness there is without mending the picture. I will however do what I can to it before I come to town in October, and will then leave it with your brother. Till then I do not forget that I am your debtor.'[38] It seems that his portrait of Clarkson, at least, was 'thought like', which was a consolation.

Sarah gave birth to another son on 26 September 1811, at twenty minutes to four in the morning. They again chose the name William – it was common practice for the father's name to be given to an eldest son, even if a previously deceased son had been given the name too. Mary Lamb's congratulatory letter had a note attached from Charles saying, 'My blessing and heaven's upon him, and make him like his father, with something a better temper and a smoother head of hair, and then all the men and women must love him.'[39] The Lambs envisaged the little boy as a 'future rich alderman or opulent merchant; painting perhaps a little in his leisure hours for amusement'. This child – hereafter referred to as William the younger – survived, to edit a book in his father's honour, and to father in his own turn a miscellaneous writer, family historian, collector, translator and gossip, William Carew Hazlitt, to whom is owed the preservation of most of what little survives of the Hazlitt family papers. Hazlitt doted on William the younger; many commented on his fond indulgence, which equally many thought spoiled the boy, one of Hazlitt's friends (Keats) calling him 'that little Nero'.

A month later Hazlitt returned to town. He was wearing a new pair of boots that pinched him horribly, and he could hardly get about. On returning to Winterslow at the end of October he sent Crabb Robinson an apology for not visiting, saying he was 'held in durance vile by one of the greatest miseries of human life, I mean a pair of tight boots'. His principal reason for being in town was that the plan to give his History of English Philosophy as lectures was now beginning to mature. Because lectures were becoming all the vogue Coleridge had decided to return to the fray also. Hazlitt's first task was to sell subscription tickets, and the second was to find a hall. It was necessary to get at least forty subscribers, at two guineas each, to make the project viable. Hazlitt's brother-in-law John helped to find a hall, suggesting the Russell Institution in Coram Fields, Brunswick Square, and persuading Hazlitt to write to the committee there. The committee agreed. It took them a long while to do so; confirmation only came in December 1811, and Hazlitt's lectures were booked to begin on Tuesday 14 January 1812, and to continue weekly for nine further weeks thereafter. Coleridge's lectures on Shakespeare and Milton were scheduled to begin earlier, on 18 November, taking place twice weekly – Mondays and Thursdays – for eight weeks at the Philosophical Society's new rooms off Fetter Lane, near Fleet Street.

While Hazlitt was in town he saw much of the Lambs, as usual. Coleridge wrote jealously to a friend complaining that Hazlitt was there almost every night, endangering Lamb's health by drinking with him. Another diarist, John Payne Collier, records the conversation at a Lambs' 'Thursday' dominated by Coleridge, who was given plenty of 'sea-room' by the others present – chief among them Lamb and Hazlitt – to 'spread his canvas and sail majestically away'.[40] Hazlitt went back to Winterslow to see Sarah and his son, and while there wrote to tell Crabb Robinson about his lecturing plans and how he had progressed in the matter of subscriptions. 'I am going (in spite of the muse that presides over eloquence, I do not know her name) to deliver lectures,' he said. 'I have got 30 subscribers, and want ten or a dozen more if I can possibly get them. If therefore you could assist me by picking up one or two names, I can only say I shall be much obliged to you, and that the lectures will be as good as I can make them.' He then listed the subjects of the lectures, and the subscription price.[41] By the time he returned to town in better boots in November, Crabb Robinson had managed to secure two more subscribers, and their guineas in advance.

Along with other familiars of the Lambs' Thursdays Hazlitt attended the opening lectures in Coleridge's series, doubtless with the added interest of one who, not having lectured before, wished to refresh his observations of a consummate speaker. But Coleridge disappointed him, by being less brilliant in the lecture theatre than in private conversation. At the Lambs' on 27 November, after the first three lectures had been delivered, the conversation turned to the start Coleridge had made – so John Payne Collier again records. Hazlitt said that Coleridge's definition of poetry was unclear, and others agreed; and he rather surprisingly questioned Coleridge's competence to be talking about Shakespeare at all: '*W. Hazlitt* did not think Coleridge at all competent to the task he had undertaken of lecturing on Shakespeare, as he was not well read in him. He knew little more than was in the Elegant Extracts, and Hazlitt himself had told him of many beautiful passages that Coleridge had never before heard of. It was owing to this ignorance that Coleridge had not exemplified any of his positions by quoting passages, and he doubted if he ever would ... Milton he was well acquainted with, and some years ago his readings of him were very fine; his natural whine gave them effect: this whine had since grown upon him and was very disagreeable. Coleridge was a man who had more ideas than any person Hazlitt had ever known, but had no capability of attending to one object.' Lamb also criticized Coleridge, and the conversation, in the manner of the Lambs' salons, moved on to embrace Johnson and Juvenal, Pythagoras and Persius.

Crabb Robinson was frequently with Hazlitt, calling on him to chat about his forthcoming lectures on one occasion, on another playing cards with him at Captain Burney's house. On 7 December he dropped by to give Hazlitt some of the advance subscription money he had raised, and found him 'alone and gloomy; he showed me a new edition of Hobbes on Human Nature'. A week afterwards Crabb Robinson wrote to his brother saying that Hazlitt was still in trouble with the portrait he owed him, but 'he is so poor and unhappy that I can't but feel more pity than displeasure.'[42] The reasons for Hazlitt's despondency were many. He was very nervous about the lectures, and his money worries meant that much turned on their proving a success. He was also embarrassed about the Robinson portrait. There were doubtless other reasons for depression – and obscure hints about another painful infatuation suggest one of them. But his year-end misery only serves to exemplify the cliché, no less true for being one, that night is darkest before dawn; for the following year saw his fortunes suddenly and handsomely change.

# CHAPTER EIGHT

# The Press of Drama

## 1812–1814

Hazlitt's first lecture at the Russell Institution was a disaster. Inexperienced and already nervous, he was further disconcerted to be told on arriving at the Institution's hall that his time was limited to one hour. He had brought material for three hours. He put his head down like a charging bull and read all of it in a scarcely audible gabble. Crabb Robinson wrote a worried report in his diary: 'I went to Hazlitt's first lecture on the History of English Philosophy. He read ill a very sensible book: and as he seems to have no conception of the difference between a lecture and a book his lectures cannot possibly be popular, hardly tolerable. He read a sensible and excellent introduction on philosophy and on Hobbes: but he delivered himself in a low monotonous voice, with his eyes fixed intently on his book, not once daring to look at his audience. He read too so rapidly that no one could possibly follow him; at the same time the matter he read was of a kind to require reflection. No subject is in itself less adapted to a lecture than Metaphysical philosophy; no manner less adapted to recommend abstruse matter than Hazlitt's. So that it is impossible H's lectures should not altogether fail of their object unless he should alter his style and delivery, which I fear is hardly in his power. With all these exceptions to his lectures, as such, the matter was in general, as far as I could force my attention to comprehend, very excellent.'[1]

The next day Crabb Robinson saw Hazlitt at the Lambs', and described him as understandably depressed, a mood made worse by a letter of advice from his brother-in-law on the correct way to give a lecture. In the first flush of his misery Hazlitt put the blame on Stoddart for suggesting the Russell Institution, which, he complained, was not suitable – the size of the room, the nature of the audience, '&c.', as Crabb Robinson puts it, being the reasons why the lecture had failed, along with the surprise injunction from Mr Flack the secretary about the one-hour limit. Crabb Robinson then adds, 'I observed on the difference between a book and a lecture, and perhaps more than I intended betrayed my opinion. I spoke of the compassion I felt beholding H so oppressed in delivering the lecture and this he misunderstood. For Miss Lamb told me the following day that he had been hurt by this, and in consequence I wrote a letter to him explaining what I had said.'[2]

Evidently the audience agreed with the diarist on the content of the lectures, for despite the unpromising beginning most of them returned on the following Tuesday – but not Lamb: he went no more, having no taste for public lectures anyway, and being thoroughly put off by the first. Hazlitt, after his anguished few days of blaming everyone but himself, paid attention to the advice given, and the transformation was remarkable. From the second Tuesday onwards he was a good lecturer. 'Lounged in my room till Hazlitt's second lecture, which I heard,' Crabb Robinson's diary continues. 'He delivered himself well; that is loud, with a tone of confidence which being forced had sometimes the air of arrogance; this however did not offend (except perhaps a few) and he was interrupted by applause several times. His lecture was on Locke.' Despite finding his brother-in-law's advice irksome, Hazlitt also found it helpful, not least in that a colleague of Stoddart's, a barrister by the name of Burrell, helped him to abridge his second lecture, and offered a few remarks about speaking in public, an art essential to his own profession. 'On the whole H improved vastly in his present lecture and I hope he will now get on. He read half his first lecture at B. Montagu's last night; he was to read the whole, but he abruptly broke off and could not be persuaded to read the remainder. Lamb and other friends were there.' That was on 21 January; on 28 January Crabb Robinson reported that the third lecture was 'not less impressively delivered than the last', and on 4 February he said that 'Hazlitt's manner is now very respectable.'

At the end of the series, during the latter part of which the diarist's dutiful and admiring attendance scarcely faltered, Crabb Robinson wrote:[3] 'At Hazlitt's last lecture. Very well delivered, and full of shrewd obser-vation. At the close, he remarked on the utility of metaphysics. He quoted and half assented to Hume's sceptical remark, that perhaps they are not worth the study, but that there are persons who can find no better way of amusing themselves. He then related an Indian legend of a Brahmin, who was so devoted to abstract meditation, that in the pursuit of philosophy he quite forgot his moral duties, and neglected ablution. For this he was degraded from the rank of humanity and transformed into a monkey. But even when a monkey he retained his original propensities, for he kept apart from the other monkeys, and had no other delight than that of eating cocoanuts and studying metaphysics. "I too," said Hazlitt, "should be very well contented to pass my life like this monkey, did I but know how to provide myself with a substitute for cocoanuts." [4] By a happy chance, coconuts were shortly to fall on his head; much of the shaking of the tree was done by Crabb Robinson and Lamb, both indefatigable friends.

Hazlitt's lectures began with Hobbes and ended with Priestley and Price. In the first he gave a survey of philosophy since Hobbes, arguing that it consisted mainly of expansion and application of the latter's views – largely unacknowledged, as Hazlitt pointed out, for Hobbes was viewed with horror as an 'atheist' and his philosophy was regarded as subversive. Hazlitt wished to give Hobbes his due, and later devoted an essay to showing how Locke's chief ideas were largely derived from Hobbes's writings, a fact which had not been (and is still not) acknowledged.

The second lecture was devoted to Locke's *Essay Concerning Human Understanding*, and focused principally on its doctrine of 'ideas', whose origin, in good empiricist fashion, Locke ascribed fundamentally to sense experience. Hazlitt argued that ideas imply a power for which perception by itself does not account, namely a 'comprehending faculty' in the mind. This is a view chiefly associated with Immanuel Kant, but Hazlitt had developed his view independently of Kant, whom he never studied in detail for the good reason that he knew no German and everything by and about Kant available in English was at that time either poorly translated or – more usually – reported second hand. (Coleridge claimed to know Kant's work; but his acquaintance with it was typical of his learning in general: unscholarly, disorganized and superficial.) Hazlitt's third lecture continued the theme of ideas and the mind's comprehending activity, concentrating on Berkeley's *Principles of Human Knowledge*, and advancing a distinctive Hazlitt thesis to the effect that the 'moderns' are wrong in their attack on general or abstract ideas, since there can in fact be no other kind; for, Hazlitt again insisted, all ideas imply at least a power of 'comprehension and abstraction' in the mind's activity.

The fourth and fifth lectures conveyed the doctrine of Hazlitt's own *Essay* on 'self-love and benevolence', including its criticisms of Hartley and Helvetius. The sixth addressed the views of an ally, Bishop Butler, with whom Hazlitt largely agreed, for both he and Butler wished to argue that sensibility, will, understanding, and the love of pleasure, truth and action, are the 'different original springs which move that various machine', the mind. In the seventh and eighth lectures he considered the debate between Price and Priestley on the question of necessity, while in the ninth he lectured on Tooke's *Diversions of Purley* as a way of canvassing theories of language and nature. He concluded, in the tenth lecture, by speaking of 'natural religion'.

At least one and possibly two of these lectures are now unfortunately lost – those on Butler and natural religion – and the published versions of the remaining lectures are not identical with their originals, for Hazlitt modified them when turning them into essays, having long since decided that because no-one would buy or read 'metaphysical choke-pears' he would always henceforth write in a way that had broader public appeal – not changing his message but packaging it more acceptably.[6] Hazlitt's philosophical opinions were accordingly often smuggled into his essays. The full essay versions of the texts of his lectures themselves lay unpublished until his son William the younger collected them for the posthumous *Literary Remains of William Hazlitt*, published in 1836. But Hazlitt tried repeatedly to publish them himself. In a letter of January 1821 he offered John Scott, the editor of the *London Magazine*, a series of eight essays on Modern Philosophy 'at five guineas apiece'. But Scott turned them down, and this is when Hazlitt probably laid them aside for good.[7]

In reproducing five of the lectures for the *Literary Remains* Hazlitt's son William the younger writes: 'I found them with other papers in an old hamper which many years ago he stuffed confusedly full of MSS. and odd volumes of books, and left in the *care* of some lodging-house people, by whom it was thrown into a cellar, so damp that even the covers of some of the books were fast mouldering when I first looked over the collection. The injury to the MSS may be imagined. Some of the Lectures indeed, to my deep regret, are altogether missing, burnt probably by the ignorant people of the house; and I have had the greatest difficulty in preparing those which remain for the press.'[8]

The lecture series was interrupted for three weeks in the middle – Crabb Robinson mentions obscurely that this had something to do with Hazlitt's debts – and when they resumed they did so fortnightly, ending on 27 April. From the point of view of Hazlitt's efforts to earn a regular income, the lectures were only a temporary expedient, aimed in large part at advertising his talents. As the series unfolded his friends made every effort to help him. To begin with, after the first lecture, Crabb Robinson set himself to make Leigh Hunt interested in Hazlitt. Hunt was an old school-fellow of Charles Lamb, and editor of the *Examiner*, a liberal-radical weekly paper which was influential enough to upset the government on a regular basis, so that when Hunt and his brother John went a step too far in criticizing the Prince Regent, they found themselves on a libel charge, followed by two years in gaol each. The Hunts were of mixed race, their English father having been a parson in the West Indies, their mother a West Indian descended from slaves. Leigh Hunt was a good essayist with a lively mind, but the exigencies of unremitting journalism prevented his reaching the heights of Lamb and Hazlitt in the art. As an editor he was excellent. The reports and discussions in the *Examiner*'s pages reveal the pressure of the times: persistent economic slump induced by the war had led to high prices and high unemployment, and that in turn prompted the Luddite riots, in which impoverished and sometimes starving workers smashed the industrial and agricultural machinery that had put them out of work. The slump also led to bank failures in the provinces. In some cases the only scrip circulating in a country town and its environs was issued by the local bank, so that if the bank failed the consequences for the local economy were disastrous. One such failure had taken place in Salisbury in 1810, and although there is no direct evidence that the Hazlitts were involved in it, it is likely that they were – and also that Sarah's mother was, which probably explains why, at her death, the annuity she had bequeathed to Sarah did not materialize. When therefore in August 1812 the Hunts' *Examiner* described the 'price of the necessaries of life' as 'enormous', no-one, least of all the Hazlitts, could disagree.[9]

At first Crabb Robinson simply wished Leigh Hunt to review Hazlitt's lectures in the *Examiner* as a way of publicizing them. As early as 17 January, just three days after the unhappy first lecture, Crabb Robinson called at the house of Barron Field and found Lamb and Hunt there, and after a while steered the conversation around to Hazlitt, hoping that Lamb would join him in extolling both lecture and the lecturer. But Lamb was already tipsy and in no mood to conceal the fact that the lecture had been an agony to him. Crabb Robinson's praises nevertheless sowed a seed, for within two years Hazlitt was the *Examiner*'s star contributor.

Hazlitt returned to Winterslow when his lectures were over, but only for a short rest. The necessity of finding a job meant that he and Sarah had to live in London. They spent the summer of 1812 rearranging their lives accordingly, taking lodgings in Southampton Buildings while looking for permanent accommodation, and with the help of John Stoddart selling some of Sarah's Winterslow property.

Hazlitt naturally wished to find work to suit his talents. He was fortunate in having the help of Lamb and Crabb Robinson. His need for a job was especially pressing because the Hazlitts' financial circumstances had not merely worsened, but had for the reasons just surmised done so dramatically. In the early part of their married life in Winterslow they were able to entertain friends, buy prints in town, travel a little – in general, live in modest comfort. Now they were poor. The war inflation had reduced their remaining income to an unlivable level, and none of Hazlitt's present resources was sufficient to remedy matters. His portrait painting was at an end, although he continued to work manfully at the Thomas Robinson picture, and at last got it to an acceptable state (acceptable to himself, as well as to the Robinsons, as their diarist member reports). He had no book project in hand other than the philosophy lectures, which no-one wished to buy. Publication of the Holcroft biography was still obstructed by Godwin, so he could not claim his fee. There was no option but regular paid employment.

It cannot have been easy for Sarah to give up her country home and friends – especially their neighbours at Winterslow, the Armsteads, with whom she was intimate.[10] She was no stranger to London, and enjoyed being there; but visiting is not the same as residing. London life was the very reverse of country life as regards tranquillity, order, fresh air and quiet – for London was a tumultuous place, crowded and bustling, which in that year saw the beginning of major building schemes, including Nash's Regent Street project – which, involving as it did the demolition of whole streets and hundreds of buildings between Soho and Mayfair, cutting a long swathe from Carlton House Terrace near St James's Park all the way to the new Regent's Park, made London not just the largest city in the world but its biggest building site too.

Hazlitt also loved living in the country, and regretted leaving it as much as Sarah did. But the return to London brought its compensations. A new acquaintance of Hazlitt who, like Crabb Robinson, kept a diary, John Payne Collier, records a conversation involving Hazlitt and Wordsworth at the Lambs' in May 1812, about Tasso's influence on Spenser, and thence of Fairfax's elegant but inaccurate translation of Tasso. Lamb complained that Fairfax's deviations from the original were 'wanton', and Hazlitt replied, 'Aye, that is an evil arising out of original genius undertaking to do unoriginal work; and yet a mere versifier, a man who can string easy rhymes, and employ smooth epithets, is sure to sacrifice the spirit and power of the poet; it is then a transfusion of wine into water, and not of one wine into another, or of water into wine. It is like setting even a tolerable artist to copy after Raphael or Titian: every light and shade, every tone and tint, every form and turn may be closely followed, but still the result is only an unsatisfactory imitation. No painter's own repetitions are equal to his original pictures.'[11] Here speaks the voice of experience and disappointment, applying the moral aptly. Collier detected no sign of unfriendliness between Hazlitt and Wordsworth, for the open breach was still two years away. Hazlitt appears in Collier's pages elsewhere too, almost always in literary discussion with Coleridge and Lamb. At this period Coleridge and Wordsworth were undergoing one of their periodic fits of enmity, painfully for the former. Hazlitt remained detached both from their quarrel and from the reconciliation which Crabb Robinson eventually arranged between them. The falling-out had multiple causes which had been accumulating over years, but it came to a head when Wordsworth called Coleridge a 'rotten drunkard'. It was not an elevated or an elevating affair, and Hazlitt was well out of it.[12] The reconciliation effected by Crabb Robinson was tearful, even hysterical, on Coleridge's side – one reason for his friable state being that he was in the worst phase of his opium addiction – and cold and self-righteous on Wordsworth's side. Their respective behaviour was altogether in character. Hazlitt had a blow-by-blow account of what was happening from Crabb Robinson, and nothing in what he heard surprised him about either man.

Crabb Robinson and Lamb were not alone in seeking to help Hazlitt find a source of income. Their mutual friend Basil Montagu, a wealthy barrister who was the natural son of the Earl of Sandwich, commissioned a pamphlet from Hazlitt on capital punishment, to be published by an anti-hanging group founded by Montagu three years earlier, called the 'Society for the Diffusion of Knowledge upon the Punishment of Death'. Montagu himself edited a two-volume work on the subject, the second volume of which had recently appeared. Hazlitt fulfilled the commission, but his pamphlet was not published until after his death – although as was usual with him the effort did not go to waste, for in 1821 he published a long essay in the *Edinburgh Review* on the same subject, again probably at Montagu's instigation, as a commentary on the 1819 report of the House of Commons Select Committee on Criminal Laws. Hazlitt was opposed to capital punishment, and glad that informed opinion had come to accept that far too many crimes carried the death penalty – at one point there were over one hundred and sixty such offences, including theft and forgery. This made victims of crime reluctant to prosecute, juries reluctant to convict, and judges reluctant to sentence.[13] As David Hume observed, severe laws make for lax observance.

If Hazlitt was paid for the pamphlet, as is likely, the fee did not solve his problems, for he still had debts he could not repay, and although he was a free borrower he hated not being able to repay loans. To add to the tensions, Sarah had yet another miscarriage on 6 September.

It was Lamb who, on the employment front, proved the most effective adjutant in the short term. On Hazlitt's behalf Crabb Robinson and he had respectively approached the editors of the country's two leading newspapers, *The Times* and the *Morning Chronicle*, citing Hazlitt's editorship of *The Eloquence of the British Senate* as proof of his knowledge of parliamentary history, and his extraordinary powers of memory, as reasons why he should be employed as a parliamentary reporter. The *Morning Chronicle*'s editor, James Perry, was persuaded by John Dyer Collier, his Foreign Editor – whose wife, in turn, had been buttonholed by

Lamb at a dinner-party and persuaded to help – to interview Hazlitt. On the strength of the interview Perry appointed Hazlitt to the job at a salary of four guineas a week.

This was the turning point at last. It is not clear whether Hazlitt's salary began at once, or only when Parliament resumed after that autumn's election; nor whether it was paid all year round or only when Parliament was sitting. Practices of paying journalists varied, not only from newspaper to newspaper but even from employee to employee within the same newspaper. But it is likely that Hazlitt's appointment formally began when the newly elected Parliament convened on 30 November 1812.

Four guineas a week – £220 a year – was handsome money for the times, and it immediately catapulted the Hazlitts from poverty to security. They could think big, and did: they rented a house in Westminster, and hired servants.

Hazlitt was no newcomer to the precincts of Parliament, having visited it often enough, not least while he was preparing his *Eloquence of the British Senate*. He would not therefore have been shocked to see Honourable Members lounging with their feet up on the seats and hats pulled over their eyes, some sleeping, some reading their newspapers, others chatting together in apparent contempt of whoever was speaking. It was technically a breach of privilege to report debates in the House, so there was no press gallery, and parliamentary reporters had to squeeze into the public seating of the Strangers' Gallery. The inconvenience of getting in and out of the gallery to go to the lavatory during debates was, allegedly, the cause of serious bladder complaints in some of the longer-serving reporters. They were a tough and cynical bunch, especially Peter Finnerty, Hazlitt's *Chronicle* colleague, an intemperate Irishman who had more than once been in gaol – and on other occasions pilloried or fined as magistrates thought fit – for believing in the freedom of the press when the government did not. When Hazlitt joined the *Chronicle* Finnerty was just home from eighteen months in Lincoln prison for libelling Lord Castlereagh, whom he had accused in print of cruel behaviour in Ireland. It is likely that, in the preceding year, Hazlitt attended the public meeting held by Sir Francis Burdett at the Crown and Anchor pub in Westminster to raise money for Finnerty's legal fees. Shelley, then an undergraduate at Oxford, was one of those who contributed money in Finnerty's support.

Finnerty and Hazlitt took to each other immediately – the latter later called Finnerty 'my old friend' – and drank together, an occupational hazard of anyone enslaved to the strange late hours kept by Parliament. But there was not much opportunity for diversions. The new Parliament had a war and an economic crisis on its hands, and the reporters in the Gallery were kept busy.

The opening debate of the new parliament, Hazlitt's first assignment, concerned the prosecution of the war in the Peninsula and in particular the battle of Salamanca – an important victory for England, since it opened the road to Madrid for Wellington's troops, and proved to be the beginning of the end for French occupation of Spain. Both Castlereagh and Canning spoke in the Commons, while in the Lords the Marquis Wellesley, Wellington's brother, castigated the ministry for slackness in its support of the Peninsular campaign. There was a stir of excitement because news was starting to reach England from Russia, which Napoleon was in the process of invading at the head of his Grande Armée, that winter had set in harsh and early, causing the French severe problems. On 17 December the Prince Regent asked the Commons for funds to support the Russian effort – which provoked an outcry from the liberal membership of the House, who said money should be voted for the starving in England instead.

Domestic news usually eclipses international news, except in special circumstances, so Napoleon's tribulations in Russia took second place to the trial of Leigh Hunt and his brother John for their libel on the Prince Regent. The outcome of the trial on 9 December was a signal event for Hazlitt, because it prompted his first meeting with Leigh Hunt. The brothers were found guilty by a special jury, and the presiding judge, Lord Ellenborough, reserved sentencing until February. The court was crowded beyond capacity; Hazlitt's paper reported that 'it was with the utmost difficulty that a great number of special constables and Bow Street officers could maintain order and tranquillity.' On the day after the Hunts were found guilty the *Chronicle* devoted eight columns to the trial. Their offence was to ask who, if otherwise uninformed about the Prince Regent, could believe that 'this *delightful, blissful, wise, pleasurable, honourable, virtuous, true* and *immortal* prince, was a violator of his word, a libertine over head and ears in disgrace, a despiser of domestic ties, the companion of gamblers and demireps, a man who has just closed half a century without a single claim on the gratitude of his country, or the respect of posterity!' The penalty for plain speaking, when handed down by Lord Ellenborough in February, was two years in gaol and a fine of £1000 each. Hazlitt was one of the first to walk across the river to the Borough of Southwark where Leigh Hunt's prison lay – in Horsemonger Lane, opposite the tenter grounds near St George's Church – to pay his respects.

The routine for *Chronicle* reporters was to cover debates in relays, a practice made necessary by the long sittings of both Houses, which sometimes lasted all night. At the end of a shift the reporter had to walk from

St Stephen's Hall in Westminster to his newspaper's office in the Strand, and there write and file his copy. Hazlitt had no illusions about Parliament, any more than he had illusions about the government, for he already knew that in a previous generation MPs used to call Burke the 'dinner bell', because they would leave in droves when he started to speak, despite the beauties of his oratory and the power of his thought. They were, said Hazlitt, incapable of appreciating the one or understanding the other.[14] Nothing had changed since Burke's day, and nothing seems to have changed since Hazlitt's day either, for his portrait of Parliament, now nearly two centuries old, is depressingly familiar. 'Not only are the topics the same; the very phrases – whole batches of them – are served up as the Order of the Day; the same parliamentary bead-roll of grave impertinence is twanged off, in full cadence, by the Honourable Member or his Learned and Honourable Friend; and the well-known, voluminous, calculable periods roll over the drowsy ears of the auditors, almost before they are delivered from the vapid tongue that utters them! It may appear, at first sight, that here are a number of persons got together, picked out from the whole nation, who can speak at all times upon all subjects in the most exemplary manner; but the fact is, they only repeat the same things over and over on the same subjects – and they obtain credit for general capacity and ready wit, like Chaucer's Monk, who, by having three words of Latin always in his mouth, passed for a great scholar ... Read over the collections of old Debates, twenty, forty, eighty, a hundred years ago; they are the same *mutatis mutandis*, as those of yesterday. You wonder to see how little has been added; you grieve that so much has been lost. Even in their own favourite topics, how much are they to seek! They still talk gravely of the Sinking Fund in St Stephen's Chapel, which has for some time been exploded as a juggle by Mr Place of Charing-Cross; and a few of the principles of Adam Smith, which every one else had been acquainted with long since, are just now beginning to dawn on the collective understanding of the two Houses of Parliament. Instead of an exuberance of sumptuous matter, you have the same meagre dishes for every day of the year. You must serve an apprenticeship to a want of originality, to a suspension of thought and feeling. You are in a go-cart of prejudices, in a regularly constructed machine of pretexts and precedents; you are not only to wear the livery of other men's thoughts, but there is a House-of-Commons jargon which must be used for everything. A man of simplicity and independence of mind cannot easily reconcile himself to all this formality and mummery; yet woe to him that shall attempt to discard it! You can no more move against the stream of custom, than you can make head against a crowd of people; the mob of lords and gentlemen will not let you speak or think but as they do. You are hemmed in, stifled, pinioned, pressed to death – and if you make one false step you are "trampled under the hoofs of a swinish multitude!" Talk of mobs! Is there any body of people that has this character in a more consummate degree than the House of Commons? Is there any set of men that determines more by acclamation, and less by deliberation and internal conviction?'[15]

Crabb Robinson was pleased to see Hazlitt's good spirits and contentment at the Lambs' just before Christmas 1812, and again at a party Hazlitt gave early in the new year: 'Hazlitt, I was gratified by finding in high spirits,' he writes in connection with the first occasion, 'he finds his engagement with Perry as Parliamentary Reporter very easy, and the four guineas per week keeps his head above water. He seems quite happy.' On 2 January he wrote, 'In the evening at Hazlitt's. The Burney and Lamb party were there, and I found H. in a handsome room and his supper comfortably set out.' He thought it remarkable that these good things had flowed from a chance conversation between Lamb and Mrs Collier: 'On what frivolous accidents do the important events of our lives depend,' he mused.[16]

Hazlitt had reason to be happy. The *Morning Chronicle* was the main Whig newspaper, the chief rival to *The Times*, and under Perry's long editorship it had a distinguished list of contributors – Sheridan, Lamb, Moore, Campbell, Byron and Hazlitt himself not least among them – and it more or less invented the system of parliamentary coverage in which Hazlitt now took part. When Perry died and editorship of the *Chronicle* passed to John Black, a man who once sat beside Hazlitt in the Commons gallery, Hazlitt wrote, 'the late Mr Perry, who raised the *Morning Chronicle* into its present consequence, held the office of Editor for nearly forty years; and he held firm to his party and his principles all that time – a long time for political honesty and consistency to last! He was a man of strong natural sense, some acquired knowledge, a quick tact; prudent, plausible, and with great heartiness and warmth of feeling.' Hazlitt's sense of justice never allowed him to stop when he had said what was good about a person, for he always felt that as every story has another side, it should be told. So he recorded that Perry was flattered by the attention of noblemen, and liked to claim all the best things in his newspaper as written by himself, and was something of a coxcomb – not that this last troubled Hazlitt, who merely observed, 'a man who does not think well of himself, generally thinks ill of others.'[17] This judgement is the more remarkable for lacking any touch of bitterness, which might be expected given the way Hazlitt's association with Perry ended a year after it began.

It was at about this time – the end of 1812 – that Hazlitt made the acquaintance of the painter Benjamin Robert Haydon. They met at the Argyll Street studio of Hazlitt's long-standing friend James Northcote. Hazlitt told Haydon that he admired his painting of 'Macbeth the instant before he murdered Duncan', which he had seen in an exhibition. Praise was opium to Haydon. Delighted, he invited Hazlitt back to his studio, and thus began a long but not always easy friendship.

Haydon was aged twenty-seven when Hazlitt met him. He was already balding, and wore a pair of small round silver spectacles on his very long, high-bridged nose. He was regarded as the rising hope of historical painting. He already had the patronage of Sir George Beaumont, who had, indeed, commissioned the 'Macbeth'. Haydon was a wilful, egocentric, erratic character, who expended more of his considerable energy on making life difficult for himself than on painting. In 1809 he foolishly made an enemy of the Royal Academy by complaining about the position in which his *Death of Dentatus* had been hung – a deliberate plot by the Academicians, he claimed, to ruin his reputation. Haydon was the painter who mistook Hazlitt's *Old Woman* for an early Rembrandt, it will be remembered; but in later years he came to think Hazlitt insufficiently appreciative of British art in general and his – Haydon's – own in particular, and he wrote some vituperative remarks about Hazlitt in his autobiography, despite also claiming him as a friend. Nevertheless Haydon included Hazlitt's head in his large canvas, completed in 1819, *Christ's Entry into Jerusalem*, along with the heads of Wordsworth, Keats, and other luminaries of the age. In it he portrayed Hazlitt as an Inquisitor, staring with intensity and scepticism at the face of Jesus as it passed by him.

The house Hazlitt rented in Westminster – his lease began in early 1813 – was 19 York Street. It had once been Milton's house, and was now owned by Jeremy Bentham, who lived next door. Extraordinarily, Hazlitt and Bentham never met, despite being landlord, tenant and neighbours for the next six years. Hazlitt used to see the great utilitarian walking in his garden, but although he admired him he also had serious reservations – for Bentham had at one point proposed demolishing Milton's house, or at any rate to put a public footpath through its garden, without any qualms about the historical importance of the place and its associations. It equally amused and exasperated Hazlitt that local people were wont to say that 19 York Street once housed '*Milford* the poet'. On Bentham's utilitarian principles the fact that Milton had lived at 19 York Street was a trifle – a view unluckily shared by the officers of Westminster City Council who, in the century between Hazlitt's occupancy of the house and the publication of Howe's biography of him, allowed it to be torn down. This was not only the house of Milton and Hazlitt, but of the early boyhood of John Stuart Mill, whose father James Mill, Bentham's collaborator and friend, had been tenant of the house immediately before Hazlitt. Mill had quitted the house on the grounds that it was damp and unhealthy.

During the six years Hazlitt lived in York Street – 1813 to 1819 – he established his public reputation as a writer and critic. By the end of that time he was famous. The Hazlitts' life there was portrayed as eccentric by some of those who knew him. When Haydon first came to dine in York Street he did not find a pleasant spread waiting for him, as Crabb Robinson had done, but a cold left-over shoulder of mutton unceremoniously banged onto the table by a sullen maid – this was Becky, the daughter of the Hazlitts' equally crab-tempered housekeeper Mrs Tomlinson. A young artist (and ardent admirer of Hazlitt) called William Bewick left a description of the place as it was some years after the Hazlitts moved in: 'The entrance was a sort of porch opening to a small anteroom, with a very red brick floor and upright posts, that one rubbed one's shoulders against, and the staircase was narrow and dark. The room where Hazlitt received us was, as he informed us, in the same condition that it had been in Milton's time; the same dull-white painted wainscot, the same windows looking out into a garden-like piece of ground, tricked out into grass-plots, shrubberies, and winding walks, with two noble trees crossing the windows. From these windows might occasionally be seen the celebrated law-giver Bentham, shuffling along in loose déshabillé, his shirt-neck thrown open, the strings of his knee-breeches hanging about his shrunk legs, his loose habit of a coat seeming too large for his short puffy body.'[18] The indoor arrangements accorded with the 'general negligence and peculiarity of Hazlitt's habits', according to Bewick: 'There was little furniture, no books, no pictures or prints of any kind whatever! – a confusion and apparent want of comfort and domestic order reigned in the apartment. Over the mantel-shelf, upon the wainscot, instead of a picture or looking-glass, there was written, in good bold hand (Hazlitt's own writing) as high up as he could reach and covering the whole space, all manner of odd conceits (as they appeared to be), of abbreviations, – words, – names, – enigmatical exclamations, – strange and queer sentences, quotations, – snatches of rhyme, – bits of arithmetical calculations, – scraps of Latin, – French expressions, – words or signs by which the author might spin a chapter, or weave an elaborate essay. The chimney piece seemed to be his tablet of mnemonics, – his sacred hieroglyphics, – all jotted down without line, or form of any kind, some horizontal, some running up to the right, some down to the left, and some obliquely. They seemed thoughts and indications of things to be remembered, put down on the instant.' Then, illogically, Bewick writes that he 'concluded that this room might not be his study, but his living-room', for what he means is the opposite – doubtless a slip of the pen or a mistake in transcription from the original.[19] For this was assuredly Hazlitt's study, his studio, his work-room, the place where he meditated and wrote. This and other descriptions of the room in which he received visitors have led some commentators to conclude that Sarah was no good at housekeeping, that the furniture was sold to defray debts, that Hazlitt was eccentric and slovenly in his habits as well as poor. The judgements are inconsistent with the evidence of comfort and good arrangements in Winterslow, so fondly remembered by Mary Lamb in her letters; and of the fact that some of Hazlitt's own paintings, and certainly the *Old Woman* which Haydon first saw in York Street, accompanied him everywhere and were displayed in his living-room, along with his bust of Napoleon, which took pride of place wherever he lived. Hazlitt was an inveterate lover of prints, and his essays are full of references to those that lay about him. If Hazlitt had had on his study wall a blackboard to write on, or a message-board to pin notes on, as does almost any writer's or academic's study you care to visit, you would see just such a sight as met Bewick's eyes – the eyes of an admirer wanting to see something unusual and cabalistic, but in fact finding nothing odder than the working arrangements of a man who wrote for his bread and butter, who jotted down memoranda, notes, ideas, quotations and felicitous phrases on his substitute for a blackboard – and although it appears eccentric and somehow disagreeable that anyone should scribble on a wall or wainscoting, the fact that either could be painted over – in those days, when coal-fires burned eight months of the year, repainting or replastering of interiors happened frequently; in great houses it was done yearly when the occupants went to their country homes after the season – shows that it was not vandalism, just a sign of constant work.

It is nevertheless clear that the Hazlitt ménage was neither an ordinary one nor by usual standards always a cosy one. Haydon gives a graphic account of the christening party for William the younger. Hazlitt, who adored his little boy, invited Haydon 'with glistening eye' to dine on Friday in celebration. Haydon arrived at four o'clock as instructed, to find Sarah in her drooping gown, unwell and huddled in front of the fire, with no Hazlitt to be seen, no other guests present, and the table unlaid. Sarah told him that Hazlitt had gone in search of a parson, not having thought to do so in advance. Haydon went to meet him, and found him marching home in a rage because all the parsons were out. Soon afterwards other guests began to arrive – 'Charles Lamb and his poor sister – all sorts of odd clever people' as Haydon put it, including a mathematician who screwed up one side of his face and 'an old Lady of Genius with torn ruffles'. Sarah was 'in an influenza, thin, pale and spitty', and the chubby baby seemed not much more appealing, 'squalling, obstinate, and half-cleaned'. Into this Rowlandson-like picture came Becky, who 'laid a cloth and put down knives and forks in a heap', followed by 'a plate with a dozen large, waxen, cold, clayey, slaty potatoes. Down they were set, down we sat also … After waiting a little, all looking forlornly at the potatoes for fear they might be the chief dish, in issued a bit of overdone beef, burnt, toppling about on seven or eight corners, with a great bone sticking out like a battering ram; the great difficulty was to make it stand upright! but the greater to discover a *cuttable* place, for all was jagged, jutting, and irregular.' Neither Hazlitt nor Lamb was in the slightest disturbed, but helped each other to meat, 'while the boy, half-clean and obstinate, kept squalling to put his fingers in the gravy'.[20] For the sake of a good story Haydon omitted a detail or two – the pheasant that followed the beef, for example, which he elsewhere reported to Bewick, and the bottles that circulated the table, for Lamb was a considerable drinker, and so in those days was Hazlitt.

The ill-tempered Mrs Tomlinson and her daughter Becky deserve their place in the history of literature. Evidently the Hazlitts were fond of them, because they tolerated their eccentricities, and when they could no longer pay Becky's wages she went to the Lambs, and served them for fifteen years, often giving them a 'piece of her mind' when they did anything she disliked. The Tomlinsons contributed much to the character of York Street life, and the Hazlitts' patient submission to their reign below stairs does credit to both – not least as the Tomlinsons were apt to eat and carouse in high style in the kitchen, especially when the soldier boyfriend of Mrs Tomlinson's other daughter came to call.[21]

The beginning of 1813 saw important related events for both Coleridge and Hazlitt. The former's tragedy *Remorse* opened at Drury Lane Theatre on Saturday 23 January, and Hazlitt had his first outing as a dramatic critic by reviewing it in the *Morning Chronicle* on 25 January. The première was a success; Coleridge began it in an agony of apprehension, but was amazed and delighted by the 'unexampled applause' – his own words – that poured from all parts of the house, and the three cheers given him by the audience at the end. The *Christian Monitor* noted that it was a fashionable occasion, as proved by 'the large number of well-dressed prostitutes doing business in the foyer'.[22] Hazlitt was still officially a parliamentary reporter, but the *Chronicle*'s drama critic, William Mudford, was away on holiday, so Hazlitt – pointing out to Perry that he had been a theatre enthusiast since childhood, and that he went to see plays whenever opportunity offered – deputized for him. He gave the production a glowing notice, not because he was still more friends than not with Coleridge but because he found something to praise in the beauty of the lines and the drama of the conception. 'In the judicious appropriation, as well as in the richness and beauty of his decorations, we have no hesitation in saying that Mr Coleridge has highly succeeded ... Mr Coleridge shews a powerful imagination ... [his] language is ... bold, elegant, natural –'. Coleridge still had an association with the *Chronicle*, and that too doubtlessly prompted Perry to tell Hazlitt to look for the good. By the Monday morning on which the review appeared Coleridge was so ecstatic about his success that he was not in the mood for anything less than unqualified praise, so he found something to carp at in the review. He wrote to Rickman, 'I know that Hazlitt in the M. C. has sneered at my presumption in entering the lists with Shakespeare's Hamlet in Teresa's description of the two brothers: when (so help me the Muses) that passage never once occurred to my conscious recollection, however it may, unknown to myself, have been the working idea within me. But mercy on us! is there no such thing as two men's having similar thoughts on similar occasions?'[23] Coleridge here protests too much: it was a common enough observation among his contemporaries, as shown by the published comments of Crabb Robinson, De Quincy, Wordsworth, and Hazlitt himself more than once, that Coleridge made liberal unacknowledged use of others' work in his own, in particular from German authors 'either literally translated or freely adapted' – plagiarism, in short.[24] But the review scarcely bears the imputation of cavilling, for it is wholly positive.

Hazlitt's début as a theatre critic did not signal the end of his reporting duties at Westminster. Parliament reassembled on 2 February, and two days afterwards John and Leigh Hunt reappeared before Lord Ellenborough to hear their sentences. Offers of help – to pay their fine, even to bring back-door pressure on the government and Ellenborough to reduce the sentence or to impose a non-custodial one – flooded in from all sides, but were rejected by the Hunts, who rightly took the view that it embarrassed the government more if they suffered the full penalty. Hazlitt admired their stand and resolved that when Charles Lamb went to visit Leigh Hunt he would accompany him.

Perry realized that he had more than a parliamentary reporter on his hands when Hazlitt had a short piece printed by the *Courier* (ironically, a

Tory paper) on 13 April, mocking the Marquis Wellesley. An unpopular figure with a questionable private life who had been Foreign Secretary and a Governor-General of India, but now (as a result of the 1812 election) in Opposition, Wellesley had been expected to make an important speech on the occasion of the East India Company's charter renewal. But despite his supposed expertise in the question his speech was a turgid disappointment, and he sank lower in informed opinion as a result – not a good moment to do so, because a grand new portrait of him by Sir Thomas Lawrence R.A. had just been hung in that year's Royal Academy exhibition, in effect putting his failure more graphically before the public. Hazlitt's professional responsibilities in the Gallery of Parliament made him an expert witness, which is what prompted the *Courier* to run his piece. Perry wanted it for the *Chronicle* too, so it was reprinted there the next day. In it a soon-to-be familiar Hazlitt appears. He quoted *Henry IV* Part II: 'And such other gambol faculties he has, as shew a weak mind, and an able body', and applied it directly: Wellesley aspires to be thought of as a great orator, Hazlitt wrote, but all he does is talk endlessly about nothing: 'We confess, those of his speeches which we have heard, appear to us prodigies of physical prowess and intellectual imbecility ... It is curious, though somewhat painful, to see this lively little lord always in the full career of his subject, and never advancing a jot the nearer; seeming to utter volumes in every word, and yet saying nothing; retaining the same unabated vehemence of voice and action without anything to excite it; still keeping alive the promise and expectation of genius without once satisfying it – soaring into mediocrity with adventurous enthusiasm, harrowed up by some plain matter-of-fact, writhing with agony under a truism, and launching a common-place with all the fury of a thunderbolt!'[25]

Later in April Crabb Robinson went to play whist at the Lambs', and there chatted to Hazlitt, who described himself as being very comfortable at the *Chronicle*. This prompted Crabb Robinson to comment in his diary that Hazlitt had 'a situation which furnishing him with the necessaries of life keeps his best faculties not employed but awake. And I do not think it is much to be feared that his faculties will therefore decline. He has a most powerful intellect and needs only encouragement to manifest this to the world in a work which could not be overlooked.'[26]

Hazlitt's talents were indeed too considerable to be overlooked, and continued to impose themselves on Perry's attention. Feeling his wings, and noting what might do for the feature pages of a newspaper, Hazlitt wrote some essays during the course of the summer, and in August showed them to Perry, telling him that he could produce as many such as required: on classical education, on the love of fame, on nature, on patriotism, on

Methodism, on envy among artists, on the characters of painters and writers &c. – in short, a prospectus of 'familiar essays', a species of literature in which he was soon to prove himself a master. Perry should have given him a column there and then, and the independence to fill it how he wished. Instead he accepted two of the essays, publishing one in early September and the other in late September.[27] But then a pair of opportunities occurred for Hazlitt to show what else his pen could do, forcing Perry to be less tentative in employing it.

One was that Southey was offered, and accepted, the Poet Laureateship. Earlier in the year news had come that Wordsworth was to receive a government sinecure as Distributor of Stamps for Westmoreland. To Hazlitt these two events were proof of the turncoat trend among the poets, and of what he perceived as the natural sympathy of poetry for power. Now that two of the poets had accepted payment from the Tory warmongers in government, he could not resist having a say, and wrote a scintillating pair of pieces for the *Chronicle* on Southey's elevation. The laureateship then as now was regarded as a poisoned chalice; everyone thought it an absurd job, which either disgraced a good poet or was disgraced by a bad one, as Leigh Hunt neatly put it. Hazlitt added: 'We fear Mr Southey will not form a splendid exception to the numberless instances which prove that there is something in the air of a court, not favourable to the genius of poetry.'[28] This marked the beginning of Hazlitt's game of reminding the poets, to their great discomfiture, of their radical past, which they all wished to forget.

The other opportunity was an anonymous piece in the *Chronicle* on 17 September bemoaning what its author described as the degeneracy of the English stage. The piece was by William Mudford, the paper's drama critic, a dull but ambitious man who wrote numerous forgettable novels and essays, and who made the mistake of theorizing about the theatre without properly formulating his views beforehand – or indeed without possessing the intellectual equipment to have views worth formulating. Hazlitt wrote a reply, which appeared on 25 September, politely but comprehensively demolishing Mudford. The startled drama critic, who knew enough about Hazlitt and his reputation for brains to guess that silence would be the better option, nevertheless ventured a reply. It was a feebler effort even than his first, and this time he made the additional mistake of annoying Hazlitt, who perceived an attempt at irony at his expense. Hazlitt responded again, this time effecting not so much a demolition as an annihilation of Mudford. In his reply to Hazlitt's first article Mudford tried to claim that his own first piece had been 'rather intended as a confession of our ignorance and an appeal to the charity of the illuminated than as a dogmatical solution of the difficulty,' to which Hazlitt now replied, 'I believe it seldom happens that we confess ourselves to be in the dark on any subject, till we are pretty well persuaded that no one else is able to dispel the gloom in which we are involved. Convinced that where our own sagacity has failed, all further search must be vain, we resign ourselves implicitly to all the self-complacency of conscious ignorance, and are very little obliged to anyone, who comes to disturb our intellectual repose. Something of this kind appears to have happened to your Correspondent on the subject of the Drama. Indeed, Sir, I should have been very cautious of attempting to remove the heap of doubts and difficulties which seem to oppress him, but that I thought so obvious a truth as the connection between the manners of the age and comedy could not startle "the plainest understanding"; but the moment this obvious truth is pointed out to him, he complains he is "dazzled with excess of light", and puts a ready moveable screen of common-places before him to keep it out.'[29]

Two decades later, with his enemy safely dead and unable to reply, Mudford raised his head over the top of the trench where he had been sheltering since the above exchange, and loosed off his riposte: 'I knew the man well, and, besides having the greatest contempt for his turgid nothings and bombastic paradoxes (which passed for fine writing with some) I thoroughly disliked his cold artificial manner, and his malignant disposition.'[30]

The exchange between Hazlitt and Mudford caused a stir and people commented that the 'H' who had so trounced Mudford obviously knew what he was talking about. Perry immediately elevated Hazlitt to the role of theatre critic of the *Chronicle*. This meteoric rise into journalistic aristocracy[31] was no less than Hazlitt's due, and it is only surprising that it took as long as nine months to happen.

There was in fact work enough for two critics, so Mudford lingered as Hazlitt's coadjutor for three more months. The seasons at the principal theatres, Covent Garden and Drury Lane, had respectively begun on 6 and 11 September, a couple of weeks before the fateful exchange of articles. Mudford's piece had been prompted by what he thought of the two houses' opening offerings. But it was not only the *Chronicle*'s readers and its editor who could see the difference in quality between Mudford's and Hazlitt's work; it was obvious enough to Mudford himself. He withdrew, which meant that by January 1814 Hazlitt was in sole charge of theatre reviewing. He had also begun to write art criticism, book reviews, and more political commentary for Perry. Commenting retrospectively on his quick rise in journalism, and the fluency in writing which pressure of work induces, Hazlitt wrote, 'Something I did *took*; and I was called upon to do a number of things all at once. I was in the middle of the stream, and must sink or swim.' He swam.[32]

Hazlitt became a theatre critic at a point in cultural history when to occupy that role carried weight. Apart from state openings of Parliament and the weddings and funerals of important persons, public entertainment was chiefly provided by sport (cricket matches and bare-knuckle boxing contests often attracted huge bets and huge crowds of spectators) and theatre. In the closing decades of the eighteenth century there was a transition to more flamboyant and dramatic Romantic theatrical styles, and as a result theatre became a major attraction. London's Drury Lane Theatre had been rebuilt in 1794, under the direction of its playwright-manager Richard Sheridan, to accommodate an audience of over three thousand. Few of London's other nine main theatres were as large, but they were quick to follow the Lyceum's lead in installing gas lighting, which introduced splendour into stage-illumination and effects. In addition to the mainstream theatres there was a rapidly growing number of 'penny theatres' for working-class audiences – eighty of them existed in London by the 1830s – which fostered a taste in some at least of their clientele for mainstream theatre. During the first decades of the nineteenth century Drury Lane, Covent Garden, Sadler's Wells and the Lyceum installed soft seats in the pit, thereby inviting quieter and more attentive audiences. The growing popularity and cultural importance of theatre explains the status accorded to the chief actors of the day – Mrs Siddons, her brother John Kemble, Edmund Kean – and the revival and growth in Shakespearian productions, for the Romantic theatre was better suited to Shakespeare's dramatic range than the confinements of eighteenth-century classic theatre had been. During the eighteenth century Shakespeare's work was read rather than performed, and some of his plays – the *Tempest*, for a famous example – were regarded as unstageable. But with the advent of the larger spirit in Romantic theatre, and under the direction of scholar-actors like John Kemble, Shakespeare came emphatically into his own. Hazlitt thus began his career as a theatre critic at a high point where public enthusiasm for theatre and its social significance coincided.

There could not have been a more spectacular difference for Hazlitt between spending his evenings in Parliament, with its members sprawling and dozing in the gloom of candlelight under a drone of jargon, and spending them in the bustle and brilliance of the theatre, surrounded by romance, tragedy, song and high emotion. If Hazlitt had been pleased with life when Crabb Robinson saw him at Lamb's in the spring, by the autumn he was in the seventh heaven of delight, a mood that shines through his account of reviewing *The Beggar's Opera*, in a performance featuring a young actress called Miss Stephens in her first appearance as Polly. Hazlitt's method of reviewing a play was to study the text beforehand, and to write an account of it which he filed before going to the theatre; then to go to see the play performed, writing his performance review immediately afterwards, and filing the copy that same night to be subjoined to the part already set by the printers. In his essay reminiscing about *The Beggar's Opera* he records that he had been to see his parents who, now retired, were living near Chertsey, 'and, on my return, had stopped at an inn at Kingston-upon-Thames, where I had got the *Beggar's Opera*, and had read it overnight. The next day I walked cheerfully to town. It was a fine sunny morning in the end of autumn, and as I repeated the beautiful song, "Life knows no return of spring", I meditated my next day's criticism, trying to do all the justice I could to so inviting a subject. I was not a little proud of it by anticipation. I had just then begun to stammer out my sentiments on paper, and was in a kind of honeymoon of authorship ... I deposited my account of the play at the *Morning Chronicle* office in the afternoon, and went to see Miss Stephens as Polly. Those were happy times, in which she first came out in this character, in Mandane, where she sang the delicious air, "If e'er the cruel tyrant, Love," (so as it can never be sung again), in *Love in a Village*, where the scene opened with her and Miss Matthews in a painted garden of roses and honeysuckles, and "Hope, thou nurse of young desire," thrilled from two sweet voices in turn. Oh! may my ears sometimes still drink the same sweet sounds, embalmed with the spirit of youth, and health, and joy, but in the thoughts of an instant, but in a dream of fancy, and I shall hardly need to complain.'[33]

Miss Stephens remained a warm favourite. In an 1820 review of a benefit evening for her Hazlitt wrote, 'Miss Stephens's Echo song seemed sung by a Spirit or an enchantress. We were glad to hear it, for we have an attachment to Miss Stephens on account of "auld lang syne" (we like old friendships better than new), and do not wish that little murmuring siren Miss Tree [a new rising star] to wean us from our old and artless favourite. – Those were happy days when first Miss Stephens began to sing! ... She came upon us by surprise, but it was to delight and charm us. There was a new sound in the air, like the voice of Spring; it was as if Music had become young again, and was resolved to try the power of her softest, simplest, sweetest notes.'[34] That Hazlitt was a master-nostalgist appears very plainly here: 'auld lang syne' meant a time just seven years earlier, yet he makes it sound a lifetime away. And in one sense it was: for in both these essays he is unable to resist saying that his 'honeymoon' as a journalist occurred just before the death of his political hopes, by which he meant the defeat of his hero Napoleon in 1814 and again in 1815, which for him was synonymous with the defeat of liberty. In the autumn of 1813 he had sat rapt in the theatre watching Miss Stephens's debut as Polly; by the autumn of 1814 the forces of reaction in Europe had erased the last remaining promise of the French Revolution – as it seemed to Hazlitt, for ever.[35] The last months of hope, coinciding with his finding at long last his voice as a writer, constituted a poignant memory for him.

One of the first and greatest results of Hazlitt's theatre criticism was that he made the career of a previously unknown actor, giving him the start to a life of legendary success. He also, thereby, saved the Drury Lane Theatre, which was in deep financial crisis, having been rebuilt after a fire two years before at such a cost that it seemed destined never to escape its debts. In the fearsome cold of January 1814 – the beginning of a 'Great Frost' in which the deep-piled snow lay frozen on the ground from January to March, and in which a Frost Fair was held on the iced-over Thames – Drury Lane staged *The Merchant of Venice* with a small, wiry, energetic, impoverished provincial player, newly arrived in London, in the role of Shylock. Because of the freezing weather the audience was small – the boxes empty, the pit less than half-full – and the management was beside itself with anxiety.[36] But the audience included Hazlitt; and the small wiry unknown actor playing Shylock was Edmund Kean. Within minutes of Shylock coming on stage – and certainly by the time he had denounced Antonio for calling him an unbeliever and spitting on his gabardine – Hazlitt was electrified. He was seeing before his eyes a new genius of the theatre, a new style of acting, an unprecedented and unparalleled phenomenon. 'For voice, eye, action, and expression, no actor has come out for many years at all equal to him,' Hazlitt wrote in the next day's *Chronicle*. He described him as a 'master in the art', a complete success as Shylock, and destined to be an even greater favourite in other parts. In his range, and in his ability to give 'perpetually fresh shocks of delight and surprise, it would be difficult to single out a competitor'. Within days, as shown by a letter from Jane Austen to her sister in the country, the rage for seeing Kean was so great that it was almost impossible to get seats in the theatre. Later an amazingly improbable story was put about that Hazlitt had been bribed (to the tune of £1500) to puff Kean and thus save Drury Lane. Hazlitt indeed saved Drury Lane, and he indeed launched Kean's career; but it was not a question of audiences blindly following the opinion of the *Chronicle*'s theatre critic, for when they saw Kean they knew Hazlitt was right, and Hazlitt's critical reputation rose further.

It could be said that the rapid ascent of Hazlitt as a critic and Kean as an actor was something of a double act.[37] But it was quite some double act: Hazlitt's notices of Kean's performances – of his Shylock, Richard III, Hamlet, Othello, Iago, Macbeth and others – figure among the most important works of dramatic criticism in the Romantic period. Hazlitt treated theatre as an art directly responsible to life, and therefore assessed both plays and the performance of them on grounds of truth – emotional as well as factual truth – and of whether they showed skill in the art of revealing truth. He paid no attention to classical rules about 'unities of time and place' and the like, nor did he wish to see theatre remote and semi-ritualistic, nor didactic, as if it were a school for inculcating loftier sentiments and a grander moral tone than is found in reality. He treated theatre as art, and moreover an art that engages the human condition, and he responded to each play and each performance as a man of intelligence and sensibility, not as a scholar laden with academic theories and pre-conceived notions.[38] By deliberate choice he was an enthusiast rather than a connoisseur, for he saw that there are many kinds of excellence, and he applauded them all.

Hazlitt was not uncritical of Kean. He more than once remarked that Kean did not adjust his exuberance and energy to the requirements of a role, and that he was sometimes tempted to over-theatricality – with pauses that were too long, for example, and too much reliance on facial expressions invisible from the pit. But Kean was a brilliant actor, and Hazlitt saw no point in stinting praise where it was merited – even the Lake Poets, for all their apostasies, always had their due from him. Kean was an actor of great power, as evidenced by the fact that his portrayal of descent into madness in Philip Massinger's *A New Way to Pay Old Debts* made Byron faint in his seat.

Factions arose on either side of the question about Kean's merits. The Tory press was muted in its opinion of him, because they disliked praising anything associated with the Whig-managed Drury Lane, and because Kean vociferously publicized his radical political views off-stage. Kean's career was not only politically but professionally controversial too. He burst into prominence just three years before the other great actor of the age, John Kemble, retired, and some argue that there is a causal connection. The caricature story goes that Kemble was classic, Kean romantic; that Kemble was gentlemanly and dignified, Kean proletarian and brash; that Kean's popularity diminished Kemble's; that his innovations as an actor put Kemble in the shade; that Kemble was anyway fading. For his part Hazlitt remained a staunch admirer of Kemble, and in print opposed the suggestion that the latter's powers had declined: 'He is no longer in exclusive possession of the Stage: but in himself he has not fallen off a jot.'[39] Kemble's scholarly interest in the theatre, especially in Shakespeare's plays, which he brought back to a central place in the English repertoire, and the fact that he was a discriminating collector of theatrical manuscripts and books, commanded Hazlitt's respect, the more so as he was a truly fine actor, who with Mrs Siddons occupied the summit of their profession throughout Hazlitt's formative years as a theatre-goer. When Hazlitt went to the theatre in Liverpool at the age of twelve, a quarter of a century before, it was Kemble he saw.

On the same day in January 1814 that his first notice of Kean appeared, Hazlitt had a second piece in the *Chronicle*, attacking the movement which had been set afoot in *The Times* for restoration of the Bourbons to the throne of France. This was a newly-begun campaign in support of the so-called 'principle of Legitimacy' – the legitimacy of royal succession, that is; a new name for the old doctrine of the 'divine right of kings'. The campaigners wished to see the 'usurper' and 'upstart' Napoleon displaced in favour of a true Bourbon monarch. They were adamant that there was to be no treating with Napoleon. He must not be left in place in France; he must go. This was the new theme of *The Times*, and the loudest voice promoting it was its leader-writer, none other than Hazlitt's brother-in-law John Stoddart. It was not, to begin with, the policy of the British government; but it was certainly the policy of Carlton House, which is to say, the Prince Regent – as was cannily pointed out by John Scott, the gifted and well-judging editor of the *Champion*. As the Carlton House–*Times* campaign gained ground, so the government began to rally behind it.

Hazlitt observed these developments with horror. He was outraged by Southey's argument, in an essay for a Tory magazine, that the French should be treated as 'the Jews of Europe – a people politically excommunicated and never to be forgiven, and above all never to be trusted'. There was much talk of exacting revenge and reparations from France, which Hazlitt argued in an article of 26 February would be both wrong and counter-productive. *The Times* on 18 January reported Marshal Blücher's proclamation to the effect that anyone failing to revoke all connection with the French Empire after Allied troops entered areas on the left bank of the Rhine 'will render himself guilty of treason against the Allied Powers; he will be carried before a Military Tribunal and condemned to death'. *The Times* (in the person of Stoddart) went so far as to relish the prospect of the Louvre being sacked by Cossacks to revenge the burning of Moscow. Hazlitt was revolted by this. His brother-in-law proclaimed: 'Our rallying cry should be "Europe as it was in 1788!" ', and, shamelessly forgetting his own early Jacobin enthusiasms, he urged the restoration to France not only of its Bourbon kings but of 'those safe and practicable principles of policy which prior to the fatal Revolution had rendered France the envy and pride of the world' – evidently forgetting that it was those very principles that had made France explode into revolution in the first place.

This battle of words in the London newspapers had begun in the previous autumn – the autumn of 1813 – after France's armies, decimated by the Russian winter, and hopelessly stretched from Spain to the Ukraine, had suffered a succession of defeats at the hands of the Allies. It was apparent that the end of the war was in sight at last. Lord Liverpool, by now Prime Minister, said in the House of Lords that England sought an honourable and reasonable peace with France, and overtures were made to Napoleon accordingly, in what came to be called the Frankfurt Proposals. If Napoleon had accepted them he would have remained Emperor. Unfortunately and unwisely, he did not, and when Castlereagh went to the continent in January 1814 the Frankfurt Proposals were no longer on the table.

Edward Sterling, the celebrated *Times* writer who used the pen-name 'Vetus', had mounted a violent attack on the Frankfurt Proposals in his column for 12 November 1813. He was moved by deep animosity towards Napoleon, whom he regarded as a blood-thirsty usurping rapacious tyrant bent on dragging all Europe into his clutches. Hazlitt sprang to Napoleon's defence in a reply. There followed a duel between them, or rather between Hazlitt on the one side and two separate adversaries on the other, Vetus and John Stoddart. *The Times* had lately acquired as its new owner John Walter II, the son of John Walter I, its founder, who had recently died. Fresh in the role and just learning his way, John Walter II was deeply under the influence of John Stoddart, whom he therefore allowed to have his head in the controversy with Hazlitt. The vituperative and violent tone of Vetus's attacks on Napoleon elicited uncompromising language from Hazlitt in response, but with it a great deal of hard excellent argument. Godwin asserted that Hazlitt's 'Illustrations of Vetus', as his series of replies was called, was the best thing he ever wrote.

The burden of Vetus's harangues was that there should be no negotiation with Napoleon. Hazlitt replied, 'We will also venture to lay down a maxim, which is – That from the moment that one party declares and acts upon the avowed principle that peace can never be made with an enemy, it renders war on the part of that enemy a matter of necessary self-defence, and holds out a plea for every excess of ambition or revenge. If we are to limit our hostility to others only with their destruction, we impose the adoption of the same principle on them as their only means of safety. There is no alternative.'[40] John Stoddart quoted Hazlitt's words in the next day's *Times* leader, and remarked, 'We copy [this] from a paper of yesterday as a proof that the keepers of St Luke or Bedlam do not keep that watch and ward over their patients which they ought to do: at least they allow them the use of pen and ink: such ravings can certainly only have proceeded from one of those receptacles of irregular genius.'[41] He here applies a trusted recipe for debate: when reason provides no answer, resort to abuse.

It was not until January 1814 that Stoddart showed his hand in supporting the endeavours of the Prince Regent and his Carlton House coterie, which had until then been covert. The 'Legitimacy' campaign, in seeking the restoration of the Bourbons, was thereby arguing that foreign armies should reimpose a monarchy on a people who had thrown out that monarchy twenty years before. Hazlitt was not alone in being appalled by the suggestion, for it suddenly transpired that Vetus, despite his hostility to Napoleon, was not therefore pro-Bourbon or pro-Legitimacy, and he shared Hazlitt's view that the French monarchy should not be restored by force. For this reason Hazlitt modified his tone in his last 'Illustration of Vetus', which appeared in January 1814. He did this even though Vetus had been using items of personal information about him, garnered from Stoddart, for purposes of *ad hominem* vilification – as for example imputing to Hazlitt a Godwinian desire to abolish marriage and thereby remove the bar to the 'unconfined embraces' of free-love. Vetus accused Hazlitt of being a votary of 'the strumpet goddess Reason' – which Hazlitt was perfectly glad to accept. But although the personal insults were not so pleasant he ignored them when he saw that Vetus was in effect an ally on the Legitimacy question, since that was by far the more important matter.[42] Vetus was sacked by *The Times* for no longer toeing the paper's line, immediately provoking Hazlitt's sympathy further.

History, in its customary way, was moving more swiftly than anyone grasped, least of all those engaged in the quarrel of the press. In the months and weeks before April 1814 John Scott in the *Champion* was still urging negotiation with Napoleon. But in the same period the Allied governments, under pressure from their royal masters, had decided that Napoleon must go, and that Louis XVIII, biding his time in London, should after all be restored to the throne of France. Late on Tuesday 5 April the completely unexpected news reached London that Allied forces had entered Paris. Five days later Napoleon abdicated. England went mad in celebration: illuminations and decorations were everywhere raised, the Bourbon royal arms and the name of Louis XVIII were displayed, and the legend 'The Triumph of Legitimate Sovereigns' was draped on the Foreign Office frontage in Downing Street.[43] For the princes of Old Regimes everywhere in Europe it was a glad day. Their uncomprehending peoples joined them in rejoicing, because the war was over; and that was all that mattered to them, for it had been a war that brought them tremendous economic hardship. Even liberals and reformers were generally pleased, because they had faced repression, censorship, imprisonment, and reaction – not least in England, in which the war amounted to a ghastly chapter in the history of a people legendarily proud of what they were wont to call their freedoms.

Napoleon's abdication and the restoration of the Bourbons set Hazlitt at odds even with his friends. Crabb Robinson noted the *Morning Chronicle*'s 'unpatriotic spirit' in his diary, and said that Hazlitt, Cobbett, and Sir Richard Phillips, editor of the *Monthly Magazine*, were among the very few who failed to rejoice. '[Hazlitt] mixes passion and ill-humour and personal feelings in his judgments on public events and characters more than any man I know,' Crabb Robinson remarked uneasily, surprised at the torment Hazlitt displayed over the events on the continent. 'And this infinitely detracts from the value of his opinions, which, possessing as he does rare talents, would be otherwise very valuable. He always vindicates Buonaparte not because he is insensible to his enormous crimes, but out of spite to the Tories of this country and the friends of the war of 1792.'[44] Hazlitt was indeed so distressed that he also quarrelled with Lamb about Napoleon, in anger saying that Lamb's 'infinite littleness' blinded him to Napoleon's greatness. It was a breach that never truly healed thereafter; at least, things could not be the same again between them. Lamb told Crabb Robinson what had happened, putting matters somewhat oddly by saying that 'Hazlitt was confounded by Napoleon's conduct and ashamed to show his face.'[45] It was in fact despair, and isolation from the general mood of rejoicing, that kept him away from company.

And, as troubles never come single spies, he had another serious problem to face: he was about to lose his job.

# CHAPTER NINE

# Waterloo

## 1814–1815

IN LATE 1814 the Lambs decided to hold their Thursday at-homes once a month only. These events had become less boisterous but not much less exuberantly intellectual than in their early heyday. This rearrangement, though, marked a change. The old spirit of the 'Thursdays' evaporated, and was never recaptured.

On 17 November Crabb Robinson went to the Lambs' after dinner to play a rubber of whist, and chatted to Hazlitt until one o'clock in the morning. Hazlitt was in an especially good mood because he had just received an invitation to write for the prince of journals, the *Edinburgh Review*. He was brought to the attention of the *Edinburgh*'s editor, Francis Jeffrey, by the second Lady Mackintosh. Impressed by a sequence of striking articles in the *Champion* she asked who had written them, and on learning that it was the author of *An Essay on the Principles of Human Action* which her husband so admired, she immediately wrote to Jeffrey.[1] On her recommendation Jeffrey read Hazlitt's work, with the result that he approached Hazlitt and 'in a very flattering manner enrolled [him] in the corps', as Crabb Robinson described it.

This development was as timely as it was welcome because, as Hazlitt told Crabb Robinson during the same conversation, he had just left the staff of the *Morning Chronicle*. Crabb Robinson already knew this piece of news, and knew too that Perry had not dismissed Hazlitt, but that Hazlitt had resigned – not in form, but simply by ceasing to write for the paper. 'He complains bitterly of Perry's treatment of him,' Crabb Robinson wrote, 'and I believe his statement, for he is too proud and high-minded to lie. He says that during the last six months he wrote seventy columns for the *Chronicle*, that Perry himself confessed to him that Hazlitt's had done more for the paper than all the other writings, and in consequence of his approbation of what Hazlitt had done, advanced him £100, of which £50 are due. I had understood from the Colliers that Perry had not actually dismissed Hazlitt, but that he abstained from coming. Hazlitt states the facts thus: Perry said to him expressly that he wished Hazlitt to *look out for another situation* – the affronting language Hazlitt could not easily forget – as he was not fit for a reporter. Hazlitt said he thought he could do miscellaneous things. Perry said he would think of it. However, when Hazlitt afterwards went to the office for his salary he was told Mr Perry wished to speak with him. He went to Perry's room. Perry was not alone, and desired Hazlitt to wait. Hazlitt went to another room. Perry then seeing Hazlitt there, went out of the house. Hazlitt, in consequence, never called again. As there [was] no express refusal either to pay or to accept his services another way than as a reporter, Perry has an excuse for saying he did not dismiss Hazlitt.'[2]

Hazlitt's explanation for Perry's change of attitude to him was the fall of Napoleon, in whose support Hazlitt had been writing, and whose exile to Elba put the *Chronicle* on the defeated side of the argument. Perry naturally had no wish to continue riding a dead horse, and no doubt found it an embarrassment to have one of the principal advocates of the deposed emperor writing leaders for his paper.

But there was an accumulation of other grounds besides. For one thing, Hazlitt made Perry nervous. His theatre criticism was such that if he wrote in praise of a performer or performance, Perry would get the credit, together with visits in his office from this or that fragrant actress to thank him in person – as when Hazlitt saw Miss Stephens come out of Perry's room on the day that the paper ran his notice of her début in the *Beggar's Opera*. But if Perry wished a play or a player to get a puff, usually because he had been lobbied in advance, he did not let Hazlitt review the play. 'I was generally sent out of the way when any *debutante* had a friend at court, and was to be tenderly handled,' Hazlitt wrote – the 'court' being Perry – 'For the rest, or those of robust constitutions, I had *carte blanche* given me. Sometimes I ran out of the course, to be sure.' When it came to politics and society matters Perry's anxieties were even greater: 'Poor Perry! what bitter complaints he used to make, that by *running-a-muck* at lords and Scotchmen I should not leave him a place to dine out at! the expression on his face at those moments, as if he should shortly be without a friend in the world, was truly pitiable.'[3] As if the content of Hazlitt's pieces were not enough, their length bothered Perry too: his friend Mary Russell Mitford, an enthusiastic admirer of Hazlitt's writing, recalled 'the doleful visage with which Mr Perry used to ... execrate "the damned fellow's damned stuff" for filling up so much of the paper in the very height of the advertisement season. I shall never forget his long face. It was the only time of day that I ever saw it either long or sour.'[4]

Another factor, and perhaps the precipitating one, was Hazlitt's criticism of Sir Thomas Lawrence's portrait of Lord Castlereagh, exhibited at the Royal Academy that summer of 1814. Hazlitt said it gave Castlereagh a 'smug, smart, upstart, haberdasher look'. It happened that Lawrence was a friend of Perry and was at that very time painting his portrait. Perry naturally found it awkward to have his own newspaper damn the work of the man he was sitting to. Mary Russell Mitford reported that Perry was incensed by Hazlitt's 'very masterly but damaging critique on Sir Thomas Lawrence, whom Mr P., as one whom he visited and was being painted by, chose to have praised'. To make matters worse, Perry had in early life worked behind a haberdasher's counter in Aberdeen, a fact he wished to forget when dining at Holland House and other grand places, and which he might have imagined was lurking maliciously behind Hazlitt's remark.

Perry acted swiftly to remedy the damage done to Sir Thomas Lawrence's feelings. He wrote a piece reprimanding Hazlitt for conflating 'the ebullition of party spirit with his ideas of characteristic resemblance'. Art and politics are independent matters, he said, and the Castlereagh portrait was one of the best in the exhibition. Hazlitt of course agreed with neither of these points, but he had had his say first, and good judges agreed with him. Crabb Robinson reported that the sculptor John Flaxman was among them: 'Lawrence's Lord Castlereagh is objected to as mean and haberdasher-like by Hazlitt and Flaxman.' The two also thought that Lawrence's social success interfered with his art; Hazlitt said, 'No good talker will ever labour enough to become a good painter' – or writer, or thinker, Hazlitt elsewhere added, with Coleridge in mind.

Perry thus found himself with an unexpectedly large cuckoo in the nest, a writer of decided opinions and great powers whom readers noticed – but who therefore sometimes rocked the boat. To save himself a ducking he attempted to loosen his connection with Hazlitt, by trying to get Hazlitt off his staff while leaving open the option of employing his talents occasionally. His attempt was ham-handed, and he lost Hazlitt completely. Mary Russell Mitford believed that Perry did not fully understand the nature and range of Hazlitt's gifts, and therefore missed a great opportunity. Later, in the winter of 1817–18, when Hazlitt's fame was established and he was adding to it with his lectures and a highly successful book, Perry invited him to dinner 'and a large party to meet him, to hear him talk, and to show him off as a lion of the day'. Hazlitt accepted the invitation, and behaved impeccably, except that he uttered scarcely a word. He was 'gracious and polite past all expression – a perfect pattern of mute elegance – a silent Lord Chesterfield,' Mary Russell Mitford reported, thinking that this was his way of getting revenge on Perry. It was probably no such thing: Hazlitt was shy, and only talked freely in congenial company.

But he had not forgotten Perry's ill-treatment. In the *London Magazine* in 1820 he recurred to it, the passage of years altering the reasons for his leaving: 'A writer whom I know very well ... having written upward of sixty columns of original matter on politics, criticism, belles-lettres, and *virtu* in a respectable Morning Paper, in a single half-year, was, at the end of that period, on applying for renewal of his engagement, told by the Editor "he might give in a specimen of what he could do!" One would think that sixty columns of the *Morning Chronicle* are a sufficient specimen of what a man can do. But while this person was thinking of his next answer to Vetus, or account of Mr Kean's performance of Hamlet, he had neglected "to point the toe", to hold up his head higher than usual (having acquired a habit of poring over books when young), and to get a new velvet collar to an old-fashioned great coat. These are "the graceful ornaments to the columns of a newspaper – the Corinthian capitals of a polished style". This unprofitable servant of the press found no difference in himself before or after he became known to readers of the *Morning Chronicle*, and it accordingly made no difference to his appearance or pretensions.'[5] The *London*'s editor felt moved to write Perry a note of apology after this, to which Perry haughtily replied that he was unmoved by personal attacks, and anyway knew that this one had come from someone on whom he, Perry, had conferred nothing but favours. There is delicious irony in his remark, for Perry cannot have been without at least some inkling that the favours went in the opposite direction, as history proves; for were it not for Hazlitt, Perry's name would be lost to memory.

For his part, Hazlitt was quite convinced that Perry had dismissed him. Writing still later, in 1823, he said that 'he was dismissed from the *Morning Chronicle* much against his inclination.'[6] It was obviously a blow; the regular salary and the connection with one of the country's two great newspapers had made a palpable difference to life. But as it turned out, the ending of the connection proved an opportunity, not a disaster, for it meant the transference of his talents to two far more congenial journals, John Scott's *Champion* and the Hunts' *Examiner*. In the former he wrote art and drama criticism, while in the latter he was given freedom to develop the literary form for which his distinctive genius was suited – the 'familiar essay', the free-style, personal, wide-ranging miscellaneous essay.

Leigh Hunt had been conducting his editorial labours from a cell in the Horsemonger Lane Gaol since the spring of 1813. He had papered his cell with roses on the walls and painted a blue sky on the ceiling. His door stood open and visitors walked in as if he was in the drawing room of his own home. His cell was in the part of the prison that housed the Governor, and there was a little garden outside, which Hunt fenced with green palings and adorned with a trellis. He planted a small lawn and bordered it 'with a thick bed from a nursery'. He wrote, 'The earth I filled with flowers and young trees. There was an apple tree, from which we managed to get a pudding the second year.'[7] The 'we' refers to his wife and son, who lived with him in his cell. Thomas Moore and Lord Byron called, and admired his snug corner. The Lambs came in all weathers, including the frightful winter of early 1814. The constraint on his liberty was not a constraint on his life.

Conditions were very different for felons of less note and lower class elsewhere in the prison, and the bodies of the executed were sometimes displayed on its roof. A decade later builders began to erect the beautiful Trinity Church Square on the tenter ground across the road, with a lovely honey-coloured neoclassical church at its centre, whose tower contains a clock with a face on each of its four sides. Legend says that the face looking towards the prison never shows the proper time because it was cursed by an innocent woman hanged in the prison yard.[8] The prison was replaced by a grand neoclassical court-house and a park in Edwardian times. Where the gibbet once stood children now play football.

It was here, in Hunt's celebrated confinement, that Hazlitt and he first met. It is surprising that they did not meet before, for Hunt had known Lamb since 1808, and Haydon records in his diary that both Hazlitt and Hunt were almost daily visitors at his studio. But they knew one another very well by reputation, so when Hazlitt arrived at Hunt's prison cell for their first encounter, both were overcome by shyness. 'William Hazlitt, who there first did me the honour of a visit, would stand interchanging amenities at the threshold, which I had great difficulty in making him pass. I know not which kept his hat off with the greater pertinacity of deference, I to the diffident cutter-up of Tory dukes and kings, or he to the amazing prisoner and invalid who issued out of a bower of roses.'[9]

Hazlitt dined with Haydon and Thomas Barnes at Hunt's cell, and there too first met John Scott of the *Champion*. Barnes, an old and close school-friend of Hunt, was just two years away from beginning his distinguished career as editor of *The Times*. At this point he was on the *Times* staff, but also writing for both Hunt and John Scott, contributing astute and well-judged theatre criticism to the *Examiner* in place of Hunt, whose office that had hitherto always been. Scott and Hazlitt admired one another's contributions to the anti-Legitimacy battle, and to begin with at least liked one another. As Hazlitt's association with Perry and the *Chronicle* faltered in the spring and early summer of 1814, these new connections came into their own. Scott ran a piece by Hazlitt in April, a feisty essay entitled 'On the Late War' which Perry was too squeamish to use. From June onwards Hazlitt began providing regular essays on art to John Scott, and on 22 May his first *Examiner* essay appeared, 'On Posthumous Fame', which argues that Shakespeare's protean ability to enter into every one of his characters bespeaks a lack of egotism, which in turn made him indifferent to future fame, showing that real genius springs from inspiration not ambition.

In his history of the *Examiner* Edmund Blunden (who is also Leigh Hunt's biographer) wrote, 'The next volume [1814] was enriched and enlivened by the accession of William Hazlitt to the list of contributors. There had never crept in any want of enthusiasm or courage in the "Examiner", the editor's writings at this stage being extraordinarily lively and challenging, but with the arrival of Hazlitt a tempestuous gale soon seemed to have sprung up.'[10]

The essay that established Hazlitt's standing as an art critic was the first of his regular pieces for the *Champion*, on Benjamin West's large academic painting entitled *Christ Rejected*. Hazlitt wrote, 'We might sum up our opinion in one word by saying, that there is in the present picture an absolute want of what is called *gusto* throughout; nor can we describe our idea of Mr West's style in general better than by saying that it is the reverse of Raphael's. The difference is this. In Raphael, every muscle and nerve has intense feeling. The same divine spirit breathes from every part; it either agitates the inmost frame, or plays in gentle undulations on the trembling surface. Whether we see his figures bending with all the blandishments of maternal love, or standing in the motionless silence of thought, or hurried into the tumult of action, the whole is bursting with expression. But Mr West makes no use whatever of the moveable frame of the countenance, the only language it possesses; he sees and feels nothing in the human face but bones and cartilages: or if he does avail himself of this flexible machinery, it is only by rule and method. The effect is not that which the soul of passion impresses on it, and which the soul of genius alone can seize; but such as might be given to the wooden puppets or pasteboard figures, pulled by wires, and taught to open the mouth, or knit the forehead, or raise the eyes with a great deal of significance. It is not the hardness of the outline, but the want of inflection in the lines themselves, that is the real and insurmountable objection to Mr West's pictures, which are not of the epic but the didactic kind; not poetry, but prose.'[11]

Crabb Robinson visited Flaxman a week later, and read aloud to him Hazlitt's 'bitter and severe but most excellent' piece. Flaxman was Professor of Sculpture at the Royal Academy, and therefore a colleague of

West. He and his wife were admirers of Hazlitt, having attended his philosophy lectures in 1812. The diarist reported that Flaxman was 'constrained to admit the high talent of the criticism though he was unaffectedly pained by its severity'.[12] Crabb Robinson would read Hazlitt's work aloud to anyone who cared to listen; not long afterwards he read this same piece to Mrs Barbauld, authoress of the poems Hazlitt had enjoyed in childhood.[13]

But it was in the *Examiner* that Hazlitt exploded with an even louder bang, first in a tormented piece on Kean's Iago, which shocked many who read it, and then in his review of Wordsworth's *Excursion*. Both these essays laid the foundations for serious difficulties later, at the same time as they confirmed his formidable intellectual stature as a critic.

Hazlitt saw Kean in the role of Iago at Drury Lane in July 1814, and on the 24th of that month and the 7th of the following month wrote a two-part discussion in the *Examiner* to explain why he thought Kean had played the character in a too light and witty vein. This meant giving his own assessment of Iago's nature, based on the textual evidence. It is a brilliant and absorbing piece of analysis which imputes to Iago a dissociation of intellectual and moral faculties, the latter practically non-existent, the former having a cast of mind that made him fascinated by possibilities and opportunities for doing intricate evil among the people about him, as if he were playing a game of human chess. Hazlitt saw in Iago a man in whom the ordinary human propensity to read about fires and murders in the newspapers, or to witness a hanging, was taken to the extreme: his interest lay not just in watching destruction, but in contriving it.[14]

To the second part of this discussion Hazlitt appended a note on Desdemona's love for the Moor, and it was this that caused the stir. Earlier in the year one 'P. G. P.' – Peter George Patmore,[15] who later became Hazlitt's friend and confidant, though they were at this time unacquainted – contributed to the *Examiner* a piece about *Othello* in which he praised the character of Desdemona in conventional terms as a virtuous and affectionate woman, who loved the Moor despite his physical appearance and his defects of character, and in particular despite the large incongruity between them in all respects of person, tradition and situation. 'Shakespeare delighted to honour the female character,' Patmore sentimentally wrote, quite forgetting Lady Macbeth, shrewish Kate, Queen Gertrude, and several besides, 'and how exquisitely he has done so in Desdemona [who] loves the Moor in spite of his personal defects ... *she* saw beauty in his goodness, *she* saw Othello's visage in his mind.'[16] To this Hazlitt responded, 'If Desdemona really "saw her husband's visage in his mind," or fell in love with the abstract idea of his "virtues and valiant parts", she was the only woman on record, either before or since, who ever did so. Shakespeare's want of penetration in supposing that those are the sort of things that gain the affections, might have drawn a smile from the ladies, if honest Iago had not checked it by suggesting a different explanation. It should seem by this, as if the rankness and gross impropriety of the personal connection, the difference in age, features, colour, constitution, instead of being the obstacle, had been the motive of the refinement of her choice, and had, by beginning at the wrong end, subdued her to the amiable qualities of her lord. Iago is indeed a most learned and irrefragable doctor on the subject of love, which he defines to be "merely a lust of the blood, and a permission of the will." The idea that love has its source in moral or intellectual excellence, in good nature or good sense, or has any connection with sentiment or refinement of any kind, is one of those preposterous and wilful errors, which ought to be extirpated for the sake of those few persons who alone are likely to suffer by it, whose romantic generosity and delicacy ought not to be sacrificed to the baseness of their nature, but who, treading secure the flowery path, marked out for them by poets and moralists, the licensed artificers of fraud and lies, are dashed to pieces down the precipice, and perish without help.'[17] In short, Hazlitt said, Desdemona's love for Othello was a profoundly sexual passion, the expression of female desire to yield itself to masculine power and difference. Poetry says that love is a thing of flowers and sentiment, but anyone who believes this is, said Hazlitt, a fool: love has its roots in lust.

It is tempting to surmise that behind the stinging bitterness of these views is a fruitless infatuation, an amorous disappointment – yet another one, for hidden behind the scenes of Hazlitt's life, as frequent hints and glimpses like this one attest, are any number of failed infatuations. In the previous autumn, walking back to London from Chertsey and humming airs from the *Beggar's Opera*, Hazlitt had seemed to be in love with someone lost to the record; these lines, written almost a year later, make him appear savage with hurt.[18] It would be in character if so – it was the self-same Patmore who later said, when he had become Hazlitt's friend, that he 'never knew him out of love'. If the surmise is right, the wound was a large one, for six months later Hazlitt wrote, as if dwelling on the same theme, 'We waste our regrets on what cannot be recalled, or fix our desires on what we know cannot be attained. Every hour is the slave of the last; and we are seldom masters either of our thoughts or of our actions. We are the creatures of imagination, passion, and self-will, more than of reason or even of self-interest. Rousseau, in his Emilius, proposed to educate a perfectly reasonable man, who was to have passions and affections like other men, but with an absolute control over them. He was to love and be wise. This is a contradiction in terms.'[19]

These painful remarks occur in Hazlitt's recounting of the sad tale of Anthony Codrus Urceus of Forli, 'a most learned and unfortunate Italian,' who was described by a biographer as a striking instance of 'the miseries men bring upon themselves by setting their affections unreasonably on trifles'. Urceus went mad when his papers were burned in a fire, and Hazlitt says of his story, 'Almost every one may here read the history of his own life.' It is a bleak assessment, explicable only on the basis of pain.[20]

Both Hunt (duly quoting sonnet 116, 'Let me not to the marriage of true minds/Admit impediments') and Barnes wrote responses in the *Examiner* to Hazlitt on Iago, and Hazlitt duelled entertainingly with Barnes for a couple of issues, the latter slyly teasing him in the piece that closed their debate, by saying that in describing an 'over-active mind dangerous to itself and others, and insatiably craving after action of the most violent kind,' Hazlitt had described not Iago but his idol Napoleon.

The poison seed that Hazlitt sowed by this analysis of Desdemona's sexual infatuation for Othello was the opportunity for his enemies, when open warfare between him and them flared in the periodicals a few years later, to brand him as an obscene and immoral writer. But what watered the seed thus planted was an entirely different venture: his review of Wordsworth's *Excursion* in three parts on 21 and 28 August and 2 October 1814. In it Hazlitt praised Wordsworth liberally: 'In power of intellect, in lofty conception, in the depth of feeling, at once simple and sublime, which pervades every part of it and which gives to every object an almost preternatural and preterhuman interest, this work has seldom been surpassed,' he began, and later continued, 'There is in his general sentiments and reflections on human life a depth, an originality, a truth, a beauty, and a grandeur, both of conception and expression, which place him decidedly at the head of the poets of the present day.' This was written at a time when Wordsworth had scarcely any reputation as a poet; when, indeed, he was regarded as a bad poet – in the *Edinburgh Review* Francis Jeffrey famously commenced his review of the same poem with the words, 'This won't do.' Hazlitt had always believed in Wordsworth's qualities. He sincerely believed him to be the outstanding poetical genius of the time, and continued to think so despite everything that ensued upon his review. But he was not capable of withholding criticism when he thought it due. There were several things about the *Excursion* that disappointed him – deeply, as it happened, for he remembered parts of earlier drafts of the poem in 1803, and he remembered Wordsworth's youthful principles. He accordingly expected more from the poem than it offered, and he could not be silent in the face of Wordsworth's public condemnation of the French Revolution, given that he had once enthusiastically supported its principles.

Hazlitt's main objections were that the subject of the poem was not equal to the genius of the poet, that Wordsworth's use of particular examples to illustrate his general theses merely distracted and impeded attention, that Wordsworth could not resist interposing his own interpretation on things, instead of letting them speak for themselves, and that he lacked imagination. He also criticized Wordsworth's strictures on Voltaire, and – quoting from years-old memory certain unpublished lines of Wordsworth's, surely a flattering attention – the poet's falling-off from the cause of liberty. In the last of the three pieces Hazlitt indulged a long digression on the stupidity and unpleasantness of country people in general and those of the Lake District in particular, whom Wordsworth had made heroes and heroines of his epic of ordinary life.

There was much here to annoy one as prickly as Wordsworth, but worst was the fact that it was Hazlitt who said them. Some latent hostility, or a feeling of *lèse-majesté* because the boy whom he and Coleridge had patronized at Alfoxden all those years before was now daring to pronounce on his work, flared in Wordsworth's soul. It is a speaking fact that Wordsworth was on the whole pleased with the review until he learned who wrote it. And, by an unfortunate coincidence, when he discovered the reviewer's identity he had staying with him a young Edinburgh man called John Wilson, who was soon to play a large part in Hazlitt's troubles.

A straw in the wind is captured in a letter of 29 October 1814 from Wordsworth's wife to his sister Dorothy: 'The conclusion of Hazlitt's Critique is come to us – a curious piece, but it must benefit the sale of the book. You will be amused greatly at the abuse he levies at the Mountaineers – he says "all country people hate each other" and these more than others, and he gives the reason why and is confirmed in his opinions by the Poet who lets it out now and then – he declaims against the Poverty of the country – that *nothing good* is to be got – speaks of the want of everything that is intellectual and elegant, enumerates these wants, and amongst the items courtezans are found. A pretty comment upon these opinions would be to relate something of the critics departure [from] this unaccommodating country.'[21] Dorothy passed on the point to Mrs Clarkson on 11 November: 'amongst other evils he has the audacity to complain that there are no Courtesans to be found in the Country.'[22]

Hazlitt had written that, lacking the amenities of a town, country folk had only 'mischief-making and backbiting for want of any better amusement. There are no shops, no taverns, no theatres, no opera, no concerts, no pictures, no public-buildings, no crowded streets, no noise of coaches, or courts of law, – neither courtiers nor courtesans, no literary parties, no fashionable routs, no society, no books, or knowledge of books. Vanity and luxury are the civilisers of the world, and sweeteners of human life. Without objects either of pleasure or action, it grows harsh and crabbed: the mind becomes stagnant, the affections callous, and the eye dull.'[23] By the reference to courtesans – prompted by alliteration with 'courtiers' and the general picture of town life – Hazlitt gave Wordsworth a tool for revenge. With the aim of discrediting Hazlitt he now told John Wilson and everyone else who would listen – including Lamb and Crabb Robinson – that Hazlitt had been involved in a disgraceful escapade in the Lake District in 1803, from which he had only narrowly escaped a ducking from the local people. John Wilson stored the information away for future use. Lamb – despite the fact that his friendship with Hazlitt was still somewhat under a cloud because of their Napoleon disagreement, and who had lent Hazlitt his copy of the *Excursion* but had not yet received it back, which was a nuisance because he was supposed to be reviewing it for another magazine – was not troubled by Wordsworth's tale: 'The 'scapes of the great god Pan who appeared among your mountains some dozen years hence, and his narrow chance of being submerged by the swains, afforded me much pleasure,' he wrote. 'I can conceive the water nymphs pulling for him. He would have been another Hylas. W. Hylas.'[24]

Nor was Haydon impressed by Wordsworth's revelations, because he had a good idea of the poet's distaste for anything associated with sensuality, and knew how to discount the violence of his language (Wordsworth described Hazlitt's interest in women as 'Satyr and *beastly* appetites') in recounting what had allegedly happened. On one occasion, Haydon wrote, he and Wordsworth looked together at a sculpture of Cupid and Psyche kissing, and Wordsworth after a long pause turned to Haydon with scandalized revulsion, saying, 'the *dev-ils*'. Haydon's comment on this remark, in reporting it to Mary Russell Mitford, was: 'There's a mind!'

But the story Wordsworth was spreading about Hazlitt was not everywhere received with equanimity. Apart from its future use in the hands of John Wilson, both John Scott and Crabb Robinson were negatively influenced by it, and this was serious, for Hazlitt's livelihood was concerned in the former case, and an old and valuable friendship was jeopardized in the latter. At just this time Crabb Robinson's admiration for Wordsworth was increasing, and they were soon close friends. Partly because of Wordsworth's hostility to Hazlitt, and partly because of growing disagreements with Hazlitt over politics, Crabb Robinson's feelings towards Hazlitt now began to change. He still admired Hazlitt's writing – he never ceased to do so – but a coolness entered his personal feelings towards him.

Wordsworth told John Scott that the 1803 incident revealed Hazlitt's 'sensations' to be 'too corrupt to allow him to understand my Poetry'. Alone among Wordsworth's acquaintance, Hazlitt himself understood the real source of the antagonism. It was old-fashioned jealousy – Wordsworth's poetry met with disdain and scorn more often than with praise, while Hazlitt's rise into prominence as a critic was spectacular. And it was old-fashioned resentment – Wordsworth was bitterly averse to sitting under Hazlitt's judgement, even if it was commendatory, for the reason given: that he viewed Hazlitt as his junior in art as in age. Hazlitt heard the full story of Wordsworth's reception of his *Examiner* review, and (with embellishments and temporal adjustments to better bring out its dramatic qualities) reported it thus: 'Mr Wilson tells, as I understand, in all companies the following story of Mr Wordsworth's particular benevolence and regard to me. Sometime in the latter end of the year 1814 Mr Wordsworth received an *Examiner* by post, which annoyed him exceedingly both on account of the expence and the paper. "Why did they send that rascally paper to him, and make him pay for it?" Mr Wordsworth is tenacious of his principles and is not less so of his purse. "Oh," said Wilson, "let us see what there is in it. I daresay they have not sent it to you for nothing. Why here, there's a criticism upon the Excursion in it." This made the poet (*par excellence*) rage and fret the more. "What did they know about his poetry? What could they know about it? It was presumption in the highest degree for these cockney writers to pretend to criticise a Lake poet." "Well," says the other, "at any rate let us read it." So he began. The article was much in favour of the poet and the poem. As the reading proceeded, "Ha!" said Mr Wordsworth, somewhat appeased, "there's some sense in this fellow too: the Dog writes strong." Upon which Mr Wilson was encouraged to proceed still farther with the encomium, and Mr Wordsworth continued his approbation; "Upon my word very judicious, very well indeed." At length, growing vain with his own and the *Examiner*'s applause, he suddenly seized the paper in his own hands, and saying "Let me read it, Mr Wilson," did so with an audible voice and appropriate gesture to the end, when he exclaimed, "Very well written indeed, Sir, I did not expect a thing of this kind," and strutting up and down the room in high good humour kept every now and then wondering who could be the author, "he had no idea, and should like very much to know to whom he was indebted for such pointed and judicious praise" – when Mr Wilson interrupting him with saying, "Oh don't you know; it's

Hazlitt, to be sure, here are his initials to it," threw our poor philosopher into a greater rage than ever, and a fit of outrageous incredulity to think that he should be indebted for the first favourable account that had ever appeared of any work he had ever written to a person on whom he had conferred such great and unmerited obligations.'[25]

To Hazlitt, this spoke volumes about what he called 'Wordsworth's egotism', which was, he said, 'in some respects a madness; for he scorns even the admiration of himself, thinking it a presumption in any one to suppose that he has taste or sense enough to understand him.'[26] That there is more than a measure of truth in this is shown by the fact that Wordsworth resented being compared unfavourably to Shakespeare and Milton. In his review Hazlitt said that whereas these two great poets had both imagination and feeling, Wordsworth possessed only the latter, being 'certainly deficient in fanciful invention'. At that moment Wordsworth was preparing a collected edition of his poems, and he was driven by this criticism to group them as 'Poems of the Fancy', 'Poems of the Imagination', 'Poems founded on the Affections' and so on. Moreover he added an 'Essay, Supplementary to the Preface' in which he wrote that his powers of imagination were on a par with those of Shakespeare and Milton, and said that in response to the 'insults ... heaped' upon his poems by the 'Ignorant, the Incapable and the Presumptuous', he would 'anticipate the judgment of posterity upon myself' and claim that his work was 'worthy to be holden in undying remembrance.'[27]

It is worth noting that Lamb told Crabb Robinson – who received the news sceptically – that Hazlitt wept over the writing of the review. Hazlitt told Lamb that he did so because he had long anticipated the poem's publication, remembered reading draft parts of it long before, and expected great things of it. His tears fell because he was not able to praise it more. Without question they were also for the fact that the poem was renewed proof of yet another failure of promise: the landscape he had glimpsed before him in the blissful dawn of his and the French Revolution's beginnings turned out, when day came, a desert after all. The poignancy is vivid in his remarks on Wordsworth's espousal of a reactionary view, which postpones to an indefinite future the day when, as Hazlitt put it, 'the triumph of virtue and liberty will be complete'. This will never be, Hazlitt wrote, until 'the nature of things is changed, till the many become as *one*, till romantic generosity shall be as common as gross selfishness, till reason shall have acquired the obstinate blindness of prejudice, till the love of power and of change shall no longer goad men on to restless action, till passion and will, hope and fear, love and hatred, and the objects proper to excite them, that is, alternate good and evil, shall no longer sway the bosoms and business of men.' These had been the dreams of the blissful dawn of 1789; these changes had then seemed in the very process of coming about. Events had proved that they are, after all, impossible. 'But,' Hazlitt went on, 'though we cannot weave over again the airy, unsubstantial dream, which reason and experience have dispelled –

> What though the radiance, which was once so bright
> Be now for ever taken from our sight,
> Though nothing can bring back the hour
> Of glory in the grass, of splendour in the flower –

yet we will never cease, nor be prevented from returning on the wings of imagination to that bright dream of our youth; that glad dawn of the day-star of liberty; that spring-time of the world, in which the hopes and expectations of the human race seemed opening in the same gay career with our own ... To those hopes eternal regrets are due; to those who maliciously and wilfully blasted them, in the fear that they might be accomplished, we feel no less than what we owe – hatred and scorn as lasting.' The lines he quotes are Wordsworth's, then still unpublished, but lodged in Hazlitt's memory from years before.[28]

While these excitements were taking place in Hazlitt's life, others of a more public kind were occurring in the city around him, and indeed under the very windows of his house.[29] The end of war, and the triumph of the 'legitimate' monarchs who had saved their skins and privileges at last, was again being celebrated, this time in high formal style. Hyde Park was a sea of booths, towers, and alcoves offering entertainment and refreshment of every conceivable kind – beer, fireworks, dancing-dogs, gingerbread stalls, slack-rope vaulters, fire-eaters – and it rapidly became 'the headquarters of drunkenness and obscenity', as one newspaper put it. All the grass disappeared, to be replaced by a desert of churned earth. On the Serpentine there were miniature re-enactments of naval battles. The Grand Jubilee (the 'Regent's Fair' as Hazlitt more aptly called it) spilled over into Green Park and St James's Park, the latter directly opposite Hazlitt's house; but this was not the only way that the celebrations, bitterly unwelcome to him, obtruded; for London was also full of visiting dignitaries, including monarchs, not least among them the King of Prussia and Tsar Alexander of Russia, both staying at the Pultney Hotel in Piccadilly. The Tsar gave out that he was an enthusiast for liberal reform, despite ruling as an absolute dictator over a vast medieval feudality of slaves, and he made a show of communing with some of the leading English liberals, inviting

Thomas Erskine – lawyer for Thomas Paine and the defendants in the 1794 Treason Trials – to meet him, saying that he had read his speech in Hardy's defence at the time. Alexander also visited Bentham in York Street, so Hazlitt had the spectacle of a state coach, accompanied by footmen and mounted Cossacks, arriving in tumult before the house next door to his own. The Tsar was contemptuous of the Prince Regent, who had stayed at home and grown fat while other princes were in the field of battle with their armies, protecting their interests against the threat of Liberty, Equality and Fraternity. This was a view shared by the Regent's own subjects; when the Tsar, the Prussian King and the Regent drove in procession through the huge crowds in the Strand on the way to the Guildhall, the visitors were cheered and the Prince Regent roundly hissed.

The peace meant that France was again accessible to travel, as after the Treaty of Amiens, so the English flocked abroad, Haydon and his fellow-painter David Wilkie among them. Haydon had just exhibited his *Judgment of Solomon* at the Water Colour Society's rooms in Spring Gardens, and Hazlitt reviewed it favourably – after looking at the picture on the gallery wall he turned to Haydon and shook his hand, saying, 'By god, Sir, it is a victory.' Haydon astutely realized that Hazlitt was – somewhat unusually – not saying everything he thought; and Hazlitt indeed had reservations, because he perceived that Haydon's genius was erratic though real, and that his approach to his professional life threatened to injure him as a painter. Hazlitt would have loved to go with Haydon to Paris, to see again the long galleries of the Louvre. But a combination of the – to him – painful circumstances that had brought peace about, and the fact that he had just left regular salaried employment and was now working as a freelance with a family to house and feed, kept him in London. The best and the worst years of his life had to intervene before he could next visit the Louvre.

Becoming a contributor to the *Edinburgh Review* at the end of 1814 was an important moment for Hazlitt. It represented recognition, it promised a significant boost to his income because it paid extremely well at £25 per article (it is worth iterating yet again that William senior began on £30 a year for preaching in the Unitarian interest at Wem, and that a small family might expect to get by on £100 a year), and it gave an influential platform to Hazlitt's views. It was the major periodical of its day, read internationally Stendhal got to know Hazlitt's work in its pages. It owed much of its authority and excellence to the gifts, the watchfulness and the skill of its redoubtable editor, Francis Jeffrey, who would rewrite contributors' copy almost completely when so minded, and who, despite his old-fashioned taste in literature, made the *Edinburgh Review* required reading for the literate classes of the day. Hazlitt was very conscious of the distinction that an association with the periodical brought – 'To be an Edinburgh Reviewer is, I suspect, the highest rank in modern literary society,' he wrote[30] – and he lavished attention on the pieces he wrote for it, especially the first few, to be sure of meriting Jeffrey's approbation. Hazlitt had been writing for only a couple of years as a periodical journalist, so his rise to the status of an *Edinburgh* reviewer is meteoric. For his part Jeffrey conceived a lifelong admiration for Hazlitt's work, although he thought him inclined to intemperance in his political partialities and his attacks on individuals – which was quite true, as Hazlitt himself acknowledged cheerfully enough. Jeffrey was generous in giving Hazlitt help, especially financial help, whenever it was needed.

The *Edinburgh* contributors regarded Jeffrey with respect verging on awe. Hazlitt described him as looking on writers with the eye of a Justice of the Peace sentencing poachers. Sydney Smith captured Jeffrey's confident, exacting, bracing editorial manner in a lampoon, in which Jeffrey reviews the solar system: 'bad light – planets too distant – pestered with comets – feeble contrivance – could make a better with great ease.'[31] Lord Cockburn wrote an appreciation of Jeffrey's achievements as an editor which many in the same trade would enjoy: 'He had not only to revise and arrange each number after its parts were brought together, but before he got this length, he, like any other person in that situation, had much difficult and delicate work to perform. He had to discover, and train, authors; to discern what truth and the public mind required; to suggest subjects, to reject, and, more offensive still, to improve, contributions; to keep down absurdities; to infuse spirit; to excite the timid; to repress violence; to soothe jealousies; to quell mutinies; to watch times; and all this in the morning of the reviewing day, before experience taught editors conciliatory firmness, and contributors reasonable submission. He directed and controlled the elements he presided over with a master's judgment. There was not one of his associates who could have held these elements together for a single year.'

Hazlitt's first piece for Jeffrey was a review of a novel by Fanny Burney, *The Wanderer*. In his characteristic way he ranged over the whole field of English and European literature in discussing it. As a result of his article the Burneys, old friends of the Lambs' evenings, refused to speak to him again. Jeffrey praised the review handsomely, and Hazlitt wrote in reply, 'You need hardly be assured of the gratification I have felt in receiving your very obliging letter.' He was already working on his second piece, a long discussion of Sismondi's *De la littérature du midi de l'Europe*, which he was reading in French. He took it with him into the country to work on it and to relax at the same time (after, as usual, a visit to his parents and Peggy), no doubt feeling that despite the loss of his post on the *Morning Chronicle* and the defeat of Napoleon, there were some compensations nevertheless as 1815 opened.

Hazlitt was still busy writing for both the *Examiner* and the *Champion*. In the former he had, among his reviews and other articles, contributed a few miscellaneous essays under the label 'Commonplaces' during the course of 1814, but now Hunt instituted a new column under the title 'The Round Table', originally intended to be a running debate by several hands, each taking turns to answer one another's essays, thus developing in print the analogue of a dinner-table conversation. In the event only Hunt and Hazlitt sat at the Round Table, with Hunt writing some, and Hazlitt most, of the essays. The Round Table gave Hazlitt his first proper opportunity to write freely and personally on a wide range of subjects. This format – the familiar essay – was his forte. As with his other periodical writings he established his voice immediately and powerfully, taking Arthur's seat at the Round Table by right.

In the *Champion* he was still writing art criticism, among other things expressing his disappointment at the pictures in the Lucien Buonaparte collection which were then on sale in London. But his relations with the *Champion*'s editor, John Scott, had become difficult. One source of tension between them was politics. Throughout the early months of 1815 Hazlitt had been annoying some of his friends by his insistence that Napoleon was manifestly a better alternative to Europe's 'legitimate' monarchs, whose reactionary behaviour since the outbreak of peace was proving an embarrassment to those who had supported their cause. Hazlitt was in a told-you-so mood over such scandalous events as the annexation of Genoa by the King of Sardinia, the use of foreign armies to foist a Prince of Orange on the Netherlands, the Russian and Prussian refusal to restore Poland, the division of Saxony, the annulment of Spain's constitution, the revival of the Inquisition, the transfer of Norway and Finland between powers as if they were chattels, and the cruel reprisals against Buonapartists in France. Crabb Robinson had a heated argument with Hazlitt on these topics at an evening party at the house of their friend Thomas Alsager.[32] So when the rupture between Hazlitt and Scott came in the spring of 1815, it was in part precipitated by the great event which then occurred – the escape of Napoleon from Elba.

But there was another more personal reason, connected with Words-worth's allegations about Hazlitt in the Lakes twelve years before, and Scott's reaction to what Wordsworth told him. Haydon recounts in his diary that Scott one night in that same spring made Hazlitt drunk, and got him to speak of his secrets and weaknesses.[33] It took very little, if any, liquor to make Hazlitt dilate on these subjects; he was perfectly happy to talk about them to anyone, for he rarely concealed anything about himself or (to the chagrin sometimes of friends) anyone else. But the very next Sunday Scott used some of these confidences in a leading article in the *Champion* in which he criticized the *Examiner*'s politics and morals, saying that its excellent editor (Hunt) had been led astray by 'the coarseness of an individual scowler', who when he speaks of the delicacies and beauties of the world perverts them in accordance with his own moral deformity.[34] Only those in the know could have recognized this as an attack on Hazlitt, but Hazlitt was so shocked by it that he ceased all connection with the *Champion* immediately, and he and Scott were not reconciled for several years.

Haydon had a surprising opinion about the reason for Scott's sudden attack on Hazlitt. He claimed in his diary that the source of Scott's action lay in his violent and misanthropic personality (he was a wife-beater, Haydon said); he had been bullied by his father as a child, and had grown up with a severe feeling of inferiority, so that people with greater talents than his own made him jealous – people, said Haydon, like Hazlitt.

The breach with Scott came not only at the same time as Napoleon's return from Elba in March, but a short time after Hunt's release from prison in February. Hunt was so institutionalized as a result of his two years' imprisonment that he found it difficult to go into London's busy streets, and still less to the crowded theatres which had once been his delight. His agoraphobia kept him at home for as nearly as long again as he had been in prison. He resigned more and more of the theatre reviewing into Hazlitt's hands, until at last the latter was officially given the *Theatrical Examiner* column later that spring. In any case Hunt had his plate full with the political debates occasioned by Napoleon's return.

Hazlitt was delighted by Napoleon's reappearance, but irritated by all those among his acquaintance who had once professed liberal sentiments but were now rallying behind 'Legitimacy' to oppose Napoleon's restitution. Crabb Robinson records another uncomfortable argument with Hazlitt at Alsager's house – he admits to having been worsted in it, but not, in his opinion, because Hazlitt's case was better, only that his skill as a debater was greater (here speaks the barrister thinking about whose eloquence had carried the cause). 'Hazlitt and I once felt alike on politics, and now our hopes and fears are directly opposed,' Crabb Robinson wrote. 'Hazlitt retains all his hatred of kings and bad governments, and believing them to be incorrigible, he from a principle of revenge, rejoices that they are punished. I am indignant to find the man who might have been their punisher become their imitator, and even surpassing them all in guilt. Hazlitt is angry with the friends of liberty for weakening their strength by going with the common foe against Buonaparte, by which the old governors are so much assisted, even in their attempts against the general liberty. I am not shaken by this consequence because I think, after all, that should the governments succeed in the worst projects imputed to them, still the evil will be infinitely less than what would arise from Buonaparte's success. I say destroy him at any rate and take the consequences. Hazlitt says, "Let the enemy of old tyrannical governments triumph, I am glad, and I do not much care how the new government turns out." Not that either I am indifferent to the government which the successful kings of Europe may establish or that Hazlitt has lost all love for liberty. But his *hatred*, and my *fear*, predominate and absorb all weaker impressions. This I believe to be the great difference between us.'[35]

Hazlitt was by no means alone in his support for Napoleon. The Liverpool banker William Roscoe was a keen Buonapartist, as was the famous Latin scholar, smoker, and member of the Lunar Society, Dr Samuel Parr (who thought Hazlitt's writings 'very ingenious'),[36] who said that he never failed to pray for Napoleon's success every night when he went to bed. Moreover Perry and the *Morning Chronicle* had returned to their old allegiance, at least to the extent of opposing any renewal of war against Napoleon, a view championed in public meetings and in Parliament by the doughty liberal Sir Francis Burdett and his allies. For all his personal failings John Scott had been a sound liberal voice in the *Champion* all along, and he too argued against resumption of war – and described John Stoddart's anti-Napoleon hysteria in *The Times* as the 'ravings of a madman'. Sir James Mackintosh wrote the very next day to congratulate Scott on his stand. The broad alliance embracing a variety of voices – the Whig epicentre of Holland House, periodicals and papers like the *Edinburgh Review, Examiner, Champion, Morning Chronicle*, individuals of influence like the Hunt brothers, Hazlitt, Burdett, Mackintosh, Dr Parr, businessmen like Roscoe – represented an impressive and powerful front at least against restarting the war, and occasionally in positive support of Napoleon. But the government and the Regent, mindful of the previous summer's triumphalisms in the Royal parks, under pressure from their allies among Europe's old regimes, and anyway in no mood to see Napoleon restored, had no ear for them. Resumption of war was declared on 23 March 1815, and events began to move towards the denouement of Waterloo.

For Hazlitt and like-minded people these events stifled the early euphoria of Napoleon's return. In the early summer Wordsworth arrived in town to see his two-volume *Poems* and *The White Doe of Rylstone* through the press, and he asked Lamb to ensure that Hazlitt would not be present whenever he was due to visit the Lambs' home. Uncharacteristically, but no doubt in an endeavour to maintain peace with his friends on both sides, Lamb agreed. The combination of Wordsworth in London and Wellington in Brussels blackened Hazlitt's mood, and in writing of Milton's *Comus* in the *Examiner* in early June – the masque had been 'splendidly got up' at Covent Garden, despite being inherently unfit for live performance – he said, 'We have no less respect for the memory of Milton as a patriot than as a poet. Whether he was a *true* patriot, we shall not enquire; he was at least a *consistent* one. He did not retract his defence of the people of England; he did not say that his sonnets to Vane or Cromwell were meant ironically; he was not appointed Poet Laureate to a Court which he had reviled and insulted; he accepted neither place nor pension; nor did he write paltry sonnets upon the "Royal Fortitude" of the House of Stuart, by which, however, they really lost something.' Hazlitt adds this footnote: 'In the last edition of the works of a modern Poet, there is a sonnet to the King, complimenting him on "his royal fortitude". The story of the Female Vagrant, which very beautifully and affectingly describes the miseries brought on the lower classes by war, in bearing which the said "royal fortitude" is so nobly exercised, is very properly struck out of the collection.'[37] These rapier-like thrusts under the ribs of Southey and, in particular, Wordsworth doubtless wounded all the more because of their simple truth.

Wordsworth called on Hunt the very day that Hazlitt's *Comus* piece appeared, and Hunt manfully drew his attention to it. Wordsworth had not seen it. Hunt apologized, saying – implausibly – that it had been printed without his knowledge. In view of Wordsworth's stated contempt for the *Examiner*, the justice of the remarks in Hazlitt's piece, and Hunt's own position on the liberal side of the argument, it is odd that Hunt felt it necessary to defer so far to Wordsworth's feelings. The latter, for his part, was doing the rounds of as many editors in London as he could in the hope currying good reviews. This was his first meeting with Hunt, whose sense of humour was not entirely quelled by Wordsworth's grand prophetic manner. 'Hunt asked the bard whether he would take any refreshment,' Blunden writes in his biography of Hunt, 'and, as he put the question, his eye was on a cart outside passing through the archway underneath their room. Wordsworth replied, "Anything which is *going forward*" with such gravity that Hunt felt like asking him to take a piece of the cart.'[38]

Haydon had Wordsworth to breakfast at his studio on 12 June to meet John Scott, as another influential editor. Scott was so impressed by Wordsworth's grand manner and genuine talents that he did not stint column inches in extolling his virtues, praising his abilities, and calling him 'the greatest poetical genius of the age'. It was on this occasion that Wordsworth suborned Scott's opinion of Hazlitt by telling him his story about Hazlitt's 1803 adventure in the Lakes.

On 20 June 1815, just over a week after Haydon's breakfast for Wordsworth, the London papers were filled with the news that Napoleon's forces and those of the Allies had clashed in open country near Brussels. The great battle had begun. Brussels itself was filled with excited English visitors, treating the resumption of war as if it were more of the previous summer's jollities in Hyde Park. The upper classes and the rich – not always the same people – fancied that they could spectate the war from a ringside of dinners and balls. Everything military was highly fashionable, and Joseph Sedley in Thackeray's *Vanity Fair* exactly represents the occasion's folly and pretension by having his tailor make him regimental-looking coats and pantaloons. Famously, news of the rapid approach of Napoleon's army, its crossing of the Sambre river and its capture of the hamlet of Charleroi not far from Brussels, reached Wellington while he was at the Duchess of Richmond's ball. The duchess had two hundred and twenty guests that night; by the end of the Battle of Waterloo fifty of the officers who danced at her ball were dead or wounded. Some died in their evening dress.

At the first news of Napoleon's approach, and more especially at the sight of convoys of carts with bloodied, exhausted, wounded troops jolting back into the city to makeshift hospitals, the festive mood turned to panic, and the gay society fled ignominiously for England, scrambling over one another for horses, donkeys, and anything with wheels, terrified that the monster Napoleon would suddenly appear in the doorway of their rented residences to tear them with his hands and grind their bones with his teeth.

On 22 June news broke in London that Napoleon had been defeated. The country went delirious with joy. Even the opposition newspapers were elated by this feat of British arms (Blücher was reserved for the small print).

Hazlitt, however, was like a man shot through the heart. He was devastated by the news. Haydon wrote: 'It is not to be believed how the destruction of Napoleon affected him; he seemed prostrated in mind and body, he walked about unwashed, unshaved, hardly sober by day, and always intoxicated by night, literally, without exaggeration, for weeks; until at length awakening as it were from his stupor, he at once left off all stimulating liquors, and never touched them after.' Shortly before this time Hazlitt had met Thomas Noon Talfourd, a lawyer who was a recently acquired friend and neighbour of the Lambs, and who in due course became one of Hazlitt's staunchest friends. Talfourd also described the effect of the news on Hazlitt: 'He was staggering under the blow of Waterloo. The reappearance of his imperial idol on the coast of France and his triumphant march to Paris, like a fairy vision, had excited his admiration and sympathy to the utmost pitch; and though in many respects sturdily English in feeling, he could scarcely forgive the valour of the conquerors; and bitterly resented the captivity of the Emperor on St Helena which followed it, as if he had sustained a personal wrong.'[39]

A little more than a decade later Hazlitt wrote a four-volume biography of Napoleon to honour and justify him. The immediate prompt for doing so was news that Sir Walter Scott was engaged on the same task, and likely to give a hostile portrait from his Tory point of view – which is precisely the portrait of Napoleon as monster that has survived in the English imagination, even among the educated, so that one finds his name bracketed with such genuine horrors as Hitler and Stalin. This is a gross historical distortion. Hazlitt knew that the victor's version of history always becomes the official one, so he felt that he would do Napoleon a service by registering a countervailing contemporary view. He did not wait until he wrote his biography to do this. At the latter end of 1815 he found himself defending Napoleon in print against critics who, naturally, picked on the worst things that had happened under the emperor's reign, an egregious example being the murder of the duc d'Enghien. In his sour post-Waterloo mood Hazlitt wrote a piece castigating René de Chateaubriand, the French Romantic writer, royalist and politician, for shifting allegiance from Rousseau to Louis XVIII – which for Hazlitt was like pushing aside a plate of caviar to dine on dog's dirt instead. In passing he alluded to the criticisms directed at Napoleon for engineering the death of the duc d'Enghien, saying that it was unfair to blame Napoleon given that d'Enghien was plotting to assassinate him, and that Napoleon's action was therefore a pre-emptive strike – in effect, self-defence. A correspondent signing himself 'Fair Play' challenged Hazlitt on this interpretation of events, on the ground that the duke had been kidnapped abroad, smuggled back to France, and killed after a hasty and doubtful trial, an unpleasant sequence that would darken any tyrant's record. Hazlitt responded in irritated vein, even questioning the correspondent's belief, expressed by his choice of pen-name, that there could be such a thing as 'fair play' in situations of the kind Napoleon faced. Politics is like war, Hazlitt said, in that 'you do not have your choice of ends or means.' Circumstances sometimes force you to do wrong in the interests of a greater right. This is an uncomfortable argument to sustain, but the realities of life compel it. Hazlitt saw Napoleon as one who was forced to many of the recourses his critics blamed him for, such as becoming Emperor, which Hazlitt argued was in part an expedient to make it possible for Napoleon to deal with the 'legitimate' monarchs who haughtily refused to treat with him on the grounds that he was a mere upstart. Napoleon thought that if he had the style and dignity of a monarch too, they would accept the situation in France and allow peace. After all, their own dynasties had begun in exactly the same way; royal dynasties do not fall out of passing clouds, but begin in the victories of the strongest man around, who places a diadem on his brow and whose posterity thereafter reaps the reward of his being the one who won the battles that mattered. If nervous monarchs elsewhere in Europe had pretended to go along with the birth of a new member of their number, said Hazlitt, there would have been peace all along. The trouble was that Napoleon was the inheritor of a revolution, many of whose principles were enshrined in the Code Napoleon. He destroyed the ancient superstitions that underlay 'legitimacy', he ended the Inquisition, dismantled the Holy Roman Empire, and emancipated Europe's Jews. Clearly, said Hazlitt with heavy irony, he was a menace and had to go.

Hazlitt's response to the anti-Buonapartists' concentration on events like the d'Enghien affair was a function of his annoyance at their refusal to see what good Napoleon had done in other spheres, not least in smashing the corrupt old system in Europe in which a few individuals inherit whole countries and populations and live in luxury off the sweated labour, the poverty, the unfreedom and the benightedness of the majority of their fellows. The mere existence of this state of injustice stung Hazlitt so fiercely all his life long that other considerations paled beside it.[40]

Despite the despair induced by Napoleon's defeat, and indeed as a way of coping with it, Hazlitt continued to pour out work, chiefly his theatre reviews and his 'Round Table' essays. He was flattered to receive an invitation, courtesy of his association with the *Edinburgh Review*, to contribute to the *Encyclopaedia Britannica*. Moreover, the publisher of both these distinguished titles, Archibald Constable, responded favourably to Hazlitt's suggestion of a collected edition of the 'Round Table' essays. Hazlitt's stock was on the rise.

To these consoling events was added the happiness of a safe birth, on 28 November, of another son. Hazlitt and Sarah named him John (each being able to claim to his and her respective brother that it was in honour of *him*.) Sarah had by now had a number of miscarriages, and her absence from the at-homes and dinner parties recorded in the diaries of Crabb Robinson and Haydon suggests that she had been keeping carefully inactive during her pregnancies.

Hazlitt was delighted to have another child. At this time William the younger was four years old, and Bewick describes how, when he was one day visiting Hazlitt in York Street, there came a sound at the door of Hazlitt's study, followed by the appearance of the little boy 'creeping on all fours'. Hazlitt 'jumped up from his seat, ran to him, and clasping his boy in his arms, hugged, and kissed, and caressed him, like some ardent loving mother with her first-born'.[41] Earlier that year Hunt had written of Hazlitt playing 'the great horse' with William the younger on his shoulders. In the previous year the child had fallen into the Thames at Millbank – playing on the beach there at low tide, near the home of one of Hazlitt's friends – and was plucked from the water by the friend's big dog; and this became a family story passed down the generations.

Although Hazlitt spent several evenings a week at the theatre in the way of business, it did not interfere with his social life. Often he went to the Lambs' straight afterwards. Talfourd wrote of one occasion, 'in *slouches* Hazlitt from the theatre, where his stubborn anger for Napoleon's defeat at Waterloo has been softened by Miss Stephens's angelic notes.' Lamb's brother John did not have Charles's equable temperament; one night he and Hazlitt fell into a dispute over the respective uses of colour by Van Dyck and Holbein, and John Lamb became so angry that he punched Hazlitt. The latter picked himself up and shook hands with his assailant, saying, 'I am a metaphysician, and do not mind a blow; nothing but an *idea* hurts *me*.'[42] He was a constant visitor at the Hunt and Haydon households also, even when Hunt moved to the Vale of Health on Hampstead Heath and Hazlitt needed someone to walk back with him at night because he was afraid of footpads. The records of Haydon and Bewick show how often his calls on friends were returned. On one visit to York Street Haydon found Hazlitt trying different arrangements of his long glossy black hair in a looking-glass, wondering whether he should show more or less of his forehead. Hunt described Hazlitt as 'a very good-looking fellow'. Talfourd, in saying that Hazlitt's 'handsome and eager' face looked 'worn with sickness and thought' after Waterloo, concurs. Evidently, like most people, Hazlitt was not without a trace of vanity; but Haydon was scathing of his taking thought about his coiffure, saying 'In that large wainscoted room Milton had conceived, and perhaps written, many of his finest thoughts, and there sat one of his critics admiring his own features.'[43] Crabb Robinson mentioned in passing, some time before this date, that Hazlitt had come to be rather well turned-out, in contrast to his youthful dishevelment. He was regarded as an ornament at the Basil Montagu home at 25 Bedford Square, where he had long been a visitor and where he often read papers on metaphysical topics at their soirées. The Montagus invited him to their country home in Yorkshire also. None of this is inconsistent with Talfourd's talk of 'slouching' (reminiscent of Coleridge's description of his 'shoe-contemplative' demeanour) or his shyness or the 'misanthropy' for which it could be mistaken (although that sentiment was sometimes real enough too), for Hazlitt was a man of moods, and anyway needed to feel quite at home to be fully himself.

One place where Hazlitt felt quite at home was the rackets court. Rackets, sometimes called 'fives', was his favourite pastime. He regarded it as an excellent relaxation both for body and mind. He devoted hours to the game every week, at which he was a vigorous, energetic and highly skilful competitor – a 'furious player', one observer wrote – whose reputation attracted crowds of watchers whenever he was on the court. His chief competition was himself; he would berate himself mercilessly for any failure to win a point. Bewick has left a vivid portrait of him in action: 'My friend, having stripped to his shirt, looked all alive, and being anxious to do his best, soon displayed himself not only an adept, but an original in his style of play. It was peculiar and characteristic of the man, and his sighs, groans and lamentations left no doubt that he was becoming warm in the spirit of the game, and sad trouble he had to hitch up his trousers, it being his custom to be free of braces. He was the only one despoiled of his upper garments, so that I had no difficulty in following his rapid movements, and as his excitement warmed in the course of the game, so his exclamations became more vehement, and with his difficulties his ardour increased, until he lashed himself up to a desperation, and looked more like a savage animal than anything human. The spectators below me appeared to be well aware of the ability and eccentricity of this hero of the game, as they peered forward to witness any extraordinary feat of play. When a difficult ball was driven to such a distance from him, and so skillfully dropped close to the wall, that it seemed an impossibility to come near it in time, or to catch it with the racket if he did, he would run with desperate speed, make a last spring, and bending down his head to meet the concussion with the wall, crushing his hat flat over his eyes, dexterously tip the ball, sending it to its intended mark with unerring truth amid murmurs of applause. Then jerking himself upright again, his eye following the ball in its lightning speed, he would pursue it, however difficult the course. Thus he would repeat his feats of agility and success, excited all the while to a desperation and madness beyond belief. It is impossible to give an idea of his expressions. His ejaculations were interlarded with unintentional and unmeaning oaths that cannot be repeated, but may be imagined. In this way he would stamp and rave: – "Nothing but my incapacity, – sheer want of skill, of power, of physical ability, – of the Devil knows what! There again! Ever see such play? Egad, I'd better not take hold of the racket again if I do not do better. Ah! well, that is better, but it is still bad enough – sheer incapacity, egad!" And so he ran on all the time he played, so that the energies of his mind and body were fretted and embittered.'

Bewick was a sensitive soul, and found Hazlitt's utter commitment to the game alarming; he doubtless knew Hazlitt's attachment to the concept of 'gusto' – intensity, passion, wholeheartedness – but seems not to have recognized the critic's application to it even in his recreations. 'The frenzy of his irritability, although curious as a characteristic, yet became, if not alarming, at least not pleasant to witness,' Bewick continues. 'And as he came occasionally to set his back against the post under me, and rub himself to and fro with the force of irascible impatience, repeating the exclamations to himself, I could not but wish that all might end well, and that the game might close in favour of my friend's party. Fortunately it was soon over, and, as I wished, William Hazlitt had won his game at tennis. I could perceive him in all the joyous triumph of his boyish pleasure, stooping low, his racket in both hands, and, bounding from the ground, throw it high up to the roof, exclaim to himself "Hurrah! Hurrah!" and as he waved his right arm over his head, catch with dexterity the falling racket, retiring with the satisfied beam of triumph in his face, to put on his coat and waistcoat.

'Hazlitt came smiling with delight, and said, "Well, we had a hard run for it, but we beat after all." When we came to the street, he pointed to his cravat, and said to me with a somewhat mock servility, "You see I am without my shirt; it was so wet with perspiration that I left it behind to get dried. You must not be seen walking with a person who has no shirt to his back, therefore we part here: you go that way, I this." '44

# CHAPTER TEN

# Fame and Infamy

## 1816–1817

As 1816 COMMENCED, some combination of a passion for fives, a new baby in the house, and the routine journalism that paid the rent, was slowing Hazlitt's work on his 'Fine Arts' article for the *Encyclopaedia Britannica*. He was obliged to write to its editor, Macvey Napier, to request an extension. As if in return, the publisher Constable was delaying over the Round Table collection, and Jeffrey had not responded to Hazlitt's review of a book by the German romantic critic August Wilhelm Schlegel. Since Constable was the publisher not only of the Round Table collection but of both the *Encyclopaedia Britannica* and the *Edinburgh Review*, Hazlitt wrote to him to find out what was happening: 'I sent off the first half of the Round Table some weeks ago, and I begin to fear some accident has happened to it or that you do not approve of the contents. Neither have I heard of the Review from Mr Jeffrey, so that I am getting *blue-devilish* on that score also. You would oblige me by letting me know at your leisure whether anything has been done with the essays, and whether I shall send off the remainder. I had a letter from Mr Napier this day giving me until the middle of March for the article on Fine Arts, a respite which is very agreeable to me.'[1] He promised to send the encyclopaedia article on 12 March, and in the event it was posted on the 20th, which is not bad by the standards of many authors. In it Hazlitt put 'the best part of what I know about art', as he told Napier, extolling the merits of his great favourites, chief among them Raphael, Titian and Rembrandt. He also gave the *Britannica* a biographical sketch of the Irish painter James Barry, and some translations from the *Biographie Universelle*.

It took another letter to Constable to elicit proof sheets of the first eight Round Table essays. In his accompanying reply Constable expressed the hope that the remainder of the proofs would be available in April. He then added an intriguing remark: that he hoped he would be able to get subscribers for Hazlitt's *Philosophy of the Human Mind*. As this shows, Hazlitt was continuing to think about philosophical matters, and continuing to seek publication of his 1812 lectures. In a letter to Napier written at just this time, responding to the latter's editorial comments on his Fine Arts piece, he says, 'I confess I am apt to be paradoxical in stating an extreme opinion when I think the prevailing one is not quite correct. I believe however this way of writing answers with most readers better than the logical. I tried for some years to express the truth and nothing but the truth, till I found it would not do. The opinions themselves I believe to be true, but like all abstract principles, they require deduction, which it is often best to leave the public to find out.'[2]

In May Hazlitt's article on Wilhelm Schlegel's *Lectures on Dramatic Literature* appeared in the delayed February number of the *Edinburgh Review*. It is a long account, with copious extracts, of Schlegel's synoptic discussion of world drama. In it Hazlitt shows an easy familiarity with classical as well as contemporary drama, and his comments on Schlegel are judicious. He had also written a review of Leigh Hunt's poem *The Story of Rimini* for Jeffrey, but it was far too partial to the author, and therefore Jeffrey rewrote it, so extensively that it eventually appeared as Jeffrey's own in his collected works.

Throughout the year Hazlitt's dramatic criticisms and 'Round Table' essays flowed regularly into the pages of the *Examiner*. Their strength and highly individual flavour made them easily recognizable to readers. He also contributed political essays: two on Robert Owen's proto-socialist principles, a consideration of the 'Distresses of the Country' as Parliament was dealing with them, and an attack on the Tory political character. His impatience with the mishandling of the country's economy, and the waste occasioned by a long war which he believed had been wrong in its inspiration from the first, expressed itself in whipping style: 'The war has cost the country five or six hundred millions of money. This has not been a nominal expense, a playing at ducks and drakes with the King's picture on the water, or a manufacturing of bank-notes, and then lighting our pipes with them, but a real *bona fide* waste of the means, wealth, labour, produce, or resources of the country, in the carrying on of the war. About one hundred million of this five or six hundred millions have been sent directly out of the country in loans to our Allies, from the year 1793 to the year 1815, inclusive, during which period there is not a single year in which we did not (from our desire of peace with the legitimate government of that country) subsidise one or other of these powers of Europe, to carry on war against the rebels, regicides, republicans, and usurpers of France. Now the interest of this money alone would be five millions yearly, which would be nearly enough to pay the amount of the poor-rates of the whole country, which is seven millions of our yearly taxes, or might at least be applied to mitigate the mild severity of Mr Malthus's sweeping clauses on that defenceless part of the subject. Here is a hundred millions then gone clean out of the country: there are four or five hundred millions more which have been sunk in the expenses of the war, and which might as well have been sunk into the sea; or what has been saved out of the wreck by those who have been most active in running the vessel aground, is in the hands of persons who are in no hurry that the public should go snacks with them in their excessive good fortune.'[3]

His attack on the Tories – and especially on the Prince Regent, gilded crest of the Tory interest, who was busy with his pavilion at Brighton – was even more scathing: 'A Tory considers boundless extravagance in certain persons as noble munificence and public spirit, benefiting the nation, by causing a circulation of money among Court tradesmen and artists; and so deems a tailor's bill, sometimes amounting to more than the annual pay of all the Admirals, Captains, and Lieutenants in the Navy, – a jeweller's, to more than the whole expense of the expedition to Algiers, – and more money expended on useless furniture, pagodas, mandarins, Chinese lanterns, sphynxes, dragons, monsters, china vases, girandoles, clocks, snuff-boxes, and French frippery, than ten times the amount of the munificent subscription of the Royal Family and Cabinet Ministers for the relief of the starving poor!'[4] For Hazlitt hypocrisy and inconsistency were good clues to each other's existence: 'A Tory in former times hated the Bourbons as the most inveterate enemies of England, execrated their bad faith, ambition, and tyranny, and despised the French nation for submitting to so vile a Government: – a Tory in these times hails their return to power with rapture, as ensuring good will and liberality towards England, and lasting peace to all the world!'[5] And it was these very Tories who, by wasting England's money in defeating Napoleon, had thereby helped to restore not just the Bourbons but the Papacy, the Inquisition, and a pack of feudal monarchies, forcing the peoples of Europe to take them back at the point of a sword.

It was in this bitter vein of satire against the governing dispensation and its triumph over liberal hopes that Hazlitt returned again and again to attack the apostate poets. It is easy to say that he singled them out for castigation because his personal connection with them made the relief to his feelings greater. Perhaps it soothed the irritation of his spirits to pillory them for their abandonment of the dreams they had once shared with him, because he knew how they would feel, and it is more satisfying to provoke a known reaction than to fire one's arrows blindly into the night. But there was an added, public, reason: Coleridge and Southey had in their different ways a quantum of influence, and in a more restricted way so did

Wordsworth. Because they were public figures, and because Hazlitt knew exactly the when, where and how of their apostasies, they made particularly suitable targets. He pulled no punches. But at the same time he was serious both in his praise and his criticism of their work when he thought either was merited. He was angry with them, but he was fair. Moreover not everything that has been construed as venom is in fact so; when for example he bracketed Wordsworth with Benvenuto Cellini and his favourite Rousseau as 'the three greatest egotists that we know of,' he did not mean it at all pejoratively; he continues, 'that is, [they are] the three writers who felt their own being most powerfully and exclusively.'[6] That remark occurred in a Round Table essay in April 1816. In June he reviewed Coleridge's 'Christabel' and 'Kubla Khan', and said, 'The fault of Mr Coleridge is that he comes to no conclusion. He is a man of so great universality of genius, that his mind hangs suspended between poetry and prose, truth and falsehood, and an infinity of other things, and from an excess of capacity he does little or nothing [– as witness these] two unfinished poems, and a fragment.'[7] He is severe but just on the merits of the poems, finding much to admire, but berating their unfocused and unfinished character, and recognizing in 'Christabel' the miasma of something unhealthy beneath the beauty of the lines. The poem received bad reviews all round, the worst from Thomas Moore in the *Edinburgh Review* who, on the basis of a careful analysis, concluded that it was incoherent, extravagant, and full of incongruities. Coleridge's career, already bedevilled by opium, faltered yet further under the weight of these responses, for his publisher John Murray lost money on him, and soon after withdrew from their relationship, leaving Coleridge to seek a publisher of less stature.[8]

Leigh Hunt, in an irenic gesture to the victims of his best writer's blows, wrote: 'O ye critics, the best of ye, what havoc does personal difference play with your judgments!' Hazlitt replied in a later issue of the *Examiner*, 'If the truth were known, the most disagreeable people are the most amiable. They are the only persons who feel an interest in what does not concern them ... They are vexed to see genius playing at Tom Fool, and honesty turned bawd. It gives them a cutting sensation to see Mr Southey, poet laureate; Mr Wordsworth, an exciseman; and Mr Coleridge, nothing.'[9] These remarks appeared on 9 June in the *Examiner*, which evidently Wordsworth was still not reading but somehow contriving to follow with assiduity, because on 11 June he wrote to his admirer John Scott at the *Champion*, perhaps to drop a hint of how Scott might reply to Hazlitt – and also to keep Hazlitt out of Scott's pages for the foreseeable future. 'What you mention about the mode in which I am treated in the Examiner does not surprise me though it accords little with Mr H[azlitt]'s verbal professions the only time I ever saw him,' he wrote. 'He is a man of low propensities, and of bad heart, I fear, but doubtless very clever – to his own injury, mostly, and to that of his readers, for he is as perverse Creature as any whom it has been my lot to know. His sensations are too corrupt to allow him to understand my Poetry – though his ingenuity might enable him to write as if he knew something about it.'[10] This is tortuous stuff: Wordsworth allows that Hazlitt is clever – but to the harm of readers, he quickly adds, to deter Scott from re-employing him. And Wordsworth finds it necessary to explain how Hazlitt can appear to be such a penetrating critic, given that he does not understand his poetry. Wordsworth's response to Hazlitt was to work behind the scenes at undermining him; Coleridge's was to rail tearfully to friends.

On 19 June Hazlitt's second son John died of measles. He was seven months old. It was a frightful blow. Hazlitt could not bear to look at the body, but asked Sarah to cut a lock of the child's hair for him. He put the lock in a twist of paper on which he wrote 'My dear little John's hair, cut off the day he died,' and kept it with him for the rest of his life.

As if in palliation of grief, but also as if to lay a salve to his rage against the apostates, Leigh Hunt published a poem to Hazlitt in the *Examiner* in July: 'Dear Hazlitt, whose tact intellectual is such/That it seems to feel truth, as one's fingers do touch ...' Whatever Hazlitt's private feelings, nothing obstructed his anti-apostate campaign. On 7 and 14 July he published the two parts of his excoriating attack on Southey's latest Laureate offering, the *Carmen Nuptiale* for Princess Charlotte's wedding. Both poem and poet came in for withering scorn. 'The poetry of the Lay is beneath criticism; it has all sorts of obvious common-place defects, without any beauties either obvious or recondite. It is the Namby-Pamby of the Tabernacle; a Methodist sermon turned into doggerel verse. It is a gossiping profession of Mr Southey's political faith' – in allusion to which, Hazlitt points out that Southey is said to have been given the Laureateship because of his championing of the cause of Spain during the Peninsular War, in that he hymned the defeat of French dominion there: 'It was understood to be for his exertions in the cause of Spanish liberty that he was made Poet-Laureate. It is then high time for him to resign. Why has he not written a single ode to a single Spanish patriot who has been hanged, banished, imprisoned, sent to the galleys, assassinated, tortured? It must be pleasant to those suffering under the thumb-screw to read Mr Southey's thoughts upon that ingenious little instrument of royal gratitude.'[11] The remarks refer to the turmoil in Spain, where liberals and reformers were being subjected to savage reprisals by the restored regime.

In September it was Coleridge's turn again. The difficult economic and social situation in England which had prompted Hazlitt's essay on the 'distresses of the country' promised to evoke – so an advertisement announced – a 'Lay Sermon' on the same subject from Coleridge, addressed 'to the Middle and Higher Orders' and published in pamphlet form. Hazlitt pounced on the announcement, 'reviewing' the pamphlet before it appeared – in fact, before it was even written: he knew his target well – saying that he could easily guess at what it would contain, confidently predicting that like Coleridge's *The Friend* it would be 'an endless Preface to an imaginary work', obscure and rambling, incoherently defending his political apostasy. He was hard on both the anticipated argument and the arguer, as usual. Hunt had described Hazlitt's Round Table pieces as examples of 'cannonade reasoning' and the allusion is aptly applied here. Coleridge, says Hazlitt, 'defines Jacobinism to be an abstract attachment to liberty, truth, and justice; and finding that this principle has been abused or carried to excess, he argues that Anti-jacobinism, or the abstract principles of despotism, superstition, and oppression, are the safe, sure, and undeniable remedy for the former, and the only means of restoring liberty, truth, and justice in the world.' As to Coleridge himself Hazlitt repeats his view that 'Mr Coleridge has great powers of thought and fancy, without will or sense. He is without a strong feeling of the existence of any thing out of himself; and he has neither purposes nor passions of his own to make him wish it to be. All that he does or thinks is involuntary; even his perversity and self-will are so. They are nothing but a necessity of yielding to the slightest motive. Everlasting inconsequentiality marks all that he attempts. All his impulses are loose, airy, devious, casual ... His mind has infinite activity, which only leads him into numberless chimeras; and infinite resources, which not being under the guidance of his will, only distract and perplex him. His genius has angel's wings; but neither hands nor feet. He soars up to heaven, circles the empyrean, or dives to the centre of the earth, but he neither lays his hands upon the treasures of the one, nor can find a resting place for his feet in the other ... We lose our patience when we think of the powers he has wasted.'[12]

Coleridge was nowhere near as hardy as Wordsworth or Southey, and Hazlitt's rough handling upset him cruelly. 'There has appeared a most brutal attack, as unprovoked as it is even to extravagance false, on me both as a man and an author, in the Examiner – written by a man named William Hazlitt, whom I befriended for several years with the most improvident kindness when he was utterly friendless,' he wrote to a friend, and there follows a version of the 1803 Keswick incident and how

Coleridge and Southey saved Hazlitt from 'infamy and transportation'. A few days later he wrote to the same friend, 'Hazlitt possesses considerable talent; but it is diseased by a morbid hatred of the Beautiful, and killed by the absence of Imagination, and alas! by a wicked heart of embruted Appetites. Poor wretch! he is a melancholy instance of the awful Truth – that man cannot be on a level with the Beasts – he must be above them or below them.' And Coleridge claimed that all the 'sparkles and originalities' in Hazlitt's essays came from Lamb, and that the striking image of the limbless angel was 'stolen from a Letter of my own to Charles Lamb, which had been quoted to him' – although it was precisely one of Hazlitt's most effective and frequently used weapons, to quote an opponent's own words against him.[13]

In July 1816 Richard Brinsley Sheridan died, and was buried with great pomp in Westminster Abbey because of his double fame as a man of the theatre and as a politician. His fame in the first capacity was assured by his authorship of *The School for Scandal* and *The Rivals*, and his long ownership of the Drury Lane Theatre. His fame in the second was assured by his even longer association with Charles James Fox at the head of the Whigs. Sheridan and Fox had once been intimates of the Prince Regent, but only while the latter was himself in opposition to his father. As soon as the Regent was de facto in his father's shoes, he inclined to the Tory side, to the immense disappointment of the Whigs. Sheridan was a brilliant orator – Hazlitt called him 'the last accomplished debater of the House of Commons', and said that he was 'an excellent dramatic writer'. Sheridan was famously incorruptible, and equally famous for his aplomb: when his theatre at Drury Lane burned to the ground in 1809, ruining him financially, he stood outside a neighbouring tavern with a glass in his hand, watching; and when an acquaintance expressed surprise at seeing him there he said, 'Can't a man take a glass of wine at his own fireside?'

This was also the year of the Byron scandal. In January of the previous year the poet had married Annabella Milbanke, partly because he needed to marry an heiress and partly because his relationship with Augusta Leigh could not provide domestic happiness for the two good reasons that she was already married and, more, was his half-sister. He and Augusta perhaps hoped that his marrying would provide a convenient mask for their love-affair, but when he brought Annabella to Augusta's home in Newmarket the two women became friends, and were equally concerned about Byron's wild behaviour – for by then he had realized his mistake in marrying Annabella, since they were completely unsuited to each other, and he began behaving very badly towards her because he felt trapped, miserable and frustrated. He was also seriously in debt. Knowledge of his scandalous relations with Augusta had got abroad, filling the newspapers and rumour sheets, and both she and he were shunned by society as a result – on one ghastly occasion Augusta was snubbed by everyone at Almacks, where the *bon ton* gathered for its recreations, and when Byron entered the entire assembly left the room. Annabella sued for a legal separation and Byron left England as an exile, seen off at Dover by scores of adoring female fans trying to catch a last glimpse of him.

Hazlitt did not address the question of Byron's moral character, because he was not inspired by it either to the public's frisson of delight or its professions of scandalized horror. But although he had reservations about Byron both as politician and poet, he was consistent in praising his 'intensity of conception and expression' and his 'wildness of invention, brilliant and elegant fancy, [and] caustic wit'. A few years later Hazlitt and Byron were briefly associated, the former writing for a journal partly managed by the latter.

In the autumn of 1816 Hazlitt went on one of his usual visits to his family, who had recently moved from Surrey to a village near Bath. For his sister Peggy it was a fortunate change, because the Hazlitts there met Catherine Emmet, niece of the Irish patriot Robert Emmet. She came to live with the family, and when she died she bequeathed to Margaret a life-interest in the small but nevertheless helpful proceeds of an investment. A break from London was always a refreshment to Hazlitt, especially if he walked at least part of the way, because walking stimulated his thinking; and when he returned to London he poured out the results in Haydon's studio. 'He said some fine things which when he writes them will be remembered for ever,' Haydon wrote. This conversation had put Haydon in a good humour with Hazlitt, and he resolved to bear with the latter's sharp intellect and criticisms for the sake of nurturing all the good that he could do, especially for art. 'All his sneers and attacks at times at my views I take as nothing. My object is to manage such an intellect for the great purposes of art; and if he was to write against me for six months, still I would be patient. He is a sincere good fellow at Bottom, with fierce passions and appetites. Appeal to him and he is always conquered and yields, and before long I'll venture to predict he shall assist the good cause.'[14] One effect of Haydon's nurturing is a set of pieces Hazlitt wrote in November 1816 on the British Institution's 'Catalogue Raisonné', which Haydon said in his diary was done 'to oblige me'. Hazlitt thought that the catalogue and the exhibition were perfidious. The British Institution existed to promote the interests of contemporary fine arts and artists, and on this occasion it attempted to do so by drawing unfavourable comparisons between Old Master works and the productions of living artists, the former offering nothing to admire, said the Catalogue, when not hanging against backgrounds of red velvet. 'This is the kind of patronage and promotion of the Fine Arts,' Hazlitt wrote, 'on which [the Institution] insists as necessary to keep up the reputation of living Artists, and to ensure the sale of their works. There is nothing then in common between the merits of the old Masters and the doubtful claims of the new; *those* are not "the scale by which we can ascend to the love" of these. The excellences of the latter are of their own making and of their own seeing; we must take their own word for them; and not only so, but we must sacrifice all established principles and all established reputation to their upstart pretensions, because, if the old pictures are not totally worthless, their own can be good for nothing.'[15]

The apostate poets were not the only ones to receive a battering from Hazlitt's pen. He also regularly attacked his brother-in-law, arch Tory and Napoleon-hater, who was now editor of *The Times*, and to whom the radical writer and publisher William Hone had attached the nickname 'Dr Slop', which stuck, and which Hazlitt delightedly used. On 1 December 1816 appeared the first of four tremendous assaults by Hazlitt on Dr Slop and his newspaper. *The Times*, said Hazlitt, 'is a nuisance which ought to be abated,' and its 'little pert pragmatical plebeian Editor [is] an apostate from principle, a sophist by profession, a courtier by accident, and a very head-strong man with little understanding and no imagination, who believes whatever absurdity he pleases, and works himself up into a passion by calling names.'[16] Obviously the brothers-in-law had long ceased to be on speaking terms, but there is no record of their personal relations since becoming in-laws, nor any of the effect it had on Sarah.

Coleridge was still smarting, and still writing unhappy letters to friends: 'The man who has so grossly calumniated me in the Examiner and the Ed. Review is a Wm Hazlitt, one who owes to me more than to his own parents,' he wrote to another friend, and whereas in the earlier letter Hazlitt had been saved from transportation in the 1803 incident, the story was growing in dramatic content: now he was saved from the gallows, and Coleridge's own life had been at risk in the attempt.[17] Coleridge might well have been anticipating another attack, which duly came on 15 December, for now that Hazlitt had warmed to his theme as regards John Stoddart, he was ready to include his other favourite targets along with him, and accordingly let fly collectively at those who were 'patriots in 1793, royalists in 1816', detailing the changes in the writings of all four men. And then he returned to *The Times*: 'All that is low in understanding, vulgar and sordid in principle in city politics, is seen exuding from the formal jaws of the *Times* newspaper, as we see in the filth, and slime, and garbage, and offal of this great city pouring into the Thames from the sewers and conduit-pipes of the scavenger's company. It is a patent water-closet for the dirty uses of legitimacy: a leaden cistern for obsolete prejudices and upstart sophistry "to knot and gender in".'[18]

In one significant respect this mounting series of cannonades against the apostates was bringing to a head a matter that Hazlitt was to regret. On 21 December Crabb Robinson visited Coleridge at Highgate, where the latter was living in the care of the Gillman family, and during the course of the visit they discussed Hazlitt's articles. Coleridge complained to Crabb Robinson that Lamb should not let Hazlitt into his house, although 'he was not displeased to hear of his being knocked down by John Lamb lately.'[19] The very next day, however, there appeared the third of Hazlitt's articles on *The Times*, in which Wordsworth received a fearful thrashing on the grounds that he was interested in nothing but himself, and that he resented anything taking precedence over him in importance or esteem: 'He hates all that others love and admire but himself,' wrote Hazlitt. 'He is glad that Bonaparte is sent to St Helena, and that the Louvre is dispersed for the same reason – to get rid of the idea of any thing greater, or thought greater than himself.'[20] That night an enraged Crabb Robinson met Hazlitt at the Montagus' house in Bedford Square, and told Hazlitt that he did not like what he had been saying about Coleridge and Wordsworth, with both of whom he was now on intimate terms. Hazlitt replied that his intention was to 'expose people who otherwise would gain credit by canting and hypocrisy'. This was a full rupture between them; they did not shake hands on parting, and it was some years before they could meet with any cordiality. One thing that incensed Crabb Robinson was that Hazlitt repeated in print what he had heard said in conversation by and about his targets. Hazlitt replied that what anyone said repeatedly and openly in different conversations was public property – and to Crabb Robinson's chagrin, Basil Montagu agreed with him.

Coleridge's 'Lay Sermon' eventually appeared in December, under a new title: *The Statesman's Manual*, by which he meant the Bible. Hazlitt reviewed it in both the *Examiner* and the *Edinburgh Review*, giving it exceedingly short shrift, in particular pointing out that the Bible does not sanction the divine right of kings, as any Dissenter could have told Coleridge in his sleep – which is where, Hazlitt unkindly said, most of the *Manual* had been composed, and none too wisely at that. With the kind of polemical panache that had become a hallmark, he began his essay by saying, ' "The privilege" (says a certain author) "of talking, and even publishing nonsense, is necessary in a free state; but the more sparingly we make use of it the better." Mr Coleridge has here availed himself of his privilege – but not sparingly.'[21]

Constable was taking an inordinate length of time over the Round Table collection, and only produced a batch of proofs if Hazlitt prompted him. As 1816 ended there was still no sign that the book would appear soon. But in the course of the year Hazlitt had the pleasure of seeing his much-delayed life of Holcroft published at last. Longman brought it out in August, and the reviews were mainly complimentary, the best coming from the *Gentleman's Magazine* which said that 'The liberal impartiality with which this Editor has accomplished his task, cannot fail meeting with the most decided approbation of all parties.'

With one book out and another shortly to appear, commendation of the former, a full harvest of work in the *Examiner*, appearance in three of the four numbers of that year's *Edinburgh Review*, and a satisfying sense of having vented his political anger – a relief to the frustration and disappointment that followed the defeat of Napoleon – Hazlitt might have felt that there were at least a few consolations to set against the great sorrow of the year, his infant son's death.

Hazlitt had been handing out journalistic beatings, but so far he was unscathed in return, save for the loss of his friendship with Crabb Robinson. But this occurrence was an augury, and the damage being done by Wordsworth in spreading the story of the Keswick incident was shortly to become apparent. Wordsworth and the others did not attempt to defend themselves in the open against Hazlitt's charges, which were all true. Instead they sought to silence him by discrediting him, for which purpose the Keswick incident was a gift. This *ad hominem* tactic is familiar at all times and places, a fact which does not make it any more just, or any less unpleasant. But even if Wordsworth had not been working against him in this fashion, Hazlitt's reputation was now in any case too large for the Tory press to ignore him for much longer.

In the autumn of 1816 Hazlitt met a young medical student at Haydon's studio, a small, slight, clever man, with large widely-set eyes and an expressive mouth. His name was John Keats. Earlier that year Haydon had made a life-mask of Keats, but the mask is very unlike its lively original. Keats was already an admirer of Hazlitt's writings, and Hazlitt for his part instantly recognized the young poet's gifts when, one evening shortly after meeting him, he heard Hunt read aloud Keats's sonnet 'On Looking into Chapman's Homer'. After their first meeting in Haydon's studio they were frequently together, a friendship ended only by Keats's fatal journey to Italy four years later.

Hazlitt began 1817 in exactly the same combative and annoyed spirit which had sustained him through the previous year. His fourth article in *The Times* series appeared in January, focusing on the 'connexion between toad-eaters and tyrants'. His target was again those who had gone over from the liberal to the 'legitimate' side – men who 'contrived to sneak over one by one to the side on which "empty praise or solid pudding" was to be got; they could not live without the smiles of the great (not they)' – and who now lie 'sunk in torpid repose (from which they do not like to be disturbed by calling on their former names or professions), in lazy sinecures and good warm berths! Such is the history and mystery of literary patriotism and prostitution for the last twenty years.'[22] In the same issue of the *Examiner* a letter appeared contrasting Coleridge's *Statesman's Manual* and his sermon in Shrewsbury in January 1798, in which the philosopher-poet had called for separation of Church and State. 'I ask Mr Coleridge, why, having preached such a sermon as I have described, he has published a sermon such as you have described?' The writer was Hazlitt himself; it was a neat piece of polemic.

Crabb Robinson visited the Lambs on 29 January 1817 and he and Lamb talked of Hazlitt's attacks on the poets. Crabb Robinson tried to persuade Lamb, in furtherance of Coleridge's desires, that Lamb should close his door to Hazlitt. Lamb emphatically refused. He claimed even to have been the object of a Hazlitt attack himself; in fact Hazlitt's reference to Lamb was a charming and affectionate one, in which he anonymously described Lamb as 'a mad wag – who ought to have lived at the Court of Horwendillus, with Yorick and Hamlet, – equally desperate in his mirth and his gravity, who would laugh at a funeral and weep at a wedding, who talks nonsense to prevent the head-ache, who would wag his finger at a skeleton, whose jests scald like tears, who makes a joke of a great man, and a hero of a cat's-paw.'[23] It was on this occasion that Lamb told Crabb Robinson that Hazlitt had wept over his review of the *Excursion*, a piece of information Crabb Robinson refused to believe.

Lamb was by no means the only friend who remained loyal. Hazlitt spent much time with the Hunts – now living in the Vale of Health at Hampstead – and the Montagus, and Haydon; and he went often, as always, to Northcote's studio, and sat and talked with him by the hour. Haydon gave regular Sunday dinners, to which Hazlitt and his son William the younger frequently went. Hazlitt would say to William the younger at breakfast on such Sundays, 'Well, sir; shall we go and eat Haydon's mutton?'[24] In February 1817 Hazlitt found that an acquaintance of long standing, Godwin's daughter Mary, was staying with the Hunts in company with her recently acquired husband, Percy Shelley. The young poet and Hazlitt were much together during the next several weeks, and on one occasion they sided together in a warm dispute over the merits of monarchy and republicanism, Shelley and Hazlitt on the republican side naturally. Despite this, Hazlitt did not take to Shelley, as he had done to Keats. His reason for being sceptical about Shelley was, he said, that he thought the latter's feet never quite touched the ground.

Towards the end of February Mary Shelley recorded in her diary that she was reading Hazlitt's *Round Table*, which Constable had at last published on St Valentine's day. Keats was another appreciative reader; he wrote to his friends Reynolds, 'How is Hazlitt? We were reading his Table last night – I know he thinks himself not estimated by ten people in the world – I wish he knew he is.' Of the fifty-two essays in the collection Hunt had written twelve, and the rest were by Hazlitt. The first review appeared in the *Scots Magazine* – which was owned by Constable, so it was more puff than review, but it well expresses the Edinburgh attitude to Hazlitt: 'Mr Hazlitt has a style of his own, which it is not very easy to characterise. Originality is one of its most distinguishing features; a rare quality in these days; especially coming, as it appears to do here, without the smallest effort. Equally remarkable is his facility; his thoughts seem to issue almost without a volition, from an overflowing fountain within. In his manner there is a singular combination of that of the oldest English writers with the gayest tone of modern conversation, and yet these opposite elements are blended so intimately, as to form quite a harmonious whole.' The *Critical Review* was likewise impressed, praising the essays' 'degree of thinking, shrewdness of observation, and depth of critical acumen' and saying that in its pages 'profound reflection, ingenious argument, and happy illustration, vie with each other'. The *Monthly Magazine* also gave the volume a warm welcome; these 'two very pleasant volumes' are, it said, 'rendered peculiarly attractive by the well-known fineness of tact of the two contributors, and the exquisite originality of mind, and breathing freedom displayed in their critical observations, especially upon the poets; and above all on Shakespeare.' It is surprising to find Hazlitt praised for tact, until one remembers that Hunt had enough of it for two. The *New Monthly Magazine*, however, which existed to oppose the *Monthly Magazine*, took the exact opposite line: its short notice says that the *Round Table* is a misleading title, for the book should have been called ' "The Dunghill", or something still more characteristically vile; for such an offensive heap of pestilential jargon has seldom come our way'; and it tells its readers that they will not wonder at the existence of this vile heap when they learn that it was 'raked together' from the 'common sewer of a weekly paper called the *Examiner*, and they who after that information can have any relish for the feculent garbage of blasphemy and scurrility, may sit down at the Round Table, and enjoy the same meal with the same appetite as the negroes in the West Indies eat dirt and filth'.

From the rest of the Tory press came yet more omens of what lay in store for Hazlitt. They showed that a storm was brewing around his head. His sharp polemics were about to be answered by a flood of invective and abuse that makes present-day journalism look like milksop in comparison. The chief of the Tory magazines was the government-sponsored *Quarterly Review*, edited by William Gifford, and it led the way. It derided Hazlitt's remark that the *Round Table* aspired to restore to English periodical journalism the tradition of Steele and Addison. The author of the review was one John Russell, who, although he did not have Hazlitt's genius for polemic, certainly displayed a knack for its alternative, namely, abuse. He focused especially upon one essay – 'On Washerwomen' – which he knew to be by Hunt, but which he attributed to Hazlitt so that he could claim that all his interests and knowledge were restricted to what is vulgar and low-class, claiming in particular that he is 'quite at home' among 'tub-tumbling viragos', to whom he 'dedicates one of his longest essays, [giving] a minute account of their appearance, their habits, and their conversation'. Russell further attacked him for his 'rancorous abuse' of all poets except Milton, and said: 'He seems to feel the warmth of a private quarrel against whole nations; but against none so strongly as his own.'

And then, in a highly significant passage, Russell gave Hazlitt a fore-shadowing of what to expect over the next few years. Hazlitt had taken a parenthetic kick at Burke – whom he still, as ever, admired for his rhetorical skills, but resented for placing them so powerfully and consequentially in the service of reaction – in a footnote to one of the essays, after describing him as 'an Irish patriot and philosopher [who] abused metaphysics, because he could make nothing out of them, and turned his back upon liberty, when he found he could get nothing more by her'. Hazlitt's footnote is full of his post-Waterloo vexation and bitterness. It reads: 'This man (Burke) who was a half poet and a half philosopher, has done more mischief than perhaps any other person in the world. His understanding was not competent to the discovery of any truth, but it was sufficient to palliate a falsehood; his reasons, of little weight in themselves, thrown into the scale of power, were dreadful. Without genius to adorn the beautiful, he had the art to throw a dazzling veil over the deformed and disgusting; and to strew the flowers of imagination over the rotten carcase of corruption, not to prevent, but to communicate the infection. His jealousy of Rousseau was one chief cause of his opposition to the French Revolution. The writings of the one had changed the institutions of a kingdom; while the speeches of the other, with the intrigues of his whole party, had changed nothing but the *turnspit of the King's kitchen*. He would have blotted out the broad pure light of heaven, because it did not first shine in at the little Gothic windows of St Stephen's Chapel [the House of Commons]. The genius of Rousseau had levelled the towers of the Bastille with the dust; our zealous reformist, who had rather be doing mischief than nothing, tried, therefore, to patch them up again, by calling that loathsome dungeon the King's castle, and by fulsome adulation of the virtues of a Court strumpet. This man, – but enough of him here.'[25]

To this Russell replied, 'We were far from intending to write a single word in answer to this loathsome trash; but we confess that these passages chiefly excited us to take the trouble of noticing the work. The author might have described washerwomen for ever; complimented himself unceasingly on his own "chivalrous eloquence"; prosed interminably about Chaucer; written, if possible, in a more affected, silly, confused, ungrammatical style, and believed, as he now believes, that he was surpassing Addison – we should not have meddled with him; but if the creature, in his endeavours to crawl into the light, must take his way over the tombs of illustrious men, disfiguring the records of their greatness with the slime and filth which marks his track, it is right to point him out that he may be flung back to the situation in which nature designed that he should grovel.'[26]

Periodicals strongly flavoured by high-minded old-fashioned Church and Crown principles were horrified by the *Round Table*. The *Eclectic Review* described it as full of 'blasphemous ribaldry'; the *British Critic* called it depraved, shallow, vulgar, presumptuous, obscure and tasteless. The *Literary Gazette* deplored its morals, which it found especially repellent given that the *Examiner* was a Sunday paper – and added, in reference to Hazlitt's animadversions on the folk of the Lake country, 'we know of no parallel to this cold-blooded malignity; this unappeasable, unprovoked, and wanton craving for the indiscriminate slaughter of public and private character; this horrid fiendlike eagerness to traduce defenceless women, and foment local hatreds and national divisions among their countrymen.'

One person who, though no longer friendly with Hazlitt, retained a rich sense of his talents and was therefore disgusted by the *Quarterly* attack, was Crabb Robinson. He was shocked by the magazine's 'very bitter and scornful review', which he read soon after it came out in the late summer of 1817. He told his diary that he hoped the article was not by Southey, or some friend of Southey, who had chosen to retaliate with this 'laboured malice', which Crabb Robinson thought defeated its own object. 'The *Quarterly* exceeds the *Edinburgh* in acrimony and vulgarity,' he wrote.[27]

The influence of the *Round Table* essays on Keats was direct and palpable. In number 14, 'On Milton's Versification', Hazlitt said that the poetic reflexes of Johnson and Pope would transform Milton's vaulting Pegasus into a rocking-horse; the figure captivated Keats, who in his poem 'Sleep and Poetry' writes, 'And sway'd about upon a rocking-horse,/And thought it Pegasus.'[28] In a letter of March 1817 to Reynolds he employs, with an acknowledgement, one of Hazlitt's speech mannerisms, 'It is the finest thing by God – as Hazlitt would say,'[23] and in a letter to Haydon in May he praises a recent *Examiner* article by Hazlitt, commenting 'I am very near agreeing with Hazlitt that Shakespeare is enough for us.'[30]

Andrew Motion has shown the depth and pervasiveness of Hazlitt's influence on Keats: 'Few people had more impact on his thinking, or on how he expressed himself,' Motion writes. 'It was an influence that he embraced freely, and was supported by the good opinion of all his other friends. The *Examiner* followed Hazlitt's doings almost reverentially, saying: "He yields only to some of the greatest poets and novelists, and he is at the head of the class in which our most ambitious wits are anxious to be enrolled." '[31] Keats was not alone in finding himself echoing Hazlitt's thought and expression; Haydon likewise imitated and paraphrased him often. But with Keats it was more than a matter of echoes: 'Hazlitt not only gave Keats phrases to borrow and ideas to develop, but mapped the whole landscape of his intentions,' Motion says. 'Keats, in turn, regarded Hazlitt's "taste" as one of "the wonders of the age", and sprinkled his letters with enquiries about his health, with fond imitations of his mannerisms, with tributes to his intellectual powers, and with comments on his writing.'[32] Especially important was Hazlitt's philosophical doctrine of the natural disinterestedness of the human mind, which Keats developed into his own doctrine of the poet's 'self-annulling character' and 'chameleon' capacity. According to Motion, Hazlitt's disinterestedness principle underlay Keats's definition of 'Men of Genius', his concept of negative capability, his understanding of the 'egotistical sublime', and his views about the relationship between 'thought' and 'sensation'.[33] 'Keats also allowed Hazlitt to affect the very fabric and movement of his writing. His letters blaze with the "fiery laconicism" he prized in Hazlitt's prose, and their pacing shows a similarly "variable speed of uncommon thoughts", as well as a similar tendency to ingest a rich mass of quotation. (Hazlitt described Milton as a writer of "centos", meaning that his works were often a collage of references. He might equally well have been speaking of himself.) Keats's mature poems are energized by the same spirit: "lively, swift to digress and return, and at home in all the possible roles of a narrator". Even when most eloquently exotic, they embody the principles that Hazlitt exemplified and analysed in his essays on "The Conversation of Authors" and "On Familiar Style". The essence of his style, he said, "is not to take the first word that offers, but the best word in common use; it is not to throw words together in any combination we please, but to follow and avail ourselves of the true idiom of the language. To write a genuine familiar or truly English style, is to write as any one would speak in common conversation who had a thorough command and choice of words, or who could discourse with ease, force, and perspicuity, setting aside all pedantic and oratorical flourishes." ' When Keats met Hazlitt in Haydon's studio in the autumn of 1816, Motion says, it 'marked a turning point in his mental life.'[34]

The first few months of 1817 found Hazlitt ill, and he remained so for many weeks. His contributions to the *Examiner* were fewer than usual, although he managed to drag himself to the theatres and to file his reviews. In March he wrote to Jeffrey, 'I have been so ill as to be unable to do almost anything,' and a few days later, apologizing to Macvey Napier for delays to further pieces for the *Encyclopaedia Britannica*, he says 'I have been very ill all the winter, and have had more to do than I could have got through properly if I had been well.'

Well or ill, Hazlitt could not miss a chance of fun at the expense of Southey and, as a bonus, Coleridge – for the latter attempted to come to Southey's rescue. An early dramatic poem by Southey called *Wat Tyler*, written in his enthusiastic Jacobin youth, was piratically published against his wishes and despite his attempts to stop it by legal injunction. A short time later the *Quarterly Review* ran an article on parliamentary reform, which Hazlitt and others recognized as Southey's work. This was far too good an opportunity; Hazlitt responded with an essay in the *Examiner* in March, contrasting quotations from *Wat Tyler* with the 'ultra-royalist' sentiments of the article. Coleridge leaped to Southey's defence in the *Courier*, saying that *Wat Tyler* was a youthful production, and that Southey could not be held to account for what he thought and said in his days of inexperience, for he had since come to maturer views. In a gem of a riposte Hazlitt answered that, in summary, Coleridge's excuse for Southey was 'That Mr Southey was a mere boy when he wrote *Wat Tyler*, and entertained Jacobin opinions; that being a child, he felt as a child, and thought

slavery, superstition, war, famine, bloodshed, taxes, bribery and corruption, rotten boroughs, places and pensions, shocking things; but now
he is become a man, he has put away childish things, and thinks there is
nothing so delightful as slavery, superstition, war, famine, bloodshed,
taxes, bribery and corruption, rotten boroughs, places and pensions, and
particularly, his own.'[35] As he had done before, using a disguised letter to
contrast Coleridge's 1798 lecture on Church and State with his *Statesman's
Manual*, he now inserted a clever letter in the 6 April *Examiner*, written
as from Bristol and signed 'Vindex', in which he identified this 'hack writer
of the *Courier*' who defended Southey's scurrilous apostasy as an apostate
in his own right, showing that he was the author of the early and highly
inflammatory *Conciones ad Populum*, originally delivered as a pair of
lectures in Bristol (hence the alleged postmark of 'Vindex's' letter). Moreover, said Vindex, he remembers Coleridge publicly burlesquing Southey
and accusing him of ignorant plagiarism from Wordsworth – but here he
is calling him 'dear friend' and defending him from the criticism he
deserves.[36] If the apostate poets flinched under Hazlitt's tongue, they
equally flinched at his unforgiving powers of memory.

In the same number of the *Examiner* Hazlitt began a two-part 'review'
of an unnamed book ('the title of which I dare not give', says Hazlitt;
Howe found no original for it, but need not have looked, for it is obviously
a spoof). The title of the article is 'A Sketch of the History of the Good
Old Times Before the French Revolution, when Kings and Priests did what
they pleased, by the Grace of God', and an adaptation serves as an
epigraph: 'Sweet are the Uses of Legitimacy'. It is in Hazlitt's most brilliant,
amusing and relishable vein. 'It is the fashion for some people to say, and
others to believe, that all crimes and sufferings began with the French
Revolution, that till that period there were neither wars, murders, treasons,
nor "sudden death"; neither slavery nor tyranny, neither want nor woe,
folly or madness in the world; that the French Revolution was a wanton,
deliberate, villainous plot to wake the world out of that "sweet sleep"
which it had enjoyed for three thousand years, by thrusting the torch of
modern philosophy in its eyes; and that the object of the "late arduous
struggle" was not at all to restore "the right divine of kings to govern
wrong", but on the contrary, to bring back the blessings of peace, plenty,
liberty, loyalty, religion, morality, and the social order, which had always
accompanied the undisputed exercise and tacit acknowledgement of the
said Divine Right.'[37] The remainder of the essay is a demolition of the
principle of monarchy – with Coleridge and Southey, as its defenders, sent
staggering off the arena under some mighty passing blows – and a summary
of the wretched and bloody history of France's crown since Capet, which

shows how justified were the French when, in desperation, they revolted against monarchy and all its evils. 'And there we close the book,' Hazlitt writes at the end, declaring himself incapable of repeating the history of the present King, Louis XVIII, 'the Desired'; 'But whoever after this sketch shall have the face to talk of "the good old times", of mild paternal sway, and the blessings of Legitimacy, that is, of power restrained only by its own interests, follies, vices, and passions, and therefore necessarily sacrificing to them the rights, liberties, and happiness of nations, we shall pronounce to be either a consummate hypocrite or "a fool indeed".'[38]

There is no question of the depth and sincerity of Hazlitt's outlook in these respects. He was not a party man, but he was a passionate believer in liberty, secular republicanism, and the rights of man, and it goaded him into a rage to think how monarchs and the privileged batten on the majority of mankind. He was incensed by hypocrisy and apostasy; he could not forgive a man who had seen and vocally sympathized with the plight of mankind, but then turned away to feather his nest by fawning on the powers that created that plight. Such were Hazlitt's views, and they explain the vehemence of his attacks.

Wordsworth wrote to Haydon, 'The miscreant Hazlitt continues, I have heard, his abuse of Southey, Coleridge, and myself, in the Examiner. – I hope that you do not associate with that Fellow, he is not a proper person to be admitted into respectable society, being the most perverse and malevolent Creature that ill luck has ever thrown in my way. Avoid him – hic niger est – And this, I understand is the general opinion everywhere he is known in London.'[39] This last was wishful thinking, but worthy of a defender of 'respectable society', which happily for Wordsworth did not know about his love-child in France and had forgotten his youthful Jacobinism. The pusillanimity of Haydon's reply to Wordsworth does him little credit; he wrote that he too expected to be attacked by Hazlitt one day soon, that Hazlitt neglected to mention him in his *Encyclopaedia Britannica* article on art, that Hazlitt attacked his friend Wilkie – and anyway, Haydon then untruthfully adds, 'I see him scarcely ever, and then not at my own house.'[40] A couple of months later Hazlitt was sitting to Haydon for a 'head' to be included in his painting *Christ's Entry into Jerusalem*, and Haydon wrote in his diary that he had 'never had so pleasant [a] sitter'.

In the wainscoted study where he scribbled his notes over the mantelpiece, Hazlitt had been working quietly at a series of studies of the characters in Shakespeare's plays. By mid-April it was finished, and he sent a copy to

Jeffrey asking him to include a notice of it in the *Edinburgh Review*. He had two connected reasons for wanting the work to get an advance puff. One was that it would secure him favourable terms with a publisher – he had decided to hold onto the copyright until something had been done to increase the work's value – and this in turn would release him from the 'necessity of circumstances', which was his 'writing for three newspapers at a time to the ruin of my health and without any progress in my finances'. This related to the second reason, which was that he earnestly desired leisure to concentrate on his 'work on Metaphysics'. Hazlitt mentions *three* newspapers because he was also now writing for *The Times* – in view of the birching he had given it at the turn of the year it seems very odd that he should suddenly begin to appear in its pages as its theatre critic, but so it was; and the explanation is that John Stoddart had been sacked, and the editorial chair had been filled by Thomas Barnes, Hazlitt's friend and one-time colleague in the Strangers' Gallery of Parliament, who immediately persuaded John Walter, the paper's owner, that Hazlitt was the best man in the country to write the theatre column. Walter consulted Crabb Robinson, whose association with *The Times* went back a long way – he had been its very first war correspondent and then its Foreign Editor – and to his great credit he advised Walter to appoint Hazlitt, after reading him one of Hazlitt's 'Round Tables' as proof of his powers – but, says Crabb Robinson, 'at the same time I did not encourage [Walter] to form a personal intimacy with him.'[41]

With a certain difficulty Hazlitt managed for a while to be a theatre critic for both the *Examiner* and *The Times*, but it was tiring work juggling the two. The season was not an especially good one, and Hazlitt was distracted by other concerns. Among them was Southey's 'Letter to William Smith Esq., MP.', in which the Laureate defended himself over the *Wat Tyler* matter, for Smith – prompted by Hazlitt's piece – had read out in the Commons comparisons between the poem and the *Quarterly Review* article on parliamentary reform. Southey re-ran the Coleridge argument about his youth and inexperience, but also, inconsistently, argued that in putting highly revolutionary sentiments into the mouth of Wat Tyler he had not thereby endorsed them himself, for it was a poet's task to make different characters express their own views forcefully. Hazlitt's reply is in his best style of contempt – 'Faugh!' he says at one point, regarding Southey's relationship with the 'foul ugly witch' of Legitimacy: he 'for very shame lays his head in her lap, paddles with the palms of her hands, inhales her hateful breath, leers in her eyes and whispers in her ears, calls her little fondling names, Religion, Morality, and Social Order ... sticks close to his filthy bargain, and will not give her up, because she keeps him, and he is down in her will. Faugh!'[42]

Keats was delighted by this piece: 'By the by what a tremendous Southean Article his last was,' he said to Haydon on 11 May, and the next day wrote in the same vein to Hunt. Coleridge was almost prostrated by it; in writing of the 'infamous Calumny' that Hazlitt was loading onto him and his friends he again related the Keswick story, which by now was getting positively exciting, for in this new version two hundred horsemen appeared in pursuit of Hazlitt, and to help him escape Coleridge gave him 'all the money I had in the world and the very shoes off my feet'.

Despite Wordsworth's belief that Hazlitt was a social outcast in London, he was in his usual way often at Basil Montagu's house, and one evening he there met the Royal Academy's professor of anatomy, Sir Anthony Carlisle. Carlisle had famously introduced naked Guardsmen performing sword exercises, and jugglers and gymnasts engaged in their tricks, to demonstrate muscular action to the students. Hazlitt was intrigued by Carlisle's reputation, and persuaded Bewick to take him to one of his lectures. In the course of it the anatomist passed around, on a dinner plate, a human heart and a human brain. Hazlitt, reported Bewick, 'shrank back in sensitive horror, closed his eyes, turned away his pale, shuddering countenance, and appeared to those near him to be in a swooning state.'[43]

Hazlitt's plan to make a pre-publication splash with his 'Characters of Shakespeare's Plays' had only partially worked. Jeffrey promised to notice the book, but there was not enough time to do it in advance of publication, so Hazlitt inserted an advertisement in *The Times* to inform lovers of the drama and, especially, Shakespeare that 'they will derive considerable pleasure from Mr W. Hazlitt's forthcoming work, &c.' – and there was an enthusiastic prepublication review by Hunt in the *Examiner*. None of Hazlitt's preparations were enough to persuade Constable to publish the book, so the successors of Joseph Johnson in St Paul's Churchyard did so instead. This was the firm of Ollier and Hunter, and they brought out the book on 9 July 1817. The dedication read: 'To Charles Lamb Esq., this volume is inscribed, as a mark of old friendship and lasting esteem'.

Hazlitt was not a scholar, not a 'literary critic' in the modern sense of this term, but a lover of literature. He was a feeling, thinking, responsive individual with a fine taste and great powers of discernment; and that is the basis of his book about the characters of Shakespeare. There is nothing in these essays about textual problems and variant readings, of first folios and bad quartos, of printer's errors and prompt copies, of dates and sources, of attributions and borrowings. He is interested in the characters and the situations they are placed in, and he thrilled to the insight and vision of the poet who was able to present such an array of humanity with such truth. For Hazlitt Shakespeare is a supreme philosopher of human nature and human experience, and his essays discuss the plays accordingly.

Hazlitt took his point of departure from Pope's observation that Shakespeare's characters 'are so much nature herself, that it is a sort of injury to call them by so distant a name as copies of her'. Profiting from his long study for the *Edinburgh Review* of Schlegel's book on the drama, he discussed the plays in turn, commenting on the principal characters in each as if discussing them at dinner after a performance. He did not approve of Dr Johnson's elephantine approach, which subdues critical sensitivity to 'the common standard of conventional propriety', and always looks for a criticism to balance a word of praise, so that the rolling progress of the Johnsonian sentences might not lose their antistrophic rhythm. Instead Hazlitt wrote with the enthusiasm of someone who has just left the pit after the curtain has fallen, full of passionate interest in the psychology of the characters, and struck by Shakespeare's genius in portraying them. The essays have been criticized as impressionistic and slight, which is to miss their point. They were quoted with appreciation by such great Shakespeare scholars as A. C. Bradley, and are quoted still; and their freshness and quickness remain undiminished.

A good example of the charm of the essays, and their penetration, is Hazlitt's response to the standard objection urged against *Romeo and Juliet* that it is 'founded on the idle passion between a boy and girl, who have scarcely seen and can have but little sympathy or rational esteem for one another, who have had no experience of the good or ills of life, and whose raptures or despair must therefore be equally groundless and fantastical'. His answer was, 'Whoever objects to the youth of the parties in this play as "too unripe and crude" to pluck the sweets of love, and wishes to see a first-love carried on into a good old age, and the passions taken at the rebound, when their force is spent, may find all this done in *The Stranger* and other German plays, where they do things by contraries, and transpose nature to inspire sentiment and create philosophy. Shakespear proceeded in a more strait-forward, and, we think, effectual way. He did not endeavour to extract beauty from wrinkles, or the wild throb of passion from the last expiring sigh of indifference. He did not "gather grapes of thorns nor figs of thistles". It was not his way. But he has given a picture of human life, such as it is in the order of nature. He has founded the passion of the two lovers not on the pleasures they had experienced, but on all the pleasures they had *not* experienced. All that was to come of life was theirs. At that untried source of promised happiness they slaked their thirst, and the first eager draught made them drunk with love and joy. They were in full possession of their senses and their affections. Their hopes were of air, their desires of fire. Youth is the season of love, because the heart is then first melted in tenderness from the touch of novelty, and kindled to rapture, for it knows no end of its enjoyments or its wishes. Desire has no limit but itself. Passion, the love and expectation of pleasure, is infinite, extravagant, inexhaustible, till experience comes to check and kill it. Juliet exclaims on her first interview with Romeo, "My bounty is as boundless as the sea,/My love as deep." And why should it not? What was to hinder the thrilling tide of pleasure, which had just gushed from her heart, from flowing on without stint or measure, but experience which she was yet without? What was to abate the transport of the first sweet sense of pleasure, which her heart and her senses had just tasted, but indifference which she was yet stranger to? What was there to check the ardour of faith, of hope, of constance, just rising in her breast, but disappointment which she had not yet felt?'

Hazlitt profoundly appreciated Shakespeare's grasp of emotional truth in this play, just as he recognized, equally profoundly, the universality of experience embodied in the person of Hamlet. Everyone knows Hamlet, the prince, and *Hamlet*, the play, as if we remembered both before we even encountered them. But who recognizes that each of us *is* Hamlet, and that his story is our own? 'Hamlet is a name; his speeches and sayings but the idle coinage of the poet's brain. What then, are they not real? They are as real as our own thoughts. Their reality is in the reader's mind. It is *we* who are Hamlet. The play has a prophetic truth, which is above that of history. Whoever has become thoughtful and melancholy through his own mishaps or those of others; whoever has borne about with him the clouded brow of reflection, and thought himself "too much i' th' sun"; whoever has seen the golden lamp of day dimmed by envious mists rising in his own breast, and could find in the world before him only a dull blank with nothing left remarkable in it; whoever has known "the pangs of despised love, the insolence of office, or the spurns which patient merit of the unworthy takes"; he who has felt his mind sink within him, and sadness cling to his heart like a malady, who has had his hopes blighted and his youth staggered by the apparitions of strange things; who cannot be well at ease, while he sees evil hovering near him like a spectre; whose powers of action have been eaten up by thought, he to whom the universe seems infinite, and himself nothing; whose bitterness of soul makes him careless of consequences, and who goes to a play as his best resource to shove off, to a second remove, the evils of life by a mock representation of them – this is the true Hamlet.'

The Edinburgh reviews of *Characters of Shakespeare's Plays* were full of praise. Jeffrey described the book as 'very pleasing – and, we do not hesitate to say, a book of very considerable originality and genius', while the *Edinburgh Magazine* said that it was a 'most animated, intelligent, and prepossessed criticism of the "great heir of fame" '; and it described Hazlitt as 'the best writer of a short essay since Goldsmith'. In the *Monthly Review* Hazlitt was praised as 'the most sparkling prose-writer of the present day', and the book was commended. Predictably, the Tory press damned it, and concentrated wholly on Hazlitt's politics; Russell in the *Quarterly Review* said that Hazlitt proved 'how very small a portion of talent and literature was necessary for carrying on the trade of sedition'.

The book was a bestseller. The first edition was gone in six weeks, and Taylor and Hessey bought the copyright and prepared a second edition. Hazlitt meanwhile had taken himself into the country for refreshment, first to see his family for a few days, and then to Burford Bridge on the river Mole, where he reported finding a copy of Thomas Chalmers's *Sermons on Astronomy* and spending a delightful morning reading them under an apple tree.[44] On returning to London he recommended the Fox and Hounds at Burford Bridge to Keats, who went there in the following November to finish writing *Endymion*.

As usual, walking in the country reinvigorated Hazlitt. The *Champion* was no longer under the editorship of John Scott, and its new management were pleased to have Hazlitt's services. In August 1817 he contributed to it an article on 'The Effects of War and Taxes'. In the *Edinburgh Review* for this same month he reviewed Coleridge's *Biographia Literaria*, and the litany of his complaints against the 'dreamer' was familiar: 'Mr C., with great talents, has, by ambition to be every thing, become nothing. His metaphysics have been a dead weight on the wings of his imagination – while his imagination has run away with his reason and common sense. He might, we seriously think, have been a very considerable poet – instead of which he has chosen to be a bad philosopher and a worse politician.'[45] From the late summer into the winter Hazlitt continued to review theatre for *The Times*, and contributed frequent articles to the *Morning Chronicle* and the *Champion*. He had stopped writing for the *Examiner*, partly because of the conflict of interest over theatre reviewing, but mainly because the other papers paid more, and were absorbing his energies – indeed too much so. Theatre reviewing was proving especially taxing, so in December, just before Christmas, he resigned from *The Times*, giving his reason as 'want of health and leisure'. The want of health and leisure was amply explained by the fact that he had a major new project in hand: a series of lectures on poetry, due to start in January 1818. It was to be the apogee of his success – and a cue for the Tory press to intensify their campaign against him.

# CHAPTER ELEVEN

# Reputation and Calumny

## 1818–1820

IN THE CLOSING months of 1817 Hazlitt wrote to the committee of the Surrey Institution offering to give a series of lectures on the English poets. His friend Thomas Alsager was a member of the committee, but Alsager did not have to exert himself on the proposal's behalf, because Hazlitt's literary reputation was more than enough to recommend him.

The Assistant Secretary of the Institution was Peter George Patmore, father of the poet Coventry Patmore. Although he had not met Hazlitt in person before this date, he was familiar with Hazlitt's work, including his fearsome polemical essays, and equally familiar with the discreditable rumours being spread about him by Wordsworth, Coleridge and the Tory press. In this respect Patmore represented a sizeable segment of public opinion about Hazlitt. He was convinced, as he made his way to the room in the Institution where Hazlitt was waiting to hear whether his lecture proposal had been accepted, that he was about to meet a monster. Writing thirty years later he said, 'I remember the time when no words could express the horror I felt at the (supposed) personal character of William Hazlitt, or were deemed too strong to openly set forth those feelings ... From all that I had heard from his enemies (and even from his so-called friends) I looked upon him personally as little better than an incarnate fiend ... my first impressions were derived not from my own observations, but from the reports of those who ought to have known better, and who certainly would have known him better, had not their personal feelings been enlisted in the cabal against him.'[1] It was therefore with 'inexpressible horror and dread' that he entered the office where Hazlitt sat waiting for him, only to find there 'a pale anatomy of a man, sitting uneasily, half on half off a chair, with his legs tucked awkwardly underneath the rail, his hands folded listlessly on his knees, his head drooping on one side, and one of his elbows leaning (not resting) on the edge of the table by which he sat, as if in fear of having no right to be there. His hat had taken as odd a position on the floor beside him, as if that, too, felt itself as much out of its element as the owner.'[2] He half rose from his chair, but said nothing. Patmore communicated to him the committee's decision about the lectures. Hazlitt told him with disarming honesty that he had not yet written them, and asked for 'whole or part' of the payment in advance.

Shortly afterwards Patmore visited Hazlitt in York Street, describing his study much as Bewick had done – bare, the wainscoting scribbled over with notes – to finalize arrangements. He asked Hazlitt's permission to review the lectures in *Blackwood's Magazine*. Hazlitt was surprised by this request, for *Blackwood's* was hostile both to him and its grand neighbour in the Scottish capital, the *Edinburgh Review*. To begin with he was not sure whether Patmore was sincere, but he agreed to let him have copies of the texts of the lectures as he finished writing them.

Leigh Hunt's brother John, whom Hazlitt always liked and admired as a quiet, staunch, unflinching friend of liberty, had begun a new weekly magazine called the *Yellow Dwarf*. Hazlitt contributed to it, continuing his attacks on Tories and apostates in accustomed style, but in the process giving his next-door neighbour and landlord, Jeremy Bentham, a good review for being the only honest man among those named in his essay 'The Press – Coleridge, Southey, Wordsworth, and Bentham'. In another essay, describing the corrupting effect of Court influence, he observed that it is difficult for anyone to be honest in politics who had not been brought up a Dissenter – whereupon he applauded Dissenters as a sturdy caste of independents who held fast to their principles despite every difficulty and discouragement. The essay was an affectionate tribute to his father, now in his eighties and declining into second childhood at his last home at Crediton in Devonshire.

On Tuesday 13 January 1818 Hazlitt gave the first of his lectures on poetry at the Surrey Institution. Bewick gives an account of its beginning: 'The friends who knew the sensitive and wayward character of Hazlitt were prepared for a disappointment from his failure in self-possession and confidence. They therefore placed themselves in readiness – but what did take place? The time arriving, and the audience expressing unequivocal signs of impatience, our lecturer, pallid as death, and hesitating, like some unhappy being about to meet his doom, approached the table, lecture in hand, and tried to clear his choking voice, but all his efforts failed to overcome his nervousness. The auditory, perceiving his timidity, clapped and applauded, crying, "Bravo, Hazlitt!" This seemed to encourage him, and he began in faint and tremulous accents; but as the noise subsided, and he became conscious of the sound of his own voice, lifting his too-observant eyes to the "sea of heads" before him, all watching and gazing at him, his small modicum of voice and confidence oozed out, and fidgeting confusedly at his waistcoat pockets, he came to a full stop, closed his manuscript, and bolted off in quick retreat. In the room he passed into, however, he found friends ready to prevent his disappearance. They came round him, encouraged and persuaded him; he heard too the hubbub of applause, the shouting of his name, with many expressions of encouragement, and he slowly returned to the lecture-table, amidst vociferous clamours of "Bravo, Hazlitt!" &c. He commenced once more his difficult task, and warming to his subject while he was stimulated by the frequent acknowledgements of his striking thoughts or brilliant language, before he had finished his first lecture he had become quite at home with the indulgent friends before him.'[3]

This opening lecture contained Hazlitt's controversial definition of poetry as 'the language of the imagination and the passions . . . the universal language which the heart holds with nature and itself . . . an imitation of nature . . . the high-wrought enthusiasm of fancy and feeling'. Poetry 'is not a branch of authorship,' he said, 'it is "the stuff of which our life is made". The rest is "mere oblivion", a dead letter: for all that is worth remembering in life is the poetry of it.'[4]

The lecture was a triumph; the audience wafted Hazlitt from the hall on a gale of applause and cheering. Patmore insisted on escorting Hazlitt home, and offered him his arm; Hazlitt pulled away, but Patmore persevered, so Hazlitt took it 'gingerly with the tips of his fingers . . . as if it had been a bar of hot iron,' and peppered his sentences with 'Sir' in the formal manner. The following weekend Keats and Hazlitt dined with Haydon at his studio, by which time news was all over town that the first lecture had been a brilliant success. Keats was determined to attend the second, which was on Chaucer and Spenser – but in the event he missed it, having mistaken the time, arriving just as the audience came pouring out, in their midst Hazlitt himself, Bewick, John Hunt and the Landseers – all of whom 'pounced upon' Keats and took him to dinner. After the third lecture, on Shakespeare and Milton, Crabb Robinson wrote in his diary that Hazlitt 'delighted me much by the talent he displayed'; the lecture was 'full of striking and beautiful observations'.[5] As the series proceeded the audience grew bigger. Bewick fell into the routine of going to York Street to accompany Hazlitt to the Surrey Institution, located in the now-lost Rotunda on the south end of Blackfriars Bridge: 'By his request I often called upon him and accompanied him to the Surrey Institution. He was generally sitting alone in front of the looking-glass putting the finishing touches to the lecture of the evening. After which he would chat away in great good-humour, making pertinent remarks upon the requirements of popular lecturing, observing that "*He* at all events must endeavour to express his own thoughts upon what he undertook to do, and not be led away by the mistake of pleasing the million, or speaking for the present hour." [6] In a letter to his brother Bewick reported, 'Hazlitt is giving lectures on poetry; they are said to be the finest lectures ever delivered. He is the Shakespeare prose writer of our glorious country; he outdoes all in truth, style, and originality – you must read his Shakespeare's characters.' [7] Bewick was a fan; but he had caught the mood of the crowded Surrey Institution, where the audiences were roused by Hazlitt's always striking and frequently provocative views into setting aside the usual decorums and voicing their responses even as Hazlitt spoke. A member of the audience who disapproved of this departure wrote to *The Times*: 'I am in the habit of attending the lectures at the Surrey Institution, and on Tuesday last was present at one delivered by Mr Hazlitt ... in the course of which he made (as he not infrequently does) an unfortunate and irrelevant political allusion, which was instantly followed by rounds of applause from some, and hissing from other parts of the audience ... I am myself very little moved by party differences, and looked upon this scene with calm composure, and was not a little shocked at seeing so well dressed and (to my own knowledge) generally respectable an audience emulating the uproar of a one-shilling gallery – behaviour totally at variance with the dignity and decorum due to the place and the occasion, and highly offensive to everyone who professes to be, with the writer, a friend to order.' [8] Hazlitt was not troubled by hissing; when it occurred, he repeated the passage that had occasioned it in a louder voice and with special emphasis. To Crabb Robinson's outrage he spoke well of Voltaire; to the sniggers of some in the audience he described Dr Johnson picking up and carrying home on his back an aged prostitute who had fainted from disease – and he silenced the sniggers by remarking on the similarity between that incident and the story of the Good Samaritan.

On the day of Hazlitt's third lecture a rival attraction began on the other side of the river, in Flower-de-Luce Court off Fleet Street – Coleridge was lecturing *ad libitum* on a wide variety of subjects, commencing at eight o'clock. Happily for the indefatigable Crabb Robinson, Hazlitt's lectures began at seven o'clock, which meant that he was able to rush from one to the other and hear most of both. He found to his dismay that Coleridge rambled and sometimes bored, in sharp contrast to Hazlitt, who sparkled. The disparity confirmed Hazlitt's own observation made some years earlier, that Coleridge's genius as a talker was better displayed at an informal fireside than in the setting of a public lecture hall, although – as the experience of Hazlitt's youth testifies – that had not always been so. Crabb Robinson now wrote, 'his speculations have ceased to be living thoughts … I fear that Coleridge will not on the whole add to his reputation by these lectures.'

Hazlitt's audiences continued to grow. At the last lecture, which was on the contemporary poets – and no doubt because people expected fireworks from Hazlitt on that subject – the hall was packed to the ceiling. Crabb Robinson had to make do with confinement to the outer margins of the crowd, so when Hazlitt cast an expected aspersion on Wordsworth his long-prepared hiss went, he reports, unheeded.

An enthusiastic presence at this as at all Hazlitt's lectures was his great admirer, Mary Russell Mitford, later to become famous as the authoress of *Our Village*, but at this time a minor contributor of verses to the journals, and busy writing plays which made her a celebrity in the 1820s. On 3 March she wrote home to praise Hazlitt's last lecture, which she had just been to hear that evening, adding, 'it was on the Modern Poets and most charmingly he trimmed the whole set of them. Nothing was so amusing.'[9] She expanded her report for a friend, Sir William Elford, a few days later: 'Mr Hazlitt is really the most delightful lecturer I ever heard – his last, on modern poetry was amusing past all description to everybody but the parties concerned – them to be sure he spared as little as a mower spares the flowers in a hayfield. I never so thoroughly thanked heaven for the double blessing of being nobody and being a woman as at this lecture.'[10] The experience left a vivid memory. The following autumn, when she had read the published version of the lectures, she wrote a fuller account of them: 'He is a very entertaining person, that Mr Hazlitt, the best demolisher of a bloated unwieldy overblown fame that ever existed. He sweeps it away as easily as an east wind brushes the leaves off a faded peony. He is a literary Warwick – "a puller down of kings". I am not so sure that he deserves the other half of Warwick's title. He is no "setter-up" of anything. He praises indeed pretty often but his praise has an unlucky air of insincerity which whether intentional or not spoils the effect. And yet he can speak well of some poets. Of Milton for instance because Johnson has abused him – Of Shakespeare because he himself has written a book about him – Of Thomson from contradiction – Of Pope from fellow-feeling – but of Swift and Voltaire only with hearty goodwill. He is very like Voltaire himself – just the same shaker to pieces of the great and the old and the severest – yet he has the same light and decisive spirit – and the same delicate and subtle wit – the same calmness – the same tact. As a critic he is too cold, too uncatchable – he has no enthusiasm – right or wrong – there is nothing like fire about him, neither flame nor smoke – he is a provoking unadmiring critic, but a most delightful lecturer – more delight-ful viva voce than in a printed book. When I read his lecture on the living poets it seemed, impudent as it is, so much civiller than my recollections that I at first thought he had softened and sweetened it from a well-grounded fear of pistol or poison, but upon reconsidering the matter I am convinced that it is unaltered and that it owed its superior effect to Mr Hazlitt's fine delivery – to certain slight inflections in his very calm and gentlemanly voice – to certain almost imperceptible motions of his graceful person and above all to a certain momentary upward look full of malice French and not quite free from malice English by which he contrives to turn the grandest compliment into the bitterest sarcasm. In short the man, mind and body, has a genius for contempt and I am afraid, very much afraid, that I like him the better for it.'[11]

A good example of the passages she had in mind is Hazlitt's comment on Southey's more ambitious poetical works: 'Of Mr Southey's larger epics, I have but a faint recollection of them at this distance of time, but all that I remember of them is mechanical and extravagant, heavy and artificial. His affected, disjointed style is well imitated in the Rejected Addresses. The difference between him and Sir Richard Blackmore seems to be, that the one is heavy and the other light, the one solemn and the other pragmatical, the one phlegmatic and the other flippant; and that there is no Gay in the present time to give a Catalogue Raisonné of the performances of the living undertaker of epics. Kehama is a loose sprawling figure, such as we see cut out of wood or paper, and pulled or jerked with wire or thread, to make sudden and surprising motions, without meaning, grace, or nature in them. By far the best of his works are his shorter personal compositions, in which there is an ironical mixture of the quaint and serious, such as his lines of Gaspar Poussin, the fine tale of Gualberto, his Description of a Pig, and the Holly-tree, which is an affecting, beautiful, and modest retrospect on his own character ... But the little he has done of true and sterling excellence, is overloaded by the quantity of indifferent matter which he turns out every year, "prosing or versing", with equally mechanical and irresistible facility.'[12]

Hazlitt repeated the series of lectures at the Crown and Anchor in the Strand from late March, and many of his friends who had not been able to make the journey across the river now came to hear him – Lamb, Godwin and his family, Charles Kemble, Alsager, Martin Burney (time had softened the blow of Hazlitt's attack on Fanny Burney's novel), and Mr and Mrs Basil Montagu. In the audience was John Taylor of the publishing firm Taylor and Hessey, who had paid £100 for the copyright of the lectures and soon thereafter published them. Hazlitt was in fact already at work correcting the proofs when the repeat series began.

Patmore sent the draft manuscript of his reviews for *Blackwood's Magazine* to Hazlitt, who was pleased with them. After reading the first one he wrote to Patmore, 'I am well satisfied with the article, and will be obliged to you for it. I am afraid the censure is truer than the praise. It will be a great service if they insert it intire, which, however, I hope.'[13] *Blackwood's* indeed ran Patmore's pieces, which he signed 'A. Z.' But elsewhere in the magazine signs of fast-impending trouble appeared, for one of the editors – John Gibson Lockhart – inserted a squib to blunt Patmore's praise:

> Of pimpled Hazlitt's coxcomb lectures writing
> Our friend with moderate pleasure we peruse.
> A. Z. when Kean's or Shakespeare's praise indicting
> Seems to have caught the flame of either's muse.

This angered Patmore. He wrote at once to William Blackwood, the magazine's owner, to say, 'Was it not a gratuitous piece of *imprudence* (to say the least of it) to admit that line in the last number about "pimpled Hazlitt"? In consequence of being one of the managers of a Literary Institution I have been led to form a slight personal acquaintance with Mr Hazlitt, and I have reason to know that such notices ... are exceedingly obnoxious to him – I suppose your Editor is not ignorant how tremendous his power is when he sets about to resent what he feels or fancies to be an injury?'[14] *Blackwood's* would have done well to heed this warning, for when they came to overstep the mark with Hazlitt they found that Patmore was right. Blackwood disingenuously replied, 'Your notices of Mr Hazlitt's lectures have been admirable, and must, I think, have been satisfactory to himself. The joke about him in the notices I do not understand nor much care about. The said Notices were written in a few hours by a gentleman of real wit, and perfect good humour. Someone had told him (it would seem erroneously) that Mr Hazlitt had a pimpled face, and he accordingly said so, without much meaning.' But then a note of bravado crept in. 'I can have no wish to offend or irritate Mr Hazlitt. But neither have I the slightest fear of him. I am mistaken greatly, if there be not a pen ready to be drawn in my service, by "one as good as he".' That *Blackwood's* was not in the mood to heed warnings was confirmed by a note appended to the last of Patmore's notices in April: 'When we undertook to give the foregoing abstract of Mr Hazlitt's Lectures, it was not our intention to have accompanied it by a single observation in the shape of judgment, as to their merits or defects; but we find, that our own opinions have been strangely supposed to be identified with those we have done nothing more than detail. We choose, therefore, to say a few words on the impression we have received from these, and from Mr Hazlitt's previous writings on similar subjects ... As we have not scrupled to declare, that we think Mr Hazlitt is sometimes the very best living critic, we shall venture one step farther, and add, that we think he is sometimes the very worst. One would suppose he had a personal quarrel with all living writers, good, bad, or indifferent. In fact, he seems to know little about them, and to care less. With him, to be alive is not only a fault in itself, but it includes all other possible faults ... In short, if you want his praise, you must die for it; and when such praise is deserved, and given really *con amore*, it is almost worth dying for. By the bye, what can our Editor's friend mean by "pimpled Hazlitt"? If he knows the gentleman's person, he cannot intend the epithet to apply to *that*; and how "pimpled" may be interpreted with reference to *mind*, we are not able to divine.' More, but worse, followed in May; the hostility was ratcheting up: 'It was indeed a fatal day for Mr Jeffrey, when he degraded both himself and his original coadjutors, by taking into pay such an unprincipled blunderer as Hazlitt. He is not a coadjutor, he is an accomplice. The day perhaps is not far distant, when the Charlatan shall be stripped to the naked skin, and made to swallow his own vile prescriptions.'

The threat implicit in these remarks was soon fulfilled. For the present, in ignorance of what these words might portend, Hazlitt said and did nothing.

In March 1818 Mary Shelley's *Frankenstein* was published anonymously. It was widely reviewed and seriously treated, its reviewers assuming that such a powerful tale must be the work of a man (Mary Shelley was then a girl of nineteen). Hazlitt read it, and doubtless knew that it was by his friend Godwin's daughter, but he did not comment on it directly. In an essay written eight years later he alludes to it by employing the phrase, which had then become a byword, 'like the monster in Frankenstein'. It was a significant year for literature, for in it 'Monk' Lewis died, Jane Austen's *Northanger Abbey* and *Persuasion* were published (posthumously; she had died the previous year), and so were Keats's *Endymion*, Scott's *Heart of Midlothian* and *Rob Roy*, and the first part of Byron's *Don Juan*, which was a runaway bestseller. Hazlitt read and admired the work of Keats, Scott, Lewis and Byron, although he liked neither the politics of Scott nor the aristocratic misdemeanours of Byron, and said so plainly. But he still did not read Jane Austen, despite the fact that her work was enjoyed and discussed in his circle. Crabb Robinson records sitting up until two in the morning reading *Pride and Prejudice*, after which he wrote in his journal, 'This novel I consider as one of the most excellent works of our female novelists. Its merit lies in the characters, and in the perfectly colloquial style of the dialogue.' Hazlitt's neglect of Jane Austen was not the product of an aversion to female novelists, for he loved the works of Mrs Inchbald and Mrs Radcliffe, the former a writer of romances, the latter of tremendous Gothic tales. Mrs Inchbald had wrung Hazlitt's heart in his youth with her affecting tales of blighted love, an unfortunately formative experience for one so ardent and sentimental. In writing of her books he said that the 'pathos and interest' of her stories was 'too great ... hardly to be borne with patience'. Mrs Inchbald comes nowhere near Jane Austen in fineness of touch, depth of perception or perfection of irony, nor can she write a quarter as well, so it is a very great pity that the age's finest critic did not read and review the age's finest novelist, for his reaction would be well worth knowing – all the more so as their moral outlooks are surprisingly similar.

The relative prosperity Hazlitt enjoyed while he was salaried on the *Morning Chronicle*, the *Champion* and *The Times* was not so easy to maintain now that he had returned to freelance work. The lectures on poetry were lucrative, but Hazlitt was a spendthrift, and what he earned from them was not enough to save him from money anxieties, which appear to have been accumulating again. The pressure to produce journalism therefore remained. He continued contributing to the *Yellow Dwarf* and the *Edinburgh Review*, although in the manner of all who write for a living, he was not averse to recycling his material. Some of his *Dwarf* pieces had appeared in earlier incarnations, and he used the text of his fourth poetry lecture as an essay for the *Edinburgh Review*. But most of what he wrote was new. It included an attack on the clergy of the Established church, and a review of Byron's *Childe Harold's Pilgrimage* which he described as 'an indigestion of the mind' because, despite his wish to think well of Byron and his work, he could not, he said, make himself like this particular instance of it. His last piece for the *Yellow Dwarf* – the last, because the journal was about to close – again vented his dislike of opera, which he thought 'artificial' and shallow. He wrote to press Jeffrey for more work in the *Edinburgh*, because he needed the money, and even sent an essay in the hope Jeffrey would use it; and he asked whether his lecture series would be likely to do well in Edinburgh. Jeffrey replied in the negative, but added, 'we cannot let a man of genius suffer,' and enclosed £100, 'a great part of which I shall owe you in a few weeks' – meaning that more commissions were on their way – and saying that the same sum again was 'heartily at your service' if required.

Taylor and Hessey published the *Lectures on the English Poets* towards the end of May 1818, on the same day that they issued the second edition of *Characters of Shakespeare's Plays*. In a letter to his brother dated 4 June Taylor described the *Lectures* as 'a work of extraordinary ability'. As if this were not enough for a public which, whatever its opinions of Hazlitt, could neither be indifferent to his views nor short of opportunities to read them, he soon afterwards brought out a collection of his theatre reviews under the title *A View of the English Stage*, published by Richard Stodart. It attracted little notice in the journals because it was overshadowed by the other volumes, but private admirers read it with pleasure. Mary Russell Mitford wrote, 'I could not help reading them altogether; though so much of Hazlitt is rather dangerous to one's taste, rather like dining on sweetmeats and supping on pickles. So poignant is he, and so rich, everything seems insipid after him.'

As usual, reviews of the *Lectures* – apart from Patmore's appreciative notices in *Blackwood's* which were published as the lectures unfolded – did not start appearing until some months later. The earliest was in the *Quarterly Review* in January 1819 (the belated July 1818 issue), and as a matter of course it attacked the lectures, but with merciless venom, describing them as meaningless, verbose, vague, unintelligible, and vacant, and mounting a personal attack on Hazlitt in the process. As usual, the *Quarterly* gave the tone to the rest of the Tory press; in the *British Critic* Hazlitt was described as belonging to 'a certain class of half-bred, half-witted geniuses, men naturally possessing a certain vivacity of thought and fancy, but whose minds are neither gifted by nature with strength sufficient for the acquisition of habits of thinking justly, or led to the cultivation of such dispositions by the useful discipline of regular education'. But even this enemy was forced to acknowledge that 'Mr Hazlitt shews often a lively and discriminating perception of the qualities of the several authors that come before him,' and he concludes – again perforce – 'Upon the whole, as we have said before, we think the volume entertaining, in spite of all its foppery and flippancy and affectation.'

But the *Edinburgh Magazine* and the *Literary Journal* were warmly appreciative. The former said: 'There are few authors to whose decision we should be more disposed to bow, when any subject of literature or of taste was in discussion ... [his lectures] contain a very interesting and luminous history of the progress of poetry in this country, interspersed with many well chosen specimens from our various authors.' The latter said: 'our partial recollection of [Hazlitt's] former productions, led us to take up the present work with considerable expectation of amusement. Nor have our hopes been disappointed.' Not just the matter but the manner greatly pleased: 'Mr H's powers of expression are unlimited. The sublime, the affecting, the simple, the flowery, and the facetious, are all the mere play-things of his pen. He draws from inexhaustible funds and lavishes on his descriptions an exuberance of imagery and diction, that might well bankrupt the boldest genius.' Hazlitt is 'second to none' in 'extent of imagination, in beauty, in brilliance, and strength of language.'

In the spring of 1820, so late that it was able to take account of several other of Hazlitt's books also, a review appeared in the *Monthly Magazine*. 'Mr Hazlitt is perhaps the most sparkling prose-writer of the present day,' it said. 'To whatever department of criticism he turns his versatile attention, he is sure of illuminating the objects in survey with the rainbow tints of fancy, and with a dazzling glitter of intellect.' His works 'will be read with luxury on account of their brilliant execution, and with instruction on account of the many delicate remarks which are interspersed among the declamations.'

In all, Hazlitt was entitled to be pleased by the reception of the *Lectures*, for even party spite had not been able to dampen the admiration they evoked. But his enjoyment of its success was diminished by what happened to the second edition of his *Characters of Shakespeare's Plays*. In Hazlitt's view the comprehensive damning given it by the *Quarterly* killed its commercial viability almost as soon as Taylor and Hessey published it. The January 1818 number of the *Quarterly* appeared in June – most periodicals ran late – with a review of *Characters* by John Russell in a highly vituperative vein: 'We should not have condescended to notice the senseless and wicked sophistry of this writer, or to point out to the contempt of the reader his "didactic forms" and "logical diagrams", had we not considered him as one of the representatives of a class of men by whom literature is more than at any former period disgraced, who are labouring to effect their mischievous purposes *non vi sed saepe cadendo*; and therefore conceived that it might not be unprofitable to show how small a portion of talent and literature was necessary for carrying on the trade of sedition. The few specimens which we have selected of his ethics and his criticism are more than sufficient to prove that Mr Hazlitt's knowledge of Shakespeare and the English language is exactly on a par with the purity of his morals and the depth of his understanding.'

Hazlitt did not like being the subject of personal abuse any more than the next man, but he was prepared to endure it as a hazard of living a public life engaged in political and literary controversy. But when an attempt to disrupt his livelihood was made in the form of a backhanded assault on his morals, he became angry. The *Quarterly* attacked him because he was an eloquent and intelligent political radical, and he knew

perfectly well that their aim was to discredit him, to discolour his reputation and cheapen his work in the opinion of the public, with the eventual
aim of neutering or even silencing him. They did it not by addressing his
arguments and proving him wrong, but by attacking his character with
innuendo and derision. He held the editor of the *Quarterly*, William
Gifford, personally responsible. Goaded by Russell's review, he took
Gifford to task in the 14 June number of the *Examiner*. 'This little person,'
Hazlitt said of him, 'is a considerable cat's-paw; and so far worthy of some
notice. He is the *Government Critic*, a character nicely differing from that
of a government spy – the invisible link, that connects literature with the
police. It is his business to keep a strict eye over all writers who differ in
opinion with His Majesty's Ministers, and to measure their talents and
attainments by the standard of their servility and meanness. For this office
he is well qualified. – The Editor of the *Quarterly Review* is also Paymaster
of the Band of Gentlemen-Pensioners; and whenever an author comes
before him in the one capacity, with whom he is not acquainted in the
other, he knows how to deal with him. He has his cue beforehand. The
distinction between truth and falsity is lost on him; he knows only the
distinction between Whig and Tory. The same set of thread-bare common-
places, the same second-hand assortment of abusive nick-names, are
always repeated; and the ready convenient lie comes in aid of the lack of
other resources, and passes off, with impunity, in the garb of religion and
loyalty. He is under the protection of *the Court*; and his zeal for his King
and country gives him a right to say what he pleases of every public writer
who does not do all in his power to pamper the one into a tyrant, and to
trample the other into a herd of slaves.'[15]

Hunt was delighted by the piece. He wrote to Shelley in August to say
'Hazlitt has written a masterly character of Gifford, much more coolly
done than these things of his in general.' But Hazlitt had not finished with
Gifford. This was just a warming up. Six months later Hazlitt dealt with
Gifford at greater length, when the belated July 1818 number appeared in
January 1919 with its review of his poetry lectures.

Because of the success of the poetry lectures Hazlitt and the Surrey Institution readily agreed that he would do another series in the following
winter of 1818–19. In part to prepare for them, and in part to refresh
himself with country air and walking, Hazlitt went to Winterslow, lodging
at the inn called The Hut on the Salisbury road. He there immersed himself
in work, reading and thinking about the subject of the new lectures, which
was the history of literature in England since Shakespeare's time, other
than Shakespeare himself and poetry. He chose to discuss Jonson, the

Restoration dramatists, the periodical essayists of the eighteenth century, and that century's novelists – and, remarkably, Hogarth, whom Hazlitt included because, he said, whereas we *see* other artists' pictures, Hogarth's we *read*. Hazlitt was the first ever critic of visual forms of narrative other than theatre; had he lived in the age of cinema, television and comic books he would have been delighted by them. His unique qualifications as a critic – a philosopher who understood painting and literature – allowed him to recognize Hogarth's true avocation as a commentator on human nature, and a teller of tales which aptly reveal it.

Hazlitt was increasingly prone to nostalgia. As he read and walked in the familiar haunts of Winterslow his revisitings of the English authors prompted comparisons with other names marinated in associations with his youth and early hopes – Cervantes, Gil Blas, Rousseau, Molière, Rabelais. The death of his youthful hopes, and his anger at the perfidy of those who had once shared them, explains his nostalgia. Nostalgia was for Hazlitt a form of spiritual retreat; the past was his utopia, now that the future had no chance of becoming one.

The fact that Hazlitt stayed at The Hut in Winterslow is the first suggestion, in an otherwise silent record, that the Hazlitts' marriage was no longer working. After the death of their son John in 1816 Sarah, already scarcely visible in the letters and diaries that mention Hazlitt, becomes even less so. The likelihood is that she was spending more time in Winterslow, and that when Hazlitt began to stay at The Hut it was because they were no longer living together. Apart from his love for that part of England, Hazlitt naturally wished to see his son, so the pattern of his country visits began to focus on Winterslow again. That pattern always involved going for a few days to Bath and later to Crediton in Devon to which his parents and Peggy had moved, and then settling at an inn for part of the summer, to read and write. From now on the inn of choice was Winterslow Hut.

One powerful indication of marital trouble is an essay Hazlitt wrote in the summer of 1818 in the form of a Shaftesburian letter of advice to his son. One of its main themes is a pessimistic reflection on the matrimonial state. 'If you every marry,' Hazlitt wrote, 'I would wish you to marry the woman you like. Do not be guided by the recommendation of friends. Nothing will atone for or overcome an original distaste. It will only increase from intimacy.'[16] And again, in an essay written in the winter of 1821, he wrote, 'How few out of the infinite number of those that marry and are given in marriage, wed with those they would prefer to all the world; nay, how far the greater proportion are joined together by the mere motives of convenience, accident, recommendation of friends, or indeed not unfrequently by the very fear of the event, by repugnance and a sort of fatal fascination: yet the tie is for life, not to be shaken off but with disgrace or death: a man no longer lives to himself, but is a body (as well as a mind) chained to another, in spite of himself – "Like life and death in disproportion met." So Milton (perhaps from his own experience) makes Adam exclaim, in the vehemence of his despair,

> For either
> He shall never find out fit mate, but such
> As some misfortune brings him or mistake;
> Or whom he wishes most shall seldom gain
> Through her perverseness, but shall see her gain'd
> By a far worse; or if she love, withheld
> By parents; or his happiest choice too late
> Shall meet, already link'd and wedlock-bound
> To a fell adversary, his hate and shame;
> Which infinite calamity shall cause
> To human life, and household peace confound.'

The lines had proved apt in Hazlitt's case.

Before going to Winterslow Hazlitt sent two pieces to the *Edinburgh Magazine* and had his say, in the *Examiner*, on the public excitement which had broken out earlier in the year over the Westmoreland by-election campaign. That county's two parliamentary seats were in the pocket of the Earl of Lonsdale, who proposed to fill them in the Tory interest with his sons Lord Lowther and the Hon. Colonel Lowther. On the principle that parliamentary representation should not be a matter of family property, the radical MP and lawyer Henry Brougham went to Westmoreland to contest one of the seats. The great majority of Westmoreland's population supported him, and wore his colours, cheering him wherever he went. But none of them had the vote; the few Westmorelanders who figured on the electoral roll were in the Earl's pay. Among them was William Wordsworth, who campaigned on the Lowthers' behalf. 'The only way for a poet now-a-days to emerge from the obscurity of poverty and genius,' Hazlitt acidly remarked, 'is to prostitute his pen, turn pimp to a borough-mongering lord, canvass for him at elections, and by this means aspire to some importance, and be admitted on the same respectable footing with him as his valet, his steward, or his practising attorney.'[17]

Now, just as Hazlitt was returning to London from Winterslow, the long-range missile that *Blackwood's Magazine* had been preparing for him was launched, and struck him with a terrific detonation. It took the form of an attack on him in its August 1818 number, in an article entitled 'Hazlitt Cross-Questioned'. It was wholly unexpected, for in addition to the commendatory character of Patmore's reports of his lectures earlier in the year, Hazlitt had been coupled with Jeffrey in the pages of *Blackwood's* in an article in June, entitled 'Jeffrey and Hazlitt', which described them as the two foremost critics of the age.

'Hazlitt Cross-Questioned' was the work of Lockhart, writing as 'Z', aided by John Wilson, his partner in running the magazine. It contained allegations about the Keswick incident of 1803 that Wilson had learned from Wordsworth and saved for this occasion. By this time, as it happens, *Blackwood's* had turned on Wordsworth and reviled him in its pages; but scandal is no respecter of sources, and neither Lockhart nor Wilson was willing to ignore what they had learned from the poet just because they now enjoyed vilifying him as much as Hazlitt. These men – to give the measure of them – were capable of much, as witness this reply from one of them to critics of *Blackwood's* habitual scurrilities: 'Let execrations gurgle in your gullets, distended with the rising gorge of your blackest bile; belch out your bitter blackguardism lest you burst; clench your fists till your fretted palms are pierced with the jagged edge of nails bitten in impotent desperation; stamp, unclean beasts with cloven feet, on the fetid flags of your sty till the mire mounts to your mouths –' and so on.[18] The author of these words was Wilson; a couple of years later he was appointed Professor of Moral Philosophy at Edinburgh University.

The magazine's owner, William Blackwood, was an ambitious, coarse, envious man whose principal desire was to outdo his long-standing and far more successful rival Archibald Constable, owner and publisher of the *Edinburgh Magazine*, the *Encyclopaedia Britannica*, and the novels of Scott – and one of whose favourite authors was Hazlitt. Blackwood gave Wilson and Lockhart their heads, delighting in their attacks and puerilities. He had been John Murray's Edinburgh agent since 1811, despite not being to Murray's personal taste. In the event, 'Hazlitt Cross-Questioned' was destined to bring the relationship between Blackwood and Murray to an end.

The August 1818 edition of *Blackwood's* is equally famous for its attack on Keats, disguised as a review of his *Endymion*. Andrew Motion disputes the claims made by Keats's contemporaries, and universally believed thereafter, that the *Blackwood's* attack killed him. Shelley, for one example, wrote: 'Poor Keats was thrown into a dreadful state [by the review] ... the agony of his sufferings at length produced a rupture of a blood-vessel in the lungs [which led to] the usual process of consumption.' But Keats was much more robust than Shelley's account implies. He knew what reviews could be like and understood that partisan spleen lay behind this one.[19] In fact the attacks on Keats and Hazlitt were connected, as both representing the 'Cockney school' which *Blackwood's* had often before attacked, chiefly in the person of Leigh Hunt. The whole number is spiked with stabs at the 'Cockneys'; apart from the articles on each of Keats and Hazlitt, there is one on Lamb's recent publications, which, *Blackwood's* notes, contains not a single word on 'pimpled Hazlitt' nor his 'coxcomb lectures'. Several other articles carry pointed references to Hazlitt, cunningly indexed to charges laid in the 'Questions' constituting the main article.

*Blackwood's* employed spies to unearth personal details about those they wished to attack. They used this ploy against Hazlitt while preparing the 'Cross-Questioned' article. A young, enthusiastic, obsequious literary dilettante called Alexander Henderson was employed by the magazine to ferret for them when he visited London in the summer of 1818. Henderson managed to get Godwin to arrange an introduction to Hazlitt, who neither then nor later suspected that Henderson was sending reports about him to *Blackwood's* principals. He welcomed Henderson at York Street, and some years later sent him a volume of his travel writings. Henderson wrote to Blackwood, 'I shall get some curious news for you respecting the operations of the enemy from Hazlitt and Godwin.'[20]

The infamous article began in jesting mode. 'Mr Editor,' it said, 'In the course of your practice as a critical sportsman, you have already had the merit of discovering, winging, and bagging some new kinds of game. Upon one of these, your addition to the sphere of amusement, I beg leave heartily to congratulate you. I mean the wild, black-bill Hazlitt. You do not, I perceive, know what a paltry creature this is, otherwise you would have said more or less about him than you have done ... he is a mere quack, Mr Editor, and a mere book-maker; one of the sort that lounge in third-rate bookshops, and writes third-rate books.' Then the mood changed, and the questions began, in lawyer's style: '1. Mr William Hazlitt, ex-painter, theatrical critic, review essay and lecture manufacturer, London, Did you or did you not, in the course of your late Lectures on Poetry, & c., infamously vituperate and sneer at the character of Mr Wordsworth – I mean his personal character, his genius even you dare not deny. 2. Is it, or is it not, true that you owe all your ideas about poetry or criticism to gross misperceptions of the meaning of his conversation; and that you once owed your personal safety, perhaps existence, to the humane and firm interference of that virtuous man, who rescued you from the hands of an indignant peasantry, whose ideas of purity you, a cockney visitor, had dared to outrage?' – and so on six more times, alleging among other things that he called Desdemona a lewd woman, that Jeffrey had sacked him from the *Edinburgh Review*, that he did not know the Greek alphabet, or English grammar, or the Latin for Goose – which, since it is *anser*, was a clever enough pun to end on, and of course a challenge.

*Blackwood's* attacks on Wordsworth are here forgotten (they were resumed a year or two later), and the whole piece is an exercise in intentional defamation and damage. Part of the design was to hurt Constable also, by driving a wedge between him and Hazlitt; one of the allegations was that Hazlitt's contributions to the *Edinburgh Magazine* contain falsehoods and errors, thus harming the journal and embarrassing its managers. In its aim of hurting Hazlitt professionally, the attack partly succeeded, for Taylor and Hessey were so unnerved by it that they withdrew their offer of £200 for the copyright of the lectures on 'English Comic Writers', just about to be delivered at the Surrey Institution, on the grounds that 'the value of his literary estate was lessened'. When Hazlitt saw that the *Blackwood's* piece was interfering with his power of earning a living he did not hesitate a moment longer. He wrote to Blackwood demanding the name of his accuser; Blackwood refused to give it to him; whereupon Hazlitt began an action for £2000 damages in the Court of Session. Jeffrey, who was an advocate, agreed to act as his counsel in Edinburgh.

This swift and determined response unnerved Blackwood, but he tried to brazen his way through. Murray wrote in agitation and annoyance from London, and Blackwood replied defending Lockhart and blaming Constable for egging Hazlitt on. But Murray knew that the article had backfired. Practically everyone who read it disapproved. *The Times* reported Hazlitt's suit against *Blackwood's*, which it described as 'a book filled with private slander'. Murray told Blackwood that 'the clamour against [*Blackwood's* is] almost universal.' Blackwood replied that an even more powerful attack on Hazlitt would appear in October, blasting him out of the water entirely, for – said Blackwood – Hazlitt was only blustering in an effort to pick up a little money in damages.

Blackwood in fact seemed not to understand the gravity of the situation. Lockhart and Wilson sent Murray a long letter explaining that they had good grounds for their allegations, and that therefore if matters came to court they would win. At just that moment a pamphlet appeared – anonymously written, but not by Hazlitt – called 'Hypocrisy Unveiled, and Calumny Detected', which attacked *Blackwood's* and defended Hazlitt, saying that the magazine had set upon him because of his fame and the advantage enjoyed by their rival the *Edinburgh Magazine* in having him among its contributors. It also revealed other dealings of the magazine and its owner, including his failed attempts to gain government influence. Foolishly, Wilson and Lockhart sent a challenge to the author of the pamphlet, thus exposing their identities. The pamphlet's author forwarded their letter, with their names, to the newspapers, and the cat was out of the bag. Murray wrote in fury to Blackwood: 'Three fourths of the talent of the Bar are in hostility to you,' he said, 'any jury will be prejudiced against you.'

Murray now took matters into his own hands. It was clear that *Blackwood's* stood to accumulate losses – certainly in reputation, probably in court too – unless Hazlitt could be brought to terms. He opened negotiations with Hazlitt through intermediaries. Hazlitt agreed to an out-of-court settlement, and accepted £100 damages and payment of all his costs. Immediately afterwards Murray severed his connection with *Blackwood's*. There was no follow-up article on Hazlitt in October; indeed, *Blackwood's* became quiescent for a while, not just on the subject of Hazlitt but in political and literary controversy in general. It concentrated on the autumn's hot weather and other such topics instead. Several years went by before its editors dared attack Hazlitt again. But some of the dirt they had flung stuck, as is always the case; towards the end of the year imitators in the *New Monthly Magazine* began calling Hazlitt a 'cankered Cockney', a 'pimpled coxcomb', and the 'dirty dandy of literature'. A decade later, in his published conversations with Northcote, Hazlitt wryly remarked, 'All the former part of my life I was treated as a cipher; and since I have got into notice, I have been set upon as a wild beast.'[21]

Hazlitt had, naturally enough, wished to answer 'Z', and wrote a detailed and dignified reply to the allegations, sending it to Jeffrey as a brief should the matter come to court. He might have contemplated publishing it also, but in the end did not.

Because Hazlitt had a pale clear complexion, the epithet 'pimpled' was a source of puzzlement then as later. The writers of *Blackwood's* on one occasion said that, since the adjective did not describe his face, it must describe his mind. The remarks about the supposed 'coxcombery' of his language was an attack on his style. The *New Monthly Magazine*'s use of these adjectives and others like 'cankered' show that they are intended to suggest sexual immorality. If the *New Monthly Magazine* hoped to gain publicity by being the subject of one of Hazlitt's famous counter-attacks, they were disappointed, for he ignored them.

Under the brooding peaks of the Lakes there had been an uncomfortable flutter. It was one thing to undermine Hazlitt privately, spreading stories and letting others make use of them to damage his character and his career;

but it was another to be publicly involved, and expected to speak in open court. 'Southey and Wordsworth may be troubled to give their evidence to the truth of the assertions in the article which would be very disagreeable,' wrote Sarah Coleridge from Keswick. 'W. spoke of it here last week and seemed vexed that his name was connected with the thing in any way.'[22] His 'connection with the thing' was that he was the source of its worst part; italicize 'name' in Sarah Coleridge's last sentence and you have a picture of the man.

'Man is the only animal that laughs and weeps, for he is the only animal that is struck with the difference between what things are, and what they ought to be.' So began Hazlitt on the evening of Tuesday 3 November 1818 in commencing his new series of lectures. The success of the previous winter's series guaranteed the success of this; the Surrey Institution's hall was filled by large admiring audiences, with here and there someone who hissed at his more controversial remarks, thereby inviting his usual response, which was to repeat the hissed passage, reading it more emphatically. This happened when he made a passing criticism of Byron, who was a favourite with many in the audience. He told them, 'If my Lord Byron will do these things, he must take the consequences.' As before, a commendatory running report was given of the lectures, this time by Keats's friend Reynolds in the pages of the *Edinburgh Magazine*. When the series ended on Tuesday 5 January 1819, the *Morning Chronicle* said 'Mr Hazlitt's reputation stood already high with the public; but we are mistaken if these Lectures will not add to it. He displayed the same boldness and originality of thinking; the same critical acuteness, eloquence, and felicity of expression for which his Lectures on the poets were so eminently distinguished. From the character which Mr Hazlitt has by universal assent acquired, of being one of the ablest and most eloquent critics of our nation (we may say of any nation) much was of course expected from the employment of his talents on a branch of literature, in which the genius of our countrymen shines perhaps with more distinguished lustre than in any other; but the warm applause which he received throughout his course of lectures from his numerous and respectable audiences, sufficiently proved that their expectations were amply realised.' Bewick and Talfourd left corroborating reports, but Crabb Robinson did not enjoy this series as much as the last.

The lectures were published in March by Taylor and Hessey – Hazlitt had accepted a lower sum from them for the copyright because of the *Blackwood's* affair – but he was able to tell Jeffrey that the copyright and the lectures themselves had cleared 200 guineas for him, with which he was reasonably satisfied. Despite his recurring money worries Hazlitt's earnings were considerable; at a rough estimate he was making £400 a year and more. But he never saved, and was always in debt and always in need of advances. He was in the habit of giving money to his son William the younger with the injunction to spend it all before nightfall, so that the boy could learn liberal ways. Sarah did not approve of the spendthrift philosophy this embodied, but at least she had a small income of her own.

One likely reason why Hazlitt always got through his money so quickly was that he regularly sent sums to his parents and Peggy, perhaps indeed even supported them to a degree. Apart from his obvious filial sense, disbursements of this kind are required to explain how he managed to spend so much, for his only known extravagance was the employment of prostitutes. He did not drink or gamble, and although he dressed well and travelled on the inside of the coach when there were seats available – the expensive option – there is nothing else that could have readily absorbed what was relatively speaking a large income for the day.

Hazlitt's lectures were repeated at the Crown and Anchor in the Strand in January and February. Hazlitt did not write much for the periodicals while lecturing, although one of the few essays dating from these months came to be a classic: his affectionate obituary of the great fives player John Cavanagh. It appeared in a March number of the *Examiner*. But he had another task in hand: in January, as noted above (see page 233), the belated July 1818 issue of the *Quarterly Review* appeared, with its violent attack on him and his *Lectures on the English Poets*. Having dealt satisfactorily with *Blackwood's Magazine*, Hazlitt decided to deal with the *Quarterly*. He did it not by suing, but by publishing a 'Letter to William Gifford Esq.' in pamphlet form, which came out at the beginning of March. 'Sir, – You have a nasty trick of saying what is not true of any one you do not like; and it will be the object of this letter to cure you of it. You say what you please of others: it is time you were told what you are.' After this beginning Hazlitt rehearses and considerably expands his *Examiner* article of the previous summer, dismantling Gifford and the *Quarterly*'s criticisms of Hazlitt's work as if with a scalpel and a hammer at the same time. Keats delightedly copied whole pages of it to send to his brother George in America, commenting 'The manner in which this is managed, the force and innate power with which it yeasts and works itself up ... is in a style of genius.' Leigh Hunt, equally delighted, reviewed it over two numbers of the *Examiner* (7 and 14 March): 'We said a little while since, that if the creature yclept Gifford did not take care, he would be picked up by the fingers of some person indignant of his perpetual creeping malice, and held out to the loathing eyes of the community, sprawling and shrieking. Here he is. Mr Hazlitt has got him fast by the ribs, forcing him, with various ingenuity of grip, to display unwillingly all the deformities of his moral structure.' Hazlitt included Gifford in his *Spirit of the Age* some years later, and benefiting from the further meditation on his character permitted by the passage of time, gave a masterly and stinging account of him, beginning 'Mr Gifford was originally bred to some handicraft: he afterwards contrived to learn Latin, and was for some time an usher in a school, till he became a tutor in a nobleman's family. The low-bred, self-taught man, the pedant, and the dependant on the great contribute to form the Editor of the *Quarterly Review*. He is admirably qualified for this situation, which he has held for some years, by a happy combination of defects, natural and acquired; and in the event of his death, it will be difficult to provide him a suitable successor.'[23]

One of those who attended the lectures on the comic writers was the radical publisher William Hone, who, in partnership with the satirical cartoonist George Cruikshank, was proving an effective scourge of the government. Hazlitt offered Hone the copyright of a collection of his political essays, and Hone accepted. The contract was drawn up and signed on 25 January 1819, Hazlitt getting £100 in two instalments, and Hone getting a promise to have all the copy within a week. This bold offer from Hazlitt, given that the essays fill over four hundred pages, with a new Preface of nearly forty pages, suggests that he had been sorting and preparing his political essays for some time, and that the projected volume was in an advanced state of readiness.

The decision to publish the essays in volume form was a significant one for Hazlitt. It was his farewell to political controversy. After the wearing political struggles of the last few years, and the sinking of his hopes with Napoleon, he had decided to write no more on the subject. Collecting his political essays was therefore a way of marking his withdrawal from the fray. It also marked the beginning of a lasting friendship: Hazlitt and Hone admired each other and found each other's company congenial. Hazlitt applauded Hone's courage in facing prosecution for his political beliefs and for defying the censorship laws. Hone had just survived two trials in a court presided over by the hated Lord Ellenborough, who as Edward Law had been one of the prosecuting counsel against Horne Tooke in 1794, and who had sent the Hunt brothers to prison in 1813. Hone ably defended himself in long speeches to the jury; Ellenborough summed up against him in a highly tendentious manner, but the jury acquitted Hone – whereupon Ellenborough resigned in rage and despair, and died not long afterwards. Hone's supporters raised over £3000 for his defence fund. Hone, for his part, applauded Hazlitt's genius, and had already published Hazlitt's 'Preface, suitable to Recent Circumstances' which introduced Hone's pirated edition of Southey's *Wat Tyler*.

Despite Hazlitt's swiftness in giving Hone the manuscript for the collection, it did not appear until August 1819. In saying goodbye to political controversy in the Preface, Hazlitt gave a statement of the credo which had guided him throughout: 'I am no politician, and still less can I be said to be a party-man; but I have a hatred of tyranny, and contempt for its tools; and this feeling I have expressed as often and as strongly as I could. I cannot sit quietly down under the claims of barefaced power, and I have tried to expose the little arts of sophistry by which they are defended. I have no mind to have my person made a property of, nor my understanding made a dupe of. I deny that liberty and slavery are convertible terms, that right and wrong, truth and falsehood, plenty and famine, the comforts or wretchedness of a people, are a matter of perfect indifference. This is all I know of the matter; but on these points I am likely to remain incorrigible.'[24] He also took the opportunity to explain his loyalty to Napoleon. 'If Buonaparte was a conqueror, he conquered the grand conspiracy of kings against the abstract right of the human race to be free; and I, as a man, could not be indifferent which side to take. If he was ambitious, his greatness was not founded on the unconditional, avowed surrender of the rights of human nature. But with him, the state of man rose too. If he was arbitrary and a tyrant, first, France as a country was in a state of military blockade, on garrison-duty, and not to be defended by mere paper bullets of the brain; secondly, but chief, he was not, nor could not become, a tyrant by divine right. Tyranny in him was not sacred: it was not eternal: it was not instinctively bound in a league of amity with other tyrannies; it was not sanctioned by all the laws of religion and morality.'[25]

Hazlitt quitted the political quarrel of the age just before it moved into the last and grossest act of the oppression which, from the early 1790s, had kept radical and reforming movements in Britain firmly under restraint. These movements were never completely submerged, and even during the war expressions of popular disquiet, such as the Luddite riots, had broken out despite the government's harsh measures to contain them. When it became clear that the end of hostilities in 1815 did not mean an end to high rates of unemployment and high food prices (kept artificially raised by the Corn Laws to protect landowners' incomes), the country's various strands of political dissent grew more vociferous, all the way from poorly organized working-class groups at one end of the spectrum to the Whigs in Parliament at the other. To some extent the government of

Lord Liverpool – he, Lord Castlereagh and Lord Sidmouth made a grim triumvirate of reaction at the government's head – was itself responsible for the worst excesses of the radicals, for they employed large numbers of spies and *agents provocateurs* to inflame mass meetings and prompt them to violence, thus giving the government an excuse for savage policing and the continuance of draconian laws. Although habeas corpus had been restored in 1817, after much pressure from the opposition in Parliament and the country, the government had no intention of instituting a liberal regime, or tolerating challenges to its authority. So when a mass meeting of radical and reform groups was organized for 16 August 1819, to be held in St Peter's Fields in Manchester, Lord Sidmouth at the Home Office sanctioned the deployment of the 15th Hussars together with the yeomanry, made up of local sons of mill owners and minor gentry, to police it. The result was the tragic event known as Peterloo, when six hundred people were hurt and eleven killed by a cavalry charge ordered by the local magistrates, who wished to teach the radicals a lesson by breaking up the meeting and arresting the speakers on the platform. There was a crowd of between sixty and eighty thousand in the Fields that day, a vast gathering for the time; and if we think (as J. B. Priestley suggests) that the figures should be multiplied by twenty to give a comparison with how it would seem if, today, troops were sent to disperse a demonstration, the result would be 220 dead and twenty thousand injured.

The outcry that followed was universal. Even *The Times*, usually on the government's side, was critical. Its owner (and now editor too) John Walter II took pride in his stance on this occasion, which provoked Hazlitt's only comment on the Peterloo Massacre. 'Mr Walter's hair stands on end, and he is in a perfect cold-sweat at the sacrifices and dangers he has been exposed to in making head against the abuses of power. He gives one desperate instance. He ventured to condemn "the Manchester massacre" – a measure that only one man in the three kingdoms was forward to applaud. Yet with public opinion at his back, with popular clamour, with the indignant scorn of all "the honest and independent part of the community" directed against this illegal, unmanly, and indecent outrage, the Editor looks back with horror at the dangers that beset him.'[26]

While the tragedy of Peterloo was first looming and then happening in the summer of 1819, Hazlitt was again at Winterslow, and again – apart from his family concerns – his purpose was to prepare a set of lectures. He and the Surrey Institution had agreed on a third series, under the title 'Lectures on the Dramatic Literature of the Age of Elizabeth'. Another new friend, Barry Cornwall, was an enthusiast in this field, and so was Charles Lamb.

They each had extensive collections of relevant books, so Hazlitt borrowed from them both and took a small library to Winterslow Hut. He was annoyed there by servants of the inn questioning whether he got any good from so much reading, and whether anyone should be allowed to make a living just by reading and writing. His irritation manifested itself as an article in the *Examiner* complaining – yet again – about the stupidity, narrowness, ignorance and temerity of country-folk.

But walking in the summer sunlight along familiar ways with William the younger, lying reading for hours on a bank on Salisbury Plain or in the woods about Winterslow village, brought some of the happiness of his youth back, as it always did. 'After a long walk through unfrequented tracks, after starting the hare from the fern, or hearing the wing of the raven rustling over my head, or being greeted by the woodsman's "stern goodnight" as he strikes into his narrow homeward path, I can "take mine ease at mine inn", beside the blazing hearth, and shake hands with Signor Orlando Friscobaldo, as the oldest acquaintance I have. Ben Jonson, learned Chapman, Master Webster, and Master Heywood, are there; and seated round, discourse the silent hours away.' Hazlitt wrote in this lecture that his first loyalty was to nature, and his second to books; for the latter are 'nearest to our thoughts: they wind into the heart: the poet's verse slides into the current of our blood. We read them when young, we remember them when old. We read there what has happened to others; we feel that it has happened to ourselves.' For this reason he could be content to spend his days walking in the country, his evenings with a book by the fire. 'I should have no objection to pass my life in this manner out of the world, not thinking of it, or it of me; neither abused by my enemies, nor defended by my friends; careless of the future, but sometimes dreaming of the past, which might as well be forgotten!'[27] In these moods of nostalgia, when he envisaged a perfect tranquillity of retreat, he forgot the one thing that he otherwise always regretted: the absence of a companion – a companion of the spirit – to share it with.

Hazlitt could try to forget his cares when he went to the country, but he could not leave money troubles behind. In September, still at Winterslow, he received a message from John Hunt asking him to settle a £50 bill which Hunt had endorsed on his behalf some time before. Hazlitt quickly wrote to Jeffrey: 'I blush when I sit down to write this letter. But you some time ago said if I wanted it and would send to you for another £100, you would let me have it. It would at this present moment interpose between me and almost ruin.'[28] Jeffrey obliged, and the difficulty passed. Before going to the country Hazlitt had been pushed to some unhappy expedients for money, one of which was the sale of his copies of Louvre pictures to Haydon for £50 (he asked £40 but Haydon magnanimously said they were worth more) and of his treasured *Old Woman* to John Hunt. Hunt so liked this picture that when, a couple of years later, he was again sent to prison for publishing what the government disliked, he took it with him and put it up in his cell. Haydon said of Hazlitt's pictures: 'They are not artistic, but as if done by a literary man with great feeling for the beauties of High Art.'

In August Hone published Hazlitt's *Political Essays*, and the reviews were predictably divided on party lines. Gifford in the *Quarterly* took revenge in the same entomological vein as Hunt, treating Hazlitt as an unpleasant glittering black insect which he was noticing only out of interest in what the recent heats had produced, by way of a plague of such things with their 'dirt' and 'noise'. Hazlitt is, he said, 'a slanderer of the human race'. It bears saying again how remarkable it is that all of the vituperation Hazlitt received is *ad hominem*, scarcely any effort being made to engage with his arguments, still less to refute them. Hostile reviews of all his books took this form, irrespective of content, but it is most noticeable in the Tory press's response to the *Political Essays* – a fact all the more striking given that, by their nature, they offered an opportunity for opponents to put the countervailing case, if they had one. The *Anti-Jacobin Review* was so incensed by the volume that it called for censorship and the strongest punishment of the law, meaning that Hazlitt should be sent to prison. That authors then risked prison for what they wrote, as happened to the Hunts and Hone among others, was a consideration that never made Hazlitt temporize or keep silence. Because he abominated the use of religion to bolster tyranny, his political strictures enraged those of orthodox sentiments in the Church, who branded him a blasphemer. The reviewer in the *Anti-Jacobin* thought that placing the press under the control of the police would be preferable to letting Hazlitt publish his 'libels against the Christian religion' and other scurrilities.

The *Monthly Magazine*, which was on Hazlitt's side of the argument, saw in the essays 'the strong hand of truth and critical sagacity', and it forgave their polemical ferocity, saying they 'severely handled the corruption, tergiversation, and interested motives of public character, wherever they have appeared; and this in an alternate indignant and satiric vein that, independent of its truth, baffles all the frivolous sophism and mysticism even of a *Quarterly Review*.' The *Champion* was likewise laudatory, saying that the essays were marked with 'all the spirit, the energy and the eccentricity of this very extraordinary writer', and that the book 'abounds with striking beauties and nervous peculiarities of composition'.

Hazlitt's third set of lectures began on Guy Fawkes Day 1819 at the Surrey Institution. They were monitored in an admiring sequence of reports by John Hunt in the *Examiner*. Crabb Robinson made grudging comments about them, complaining that neither of Hazlitt's second or third lecture series matched the first. The lectures were published the following February by Richard Stodart and were well reviewed, most critics repeating the familiar litany of praises for Hazlitt's astuteness. There were reservations about the way he had organized the material; but it was a deliberate feature of Hazlitt's method to write, and to lecture, as if he were a dinner guest invited to speak his mind on a given topic, and therefore he allowed the digressive and evolutionary spirit of informal discourse to direct his remarks, as part of their attraction to the open-minded listener. One critic, in the *Monthly Review*, thought his manner verged too much on mannerism: 'He presents himself as before; he persists in the swimming walk and spangled shoes, and pushes elegance of step almost to affectation; he advances in the same luxurious dress, in which the flowers of fancy, the jewels of allusion, the tinsel of conceit, and the ribbands of sentiment, mingle in gay embroidery, with too much ostentation to be either entirely unheeded or entirely approved.' The passage is almost worthy of Hazlitt himself. John Scott, once editor of the *Champion* and once motivated by Wordsworth to attack Hazlitt in print, was now in charge of the newly launched *London Magazine*, and commended Hazlitt's originality, his 'comprehension of innate character, absolutely unequalled by any of his contemporaries ... [his] finer and more philosophical taste than any other critic on poetry and art ... [his] intense feeling of the pathetic, the pure, the sublime, in quality, action, and form'. In an apposite comment on Hazlitt's struggles with his opponents in the periodical press, the *Monthly Magazine* remarked: 'We may safely appeal to the judgment of the literary public whether the articles contained in the *Quarterly Review* upon similar subjects, are at all comparable in the enlightened spirit of truth, and critical discrimination which abound in the single volume before us.'

It has to be asked whether these positive contemporary judgements of Hazlitt's gifts as a writer and critic are worth much, or whether they should be discounted on grounds of the hyperbole of the time, the zealousness of party spirit, and the rudimentary, amateur, and unscholarly state of literary criticism as it then existed. After all, reading Hazlitt now on these subjects is an experience quite different from reading academic criticism of the last century or so, and especially of the Post-modern era.[29] The answer lies in the respect in which the Shakespeare critic A. C. Bradley held Hazlitt, and in George Saintsbury's comment that 'To anyone who has made a little progress in criticism for himself, to anyone who has either read for himself or is capable of reading for himself, of being guided by what is helpful and of neglecting what is not, there is no greater critic than Hazlitt in any language . . . he is the critic's critic as Spenser is the poet's poet.'[30] Saintsbury wrote before the twentieth-century turn to academic criticism, whose source, as David Bromwich perceptively remarks, is not Hazlitt but Coleridge, and which, in making and continually widening the gulf between 'the world of journalism, where new literature is fostered or starved, and the world of scholarship, where old literature is interpreted and canonized,' is not concerned with taste, but with technique;[31] not with the common readers' or viewers' response to books read or plays or paintings seen, and their connection with life as lived, but with specialist academic interest in methods and classifications, schools and '–isms', unconscious influences, supposed hidden meanings, patriarchal oppressions, deconstruction of texts, and multiple readings. For Hazlitt this latter enterprise would have seemed futile pedantry. Literature, theatre, art and philosophy were in his view matters of direct concern to the experience of life; they made a practical difference; therefore they were to be encountered, and evaluated, and responded to, not only with discrimination and thought, but with feeling. They were to be tested on the pulses, and everything they taught of character and the human condition made a difference to the perceiver's heart and mind. This is not to say that Hazlitt was a utilitarian; *very* far from it, for he despised the view that something could only qualify as art if it had some usefulness other than its value to the quality of the experience – the life – that encountered it. In this Hazlitt anticipates Pater, whose remark that 'it is only the dulness of the eye that makes any two things seem alike' is pure essence of Hazlitt.

For an assessment of Hazlitt as a critic nothing compares with David Bromwich's fine study.[32] One large inference that can be drawn from it is that Hazlitt's contemporary reviewers accurately reflect his power, and remind us of the much he has to offer. Wherever discussion of literature and the arts is addressed to an audience beyond the recent cabalization and Balkanization of academic speciality, where don speaks only to don – with the sole aim of lengthening a publications list by disagreeing with other dons – Hazlitt's name occurs, without need of introduction or apology, as one of the most distinguished voices on the topic in hand.[33] This is the true mark of lasting value.

*

Hazlitt did not repeat the lectures in the Strand as with the previous two series. They ended on a very tired note. 'In youth we borrow patience from our future years: the spring of hope gives us courage to act and suffer. A cloud is upon our upward path, and we fancy that all is sunshine beyond it. The prospect seems endless, because we do not know the end of it. We think that life is long, because art is so, and that, because we have much to do, it is well worth doing: or that no exertions can be too great, no sacrifices too painful, to overcome the difficulties we have to encounter ... But as we approach the goal, we draw in the reins; the impulse is less, as we have not so far to go; as we see objects nearer, we become less sanguine in the pursuit: it is not the despair of not attaining, so much as knowing there is nothing worth obtaining, and the fear of having nothing left even to wish for, that damps our ardour, and relaxes our efforts; and if the mechanical habit did not increase the facility, would, I believe, take away all inclination or power to do any thing. We stagger on the few remaining paces to the end of our journey; make perhaps one final effort; and are glad when our task is done.'[34] It is a fitting note for the last lecture he ever gave, and it seemed to have even more of a valedictory air given his recent decision to withdraw from political battles too. He had made his reputation – at a great cost. He could not of course know that something catastrophic was about to happen in his life, nor that later judges would say that the very best of his work was yet to come. But so it was; and the catastrophe came first, preparing the way for the work that followed.

# CHAPTER TWELVE

# Love and Disaster

## 1820–1823

IN THE WINTER of 1819–20, on the unexceptionable grounds of non-payment of rent, Jeremy Bentham evicted William Hazlitt from 19 York Street. The commonplace air of this transaction is singularly at odds with the significance for literary history of the parties and the place. Bentham and Hazlitt never met, and the former, such was his abstraction from the world, quite likely did not know that his tenant was a famous literary lion. During the Alliance's celebrations in 1814 the Tsar of All The Russias had, after all, been obliged to come to Bentham – like Muhammad to the mountain – and not the other way round, for the great utilitarian was as remote from the society he was busy trying to reform as Pluto from the sun. And Bentham was no more impressed by the fact that 19 York Street had once been Milton's home than he was by the reputation of his current tenant. What he did or did not do with his lettable property was governed solely by considerations of utility. If evidence were needed that Hazlitt was in difficulties over money, at least the eviction confirms the fact.

It was another severe winter, as bad if not worse than the winter of 1814 when a Frost Fair was held on the Thames and Kean made his début as Shylock. The weather might have been implicated in January's two royal deaths: that of the Duke of York, young and apparently well at fifty-three, who had seemed to have no worse than a cold and – much more significantly – that of his father, the half-forgotten mad old King George III. 'In consequence of [these] two great public calamities,' was Hazlitt's only, but venomously ironic, remark, 'the theatres were closed for some weeks together.'[1]

Hazlitt was once stopped on his way home, while still living in West-minster, by a crowd of people waiting in Horse Guards Parade to see the Duke of York. They were 'some of the lowest and most wretched of the people,' he recalled, there to gratify their need to admire the famous. They came to see the Commander in Chief of the British Army, who had led the troops at Dunkirk, and who earlier had been the subject of a great scandal in which his mistress sold army commissions that she had wheedled out of him in bed. At this time he was heir-presumptive after the Regent. But all that the crowd saw when this 'metaphysical and political abstraction' at last emerged, said Hazlitt, was 'a ruddy face and a frock-coat.'[2]

The old King's death, in the irrational way of these things, provoked a large public response of sympathy and grief. It meant of course that the Prince Regent had at last become George IV. When news of his father's death reached him he too was ill in bed, with pleurisy, being 'cupped' by his physicians, who reported that they cured him by letting 50 ounces of his blood. In one respect at least the news was most unwelcome to him, for it meant trouble with his estranged wife, the embarrassing and vexatious Princess Caroline of Brunswick, who had always stated her determination to become Queen when he became King, and whom he now, rightly, expected to make trouble.

The Caroline affair annoyed Hazlitt because of what it showed about the public mind. Caroline had been living on the Continent since 1814, making a spectacle of herself. Plump and in her forties with dyed black hair, she dressed in transparent *décolleté* and short skirts that showed her fat white legs, and she danced and flirted as she travelled around Europe, eventually taking as her lover one Bartolomeo Bergami, who in addition to warming her bed served as manager of her entourage, which soon therefore contained a dozen of his relatives. Caroline went where English tourists went, with the express intention of making sure that news of her doings reached the Prince Regent and embarrassed him. Lady Bessborough – herself no model of virtue – was scandalized by her at a ball in Genoa: 'I cannot tell you how sorry and ashamed I felt as an Englishwoman,' she wrote home. 'The first thing I saw in the room was a short, fat, elderly woman, with an extremely red face (owing, I suppose, to the heat) in a girl's white frock looking dress, but with shoulder, back and neck, quite low (disgustingly so) down to the middle of her stomach; very black hair and eyebrows, which gave her a fierce look, and a wreath of light pink roses on her head.' Caroline nodded at Lady Bessborough, who did not recognize her at first and tried to ignore her, until her husband whispered 'Do you not see the Princess of Wales nodding to you?'

Determined to make a scene, Caroline set off for England as soon as news of the old King's death reached her. The new King was equally determined to get rid of her, and immediately instructed his ministers to find a way. Using the evidence of adultery collected by their spies, the government set about arranging a divorce by Act of Parliament.

The resulting débâcle, known to history as 'the trial of Queen Caroline', reinforced Hazlitt's view that 'Mankind are an incorrigible race. Give them but bugbears and idols – it is all that they ask.'³ When Caroline arrived in England she was fêted by everyone opposed to George IV – from ordinary folk to Opposition politicians. Her 'trial' was not a trial in the ordinary sense but a debate in the House of Lords over a Bill of Pains and Penalties aimed at ending the marriage and thereby barring her accession as Queen Consort. Nevertheless it took the form of a trial, with counsel addressing the House on either side of the question. Henry Brougham, who had served as Caroline's attorney while she travelled abroad, now undertook her defence. As the debate unfolded through the autumn Caroline's house at Kew became a centre of pilgrimage for enormous crowds. Livery companies made loyal addresses to her from barges in the river, and – a sight to sicken Hazlitt's eyes – radicals of long standing knelt to 'sip loyalty', as he put it, from the back of her hand. 'Mr Place, Mr Hone, Mr Thelwall, Sir Richard Phillips, kissed Her Majesty's hand; Mr Cobbett alone was not invited, – it was thought he might *bite*,' he wrote.⁴

The whole country was avid in following the event. For Hazlitt both the nature of the affair and the attention it commanded were a sad comment on the character of public debate. 'The Queen's trial gave a deathblow to the hopes of all reflecting persons with respect to the springs and issues of public spirit and opinion,' he said. 'It was the only question I ever knew that excited a thorough popular feeling. It struck its roots into the heart of the nation; it took possession of every house or cottage in the kingdom; man, woman, and child took part in it, as if it had been their own concern. Business was laid aside for it; people forgot their pleasures, even their meals were neglected, nothing was thought of but the fate of the Queen's trial. The arrival of the *Times Newspaper* was looked upon as an event in every village, the Mails hardly travelled fast enough; and he who had the latest intelligence in his pocket was considered as the happiest of mortals. It kept the town in a ferment for several weeks: it agitated the country to the remotest corner.' What Hazlitt chiefly regretted was that this degree and intensity of public feeling had been prompted by such a trivial matter. 'The public mind was electrical. So it should be on other occasions; it was only so on this. An individual may be oppressed, a nation may be trampled upon, mankind may be threatened with the annihilation of their rights, and the threat enforced; and not a finger is raised, not a heart sinks, not a pulse beats quicker.'⁵ The uselessness of hoping that things might be otherwise was the chief reason he gave up writing about politics.

The Bill failed, so Caroline 'won'; she was given a pension of £70,000 a year and a royal residence to live in. When she went to St Paul's to give thanks – a proceeding pointedly boycotted by the senior clergy – vast mobs cheered her en route. 'What was it then in the Queen's cause that stirred this mighty "coil and pudder" in the breast?' asked Hazlitt. 'Was it the love of truth, of justice, of liberty? No such thing! Her case was at best doubtful, and she had only suffered the loss of privileges peculiar to herself. But she was a Queen, she was a woman, and *a thorn in the King's side*. There was the cant of loyalty, the cant of gallantry, and the cant of freedom mixed altogether in a delightful and inextricable confusion.' And Hazlitt could not forbear remarking that within a very short time the new King, so unpopular while Caroline was being fêted, was in his own turn loudly cheered when he entered his box at the theatre, as if nothing had happened and he was 'not only the most graceful man in his dominions, but the best of monarchs and of husbands.'[6] So the brouhaha had been for nothing, except to prove the fickleness, the shortness of memory, and the vacuity of the mass mind.

While the public had these excitements to occupy them Hazlitt was otherwise engaged. At the end of February 1820 he went down to the West Country to see his family at Crediton, and then, on the way back, to stay with John Hunt in Somersetshire.[7] His family visit was made despite exceptionally bad winter weather, suggesting a moment of emergency in the health of William senior, then aged 82.

In staying with John Hunt in Somersetshire Hazlitt was visiting that county for the first time since his sojourn with Coleridge at Nether Stowey. John Hunt continued to be a favourite with Hazlitt. He was a man who, in his principles and actions – and despite welcoming most opportunities to strike at the monarchy – was the very opposite of those radicals who fawned around Queen Caroline during her 'trial'. Hazlitt dedicated his *Political Essays* to him with the words, 'To John Hunt Esq. The tried, steady, zealous, and conscientious advocate of the liberty of his country, and the rights of mankind – One of those few persons who are what they would be thought to be; sincere without offence, firm but temperate; uniting private worth to public principle; a friend in need, a patriot without an eye to himself; who never betrayed an individual or a cause that he pretended to serve – in short, that rare character, a man of common sense and common honesty – This volume is respectfully and gratefully inscribed by THE AUTHOR'. In praising him in these terms Hazlitt was of course giving the world another taste of his opinion about people who betrayed individuals and causes; but the dedication was sincerely meant. Indeed a large part of the reason for Hazlitt's loyalty to the *Examiner* was his regard for John Hunt. He liked and admired Leigh Hunt, though he knew his limitations, and the two of them had their fallings-out at times. But he was not as close a friend of Leigh Hunt as he was of John Hunt. In the records left by keepers of diaries and writers of letters, Hazlitt is seen more often at Leigh Hunt's hospitable table than at John Hunt's, not because he was in fact so but because John Hunt was a quieter man than his brother, less gregarious, a less brilliant conversationalist, and less often host to the likes of Keats and Haydon; and therefore less present in the records they kept.

The steady zeal of John Hunt in the interest of reform, and the rationale behind Hazlitt's decision to withdraw from political controversy, was thrown into relief this February by the farce and tragedy of the Cato Street Conspiracy. A group of politically radical working men, gathered under the leadership of one Arthur Thistlewood, planned to murder the entire Cabinet as it sat at dinner. Thistlewood was an ex-soldier who had served as a volunteer officer in the French republican army. He recognized that Peterloo and the ensuing collapse of the radical movement meant that oppression was winning and reform was in retreat. He therefore decided that desperate measures were required, in the form of one mighty blow that would rouse the whole country. When a government spy called Edwards persuaded the group to deliver such a blow by murdering the Cabinet *en masse*, Thistlewood and his fellow-conspirators eagerly agreed.

They were led into a trap. The putative Cabinet dinner was a bait; notice of it was inserted in the newspapers although no such event was planned. The conspirators were arrested, and their leaders were first hanged and then decapitated in public – or would have been, had not the crowd begun to boo and hiss when the decapitations started. The rest of the gang were transported. It was suspected then, and has been proved since, that incitement by government spies was a stratagem to keep the public hostile towards radicals, and to boost the government – in this case, helping it to win the election of 1820 which followed soon after the Cato Street trials. The ploy worked, for Lord Liverpool's government was returned to office. Not long after the election John Hunt was again locked up, this time for a year, for publishing Byron's attack on the recently deceased King George III. Hazlitt thought the Cato Street affair a shabby put-up job. Had he still been writing about politics he would doubtless have returned to his strictures on the spy system, in a *Morning Chronicle* article of 1817, where he pilloried the government for its use of *agents provocateurs*: 'Lord Castlereagh, in the debate some evenings ago, appeared in a new character, and mingled with his usual stock of political commonplaces, some lively moral paradoxes, after a new French pattern. According to his Lordship's comprehensive and liberal views, the liberty and independence of nations are best supported abroad by the point of a bayonet; and morality, religion, and social order, are best defended at home by spies and informers. It is a pretty system, and worthy of itself from first to last ... Lord Castlereagh may say with *Lingo* in the play, who boasts that "he is not a scholar but a master of scholars," that he is not a spy, but a creator of spies and informers – not a receiver, but a distributor of blood-money – not a travelling companion and scurvy accomplice in the forging of sham treasons and accommodation plots, but head of the town-firm established for that purpose – not the dupe or agent of the treason hatched by others, but chief mover and instigator of the grand plot for increasing the power of the Sovereign, by hazarding the safety of his person.'[8]

Hazlitt was back in London by 25 March when Haydon's picture *Christ's Entry into Jerusalem* was exhibited. Hazlitt and Keats went together to see it – and to admire their own portraits, included in it along with those of Wordsworth and Haydon himself. Haydon wrote in his diary that Hazlitt and Keats were 'really rejoicing' as they looked at his picture. Hazlitt was indeed pleased that the painting was finished, for it had taken Haydon many years; but he thought it no more than 'the foundation, not the superstructure of a first-rate work of art. It is a rude outline, a striking and masterly sketch'. But it had, he said, 'spirit, conception, force, and effect,' and Haydon was 'a young artist of great promise'. While Hazlitt and Keats were looking at the picture the Persian Ambassador arrived, and announced to his train that he liked the elbow of a soldier in the lower part of the canvas. Haydon was afraid that Christ's head would attract criticism, for he had given it a pale, modern, troubled face, quite unlike traditional representations. When the great actress Mrs Siddons arrived a hush fell on the room. She inspected Christ, and announced, 'It is a triumph.' Thereafter the success of the picture was assured. Hazlitt reported that it prompted 'universal admiration' and 'deserved applause'.[9]

Hazlitt and John Scott had patched their differences in January 1820, so Hazlitt began writing a theatre column for Scott's *London Magazine*. Because the magazine appeared monthly Hazlitt's pieces were not reviews in the ordinary sense, but meditations and comments on the current state of the English stage. But the renewed connection with Scott provided an opportunity for a significant development in Hazlitt's work. In April he tried to sell Scott his eight philosophy lectures, and when Scott refused them Hazlitt suggested instead a series of miscellaneous essays under the title 'Table Talk'. Scott agreed, and thus, beginning in June 1820, came into existence a body of classic writings.

These essays are a development of Hazlitt's *Round Table* style of 'familiar essay', but longer, more searching and more personal. The subjects are Hazlitt's own, the handling of them is free, the style is flowing, vigorous, felicitous and striking – Hazlitt at his best. Together with the essays written later and collected as *The Plain Speaker* and *The Spirit of the Age*, 'Table Talk' constitutes Hazlitt's finest achievement.[10] Part of the reason for this upward change of gear from 1820 onwards is Hazlitt's disengagement from current politics, allowing more perspective in his work, and an even more reflective because less immediately polemical manner. His reputation as a writer meant that he could choose his topics and write about subjects that mattered most to him. His literary reputation gave him freedom, and his freedom allowed him to add immeasurably to his literary reputation.

The first 'Table Talk' was entitled 'On the Qualifications Necessary to Success in Life', and it concluded 'The way to secure success is to be more anxious about obtaining than about deserving it.'[11] It also helps, Hazlitt said, if you are a nobleman, or rich: 'the simple literary character is not enough. "Such a poor forked animal" as a mere poet or philosopher turned loose upon public opinion, has no chance against the flock of bats and owls that instantly assail him. It is name, it is wealth, it is title and influence that mollifies the tender-hearted Cerberus of criticism – first, by placing the honorary candidate for fame out of the reach of Grub-street malice; secondly, by holding out the prospect of a dinner or a vacant office to successful sycophancy. This is the reason why a certain Magazine praises Percy Bysshe Shelley and vilifies "Johnny Keats": they know very well that they cannot ruin the one in fortune as in fame, but they may ruin the other in both, deprive him of a livelihood together with his good name, send him to *Coventry*, and into the Rules of a prison; and this is a double incitement to the exercise of their laudable and legitimate vocation.'[12] The 'certain magazine' was *Blackwood's*. Hazlitt attacked it out of a sense of outrage at its treatment of Keats and himself, but there is also irony in these remarks, for by 1820 Hazlitt was famous among the reading classes, and according to Patmore he 'had only to lift his pen to coin money' – an exaggeration, to be sure, but an indication that editors were generally ready for something from his pen, and he knew he could if he wished earn up to 'thirty guineas a week' at times if, by hard work, he wrote ten pages a day.[13]

In his now accustomed way Hazlitt went to Winterslow for the summer to see William the younger and to write, staying at The Hut. While enjoying the season's first warm days he received a letter from Bryan Procter (the poet 'Barry Cornwall') telling him that the management of Covent Garden had accepted a play by his young but long-standing friend James Sheridan

Knowles, and that it was soon to be staged. Procter also wrote about it to Leigh Hunt: 'A new Tragedy on a subject of Roman History is accepted and forthcoming at Covent Garden . . . As the author is an old acquaintance of Hazlitt's you will I know be glad to mention the thing.'[14] Hazlitt went up to town to see the play, called *Virginius*, and wrote in his drama column: 'We came, we saw, and were satisfied. *Virginius* is a good play: – we repeat it. It is a real tragedy; a sound historical painting.' This was not mere puff, for just a few months earlier Hazlitt used his column to complain that no good tragedies had been written in recent years. William Macready played the lead, and Hazlitt praised him too. His one cause for complaint was that Covent Garden's Tory management had required the cutting of some politically liberal passages – which, he told his readers, they could however find in the printed version of the play.

Macready, Knowles and Hazlitt dined together one night after the show, sharing salmon and boiled mutton at a coffee-house near the theatre. The occasion is remembered by Macready in his autobiographical notes: 'Hazlitt was a man whose conversation could not fail to arrest attention. He found in me a ready listener, and in the interest of our discussion became irritated by the boisterous boyish sallies of Knowles's irrepressible spirits, rebuking him for his unseasonable interruptions, and, as one having authority, desiring him not to "play the fool". The poet was in truth a very child of nature, and Hazlitt, who knew him well, treated him as such.'[15] Hazlitt was fond of Knowles. He had painted his portrait when he was a boy, and the two had attempted to learn rope-dancing together. Knowles told Macready that he 'considered himself greatly indebted' for Hazlitt's 'early advice and tutorship'. As if in confirmation of this aspect of Hazlitt's friendship with younger men, Keats shortly afterwards sent him a copy of *Lamia*, just published, inscribed 'To Wm Hazlitt Esq. with the Author's sincere respects'.

After attending Knowles's début Hazlitt returned to The Hut at Winterslow, and there resumed work on his pieces for the journals which were now his main outlets, the *London Magazine*, the *Edinburgh Magazine* and the *Edinburgh Review*. He had no lodgings in London at this point, but was happy to be rusticating among his old haunts on the edge of Salisbury Plain, where he had quiet and solitude. But no sooner had he settled himself back at The Hut than the sad but not unexpected news reached him of his father's death.

William senior had died some weeks earlier, on 16 July 1820, but the news took time to reach Hazlitt because Peggy wrote to him in London and the letter was slow in being forwarded. 'I did not see my father dead,

but I saw death shake him by the palsied hand and stare him in the face,'
he wrote later, in a passage deleted from the manuscript of his essay 'On
the Fear of Death'. 'He made as good an end as Falstaff; though different,
as became him. After repeating the name of his Redeemer often, he took
my mother's hand, and looking up, put it in my sister's, and so expired.
There was something graceful and gracious in his nature, which showed
itself in his last act.'[16] William senior had placed his wife's hand in Peggy's
in Boston just before he returned to England thirty years before, imposing
on the daughter a duty of care for the mother. That affecting action had
bound poor Peggy to a spinster's lifelong service to her parents, and if she
had ever felt a pang about that fact, she must have remembered it again
then – although by this time, as a woman in her late forties (which in that
period meant she was already an old lady) the time for repining had passed.

A notice of William senior's death appeared in the *Examiner* on 1
August, describing him as 'a man who through his whole life was a friend
to truth and liberty'. In a 'Table Talk' essay written later that year, 'On the
Pleasure of Painting', Hazlitt paid a fuller tribute in his own way: he
recalled the time he had painted his father in the dim light of the chapel at
Wem, an activity that drew them together after the constraint caused by
Hazlitt's decision not to become a preacher.

It might be pure coincidence, and there is no obvious connection between
the two events, but the death of William senior marked the beginning of
a Dantesque journey for Hazlitt into heaven and hell – the latter more
thoroughly, and for far longer, and in a way that marked the remainder of
his life and marred his reputation after his death.

Hazlitt went to Crediton despite being too late for the funeral, to spend
a little time with his mother and Peggy. By mid-August he was back in
London, having decided to return to his familiar stamping-ground in
Southampton Buildings. He had lived at No. 34 before; this time he took
a pair of rooms on the second floor of No. 9. He had a quiet rearward
view over the inner gardens of Staple Inn from the windows of both rooms.
He moved in on 13 August. It proved to be a profoundly unlucky day.

His landlord was a tailor called Micaiah Walker, whose wife took
lodgers – usually about three or four in number – and looked after them
with the help of her daughters and a maid. Hazlitt already had a slight
connection with the household, in that the Walkers' eldest daughter
Martha was married to an acquaintance of his, one Robert Roscoe, the
fourth son of the Liverpool banker William Roscoe whose portrait Hazlitt
had painted nearly twenty years before. Robert Roscoe was a Cambridge
graduate and now a solicitor. He had met Martha while residing at No. 9

Southampton Buildings, and he told Hazlitt that he was well pleased with the outcome of his decision to lodge there. He and Martha were living nearby, and their first child was born shortly after Hazlitt moved in.

Two sons and two daughters still lived at home with Micaiah Walker and his wife. One of the sons was a sixteen-year-old called Cajah (an abbreviation of Micaiah), the other a two-year-old called John, destined to live only until the following spring. The elder of the two daughters was called Sarah, who was nineteen, and the younger was called Betsey, who was about ten.

The fateful element in these arrangements was Sarah Walker. On Hazlitt's third day in his new lodgings – 16 August 1820 – she brought him his breakfast. As she left the room after putting down his tray he watched her go, mesmerized by the way she walked, for she had a waving, gliding step, which he found graceful beyond description. At the door she turned and looked him full in the eye, her strange dark gaze burning him to the core of his soul. He was stunned, amazed – and in love in an instant.

It might seem that for one who suffered frequently from infatuations (until now, mainly behind the scenes; recall Patmore's remark that 'he was always in love with somebody or other') and who therefore understood their nature, Hazlitt should have been well armed against taking them too seriously. But his own views explain why he allowed himself to become besotted in this case. Love and desire, he said, are blessings when mutual (if ever they are, outside the covers of a novel), but are like the Furies when unrequited. Either way they are inescapable. They are non-rational, and the will cannot oppose them. They take hold and run their course, and the subject of them can do nothing but survive as best he – usually, in Hazlitt's book, he – can. Hazlitt accordingly never attempted to fight against them. He gave in to his feelings at their first impulse, and invariably suffered the consequences. In the case of Sarah Walker, 'suffered' is a wholly inadequate word. His obsession with her drove him almost mad.

Hazlitt also therefore believed in love at first sight. More accurately, he believed that what goes by that name is only a recognition of an antecedently cherished ideal, so in one sense it is not really 'first sight' at all – and he knew that time has nothing to do with it. 'I do not think that what is called *Love at first sight* is so great an absurdity as it is sometimes imagined to be,' he wrote soon after meeting Sarah Walker, in self-justifying vein. 'We generally make up our minds beforehand to the sort of person we should like, grave or gay, black, brown or fair; with golden tresses or with raven locks; – and when we meet with a complete example of the qualities we admire, the bargain is soon struck. We have never seen any thing to come up to our newly discovered goddess before, but she is what we have been all our lives looking for. The idol we fall down and worship is an image familiar to our minds. It has been present to our waking thoughts, it has haunted us in our dreams.'[17]

A few years before, in his article for the *Edinburgh Review* on Sismondi's *De la littérature du midi de l'Europe*, Hazlitt had pointedly disagreed with its author's regret that Petrarch and his Laura had not been able to enjoy a longer intimacy. 'The whole is in better keeping as it is,' Hazlitt wrote. 'The love of a man like Petrarch would have been less in character, if it had been less ideal. For the purposes of inspiration, a single interview was quite sufficient. The smile which sank into his heart the first time he ever beheld her, played round her lips ever after, the look with which her eyes first met his, never passed away. The image of his mistress still haunted his mind, and was recalled by every object in nature. Even death could not dissolve the fine illusion: for that which exists in the imagination is alone imperishable. As our feelings become more ideal, the impression of the moment indeed becomes less violent; but the effect is more general and permanent. The blow is felt only by reflection; it is the rebound that is fatal.'[18] These words struck deeply home to a reader in Paris who felt that they described his own biography exactly. The reader was Stendhal, who, in making a note of this passage, was for a second time copying out words written by Hazlitt without knowing who their author was or that the two passages were by the same hand – for he had annotated an earlier *Edinburgh Review* essay in which Hazlitt says of *Don Quixote*, 'The whole work breathes the air of romance – that aspiration after imaginary good.' The two met in Paris years later, in 1825.

Those words – 'The smile which sank into his heart the first time he ever beheld her, played round her lips ever after, the look with which her eyes first met his, never passed away' – could scarcely have been more prophetic or insightful, given the beginning and the manner of Hazlitt's passion for Sarah Walker. She made him dithyrambic: 'Oh! thou, who, the first time I ever beheld thee, didst draw my soul into the circle of thy heavenly looks, and wave enchantment round me, do not think thy conquest less complete because it was instantaneous; for in that gentle form (as if another Imogen had entered) I saw all that I had ever loved of female grace, modesty, and sweetness!'

The young woman who thus conquered Hazlitt's heart and reason so completely was described by Procter in unflattering terms. 'Her face was round and small,' Procter wrote, 'and her eyes were motionless, glassy, and without any speculation (apparently) in them. Her movements in walking were very remarkable, for I never observed her to make a step. She went onwards in a sort of wavy, sinuous manner, like the movement of a snake. She was silent, or uttered monosyllables only, and was very demure. Her steady, unmoving gaze upon the person she was addressing was exceedingly unpleasant. The Germans would have extracted a romance from her, endowing her perhaps with some diabolic attribute.'[19] Although this description was written after the event, in pity for Hazlitt and dislike of Sarah Walker – though it is not as unfriendly as Sarah Stoddart's characterization of her as 'thin and bony as the scrag end of a neck of mutton'[20] – it tallies exactly with Hazlitt's own descriptions, except that he gave them a different cast. Her waving walk, her sphinx-like eyes, her demure silence, and her round face and slender figure, all recur in Hazlitt's accounts of her as matters for celebration, and as the barbs that snagged his soul and would not let him go.

Hazlitt longed for the kind of romantic love he had read about in novels. He was sceptical about whether it could exist, for such love would amount to something metaphysical: to a companionship of hearts and souls that would cure the inexpressible loneliness of being. Yet he hoped for it anyway, and sought it endlessly. By the time he fell in love with Sarah Walker his longing for the realization of this dream had grown acute, and any girl who walked with what he saw as Sarah Walker's undulating grace, and who turned at the door to look him directly and meaningfully in the eye for a long, surprising, lingering moment before leaving the room, would have made him project all his hope and yearning onto her, whoever she was. He was ripe for love, and fell hopelessly into it at the first faint imagined touch of its presence.

For eighteen months after Sarah Walker's sinuous walk and meaningful look captivated Hazlitt, she spent hours every day in his room, sitting on his knee, kissing and fondling him endlessly, and being fondled in return. He did not try to have actual sexual intercourse with her, because he idealized her and wanted to marry her, and therefore wished to believe her 'pure'. But their intimacy did not fall far short. During the first year he was often blissfully happy. She was 'the only woman that ever made me think she loved me, and that feeling was so new to me, and so delicious, that "it will never from my heart".'[21] She made him think that she loved him without ever telling him so directly – on the contrary, she refused to say that she loved him, nor would she promise him anything for the future. She merely said, 'You should judge by my actions' and 'Do I seem indifferent?' when he asked 'Do you love me? Could you love me?'[22] And indeed her actions made Hazlitt hope, and hope was enough at the outset. He showered her with gifts, some of them expensive: an ivory flageolet, a gold heart-shaped locket, a cap and gown, silk cloth, tickets for the theatre, copies of his books, even his most treasured little miniature statue of Napoleon.

The honeymoon period of the affair coincided with Hazlitt's writing most of the first volume of his 'Table Talk' essays. He went to Winterslow at the end of October to see his son and to work. He was tired of reviewing drama, so he bequeathed his theatre page to Thomas Noon Talfourd (the lawyer he had met at the Lambs' five years earlier, and had been friends with since), and concentrated on his essays instead. Crabb Robinson was sorry to see the change of authorship on the theatre page – 'it will be, I fear, a falling-off, for Hazlitt, though a mannerist in style, is a thinker at least,' he remarked. But he was delighted by the essays: 'Hazlitt's *Table Talk* in the *London* is full of acute observation ... I read all he writes with zest.'[23] The two were not yet reconciled, so the compliment is a handsome one.

In January 1821 Hazlitt wrote the most contented essay ever to come from his pen. He was in Winterslow again, comfortably installed before the fire at The Hut, after a New Year's visit to his mother and Peggy in Crediton. He was in love, and believed himself loved; he was pleased with his work, and the first collected volume of *Table Talk* essays was shortly to appear. The contented essay is 'On Living To One's Self', by which he meant being in, but not of, the world: 'it is to be a silent spectator of the mighty scene of things, not an object of attention or curiosity in it; to take a thoughtful, anxious interest in what is passing in the world, but not to feel the slightest inclination to make or meddle with it.'[24] The essay begins: 'I never was in a better place or humour than I am at present for writing on this subject. I have a partridge getting ready for my supper, my fire is blazing on the hearth, the air is mild for the season of the year.'

It was a brief respite. When he returned to London and had Sarah Walker on his knee again, she told him something he had not known before. The reason she could never feel more than friendship towards him, she said, was that she still nurtured a tenderness for a former love, a man who had lodged for a while at 9 Southampton Buildings but, because of a 'difference of station', had been obliged to leave to prevent their mutual feelings going further. This continuing attachment posed a barrier, she said, to her ever loving anyone else.

This was a severe blow. Instead of answering his question 'Do you love me? Can you love me?' with 'Do I seem indifferent?' and 'You should judge by my actions,' she was now, Hazlitt reported, saying 'No, never.'[25] He was hurt and troubled by the news, but it did not stop him from continuing to hope. He thought that his feelings for her must surely one day make her love him in return, so exalted and passionate were they, and so profound. And then he found that he was charmed by her fidelity to one she had loved, and he honoured her for it. And she still sat in his lap daily, twining her arms round his neck, kissing him, enjoying his caresses.

The last ten days of February 1821 proved eventful and distressing for reasons unconnected with Sarah Walker. On the 21st Crabb Robinson called at the Lambs' house with some Raphael prints he had purchased at Sotheby's, and found Hazlitt there, who joined him in admiring the pictures and pronounced them fine. 'Hazlitt and I now speak again,' Crabb Robinson reported, 'but he does not omit the *Sir* when he talks to me. I think he behaves with propriety and dignity towards me, considering the severity of my attack on him, which though warranted by my friendship with Wordsworth was not justified according to the customs of society.' Thus did Crabb Robinson make amends to a writer whose work he could not help admiring.

But then came news that saddened Hazlitt profoundly. Keats had just died at Rome. 'Poor Keats,' he wrote; he was a 'bud bit by an envious worm,' who 'gave the greatest promise of genius of any poet of his day.'[26] He knew that his liking for Keats had been reciprocated, but he did not know the extent of Keats's good opinion of him, nor of his influence in helping Keats to forge his own views.

There was scarcely time to mourn Keats because, less than a week after news of his death reached London, there occurred a shocking event that absorbed much of Hazlitt's public attention for the next few months. This was the death of John Scott as a result of a duel caused by the hostility between the *London Magazine* and the intemperate *Blackwood's Magazine*.

Each magazine had been attacking the other with increasing violence over preceding months, *Blackwood's* in its usual coarse and brutal way. But it was Lockhart who lost his temper with Scott for naming him explicitly in a *London* article, and he demanded that Scott should give him either an apology or 'satisfaction'. Scott in his turn demanded to know Lockhart's exact connection with *Blackwood's*. The quarrel turned on the fact that magazine management and editorship was then a putatively anonymous matter, although it was in practice almost always an open secret. As an excuse to escalate rivalry between the two magazines Lockhart accordingly chose to treat Scott's revelation of his identity as an insult.

In January 1821 Scott was visited by a young barrister called Christie, who came on Lockhart's behalf to demand either the apology or the satisfaction required. Demands and counter-demands flew between the two principals; John Stoddart became involved on Lockhart's side, Patmore and Horace Smith on Scott's. By dint of anger and misunderstanding the matter grew more heated, until finally Christie accused Scott of cowardice for not going to Edinburgh to duel with Lockhart. Scott promptly challenged Christie over this supplementary insult, and the two men fought with pistols at Chalk Farm near Hampstead in the dawn light of 16 February 1821.

Christie was unscathed, but Scott was wounded. The wound proved fatal. He died eleven days later, on 27 February. After the inquest blame was heaped on Patmore for his ineptitude as Scott's second; if Horace Smith had filled the office, people said, an actual fight would have been avoided.

During the quarrel Hazlitt wrote to Scott praising him for giving *Blackwood's* some well-deserved blows in the pages of the *London*, and urging him not to back down. But he did not mean by this that Scott should literally fight Lockhart or one of his supporters, and he was horrified both by the duel and its consequences. Upon news of Scott's death he wrote to Robert Baldwin, the publisher of the *London*, offering his help. Baldwin replied, 'Dear Sir, I must not any longer neglect to avail myself of your kind offer to assist in filling up the chasm made by the death of our lamented friend in the Magazine.' Hazlitt's offer was to write as much as needed, but Baldwin had a further wish: that Hazlitt would become the magazine's editor.

Hazlitt was not interested in an editorial post. Reluctantly he agreed to undertake the role temporarily while Baldwin sought a successor. He recruited contributors, including Leigh Hunt and Barry Cornwall, and persuaded a one-time regular columnist, Thomas Wainewright, to resume his labours. He himself wrote four essays for the May number.

While he was thus engaged the first volume of *Table Talk* was published. An immediate consequence was a falling-out with Leigh Hunt, because the essays contained some kicks both at him and his protégé Shelley. Hazlitt characterized the latter as one for whom 'whatever is, is wrong ... he has a fire in his eye, a fever in his blood, a maggot in his brain, a hectic flutter in his speech, which mark out the philosophic fanatic. He is sanguine-complexioned, and shrill-voiced'. Leigh Hunt is made to figure as an example of the type of person who, though vivacious, loquacious, and interesting, has only one idea, and one subject of conversation: himself.

Leigh Hunt was genuinely hurt. He wrote, 'I think, Mr Hazlitt, that you might have found a better time, and place too, for assaulting me and my friends in this bitter manner ... the sight of acquaintances and brother-reformers cutting and carbonadoing one another in public is, I conceive, no advancement to the cause of Liberal opinion ... in God's name, why could you not tell Mr Shelley in a pleasant manner what you dislike in him? ... Is it possible that a misconception of anything private can transport you into these – what shall I call them? – extravagances of stomach? ... I have faith enough in your disinterestedness and suffering to tell you so privately instead of publicly; and you might have paid as decent a compliment to a man half killed with his thoughts for others if you had done as much for me, instead of making my faults stand for my whole character.'

Hazlitt was chastened by this, and wrote back immediately, 'My dear Hunt, – I have no quarrel with you, nor can I have. You are one of those people I like, do what they will; there are others that I do not like, do what they may. I have always spoken well of you to friend or foe – viz. I have said you were one of the pleasantest and cleverest persons I ever knew; but that you teased anyone you had to deal with out of their lives.' But there was a reason why he had done it. If there was one thing Hazlitt could not bear, it was a personal slight – being cut in the street, being offered an insult by an acquaintance, being let down by friends. For a variety of reasons he thought some of his longest-standing friends – Lamb and Leigh Hunt among them – were guilty of the latter; they had, he thought, failed to support him when he needed them, for example by not coming to his lectures, and by not intervening on his behalf with Bentham in the matter of his eviction from York Street. These were events of a year and more ago, but they had sufficiently rankled with Hazlitt for him to do what was entirely characteristic, which was to express his displeasure publicly. Leigh Hunt had indeed correctly identified the source of the problem: 'a misconception of something private'. He knew his man. He replied, 'Dear Hazlitt, If you do not want to quarrel with me, I certainly do not want to quarrel with you. I have always said, to my own mind and to those few to whom I am in the habit of speaking on such things, that Hazlitt might pay me more tricks than any man; and I conceive you have played me some. If I have teased you, as you say, I have never revenged myself by trampling upon you in public ... I have often said, I have a sort of irrepressible love for Hazlitt, on account of his sympathy for mankind, his unmercenary disinterestedness, and his suffering; and I should have a still greater and more personal affection for him if he would let one; but I declare to God I never seem to know whether he is pleased or displeased, cordial or uncordial – indeed his manners are never cordial – and he has a way with him when first introduced to you, and ever afterwards, as if he said, "I have no faith in anything, especially your advances: don't flatter yourself you have any road to my credulity: we have nothing in common between us." '[27]

\*

In the summer Hazlitt gratefully relinquished the editorship of the *London Magazine*, and wrote little. At the magazine's regular dinners he seemed to his colleagues withdrawn, participating in conversations only when they turned to politics. Among the topics of the day was the coronation of George IV, who was crowned on 19 July 1821 at enormous expense and with great magnificence – except that the proceedings were threatened with farce by the efforts of Caroline to gain admission to Westminster Abbey so that she could be crowned too, trying all its doors to the derisory hoots of the spectators. Two weeks later she was taken ill while at Drury Lane Theatre, and died on 7 August. The reason given was an abdominal obstruction complicated by 1821-style medical treatment; conspiracy theories about a different cause were not mooted at the time. The more romantically inclined – they were now few in number, as regards her – said that she had died of a 'broken heart' because of her exclusion from the throne. She was buried in her native Brunswick, unmourned by most despite her vast popularity in the preceding year.

For Hazlitt the coronation was a text for a sermon. 'Let us take the Spirit of Monarchy in its highest state of exaltation, in the moment of its proudest triumph – a Coronation-day,' he wrote. 'We now see it in the mind's eye: the preparation of weeks – the expectation of months – the seats, the privileged places, are occupied in the obscurity of night, and in silence – the day dawns slowly, big with the hope of Caesar and of Rome – the golden censers are set in order, the tables groan with splendour and with luxury – within the inner space the peeresses are set, and revealed to the eye decked out in ostrich feathers and pearls, like beds of lilies sparkling with a thousand dew-drops – the marshal and the heralds are in motion, the full organ, majestic, peals forth the Coronation Anthem – everything is ready – and all at once the Majesty of kingdoms bursts upon the astonished sight – his person swelled out with all the gorgeousness of dress, and swathed in bales of silk and golden tissues – the bow with which he greets the assembled multitude, and the representatives of foreign kings, is the climax of conscious dignity ...'[28] The description is so accurate, as a comparison with contemporary pictures shows, that it prompts one to think Hazlitt was present.[29] 'What does all this amount to?' he continues. 'A shew – a theatrical spectacle! What does it prove? That a king is crowned, that a king is dead! What is the moral to be drawn from it, that is likely to sink into the heart of a nation? That greatness consists in finery, and that supreme merit is the dower of birth and fortune! ... Does it depend on the inheritance of virtue, on the acquisition of knowledge in the new monarch, whether he shall be thus exalted in the eyes of the people? No; – to say so is not only an offence in manners, but a violation of the law.'[30] As his epigraph for the piece Hazlitt chose 'Strip it of its externals, what is it but a *jest*? (*charade on the word "Majesty"*).'

These externals had little relevance to the tribulations gathering in Hazlitt's private life. As his *London* colleagues sensed from his dinner-table demeanour, Hazlitt was not himself, for as the months of 1821 advanced his relationship with Sarah Walker did not. They still spent intimate if unconsummated hours together, but she was stalling him, invoking her past attachment as a bar, insisting that they could only be friends. Nevertheless when he was in her company, holding her in his arms, he was happy. Trouble really began in October 1821 with the arrival of a new lodger at 9 Southampton Buildings, one John Tomkins.

Sarah Walker was immediately infatuated with Tomkins. She blushed when she saw him, darted to his room when he rang, waited for him on the landing, forbade Hazlitt to kiss her on the stairs in case he saw them. From then on an emphatic note entered her avowals when she told Hazlitt that friendship was the most he could ever expect from her.

Hazlitt was plunged into a torment of jealousy and pain. The turn of events made him suspect that she was not the little angel he wished her to be. He started to hear, see and guess uncomplimentary things about her relations with other and previous lodgers. Then, one night, he overheard her talking with her mother and siblings in their kitchen about the length of another lodger's penis. He was shocked, not because he was a prude but because he had thought her above such things. Jealousy, anger, frustration and helpless devotion mingled painfully in him. Their relationship changed. He began to plead with her, even on his knees, to love him, or at least to belong to him. His pleadings sometimes extorted crumbs of hope from her, by forcing her to say that she was not indifferent to him. It kept his mania alive. But if ever she had been more than merely toying with him, which is not very likely, Sarah Walker was certainly now no longer interested.

In his desperation Hazlitt concluded that Sarah Walker was behaving in this difficult way because he was not free to marry her. He resolved to overcome that problem by asking Sarah Stoddart for an Edinburgh divorce.

Before putting this plan into execution Hazlitt had much to do. First, he had quarrelled with the new owners of the *London Magazine*, his old publishers Taylor and Hessey, because they objected to his defence of Guy Fawkes in an eponymous essay. The only person from whom Hazlitt tolerated editorial interference was Francis Jeffrey of the *Edinburgh Review*. Taylor and Hessey wished him to write a series of 'Living Authors' essays, and indeed he had already produced a few such, which later became part of his *Spirit of the Age* collection. But at this point he was far more interested in his *Table Talk*, which he wished to write in his own way on subjects of his own choosing. When Hessey called on him in Southampton Buildings in early October 1821 he found Hazlitt in a vexed mood over the matter. 'On my asking him if we were to expect a no. of the Living Authors he observed that he felt no interest in them or their works and that he considered such papers as mere fat work which cost him no effort and brought him no fame. He then spoke of the Table Talks as being the papers on which he valued himself and which he wished to continue but said that he felt so annoyed and cramped in his mind by the fear of alteration or objection or perhaps rejection altogether that he could not write freely as he was accustomed to do.' Hessey and Taylor were afraid of the consequences of publishing so incendiary an article as a defence of Guy Fawkes; Hazlitt was insistent; eventually the article came out in three parts in Leigh Hunt's *Examiner*, and Hazlitt's relationship with the *London Magazine* was no longer as close as it had been. He looked for another home for his work and found it in Colbourn's *New Monthly Magazine*, on very satisfactory terms, for Colbourn agreed to take his new series of 'Table Talks' and thereafter to produce them in book form as Volume Two.

In December 1821, seeking distraction from the growing frustrations of his relations with Sarah Walker, Hazlitt allowed a friend to persuade him to an entirely new experience: attendance at a boxing match. The result was his famous essay 'The Fight'. In that age boxing, called 'the Fancy', was a sport that roused strong emotions and attracted mammoth bets, and its classic moments established themselves in the social history of the country as legends, paintings, prints, and even illustrations on chinaware. There was a famous battle in 1810 between Tom Cribb, a coal-heaver nicknamed the 'Black Diamond', and Tom Molyneux from Virginia in the United States, which people still talked of, and which decorated the sides of milk-jugs and mugs from London to Newcastle. Now, as the nights drew in at the end of 1821, news was circulating that two celebrated pugilists were to meet for a large purse on the downs near Hungerford in Berkshire, and it was to be a fight to the finish. They were Bill Neate and Tom Hickman, the 'Gas-man'. Hazlitt had never seen a fight, but, inspired by Patmore who was a keen follower of the Fancy, he decided to go.

Hazlitt's account of the experience is both a literary classic and a boxing classic. Gene Tunney – who himself won the world heavyweight championship in a celebrated bout against Jack Dempsey in 1927 –

included 'The Fight' in his collection of essays on boxing, and praised it highly; which is a remarkable judgement given that the essay contains relatively little about the actual trading of punches, and much more about the journey to the fight and the journey home, with asides on Sarah Walker. 'Reader, have you ever seen a fight?' Hazlitt asks, after several amusing pages describing the journey by coach from London to Berkshire. 'If not, you have a pleasure to come, at least if it is a fight like that between the Gas-man and Bill Neate. The crowd was very great when we arrived on the spot; open carriages were coming up, with streamers flying and music playing, and the country-people were pouring in over hedge and ditch in all directions, to see their hero beat or be beaten. The odds were still on Gas, but only about five to four. Gully had been down to try Neate, and had backed him considerably, which was a damper to the sanguine confidence of the adverse party. About two hundred thousand pounds were pending.' As to the arrogant Gas-man, 'this spirited and formidable young fellow seems to have taken for his motto the old maxim that "there are three things necessary to success in life – *Impudence! Impudence! Impudence!*" ' Like Muhammad Ali after him, Hickman was apt to start his fights beforehand by psychological means, in this case by accosting Neate at the fives-court in London and telling him 'I'll knock more blood out of that great carcase of thine, this day fortnight, than you ever knocked out of a bullock's!'

As to the fight itself, Hazlitt's natural squeamishness – recalling his reaction to the human heart handed round on a dinner plate at the Royal Academy anatomy lecture – was engaged from the outset. A great hush fell over the crowd as the combatants stripped off their shirts and swung their arms to loosen them. They shook hands at the mark, and then the fight was on. 'In the first round everyone thought it was all over. After making play a short time, the Gas-man flew at his adversary like a tiger, struck five blows in as many seconds, three first, and then following him as he staggered back, two more, right and left, and down he fell, a mighty ruin. There was a shout, and I said, "There is no standing this." '[31] But Neate was made of stern stuff. He leaped up, he rallied; the fight went on round after round; the two men were prodigies of strength and resolution. 'To see two men smashed to the ground, smeared with gore, stunned, senseless, the breath beaten out of them, rise up with new strength and courage, stand ready to inflict or receive mortal offence, and rush upon each other "like two clouds over the Caspian" – this is the most astonishing thing of all: – this is the high and heroic state of man!' exclaimed Hazlitt. It ended suitably: Neate, the under-dog, caught the Gas-man a full-bodied blow in the middle of the face, and the Gas-man flung his arms in the air, hung suspended for a moment, then crashed to the ground. 'I never saw anything more terrific than his aspect just before he fell,' Hazlitt wrote. 'All traces of life, of natural expression, were gone from him. His face was like a human skull, a death's head, spouting blood. The eyes were filled with blood, the nose streamed with blood, the mouth gaped blood. He was not like an actual man, but like a preternatural, spectral appearance, or like one of the figures in Dante's *Inferno*.'[32]

Hazlitt was exhilarated. He had never seen anything like it, and he never went to another boxing match afterwards. He responded to it as a sportsman, and even as an artist: he described the muscled backs and shoulders of the two big men catching the December sunlight as they prepared to fight, as if he were going to draw them from life.

But the excitement of the excursion and the fight was only a half-holiday from the growing desperation of his feelings. In the published version of the essay he allows some of the torment to spill out, as if it were a liquid too hot to hold in for long: 'I will not libel any life by comparing it to mine, which is (at the date of these presents) bitter as coloquintida and the dregs of aconitum,' he remarked sadly.[33] But in the manuscript of the essay there are several deleted passages freighted with much harder emotions to bear. 'No tongue can tell the heaviness of heart I felt at that moment ... every step that carried me nearer to Brentford, bore me further from her with whom my soul and every thought lingered ... Oh! thou dumb heart, lonely, sad, shut up in the prison house of this rude form, that hast never found a fellow but for an hour and in very mockery of thy misery, speak, find bleeding words to express thy thoughts ...'[34] On the journey back from the fight Hazlitt was accompanied by Patmore, and found him a willing and sympathetic listener. Patmore had a copy of Rousseau's *La Nouvelle Héloïse* in his pocket, which endeared him to Hazlitt further. Patmore proved an important adjunct to Hazlitt in the remainder of the Sarah Walker affair, which was now reaching crisis point.

This was so much so that Hazlitt found it hard to keep his experience out of what he was writing. In his February 1822 'Table Talk' in the *New Monthly Magazine* he gave what was in effect an emotional autobiography. 'I always was inclined to raise and magnify the power of Love. I thought that his sweet power should only be exerted to join together the loveliest forms and fondest hearts; that none but those in whom his Godhead shone outwardly, and was inly felt, should ever partake of his triumphs; and I stood and gazed at a distance, as unworthy to mingle in so bright a throng, and did not even (for a moment) wish to tarnish the glory of so fair a vision by being admitted into it. I say this was my notion once, but God knows it was one of the errors of my youth. For coming nearer to look, I saw the maimed, the blind, and the halt enter in, the crooked and the dwarf, the ugly, the old and impotent, the man of pleasure and the man of the world, the dapper and the pert, the vain and shallow boaster, the fool and the pedant, the ignorant and the brutal, and all that is farthest removed from earth's fairest-born, and the pride of human life. Seeing all these enter the courts of Love, and thinking that I also might venture in under favour of the crowd, but finding myself rejected, I fancied (I might be wrong) that it was not so much because I was below, as above the common standard. I did feel, but was ashamed to feel, mortified at my repulse, when I saw the meanest of mankind, the very scum and refuse, all creeping things and every obscene creature, enter in before me. I seemed a species by myself. I took a pride even in my disgrace: and concluded I had elsewhere my inheritance! The only thing I ever piqued myself upon was the writing of the *Essay Concerning the Principles of Human Action* – a work that no woman ever read, or would comprehend the meaning of ... And thus I waste my life in one long sigh; nor ever (till too late) beheld a gentle face turned gently upon mine!' And then the goads of hope drive again, and Hazlitt concludes, 'But no! not too late, if that face, pure, modest, down-cast, tender, with angel sweetness, not only gladdens the prospect of the future, but sheds its radiance on the past, smiling in tears.'[35] The spark of hope had been lit by Sarah Walker's delicious behaviour towards him when he took her and her mother to see *Romeo and Juliet* – what else? – at Covent Garden on 24 January 1822: 'Oh! my sitting down beside you, you whom I loved so well, so long, and your assuring me I had not lessened your pleasure at the play by being with you, and giving me that dear hand to press in mine – I seemed to be in Heaven, – that slight, exquisitely turned form contained my all of heaven upon earth – I sat beside the adorable creature by her own permission – and as I folded you, yes, you, my best Sarah, to my heart, there was, as you say, "a tie between us," you did seem to be mine for a few short moments, in all truth and honour and sacredness. Oh! could we but be always so – do not mock me, for I am indeed a very child in love.'[36]

By the time this essay and 'The Fight' appeared in February 1822, Hazlitt was in Scotland. Sarah Stoddart had agreed to a divorce, and Hazlitt, driven by passion and hope, hurried north. Filing for divorce in Scotland required a forty-day residence qualification, and Hazlitt chose to spend it at Renton in the Borders, working on the extra essays required to make up a second *Table Talk* volume.

On the way north Hazlitt stopped at Stamford to see the pictures at Burleigh House. In the inn there he began to make a record of his conversations with Sarah Walker, beginning at a point after she told him that she would not and could never be his. The conversations form the first of the three parts of his account of the affair – his strange, notorious, uncomfortable and unique confession called *Liber Amoris*. In the sixth conversation he taxes her with his new and agonizing doubts about her – that she is leading him on, toying with him, that she does the same with other lodgers as she does with him. 'Oh! my God! after what I have thought of you and felt towards you, as little less than an angel, to have but a doubt cross my mind for an instant that you were what I dare not name – a common lodging-house decoy, a kissing convenience, that your lips were as common as the stairs.'[37] In a letter written at the same time to Patmore he wrote what he could not publish: the basis for these dreadful fears:

> *Betsey*: 'Oh! if those trowsers were to come down, what a sight there would be!' (*A general laugh.*)
> *Mother*: 'Yes! He's a proper one. Mr Follett is nothing to him.'
> *Cajah* (aged 17): 'Then I suppose he must be seven inches.'
> *Mother W.*: 'He's quite a monster. He nearly tumbled over Mr Hazlitt one night.'
> *Sarah*: (At that once, that still and ever dear name, ah! why do I grow pale, why do I weep and forgive?) said something inaudible, but in connection.
> *Cajah* (laughing): 'Sarah says...'
> *Sarah*: 'I say, Mr Follett wears straps.'[38]

It is the first part of the *Liber Amoris* which strikes the unprepared reader as so repellent because of the cringing, fawning adulation of the man and the obvious dispassion of the woman:

> *H*. Thy sweet image has taken possession of me, haunts me, and will drive me to distraction. Yet I could almost wish to go mad for thy sake: for then I might fancy that I had thy love in return, which I cannot live without!
> *S*. Do not, I beg, talk in that manner.[39]

But there is art in this: Hazlitt wished to prove how little effect eloquence and high feelings have in matters of love, for whatever explains attraction and affection – so he believed – they are not to be won by any arts if they do not exist of their own accord. 'All your fine sentiments and romantic notions will (of themselves) make no more impression on one of these delicate creatures, than on a piece of marble,' he bitterly remarked.

Hazlitt's doubts about Sarah, and his accusations, made her angry and cold. He was contrite: 'The words I uttered hurt me more than they did you ... – Ah, Sarah! I am unworthy of your love: I hardly dare ask for your pity; but oh! Save me – save me from your scorn: I cannot bear it – it withers me like lightning!'[40] He told her that he would be happy to be married to her even if she did not love him, so long as she gave him the kindness he had enjoyed from her in their first year and a half together. They could even, he said, live together 'as friends' – meaning without sexual relations – to which she replied, 'I don't know; and yet it would be no use if we did, you would always be hankering after what could never be.' In telling Patmore of these exchanges Hazlitt went on, 'I asked her if she would do so at once – the very next day? And what do you guess her answer was – "Do you think it would be prudent?" As I didn't proceed to extremities on the spot, she began to look grave, and to declare off.'[41]

Hazlitt arrived in Edinburgh on 4 February 1822, hired a solicitor, and made arrangements at a brothel run by one Mrs Louisa Knight, to be caught in an adulterous situation with a prostitute called (ironically) Mary Walker. That was for later, when Sarah Stoddart arrived, to provide her with evidence of his adultery as her grounds for divorce. They had to agree these arrangements in secret, because any sign of collusion between them would not only prevent a divorce being granted, but could result in arrest and imprisonment or transportation.

When all was in place he took himself down to Renton, to work out his month of residency by writing 'Table Talk' essays, and letters to Sarah Walker and Patmore, alternately in hope and agony. Before going he delivered an essay on Byron to Jeffrey at the *Edinburgh Review*, and Jeffrey kindly invited him to call when he returned.

He worked well and steadily at Renton, which he had chosen because, passing through it on his northward journey, he had noticed that it was like Winterslow in its setting in open country. To Sarah Walker he wrote, 'I regularly do ten pages a day, which mounts up to thirty guineas' worth a week, so that you see I should grow rich at this rate, if I could keep on so; *and I could keep on so*, if I had you with me to encourage me with your sweet smiles, and share my lot.' And he wistfully adds, 'The Berwick smack sails twice a week, and the wind sits fair. When I think of the thousand endearing caresses that have passed between us, I do not wonder at the strong attachment that draws me to you.'

Sarah Walker's few letters to Hazlitt were short, formal and non-committal, exclusively about practical matters, such as arrangements for forwarding mail. Their lack of warmth alternately hurt and goaded him. She signed them 'Yours respectfully, S. Walker.' He wrote copiously and tenderly to her; to Patmore he wrote equally copiously, venting his anger, his anxieties, his cravings and doubts. But somehow he managed to work at the 'Table Talk' essays for Colbourn, taking time off only to walk. He slept badly, dreaming of returning to the Louvre and finding all his favourite pictures gone – and dreaming also of reading *La Nouvelle Héloïse*, in particular the lines written by Julia on her death-bed: 'Trop heureuse d'acheter au prix de ma vie le droit de t'aimer toujours sans crime et de te le dire encore une fois, avant que je meure!'[42]

On 7 March 1822 he finished the last of the 'Table Talk' essays, and noted at the end of the manuscript that he had written the entire volume in a month, beginning on Monday 11 February and finishing on Thursday 7 March. Sarah Stoddart was due to arrive in Edinburgh in mid-March, when his required period of residency would be complete. As soon as he had posted the manuscript to Colbourn he therefore returned to Edinburgh to await her arrival.

But Sarah Stoddart was in no hurry to travel to Edinburgh, for she had responsibilities at home. William the younger was at Mr Dawson's boarding school in London, but was to be home for Easter, and she had no intention of leaving him until the holiday was over. That meant a delay until mid-April. Hazlitt found the waiting intolerable. And then something Patmore wrote to him about Sarah Walker – the letter is lost; Hazlitt's reply indicates only the tenor of its contents – threw him into agony. He wrote to Patmore 'I doat on her' and 'When I touch her hand, I enjoy perfect happiness and contentment of the soul'; and then, in another letter, 'To think that I should feel as I have done for such a monster.' Patmore's news must have concerned Sarah's dealings with Tomkins, inflaming Hazlitt's jealousy.

In April he could not work with the fluency which had inspired his pen at Renton. He received the proofs of *Table Talk*, and a request for another essay to make up the volume to full length. He also had to complete a long-standing commission for the *London Magazine*. He struggled, and eventually managed to do what was required. To beguile the waiting he visited the Jeffreys – Mrs Jeffrey was very kind to him, he told Patmore, and he apologized to her for being out of spirits. He also dined with William Ritchie, editor of the *Scotsman*, for whom he had written a review of Scottish painters. Ritchie was helpful to him during his Edinburgh stay, but Hazlitt's distraction and unhappiness led to an inattention or inadvertency which gave Ritchie offence, so that when the *Liber Amoris* appeared Ritchie was one of those who attacked it most bitterly.

At Ritchie's dinner party was a lawyer called George Combe, who was an enthusiastic amateur phrenologist, and especially keen to examine the craniums of famous persons. He asked Hazlitt if he could feel his bumps, and Hazlitt obligingly gave him permission, despite being a complete

Henry Crabb Robinson in 1855, by Henry Darvall

Charles Lamb in Venetian costume in 1804, by William Hazlitt

Charles and Mary Lamb in 1834, by Francis Stephen Cary

Leigh Hunt in 1837, by
Samuel Laurence

The Hazlitt home in Wem, Shropshire

John Keats in 1819, by Benjamin Robert Haydon

*The Fight*: Tom Cribb,
'The Black Diamond',
and Tom Molyneux of
Virginia, 1812

Francis Jeffrey in
the 1820s, by
Andrew Geddes

Hazlitt drawn on his honeymoon in Melrose, Scotland in 1825, by William Bewick

Benjamin Robert Haydon in
1845, by Sir David Wilkie

Napoleon Bonaparte in
1914, by Thomas
Heaphy

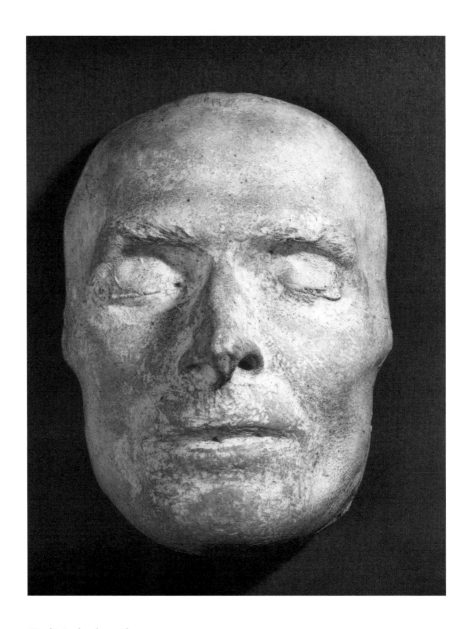

Hazlitt's death mask

sceptic about phrenology, as he several times showed in print. After feeling Hazlitt's bumps Combe made careful notes in his journal: 'I met Hazlitt in Ritchie's at supper. He appears to be about forty. He drank no wine or fermented liquor, but an enormous quantity of tea. [Some phrenological technicalities follow. Then:] The forehead retreats slightly but is decidedly capacious, and as the face is small it has a fine effect. The expression of the eyes is that of benevolence, veneration, hope, and ideality. The mouth indicates combativeness and destructiveness; lips thin and sharp. When he talks, the manner is bland and destitute of ostentation; clear rather than vehement or sparkling. When he laughs, the features become cuttingly sharp. He is a well-bred man, does not monopolize conversation, listens with attention and interest to any one who speaks, and affects nothing. The sparkling corruscations which gleam in his works are to be traced in his conversation; but they require to be looked for to be discovered, for the manner is so smooth and they flow so much in the current of his ordinary thoughts, that they do not attract attention by their prominence in delivery. If you pause in the conversation and reflect on what has been said in the last five minutes, you perceive you have been talking with an uncommon man.'[43] Thinking of *Blackwood's* allegations about Hazlitt, Combe noted, '[Hazlitt] is quite a gentleman in his manners and did not utter one sentiment which the most delicate and scrupulous female might not have listened to.'[44]

The agony induced in Hazlitt by Patmore's earlier letter was abated by another from him, this time defending Sarah Walker from Hazlitt's accusation that she was a 'common boarding-house jilt'. At the same time Hazlitt learned that his wife was about to arrive in Edinburgh at last. The letter and the news were a double relief, and he felt cheerful for the first time since leaving London.

When Sarah Stoddart arrived at Edinburgh she found herself a room at the Black Bull Inn, and the next morning went to consult a barrister. Her first question concerned the oath she had to swear to the effect that she was not colluding with Hazlitt over the divorce. She was filled with scruples about it, because she had been warned by friends in England of the serious penalties that would follow if they were found out. It took the combined and repeated efforts of the barrister and Ritchie to persuade her that she was not at risk of perjury. But her doubts induced yet further delays, to Hazlitt's frustration.

Moreover Sarah Stoddart needed money. Hazlitt had promised to pay her expenses, but now his own pockets were practically empty, and he had not yet been paid by Colbourn. Because she was in serious straits Sarah

Stoddart took the risk of going to Hazlitt's lodgings one night to tell him that unless he gave her some money the divorce was off and she would return to London.

Sarah Stoddart kept a journal of her trip to Scotland. In it she recorded the conversation of that night in detail, and it is revealing. 'In the evening, after some hesitation, went to Mr Hazlitt myself for an answer [about money]. He told me he expected thirty pounds from Colbourn on Thursday, and then he would let me have five pounds for present expences, that he had but one pound in his pocket, but if I wanted it, I should have that. That he was going to give two Lectures at Glasgow next week, for which he was to have £100 and he had eighty pounds beside to receive for the Table Talk in a fortnight out of which sums he pledged himself to fulfil his engagements relative to my expences: and also to make me a handsome present when all was over (£20) as I seemed to love money. Or it would enable me to travel back by land, as I said I should prefer seeing something of the country to going back in the steam boat, which he proposed. Said he would give the note of hand for fifty pounds to Mr Ritchie for me, payable to whomever I pleased; if he could conveniently, at the time, it should be for three months, instead of six, but he was not certain of that. Said that Mr Ritchie was a most respectable man, a lawyer, and one of the Editors of the Scotsman. Enquired if I had taken the Oath. I told him I only wanted a summons from Mr Gray, if I could depend upon the money, but I could not live in a strange place without: and I had no friends, or means of earning money here, as he had; though, as I still had four pounds, I could wait a few days. I asked him how the child's expences, or my draught, were to be paid, if he went abroad. And he answered, that if he succeeded in the divorce, he should be easy in his mind, and be able to work, and then he should probably be back in three months; but otherwise he might leave England forever. He said that as soon as I had got him to sign a paper giving away a hundred and fifty pounds a year from himself, I talked of going back, and leaving everything, as if I meant to bamboozle him. I told him to recollect that it was no advantage to myself that I sought, nor should I get a halfpenny by it; it was only to secure something to *his* child, as well as mine. He said he could do very well for the child himself; and that he was allowed to be a very indulgent kind father; some people thought too much so. I said, I did not dispute his fondness for him; but I must observe, that though he got a great deal of money, he never saved, or had any by him; or was likely to make much provision for the child. Neither could I think it was proper, or for his welfare, that he should take him to the Fives-court, and such places; and carry him out with him when he went picking up the girls on the town; it was likely to corrupt and vitiate him, and bring him up to like such ruinous practices. He said perhaps the last was wrong; but that he did not know that it was any good to bring up children in ignorance of the world. I observed that he was a very affectionate, kind-hearted and good child, both to him and to me; and he replied that he had taught him all that; but that I was frequently telling him that his father did not behave well to his mother. I told him the child made his own observations, and was pretty competent to judge of the matter; but that I had told him he was a very kind father to him, though he did not behave well towards me. He said I had always despised him, and his abilities. I asked him if the women with whom he associated were any better judges of them, and told him, in spite of his assertion, that he did not wish them to know or understand that he had abilities; nobody was more sore on that point; but, I added, that all recrimination was now useless, as probably all intercourse between us had for ever ended; he said he should be very good friends with me, and acknowledge himself obliged, if I carried through the business; if not, he would never see me again. I told him, I should certainly not want to see him in that event. He said that a paper had been brought to him from Mr Gray that day; but that he was only just come in from Lanark, after walking thirty miles, and was getting his tea. Said, I had better not come there again; and I told him I did not intend it, without a necessity; and observed to him that I had come in the dusk of the evening, and in a veil.'[45]

There is poignancy discernible between some of these lines. At the same time Sarah Stoddart seems to have had a robustly pragmatic attitude to the divorce. They had, after all, ceased to live together several years before – perhaps as many as five years before, so the arrangement was chiefly a matter of business. She treated her visit to Scotland as an opportunity for sightseeing, and in the event travelled far afield, even taking ship for a brief look at Ireland.

Sarah Stoddart's journal is disarming and brave. From her travel guide she transcribed information about the places she saw. She fearlessly undertook walking journeys for scores of miles, and visited great houses to see their picture collections. At Dalkeith Palace she unexpectedly encountered Hazlitt again, there on the same errand. Hazlitt was amazed by one of the pictures at Dalkeith, *Truth Finding Fortune in the Sea* by Luca Giordano, which contained a nude that looked exactly like Sarah Walker. Sarah Stoddart noticed that he thought it a likeness to his 'Sally', and commented on it in her diary. Hazlitt was so overcome by the painting that he walked back to Dalkeith a few days later to gaze at the Sarah Walker image in it again.

The reason why Sarah Stoddart could go on walking tours, and Hazlitt could lecture in Glasgow, and both could make visits to picture collections, was that the proceedings required a further delay of two months. Hazlitt went through the process of being formally identified as committing adultery with Mary Walker, and Sarah Stoddart thereafter 'deponed' to the effect that she was desirous of being divorced from him on the grounds of his various adulteries in London, Edinburgh, and their suburbs, as well as in unknown towns and their suburbs too, but especially with the said Mary Walker (such was the legal style of the Scottish deposition) – and yet still they had to wait.

Hazlitt's Glasgow lectures were arranged by Sheridan Knowles, now resident there as a teacher of elocution and owner of a local newspaper, the *Glasgow Free Press*. Hazlitt's two lectures were repeats of his Surrey Institution series, one on Shakespeare and Milton, the other on Thomson and Burns. After the first, given on Monday 6 May 1822, Hazlitt and Knowles went on a walking tour to Loch Lomond. Hazlitt afterwards recalled the sight of Ben Lomond from Dumbarton bridge, 'clad in air and sunshine'. He was a man of note, and the *Glasgow Chronicle* duly reported, 'Mr Hazlitt, we understand, is employing the interval between his first and second lectures in an excursion to Loch Lomond and the Trossachs. That strong feeling of the sublime and picturesque which manifests itself in his writings, must fit him peculiarly for appreciating the beauties of the scenery ... We may doubtless expect a sketch of the highland landscape, from his original and powerful pen.'[46]

But Hazlitt was missing Sarah Walker too much, and he was too tormented by uncertainty and jealousy, to be able to stomach the delays without seeing her, at least briefly. On the day after his second lecture, given on Monday 13 May, he hurried back to Edinburgh and secured himself a berth on the next morning's sailing to London.

The ship reached London's Blackwall dock on Friday evening. As it sailed up the Thames 'the air thickened with the consciousness of being near her,' Hazlitt wrote, 'and I "heaved her name pantingly forth".' He ran eagerly through the dark tangled streets of the East End and the City to Southampton Buildings, hoping that Sarah Walker would be delighted to see him, and would fall into his arms, and promise to marry him as soon as he was free.

But at the first glance he saw that something was wrong. 'It was with much difficulty and after several pressing intreaties that she was prevailed upon to come up into the room; and when she did she stood at the door, cold, distant, averse; and when at length she was persuaded by my repeated remonstrances to come and take my hand, and I offered to touch her lips, she turned her head and shrank from my embraces, as if quite alienated or mortally offended.'[47] Anxiously and tenderly he asked her what her behaviour meant, but she would not or could not reply. 'I hardly knew how to bear this first reception after so long an absence, and so different from the one my sentiments towards her merited; but I thought it might possibly be prudery (as I had returned without actually accomplishing what I went about) or that she had taken offence at something in my letters.' Pressed, Sarah Walker said it was none of these things, nor had she fallen in love with someone else in his absence.

Hazlitt had to let her go without getting an explanation for her behaviour, and she continued to be cool towards him on the next day too. But then, on Sunday, when William the younger was with him on his exeat from school, Sarah Walker seemed to soften, and for a while something of the old easiness between them returned. 'I walked out with my little boy, intending to go and dine out at one or two places, but I found that I still contrived to bend my steps towards her, and I went back to take tea at home. While we were out, I talked to William about Sarah, saying she too was unhappy, and asking him to make it up with her. He said, if she was unhappy, he would not bear her malice any more. When she came up with the tea-things, I said to her, "William has something to say to you – I believe he wants to be friends." On which he said in his abrupt, hearty manner, "Sarah, I'm sorry if I've ever said anything to vex you" – so they shook hands, and she said, smiling affably, "*Then* I'll think no more of it!" '[48] Hazlitt had given Sarah Walker his prized statuette of Napoleon, and that morning found it returned to the mantelpiece in his sitting-room. 'I added – "I see you've brought back my little Buonaparte" – she answered with tremulous softness – "I told you I'd keep it safe for you!" – as if her pride and pleasure in doing so had been equal, and she had, as it were, thought of nothing during my absence but how to greet me with this proof of her fidelity on my return. I cannot describe her manner. Her words are few and simple; but you can have no idea of the exquisite, unstudied, irresistible graces with which she accompanies them' – and Hazlitt quoted the lines in the play *Mirandola* by his friend Bryan Procter, which had indeed been written with Hazlitt's vision of Sarah Walker as their model –

> See with what a waving air she goes
> Along the corridor. How like a fawn!
> Yet statelier. No sound (however soft)
> Nor gentlest echo telleth when she treads,
> But every motion of her shape doth seem
> Hallowed by silence. So did Hebe grow
> Among the gods a paragon! Away, I'm grown
> The very fool of Love!

Sarah Walker's remark about the little Napoleon figure, and her demeanour as she said it, fired all Hazlitt's hopes again. That evening he asked her to come to see him, but when she did she had resumed her coldness, and would not come further into his room than the doorway. He placed a chair there and sat talking to her, holding her hand, and after a while she began to listen 'patiently, thoughtfully, and seemed a good deal affected by what I said. I told her how much I had felt, how much I had suffered for her in my absence, and how much I had been hurt by her sudden silence.' He looked back to the first year of their relationship, when he had been happy. ' "Ah! Sarah, when I think that it is only a year ago that you were everything to me I could wish, and that now you seem lost to me forever, the month of May (the name of which ought to be a signal for joy and hope) strikes chill to my heart. – How different is this meeting from that delicious parting, when you seemed never weary of repeating the proofs of your regard and tenderness, and it was with difficulty we tore ourselves asunder at last! I am ten thousand times fonder of you than I was then, and ten thousand times more unhappy." "You have no reason to be so; my feelings towards you are the same as they ever were." I told her, "She was my all of hope or comfort: my passion for her grew stronger every time I saw her." She answered, "She was sorry for it; for *that* she could never return." '[49]

Hazlitt was under tremendous strain. The Edinburgh journey with its delays and frustrations, the sudden journey back to London to see his adored Sarah Walker, her coolness and contrariness, all conspired to ratchet his state of mind to a pitch. 'All this time she was standing just outside the door, my hand in hers (would that they could have grown together!) she was dressed in a loose morning-gown, her hair curled beautifully; she stood with her profile to me, and looked down the whole time. No expression was ever more soft or perfect. Her whole attitude, her whole form, was dignity and bewitching grace. I said to her, "You look like a queen, my love, adorned with your graces!" I grew idolatrous, and would have kneeled to her. She made a movement, as if she was displeased. I then got up, and offered to kiss her at parting. I found that she obstinately refused. That stung me to the quick. It was the first time in her life she had ever done so. There must be some new bar between us to produce these continued denials; and she had not even esteem enough left to tell me so. I followed her halfway downstairs, but to no purpose, and returned into my room, confirmed in my most dreadful surmises.'

And then the stress, the frustration, the misery of his situation overwhelmed him. 'I could bear it no longer. I gave way to all the fury of disappointed hope and jealous passion. I tore the locket which contained her hair (and which I used to wear continually in my bosom, as the precious token of her dear regard) from my neck, and trampled it to pieces. I then dashed the little Buonaparte on the ground, and stamped upon it, as one of her instruments of mockery. I could not stay in the room; I could not leave it; my rage, my despair was uncontroulable. I shrieked curses on her name, and on her false love; and the scream I uttered (so pitiful and piercing was it, that the sound of it terrified me) instantly brought the whole house, father, mother, lodgers and all, into my room. They thought I was destroying her and myself. I had gone into the bedroom, merely to hide away from myself, and as I came out of it, raging-mad with the new sense of shame and lasting misery, Mrs F— said, "She's in there! He has got her in there!" thinking the cries had proceeded from her, and that I had been offering her violence. "Oh! No," I said, "she's in no danger from me; I am not the person"; and tried to burst from this scene of degradation.'[50] Mrs Walker did not want to let him pass; Mr Walker angrily said, 'Let him go! Why should he stay?' As Hazlitt ran down the stairs they called, 'What has she done to you?' and he shouted back, 'She has murdered me! – She has destroyed me forever! – She has doomed my soul to perdition!' He fled into the night, thinking never to go back; 'but I was no sooner in the street, than the desolation and the darkness became greater, more intolerable; and the eddying violence of my passion drove me back to the source from whence it sprung.' Mr Walker stood angrily at the door, barring the way. Hazlitt said, 'I have to beg pardon, Sir, but my mad fit is over, and I wish to say a few words to you in private.' Walker hesitated, but then – perhaps, Hazlitt surmised, because he was anxious to know what trouble Sarah was in – let him in, and followed him upstairs.

They went to Hazlitt's room, and Hazlitt told him everything. 'It is true, Sir, that I have lost my peace of mind forever,' he said, 'but at present, I am quite calm and collected, and I wish to explain to you why I have behaved in so extravagant a way, and to ask for your advice and intercession.' Walker agreed. 'Sarah told me, Sir (and I shall never forget the way in which she told me, fixing her dove's eyes on me, and looking a thousand tender reproaches for the loss of that good opinion, which she held dearer than all the world) she told me, Sir, that as you one day passed the door, which stood a-jar, you saw her in an attitude which a good deal startled you; I mean sitting in my lap, with her arms around my neck, and mine twined round her in the fondest manner. What I wished to ask was, whether this was actually the case, or whether it was a mere invention of her own, to enhance the sense of my obligations to her; for I begin to doubt everything?' – 'Indeed, it was so; and very much surprised and hurt

283

I was to see it.' 'Well then, Sir, I can only say, that as you saw her sitting then, so she had been sitting for the last year and a half, almost every day of her life, by the hour together; and you may judge for yourself, knowing what a nice modest-looking girl she is, whether, after having been admitted to such intimacy with so sweet a creature, and for so long a time, it is not enough to make any one frantic to be received by her as I have been since my return.'[51]

This news shocked Walker, who seemed genuinely unaware of his daughter's relationship with Hazlitt. Hazlitt went on, detailing everything, explaining everything, including the current proceedings in Edinburgh. Then he told Walker that his friend Patmore had advised him to complete the divorce and afterwards return to London to ask Sarah Walker to marry him. If she refused, that would be the end of the matter. Walker said, 'Well, Sir, and I don't think you can follow better advice.'

Calmed by this conversation, and buoyed by Walker's response, Hazlitt stayed in Southampton Buildings for another week, alternately happy and despairing. Sarah's sister and mother delighted him by hinting that Sarah was not indifferent to him – they told him that she treasured the books he had given her, and had never sat with other lodgers as she sat with him, for hours together. But then he saw Sarah herself, and she behaved coldly, repeating emphatically that she could never love him; and he collapsed into despair again, and had visions of her sitting on other lodgers' knees. It was in this state of jealousy, uncertainty, hope, despair, devotion, and more jealousy, that he caught ship back to Edinburgh on 30 May for the last stages of the divorce proceedings.

On board ship jealousy got the upper hand. He wrote to Patmore: 'A raging fire is in my heart and in my brain, that never quits me.' He had been dwelling on the other lodgers, and on his visions of her with them, and on the conversation about the seven-inch penis. He told Patmore that 'the iron had entered my soul – forever. I have since thought more profoundly about it than ever before and am convinced beyond a doubt that she is a regular lodging-house decoy, who leads a sporting life with every one who comes in succession, and goes different lengths according as she is urged or inclined. This is why she will not marry, because she hankers after this sort of thing. She has an itch for being slabbered and felt, and this she is determined to gratify upon system, and has a pride in making fools of the different men she indulges herself with and at the same time can stop short from the habit of running the gauntlet with so many. The impudent whore to taunt me that "she had always told me that she had no affection for me" as a salvo for her new lewdness – and how did she tell me this, sitting in my lap, twining herself round me, letting me enjoy her through her petticoats, looking as if she would faint with tenderness and modesty, admitting all sorts of indecent liberties and declaring "however she might agree to her own ruin, she would never consent to bring disgrace on her family".' The thought of what this had once meant to him enraged Hazlitt. She was, he told Patmore, a 'monster of lust and duplicity ... a hardened, impudent, heartless whore.' He suspected her of having played a double game with himself and Tomkins, and now it seemed to him that she was on suspiciously intimate terms with another lodger, one Griffiths, a pharmacist, a blackguardly-looking strongly-built man – the man, indeed, of the seven inches – just suitable for Sarah, Hazlitt railed to Patmore, because 'the bitch wants a *stallion*.' His suspicions alighted on Griffiths because of the conversation he had overheard in the kitchen. 'Can there be a doubt,' he railed to Patmore, 'when the mother dilates in this way on codpieces and the son replies in measured terms, that the girl runs mad for size. Miss is small, and exaggerates dimensions by contrast. Misjudging fair! Yet it is she whom I have spared a hundred times from witnessing this consummation devoutly wished by the whole kitchen in chorus, after she has been rubbing against me, hard at it for an hour together; [and I] thinking to myself, "the girl is a good girl, and means no harm – it is only her fondness for me, not her lech after a man." ' He now thought that Sarah Walker had never wanted to be courted as a bride, only as 'a common wench ... She would not agree to a "tie", because she would leave herself open to any new pretender that answered her purpose better, and *bitch* me without ceremony or mercy, & then say – "she had always told me that she had no regard for me" – as a reason for transferring her obscenities (for such they were without doubt) from me to her next favourite. Her addicting herself to Tomkins was endurable, because he was a gentlemanly sort of man, but her putting up with this prick of a fellow, merely for bone & measurement & gross manners, sets me low indeed.'

He reached Edinburgh in a state of feverish misery. He could not keep still; he went down to Renton, then hurried back to Edinburgh, unable to work, unable even to think. The city was in a ferment because of a murder trial over another fatal duel prompted by scurrilities in *Blackwood's Magazine*, and when a verdict was reached the trial judge roundly criticized the magazine for its part in the affair. Such events would normally have been venison to Hazlitt, but now he was indifferent to them. All he could do was to pour out his suffering to Patmore in letters.

Sarah Stoddart meanwhile went on a trip to Ireland. She had had to borrow money from local acquaintances because Hazlitt, in his confusion and distress before going to London, had not paid her what he promised, but he now gave her ten pounds, which was ample for the canal boat fare to Glasgow and a passage across the Irish Sea. She had taken her oath on 11 June, and the final hearing was scheduled for 28 June. But when this hearing drew near Hazlitt's solicitor advised him to defend the action in order to avoid all suspicion of collusion. That meant yet a further delay. Sarah Stoddart went on another tour, this time walking in the Highlands, and Hazlitt – accompanied by Henderson, the *Blackwood's* spy of whom he suspected nothing – tried to quieten himself by visiting collections of pictures. Before going he wrote to Sarah Walker in penitent mood: ' "Evil to them that evil think" is an old saying; and I have found it a true one. I have ruined myself by unjust suspicions of you. Your sweet friendship was the balm of my life, and I have lost it, I fear, forever, by one fault and folly after another. What would I give to be restored to the place in your esteem, which, you assured me, I held only a few months ago! ... Can you not forget and forgive the past, and judge of me by my conduct in the future? Can you not take all my follies in the lump, and say like a good, generous girl, "Well, I'll think no more of them"? In a word, may I come back, and try to behave better?'[52]

Viewing pictures might have helped calm him briefly, but it was on this tour that he visited Dalkeith Palace and saw the painting with a nude vision of Sarah Walker in it, an accident hardly calculated to calm him. On the contrary, it revived and exacerbated his jealous anxieties. It suddenly became a matter of urgency that he find out for certain whether Sarah Walker was indeed merely a 'boarding-house jilt'. He now regretted not having tried to sleep with her – 'I spared her so often because I hoped better things of her & to make her my future wife,' he told Patmore – but his torment at the thought of her having intercourse with Griffiths and Tomkins, and anyone else who had been less scrupulous than he, made him think that she indeed preferred such men for that reason, and laughed at him for his timidity. To Patmore he wrote, 'I intreat you get someone to work to ascertain for me, without loss of time, whether she is a common sporter, or not. Nothing else but the knowledge of her being common can reconcile me to myself, after what has passed.' The idea was to have someone take lodgings in the Walker household, and while there to try to seduce her. 'I see the young witch seated in another's lap, twining her serpent arms around him, her eyes glancing, her cheeks on fire – Damn the unnatural hag! Oh! oh! Why does not the hideous thought choake me?' He even suggested that Patmore himself might assay her: '*You* may try her, if you like – a pot-belly and a slender waist match by contrast. Do they not? I shall soon be in town, and see. Pity me ... Life is hideous to me, and death horrible. What shall I do? Oh! That I knew she was a strumpet, and that she knew I did.'

But then he received a letter from Patmore telling him that the Walker and Roscoe families were not averse to his marrying Sarah, if she would have him, and that although she was 'at present indisposed' to do so, it was 'by no means certain that she may not, at some future period, consent to it'. And moreover, Roscoe had assured Patmore that Sarah Walker was a 'good girl, and likely to make any man an excellent wife'. All might still be well, Patmore wrote, if only Hazlitt would be patient and well behaved. Hazlitt's heart soared. 'I can only say you have saved my life!' he replied in a delirium of delight, adding, 'She is an angel from heaven, and you can never say that I said to the contrary! . . . She is a saint, an angel, a love . . .'

The divorce was finally granted on 17 July. That evening Sarah Stoddart came to Hazlitt's lodgings to try to get the money he owed her, and they drank tea together, rather companionably. She recorded this conversation in detail too, for in it Hazlitt told her the whole story of his infatuation with Sarah Walker. It sheds light on the marriage just ended, confirming Hazlitt's claim that Sarah Stoddart was sexually experienced when she and Hazlitt married, and that she had had her adulterous 'intrigues' too; and that the nude in the picture at Dalkeith Palace was in her opinion more like herself than Sarah Walker – 'I said it was much nearer my form in the thighs the fall of the back and the contour of the whole figure. He said, I was very well made,' she wrote, pleased at the compliment. He told her that he sometimes thought Sarah Walker was an angel, and sometimes a common strumpet. He said, 'The mother was the most disgusting, vulgar old wretch that could be and corrupted her children's minds by her bawdy indecent conversation, though he had never heard an improper or indelicate word from the girl; yet it had often struck him, that they had never objected to the girls of the town coming up to him continually, and that Sarah would often send them up when her mother had said he was not from home, for which they praised her and said she was a nice girl.' Sarah Stoddart commented, 'I told him it showed what the house and the people were well enough.'[53]

The day after the divorce was granted, without pausing to say goodbye to anyone, Hazlitt hurried back to London and Southampton Buildings. He was free, and wanted to be near Sarah Walker – but on Patmore's advice he resolved to let time elapse before proposing to her. At their first re-encounter Sarah gave him a friendly welcome – unknown to him she was under instructions from her mother not to inflame him, for he had told

Mrs Walker that he wished to rent all the apartments in the house for a total of a hundred guineas a year, ostensibly to lighten Sarah's work but in reality to keep other lodgers away. When his attentions began to grow warm Sarah deflected them by bursting into tears. But she did not immediately dampen his revived hopes. She sewed some frills onto a shirt for him, and took his little statue of Napoleon to be mended. She brought it back to him in one piece, and they 'shook hands in token of reconciliation'. And then, wrote Hazlitt, 'she went waving out of the room, but at the door turned round and looked full at me, as she did the first time she beguiled me of my heart.'[54]

Hazlitt's decision to be cautious and patient, behaving well towards Sarah and not forcing matters, was intended to give her time to come round to him. But he was also hungry to possess her entirely and exclusively as his own, and after a few days he became nervous about something going wrong – another attack of coldness on her part, or frenzy on his; or the arrival of a new attractive lodger. Several times he was on the point of going downstairs to ask Sarah and her mother to come with him to Scotland immediately so that they could marry. He managed to stop himself. But one day he found he could wait no longer. He plucked up his courage and went downstairs to speak to them. In the kitchen Betsey told him that Sarah had gone to visit her grandmother in Somers Town, near Euston. Determined to see his resolution through, he went out in the hope of meeting her.

It was a fateful decision. As he walked he saw her coming towards him, and at first he thought she was alone. But then, as the crowd parted, he saw that she was with a tall good-looking young man. It took him a moment or two to recognize who it was. It was Tomkins, the lodger who had taken Sarah's fancy, and whose arrival had marked the beginning of the end of Hazlitt's intimacy with her. He passed them without speaking, and when he turned to look back he saw that they had turned to look back too. He retraced his steps, and they did likewise, and again they crossed without speaking. It was clear that Sarah and Tomkins were lovers, and by this dumb show were telling him so. 'The murder was out!' Hazlitt afterwards wrote in describing this devastating moment. In terrible, speechless, utter despair he stumbled back to Southampton Buildings.

According to the closing pages of the *Liber Amoris*, this encounter marked the end of the wretched story. Hazlitt said that he had one more interview with Sarah, in which she told him all about her relationship with Tomkins, thus giving Hazlitt his explanation at last of why she had rejected him. 'I felt deep grief, but no enmity towards her,' Hazlitt wrote. After their interview Hazlitt went out for a walk to calm himself, and by chance met Tomkins, and asked him for a few minutes' talk. In the event they talked for four hours, very frankly, and learned to their mutual amazement that there had been a long period when Sarah was alternating between Hazlitt's lap and Tomkins's, playing a dangerous game which now explained why sometimes, when cuddling with Hazlitt, she would suddenly colour violently and hurry away: it was because she had heard Tomkins return – she knew his tread on the stairs – and she did not want him to find her out.

'I did not sleep a wink all that night,' Hazlitt concluded the *Liber Amoris*, 'nor did I know till the next day the full meaning of what had happened to me. With the morning's light, conviction glared in upon me that I had not only lost her for ever – but every feeling I had ever had towards her – respect, tenderness, pity – all but my fatal passion, was gone.' And then, at the end, he wrote, 'The agony, the conflict of hope and fear, of adoration and jealousy, is over; or it would, ere long, have ended with my life.'[55]

But the wretched story was not quite over. There were several more scenes to play, among them one especially pitiable and another especially ugly. The pitiable one was that Hazlitt found himself unable to refrain from telling every one he met the whole story of the catastrophe. He did it out of sheer pain, coping with it by publicizing it. Haydon recorded in his diary on 9 August 1822, 'Hazlitt called last night in a state of absolute insanity about the girl who has jilted him.' He added, 'Poor Hazlitt's candour is great and his unaffected frankness is interesting.'[56] Barry Corn-wall reported that 'on one occasion I know he told the story of his attachment to five different persons in the same day, and at each time entered into minute details of his love story. "I am a cursed fool," he said to me. "I just saw J— going into Wills' Coffee-house yesterday morning; he spoke to me, I followed him into the house; and whilst he lunched, I told him the whole story. Then" (said he) "I wandered into the Regent's Park, where I met one of M—'s sons. I walked with him some time, and on his using some civil expression, by God! Sir, I told him the whole story. Well, sir, then I went and called on Haydon, but he was out. There was only his man, Salmon, there; but by God! I could not help myself. It all came out; the whole cursed story! Afterwards I went to look at some lodgings at Pimlico. The landlady at one place, after some explanations as to rent, etc., said to me very kindly, "I am afraid you are not well, sir?" – "No, Ma'am," said I, "I am not well"; and on her enquiring further, the devil take me if I did not let out the whole story, from beginning to end!'[57]

To say that he was not well was an understatement. When Mary Shelley,

Godwin's daughter, saw Hazlitt after the affair – she had been in Italy, and had not seen him for several years – she was appalled by the change it had made in him: 'I never was so shocked in my life – gaunt and thin, his hair scattered, his cheek bones projecting – but for his voice and smile I should not have known him – his smile brought tears into my eyes, it was like a sun beam illuminating the most melancholy of ruins – lightning that assured you in a dark night of the identity of a friend's ruined and deserted abode.'[58]

The affair was a matter of open comment among all who knew Hazlitt, whether personally or by repute. Crabb Robinson was disgusted by it, and so (he claimed) was Mary Lamb and Mrs Montagu. Haydon wrote to Mary Russell Mitford, 'Hazlitt at present gives me great pain by the folly with which he is conducting himself. He has fallen in love with a lodging-house hussy, who will be his death. He has been to Scotland and divorced his wife although he has a fine little boy by her; and after doing this to marry this girl, he comes back and finds that she has been making a fool of him in order to get presents, and in reality has been admitting a lover more favoured. Hazlitt's torture is beyond expression; you may imagine it. The girl really excited in him devoted and intense love. His imagination clothes her with that virtue which her affected modesty induced him to believe in, and he is really downright in love with an ideal perfection, which has no existence but in his own head! He talks of nothing else day and night.'[59]

The other scene – the ugly one – was, perhaps, a necessary catharsis for Hazlitt, and it at last taught him what Haydon and his other friends already guessed about Sarah Walker, which was that she was neither an angel nor a slut – these being the only alternatives Hazlitt could envisage until then – but merely a girl who, brought up with bachelor lodgers, had learned how to flirt and tease, and who usually had a pretty good idea how far to go. In this case, however, she had miscalculated, having no means of guessing in advance the power and distortion of Hazlitt's emotions, and no means of dealing with them properly once they were unleashed.

Sarah Walker was, in truth, not really the object of Hazlitt's grand passion, so much as the occasion for it. She fitted a preconception of his, and he was mesmerized by a few accidents of her walk and manner, so that, as Haydon recognized, he saw and loved an illusion. The real damage was done in the early months, when Sarah Walker sat on his knee with her arms around his neck, cuddling and fondling him, leading him to believe that what he longed for had at last happened: he was loved, and by a sweet modest graceful feminine creature who summoned all his masculine powers of love, desire and protectiveness in response. When the reality began to conform less and less to the illusion, he began more and more violently to wish to believe in it. So tremendous was the desire, and so shattering the disappointment, in this three-year-long ecstasy and agony, that he became as Mary Shelley described: emaciated, pale, his hair thinning and greying, his gaze half-obliterated by sorrow.

The ugly scene consisted of Hazlitt's putting into effect the plan he had mooted to Patmore, of having someone lodge at the Walkers' with a view to seducing or trying to seduce Sarah, to see what she was really made of. It is a mark of his obsession that this happened in March 1823, eight months after the final talk, recorded above, with Sarah herself, and the ensuing talk with Tomkins. Hazlitt kept a journal of the period between 4 and 16 March when his decoy, whom he calls 'F', was residing at Southampton Buildings. In it he detailed everything F told him of his dealings with Sarah, together with bitter comments on Sarah's too-familiar doings and sayings, each of which gave him a terrible pang.

F moved into the Walkers' house on 4 March. On 5 March he took off his trousers in Sarah's presence and 'naked' gave them to her for brushing. Later he asked her for a kiss, which 'very gracious & smiling' she refused. Her refusal was only temporary; on 8 March F kissed her several times, 'and while this passed he had hold of one hand, & the other was at liberty, but she did not once attempt to raise it so as to make even a show of resistance.' On 9 March F saw her whispering with Tomkins, and later had her in his room to talk, where he kissed her again. The next morning she brought F his breakfast tray dressed in her finest gown, saying that she was going out – but Hazlitt saw this as a ploy to appear at her best. 'Decoy! Damned, treble damned ideot! [several words inked out] When shall I burn her from my thoughts? – Yet I like to hear about her – that she had her bed-gown or her ruff on, that she stood or sat, or made some insipid remark, is to me to be in heaven – to know that she is a whore or an ideot is better than nothing. Were I in Hell, my only consolation would be to learn of her. In Heaven to see her would be my only reward.'[60] F was convinced that Sarah had no conversation, and had not read any of the books Hazlitt gave her. When Hazlitt asked F if he would like to set up Sarah as his mistress, at Hazlitt's expense, F declined, saying that he preferred a woman who could read and talk.

The saga continued. F kissed Sarah, then progressed to laying a hand on her thigh without her protest, and then sat with his arm around her neck playing with her necklace and stroking her throat, which she enjoyed. On 14 March 'F got her between his legs so that she came right into contact with him. She made no resistance or complaint ... He said "Miss

I will kill you with kissing, if I catch you," "But you must catch me first," she said, and bounded down stairs and stood looking up and laughing at the first landing place.'[61] Hazlitt began to worry that F was falling in love with Sarah. F asked Sarah if she would live with him, and Sarah asked whether it would be proper, or seemly, 'and kept sobbing and crying all the time & said at last she must go now. But she could come and sit with him when they were all gone to bed.'[62] On 15 March F put his hand between her legs; 'She only said, "Let me go, Sir," and retired to the door, where she asked whether he would have the fire lighted.' On 16 March she would have nothing to do with F, who tried to offer her his arm as she was walking out – to meet Tomkins, as it transpired, although she had told her family she was going to her grandmother. And there the journal ends, with Hazlitt scribbling desperately up one side of the margin, 'I also am her lover & will live and die for her only, since she can be true to any one . . . Let her be to hell with her tongue –. She is as true as heaven wished her heart and lips to be.'[63]

# CHAPTER THIRTEEN

# The Traveller

## 1823–1825

To escape Sarah Walker, and to escape the William Hazlitt who was besotted by her and whose heart she had broken, Hazlitt pieced together a carefully arranged and astonishing little book, a book which is repulsive to any reader who does not know the story of his enchantment and destruction, and unbearably poignant to anyone who does. The book is the *Liber Amoris, or, The New Pygmalion*.

It was a book Hazlitt had to write. Dr Johnson said that no-one would be a writer unless he had no alternative way of earning money. If he spoke for anyone other than himself, he spoke for a minority. Most writers write out of inner necessity. Their urge towards published expression has any number of sources, including a desire to make sense of the world, and to have their say about it. And at times they write to heal themselves, by translating what is internal into something objective, projecting it into the public domain where, by becoming the possession of others too, it detaches itself, wholly or partially, from its roots in the writer's soul. This was Hazlitt's motivation in writing *Liber Amoris*. But his aim was not merely personal purgation. *Liber Amoris* was also intended to be a psychological study, and a cautionary tale.[1]

Hazlitt certainly wrote to make a living, and there was nothing incidental about the practicalities involved. But it had always, and far more importantly, been the case that he wrote because he had to open the overflow of his mind and sentiments, to release the pressure of their abundance within. He once said, in connection with Leigh Hunt's obsession over some or other pet theory, 'Damn him, it's always coming out like a rash. Why doesn't he write a book about it and get rid of it?'[2] Haydon therefore understood Hazlitt's motivation perfectly. In a letter to Mary Russell Mitford in August 1822 he wrote, '[Hazlitt] has written down all the conversations without colour, literal as they happened; he has preserved all the love-letters, many of which are equal to anything of the sort, and are really affecting; and I believe, in order to ease his soul of this burden, means with certain arrangements, to publish it as a tale of character. He will sink into idiotcy if he does not get rid of it.'

When Hazlitt began work on *Liber Amoris* at Stamford on his first journey to Scotland in 1822, he still of course hoped that Sarah Walker would become his wife, and therefore his aim was to give an account of how hard won she had been, written as much for her – to prove the strength of his passion – as for publication. Its final character can only have been decided after the day Hazlitt saw Sarah Walker and Tomkins together in the street.

The book was published at the beginning of May 1823, two months after the unedifying episode of F's attempted seduction of Sarah Walker. It immediately caused a tremendous storm. It did so at an especially inopportune moment for Hazlitt, who was just about to sue *Blackwood's* again. What the disaster of his passion for Sarah Walker began, the scandal over *Liber Amoris* completed: by publishing the unhappy story to the world he gave his critics the right to claim that their imputations of moral irregularity were true, that he was a dangerous radical in social as well as political ideology – that he was, in short, a tainted man, a proven enemy of order and decency.

For some weeks after that fateful day in July 1822 when Hazlitt saw Sarah Walker and Tomkins together, he was in too much misery to work – and indeed in too much misery to notice the tragedy that month of Shelley's death by drowning in Italy. He had met all his and Sarah Stoddart's expenses for the Scottish divorce in part from his advance for the feverishly written second volume of *Table Talk*, and in part through a generous £100 subvention from Francis Jeffrey. But necessity is no respecter of sorrow, and Hazlitt was not in a position to afford a lengthy mourning. He wrote to Jeffrey in August 1822 soliciting work, suggesting books he might review, and adding in his letter, 'I have since I returned found out the person I told you of to be a regular lodging-house decoy. I hope the state of distraction I was in about the affair will plead my excuse for any oddnesses I might be guilty of while in Edinburgh. I am better a good deal, but feel much like a man who has been thrown from the top of a house.'

Resumption of work helped, and very soon he was filled with ideas for various projects. In October he suggested to Jeffrey an article surveying the chief newspapers and journals of the day. Jeffrey agreed. In this letter Hazlitt told him, 'I am better than I was, and able to work ... I have come away *alive*, which in the circumstances is a great deal.' The letter's address shows that he had taken lodgings at No. 4 Chapel Street West, Curzon Street, in the West End of London. In his accustomed way he went at the first opportunity to Winterslow, and from there corresponded with Taylor and Hessey about articles he was currently writing for their *London Magazine*. His letters also mentioned a new project he had agreed to undertake for them: a series of pen-portraits of the picture collections of England. This idea grew from his account of the Earl of Exeter's collection, published by the *New Monthly Magazine* in the preceding April. He now proposed to visit all of the country's principal collections, with as usual a view to publishing his accounts of them in book form afterwards. He had also conceived an idea for a series of 'Maxims and Reflections' in the style of La Rochefoucauld, and when he returned to London in November he sat into the early hours of the morning discussing it with Hessey.

Hazlitt made a start on the picture galleries immediately. While in Winterslow he wrote about John Julius Angerstein's superb collection – subsequently bequeathed to the nation as the nucleus of the National Gallery – and visited Fonthill Abbey, whose new owner had just opened it to the public. While in London in November he revisited Dulwich, and afterwards went to Blenheim on the same errand, finding as much solace, or at least distraction, in writing about pictures as in looking at them.

As he was thus returning to work and finding that it calmed him somewhat, Hazlitt received a letter from Leigh Hunt in Italy, asking him to join Hunt and Byron in writing for a journal they and the lately deceased Shelley had started. Called *The Liberal: Verse and Prose from the South*, it was edited by Hunt and Byron in Italy and published by John Hunt in London. Leigh Hunt told Hazlitt that Byron admired his writing, and (so claimed a contemporary reviewer of the magazine) wanted him to join them in Pisa 'to throw a little spirit into future Numbers.'[3] There was no question of Hazlitt emigrating to Italy, but he was happy to write for them. Despite Leigh Hunt's claim that Byron admired Hazlitt's work, an acquaintance of the poet's, Dr Henry Muir, gathered a quite different impression in October of the following year. 'Speaking of Hazlitt, Lord B. expressed himself in the most bitter terms, and would not allow that he could write good English,' he reported.[4] Leigh Hunt himself explained the contradiction later by saying that Byron 'in truth was afraid of Mr Hazlitt; he admitted him like a courtier, for fear that he should be treated by him as an enemy.' He was, said Hunt, alarmed by the essays Hazlitt contributed to the *Liberal* because they dealt blows (actual and imagined) at aristocracy in general and Byron in particular.[5]

The picture gallery articles ran in the *London Magazine* during the winter of 1822–3, and in one of them Hazlitt allowed himself an auto-biographical indulgence, remembering himself as a boy sitting reading in the winter sun with his back against a wall, dreaming of literary fame, blissfully unaware of sorrows and difficulties to come. 'Come hither, thou poor little fellow, and let us change places with thee if thou wilt,' wrote Hazlitt; 'here, take the pen and finish this article, and sign what name you please to it; so that we may but change our dress for yours, and sit shivering in the sun, and con over our little task, and feed poor, and lie hard, and be contented and happy, and think what a fine thing it is to be an author, and dream of immortality, and sleep o' nights!'[6]

In the same month – January 1823 – the first two of Hazlitt's contributions to the *Liberal* appeared, the first, 'On the Spirit of Monarchy', containing some of the *lèse-majesté* that affronted and affrighted Byron. The other article was a short attack on 'The Scotch Character', with blistering asides on *Blackwood's* – describing it as impudent, dull, and run by 'a troop of Yahoos' – and Sir Walter Scott, whom he called a bigot and a coward.[7] The wormwood embittering these sentiments is the pain of Hazlitt's months in Scotland. To soften the venom of the piece Leigh Hunt added, as an editorial postscript, the words, 'A defence of the Scotch, surely.'

Despite the number of articles he was writing Hazlitt was in deep money trouble. In February he was arrested for debt, and asked Thomas Noon Talfourd, his lawyer friend, to help negotiate 'terms of accommodation' for him. At the same time he asked Taylor and Hessey for a £30 advance on the copyright of his picture galleries articles. Confinement for debt at the instigation of creditors often then took the form of house arrest, with a bailiff posted to prevent escape. While stuck in these circumstances in the February cold Hazlitt wrote one of his finest essays, 'My First Acquaintance With Poets', recalling his meeting in 1798 with Coleridge and his subsequent visit to the poets in the West Country. The essay was in Leigh Hunt's hands by the end of the month. Payment from Hunt and the advance from Taylor and Hessey helped Hazlitt to reach terms with his creditors, and he was at liberty again by the beginning of March – in time to put into effect his unfortunate plan to test Sarah Walker's virtue by means of F.

The tone of Hazlitt's essays during this stretch of months reveals his vexed state of mind. He was suffering a mixture of jealousy and loss, resentment and lonelines – which explains although it does not excuse the F episode. Only the 'First Acquaintance' essay is free from the prevailing bitter taint, but it contains a remark of great poignancy: 'I have loitered my life away, reading books, looking at pictures, going to plays, hearing, thinking, writing on what pleased me best. I have wanted only one thing to make me happy; but wanting that, I have wanted everything!'[8]

But he would have done well to mask the irritation of his feelings, especially as expressed in such unmitigated terms in his *Liberal* essay on the 'Scotch Character', because, as so often before, it proved an invitation to trouble. *Blackwood's* was not only annoyed at being called 'a troop of Yahoos', but one of its conductors, Lockhart, was Scott's son-in-law and future biographer, and he was in no mood to let Hazlitt's attacks pass. In its January 1823 review of Byron's 'Heaven and Earth', which had appeared in the *Liberal's* second number, *Blackwood's* described the magazine as 'a lion with a fine shagged king-like head, a lean body, hungered lips, and a tawdry tail – Byron – Hazlitt – Hunt. We shew now the lion's head Carcase, hips, and tail by and bye.' The promise was fulfilled in the March issue, in which *Blackwood's* alluded to Hazlitt's immoralities and his Scottish divorce. Incensed, Hazlitt wrote to *Blackwood's* London agent, Thomas Cadell, threatening to sue. In a fright Cadell immediately wrote to William Blackwood asking him how they were to 'avert the impending storm'. But there was no need: Hazlitt himself made it impossible for matters to go further – and in doing so handed *Blackwood's* and all his enemies a rod to beat him with. He did it by giving them and the world *Liber Amoris*.

*Liber Amoris* was published by John Hunt. It was issued anonymously, and in an effort to cover tracks further it was prefaced by the claim that its author was a 'North Briton' (a Scot) who had since died of his broken heart in the Netherlands.[9] Hazlitt did not really suppose that the book's authorship could remain a secret, because far too many people knew the story, and he had anyway openly informed his friends that he was about to publish it. Given this, it is surprising – even by the standards of Hazlitt's usual indifference to the consequences of what he said or did until it was too late – that he did not anticipate the trouble that the book would cause.

   *Liber Amoris* is an extraordinary work not only in its confessional character and unsettling honesty, but in its structure. It does not follow the chronology of events as they actually happened, but impressionistically weaves backwards and forwards in time, giving a painful, disturbing inevitability to the tragedy it reveals – the tragedy of an intelligent, sensitive man prostrated into absurdity, folly, disgrace and nervous collapse by his obsession with a girl whose power of enchantment was a function more of the man's imagination than her actual graces.

   The first review was, as it happened, a friendly one, because it appeared in the *Examiner*, and was written in an effort to pre-empt hostile criticism. The author of the review was Leigh Hunt's successor as the *Examiner's* editor, Albany Fonblanque, who discussed an advance proof of the book with John Hunt – publisher both of the book and the magazine – and with him decided how best to prepare the public for the strange and painful effusion about to be put before them. He did so by placing *Liber Amoris* in a confessional and passional tradition including Le Sage, Rousseau and Goethe, and told his readers that it was 'a novelty in the English language'. On all counts he was right, although his principal motive for making the book seem – so to speak – foreign in manner and content, was to protect it by distancing it from the usual expectations of English readers. Fonblanque played along with the pretence that the author had died abroad, saying: 'We are of opinion … that had he lived for some time longer he would have survived his passion.' The remark was doubtlessly intended as a word of comfort from Fonblanque to Hazlitt, and perhaps from John Hunt too.

Less than a week later the *Literary Register* identified Hazlitt as the book's author, and launched into a violent attack – 'behold Billy again; it can be no one else. A dukedom to a ducat it is Billy … "A native of North Britain, who died in the Netherlands?" Pooh! – no such thing. It is he of the "Liberal" … [he fell in love with] his landlord's daughter, a pert, cunning, coming, good-for-nothing chit, who amuses herself with Silly Billy's tomfoolery, till she draws him on to an exposure of himself in all the nakedness of his conceit, selfishness, slavering sensuality, filthy profligacy, and howling idiotcy; and all this, the poor mistaken man has deemed fit to publish to the world, with a studied minuteness of detail.' The book is one 'from which every mind, with one single spark of good sense and right feeling left in it, will turn with horror, loathing, and contempt … [it is] indecent trash … the ordure of a filthy mind.' The article has no hesitation in identifying and traducing Sarah Walker, not just in the terms above but as 'a tradesman's daughter – a common flirt – a common lodging-house servant, nay, a common trader in indecencies with every fellow in the house.' A continuation of the review appeared in the next number of the magazine, fulminating against Hazlitt's 'hateful and nauseous depravity', in the process reprinting almost all of the text of the *Liber Amoris* to prove the point.[10]

Hazlitt's authorship was also publicized by the *Literary Gazette*. 'This horrible book,' it slyly said, 'has been cruelly ascribed by some malignant enemy to Mr Hazlitt,' and expressed surprise that, given his sensitivity to attack, he had not 'leaped forth to disclaim the foul reproach.' Worse followed in June at the hands of the *John Bull*. 'The dirty abominations of the raffs of literature are far below notice,' it said, 'but when to innate stupidity, grossness, vulgarity, and impudence are added the most degraded sensuality, the most inveterate ignorance, and the most depraved principle, it becomes necessary to take a double view of their abominable struggles against, taste, decency, and morality.' The conductors of the *John Bull* had spared no efforts in mounting their attack. The review was followed by a spoof account of the affair between 'Mr Billy Hazlitt' and his 'Sally' in 'The Tailor's Lodging-House', in which Hazlitt figures as an ugly middle-aged man and Sarah Walker as 'a poor plebeian girl'. In a follow-up in the next issue, *John Bull* played its ace. Somehow it managed to acquire the letter Hazlitt wrote to Sarah Walker from Renton in March of the preceding year, and now it published the text in full (a shortened version of it appears in *Liber Amoris* itself). It is puzzling to know what either *John Bull* or its readers made of this tender and moving letter, given that it was offered as an example of Hazlitt's alleged vileness and obscenity. It therefore merits quoting again: 'Not for the world would I send thee an unkind word so far away,' it reads; 'I may be rash and hasty when I am with thee, but deliberately can I never say or do aught to cast the slightest blame upon thee. You are my idol – the dear image in my heart as "that little image" on the mantelpiece (*or somebody like it*) is thine ... can I ever forget [taking you and your mother to see *Romeo and Juliet*] – your sweet modest looks, your infinite propriety of behaviour, all your sweet ways – your hesitating about taking my arm as we came out until your mother did – your laughing about losing your cloak – your stepping into the coach without my being able to make an inch of discovery – and oh! My sitting down beside you, you whom I loved so well, so long, and your assuring me I had not lessened your pleasure at the play by being with you, and giving me that dear hand to press in mine – I seemed to be in Heaven, – that slight, exquisitely turned form contained my all of heaven upon earth – I sat beside the adorable creature by her own permission – and as I folded you, yes, you my best Sarah, to my heart, there was, as you say, "a tie between us," you did seem to be mine for a few short moments, in all truth and honour and sacredness. Oh! could we but be always so – do not mock me for I am indeed a very child in love.'[11] The abasement in the letter might be unattract-ive, but the sentiments are true and touching, and one would have thought that any reader capable of a modicum of human sympathy would see it as giving the lie to *John Bull's* brutal portrayal of Hazlitt as a monster.

No-one now knows how the letter fell into the hands of Theodore Hook, the editor of *John Bull*, but his methods were even more unscrupulous than those of present-day tabloid newspapers. It is not impossible that he bought it directly from Sarah Walker herself, for what would have seemed to her a very large sum – and she might not have grasped the full significance of what she was doing.

Review after review brought execrations down on Hazlitt's head. One reviewer called the book an 'insult to public decency and morals', another described it as 'disgraceful and disgusting'. In delight, *Blackwood's* had a field day – or field months: references to Hazlitt and the book were a running theme in the magazine for long afterwards. One specimen of the references occurs in yet another attack on the 'Cockney School', in which, says the magazine, 'Hazlitt is the most loathsome, Hunt the most ludicrous. Pygmalion is so brutified and besotted now, that he walks out into the public street, enters a bookseller's shop, mounts a stool, and represents Priapus in Ludgate Hill.'

For the rest of his life Hazlitt found references to *Liber Amoris* in reviews of all his work, usually hostile. He had been an object of political attack and character assassination before; here he had sold the pass to his enemies, and his reputation never recovered – not during his life, nor for nearly a century after his death. The *New European Magazine* expressed the anti-Hazlitt consensus perfectly in saying, '[Hazlitt] sets himself up as a critic, a moralist, a judge of human nature, and – *horresco referens* – a reformer of the morals and the politics of the people! But what will the majority of his countrymen now think of this virtuous Essayist? Will they not regard him with all the horror and detestation which he deserves? Will they not, when they hear even his name mentioned, shudder at the sound, and pray to Heaven that their children may die ignorant of his name?'

Those who knew Hazlitt personally were divided in their views. Crabb Robinson, by now perhaps predictably, was scandalized. He thought the book 'disgusting ... nauseous and revolting ... low and gross and tedious and very offensive ... it ought to exclude the author from all decent society.'[12] De Quincey, despite the coolness in the relations between the two men, remarked that the book increased his esteem for Hazlitt, because it showed that he possessed 'stronger and more agitating passions than I believed to be in the range of his nature.'[13] Mary Russell Mitford was sympathetic. She wrote that Hazlitt had found himself in love 'for the first time in his life, to desperation and folly; but it is a fine passion, and therefore affecting.'[14] She reported that an Archdeacon of her acquaintance hurried to buy the book, thinking that a first edition of it would one day prove valuable. In fact the book sold poorly, and later collectors found first editions easy to buy.

While being pelted by this pitiless storm Hazlitt saw the publication, in the summer of 1823, of his *Characteristics: In the Manner of Rochefoucauld's Maxims*. The book was not published by Taylor and Hessey after all, but by Simpkin and Marshall. The entries, over four hundred in number, are not really maxims but very short essays – essays in *haiku* form, so to say. They distil many of Hazlitt's attitudes and views, and it is remarkable to find him retaining his belief in the natural disinterestedness of man, despite the air of disillusionment that pervades most of the entries. A recurrent theme was of course provided by his late and continuing miseries. In number 126 he says, 'The affected modesty of most women is a decoy for the generous, the delicate, and unsuspecting; while the artful, the bold, and the unfeeling either see or break through its slender disguises.' In number 278 he cites as an example of people who are 'ruined with their eyes open by some whim or fancy' the man who 'divorced his wife to marry a wench at a lodging-house, who refused him, and whose cruelty and charms are the torment of his own life and that of his friends.'[15]

The *Characteristics* attracted scarcely any notice because it was swamped in the turbulent wake of *Liber Amoris*. Although Hazlitt continued to write his art-collection essays for the *London Magazine*, and full-length essays for the *Liberal*, he felt so battered by criticism, and so wretched still about Sarah Walker, that he fled London to the refuge of Winterslow. In a letter from there to Tom Hood of the *London Magazine* he said that recent events had 'hurt my mind ... I had only the heart to come down here and see my little boy.' Referring to the delay in producing some of his art-collection articles he added, 'I used to think she read and perhaps approved these articles. But whatever I do, implying an idea of taste or elegance, only makes me more odious to myself, and tantalizes me with feelings which I can never hope to excite in others – wretch that I am, and am to be, until I am nothing!'[16] He remained in Winterslow until William the younger returned to school in London, and then went to Devon to visit his mother, Peggy, and his brother John, who had recently moved to the West Country to be near his mother – not for her sake but his own, for he was an alcoholic, his marriage had ended, and he was not coping well with life. For old Mrs Hazlitt and Peggy the spectacle of their Hazlitt menfolk during the last two or three years was unquestionably a painful one, and they doubtless gave silent thanks that William senior was no longer present to witness it.

That Hazlitt was still sufferingly in love with Sarah Walker, despite his bitterness towards her, is amply proved by the fact that when he went to London for a few days in September 1823 he spent, according to Haydon, 'nearly the whole of each [night] watching Sally's door.' But he had formed a plan of action to drag himself out of his mess. To assuage the pain of loneliness while at the same time overcoming the practical difficulty of not having a regular income, he resolved to find a wife with money.[17] Others could do it – the halt, the infirm, the ugly, the boring: why not he? In August 1823 Mary Shelley wrote to Leigh Hunt in Italy: 'I asked ... about Hazlitt – This love-sick youth, jilted by Infelice, has taken to falling in love. He told Kenny that whereas formerly he thought women silly, unamusing toys, and people with whose society he delighted to dispense – he was now only happy where they were and given up to the admiration of their interesting foibles and amiable weaknesses. He is the humble servant of all marriageable young ladies ... K. met H. in the Hampstead fields – Well, sir – he said – I was just going to Mr — there's a young lady there – I don't know – But said K there was another a young lady of colour you were about to marry – has she jilted you like Infelice? – No Sir, but you see sir, she had relations – kind of people who ask after character, and as mine smacks, sir, why it was broken off.'[18] His campaign was confirmed by Haydon in a letter to Mary Russell Mitford: 'He had another flame, who is at Hampton; down he went to tempt her for Gretna; but her brother, an officer in the Navy, happened to be with her; and "officers," said Hazlitt, "you know, are awkward fellows to deal with." Oh, the gallant, gay Lothario!'[19]

Hazlitt was still working on his series of articles about picture-collections, and as it was contracted to appear in book form when finished he needed to expedite matters. He resumed his visits to great houses, this time in company with Patmore, who was undertaking a similar task for the *New Monthly Magazine*. Patmore recorded how he and Hazlitt spent ten days at Fonthill Abbey – the house and its contents were about to be auctioned – and together visited Stourhead to see Sir Richard Colt Hoare's pictures. Hazlitt greeted 'with childish delight' old favourites among the paintings they saw, and enjoyed introducing Patmore to them. One day, 'in broiling sunshine,' the two men walked twelve miles together, and Patmore was struck by 'the extraordinary physical as well as moral effect produced on Hazlitt by the sight and feel of the country ... he was like a being of another species; his step firm, vigorous and rapid; his look eager and onward, as if devouring the way before it – and his whole air buoyant and triumphant.'[20]

As another distraction from his present troubles Hazlitt had begin putting together a poetry anthology, including in it work by contemporaries. The *Liberal* foundered after just four numbers, but Hazlitt was again writing 'Table Talks' and contributing them to the *New Monthly Magazine*. His long piece on the 'periodical press' – a survey of contemporary journalism – had appeared in the *Edinburgh Review* in May, at the same time as *Liber Amoris*, and now as 1823 ended responses to it began to appear. *Blackwood's* lamented the fact that Francis Jeffrey 'has suffered William Hazlitt, author of the *Liber Amoris*, an old newspaper-monger – a gentleman of the press, that has lived all his days scribbling dramatic criticisms, and leading paragraphs, and so forth, for the different London newspapers and magazines; – he has suffered this low, vulgar impudent gentleman of the press – the writer of that filthy book, which, but for its dulness, and the obscurity of its author, must long ere now have been burnt by "the hands of the common hangman;" – he has suffered this despicable member of the Cockney School to write an Essay in the Edinburgh Review on "the Periodical Press of Britain".' What must have especially galled *Blackwood's* is that Hazlitt did not mention it.

Publication of the *Characteristics* did not quench Hazlitt's new-found attachment to writing in a lapidary aphoristic style, so the Hunts ran eighty-six 'Common Places' by him in their *Literary Examiner* during the last months of the year. Number 64 said, 'If a man were refused by a woman a thousand times, and he really loved her, he would still think that at the bottom of her heart she preferred him to every one else. Nor is this wonderful, when we consider that all passion is a species of madness; and that the feeling in the mind towards the beloved object is the most amiable and delightful thing in the world. Our love to her is heavenly, and so (the heart whispers us) must hers be to us – though it were buried at the bottom of the sea; nay, from the tomb our self-love would revive it! We can never persuade ourselves that a mistress cares nothing about us, till we no longer care about her. No! It is certain that there is nothing truly deserving of love but love, and "In spite of pride, in erring reason's spite," we still believe in the justice of the blind God!' But Hazlitt's sanity and sense of proportion was beginning to return; number 65 tersely adds, 'It would be easy to forget a misplaced attachment, but that we do not like to acknowledge ourselves in the wrong.'[21]

De Quincey published an article on Malthus in the October issue of the *London Magazine*, containing arguments which closely – even to wording – followed Hazlitt's refutation of Malthus written years before. Hazlitt sent Hessey a 'Letter to the Editor', calmly saying that he was 'glad to find our ingenious and studious friend the *Opium-Eater* agrees with me on this point ... almost in so many words,' but remarking that because he had received such vilification for advancing those arguments, he might as well retain the credit for devising them. De Quincey replied apologetically in the December issue, acknowledging Hazlitt's priority, but disclaiming intentional plagiarism. Hazlitt let the matter rest.

There was one real consolation for Hazlitt's recent turmoils in a warm public gesture from Lamb. During the preceding few years Hazlitt and Lamb had seen less of each other, Hazlitt believing that Lamb had been neglectful in the offices of friendship when he most needed them. He said as much during his spat with Leigh Hunt in April 1821: Lamb, he told Hunt, 'seemed struck all of a heap, if I ever hinted at the possibility of his giving me a lift at any time.' Now that Hazlitt needed a lift more than ever, Lamb gave him one, in the form of a response to an article by Southey in the *Quarterly Review* of January 1823, which among other things questioned the propriety of Lamb's friendship with Hazlitt and Leigh Hunt. In the October *London Magazine* Lamb replied: 'What hath soured [Hazlitt], and made him suspect his friends of infidelity towards him, when there was no such matter, I know not. I stood well with him for fifteen years (the proudest of my life), and have ever spoken my full mind of him to some, to whom his panegyric must naturally be least tasteful ... I wish he would not quarrel with the world at the rate he does; but the reconciliation must be effected by himself, and I despair of living to see that day. But, protesting against much that he has written, and some things which he chooses to do; judging him by his conversation, which I enjoyed so long, and relished so deeply; or by his books, in those places where no clouding passion intervenes – I should belie my own conscience, if I said less, than that I think W. H. to be, in his natural and healthy state, one of the wisest and finest spirits breathing. So far from being ashamed of that intimacy, which was betwixt us, it is my boast that I was able for so many years to have preserved it entire; and I think I shall go to my grave without finding, or expecting to find, such another companion.' Lamb cemented this beautiful gesture by quoting Hazlitt in the very next issue of the *London*, describing him as 'a very ingenious and subtle writer'.

Hazlitt profoundly appreciated this gesture, coming as it did – and deliberately so – even as the *Liber Amoris* furore rumbled on. Evidently Lamb learned from Sarah Stoddart how pleased Hazlitt was, for at the bottom of one of Mary's letters to her he scribbled 'I am pleased that H. liked my letter to the Laureate.' Soon afterwards Crabb Robinson wrote in his diary on 25 January 1824 that he saw (but ignored) Hazlitt at the Lambs' home – they now lived in a cottage in the suburb of Islington in north London.

The new year opened with Hazlitt in an improved state of mind. He had two commissions from Jeffrey for the *Edinburgh*, and he was about to begin a fresh series of essays in the *New Monthly Magazine*. Although his resumed series of 'Table Talk' essays had flowed easily from his pen, he now replaced them with pen-portraits of people he thought were especially representative of the age and whose names – in his judgement – would survive into history. A year later his essays on this theme were collected and published in book form as *The Spirit of the Age*. It is one of Hazlitt's finest achievements. The first essay, published in January 1824, was an account of his old landlord Jeremy Bentham, and its impartiality and fairness set the tone for most (but not all) of the remainder. Of course

Hazlitt was unable to resist kicking the ankles of such as William Gifford, the apostate poets, and various Tory politicians, as was his way; but at the same time he was fair to almost all of them, acknowledging their gifts and successes as well as unblinkingly nominating their faults. One of Hazlitt's 'spirits of the age' was Francis Jeffrey, and although Hazlitt lauded his achievements as a great editor, and praised him fulsomely as a man – which he had every reason to do, owing him much, and being sincere in his respect for his powers – nevertheless he gave his opinion of Jeffrey's faults also, and with them those of the *Edinburgh Review*. Jeffrey wrote like a public speaker, said Hazlitt; he was balanced to a fault in his assessments and analyses, not coming down strongly enough on one side of a case; he was not good in a tête-à-tête but preferred to talk in company. As to the *Edinburgh Review*, although it was on the Whig side of the question it was insufficiently robust in its party spirit, always – like its editor – straining too far to accommodate both sides, to the point of weakening its effect. Thus Hazlitt's view; and he was to learn Jeffrey's response when the great man himself reviewed *The Spirit of the Age* in the following year.

Another reason for Hazlitt's improved state of mind was that his deter-mined search for a wife had met with unexpectedly rapid and handsome success. While travelling by coach in the summer of 1823 on one of his picture-viewing expeditions he fell into conversation with a good-looking, intelligent, well-read woman in her early thirties, who was expensively dressed and had pleasing manners. It turned out that she was an avid and admiring reader of Hazlitt's work, and was delighted to meet him in this accidental way. She was not alarmed by his reputation as an alleged blackguard – rather the contrary – and certainly did not think the worse of him for *Liber Amoris*, her attitude to which was the same as Mary Russell Mitford's. It further transpired that she was a widow with a competence as handsome as her person: three hundred pounds a year. Evidently when Hazlitt was not in love with a woman he could be pleasing to her, for the two rapidly came to an understanding, and in the early spring of 1824 Hazlitt and Isabella Bridgwater – for that was her name – went together to Scotland and were married.

Isabella Bridgwater was quite likely *all* the women mentioned earlier by Mary Shelley and Haydon. The phrase 'woman of colour' was equally likely a misrepresentation, by Mary Shelley's interlocutor, of the fact that Isabella Bridgwater, a Scotswoman born Isabella Shaw in Muirtown in 1791, had lived since her teenage years in Grenada in the West Indies. There she had married one Henry Bridgwater, a prominent lawyer and local militiaman from a long-standing colonial family.[22] In 1820, after rising to the rank of chief justice for the island and lieutenant colonel in its militia, Henry Bridgwater died, leaving Isabella childless, young, and comfortably off. She returned to Britain independent enough in mind and purse to dispose of herself as she wished.

Her ancestry was distinguished, for on her father's side she was descended from Sir Robert Gordon, and on her mother's from the Earls of Athole and the Barons of Kintail. She was the ninth of thirteen children. Her brothers became army officers, and at least one of her sisters married and went to the West Indies. Her father, James Shaw, was wealthy, but the family suffered hardship after his early death and the profligate dispersal of his estates by his heir. That is the reason Isabella went to the West Indies: to join her married sister there, and to find a husband.

Hazlitt and Isabella were obliged to marry in Scotland because Hazlitt's divorce was not recognized in England. As Stanley Jones ingeniously discovered, they were married at Coldstream, and went from there to Melrose for their honeymoon. Jones's identification of their wedding-place rests on the fact that because they had travelled from London by coach and married at the first possible place across the border – a 'Gretna'-style smithy wedding indeed, although not at Gretna Green itself – Hazlitt had to think of where to go for a honeymoon. He saw a pair of hills in the distance, and asked the coach driver what place they were near. 'Melrose,' said the driver, and Hazlitt said, 'Take us there.' As Jones points out, the only place that a coach from London could have stopped for a smithy wedding, and at the same time afford its passengers a view of the Eildon Hills near Melrose, is Coldstream.[23]

At Melrose, while the couple honeymooned, Hazlitt wrote several articles for the *Edinburgh Review,* and corrected the proofs of *Sketches of the Principal Picture-Galleries of England.* Sheridan Knowles and William Bewick visited from Glasgow, and Bewick wrote an account of their visit. He also drew Hazlitt's 'pale and contemplative face,' as he describes it, 'his head on one side, and his searching expressive eyes bent in meditation ... his long black hair clustering in massy locks about a forehead and features the very image of intellectual refinement, of deep or critical investigation.'[24] The description tallies with Patmore's pen-sketch of Hazlitt's appearance, but not with Mary Shelley's shocked account of 'scattered hair and projecting cheek-bones'. Hazlitt was delighted with the sketch, which Bewick fixed to the wainscoting with a pair of forks opposite Hazlitt's place at table, so that he could look at it. 'He frequently laid down his knife and fork to contemplate the likeness,' wrote Bewick, 'gazing earnestly and long, asking if really his own hair was anything like that of the drawing.' Isabella said, 'Oh! It is exactly your own hair, my dear.' Hazlitt said, 'Well, that surely puts me in mind of some of Raphael's heads in the cartoons. Ah! It is, however, something to live for, to have such a head as *that*.' Knowles was as impressed by the drawing as Hazlitt himself, and wrote a sonnet on it, which – helpfully for history if not for literature – begins, 'Thus Hazlitt looked!'[25]

Melrose is close to Abbotsford, the home of Sir Walter Scott. Hazlitt had no wish to meet him, but Bewick walked over to see the place and its pictures, and while there was attracted by a portrait of Mary Queen of Scots. He wrote to Scott asking if he could copy it, and Scott agreed. He therefore met Scott himself, who asked how it came about that Hazlitt was at Melrose. Bewick told him of the wedding, and Scott 'observed, with great apparent sincerity, that "Mr Hazlitt was one of our most eloquent authors, and a man, as far as he could be allowed to judge, of great natural and original genius; that it was a pity such great powers were not concentrated upon some important work, valuable to his country, to literature, and lasting to his fame".'[26] Bewick hastened back to Melrose to tell Hazlitt what Scott had said, only to find that the newlyweds had left for London, leaving behind a note and a gift of books.

The Hazlitts had taken a house at 10 Down Street, Piccadilly, and there Sarah Stoddart met her successor and declared herself 'much taken' with her. John Hunt and his wife dined with them too, and found Isabella 'pleasant and ladylike'. Haydon did not meet her until later, but he bumped into William the younger in the street, looking 'better-dressed, cleaner, more modest and more respectable than I had ever met him before,' which he attributed to the new domestic regime.

Hazlitt and Isabella returned early from their honeymoon because they had decided to make a long tour on the Continent, and there were various matters to be settled. First, William the younger was to be moved from his school in London to one in Tavistock, closer to his grandmother and aunt Peggy. At about this time the boy received a letter from his grandmother saying that she was happy to hear that his father and the new Mrs Hazlitt were 'comfortable together'. Having had her fill in America, she did not like the idea of foreign travel: 'I don't like his going [abroad],' she told her grandson querulously, 'so many die there; such stagnant waters surrounding the towns, and all over the country.'[27] Second, Hazlitt proposed to fund the continental tour by writing it up as he went, and to this end he needed to find a taker in one of the journals or newspapers. In the end he sold the idea to the *Morning Chronicle*. While he was busy with these preparations his anthology of poetry, *Select British Poets*, was published, but had to be withdrawn immediately because it included the work of contemporary poets from whom he had not secured permission to reprint.

The volume was reissued in the following year without the contemporary poets. It is a judicious volume, arguably one of the best anthologies of poetry in English ever made. There was nothing mistaken in the praise Keats had heaped on Hazlitt's poetical taste.

When all arrangements were in place Hazlitt and Isabella caught the coach to Brighton, from whence they were booked on the steam packet to Dieppe. It was the end of August 1824, and Hazlitt began producing his travel articles straight away, even before leaving England's shores. 'The rule for travelling abroad is to take our common sense with us, and to leave our prejudices behind,' he wrote in relishing mood, for before him lay Paris and Italy, and behind him lay years of durance and pain which he was glad to leave in his wake.

Hazlitt and Isabella were away from England for just over a year, returning in October 1825. The trip was a project long meditated and desired by Hazlitt. In 1821 he had suggested to Taylor and Hessey that he write a book about just such a journey. He had wanted to go with Sarah Walker, and hoped – as he told her – that it would be their wedding trip. The ache to return to Paris was as old as his first visit there; his desire to see the art of Italy, and to visit the scenes of Rousseau's romances in Switzerland, was even older. As the steam packet pulled away from Brighton on the first day of September 1824 the dream was at last being realized.

When Hazlitt was in Scotland for his divorce, during his lecture visit to Glasgow, the local newspaper commented on his walking tour along Loch Lomond, saying that readers could look forward with anticipation to seeing something from his pen about the tour one day, which, because of his powers of observation and mind, would be well worth reading. He did indeed write about it, briefly, adverting to the air-clad peak of Ben Lomond, as he had often written about travelling in England. But this Continental journey was an opportunity on a different scale. No-one would expect a straightforward or conventional travel guide from Hazlitt, and the readers of the *Morning Chronicle* and the subsequent book version, *Notes of a Journey through France and Italy*, were not disappointed. His record of his time on the Continent is personal, idiosyncratic, surprising, full of strong judgements and brilliant perceptions, liberally interwoven with characteristically dogmatic generalizations that always carry more than a tincture of truth – all served in his marvellous prose.

Hazlitt began as he intended to go on, capturing impressions with bold deft strokes of the pen: 'We had a fine passage in the steam-boat ... Not a cloud, scarce a breath of air; a moon, then starlight, till the dawn, with rosy fingers, ushered us into Dieppe. Our fellow-passengers were pleasant and unobtrusive ... A Member of Parliament, delighted to escape from "late hours and bad company", an English General, proud of his bad French; a Captain in the Navy, glad to enter a French harbour peaceably; a Country Squire, extending his enquiries beyond his paternal acres; the younger sons of wealthy citizens, refined through the strainers of a University education, and finishing off with foreign travel; a young lawyer, quoting Peregrine Pickle, and divided between his last circuit and projected tour. There was also a young Dutchman, looking mild through his mustachios, and a new-married couple (A French Jew and Jewess) who grew uxorious from the effects of sea-sickness, and took refuge from the qualms of the disorder in paroxysms of tenderness.'[28] At Dieppe they found a hotel room with a delightful view over the river, but the bed 'had that kind of odour which could not be mistaken for otto of roses', and they immediately remarked on the strong smells everywhere apparent, which is why, Hazlitt surmised, the French call the nose 'the organ of sense'.

Little escaped Hazlitt's eager scrutiny on the road from Dieppe to Paris – the peasants, the state of agriculture, the condition of the road, the advantages and disadvantages of the 'diligence', which was the French version of a stage-coach. 'There is as much difference [between a diligence and a coach] as between a barge and a pleasure-boat,' said Hazlitt, 'but then it is roomy and airy, and remarkably easy in its motion.' He liked the look of the girls he saw from the diligence window – 'handsome, healthy-looking, animated; a better sort of English country girls' – but not the older women with their 'Albert-Durer chins and noses, that have been coming together for half a century'.

Rouen pleased by its beauty and antiquity, and its handsome Gothic cathedral. By this time the Hazlitts were finding their way round French cuisine, and had concluded that game and poultry dishes were the safest compromise between what they were used to – the dry cookery of England with its 'solid, unsavoury morsels, beef steaks, and mutton chops' which stick in French throats as well as being 'repulsive to their imaginations' – and 'French receipts and ragouts'. If an Englishman wishes to experiment on these latter, said Hazlitt, let him sit near the door so that he can 'make his exit suddenly'.[29]

'The first thing I did when I got to Paris,' Hazlitt wrote, justifiably allowing himself some poetic licence, 'was to go to the Louvre,' which in all the years since he had last been in Paris was 'first and last and midst in my thoughts'. The prospect of revisiting that memory-hallowed treasure-house filled him with excitement – and trepidation: for what if it was all different? It was a symbol of his youth, of Napoleon, of the failure of the endeavour of freedom, of the return of the yoke of monarchical servitude. He became dithyrambic. 'Thou sacred shrine of God-like magnificence, must not my heart fail and my feet stumble as I approach thee? ... for here still linger the broken remains and the faded splendour of that proud monument of the triumphs of art and of the majesty of man's nature over the mock-majesty of thrones!' He was filled with memories, regrets, nostalgia, and a sad satisfaction that 'in all the time that I had been away from thee, and amidst all the changes that have happened in it, did I ever forget, did I ever profane thee? Never for a moment or in thought have I swerved from thee, or from the cause of which thou wert the pledge and crown.'[30]

This was a serious and deep passion. Artistic values and political principles were inseparably mixed in Hazlitt with the hopes of his youth. The Louvre was the symbol of everything that mattered to him, because it was a treasure-house of art which, when he had dwelt in it at its finest and completest moment as a young man, had been gathered together as a result of the conquests of Napoleon over 'legitimate' monarchs. Paris promised to be the capital of a new world, and the Louvre was the shrine at its heart where man's highest achievements – his works of art – were deposited, like the Ark of the Covenant in the Holy of Holies. In the two decades since his first visit Hazlitt kept the Louvre vividly in his head, and could wander its galleries in thought, seeing the pictures as if they hung before his face. 'I had but to touch a certain spring,' he said, 'and lo! ... the divine grace of Guido appeared free from blemish – there were the golden hues of Titian, and Raphael's speaking faces, the splendour of Rubens, the gorgeous gloom of Rembrandt, the airy elegance of Van Dyke, and Claude's classic scenes lapped the senses in Elysium, and Poussin breathed the spirit of antiquity over them. There, in that fine old lumber-room of the imagination, were the St Peter Martyr, with its majestic figures and its unrivalled landscape background. There also were the two St Jeromes, Domenichino's and Correggio's – there 'stood the statue that enchants the world' – there were the Apollo and the Antinous, the Laocoon, the Dying Gladiator, Diana and her Fawn, and all the glories of the antique world.' Anxiously, thinking that much must have gone since Napoleon's fall, Hazlitt entered the coolness and stillness of the Grand Gallery, leaving the bustling heat of the common rooms behind – and found to his delight that almost everything was still there, and in its place. 'I cast a glance forward, and found that the Poussins were there. At the sight of the first ... the tears came into my eyes, and I passed an hour or two in that state of luxurious enjoyment, which is the highest privilege of the mind of man, and which perhaps makes him amend for many sorrows.'[31]

Hazlitt's taste in art was not restricted to Old Masters. At an exhibition

of contemporary French painters he defended their merits against a sceptical Frenchman, who said that the paintings looked 'unfinished', to which
Hazlitt replied that they were 'unfinished as nature is unfinished'.[32]

He loved Paris, despite its dirty streets and narrow pavements, and the
slop-buckets being emptied from upper windows. He thought the Tuileries
beautiful, and delighted in walking to the Champ de Mars, the Jardin des
Plantes, and Montmartre with its 'vivifying air and inspiring view'. He
and Isabella were constantly at the theatre – the Théâtre Français, the
Théâtre des Variétés, the Salle Louvois, the Opéra. He saw Mademoiselle
Mars play Célimène in Molière's *Le Misanthrope*, and thought her 'accomplished' and the rest of the cast 'flawless'. He was surprised at the poor
attendance at the opera, which he believed French audiences disliked
because the music interfered with their conversation. And he did not take
to the new-fangled dance called 'ballet' on show in Paris: 'The French
Opera-dancers think it graceful to stand on one leg or on the points of
their toes, or with one leg stretched out behind them, as if they were going
to be shod, or to raise one foot at right angles with their bodies, and twirl
themselves round like a *te-totum*, to see how long they can spin, and then
stop short all of a sudden; or to skim along the ground, flat-footed, like a
spider running along a cobweb, or to pop up and down like a pea on a
tobacco-pipe, or to stick in their backs till another part projects out behind
*comme des volails*, and to strut about like peacocks with infirm, vain-
glorious steps, or to turn out their toes till their feet resemble apes, or to
raise one foot about their heads, and turn swiftly round upon the other,
till the petticoats of the female dancers (for I have been thinking of them)
rise above their garters, and display a pair of spindleshanks, like the
wooden ones of a wax-doll, just as shapeless and as tempting.'[33]

It impressed him that the Parisians were great readers. He saw a girl
minding a stall on the street, with her feet on a stove in the cold weather,
reading Racine and Voltaire. He saw a grisette in a shop reading Mar-
montel's tales in her spare moments. 'The French read with avidity whenever they can snatch the opportunity,' he approvingly noted. 'They read
standing in the open air, into which they are driven by the want of air in
their homes. They read in garrets and in cellars.'[34]

The indomitable Sarah Stoddart was also on a European tour, and called
on the Hazlitts in their Paris hotel, the Hôtel des Étrangers, not solely for
social reasons, but to get from Hazlitt money he owed her. She found
him – as she reported by letter to William the younger – 'splendidly situated
as to rooms', getting his food prepared 'in the English way, which is a very
great object to him; but, as may be supposed, it is terribly expensive.' Art,

theatre and sightseeing kept the Hazlitts busy, but not too busy to enjoy a social life also. Hazlitt met Stendhal, almost certainly at the home of his fellow-student from Hackney, William Edwards, now Dr William Edwards, who had earned a considerable reputation as a scientist during his long sojourn in Paris.[35] Hazlitt and Williams were chums at school, and their re-encounter was a glad one: 'It is wonderful how friendship, that has long lain unused, accumulates like money at compound interest,' Hazlitt remarked. Mrs Edwards hosted a Wednesday evening salon, at which Stendhal was a regular visitor. Hazlitt saw a good deal of him during the remainder of his stay, and frequently thereafter alluded to Stendhal's writings in his own, referring to him as 'my friend Monsieur Beyle'. And to cap it all, Hazlitt was also present at a reception given by the Duchess of Noailles 'in her bedroom'; but alas, he left no further record of the occasion, which was just made for his pen.[36]

In addition to his pieces for the *Morning Chronicle* Hazlitt wrote a number of longer essays for the *New Monthly,* one of which displays the good effect on him of his change of scene. 'Upon the whole, there are many things to prop up and reinforce our fondness for existence, after the intoxication of our first acquaintance with it is over; health, a walk and the appetite it creates, a book, the doing a good-natured or friendly action, are satisfactions that hold out to the last; and with these, and any others to aid us that fall harmlessly in our way, we may make a shift for a few seasons, after having exhausted the short-lived transports of an eager and enthusiastic imagination, and without being under the necessity of hanging or drowning ourselves as soon as we come to years of discretion.'[37] To boost his genial mood he received copies in January 1825 of his just-published *Spirit of the Age* from London, and arranged with the Paris publisher Galignani for a French edition both of it and his *Table Talk*. The latter was not exactly parallel in content to its London cousin, for it included some new pieces and excluded others. For *The Spirit of the Age* he used five of his previously published pieces under that title, and thirteen new ones. Most of them concerned people he had written about before, but he did not use the older material, choosing instead to start afresh and to give a fully considered final view of his subjects. It involved changing some of his previous opinions, and redressing the balance of earlier attacks, most notably those against Wordsworth and Sir James Mackintosh.

That *The Spirit of the Age* is one of Hazlitt's finest works was recognized by his contemporaries, who bought and read it even if the reviews – most of them by writers animated by party feeling, none of whom could see the book otherwise than through the smoke rising from the *Liber Amoris* scandal – were mixed. It went into a second edition in London before the end of the year. Vituperation of the familiar sort to be found in *Blackwood's* and elsewhere can be taken as read, but even some of the hostile reviewers had to admit Hazlitt's virtues as a writer; the *Gentleman's Magazine* in March 1825 attacked the book, but added, 'Still, however, it must be confessed that Mr Hazlitt is a man of no ordinary powers ... His style is peculiar to himself, it is deeply impregnated with the spirit of the masters of our language, and strengthened by a rich infusion of golden ore dug from the pure mine of classic antiquity.' The *European Magazine* praised the book's 'abundance of eloquent writing'. From the *Examiner* Hazlitt got an expectedly good review, Albany Fonblanque taking up cudgels on his behalf to criticize *Blackwood's* and *John Bull* for their violent antipathy to him.

But two other reviews were more significant. One was by William Ritchie, editor of the *Scotsman*, who had been helpful to Hazlitt during his divorce in Edinburgh, but who in the interim had changed his attitude to Hazlitt, most likely because of the latter's bitter *Liberal* attack on the Scottish character. It is also likely that *Liber Amoris* upset Ritchie's moral sensibilities. 'It is not long possible to serve him who is bent on dis-serving himself,' he wrote. 'It is weakness to persevere in being generous to one who can be just to nobody.' He thought Hazlitt treated his subjects with 'indelicate freedom', and that he had only spared Jeffrey because, as an editor, he had the power to influence Hazlitt's earnings. He criticized Hazlitt's 'imposing swagger of style', and then turned his guns on Hazlitt himself: 'He likes talking about himself. Tête-à-tête, you can have nothing else, and there you have both the selfishness of the Englishman and the self-love of the small author; while in general company, you have either silence, or a straining after something trenchant, or striking. He cannot act as if he were one string of a large instrument, which, by the subordination and proper working of the parts, is to produce one harmonious whole, he must play a *solo*; and then he hits as if *intensity* were every thing. He abandons himself, upon system, to the feeling of the moment; but although he thus gains in force of conception, he loses in power of discrimination, to say nothing of relief, repose, or graduation.'[38] Ritchie here makes no allowances for the misery and strain Hazlitt was under in Edinburgh during the divorce, and he certainly did not know the Hazlitt of Lamb's Thursdays. But the sketch throws light on that awful period in Hazlitt's life, showing how much the metal of his character was bent under the weight of the disaster.

Far more seriously, Jeffrey had taken it on himself to review the book in the *Edinburgh Review*. Hazlitt did not see Jeffrey's review until later in the year, when he was in Geneva visiting Rousseau's house. There in the hall of the house lay a copy of the April 1825 *Edinburgh Review*, and in it was Jeffrey's response to his book. It was a shock. Hazlitt would not have counted on his decade's service as a regular of the magazine to get a good review, but he might have expected Jeffrey to read the book with a sympathetic eye. He reported that when he told Jeffrey about the book before publication the latter had replied that 'out of twenty men he would have one for him and nineteen against him'. And so it proved. In his review Jeffrey praised Hazlitt as 'a man not merely of talents, but of genius', but said that his work was marred by 'bad taste and affectations'. He praised him for being 'an advocate of liberty and human improvement', but said that the whole project of *The Spirit of the Age* was misconceived, and anyway contained a number of factual errors, which he proceeded to list. 'His writing is often powerful,' said Jeffrey, 'and his ideas are generally original – sometimes valuable, not seldom brilliant. But a perpetual hunting after originality, and a determination to say every thing in a strange manner, lead him into paradox, error, and extravagance; and give a tinge of affectation to his style, which is far from captivating. His besetting sin is self-sufficiency, and this in all its branches, whereof dogmatism is the most prevailing. Whatever he writes is likely to be read, and either praised or censured beyond its deserts. But it is his own fault that he does not write better than he ever has done. Let him be only somewhat more humble and diffident. Let him reflect, that fine writing really cannot exist without good sense, and an earnest pursuit of "whatsoever things are just, and whatsoever things are true"; let him be assured, that the first object with every rational writer is to be in the right, rather than to strike by some novelty; and that no degree of brilliancy will ever make up for want of sense and nature; and with his talents, nay with far less than his talents, far more valuable books will be produced.'

Hazlitt never again wrote for the *Edinburgh Review* while Jeffrey was its editor. He was both hurt and taken aback by Jeffrey's strictures, not because he was worried that they might be right – he knew his own strengths and weaknesses well enough, and wrote as he did because it expressed his nature and his views as tellingly as he knew how, which was his main aim – but because it was unpleasant to find that he had not been right in the degree to which he thought Jeffrey was a friend to his work. Perhaps Jeffrey wrote as he did because he felt exactly the same way.

Hazlitt's immediate response was to write a poem – it is the only poem of his that survives:

The rock I'm told on which I'll split
Is bad economy of wit –
An affectation to be thought
That which I am and yet am not,
Deep, brilliant, new, and all the rest:
Help, help, thou great economist
Of what thou ne'er thyself possest,
Of financiers the ruthless Moloch
Dry, plodding, husky, stiff Maculloch!
Or to avoid the consequences
I may incur from corporate dunces,
I'll write as Allen writes all day;
Whate'er his Lordship says, I'll say –
(To hint what ne'er was said before
Is but to be set down a *bore*
By all the learned Whigs and Dames
Who fear you should out-write Sir James) –
I'll swear that every strutting elf
Is just what he conceives himself,
Or draw his picture to the life
As all the world would – and *his wife*!
From Mackintosh I'll nature learn
From Sidney Smith false glitter spurn;
Lend me, oh! Brougham, thy modesty,
Thou, Thomas Moore, simplicity;
Mill, scorn of juggling politics;
Thy soul of candour, Chevenix;
And last, to make my measure full,
Teach me, great Jeffrey, to be dull![39]

He sent it to the editor of the *Morning Chronicle*, who did not print it.

As his famous 'This will never do!' judgement on Wordsworth shows, Jeffrey was not enough in tune with the spirit of the age, despite being a good, thinking writer as well as a truly great editor, fully to grasp the character of Hazlitt's work. Hazlitt did not write in conventional ways, did not tackle his subject as an historian or journalist, and did not see things from the viewpoint of any orthodoxy. His remit was that a man of sensibility responding to his world. He is a conversational writer, anticipating by nearly two centuries the kind of columnists who write in highly personal and miscellaneous vein in today's newspapers. At the same time the power of his intellect, the range of his interests, and the depth of his passions – including his political ones, though in this one respect he was not unusual in that fiercely political and quarrelsome time – meant that he was a new force in literature, and not fully understood by his contemporaries. The review which then most closely anticipated the judgement of posterity – and posterity's judgements are more discerning because they can afford to be, since they lie out of range of the personal and party spite that inevitably colours contemporary opinion – appeared in the *Philomathic Journal*, which said that the book 'displays extraordinary talent', and that in it the reader 'will find many happy illustrations, many ingenious thoughts, excellent sentiments, and brilliant displays of imagination'.[40]

When the first copies of *The Spirit of the Age* reached him, Hazlitt's encounter with Jeffrey's review lay several months in the future. He and Isabella were still enjoying Paris, but the aim was to see Italy too, so with a mixture of regret and anticipation they took their places in a diligence in mid-January, and headed south. The vicissitudes of travelling in a French winter in 1825 provided amusing copy for the *Morning Chronicle*'s readers, not least on the comedy of life in French inns, and the 'purgatory of heat, closeness, confinement, and bad smells' inside a diligence. It was a relief to the Hazlitts to find themselves relegated, on one leg of the journey, to the coupé, a leather-curtained outside portion of the diligence where they had plenty of fresh air, although in the form of an icy wind whipping round them. Their outside seat gave them a grandstand view of what they had come a thousand miles to see: the Alps. Hazlitt was thrilled by them, and even more so by the valleys and rocky steeps as they wound their way up into the Alpine passes. But after a while the barren, desolate, brooding peaks began to press on him: 'The wind cut like a scythe through the valleys, and a cold, icy feeling struck from the sides of the snowy precipices that surrounded us, so that we seemed enclosed in a huge well of mountains ... Let no one imagine that the crossing the Alps is the work of a moment, or done by a single heroic effort – that they are a huge but detached chain of hills, or like the dotted line we find in the map. They are a sea or an entire kingdom of mountains.'[41]

To get to Turin from the high passes of the Alps necessitated entering the King of Sardinia's mainland territories. At the border the diligence's passengers were let out into the fresh air, and the Hazlitts took tea with a Spanish fellow-traveller, who complimented Isabella on her handling of the tea-pot. In the ensuing conversation Hazlitt praised Murillo and Velazquez, to the surprise and delight of his companion – 'here was sympathy!' – and multiplied it by praising *Don Quixote*. 'What a thing it is to have produced a work that makes friends of all the world that have read it,' Hazlitt wrote. 'There is no French work at the name of which (as at a talisman) the scales of national prejudice so completely fall off; nay more, I must confess there is no English one.' Before they could set forward again the diligence's occupants had to submit to inspection by the customs officials. Hazlitt had two trunks, one of them filled with books. When the book-filled one was unlocked 'it was as if the lid of Pandora's box flew open. There could not have been a more sudden start or expression of surprise, had it been filled with cartridge-paper or gun-powder. Books were the corrosive sublimate that eats out despotism and priestcraft – the artillery that battered down castle and dungeon-walls – the ferrets that ferreted out abuses – the lynx-eyed guardians that tore off disguises – the scales that weighed right and wrong – the thumping make-weight thrown into the balance that made force and fraud, the sword and the cowl, kick the beam – the dread of knaves, the scoff of fools – the balm and the consolation of the human mind – the salt of the earth – the future rulers of the world! A box full of them was a contempt of the constituted authorities; and the names of mine were taken down with great care and secrecy – Lord Bacon's "Advancement of Learning", Milton's "Paradise Lost", De Stutt-Tracy's "Ideologie" (which Buonaparte said ruined his Russian expedition), Mignet's "French Revolution", (which wants a chapter on the English Government), "Sayings and Doings" with pencil notes in the margin, "Irving's Orations", the same, an "Edinburgh Review", some "Morning Chronicles", "the Literary Examiner", a collection of Poetry, a Volume bound in crimson velvet, and the Paris edition of "Table-Talk". Here was some questionable matter enough – but no notice was taken. My box was afterwards corded and *leaded* with equal gravity and politeness, and it was not until I arrived at Turin that I found it was a prisoner of state, and would be forwarded to me anywhere I chose to mention, out of his Sardinian Majesty's dominions. I was startled to find myself in the smooth grasp of legitimate power, without suspecting it.'[42]

Hazlitt thought Turin splendid, except for its beggars and inept opera, but they did not stay long because a week's journey lay before them to Florence, by way of Parma and Bologna through fertile country that was as well tended as a garden. It was carnival time, and in both towns they watched cheerful noisy processions from their hotel windows. Bologna's arcades and porticos were 'a perpetual feast to the eye', and the Academy gallery was rich in Raphaels, Caraccis, Domenichinos and Guidos. Florence could not be reached without an arduous haul over the Apennines, in a coach pulled by straining oxen through sleet and icy rain. But the view of Florence, when at last they were clear of the passes, was breathtaking; it was 'a scene of enchantment, a city planted in a garden'.

They took apartments for two months, and saw much of Leigh Hunt and his family, living in Maiano with its views over Florence and the neighbouring country. Leigh Hunt was in a depressed state – Hazlitt said he was 'moulting', and described him to Haydon as 'dull as a hen under a pent-house on a rainy day'. The deaths of Shelley and Byron, especially the former, had hurt Hunt, and the failure of the *Liberal* left him unable or unwilling to pay his way back to England. Hazlitt invited him to come to Venice or Rimini (at Hazlitt's expense), but he refused.

Hazlitt was enchanted with Maiano. From the Hunts' home could be seen Machiavelli's house, and the village of Settignano where Michelangelo was born, and Fiesole where among others Milton stayed, with near it a house that figures in Boccaccio; and on the other side of the *Decameron*'s 'Valley of Ladies' stood Dante's house, and from the terrace Florence could be viewed, and beyond it the Villa of Arcetri, where Galileo had lived. Hunt wrote that Hazlitt 'beheld the scene around us with the admiration natural to a lover of old folios and great names, and confessed, in the language of Burns, that it was a sight to enrich the eyes.'

Florence's art enriched Hazlitt's eyes too, although he did not like quite all the things that have since become fashionable. Michelangelo's *David* looked to him 'like an overgrown actor at one of our minor theatres, without his clothes: the head is too big for the body, and it has a helpless expression of distress.' The Venus de Medici seemed to him 'a little too much like an exquisite marble doll'. And the Apollo Belvedere was 'positively bad, a theatrical coxcomb, and ill made'.[43] But he was in ecstasies at the Pitti palace, where he found some of his favourite works from the Louvre, among them Titian's *Ippolito de Medici*. The Pitti's walls swarmed with Raphael, Rubens, Correggio, Giorgione, Andrea del Sarto, Schiavoni, Guido. 'Those who come in search of high Italian art will here find it in perfection,' he enthusiastically told his readers.[44]

Cheered by these delights, Hazlitt decided to call on Walter Savage Landor, also staying in Florence. He had not done so at first for the two reasons that Landor was reputed to dislike uninvited guests, being jealous of his privacy, and – worse – Hazlitt had given his *Imaginary Conversations* a bad review in the *Edinburgh Review*, saying that it was written for 'fools and knaves'. Nevertheless Hazlitt – curiously attired in a 'dress-coat and nankeen trousers halfway up his legs, leaving his stockings well visible over his shoes' as Mrs Landor reported to a correspondent – presented himself at the Palazzo Medici where the Landors were lodging, and intro-duced himself without ceremony. The two men took to each other imme-diately, despite each thinking the other a little odd. Landor wrote, 'A funny fellow he was. He used to say to me, "Mr Landor, I like you, sir – I like you very much, sir – you're an honest man, sir; but I don't approve, sir, of a great deal that you have written, sir. You must reform some of your opinions, sir." ' Landor had never seen Wordsworth, and asked Hazlitt to describe the poet to him, receiving a reply that delighted him: ' "You have seen a horse, I suppose," he said; "well sir, if you have seen a horse, sir, I mean his head, sir, you have seen Wordsworth." '

Hazlitt, Landor and Leigh Hunt, together with other British denizens of Florence, among them Seymour Kirkup the artist, an Irish peer called Lord Dillon who liked to read his own poetical effusions aloud and at length, and Keats's friend Charles Armitage Brown, formed a congenial circle which met frequently. Hazlitt amused the company one evening with an account of his Edinburgh divorce, claiming that he and the prostitute he hired to establish his adultery lay side by side in his hotel bedroom waiting for Sarah Stoddart to walk in on them, as arranged, with two witnesses. She did so, identified him, made him a curtsey, and went out again, leaving him 'in statu quo' with his assistant (described, in the account Haydon claimed Hazlitt had given him, as 'a strumpet one-eyed from disease').

Florence's answering of expectations made Hazlitt eager to see Rome. He and Isabella travelled south by way of Sienna – 'more a receptacle of the dead than the residence of the living' – and reached Rome after a journey of six days. Their first sight of the eternal city was the dome of St Peter's wavering in a haze across a distant plain. They took lodgings in a house once occupied by Salvator Rosa in the Via Gregoriana, a location that enabled them to look out over the city and 'indulge in sentiment, without being poisoned by bad air'. Hazlitt was impressed by the Pantheon, the Colosseum and the Arch of Constantine, but the rest disappointed him. The Tiber was a muddy stream, St Peter's was not as grand as St Paul's, the city itself was a mess of tumble-down buildings and dung-hills. The stranglehold of Catholicism was overpoweringly evident, and he was angered by the fact that the Jews of the Rome ghetto were obliged to listen to a sermon every Sunday on the virtues of Christianity. On Easter Sunday he and Isabella went to St Peter's and saw the Pope officiating, 'a harmless, infirm, fretful old man'. Almost the only thing he liked among the art treasures of the Vatican was the ceiling of the Sistine Chapel.

They left Rome somewhat disillusioned, and headed for Venice, stopping briefly at Florence again on the way. The further north they travelled, the more cheerful Hazlitt became. He applauded Lombardy, 'the Garden of Italy, or of the World', and was especially delighted by Ferrara, whose antique beauty was such that he said it was the city he would most like to live in if he were ever to settle in Italy.

He loved Venice. Its 'magical, dazzling, perplexing effect' made one feel 'at first a little giddy', he wrote, but its luxury and lavishness, its irregular and overblown decorativeness, seemed exactly right. He attributed Venice's strange and ornamental character to the sea, of which she is the 'nominal bride ... [to] which she owes her all, and the very essence of which is caprice, uncertainty, and vicissitude.'[45] The high point was his visit to Titian's studio – 'an event of one's life' – and seeing again the St Peter Martyr, which Hazlitt thought 'probably ... the finest [painting] in the world.'

Like Titian's great painting, the city itself was in Hazlitt's view 'without a rival'. 'Venice is loaded with ornament, like a rich city-heiress with jewels. It seems the natural order of things. Her origin was a wonder; her end is to surprise. The strong, implanted tendency of her genius must be to the showy, the singular, the fantastic. Herself an anomaly, she reconciles contradictions.'[46]

When it was time to leave they did so with 'mingled satisfaction and regret'. They travelled by way of Padua and Verona to Milan through 'cultivated beauty and smiling vegetation'. At Verona they paused to enjoy the associations with *Romeo and Juliet*, visiting Juliet's tomb and having their suspicions roused when their guide showed them the section of wall Romeo leaped over, and the spot in the garden where he fell. 'This gives an air of trick and fiction to the whole,' Hazlitt remarked. They were annoyed in Milan to find that their arrival coincided with that of the Emperor of Austria. Opera at La Scala – 'Gran Scala' – disappointed, but not the theatre itself, which Hazlitt admired for its size and beauty. And then he flatly, but astonishingly, remarked, 'I did not see the great picture of the Last Supper by Leonardo nor the little Luini, two miles out of Milan, which my friend Mr Beyle charged me particularly to see,' giving no reason for either sin of omission.

Their last stops in Italy were Como and then Lake Maggiore, where they considered spending the rest of the summer. But Hazlitt was anxious to pay his tribute of pilgrimage to Rousseau, so they pressed on over the Simplon Pass and thence to Vevey on Lake Geneva – a place rich in iconic significance for Hazlitt, for it is the scene of *La Nouvelle Héloïse*, the setting for Julie, Madame de Warens, and the deepest and most speaking of Rousseau's emotions.

Hazlitt and Isabella took seven rooms in a farmhouse called Gelamont, situated in quiet vineyards sloping to the lake. It was extremely comfortable and pleasant. 'Days, weeks, months might have passed on much in the same manner with "but the season's difference". We breakfasted at the same hour, and the tea-kettle was always boiling (an excellent thing in housewifery) – a *lounge* in the orchard for an hour or two, and twice a week we could see the steam-boat creeping like a spider over the surface of the lake ... [reading] amused us until dinner-time; then tea and a walk till the moon unveiled itself, "apparent queen of the night", or the brook, swoln with a transient shower, was heard more distinctly in the darkness, mingling with the soft, rustling breeze; and the next morning the song of peasants broke upon refreshing sleep, as the sun glanced among the clustering vine-leaves, or the shadowy hills, as the mists retired from the summits, looked in at our windows.'[47]

Hazlitt read *La Nouvelle Héloïse* again, and visited Julie's supposititious birthplace at Clarens. They went round the shores of the lake to the Castle of Chillon near Montreux, and thought of Byron and the Prisoner. An elderly physician in Vevey called La Varde had known Rousseau personally, and Hazlitt talked with him. Despite claiming that his days were given to laziness and relaxation, Hazlitt was busy, writing at Vevey eleven travel pieces and several other essays in addition – and beginning to plan, as the contents of his trunk of books demonstrates, a biography of Napoleon. This project was in a very preliminary state, but Hazlitt intended it to be a major work, the crowning achievement of his literary life.

He was happy at Vevey; in one of the essays written there he said, 'As I write this, I am sitting in the open air in a beautiful valley, near Vevey; Clarens is on my left, the Dent de Jamant is behind me, the rocks of Meillerie opposite: under my feet is a green bank, enamelled with white and purple flowers, in which a dew-drop here and there glitters with pearly light ... Intent upon the scene and upon the thoughts that stir within me, I conjure up the cheerful passages in my life, and a crowd of happy images appear before me.'[48] This is a rare Hazlitt, but it shows that time and distance had dissolved at least some of the residues of bitterness that a hard, struggling, marginal and unloved life had left.

Some of the residues – but not all. The Hazlitts were twice visited by Thomas Medwin, a relation of Shelley's, who had married a Swiss countess and was living near Vevey. He was moved by Hazlitt's appearance to make a note of it: 'The lines of his countenance are regular, but bear evident marks of late and intense application, and there was an habitual melancholy in the expression, as though he had been chewing the cud of past miseries, or brooding bitter anticipation of the future. His figure was emaciated; and it is evident his mind has preyed upon and consumed much of the vital energies of his frame; and this last, as was said of Shelley, seemed only a tenement for spirit.'[49]

On both of Medwin's visits, and probably at his instigation, the conversation turned on recent or contemporary literary figures – Byron first, then Scott, then the reviewers – and Medwin was struck by the bitterness of Hazlitt's remarks about them. His loathing of *Blackwood's* was especially noticeable, Medwin reported. Hazlitt said that Scott was the 'high priest of legitimacy' because by giving his readers enchanting portraits of bygone ages he had 'done more to put back the age than any writer of the day, the political writers and Malthus only excepted'.

It was on a visit to Geneva to see Rousseau's house that Hazlitt saw Jeffrey's review of his *Spirit of the Age*. It jarred, but it was a call from the outside world. Hazlitt felt that it was time to return home. The thought of home filled him with a rush of relief; suddenly he was anxious to quit the itinerant life, to give up the existence of a stranger, even though it had healed him. It was now October 1825. He and Isabella packed and took the *char-à-banc* to Basle – 'an aeriel voyage' with a view of Mont Blanc receding behind them – and went from there by diligence along the Rhine to Amsterdam. Hazlitt was tired of writing about travels, he now frankly informed his readers, and therefore skimped the details of the Rhine journey. By the time they reached Amsterdam they were clearly weary, for the city seemed to them 'a kind of paltry, rubbishy Venice', and they were disappointed by the art, Hazlitt claiming that the Rembrandts on show were less good than those in English collections. Although Holland looked neat and prosperous it was, said Hazlitt, boring – 'perhaps, the only country which you gain nothing by seeing ... What is to be gained by seeing a hundred wind-mills, a hundred barges, a hundred willow-trees, or a hundred herds of cattle all at once?'[50]

This inability to appreciate the subtle and distinctive charms of the Netherlands is evidence of a jaded palate. So too was Hazlitt's grumpiness – he was annoyed by a waiter in Calais, by the dreadful food in the inn at Dover, and by the muddy and straggling appearance of London as they passed through its suburbs. But he told his readers, 'I am not sorry that I have got back. There is an old saying, *Home is home, be it never so homely*. However delightful or striking the objects may be abroad, they do not take the same hold of you, nor can you identify yourself with them as at home.'[51]

It was not however only travel-weariness that afflicted Hazlitt on his return. When he called on Haydon soon afterwards the painter found him looking gaunt, and much greyer than before he left, wearing his hair cropped close to his head because of it. He was unwell, complaining that his old and chronic disability of indigestion was plaguing him and forcing him to a diet of 'brown bread, beef, and tea'. Haydon was pleased to see him; he wrote to Mary Russell Mitford that they had talked 'with great delight' for several hours, and said that despite being physically ill Hazlitt was psychologically much better. 'I like Hazlitt, in spite of all,' Haydon told her; 'everybody must.' Shortly afterwards, on a grey December day, Haydon 'called on Hazlitt, as being all in character with the day, and had a regular groan.'[52] One thing he learned from Hazlitt in these conversations was that the grand project of a biography of Napoleon had now taken full shape in Hazlitt's mind and he was about to begin work on it in earnest.

# CHAPTER FOURTEEN

# Napoleon and Twilight

## 1826–1830

BECAUSE OF THE perspective induced by his leisurely year abroad, Hazlitt returned to England in a subtly but significantly altered frame of mind. There had always been introspection and retrospection in his writing, but now there was even more, as he visited his past with increasing nostalgia, and weighed his life and work. He wrote more frequently in dialogue form too, finding it apt for the expression of his still passionately held political and ethical beliefs, but in more measured and sometimes in more exact terms. He started – at first as occasional pieces, then as a series which saw publication in book form as *Conversations of James Northcote RA* – a semi-fictionalized record of his long, meandering but fascinating discussions with the old artist in the comfortably familiar litter of his studio. The book bore the epigraph 'The precepts here of a divine old man I could recite.' The *Conversations* were not an historical reconstruction of their talk, but a vehicle for Hazlitt to have his say. Opinions and anecdotes were elicited from the old man by clever questioning designed by Hazlitt to steer their conversations in directions he wanted. In the preface to the book Hazlitt acknowledged that he had made free with the form, and that therefore the *Conversations* were to be considered 'as good as real'. A striking feature of them is Hazlitt's merciless self-exploration, giving Northcote criticisms, sometimes savage ones, which offered him a chance to justify himself. An early example is the conversation 'On Envy' published in 1826.

N: Did you never feel envy?
H: Very little, I think. In truth, I am out of the way of it; for the only pretension, of which I am tenacious, is that of being a metaphysician; and there is so little attention paid to this subject to pamper one's vanity, and so little fear of losing that little from competition, that there is scarcely any room for envy here. One occupies the niche of eminence in which one places oneself, very quietly and contentedly! If I have ever felt this passion at all,

it has been when some very paltry fellow has by trick and management contrived to obtain much more credit than he was entitled to. There was — — , to whom I had a perfect antipathy.[1] He was the antithesis of a man of genius; and yet he did better, by mere dint of dulness, than many men of genius. This was intolerable. There was something in the man and in his manner, with which you could not possibly connect the idea of admiration, or of any thing that was not merely mechanical – 'His look made the still air cold'[2] – he repelled all sympathy and cordiality. What he did (though amounting only to mediocrity) was an insult to the understanding ... Who is there that admires the Author of Waverley more than I do? Who is there that despises Sir Walter Scott more? I do not like to think there should be a second instance of the same person's being 'The wisest, the meanest of mankind' – and should be heartily glad if the greatest genius of the age should turn out to be an honest man. The only thing that renders this *mis-alliance* between first-rate intellect and want of principle endurable is that such an extreme instance of it teaches us the great moral lesson of moderating our expectations of human perfection, and enlarging our indulgence of human infirmity.

N: You start off with an idea as usual, and torture the plain state of the case into a paradox. There may be some truth in what you suppose; but malice or selfishness is at the bottom of the severity of your criticism, not the love of truth or justice, though you may make it the pretext. You are more angry at Sir Walter Scott's success than his servility. You would give yourself no trouble about his poverty of spirit, if he had not made a hundred thousand pounds by his writings. The sting lies there, though you may try to conceal it from yourself.

H: I do not think so. I hate the sight of the Duke of Wellington for his foolish face, as much as for any thing else. I cannot believe that a great general is contained under such a paste-board vizor of a man. This, you'll say, is party-spite, and rage at his good fortune. I deny it. I always liked Lord Castlereagh for the gallant spirit that shone through his appearance; and his fine bust surmounted and crushed fifty orders that glittered beneath it. Nature seemd to have meant him for something better than he was. But in the other instance, Fortune has evidently played Nature a trick, 'To throw a cruel sunshine on a fool.'

N: The truth is, you were reconciled to Lord Castlereagh's face, and patronised his person, because you felt a sort of advantage over him in point of style. His blunders qualified his success; and you fancied you could take his speeches in pieces, whereas you could not undo the battles that the other had won.

H: So I have been accused of denying the merits of Pitt, from political dislike

and prejudice; but who is there who has praised Burke more than I have?
It is a subject I am never weary of, because I feel it.

N: You mean, because he is dead, and is now little talked of; and you think
you show superior discernment and liberality by praising him. If there was
a *Burke-Club*, you would say nothing about him. You deceive yourself as
to your own motives, and weave a wrong theory out of them for human
nature.

Hazlitt gave himself a pasting in these conversations, but stood up to it.
He seemed to be in private dialogue with himself, examining his conscience
and his actions, seeking to vindicate himself as much to himself as to
anyone else. The conversation turned to a man Hazlitt profoundly disliked,
the Tory critic John Wilson Croker, who had been behind some of the
more vituperative attacks on him in the party press, and who was known
for his sneering disparagement of the fine arts. Northcote's mention of him
prompted Hazlitt to anathematize his character and taste in blunt terms –
'his conceit and ill-humour ... his want of taste in art ... cunning, servile
...' were the words, and Northcote said, 'Come, this is always the way.
Now you are growing personal. Why do you so constantly let your temper
get the better of your reason?' Hazlitt replied, 'Because I hate a hypocrite,
a time-server, and a slave.'

This dialogue was written before Hazlitt formulated his idea of an entire
series of *Conversations*. It was intended for a new collection of essays,
under the title *The Plain Speaker* – the third in the magnificent set he wrote
in the 1820s, commencing with *The Round Table* and continuing with
*The Spirit of the Age*. The new collection was markedly more introspective
and nostalgic than any of his earlier work. A number of themes recur: he
meditates on his art as a writer, reprises his outlook as a philosopher, even
revisits the political concerns that had animated him a decade before and
which he had officially put behind him. In particular he iterates his belief
that imagination is central to morality and an understanding of the world,
a view that had informed his thinking from before his years at Hackney
New College.

*The Plain Speaker* was published by Colbourn in two volumes in May
1826, the same month as his *Notes of a Journey through France and Italy*
was published by John Hunt's son, Henry Leigh Hunt, and his new partner
Charles Cowden Clarke. The response to both books showed what a
knock Hazlitt's reputation had taken because of *Liber Amoris*. The
*Monthly Review* described the *Journey* as 'puerile', and the *Monthly
Magazine* said, 'Adventures, there are none; novelty of object, there is
none: he has an eye mainly for pictures – picture after picture is inflicted

upon us, without measure or mercy – but a reflection for any thing and everything.' Nevertheless the reviewer had to admit, 'the book is full of remarks, more or less lively, some sagacious, but oftener fantastic – in the writer's usual rambling, but still agreeable manner – governed by no law of association that we ever heard of before, though never forgetting his contempt for Sir W. Scott, his abhorrence of Croker and the Quarterly, or a smile at the charlatannerie of our classical Foreign Minister. Let nobody be repulsed by the introductory letter, full of *naiseries* as it is; they will find compensation for a little perseverance.' The book did not sell well. It was an almost exact reprint of his newspaper articles, and there were increasing numbers of straightforward guides and travel accounts which prospective travellers chose because they gave information about coach times and hotels and other matters which Hazlitt only fitfully mentioned, and then usually to make a point about some quite other matter than the practicalities of the journey.

Previous works by Hazlitt had been widely reviewed, but *The Plain Speaker* got only six mentions, and only the one by Leigh Hunt was positive. In the dismissiveness of the others there is a new and disquietingly patronizing tone. Whereas once Hazlitt was thought dangerous, and had to be answered fiercely, now there is an air of condescension, as if Hazlitt has become irrelevant. It is 'quite amusing' to see the 'strange miscellany' of his 'poor and feeble abuse, of mawkish vulgarity,' said the *Monthly Magazine*. The book sold badly, and was still available in its first edition in 1840, when its price was halved to help move it from the shelves.

It would have been surprising if Hazlitt did not somewhere in *The Plain Speaker* say something that reflected his state of mind or health. 'Suppose a man to labour under an habitual indigestion. Does it not oppress the very sun in the sky, beat down all his powers of enjoyment, and imprison all his faculties in a living tomb? Yet he perhaps long laboured under this disease, and felt its withering effects, before he was aware of the cause.' Hazlitt had suffered from indigestion for many years. It was growing more severe, which explains the diet he reported to Haydon. What he did not know was that the affliction either had already changed or was in the process of changing into something much more serious.

Hazlitt and Isabella were comfortably settled in Down Street. For-tunately for them Isabella's income was unaffected by the bank failures and economic recession in England in 1825, which must have seemed remote to them as they travelled in Italy, although one piece of news no doubt afflicted even if it did not affect Hazlitt: the bankruptcy in the same year of the publisher Constable, owner of the *Edinburgh Review* and the

*Encyclopaedia Britannica.* Constable was a man Hazlitt respected and to whom he owed a great deal.

In the spring and early summer of 1826 Hazlitt and Isabella entertained a stream of friends in Down Street. Leigh Hunt and his family had returned from Florence in the previous autumn, reaching England at about the same time as the Hazlitts, and Hunt was now a frequent visitor at their home. He wrote from Highgate, 'I know but one thing that would take me to town sooner than the pleasure of passing an evening with your masculine discourse on one side the table and "the calm of pleasant womankind" which you have on the other. Pray forgive my saying this, and let Mrs Hazlitt forgive me, but I am more at ease with you in your own house than anywhere else, and have felt so comfortable there both in Florence and in Down Street, that I trust to please you by saying what I do, and think you should be pleased because it is true.' Charles and Mary Lamb were frequently there too, and Patmore. Hazlitt and Godwin went to the theatre together with Mary Shelley, and doubtless father and daughter were visitors in Down Street too.

It was at the Hazlitts' that Patmore first met the Lambs, and was given special reason to remember the occasion by the embarrassment it brought. He had just published his *Rejected Articles*, the first of which was an imitation of an essay by Elia, and Hazlitt showed it to Mary Lamb, who immediately began to read it, 'evidently', Patmore uncomfortably recalled, 'with no very good will'.[3]

One person who visited only during the day, and without his wife, was Haydon. He was surprisingly strait-laced in some of his attitudes, and did not think the Hazlitts' marriage seemly. Because Hazlitt had both divorced and remarried in Scotland, neither ceremony being recognized in England, his marriage to Isabella was notionally bigamous, although no action for bigamy was at all likely to be taken. Nevertheless Haydon would not let his wife Mary meet the new Mrs Hazlitt, a circumstance which naturally led to a certain distancing between the two men.

But what gave Hazlitt most pleasure was the resumption of his favourite long-standing practice of visiting Northcote ('the person whose doors I enter with most pleasure, and quit with most regret') in his dirty untidy studio, and talking with him for hours. 'I know that I can get there what I get nowhere else – a welcome, as if one was expected to drop in just at that moment, a total absence of all respect of persons and of airs of self-consequence, endless topics of discourse, refined thoughts, made more striking by ease and simplicity of manner – the husk, the shell of humanity is left at the door, and spirit, mellowed by time, resides within! All you have to do is sit and listen; and it is like hearing one of Titian's faces speak!' Northcote was legendarily crusty and difficult – Peter Pindar called him 'that walking thumb-bottle of *aqua fortis*' – but he had a soft spot for Hazlitt, who had been coming to the studio since he was a boy. In any case Hazlitt was happy to put up with Northcote's asperities for the sake of his conversation. 'What, do you still praise that little old withered wasp?' he asked himself, and answered 'Yes: spleen before everything but truth; but truth before everything.'[4] His talks with Northcote in the summer of 1826 were the basis of 'On Envy' quoted above, and for the series that eventually became *Conversations*. Pleased by 'On Envy' Hazlitt wrote a half-dozen more based on the visits of 1826, and before the summer was out sold them to the *New Monthly Magazine* under the title 'Boswell Redivivus'.

Hazlitt's mind was now firmly fixed on his projected *magnum opus*, the biography of Napoleon. To do the research for the book meant returning to Paris for a lengthy stay. The Hazlitts were pleased about that, because they loved Paris, and although their travels in the previous summer and autumn had tired them, this was not the same thing – it was going, staying, and coming back.

They were in Paris by the beginning of August 1826, and rented a house at 58 Rue Mont-Blanc an appropriate name given their sojourn within sight of that mountain's peak the previous summer. The street lay in the newly fashionable Chaussée d'Antin where, Balzac wrote, 'the boulevards were thronged with elegance, where the world of pleasure, the opera, and the theatre, were close at hand.'[5]

Hazlitt set to work on his research, and refreshed himself with long visits to the Louvre. On one of them he decided to try copying one of the pictures he had copied twenty-five years before, Titian's *Man in Black*, partly to show a friend at home what the picture he so admired looked like, and partly to see whether he retained any of his old facility. It turned out that he did not, and the discovery depressed him terribly. 'I lately tried to make a copy of a portrait by Titian (after several years' want of practice), with a view to give a friend in England some notion of the picture, which is equally remarkable and fine. I failed, and floundered on for some days, as might be expected. I must say the effect on me was painful and excessive. My sky was suddenly overcast. Every thing seemed of the colour of the paints I used. Nature in my eyes became dark and gloomy. I had no sense or feeling left, but of the unforeseen want of power, and of the tormenting struggle to do what I could not. I was ashamed ever to have written or spoken on art: it seemed a piece of vanity and affectation in me to do so – all whose reasonings and refinements on the subject ended in an execrable daub.'[6] It was a severe blow. For a time he shrank from visiting his favourite places in Paris because his failure seemed to poison the memories associated with them – 'I was even afraid to walk out of an evening by the barrier of Neuilly, or to recall the yearnings and associations that once hung upon the beatings of my heart. All was turned to bitterness and gall.' Then he remembered that he had once 'copied this very picture very well formerly', and that when he had done so 'I had no other resource, no other language. My tongue stuck to the roof of my mouth: now it is unlocked, and I have done what I then despaired of doing another way. Ought I not to be grateful and contented? Oh yes! – and think how many there are who have nothing to which they can turn themselves, and fail in every object they undertake.' These calmer thoughts helped the painting along at last, and Hazlitt finished the copy, and hung it up in the house in the Rue Mont-Blanc. 'The copy went on better afterwards, and the affair ended less tragically than I apprehended. I did not cut a hole in the canvas, or commit any other extravagance; it is now hanging up very quietly facing me; and I have considerable satisfaction in occasionally looking at it, as I write this paragraph,' he said.[7]

The six 'Boswell Redivivus' articles began to appear in the autumn in the *New Monthly Magazine*. Hazlitt was lucky to be in Paris when the first appeared, because it immediately infuriated Leigh Hunt, and probably a few other people besides, including Mary Shelley. Earlier in the year, when Godwin and Mary Shelley accompanied Hazlitt to the theatre, Mary Shelley had spoken freely about Byron, about Shelley's attitude to Byron, and about Leigh Hunt's capacity to judge Byron's character. These remarks featured in the very first of the Northcote conversations, along with other matter scarcely calculated to please anyone involved: 'I had been to the play with G. and his daughter, from the last of whom I had learnt something about Lord Byron's conversation. "What!" he said, "the beauty-daughter?" I said, "Do you think her a beauty, then?" – "Why, no, she rather thinks herself one, and yet there is something about her that would pass as such. Girls generally find out where to place themselves. She's clever too; isn't she?" – "Oh! Yes" – "What did she tell you about Lord Byron? Because I am curious to know all about him." – I asked her if it was true that Lord Byron was so poor a creature as H— represented him? She at first misunderstood me, and said, nothing could be meaner than he was, and gave some instances of it. I said, that is not what I meant; that I could believe any thing of that kind of him; that whatever he took in his head he would carry to extremes, regardless of every thing but the feeling of the moment; but that I could not conceive him to be in conversation, or in any other way, a flat and *common-place* person. "Oh! No," said she, "he was not. H— was hardly a fair judge. The other had not behaved well to him, and whenever they met, H— always began some kind of argument, and as Lord Byron could not argue, they made but a bad piece of business of it, and it ended very unsatisfactorily for all parties." I said, H— was too apt to put people to their trumps, or to force them upon doing not what *they* could do, but what he thought *he* could do. He, however, not only gave his own opinion, but said, Mr S— could only just endure Lord Byron's company. This seemed to me odd; for although he might be neither orator nor philosopher, yet anything he might say or only stammer out in broken sentences, must be interesting: a glance, a gesture would be full of meaning; or he would make one look about one like the tree in Virgil, that expressed itself by groans. To this she assented, and observed – "At least S— and myself found it so; for we generally sat with him till morning. He was perhaps a little moody and reserved at first; but by touching on certain strings, he began to unbend, and gave the most extraordinary accounts of his own feelings and adventures that could be imagined. Besides, he was very handsome, and it was some satisfaction to look at a head at once so beautiful and expressive." ' In the later parts of the conversation Hazlitt told Northcote that Hunt ('H—') wished to make Byron 'tributary' to himself, and that he had been spoiled by flattery when young. The unpleasing light in which these remarks cast Hunt was not sweetened by Hazlitt then saying to Northcote: 'I promised H— I would bring him to see him; and then, said I, you would think as favourably of him as I do, and every body else that knows him.'

Evidently Hazlitt did not see how his reported conversation with Mary Shelley might strike Hunt himself (or for that matter Mary Shelley, who might not have liked hearing that Northcote thought she was a beauty only in her own estimation). Hunt was certainly hurt on his own account, but more so in regard to the memory of Shelley, of which he was always tenderly jealous. He wrote in indignation to the editor of the *New Monthly Magazine*, Thomas Campbell, who immediately replied in contrition: 'For this detestable passage in Hazlitt's paper I am, as I deserve to be, visited with much regret ... There was, I must say, a culpable negligence in my not rejecting what relates to Mr S ... I am truly indignant at being made the means of annoying you ... If I can say or write anything that can make a shadow of satisfaction, I am willing to do so; but I suppose you will despise this devil's aspersions.'' Campbell's prompt and fulsome apology satisfied Hunt – and the rest of the 'Boswell Redivivus' papers continued to appear as scheduled.

But the Hunt irritation was not the last of the problems to face the series. In the sixth one, which appeared in March 1827, Northcote made free reference to one Reverend Zachariah Mudge, who 'ran away from the Academy where he was brought up, because Moll Faux the housemaid, would not have him,' and who, having commenced as a Dissenter, transferred to the Church of England in dudgeon at not being given, by his Dissenting brethren, a position he particularly desired. The Mudge family of Plymouth learned of these remarks, and were incensed. The Mudges and Northcotes been acquainted since the depths of the eighteenth century, so their severe irritation both alarmed and mortified the old painter. He had been enjoying the late bloom of fame which the series was bringing him, but he now realized what he had let himself in for, and he was suddenly angry with Hazlitt for his excessive frankness. He wrote in a hurry to Thomas Campbell, describing 'Boswell Redivivus' as 'despicable and worthless trash', and vituperating Hazlitt as 'a wretch who has betrayed me, and who is gone to France to escape the vengeance of those he has annoyed.' Campbell replied that 'the *infernal* Hazlitt shall never more be permitted to write for the "New Monthly".'[9] The series accordingly came to an end – for the time being. For all his annoyance at being attacked by the Mudges, Northcote was too fond of Hazlitt to be annoyed with him long – as soon as Hazlitt was back from Paris they were once more conversing, and not long afterwards their 'Conversations' began to appear in print again. Neither was it the end of Hazlitt's association with the *New Monthly Magazine*, whose editor no doubt execrated Hazlitt to irate correspondents, but who was secretly pleased at the effect on his magazine's circulation. No sooner had the '*infernal* Hazlitt' been banned from its pages than his marvellous essay 'On the Feeling of Immortality in Youth' appeared in it, with the poignant paragraph beginning 'For my part, I set out in life with the French Revolution.'[10]

In the summer of 1827 Hazlitt's son William the younger, by now a full-fledged adolescent of fifteen, joined him and Isabella in Paris. It is not hard to guess what kind of changes a year had made in the boy, given that in the previous summer Haydon thought him newly clean and neat, whereas he was now difficult and sulky, resentful towards Isabella and towards his father because, he said, the latter had not treated his mother well. Hazlitt wanted William to see Italy, so the three of them set off along the route Hazlitt and Isabella had taken two years earlier. None of the three left a record of the journey, but the sequel makes it plain that it did the opposite of resolving the stresses and tensions that had arisen in Paris – it made domestic life intolerable. Accordingly, when the journey was over and the party had returned to Paris, Hazlitt took William back to England, leaving Isabella in the Rue Mont-Blanc reflecting on whether their marriage was sustainable in light of the difficulties. William the younger was the main, though probably not the only reason why she decided it was not, but the other reasons – Hazlitt's too intermittent contributions to the family budget, his habits with women of the street, the fact that it had been a marriage of convenience and comradeship rather than love, which is the only tie that will bind when difficulties arise – are simply not known. She wrote to say that she was not going to rejoin the two Williams, but had decided to go instead to Switzerland with her sister. With that she vanished from Hazlitt's life and the record.

The only comment that came from Hazlitt's pen at about this time which might obliquely refer to these eventualities was, 'Gallantry to women (the sure road to their favour) is nothing but the appearance of extreme devotion to all their wants and wishes – a delight in their satisfaction, and a confidence in yourself, as being able to contribute towards it. The slightest indifference with regard to them, or distrust of yourself, are equally fatal.'[11] If this is a comment on part of the reason for the ending of the marriage, it leaves untouched the question whether Hazlitt felt any kind of regret. From the accounts left by his friends, Isabella brought 'the calm of pleasant womankind' into his life, and he cannot but have missed that, together with the financial security she brought too.

Hazlitt left the Down Street house and took rooms in Half Moon Street. He had made good progress with the first two volumes of his 'Life of Napoleon Buonaparte' while in Paris, and had been promised £400 by Hunt and Clarke for the copyright of the complete work – including the third and fourth volumes, yet to be done. He continued to write for the *New Monthly Magazine*, the *Examiner*, and a new journal called *The London Weekly Review*, as he brought the first volumes to completion. Just as he was about to do so his rooms were burgled, much to his alarm – time had done nothing to diminish his constitutional timidity, and he was afraid not only for his own safety – he thought the robbers would have killed him because they would not have believed that he had neither money nor a watch to give them, which was true – but also for his manuscript, which he fancied they might wish to steal.

His lack of a watch was nothing to do with having left it at a pawn-broker's, for as he wrote in his essay 'On a Sun-Dial' at about this time, he had never owned one: 'I have never had a watch nor any other mode of keeping time in my possession, nor ever wished to learn how time goes. It is a sign I have had little to do, few avocations, few engagements ... I confess, nothing at present interests me but what has been – the recollection of the impressions of my early life, or events long past, of which only the dim traces remain in a smouldering ruin or half-obsolete custom.'[12]

In December 1827 he was ill – a 'violent spasm' which he put down to walking fifteen miles in the mud, followed by sitting in a draughty coach because he was too polite to ask a lady in the carriage whether she would mind if he shut the window – an incident which, despite being made ill by it, he passed off with piquant but profound irony: 'Delicacy, moderation, complaisance, the *suaviter in modo*, whisper it about, my dear Clarke, these are my faults and have been my ruin,' he told Charles Cowden Clarke in a letter from his sick-bed.

He had delivered the manuscript of the *Life* to Clarke and Hunt, and was annoyed at their objection to his 'Preface', in which he explained why he had written the book, and defended his championing of Napoleon. The publishers had said that it was 'impolitic' to offer the book as an unapologetic apology for Napoleon, and Hazlitt crossly replied, 'I thought all the world agreed with me at present that Buonaparte was better than the Bourbons, or that a tyrant is better than tyranny. In my opinion no one of an understanding above the rank of a lady's waiting-maid could ever have doubted this, though I alone said so ten years ago.' And he pointed out that it was surely appropriate to state the difference between his account of Napoleon and the one currently being written by Sir Walter Scott.

In the event the 'Preface' appeared as the exordium to volume three of the *Life*, which was a compromise of sorts. 'Of my object in writing the LIFE here offered to the public, and of the general tone that pervades it, it may be proper that I should render some account in order to prevent mistakes and false applications,' Hazlitt there wrote. 'It is true, I admired the man; but what chiefly attached me to him, was his being, as he had been long ago designated, "the child and champion of the Revolution". Of this character he could not divest himself, even though he wished it. He was nothing, he could be nothing, but what he owed to himself and his triumphs over those who claimed mankind as their inheritance by a divine right, and as long as he was *a thorn in the side of kings*, and kept them at bay. His cause rose out of the ruins and defeats of their pride and hopes of revenge. He stood (and he alone stood) between them and their natural prey. Her kept off that last indignity and wrong offered to a whole people (and through them to the rest of the world) of being handed over, like a herd of cattle, to a particular family, and chained to the foot of a legitimate throne. This was the chief point at issue – this was the great question, compared to which all others were tame and insignificant – Whether mankind were, from the beginning to the end of time, born slaves or not? As long as he remained, his acts, his very existence, gave a full and proud answer to this question ... he did many things wrong and foolish;

but they were individual acts, and recoiled upon the head of the doer ...
In fact, Buonaparte was not strictly a free agent. He could hardly do
otherwise than he did, ambition apart, and merely to preserve himself and
the country he ruled ... There were two other feelings that influenced me,
in this subject; a love of glory, when it did not interfere with other
things, and the wish to see personal merit prevail over external rank and
circumstance. I felt pride (not envy) to think that there was one reputation
in modern times equal to the ancients, and at seeing one man greater than
the throne he sat upon.'[13]

The two volumes were published in January 1828. His ambitions for
the book made him apprehensive about its reception: what would people
think of a book in which the immoral blackguard and splenetic critic
William Hazlitt defended the evil enemy Napoleon Buonaparte – two very
different public enemies, in character and scale, but both public enemies
anyway? In an effort to get the book widely noticed Hazlitt wrote to
acquaintances in the months leading up to publication, urging them to
arrange for reviews and excerpts. The response, when it came, was a
disappointment. The hostile press was predictably hostile, but even friends
found it hard to praise a book which, as it proved, was very uneven in
quality – lit by the flashes of Hazlitt's genius in passages of great beauty
and eloquence, but bogged down by long, turgid accounts of politics and
battles which Hazlitt had laboriously transcribed from his French and other
sources, practically without editing or arrangement. Lamb, in dismay,
confidentially told friends that he 'skipped the battles', although he was
impressed by the 'speculative episodes'. The reviewer in the *New Monthly
Magazine* summed it up for friends and foes alike by saying, 'this kind of
historical and lofty detail, this epic in writing we do not think Mr Hazlitt's
forte. He is a clever man, but on a different scale, and Teniers or Wilkie
might as well attempt the style of the cartoons of Raphael.'[14]

Hazlitt waited for the first reviews in Winterslow, walking in the bare
winter woods, and writing his contributions to the *London Weekly Review*
and the *Monthly Magazine*. For the first he aired a long-standing vexation:
the way false and unfair calumnies stick, harming their victims for a long
time thereafter. He was thinking of *Blackwood's* libel on his appearance
and by that means his moral character – the 'pimpled Hazlitt' charge.
'Suppose an individual of whom it has been repeatedly said that he has
warts on his nose, were to enter ... is there a single red-faced country
squire who would not be surprised at not finding this part of the story
true – would not persuade himself five minutes after that he could not
have been seen correctly, or that some art had been used to conceal the
defect, or would be led to doubt, from this instance, Mr Blackwood's

general candour and veracity? On the contrary, the gentleman would be obliged to disbelieve his senses rather than give Mr Blackwood the lie, who is read and believed by the whole world. He would have a host of witnesses against him: there is not a reader of Blackwood who would not swear the fact. Seeing is believing, it is said. Lying is believing, say I.'[15]

In the *Monthly Magazine* he let slip the fact that an old but deep wound had not healed after all. 'I believe there is one character that all the world would be glad to change with – which is that of a favoured rival. Even hatred gives way to envy. We would be any thing – a toad in a dungeon – to live upon her smile, which is all our earthly hope and happiness; nor can we, in our infatuation, conceive that there is any difference of feeling on the subject, or that the pressure of her hand is not in itself divine, making those to whom such bliss is deigned like the Immortal Gods!'[16]

But when these troubling reflections had quietened under the influence of Winterslow's familiar and pleasing haunts, he wrote the essay which his son later published as 'A Farewell to Essay-Writing' but which he called 'Recollections'. In it he said – writing in increasingly Horatian vein – that he was happy in the quiet and simplicity of his rural retreat, pleased to have 'food, warmth, sleep and a book', and happy in the memories that the place held for him – not least his memories of reading and painting in Winterslow's woods, and of walking across the neighbouring meadows with Charles and Mary Lamb. 'It is in looking back to such scenes that I draw my best consolation for the future. Later impressions come and go, and serve to fill up the intervals; these are my standing resources, my true classics. If I have had few real pleasures or advantages, my ideas, from their sinewy texture, have been to me in the nature of realities; and if I should not be able to add to the stock, I can live by husbanding the interest. As to my speculations, there is little to admire in them but my admiration of others; and whether they have an echo in time to come or not, I have learned to set a grateful value on the past, and am content to wind up the account of what is personal only to myself and the immediate circle of objects in which I have moved, with an act of easy oblivion.'[17]

Despite the valedictory tone of this essay, full of resignation and melancholy, Hazlitt was still busy with the next two volumes of the *Life*, and yet again thinking about arranging and publishing his philosophical work. To David Constable he offered a series of 'Outlines' – of which 'Outlines of Morals', 'Outlines of the Human Mind' and 'Outlines of Political Economy' are representative examples. Most of these were papers written long before, but they still expressed Hazlitt's views, for his principles were stout, strongly held, and not likely to change unless very powerful arguments came along to show him why they should.

In March 1828 Hazlitt resumed his old post as drama critic of the *Examiner*. It was ten years since he had done this kind of journalistic hard labour, and it signifies that he was once again in the unenviable position of living hand-to-mouth. But he took friends to the theatre, especially young friends like Charles and Mary Cowden Clarke, who delighted in what he told them about the stage and its personalities then and in the past; and he always sat in the same seat, his back propped against a pillar, and enjoyed himself as of old. His articles were not straightforward reviews, but had a more general, discursive air, in which he dilated on subjects other than theatre if the mood took him.

The work for the *Examiner* was a makeshift while he gathered resources for another stay in Paris to finish his research for the last two volumes of the *Life*.[18] By June he was there again, this time staying at a cheap *pension* which he amusingly portrayed in an essay for the *New Monthly Magazine*, describing its inedible food, the pile of dirty washing 'stewing in the window', a baby being changed at table, and one of the residents wiping his gravy with his bread and picking his teeth with the point of his knife. Hazlitt wrote, 'What scenes we have (fit to make us die with laughter) in going over the messes and manners of the place!' – but it sounds ghastly, and although there was nothing precious about Hazlitt, he was a man of keen sensibility, and is unlikely to have laughed about it much or for long.

He remained in Paris for a couple of months only, returning to England in the autumn and going straight away to Winterslow to be near William the younger and to finish writing the remaining two volumes of the *Life*. All the while he kept up the flow of essays on which his daily bread depended, and also began to write a column for a weekly paper called the *Atlas*. This routine persisted through the winter, supplemented in March 1829 by a resumption of his conversations with Northcote – somewhat disguised, with he and Northcote appearing, doubtlessly at the old man's request, under a variety of letters of the alphabet other than 'N' and 'H'. Hazlitt now called them 'Conversations as Good as Real', and because of their shorter format in the *Atlas* he focused on a single subject, or a small range of subjects, each time.

Disaster struck in May 1829. The publishing venture of Henry Leigh Hunt and Charles Cowden Clarke failed, leaving Hazlitt without a publisher for the final volumes of the *Life*, and – even more to the point – with no prospect of collecting the large sum of money owed him by the firm: two hundred pounds, an income for a year or more.

The bankruptcy could not have come at a worse time for Hazlitt. His stomach trouble was growing worse, and the sudden loss of prospects meant that he had to retrench. He left his rooms in Half Moon Street in Mayfair, and moved to 3 Bouverie Street off Fleet Street, a cheaper area, a place of digs for clerks and young bachelors, not far from the dangerous territory of Southampton Buildings.

William the younger was living with him now, no longer at school, and already courting the young woman he later married – Catherine Reynell, daughter of the printer C. H. Reynell whom Hazlitt had known for years. Because of the connection between William the younger and Catherine, Hazlitt was often at the Reynells' house, and he took the younger members of the family to the theatre with him – a treat he was able to afford because he had free access to both of the major theatres for life, in honour of his eminence as a drama critic. Catherine Reynell was particularly fond of him, and was one of the few people he deferred to in private matters. He once told her that he had dined on pheasant, a very expensive dish (ten shillings apiece at 1829 prices). ' "Don't you think it was a good deal to give?" she asked. "Well, I don't know but what it was, Kitty," he replied, opening his eyes in his way, and tucking his chin into his shirt collar.'[19] The Reynells lived on the Oxford Road – on what is now called Bayswater Road, alongside Hyde Park; it was then a stretch of country lane beyond Tyburn, where the gallows stood, and Hazlitt was afraid enough of robbers to buy a pair of pistols to protect himself and William the younger on their journeys by foot along it. But he soon afterwards sold the pistols again, finding that he was more afraid of them than he was of prospective criminals.

As a way of thanking Northcote for his part in the 'conversations' series, still running intermittently in the *Atlas* in its new guise, Hazlitt agreed to help the old man in preparing a volume for the press, called *One Hundred Fables*. It involved Hazlitt in a mixture of editing and ghost writing. But in July 1829, just as he seemed to be sinking under the weight of hack-work and fiddling with other men's copy, he received a letter from Macvey Napier, who had taken over from Francis Jeffrey as editor of the *Edinburgh Review*, asking him to resume his position as a contributor. Hazlitt was both delighted and relieved. He wrote at once to accept, and to suggest various things he might review. The invitation was a sign that his stock was still good in quarters which mattered, and indeed he was never without a resource in one or other of the liberal periodicals when he wanted it. But the *Edinburgh* connection meant good fees, and in January 1830 he was able to move from Bouverie Street to Frith Street in Soho, taking a pair of rooms on the second floor at the back of the house. It was closer to the Reynells, and a little closer to the theatres of Covent Garden.

By an unhappy irony Hazlitt's improvement in circumstances led to his being arrested for debt not long after moving into Frith Street. He was misled into endorsing a bill by an accountant he had employed to help him arrange his affairs, and when the bill failed he was carried off to a 'Lock-Up House'. Talfourd told Mary Russell Mitford that 'Poor Hazlitt has been arrested on one of those detestable Bills of the detestable firm Hunt and Clarke for £150, all honestly earned by him ... but I have endeavoured by the aid of Procter, who is a good fellow despite his verses, to induce Basil Montagu to procure bail for him, and I hope I have succeeded.'

If hints and fragments of evidence are to be believed, Hazlitt was again in love – or at least, had formed an 'attachment'. It was a 'girl of the theatre', by which is not meant an actress but one of the prostitutes who frequented theatre foyers and lobbies. Jones quotes an undated entry in the notebook of John Mitford, which reads: 'Collier mentioned Hazlitt's attachments to one of the girls of the Theatre. She was passée, not handsome. He owned that these [illegible] etc. but was infatuated. Made her presents of necklaces etc.' Crabb Robinson said he had learned from conversations with various of Hazlitt's friends that he was 'fascinated with a worthless woman'.[20] There is no reason to think it anything but likely that Hazlitt's incorrigible heart was again in pawn; it was another instance of the truth of Patmore's observation that he was 'never out of love'.

Hazlitt's stomach problem, most probably either cancer or a serious ulcer, was worsening steadily. He was now definitely ill, and the experience of arrest and detention had not helped matters. But he was anxious for work, and wrote to Macvey Napier soliciting it. As the summer drew on he began to prepare his 'Conversations of James Northcote' for the press, and wrote an essay entitled 'Emancipation of the Jews', in which, in arguing that restrictions and civil disabilities should be lifted from the Jews, he said, 'it is the test of reason and refinement to be able to subsist without bugbears.' He was horrified to find that William the younger was contemplating a career as a singer, and that he and his mother Sarah Stoddart had been canvassing various of Hazlitt's friends to get them to approach him on the subject – which they knew would not be agreeable to him. It was not: and the matter ended there. The friends approached were Lamb, Ayrton, and Martin Burney, and it was Lamb who cautiously mooted the idea to Hazlitt, only to be greeted with such evidence of the latter's 'horror and aversion' to the idea that he refused to meddle further.

The *Conversations of Northcote* were ready for publication in July. Just as it was about to appear Hazlitt received a panic-stricken letter from the old man, saying that he had again been approached by the Mudges, who, advised that the volume was imminent, were determined that no further aspersions were to be cast on the sainted Zachariah. Northcote demanded that no mention of Mudge be allowed to appear in the book; Hazlitt assured him that Mudge had been removed; but Northcote insisted on a further six pages being excised – rather like removing healthy tissue in the vicinity of a cancer, as if to protect against spread of the disease. Hazlitt, frustratedly, had to agree.

Hazlitt's essay 'The Free Admission' appeared in the *New Monthly Magazine* for July 1830, celebrating the pleasures of theatre-going, and recalling the many years of delight he had experienced in gazing up at the stage. For him the theatre was, he wrote, 'a relief, a craving, a necessity'. But in August the deterioration in his health had reached the point where he could no longer go out, and after unequal struggles to resist the move, he finally took to his bed. He was 52 years of age, gaunt and grey, scarcely able to eat, weak and getting weaker. Even the joy of the Revolution of the Three Days in Paris, which drove the Bourbons out of France once and for all, was insufficient to rally him other than briefly. A few days after news of these events came he wrote, 'The Revolution of the Three Days was like a resurrection from the dead, and showed plainly that liberty too has a spirit of life in it; and the hatred of oppression is "the unquenchable flame, the worm that dies not".'[21] But privately he said to Charles Reynell, 'Ah, I am afraid, Charles, things will go back again.'

For Hazlitt himself in his worsening illness there was now no going back. His August contribution to the *New Monthly* was an essay very different in character from 'The Free Admission'. Called 'The Sick Chamber' it began: 'What a difference between this subject and my last ... Yet from the crowded theatre to the sick chamber, from the noise, the glare, the keen delight, to the loneliness, the darkness, the dulness, and the pain, there is but one step.'[22] For a while he tried to keep on working, sitting up in bed, but increasingly fitfully. As the hot days of August passed into September it was increasingly evident to everyone, and to himself, that he was fading. Basil Montagu, living just a few hundred yards away in Bedford Square, was a frequent visitor, and he called in Dr George Darling to serve as Hazlitt's physician. As Hazlitt grew feeble, his voice disappearing into a whisper and his energy sinking so low that he could scarcely cope with visitors, he became anxious about money. One reason for this was that, trapped helplessly in bed by illness, he could not provide for the 'worthless woman' he was in love with. William the younger wrote to Catherine Reynell saying that Hazlitt was very uneasy in mind, fretting and worrying so much that the anxiety was worse than his physical disease. In the gathering darkness of approaching death Hazlitt forgot that he had not been in touch with Francis Jeffrey since reading Jeffrey's review of his *Spirit of the Age* in Geneva, and he forgot too that Jeffrey was no longer editor of the *Edinburgh Review*. He only remembered that he was himself an *Edinburgh* reviewer, and with a quivering hand he wrote to Jeffrey: 'Dear Sir, I am dying. Can you send me £10, and so consummate your many kindnesses to me?' Jeffrey sent him £50.

Bryan Procter described Hazlitt at the last: 'he lay ghastly, shrunk, and helpless, on the bed from which he never afterwards rose. His mind seemed to have weathered all the dangers of extreme sickness, and to be safe and strong as ever. He could not lift his hand from the coverlet; and his voice was changed and diminished to a hoarse whisper, resembling the faint scream that I have heard from birds. I never was so sensible of the power of death before.' On Wednesday 15 September Hazlitt's old friend and publisher James Hessey wrote to the poet John Clare, 'Poor Hazlitt is very ill indeed – I fear on his death bed.' On Friday he seemed to his son a little better; but by the morning of Saturday 18 September it was clear that he was dying. Charles Lamb, his friend Edward White, William the younger and James Hessey were with him, remaining through the heavy hours as they wore into afternoon. He could talk very little, but what he said – what he whispered faintly, in the rough shrill whisper which was all he could manage – was remembered by them all: that he wished to see his mother, and that he was pleased his son was to marry Kitty Reynell. And then, to their astonishment and that of posterity, he whispered, 'Well, I've had a happy life.'

Death came soon afterwards, so imperceptibly and subtly that for several moments no-one was aware that his breathing had ceased, and that he was at last, and finally, beyond all passion and pain.

# CHAPTER FIFTEEN

# The Opinion of Death

HAZLITT'S FUNERAL was arranged by Lamb. It took place five days after his death on Thursday 23 September, in the churchyard of St Anne just around the corner from Frith Street. Today Hazlitt's is the only gravestone still in its place in the churchyard, near the curious onion-domed steeple which is all that remains of the church after its destruction in the blitz of 1940. The funeral was sparsely attended – Lamb, William the younger, and a few other friends gathered to lower his coffin into the damp clay, and to see the earth fall on it. Neither Peggy nor old Mrs Hazlitt were there, because Crediton was too far away for the old lady to make the journey, or for Peggy to leave her. The death notice in *The Times* was written by Sarah Stoddart, who, in her curious way, had remained attached to Hazlitt throughout, reading all that he wrote and keeping cuttings of his essays. The press was surprisingly warm in its notices of his passing, even *Blackwood's* allowing him to have been 'an ingenious author'. The warmest obituary came from the pen of Leigh Hunt. 'Mr Hazlitt was one of the profoundest writers of the day, an admirable reasoner (no one got better or sooner at the heart of a question than he did), the best general critic, the greatest critic on art that ever appeared (his writings on the subject cast a light like a painted window), exquisite in his relish of poetry, an untameable lover of liberty, and with all his humour and irritability (of which no man had more), a sincere friend and a generous enemy.'

Hazlitt had passionate admirers in his own day, one of whom arranged for a large tombstone to be raised above his grave, with the following elaborate inscription:

Here rests
WILLIAM HAZLITT
Born April 10, 1778, Died 18 September, 1830
He lived to see his deepest wishes gratified

As he has expressed them in his Essay,
'on the Fear of Death'.
Viz.:
'To see the downfall of the Bourbons,
And some prospect of good to mankind':
(Charles X
was driven from France 29<sup>th</sup> July, 1830).
'To leave some sterling work to the world':
(He lived to complete his 'Life of Napoleon')
His desire
That some friendly hand should consign
Him to the grave was accomplished to a
Limited but profound extent; on
These conditions he was ready to depart,
And to have inscribed on his tomb,
'Grateful and Contented'.
He was
The first (unanswered) Metaphysician of the age.
A despiser of the merely Rich and Great:
A lover of the People, poor or Oppressed:
A hater of the Pride and Power of the Few,
As opposed to the happiness of the many;
A man of true moral courage,
Who sacrificed Profit and present Fame
To Principle,
And a yearning for the good of Human Nature.
Who was a burning wound to an Aristocracy,
That could not answer him before men,
And who may confront him before their maker.
He lived and died
The unconquered Champion
Of
Truth, Liberty, and Humanity,
'Dubitantes opera legite'.
This stone
Is raised by one whose heart is
With him, in his grave.

The author of this encomium – much of it true and just, some of it hyperbolic, all of it constituting an essay in stone justifying Hazlitt against his enemies – is unknown, but thought to be a lawyer called Charles Wells, who had first come to know Hazlitt while attending his lectures at the Surrey Institution twelve years before, and who remained a devoted acolyte thereafter, without emerging from the shadows of Hazlitt's private life.[1] The Latin tag and the oratorical language suggest just such a follower, and make the attribution plausible. But there is another candidate for the anonymous encomiast, less likely but not absolutely impossible, in part suggested by the surprising warmth and grief of the closing words, 'This stone is raised by one whose heart is with him, in his grave.' The candidate is Sarah Stoddart. Despite the intermittent character of her appearance in Hazlitt's story after the Edinburgh divorce, it was she who wrote the death notice for *The Times*, which is unsurprising when it is remembered that whenever Hazlitt went to Winterslow to see William the younger he of course saw her too, and that she visited him often when William the younger lived with him in London after the end of his second marriage. She remained lifelong friends with his mother and his sister Peggy. Another factor that prompts the suggestion is a comparison of the style – allowing for the artificialities of lapidary inscription – with the journal Sarah Stoddart kept in Scotland. She had read and heard so much Hazlitt that the summary statement of what he was in political and philosophical terms would have come very easily to her.

If it was indeed Sarah Stoddart who raised the stone, there would be something touching about the observance that would do credit both to her and to him.


It is not altogether odd that a man who had such an emotional and intellectual struggle with himself and his world should nevertheless say, as his last words, 'I have had a happy life.' After all, Hazlitt spent his days as he chose: 'I loitered my life away, reading books, looking at pictures, going to plays, hearing, thinking, writing on what pleased me best,' he wrote. But it was not an idyll. He never found the love he longed for, although – a fact that makes things worse, not better – for a time of madness he thought he had found, or rather, narrowly missed it. 'I have wanted only one thing to make me happy; but wanting that, have wanted everything!' He knew that Sarah Walker had become pregnant by Tomkins shortly after the F episode, and had gone to live with him, unmarried. They had a son they called Frederick, who died at the early age of 28. Hazlitt was not to know that Sarah Walker and Tomkins separated about ten years before the latter's death (which happened in 1858), and that she herself lived to the age of 78, dying on 7 September 1876 in Newington, London – nine years after Hazlitt's grandson W. C. Hazlitt published the *Memoirs* which told over again, in detail, the story of the dreadful disappointment she gave her famous lover.

One might almost say that after the Sarah Walker débâcle something in Hazlitt – some silent spiritual part of himself, broken and dissipated by the emotional disaster – in effect turned its back on England, and on life. He lived only seven years longer, and spent a considerable portion of it on the continent of Europe. But in that time he added to the corpus of his writings two great works: *The Spirit of the Age* and *The Plain Speaker*.

In his very last essay, a nostalgic, retrospective, valedictory piece called 'The Letter-Bell' completed just weeks before his death, Hazlitt wrote both of his early years and of the recent events in France which had once again driven out the Bourbons (the 'Three Glorious Days' of 27–29 July 1830). And he recurred to the theme of his other great disappointment: the apostasy of those whose gifts should have served oppressed mankind. He said that in his youth 'the light of the French Revolution circled my head like a glory, though dabbled with drops of crimson gore: I walked comfortable and cheered by its side –

> And by the vision splendid
> Was on my way attended.

It rose then in the east: it has risen again in the west. Two suns in one day, two triumphs of liberty in one age, is a miracle which I hope the Laureate will hail in appropriate verse. Or may not Mr Wordsworth give a different turn to the fine passage, beginning –

> What though the radiance which was once so bright,
> Be now for ever vanished from my sight;
> Though nothing can bring back the hour
> Of glory in the grass, of splendour in the flower?

For it is not brought back, "like morn risen on mid-*night*"; and may he not yet greet the yellow light shining on the evening bank with eyes of youth, of genius, and freedom, as of yore? No, never! But what would these persons not give for the unbroken integrity of their early opinions – for one unshackled, uncontaminated strain – one *Io paean* to Liberty – one burst of indignation against tyrants and sycophants, who subject other countries to slavery by force, and prepare their own for it by servile sophistry, as we see the huge serpent lick over its trembling, helpless victim with its slime and poison, before it devours it! On every stanza so penned should be written the word RECREANT! Every taunt, every reproach, every note of exultation at restored light and freedom, would recall to them how their hearts failed them in the Valley of the Shadow of Death. And what should we say to *him* [Coleridge] – the sleep-walker, the dreamer, the sophist, the word-hunter, the craver after sympathy, but still vulnerable to truth, accessible to opinion, because not sordid or mechanical? The Bourbons being no longer tied about his neck, he may perhaps recover his original liberty of speculating; so that we may apply to him the lines about his own *Ancient Mariner* –

> And from his neck so free
> The Albatross fell off, and sank
> Like lead into the sea.

This is the reason I can write an article on the *Letter-Bell*, and other such subjects; I have never given the lie to my own soul. If I have felt the impression once, I feel it more strongly a second time; and I have no wish to revile or discard my best thoughts. There is a thorough *keeping* in what I write – not a line that betrays a principle or disguises a feeling. If my wealth is small, it all goes to enrich the same heap; and trifles in this way accumulate to a tolerable sum.'[2]

This is all true; Hazlitt was steadfast to his principles, which were altruistic and humane; and he was steadfast to his personal cost, for it meant being always excluded from the comfortable inner circles where patronage and pensions were on offer. The sincerity and depth of Hazlitt's feelings explain the bitterness of his anger at the apostates. He had heard Coleridge's eloquence in the chapel at Shrewsbury with delight and a soaring heart; it appalled him to find that those beautiful and rousing sentiments were so shallowly worn, so discardable and betrayable. Southey and Wordsworth had been likewise filled with the bliss of that dawn, likewise public and eloquent in their championing of what it promised; and they had become placemen, pensioners of a reactionary government, which had wasted the country's resources in a laborious and bloody effort to extirpate those principles, in order to preserve the privileges that the fortunate classes in England felt were threatened by them. Hazlitt was shocked and mortally hurt as much by what they had done as by the failure of those hopes, and the only way to appease his agony was to castigate them endlessly, even in the last weeks of his life, neither letting them forget their apostasy, nor letting the memory of the blissful dawn fade and die.

At Crediton in Devon where Peggy and her now very old mother still lived, the local Dissenting minister, the Reverend John Johns, gave a sermon on Sunday 10 October to comfort them in their loss. He subsequently published it under the title, 'The Season of Autumn, As Connected with Human Feelings and Changes. A Sermon Occasioned by the Death of William Hazlitt'. After an eloquent and pleasing set of reflections on the nature of autumn, distinguishing the 'autumn of the harvest' from the 'autumn of the fall', and the latter's lesson that 'We all do fade as a leaf,' Johns said, 'I should not, my bretheren, have brought these recollections before you, had it not again become my unwelcome duty to say a few words over another leaf that has fallen from the human life-tree, and rested upon the grave. A distinguished individual, a stranger but not an alien, will henceforth exist only as a distinguished name. One who has always been an object of attachment to the few, – and who by a strange involution of hostilities has been battling with the Many, while he was contending for Mankind, – has been laid at length in the peaceful resting-place, "where they shall not learn war any more" … In any age, when the general diffusion of knowledge has made it no easy matter for one man to rise greatly above the educated thousands around him, he has been one of those who have achieved the difficult undertaking, and whose thoughts have sparkled upon the topmost waves of the world. He felt it to be a proud distinction – perhaps he felt it *too* proudly – to be the owner of a luminous and vigorous mind. He could not be reproached with suffering the ploughshare to rust in the generous soil: It was rather his glorious but disastrous error, to suffer that soil too rarely to lie fallow. There is a mean, which he did not, or would not, discover; and Study may add *his* name to her long list of martyrs.'

True to the Dissenting tradition of reform, Johns also wished to draw his congregation's attention to Hazlitt's struggle in that cause, and the sacrifice it entailed in the material character of his life. Johns was a worthy instance of his caste, who in this peroration seems almost to be William senior come back to life. 'But the name of Hazlitt is associated with far nobler recollections. Whatever might be his speculative, whatever his practical errors, he was the fearless, the eloquent, and disinterested advocate of the rights and liberties of Man, in every cause and in every clime. His opinions were such as to make him one of a party, whom the brilliant and influential Administration, under which he commenced his career, honoured with no small portion of political and personal hatred. And they did not want either means or instruments to make the effects of that hatred felt, even by those, who were too haughty to show any pain, when "the sword had pierced through their souls" … A whisper went forth against them, which was, in its effects, more appalling than the thunder. Calumny

(I cite the verses for the sake of the powerful contrast), "seeing the multitudes, went up into a mountain, and when she was set, her disciples came unto her; and she opened her mouth, and taught them," saying, "These men are the enemies of the peace and happiness of Mankind. They speak of liberty; but they think of licence: they prate of the rights and wrongs of Man, while they are undermining the foundations of social justice and order. They have no true regard for the prosperity of the people, for the sanctity of the altar, or the majesty of the throne. They are impatient of all restraints upon their turbulent aspirings; and would 'turn the world upside down' in order to see how the pyramid would stand upon its head. Beware, therefore, how you join these friends of sedition and blasphemy, these enemies of peace and piety, wherever they are found. Listen not to the subtle voice of the serpent. Read not their writings, nor mix in their society; but rather unite with the true friends of your country, in banishing all such, by a silent ostracism, from the dwellings of the pious, the prudent, and the peaceful." These assertions and insinuations, enforced by an ascendant faction, made it once a dangerous and a daring thing, for any man to avow himself the partizan of liberty and reform . . . [H]e who dared to advocate these principles, was overwhelmed with a foaming deluge of obloquy and opprobrium. The step was, of itself, almost enough to blast his public hopes, and his private fame. Detraction followed him – Derision went with him – and Persecution lay in ambush for him. Let us therefore, my bretheren, look back with honour upon the few, who once lifted the sacred standard of Liberty, amid the "fiery darts of the wicked" and of the world.'

Without question, it would have meant much to Hazlitt to know that there were those among his contemporaries who understood what he had suffered for his political and social principles, and honoured him for it. He remains a great example of a democrat, a liberal, and a humanist, in the finest independent-minded traditions of all three. What he has to say of general purport on the rights and liberties of mankind remain wholly and unequivocally valid to this day.

The storms of political controversy fade or change – although the principles at stake rarely do either – and in their rootedness in historical circumstance seem not to have the permanence of art. It is in art, as a writer, that Hazlitt keeps his place – and as a critic. In this latter capacity his discernment was extraordinary. He recognized who and what was best in his day, and his insights have not been modified by posterity. His judgements of Shakespeare and other earlier writers are as good now as when he wrote them, and have commanded the respect of the greatest critics since his time. His views struck his contemporaries as original and controversial, but his attitudes have so much become part of the intellectual vocabulary of our own opinions that we no longer see how fine his insights are. But we need only reflect that in, for example, *The Spirit of the Age* he nominated such as Wordsworth and Godwin – figures of minority interest at the time he wrote – as men whose reputations would survive into history, to recognize how acute his judgements were.

What no-one then saw clearly, but many then and since have sensed, is that Hazlitt was a new phenomenon in literature. He was a prose-poet and a philosopher, who wonderfully combined and embodied in his robust, distinctive, energetic sensibility both the Enlightenment value of reason and the Romantic values of autonomy and expressiveness. He is an essayist, and a great one – perhaps the greatest of them all, if such comparisons make sense – but his essays are not as other people's. They are more accurately described as intellectual soliloquies, as streams of reasoned consciousness, rather than as concealed epistles, which is what the standard essay form fundamentally is. Where the models of Cicero and Seneca underlie most work in the form, in Hazlitt it is as if the model were Hamlet. His work in sum represents a large, copious intellectual autobiography, an account of a life lived vividly in response to the world around it, and to the art in it, with both world and art intensely mattering in life, as being what constitutes its point.

To read Hazlitt is therefore not just to hear and see him, but thereby to witness his mighty struggle to discover and state the truth about everything that engaged him. 'Life is indeed a strange gift,' he wrote, 'and its privileges are most miraculous.'[3] Writers like Hazlitt never lose or forfeit that strange gift, not even to death, because they live on in their work, and by its means pass onward a sense of life's miraculous privileges to all who come after them.

# APPENDIX ONE

# The Hazlitts in America

## 1783–1786

IN THE SPRING of 1783 England and its erstwhile colonies in the New World made peace. News of the treaty was carried to America by the *Henry*, whose captain was vehemently anti-peace, and who knew that the expectant British officers at New York would profoundly dislike what he had to tell them. This made him ill-disposed towards passengers who supported the American cause. The *Henry* called briefly at Cork to take on just such passengers, weighing anchor again on 3 April to front the Atlantic swells. The passengers in question were the Reverend William Hazlitt senior and his wife Grace, with their children John, aged fifteen, Margaret, usually called 'Peggy', aged twelve, five-year-old William the future essayist, an infant called Harriet, and a maid who, though called Honour, proved to have none. Behind them they left the bodies of two small sons: Loftus, who had died at Maidstone in England before reaching the age of two, and Thomas, who had died at Bandon in Ireland a few weeks after his birth.

The crossing took two months. The *Henry* reached New York on the morning of Monday 26 May, to be mobbed by the military as its captain had expected. Such was the clamour that the Hazlitts could not leave the boat until six in the evening. They then suffered the opposition's resentment; their letter of introduction was addressed to a Mr Trench Cox, who was so well known for his pro-British sentiments that the anti-British householders of New York would not oblige when he knocked on their doors seeking temporary accommodation for the Hazlitts. Mrs Hazlitt, Peggy and the small children had to take exhausted shelter in a porch while Cox, William senior and John continued the search for lodgings.[1]

The Hazlitts remained two days in New York while their luggage was disembarked – they were immigrants, after all, and had brought their whole world with them. Mrs Hazlitt was ill; she was six months pregnant, and sea-travel violently disagreed with her. Honour the maid stole what she could and decamped on the very first morning, leaving Peggy to do her untried best as housekeeper and cook.

On the third day the family set off for Philadelphia, which William senior had chosen not just for its fine optimistic name but because it was the principal city of the new country, its largest in size and population, and its first capital. Their route took them first to Burlington via Perth Amboy, where they made a pause, enjoying the view across the water to the hamlets of Bath and Bristol, standing handsomely in green woodland. Their names filled Mrs Hazlitt with homesickness. The New Jersey Assembly was sitting at Burlington at the time, and its members invited William senior to preach to them. Benjamin Franklin's natural son owned a house in the town, and it was to let; Mrs Hazlitt suggested renting it and settling right there, given William senior's auspicious reception and the possibilities for founding a congregation and school in the vicinity. But William senior was determined to settle in Philadelphia, so they pushed onward, travelling in a covered wagon through beautiful Jersey woods 'full of majestic trees', Peggy later wrote, 'mingled with the blossoms of the wild peach and apricot, and sweet-scented yellow flowers of the locust trees perfuming the air'.

In Philadelphia the Hazlitts took a house with a parlour, two bedrooms, two attics, and a kitchen, with 'cupboards in every room and a good cellar', where food had to be stored in pails of water to protect it from being instantly devoured by ants. There was a yard at the front and a plot of uncultivated ground at the back. For this small empire William senior paid fifty pounds a year of American money (thirty pounds British), which was a lot; their Maidstone house had cost twelve pounds a year.

On 25 June Harriet, aged eighteen months, died of croup. Six weeks later Mrs Hazlitt gave birth to another daughter, whom they named Esther. Six further weeks later Esther too died, as the result of falling from the arms of a negligent nurse.

As these events augured, the Hazlitts' sojourn in Philadelphia was eventful, and not particularly happy. On the plus side William senior and his son John saw George Washington at a service in St Peter's Church (it took a special occasion to entice them onto Episcopalian ground); and while preaching at nearby New London William senior met some distant Hazlitt relatives, one of whom was a hero for American independence, having served as a colonel in the militia. On the minus side were William senior's difficulties in finding a job. He preached in Philadelphia itself, to rising murmurs of disapprobation from the 'orthodox' who did not like what they heard of his liberal Unitarian views and his defence of 'rational religion', which set human reason as a judge over scripture. At Carlisle, not far from Philadelphia, he was offered a magnificent opportunity: a living of four hundred guineas a year, together with the presidency of a college just then being founded. He was recommended for the post by the Provost of the University of the State of Pennsylvania, Dr John Ewing. But even before he arrived to give his probationary sermons – it was the Dissenting way for a prospective minister to preach a few times to the local parishioners to see whether he and they suited each other, before any commitment was made – he found himself at the centre of controversy. Dr George Duffield of Philadelphia, author of the rousing hymn 'Stand Up, Stand Up for Jesus', took the view that William senior was a heretic, and sent word ahead to Carlisle accordingly. In his first two sermons William senior defended himself against the charge, only to find a local preacher, the Reverend William Linn, rancorously attacking him from another pulpit as 'a greater danger than they [the Americans] had faced in the late war'. This part of the accusation had a special sting for William senior, who later remarked, in a mixture of anger and sorrow, 'such was [Linn's] rude treatment of a stranger, who, to his own hurt, had released some hundreds of his countrymen from a loathsome prison, and from famine'. The problem was a simple one: the dominant strand of Protestantism in America was Calvinistic Presbyterianism, a hard-line blood-and-thunder ethos which preserved much of the Founding Fathers' original Puritanism, and survives in the outlook and practices of the religious Right in today's America. William senior's Unitarian opinions – rationalistic, tolerant and undogmatic – were by a long way too liberal in comparison.

Despite the controversy, or perhaps because of it, Carlisle's congregation decided to appoint William senior, if he would agree to subscribe 'the confession of faith, as far as it was agreeable to the word of God'. He refused; he said he would not even sign a confession of his own most cherished beliefs 'lest it be a stumbling block in my brother's way'. He could not accept that anyone's faith should be subject to a formula devised by other men: 'he would sooner die in a ditch,' he said, 'than submit to human authority in matters of faith'. He thus turned down by far the best opportunity of his life, and hastened back to Philadelphia in chagrin. Dr Ewing was later told that William senior had quitted the field too hastily, for if he had held out two weeks longer 'he would have been accepted on his own terms'.[2]

The family was not however short of friends in Philadelphia. In addition to the preachers of Dissenting persuasions, with whose families they regularly visited, they had delightful neighbours – a Jewish family on one side, and on the other side a family with a son William junior's age. There were picnics and pleasures; on one picnic Peggy nearly stepped on a snake, like Eurydice, but was saved by a stranger who pulled her back and, without speaking, shot it. 'Thus was I providentially preserved (by the accidental passing of this stranger) from a fearful death!' her *Journal* breathlessly reports.

Other advantageous offers came William senior's way, among them the headship of a school, but since it meant giving up preaching he declined. In August 1783, not long after Esther's death, he was invited to preach in Maryland. He found a congenial community there, and as usual prepared to stay for a few weeks to see if he and the congregation could agree. On the second Sunday, in mid-sermon, he collapsed in the pulpit. It was yellow fever. He was very seriously ill, and had to be taken to the home of a local family, the Earls, to be nursed. 'Two black men sat up with him every night,' Peggy wrote, 'and he partly ascribed his recovery to a large draught of water that he prevailed on them to let him have, which, however, had been strictly forbidden.' The Hazlitts at home in Philadelphia did not know what had become of him, and when at length friends brought news that he had fallen ill Mrs Hazlitt became hysterical, convinced – in the shadow of two recent burials in the family – that he was dead. It took hours to calm her.

The next day John, then just sixteen years of age, mounted his horse and in fifty-six hours traversed one hundred and sixty miles of unfamiliar marsh and woodland in search of his father. He found him recovering, but far too weak to travel. They waited several weeks, and then slowly ventured back. On reaching home William senior was too feeble to dismount, and had to be lifted from his horse and carried indoors. It was November by this time, and the day of his return saw the first snowfall. For the rest of the winter he sat huddled in his greatcoat by the fire, looking yellow in the face and medicating himself with Columbo root. It was an especially severe winter, further distinguished by an earthquake.

By the following spring William senior had recovered enough to accept an invitation to lecture at the State University of Pennsylvania on the 'Evidences of Christianity'. The lectures were well attended to begin with, and Peggy asserts in her journal that they saved many who, so disaffected by the harshness of Calvinism that they were on the point of renouncing Christianity altogether, were rescued by the reasonableness, mildness and cogency of Unitarianism's 'rational religion'. She adds, 'Here I cannot help remarking how strange it seems that my father, who openly preached the doctrine of the divine Unity from Maryland to Kennebeck, should have been so entirely overlooked and the whole work ascribed to Dr Priestley, who went there so many years after him.'[3] Joseph Priestley arrived in America in 1794, eight years after the Hazlitts returned to England. Peggy's comment is just: William senior was the first clear voice of Unitarianism in America; he laid the foundations for those who followed him, a fact which is insufficiently acknowledged. William senior was not much given either to bitterness or repining, but years later he commented sadly that it was he who had first tilled and sowed for Unitarianism in America, while others had reaped the credit.[4]

It was, though, very uphill work; the audiences at his University lectures began to dwindle as Dr Duffield and other enemies worked to undermine them, despite Dr Ewing's countervailing efforts at persuasion from his own pulpit. Dr Benjamin Rush, professor of medicine at the University, attacked the lectures in the local newspapers, at the same time criticizing his own Provost, Dr Ewing, for having recommended a 'Socinian' (the name given, usually by their enemies, to believers in rational religion, after a leading thinker in their tradition called Socinius) to be a pastor and the president of a college.

One of the University's trustees, Dr John Carson, tried to persuade William senior to publish the lectures, assuring him that five hundred subscribers would readily be found to make an edition possible. But William senior had already decided to leave Philadelphia. Invitations were still coming in, first to Charlestown in South Carolina, then to Pittsburgh, but he declined both, the first because of its inhospitable climate – the heat was so great that for two months every year the places of worship were closed – and the second because it was three hundred miles deeper into the wilderness.[5] The two Pittsburgh farmers who came to persuade him painted a delightful picture of their home as a paradise set deep among beautiful forests. Their description filled Peggy with hunger to see it. But William senior had been invited to preach at the Brattle Street Chapel in Boston, an opportunity so much to his taste that he lost no time in accepting.

William senior found that he liked Boston enormously, and was liked by the congregation in return. Not yet knowing that the Calvinists of Pennsylvania had warned their New England brethren against him, and that his early hopes of Boston were soon to be disappointed, he immediately sent for his family, confident that he had found a settlement at last. Accordingly Mrs Hazlitt and the children packed up their Philadelphia home and went to join him.

The first part of their journey to Boston followed in reverse their route of fifteen months before, again in a covered wagon pioneer-style. This time, reports Peggy in her journal, the woods were in fruit, rich with wild peaches and apricots, grapes and many kinds of nuts. From Perth Amboy on the New Jersey shore they took ship first for New York and thence to

Rhode Island. On the first leg of the sea voyage their ship ran aground on a sand bank, and was stuck for five hours, buffeted by waves. William junior, now aged six, joined the other children and most of the women in bawling with fear at the prospect of drowning. They had to wait two days in New York for the Rhode Island packet, and passed the time with their Jewish neighbours from Philadelphia, now resettled in Manhattan. 'This was the last time we saw these good and friendly Israelites,' Peggy wrote. 'Of how many kind and excellent friends have we, both before and since, taken a last and sad farewell.'

When the Rhode Island packet reached Newport the family were aghast to see the island denuded of trees, every last one felled for fuel by British troops during the recent war. The wooden floors of the houses still bore axe marks where troops had chopped mahogany furniture to feed their camp-fires when the trees ran out.

After two days at Newport the family sailed to Providence, there transferring to a coach for the last leg to Boston. When they arrived it was to find that William senior had not after all been given the Brattle Street job, nor any other job, despite his optimistic beginnings there, but he tempered their disappointment by telling them that he had at least found a house.

Peggy's reminiscence is lyrical in its description of the house and its setting in the village of Weymouth, fifteen miles from Boston. It belonged to the wife of John Adams, then ambassador to England from the United States Congress, and soon to be his country's second President. The Hazlitts believed themselves to be related to the Quincy and Adams families through their American cousin Colonel John Hazlitt, but the evidence is inconclusive. Peggy certainly believed it at the time, and the whole family recognized as relations their neighbour Dr Tufts at Weymouth, and the wife of Governor Hancock at Boston, both members of the Quincy clan.

The looked-for post at Brattle Street chapel had not materialized because of the doctrinal objections urged against William senior by the minister of the Jamaica Plain chapel in Roxbury, a 'busy bigot' called William Gordon. In consequence William senior had to resort to his now usual expedient of locum preaching, lecturing – he gave his 'Evidences of Christianity' series again – writing articles, and republishing some of Dr Priestley's works for the American readership. To preach and lecture he had to walk many miles around Boston and the neighbouring parishes, especially to Hingham, whose nonagenarian minister Reverend Ebenezer Gay was pleased to have an assistant. William senior was often accompanied on these tramps by William junior. In the course of describing the views from their Weymouth home Peggy wrote in her journal: 'To the north [lay] King

Oak Hill, which in the winter, when covered with snow, reflected the golden and purple tints of the setting sun. Over this hill the road leading to Hingham was seen. How often have we stood at the window looking at my father as he went up this road with William, in his nankeen dress, marching by his side like one that would never be tired!'[6] William senior liked Hingham, and the congregation liked him in return, many of them wishing that Gay would retire in his favour. Had he persisted in Boston he might have inherited Gay's ministry when, just two years later in 1788, the old man died.

But William senior's stars had other ideas. He was offered a living on Cape Cod, ministering to a small community of hardy fisherfolk. He found the place desolate and uncongenial; William junior, who accompanied him, noted that scarcely any of the usual birds were in evidence there, and surmised that they avoided it because, like him, they found it disagreeable. Then William senior was invited to spend the winter of 1785–6 ministering to a new settlement up the coast in Maine, at Hallowell on the Kennebeck river. A muddle over arrangements brought another prospective preacher to the settlement simultaneously, which made for awkwardness. Nevertheless William senior liked both people and town, but decided against the job because, Peggy said, he recognized that Hallowell would be a hard place for his family to live in, and an impossible place for John to ply his just-beginning trade of portrait painter.

So William senior made the long journey back to Boston – by ship, which nearly sank in a storm – to resume his hand-to-mouth freelance life. But he was weary of it, and by the summer of 1786 was convinced that his efforts to find a foothold in America were hopeless, and that he and his family should cut their losses and return to England. The New World had come to seem a stony ground after all. He was shocked to find even more vitriolic disagreements in religious matters, even greater personal animus, and even more devious machinations and plots, than he thought he had left behind in England. He perfectly understood that his opponents were determined to prevent him from getting a good settlement because of their doctrinal objections to his views, but he would not and could not adopt the remedy, which was to compromise. His landlady – the woman who owned their Weymouth house, Mrs Mary Cranch – wrote to her sister Abigail Adams: 'He is a very sensible fine preacher but alas is not orthodox, and takes no pains to secrete it – He wishes to be settled in this State but unless he will be more prudent (I call it; he says cunning) he will never get a Parish. He has a Family, a wife a very pretty sensible well bred woman & three very likely children ... He has been preaching at Hingham and Scituate. The people like him much. The people at Weymouth I hear wish to hear him but however they might like him as a preacher, I fear his freedom of speech would prevent their ever settling him let his Heart and his Head be ever so good.'[7] Her summing up was exact. And William senior had at last recognized the same facts. Moreover, he was anxious about his family, whom he would not subject to the durance of frontier conditions – the frontier was the only place he seemed likely to find a foothold – and whom he could not support indefinitely on the basis of locums and donations.

Having made up his mind, he resolved that he should go back to England alone to find a post, and that the family would rejoin him once he was settled. In late October 1786, after three hard years in America, he accordingly bid farewell to his wife and children and set sail for England on the *Rebecca* under Captain Folger.

Years later Peggy transcribed his journal entries recording the hideous crossing that followed. The *Rebecca* made a poor start; she was so leaky and unsound that she had to return to Boston within days of setting out, which meant that William senior was briefly reunited with his family and then again painfully separated from them. Repaired, the *Rebecca* ventured out to sea again only to be greeted by a succession of terrifying storms, which battered her mercilessly all the way across the Atlantic and up the English Channel. William senior was in terror of his life, and filled his journal with lamentation at his separation from his family and his fear of never seeing them again: 'At four p.m. the 21st the wind blew from the N. E., according to the testimony of the sailors, with the violence of a West Indian hurricane, 46 hours, during which time we ran before the wind, with a close-reefed top sail, at the rate of seven knots an hour, in a most tremendous situation,' he wrote. 'It then abated a little, but still continued to blow with great fury from the S. W. twenty hours longer. We lay to all this while, tossed about by the dreadful billows and sick at heart that we could not set our feet on any land.' A few days later: 'Squalls, tempests, and hurricanes in succession for three days, with heavy rain, hail, and lightning, etc. are sufficiently terrifying. We sometimes shipped horrible seas. One broke the chain which confined the boats and had almost carried them away. I can write no more.' Some days later again: 'At two yesterday morning a violent gale came on from the south, which blew with unabating fury until 10 last night, whilst heavy rains poured down upon us, and the weather was so foggy we could not see a mile from us.' Even when they reached the Channel their predicament remained: 'The wind blew all night and this morning, to use the sailors' phrase, *like guns*. The night was dreadful, as we lay in a narrow sea and heavy waves were continually breaking upon us, and we knew not but we might drift upon the coast on one side or the other.'[8] At last, on 14 December 1786, the *Rebecca* staggered into Dover, and William senior's great journeyings were over for ever.

Nine months later, after sad leave-takings of the many friends they had made in New England, and an almost uneventful Atlantic crossing which nevertheless prostrated Mrs Hazlitt because of her martyrdom to sea-sickness, the rest of his family joined him. They had set sail on the *Nonpareil* on the fourth of July 1787, as their once-British brethren celebrated independence on the shores behind them. Peggy was the only one of them who was sorry to leave. The single event that made the crossing memorable was the death by drowning of a boy sailor, who fell into the sea from high on a mast, and sank before the boat that was sent to his rescue could reach him.[9]

# The Essay

ENGLISH LITERATURE is incomparably rich in the art of the essay, to which a significant portion of its greatest treasure belongs, and in which Hazlitt occupies a leading place if not indeed the first place. A sketch of its history runs as follows – and I mention the titles of famous essays so that the interested reader can seek them out.

The first essays, in character though not in name, are to be found among the works of classical antiquity. Typical examples are the discourses of Epictetus and Plutarch, the orations of Cicero, and the letters of the younger Pliny. Between the Hellenistic and modern periods (the latter beginning in the seventeenth century), religious and philosophical discourses had the length and shape of essays, but passed under another name. With the *essais* – attempts, informal forays, literary sallies – of Montaigne the essay proper was born. The contents of Montaigne's essays rarely correspond to the titles he gave them; they roam about in subject matter, are personal and aleatory in character, and miscellaneous in content and structure. Their informality of style and their colloquial, conversational manner are easily appreciated in the original French (which is easier to read than contemporary French), and the only translation which captures their original feel is the most recent one, by M. A. Screech.

The model offered by Montaigne's essays was quickly adopted in England by Francis Bacon (1561–1626) and Abraham Cowley (1618–67). Bacon's essays are the product of acute observation; his 'Of Studies' contains the much-quoted 'Reading maketh a full man, conference a ready man, and writing an exact man'. Cowley once was more famous than his contemporary Milton. In 'Of Myself' he relates his childhood joy in reading Spenser, and the blighting of his youth by the Civil War.

An outstanding triumvir inaugurated the eighteenth century: Joseph Addison (1672–1719), Jonathan Swift (1667–1745) and Richard Steele (1672–1729). The supple, almost Greek, purity of Addison's prose is evidenced in his 'Meditations in Westminster Abbey', and the comic pungency of Swift's satire is likewise apparent in 'A Meditation upon a Broomstick'. Steele's autobiographical method, exemplified in his graphic 'A Prize Fight', is far ahead of its time. The century's achievements also include David Hume's intellectual acuity (1711–76) and Samuel Johnson's Latin monumentality (1709–84), as demonstrated by the former's 'The Stoic', which proves the superiority of the philosophical to the sybaritic life, and the latter's elephantinely but bitterly humorous 'On the Advantages of Living in a Garret'.

The supreme English essayist is William Hazlitt (1778–1830). Not only a wondrous writer, but a fiercely independent and muscular thinker, he is the star of the great age of periodical reviews. Modern criticism of art, drama and literature have at least some of their roots in him, as do political polemic and psychological autobiography. 'My First Acquaintance with Poets', recording his early meetings with Coleridge and Wordsworth, is one of many masterpieces. Honouring his debt long after the two had quarrelled, Hazlitt wrote that before meeting Coleridge he was dumb, but as a result of his inspiration 'my ideas float on winged words, and as they expand their plumes, they catch the light of other years.'

For some, Charles Lamb (1775–1834) vies with Hazlitt for the essayist's crown. Whimsical, unworldly, his work is irresistibly charming and exquisitely wrought. For an introduction to the delights of the essay in general nothing can outdo his hilarious 'Dissertation upon Roast-Pig', from which it is impossible to quote less than the whole.

Leigh Hunt (1784–1859) and Thomas De Quincey (1785–1859) unfairly suffer in the shadow of these Olympians. Hunt is a good craftsman, as his 'World of Books' shows, with its exact remark about the Westerner's miniaturist conception of the Chinese as 'people with little names, little eyes, and little feet, who sit in little bowers, drinking little cups of tea, and writing little odes'. De Quincey's marvellous ability to elaborate the fascinating and forgotten is well displayed in his 'On Murder, Considered As One of the Fine Arts'.

Leslie Stephen (1832–1904), father of Virginia Woolf, conductor after Thackeray of the *Cornhill Magazine* and first editor of the *Dictionary of National Biography*, is an intellectual historian and essayist of the first rank. Both talents shine in 'Cowper and Rousseau', in which he dissects the 'return to nature' reaction of Romanticism to the Enlightenment.

Matthew Arnold (1822–88) flayed his age in 'Culture and Anarchy', coining the pejorative 'Philistinism' in the process. Some of his arguments are even more relevant today. Robert Louis Stevenson's (1850–94) essays contain his best writing. He crafts his periods beautifully, but on casual themes; still, every maiden and youth should read 'Virginibus Puerisque' long before contemplating marriage or its modern variants.

George Saintsbury (1845–1933), least polished stylist of these named, is among the most perceptive, as his 'Carlyle' proves. Augustine Birrell (1850–1933), like Stevenson more entertainer than thinker, is standardly enjoyable, as in 'The Defamation of Genius' (Professor Lombroso ... is hopelessly sane, and the attributes of his book are those well-known attributes of perfect sanity: dullness beyond belief, and stupidity beyond measure'). Hilaire Belloc (1870–1953), despite his attraction to Fascism, is the most various and unexpected of writers, as 'On Rasselas' shows. Lytton Strachey (1880–1932) is perennially delicious: in 'The End of General Gordon' he describes how in the thick of battle this hero 'passed through every danger with the scatheless equanimity of a demigod', armed only with a cane and a faint smile.

Desmond MacCarthy (1877–1952) and Neville Cardus (1889–1975) continue the great tradition, as 'Bohemia' and 'Cricket Fields and Crick-eters' respectively show. (That cricket can be a subject for heroic prose is amply proven by Cardus: 'It was a day of lowering clouds and Australia was in an inimical situation. Darling came in and played a death or glory innings, the fitful sun glinting on his bat.' It stands comparison with Hazlitt's 'The Fight', which Gene Tunney commended as the best ever essay about boxing.)

The fact that the foregoing sketch omits the names of Dryden, Isaac Disraeli, Washington, Lord Macaulay, John Stuart Mill, Robert Louis Stevenson, Emerson, Lowell, and many more besides, shows how rich the English language is in the tradition of the essay.

There are still essayists; but the exigencies of their trades, whether in journalism or academic pursuits, mostly oblige them away from the essay to write 'articles' and 'papers' instead. The difference, though subtle, is definite.

# Appendix Three

# Hazlitt's Philosophy: The Argument of the *Essay on the Principles of Human Action*

As briefly described in the main body of the text, the thesis of Hazlitt's *Essay* is that the human mind is 'naturally disinterested', that is, that people are interested in the welfare of others in the same way and for the same reasons as they are interested in their own welfare.[1] Hazlitt urged this in opposition to the view, then prevailing in moral philosophy, and still believed by some philosophers and most non-philosophers, that not only is it a matter of psychological fact that the fundamental motivation for people's (morally evaluable) actions is self-interest – that even their acts of benevolence towards others have a self-regarding inspiration – but that there is no other sound basis of justification for such action.[2] His argument refuting this view and urging its opposite is, although apparently implausible at first encounter, on closer examination an ingenious and persuasive one. It proceeds as follows.

We are interested in what has happened in the world around us in the past, we are interested in what is happening now in the present, and we are interested in what will happen in the future. But it is only future events that can be the object of 'rational or voluntary pursuit', because we cannot by any act of will alter the past or the now actually occurring present. We are therefore moral agents with respect to the future alone: we will, desire, plan and make choices about what is to happen in the next few minutes, or days, or years.

But when a person chooses or makes plans about the future, he does so for his future self, which is in a crucial sense another person, a different person in virtue of being one that does not yet exist; and who is therefore a person on a par with other future selves – that is, with other people. Hazlitt of course allows that we tend to prefer our own future interests over those of others, because we anticipate them with 'greater warmth of present imagination', a fact that helps to explain why we think that a person's self-identity stretches into the (as yet non-existent) future just as it stretches into the past: the 'greater liveliness and force with which I can enter into my future feelings ... identifies them with my present being; and this notion of identity being once formed, the mind makes use of it to strengthen one's habitual propensity, by giving to personal motives a reality and absolute truth'.[3] But because the future does not exist, and therefore one's future self does not exist, there is in strict truth nothing for one to be identical with in the future; the projection of our past and present selves into the future is no more than that: a mere projection, an habitual fiction, an imagining of a possible future self which, for each of us, we conceive as the continuation of the self which we are presented with by memory and present experience. But the fact is that our only means of envisaging this possible future self is an act of sympathetic imagination. Yet – and this is the key point for Hazlitt – this is precisely how one understands other people too. He puts the point in a particularly interesting way by saying: understanding my future self, and being interested in its welfare, is exactly like understanding or sympathizing with another person; so if I were not able to do the latter, I could not do the former. My interest in my own welfare, therefore, is essentially linked with my interest in the welfare of others.[4]

Two points merit comment at this juncture. One is to stress the interest of Hazlitt's view that consciousness of one's personal identity – one's consciousness of the continuance and integrity over time of one's selfhood – exists only through sensation in the present and memory of the past, and that because the future does not exist, neither does a future self with whom one can literally be identical.[5] The point is central to Hazlitt's claim that whatever one thinks about or hopes for one's future self, it is strictly speaking *another* self one is thinking about, logically on a par with any other self; and that the capacity to think about one's future self requires that one be able to think about other selves in general.

The other – related – point is that Hazlitt's argument anticipates certain debates in later philosophy, one of which centres on the counter offered by P. F. Strawson to scepticism about other minds. In essence Strawson's argument is that one can only ascribe states of consciousness to oneself if one can ascribe them to others. For, to doubt the existence of other minds a sceptic must employ the concept of other minds, but he can only do this if he can distinguish between 'my states of consciousness' and 'others' states of consciousness'; and this can only be done, in turn, if others exist, because the identification of conscious states can only be effected by reference to particulars of a special kind, viz. 'persons', the concept of which – in turn again – demands that there be criteria for distinguishing one person from another, for otherwise the identification of states of consciousness would not be possible. So one can talk of 'my experiences' only if one can talk of others' experiences; this is possible only if there are criteria for distinguishing between persons; and since one *does* talk significantly about one's own experiences, there must be such criteria. Then if there are such criteria, bodily behaviour constitutes logically adequate criteria for ascribing states of consciousness to others. So the sceptic's doubts about the existence of other minds are idle, because even to articulate doubt about their existence he has to employ the discourse whose very conditions of employment legitimize what he wishes to call into question.[6]

The parallels between Strawson's and Hazlitt's argument are noteworthy. Like Strawson, Hazlitt is in effect giving what is called a 'transcendental argument', a form of argument aimed at specifying the conditions necessary for something to be possible. Hazlitt's argument states that it is a condition of being able to have an interest in one's future self that one is capable of having an interest in others; and that since the interests served by action are all future, that is, all relate to our future selves, it follows that all interest is other-regarding, which is to say 'disinterested', for the reason that ones future self is, literally as well as logically speaking, another self.

The primary application of the argument was, for Hazlitt, a practical one. It implied that the currency of the mistaken self-interest thesis was a matter of social rhetoric or persuasion, which had distracted attitudes and practices from the natural benevolence that would dictate quite different social policies if allowed their natural expression. He took the doctrines of Malthus to be just such a pernicious outcome of allowing the erroneous self-interest theory to stand unchallenged. Without saying so in so many words, the idea of universal benevolence based on the natural disinterestedness of human nature most closely approximates the kind of rational morality that would be associated with the rational theology espoused by Unitarians of Hazlitt's father's stamp. The 'rational' in both phrases denotes the subjection to human reason of the standards of acceptability of theses in both spheres. A variant of Hazlitt's disinterestedness thesis is a familiar one expressible in terms of the natural goodness of human nature – a view shared by philosophers as different in tradition and historical setting as Mencius and David Hume. With them the thesis serves as an assumption; Hazlitt gives an argument for it.

Hazlitt's argument is a good one, in all respects of its view about the metaphysics of time – the future does not exist – the nature of personal identity as consciousness of self through memory and present experience, and the transcendental argument showing that the possibility of being interested in one's own future self rests on the capacity to be interested in other selves, for the excellent reason that one's own future self is one such. And in line with Aristotle's dictum that a philosophical theory must save the *endoxa*, it accords with other things we think and believe: for example, that altruistic tendencies are biologically adaptive, having evolutionary advantages for our species.

# NOTES

ABBREVIATIONS USED IN NOTES:

8.257 (e.g.) = *The Complete Works of William Hazlitt*, ed. P. P. Howe, 21 vols.,
    vol. 8, p. 257

Haydon, *Diary* = Benjamin Robert Haydon, *Diary of Benjamin Robert Haydon*

*The Hazlitts* = W. C. Hazlitt, *The Hazlitts: An Account of their Origins and Descent*

Howe = P. P. Howe, *The Life of William Hazlitt*

*Letters* = *The Letters of William Hazlitt*, eds H. M. Sikes, W. H. Bourne, G. Lahey

*Memoirs* = W. C. Hazlitt, *Memoirs of William Hazlitt*

MH *Journal* = Margaret Hazlitt, *Journal*, ed. E. J. Moyne

Robinson = Henry Crabb Robinson, *Henry Crabb Robinson on Books and their
    Writers*, Ed. Edith J. Morley

## PREFACE

1. See Appendix 2, p. 359, for a sketch of the essay in English literature.
2. P. P. Howe (ed.) *The Complete Works of William Hazlitt*, The Centenary Edition,
   21 vols., London, 1930–34; Duncan Wu (ed.), *The Selected Writings of William
   Hazlitt*, 9 vols., London: Pickering & Chatto, 1998. Useful too is Wu's edition
   of the key essays from Hazlitt's *Plain Speaker*, with an introduction by Tom
   Paulin (who also introduces the *Selected Writings*). The biographical sketch given
   by Wu at the entrance to the latter is inaccurate in certain points, but this is a
   minor blemish in what is otherwise an extremely well-researched and helpful
   edition.

## INTRODUCTION

1. Published for the first time in extenso in Duncan Wu (ed.) Hazlitt, *The Plain
   Speaker*, Oxford: Blackwell, 1998, pp. 198–9. Earlier partial appearance in e.g.
   Andrew Motion, *Keats*, 1997, p. 124.
2. Thomas De Quincy, quoted in Howe, p. 299.
3. James Smetham, *Letters* (1891), quoted in Howe, p. 300.
4. Charles Lamb, 'Reply to Southey', *London Magazine*, October 1823.

## CHAPTER ONE A Line of Blue Hills

1. Letters.
2. 8.257.
3. Warwick Wroth, *Cremorne and the Later London Gardens*, London, 1907,
   p. 81.
4. MH *Journal*, p. 101.

5. Ibid., p. 102.
6. Ibid., p. 90.
7. 17.110.
8. Louis Philippe, Comte de Ségur, quoted by Adam Zamoyski in *Holy Madness*, London, 1999, p. 57.
9. 17.196–7.
10. MH *Journal*, pp. 106–7.
11. All letters quoted in extenso by W. C. Hazlitt in *The Hazlitts*, 1911.
12. *The Hazlitts*, p. 384.
13. Ibid., p. 300.
14. H. W. Stephenson, *William Hazlitt and Hackney College*, London: The Lindsay Press, 1930, p. 57.
15. *The Hazlitts*, pp. 397–9.
16. Paulin, p. 10.
17. 19.302.
18. 5.147.
19. 12.222–3.
20. Quoted in Howe, pp. 12–13.
21. Ibid., pp. 406–7. W. C. Hazlitt dates this letter to 1793, which would place it right at the beginning of Hazlitt's period at the New College in Hackney. The date is impossible: first, Hazlitt began his close study of Hartley on association of ideas only after starting at the college, and this letter is steeped in that idiom. Second, the later part of the letter refers to his progress, or lack of it, in writing his 'essay'; if this referred to his political essay, he had not yet properly begun to enlarge it for his tutor John Corrie; but it much more likely refers to the early work on his 'Principles of Human Action', to which he devoted most of his intellectual energies from the time of leaving the New College until its publication in 1805.

CHAPTER TWO Hackney Radicalism
1. New College Annual Report 1787, quoted in Wardle, p. 41.
2. Ibid.
3. *The Hazlitts*, p. 405.
4. Ibid., pp. 398–400.
5. Ibid., p. 401.
6. Ibid., p. 403.
7. 19.304.
8. *The Life of Thomas Holcroft* 3.150–1.
9. 3.156.
10. Robinson 1.6.
11. Robert Southey, 'The Rise and Progress of Popular Disaffection', *The Quarterly Review*, January 1817.
12. *Table Talk*, 'On the Knowledge of Character'.
13. 1.46.
14. 9.54.

15. 8.64.
16. 12.98.
17. 'On the Causes of Popular Opinion'.
18. S. T. Coleridge, *Biographia Literaria*, ed. Shawcross, 2:214.
19. 'Reply to Z'.
20. Hazlitt's philosophy is described in Chapter Six below, and discussed in Appendix 3.
21. 12.126. The identity of 'Junius' is still unknown. His 'Letters' appeared in the press between 1767 and 1772, excoriating the government from a position of obvious insider knowledge; not only did he know the gossip in ministers' offices, but details of their private lives, all of which he used to excellent – which is to say embarrassing – effect. Various suggestions have been made about the true identity of this formidable writer, admired by Burke and feared by the King's ministers: they include among many others John Wilkes, Henry Grattan, George Grenville, Lord Temple, the Earl of Chatham, Edward Gibbon, even Burke himself. The most plausible candidates are Lord Shelburne and Philip Francis, but the evidence points chiefly at the latter. Francis served in the War Office and was privy to the houses of leading politicians. In 1772, at just the point when the Letters ceased to appear, Francis received a sudden, unexpected, and handsome promotion.
22. 12.304.
23. Howe, p. 24.
24. 17.65.
25. 11.26–7.
26. 3.171.

CHAPTER THREE The Reader and the Poets

1. Richard Holmes, *Coleridge: Early Visions*, Penguin, 1989.
2. Ibid., pp. 177–8.
3. 17.109.
4. 17.111.
5. 17.110–12.
6. 17.113.
7. Holmes, op. cit., p. 179 note.
8. 17.114.
9. 8.186.

> – Here be woods as green
> As any, air likewise as fresh and sweet
> As when smooth Zephyrus plays on the fleet
> Face of the curled stream, with flowers as many
> As the young spring gives, and as choice as any;
> Here be all new delights, cool streams and wells,
> Arbours o'ergrown with woodbine, while I sit by and sing,
> Or gather rushes to make many a ring
> For thy long fmgers; to tell thee tales of love,

How the pale Phoebe, hunting in a grove,
First saw the boy Endymion, from whose eyes
She took eternal fire that never dies;
How she conveyed him softly in a sleep,
His temples bound with poppy, to the steep
Head of old Latos, where she stoops each night,
Gilding the mountain with her brother's light,
To kiss her sweetest. –

10. 17.115.
11. Holmes, op. cit., pp. 186-8.
12. Ibid., p. 118.
13. Ibid., p. 119.
14. The suggestion that Matthew is Hazlitt and that this poem is addressed directly to the latter is plausibly argued by Ralph Wardle in his *Hazlitt*, p. 57.
15. Holmes, op. cit., p. 120.
16. Ibid., p. 121.
17. 9.3-4.

CHAPTER FOUR Painting and Philosophy

1. 11.269, 320.
2. 8.15.
3. 8.14.
4. 10.32-3.
5. 9.320.
6. 17.379.
7. 8.14.
8. Maclean, *Born Under Saturn*, p. 134.
9. W. C. Hazlitt, *Four Generations of a Literary Family*, 1:235-6.
10. R. S. Knowles, *Life of James Sheridan Knowles*, London, 1872, pp. 10-12.
11. Robinson, 1.6-7.
12. 11.255.
13. 1.64.
14. Cameron, *Shelley and his Circle*, 1.219-20.
15. 8.12-13.
16. 17.180.
17. 12.303-4.
18. 12.303.
19. 8.103.
20. *The Hazlitts*, p. 205. Jones has a different and more convincing candidate for the Miss Shepherd whom Hazlitt loved: see Chapter 8.
21. 8.188-9.
22. Quoted in Maclean, op. cit., p. 159.
23. *The Hazlitts*, pp. 411-12.
24. 8.15-16.
25. *The Hazlitts*, pp. 418-19.

26. 1.171.
27. 10.111.
28. Ibid.
29. 17.139.
30. 8.319.
31. 10.254.
32. 18.87 n; 17.218.
33. 8.303.
34. 8.16–17.

CHAPTER FIVE Arts and Metaphysics

1. Holmes, *Coleridge: Early Visions*, p. 85.
2. 17.122.
3. Coleridge, *Letters*, 2.949–50.
4. Ibid. 957–8. The Lamb portrait, in the style of Titian, is included among the illustrations in this book.
5. Kenneth R. Johnston makes a convincing case for the portrait in question indeed being Hazlitt's depiction of Wordsworth: compare the picture to the description Southey gives in the text. See K. R. Johnston, *The Hidden Wordsworth*, New York, 1998, esp. pp. 3–5.
6. R. C. Southey, *Life and Correspondence of Robert Southey*, 2:238 & 291.
7. *Letters of William and Dorothy Wordsworth: The Later Years* (2nd edn) ed. A. Hill, Oxford, 1978–93. Quoted Johnston, op. cit., p. 5. The joke anticipates Oscar Wilde's *Dorian Gray*.
8. 8.204 n.
9. 17.115–6.
10. Coleridge, *Letters*, 2:990–1.
11. 1.281. This was one of the passages – his comments on the sexual attraction between Desdemona and Othello was another, and the entire *Liber Amoris* of course a third – which gave him the reputation in his own lifetime and for a century afterwards of being obscene; which is the chief reason why recognition of his stature in English letters was once so equivocal.
12. Patmore 2:275–7, 301–2, 343; 3:88–9.
13. 8.236.
14. 1.46.
15. Coleridge, *Notebooks*, ed. K. Coburn, 4 vols., New York, 1957–61, 1:1610.
16. Ibid., 1:1616–19.
17. Haydon, *Diary*, 2:470.
18. *Letters of William and Dorothy Wordsworth: The Later Years*, ed. de Selincourt, 3:1349–50.
19. Southey, *Correspondence*, 2:237–8.
20. See Appendix 3 for more discussion of Hazlitt's philosophical views.
21. 17.312; 8.237; 9.3; 9.51.
22. Douglas Grant, letter to the *Times Literary Supplement*, 19 September 1968, p. 1062.

23. W. C. Hazlitt, *Four Generations of a Literary Family*, 1:92–3.
24. William senior died in 1820. The reason for party fluidity at this period was that the harsh reactionary years of the Liverpool and Castlereagh governments were over, and the dangerous but inexorable pressure for reform was growing, pressure that led to repeal of the Test and Corporation Acts in 1829 (finally removing disabilities from members of denominations other than the Church of England; one recalls Hazlitt's boyhood harangues against it) and then reform of Parliamentary representation in 1832, the approach to which was filled with the risk of revolution in England.
25. 11.191.
26. Hazlitt's grandson mistakenly dates the letter a year later, 1806.
27. Lamb, *Letters*, op. cit., pp. 409–11.
28. Lamb, *Letters*, pp. 423–4.
29. See J. R. Barker, 'Some Early Correspondence of Sarah Stoddart and the Lambs', *Huntington Library Quarterly*, 24 (1960–61) which reveals at least half a dozen of the earlier prospective husbands; Sarah thought she was handicapped by having only £500 and her expectations at that juncture.
30. Lamb, *Letters*, 2:15.
31. 1.283.


CHAPTER SIX Towards Winterslow
1. Lamb, *Letters*, 2:16–18.
2. Ibid., 2:23.
3. Technically, the country should be called the United Kingdom of England, Wales, Scotland and Ireland; but Hazlitt and his contemporaries all called it 'England' and I follow suit here, since doing otherwise sounds anachronistic.
4. Lamb, *Letters*, 2:15.
5. 1.98; 4.125–8; 7.322–6.
6. 1.112 n.
7. G. M. Trevelyan, *A Short History of England*, Pelican Books, 1959, p. 424.
8. 12.34–5.
9. Ibid.
10. 12.36.
11. 12.36–7.
12. 17.123–4. Lamb and Ayrton figure as 'L—' and 'A—' respectively in the original text, but there is no doubt about the identifications. I give the names in full because the abbreviations are uncomfortable to the eye, and the *raison d'être* for Hazlitt's use of them no longer exists.
13. 17.126.
14. 'Locke a Great Plagiarist', 20:69, 74.
15. 17.131.
16. 17.134.
17. Lamb, *Letters*, 2:31.
18. E. V. Lucas, *The Life of Charles Lamb*, London, 1905, p. 341.
19. Ibid.

20. *The Hazlitts*, pp. 421–3.

21. 7.316.

22. 7.306.

23. 8.59 n.

24. 1.179.

25. *The Hazlitts*, p. 423.

26. See Jones, p. 11, for an account of the service performed by J. R. Barker and R. S. Woof with respect to the Pinney Papers at Bristol University Library and the light they throw on the Stoddarts and Sarah's relationship with the Lambs. Jones makes excellent use of the Pinney Papers and I profit from his work on them. Discerningly, Jones likens John Stoddart to the Reverend Mr Collins in *Pride and Prejudice*, a very apt comparison (Jones ibid.). He was however in many ways a kind and attentive brother, as Jones shows, and later was helpful to the only surviving child born to his sister and Hazlitt – William Hazlitt the younger – after Hazlitt's death.

27. The details of Sarah Stoddart's property are not clear. Before her father's death – which happened in 1803 – her prospective inheritance included capital in the five per cents and two houses in Salisbury, and perhaps she already owned one or, more probably, two cottages in Winterslow left by her grandparents (it seems she sold one to raise capital at the beginning of her marriage to Hazlitt, and lived in the other, which was larger). But her brother rearranged the family finances, hers included, at the end of the 1790s, and it is possible that the Winterslow cottage she and Hazlitt occupied was owned by John and either given or nominally rented to Sarah, and that the cottage or small house she sold on getting married was one of the Salisbury properties inherited from her father. However, my opinion is that Sarah's earlier refitting, at her own expense, of a Winterslow cottage in prospect of a possible marriage to a local farmer's son (William Dowling), suggests that the cottage was her own property.

28. Lamb, *Letters*, 2:39.

29. Ibid., 2:39–40.

30. The whole 'suicide joke' exchange can be found in W. C. Hazlitt's *Lamb and Hazlitt*, pp. 64–102; Lamb's letters occur at Lamb, *Letters*, 2.41–44.

31. See. W. B. Ober, *Boswell's Clap and Other Essays: Medical Analyses of Literary Men's Afflictions*, New York, 1979, pp. 1–42 and esp. p. 22.

32. *Memoirs*, 1:153–5.

33. 17.185.

34. Lamb, *Letters*, 2:44–5.

35. Ibid., p. 48.

36. Ibid., p. 57.

37. *Letters of William and Dorothy Wordsworth: The Middle Years*, ed. Mary Moorman, Oxford, 1969–70, 1:196–7.

CHAPTER SEVEN The Winterslow Years

1. Until Jones proved otherwise, all previous biographers thought that the Hazlitts moved to Winterlsow immediately after their wedding in May. Characteristically, Jones's deductions about their movements in 1808 are wholly persuasive. See Jones, p. 1 and note 1.

2. That there was livestock in the case is suggested by the fact that the Hazlitts sent the Lambs a pig as a present (a ready-butchered one) in 1810.

3. MH *Journal*, pp. 109–10.

4. *Plain Speaker*, 'Whether Genius is Conscious of its Powers', 12:117.

5. 10.55 6.

6. Lamb, *Letters*, 2:41–2.

7. See Sarah Stoddart Hazlitt's record of her miscarriages, births, and the deaths of her children – only one survived – in the British Library (Add. MS 38898 folios 3–4).

8. Jones, p. 43.

9. Lamb, *Letters*, 2:66–7.

10. 8.326.

11. C. Kegan Paul, *William Godwin: His Friends and Contemporaries*, 2 vols. (1876), 2:175.

12. *Letters* 108, following the dating suggested in Jones, p. 37 and see footnotes.

13. F. K. Brown, *Life of William Godwin*, London, 1926, pp. 235–6.

14. 2.6. Hazlitt was taking his lead from Horne Tooke in his *Diversions of Purley* on this head; he remarks that grammarians have wholly failed to notice Tooke's views, which – though he cannot himself subscribe to all of them – represent an important advance over previous theories of grammar.

15. Lamb, *Letters*, 2:91.

16. 17.320; the reference is to Amelia's hashed mutton.

17. Miranda Seymour, personal communication.

18. Lamb, *Letters*, 2:85–7.

19. *PMLA* 77 (1962), p. 342. See Wardle, p. 118.

20. Kegan Paul, op. cit., 2:176–7.

21. Lamb, *Letters*, 2:97–8.

22. Quoted in Howe, p. 112. Ref in *Letters*.

23. *The Hazlitts*, pp. 432–4.

24. See Jones, 'Hazlitt and the Walsh Porter Sale', EA 26 (1973), p. 452 et seq.

25. This account is based on the discovery made by Stanley Jones, the encyclopaedic Hercule Poirot of Hazlitt studies, which convincingly clears up what had long been the 'Sally Shepherd' mystery. Until Jones, Sally Shepherd had been a puzzle to students of Hazlitt's life; almost all thought she must be the daughter of Dr Shepherd of Gateacre near Liverpool, and therefore an object of Hazlitt's youthful interest. But Jones puts the question practically beyond doubt (Jones, p. 53). Jones points out that Sally Shepherd must have been 'extremely well-favoured', because in 1825, a widow aged 37 with an eleven-year-old son, she married a Winterslow man nine years her junior, becoming Mrs Judd. She died in Winterslow in 1864.

26. Patmore, 3:88–9.
27. *The Hazlitts*, pp. 433–4.
28. 17.66–7.
29. 8.188.
30. 7.408–9; 7.360–1.
31. Lamb, *Letters*, 2:111–12.
32. So Sarah's son William Hazlitt the younger reported; *Memoirs* 1.259.
33. *Spirit of the Age*, 12:1. See also Holmes, *Darker Reflections*, p. 240.
34. Robinson, 1:23–9.
35. Ibid., 1:30.
36. 12.56–7.
37. 18.42.
38. Howe, p. 122.
39. Lamb, *Letters*, 2:118.
40. J. P. Collier, *Seven Lectures on Shakespeare and Milton by S. T. Coleridge* (1856), p. xxi.
41. Howe, pp. 124–5.
42. Howe, p. 126.

CHAPTER EIGHT The Press of Drama

1. Howe, pp. 127–8.
2. Ibid., p. 128.
3. Ibid., pp. 129–30.
4. Ibid., pp. 131–2.
5. These themes are central to debate about the relation of mind and world, and in contemporary philosophy Hazlitt would find considerable support for his view from one side of the great debate on these matters. It is a pity that he did not have the opportunity – as he might do if he were living now, for he would assuredly have been fitted to an academic career in the now contemporary sense – to develop these ideas more, because they represent an endeavour to bring a broadly empiricist approach in the theory of knowledge under constraints supplied by theses about the nature of concepts and their role in governing experience. See Appendix 3.
6. A sentence Hazlitt used in his *Grammar* as a parsing exercise reads: 'To endeavour to work upon the vulgar with fine sense, is like attempting to hew blocks of marble with a razor' (2.110). The word 'vulgar' did not then have the pejorative connotation it now has; it simply meant: ordinary folk in the mass – although it was *used* pejoratively by snobs, often enough. Hazlitt was as far from being a snob as one can get. All the sentences he chose for parsing exercises come from the elementary school book he had used in his earliest youth, William Enfield's *The Speaker*, which in the then standard way used improving aphorisms as the examples on which children practised their elocution and reading skills. Hazlitt's choice of examples is interesting.
7. 20.402. I think this is the likely explanation. I think it is possible also that this lecture appears in new disguise as 'Mind and Motive', 20.43 et seq.

That Hazlitt had eight to offer suggests that he had abandoned or lost the
Butler and natural religion lectures already – or perhaps, as a note in Howe
hints, the Butler lecture had already been transformed into a pair of essays and
published as the ninth and thirteenth contributions to the 'Round Table' series
in Leigh Hunt's *Examiner* in 1814.

8. 2.289. The imputation of literary arson is unfounded, as the fact that the Butler
   and the natural religion essays were already absent in 1821 shows.
9. *Examiner*, 16 August 1812.
10. Jones, p. 68, makes a good case for this.
11. Collier, p. xxxiii.
12. See Holmes, *Darker Reflections*, almost passim but especially pp. 299–306.
13. 19.216–55; 19.324–9.
14. 12.266–7.
15. 12.270–71.
16. Howe, pp. 134–5.
17. 16.223–4.
18. Wardle, p. 133.
19. Ibid., p. 134.
20. Haydon, *Diary*, 1:303.
21. W. C. Hazlitt, *Memoirs of William Hazlitt*, 1867, pp. 215–16.
22. Holmes in *Darker Reflections*, p. 335.
23. *Life and Letters of John Rickman*, 1912, p. 166, quoted 18.465. There is, it
    should be mentioned, some controversy over the question whether the
    *Chronicle* notice of *Remorse* on 25 January 1813 is indeed by Hazlitt. Jones,
    whose opinion in these matters always commands respect, says not; and in
    this he agrees with Howe's first opinion of the matter. But Howe changed his
    mind, and other writers have agreed with his maturer thoughts. What suggests
    that Howe's second thoughts are indeed right is that Coleridge was well
    acquainted with the *Chronicle* and its editor Perry, and was no doubt told by
    Perry, or one of the staff, or indeed by Hazlitt himself, who the author of the
    piece was. Jones denies it to Hazlitt on the grounds of the insipidity of its style,
    and it is true that the piece is not vintage Hazlitt; it is too uniformly nice, and
    too colourlessly written, to be an example of his normal manner. But as his
    first contribution of the kind, written under a remit, it is a perfectly plausible
    product of his pen, and nothing about it is nearly enough to weigh against the
    fact that Coleridge speaks as if he unequivocally knew who wrote it. It would
    scarcely be worth airing the minutiae of scholarship on this question were it not
    that this is the prime candidate for Hazlitt's first critical essay in the arts, therefore
    making the beginning of 1813 an epoch in his career and in letters generally.
24. Holmes, *Darker Reflections*, p. 280 n.
25. 7.23.
26. Robinson, *Diary*, 29 April 1813.
27. 'The Love of Life', 4 September; 'On Classical Education', 25 September.
28. 7.25.
29. 20.1.

30. Mudford as 'Geoffrey Oldcastle', 'The Late S. T. Coleridge', *The Canterbury Magazine*, September 1843, quoted in Jones, pp. 109–10.
31. To be a columnist or reviewer for a great newspaper is regarded as such by those who aspire to either role.
32. 11.288.
33. 8.292–3.
34. 18.342–3.
35. In the 1820 review for the *London Magazine* Hazlitt followed his account of first hearing Miss Stephens sing by saying, 'They were the sweetest notes we ever heard, and almost the last we heard with pleasure! For since then, other events not to be named lightly here ... have stopped our ears to the voice of the charmer. But since the voice of Liberty has once more risen in Spain, its grave and its birth place, and like a babbling hound has wakened the echoes in Galicia, in the Asturias, in Castile and Leon, and Estremadura, why, we felt as if we "had three ears again" and the heart to use them.' 18.343.
36. 5.175.
37. See Jones, p. 134.
38. Gillian Russell describes Hazlitt's notices as 'among the most significant works of dramatic criticism in the period', and Duncan Wu says of Hazlitt's dramatic criticism, as collected in his *A View of the English Stage* published in 1818, that it constitutes 'unquestionably the most important book about drama in the Romantic period'. Gillian Russell, *The Oxford Companion to the Romantic Age*, 1999, p. 570; Duncan Wu, 'Editor's Note', *The Plain Speaker*, ed. Duncan Wu, Oxford, 1998, p. xxvi.
39. 5.375.
40. 7.33.
41. Jones, pp. 120–21; who very aptly points out that these remarks, and those that follow about 'wandering intellect' and strait-jackets, come from a man who regularly visited the Lambs where thoughts of both loomed tragically over daily life, and whose own mother had died in a lunatic asylum. There is an instructive variety in the character of Stoddart; his concern for the financial well-being of his sister and nephew sits at odds with his veering principles and ugly politics and polemics.
42. 7.33 et seq. See Jones, pp. 120–26.
43. Jones, pp. 137–9.
44. Robinson, *Diary*, p. 133.
45. Ibid., p. 142.

CHAPTER NINE Waterloo

1. Mackintosh admired the *Essay*, but had ceased to like its author, having been given one or two rough handlings by Hazlitt in the interim. He and Lady Mackintosh were not on easy terms, so when she promoted Hazlitt's interests with Jeffrey, Mackintosh demurred.
2. Robinson, pp. 153–4.
3. 8.292.

4. A. G. L'Estrange, *Life of Mary Russell Mitford*, 1870, 2:47–8. How things change: advertisements now take absolute priority, and not only dictate length of copy but, often enough, their content.
5. 12.204–5.
6. 20.143.
7. Hunt, p. 244.
8. I can testify that that particular clock-face never shows the right time, because I lived in Trinity Church Square for fifteen happy years, and began the writing of this book there; and always thought of Leigh Hunt and the innocent woman when turning into Horsemonger Lane, now called Harper Road.
9. Ibid., p. 246.
10. Edmund Blunden, *The 'Examiner' Examined*, London, 1928, p. 41.
11. 18.33–4.
12. Robinson, p. 63.
13. Ibid., p. 153.
14. 5.211–20.
15. P. G. Patmore was father of the poet Coventry Patmore.
16. *Examiner*, 15 May 1814, quoted in Jones, p. 153.
17. 20.401, emending Howe's reading according to Jones's revision of 'securely' to 'secure'.
18. Jones has made a plausible case for just such a surmise.
19. 20.43.
20. Ibid. The tale of Urceus opens the first of the two essays which, plausibly, constitute the missing Sixth Lecture of Hazlitt's philosophy series, concerning the motives to action. They are reprinted in Howe as 'Mind and Motive' although in their original Round Table appearance they had no title. The Urceus tale was no doubt added as providing an easier opening to the themes to follow – and it is characteristic of Hazlitt to write autobiographically in his asides, introductory remarks, envois and notes.
21. *Letters of Mary Wordsworth*, ed. Mary Burton, Oxford, 1958, p. 24.
22. *Letters of William and Dorothy Wordsworth: The Middle Years*, 2:607.
23. 19.22.
24. Lamb, *Letters*, 2:146.
25. 9.6.
26. 5.163.
27. *Poems*, 1815, I.xxxi.
28. 19.17–18.
29. See Jones, pp. 150–51 for the following and references.
30. 12.365.
31. G. Bullett, *Sydney Smith*, 1951, p. 272.
32. Robinson, *Diary*, pp. 161–2.
33. Jones, p. 168.
34. Quoted ibid., p. 169.
35. Robinson, 15 April 1815.
36. Jones, p. 196.

37. 5.233.

38. Edmund Blunden, *Leigh Hunt – A Biography*, London, 1930, p. 91.

39. Talfourd, *Memorials*, 2:170.

40. See 17.36–40; for the duc d'Enghien controversy see 19.129 et seq. The exchanges took place in the *Examiner*, September–December 1815; Hazlitt did not reprint his pieces in his *Political Essays* or anywhere else. He recurs to the controversy in a different vein in his biography of Napoleon.

41. Landseer, 1:118.

42. The story is recorded in several places: Robinson, 1:200, Haydon, 3:319–200; *Memoirs (etc) of Thomas Moore*, ed. Lord John Russell, 1853, 3:146.

43. Haydon, p. 200.

44. Landseer, 1:136–40.

CHAPTER TEN Fame and Infamy

1. Jones, 'Nine New Hazlitt Letters', p. 269.

2. Quoted in Wardle, p. 165.

3. 7.104–5.

4. 19.176.

5. Ibid.

6. 4.92–3.

7. 19.32.

8. Holmes, *Darker Reflections*, p. 439.

9. 4.101–2.

10. Quoted in Wardle, p. 171.

11. 7.87, 95.

12. 7. 116, 117–18.

13. Coleridge, *Letters*, 4:669–70.

14. Haydon, 2:64–5.

15. 4.142.

16. 19.182.

17. Coleridge, *Letters*, 4:692–3.

18. 19.356.

19. Robinson, 1:200.

20. 7.144–5.

21. 16.99–100.

22. 7.147.

23. 7.96, n.

24. *The Hazlitts*, p. 168.

25. 4.105.

26. *Quarterly Review*, 19 (July 1818), pp. 424–34.

27. Robinson, 1:210.

28. 4.40.

29. *Letters of John Keats 1814–1821*, ed. H. E. Rollins, 2 vols., Harvard University Press, 1958, 1:123.

30. Ibid., p. 124.

31. Motion, *Keats*, 1997, p. 124.
32. Ibid., p. 125.
33. Ibid.
34. Ibid., p. 126. Both Motion and Wardle give references to further studies of Hazlitt's influence on Keats.
35. 7.181.
36. 19.198.
37. 19.182.
38. 19.196.
39. *Letters of William and Dorothy Wordsworth: The Middle Years*, 2:781–2.
40. *Life, Letters and Table Talk of Benjamin Robert Haydon*, ed. R. H. Stoddart, New York, 1876, p. 196.
41. Quoted by Wardle from the official history of *The Times* (1935–47), p. 192.
42. 7.193–4.
43. Landseer, 1:141–2.
44. 11.45 n.
45. 16.137.

CHAPTER ELEVEN Reputation and Calumny

1. P. G. Patmore, *My Friends and Acquaintances*: 'Many extravagant and ridiculous stories were related, or rather whispered about vaguely, all of them discreditable to the personal character of Hazlitt, as the *immediate* cause of his alienation from the distinguished friends of his early life; and in the most discreditable of them there was, I have been led to believe, some truth. I allude to a story relating to Hazlitt's alleged treatment of some pretty village jilt, who, when he was on a visit to Wordsworth, had led him (Hazlitt) to believe that she was not insensible to his attentions: and then, having induced him to "commit" himself to her in some ridiculous manner, turned round upon him and made him the laughing-stock of the village. There is, I believe, too much truth in the statement of his enemies, that the mingled disappointment and rage of Hazlitt on this occasion led him, during the madness of the moment (for it must have been nothing less) to acts which nothing but the supposition of insanity could account for, much less excuse.' 2:250.
2. Ibid.
3. Landseer, 1:144.
4. 5.6.
5. Robinson, 1:218.
6. Landseer, 1:144–5.
7. Ibid., 1:141–2.
8. Quoted in Maclean, pp. 372–3.
9. Mitford, *Letters*, 3:324.
10. Ibid., 3:325.
11. Ibid., 3:350. Jones discovered this trove of contemporary comment, and notes that in Miss Mitford's manuscript the words 'such as Johnson's' are crossed out after 'overblown fame'. See Jones, p. 285 n. 29.

12. 5.164–5.
13. Patmore, 2:278 n.
14. Jones, p. 297.
15. 19.210–11.
16. 17.98.
17. 12.364.
18. *Blackwood's Magazine*, 14 (1823), quoted in Jones, pp. 289–90.
19. Motion, *Keats*, p. 302.
20. Jones discovered Henderson's spying activities by a piece of brilliant detective work; see his p. 296.
21. 11.318.
22. Quoted in Wardle, p. 232.
23. 11.114.
24. 7.7.
25. 7.12.
26. 20.142.
27. 6.257.
28. Baker, pp. 261–2.
29. By a happy chance I saw once some works of literary theory displayed on a shelf in Blackwell's Bookshop, Charing Cross Road, London, marked 'EFL', which means 'English as a Foreign Language'.
30. Saintsbury is especially perceptive about Hazlitt's critical acumen. See the sections on Hazlitt in Saintsbury, George, *A History of Nineteenth Century Literature*, 1917.
31. David Bromwich, *Hazlitt: The Mind of a Critic*, Oxford, 1983, p. 14. See also the works by Kinnaird, Park, Paulin and others listed in the bibliography.
32. David Bromwich, *Hazlitt: The Mind of a Critic*.
33. For further witnesses see, for example, Michael Schmidt on the poets' lives or Kenneth Clarke on art. Michael Schmidt, *Lives of the Poets*, London, 1998, e.g. pp. 98, 334, 405 et seq., 417 et seq., 462, 957. Clarke described Hazlitt as the 'best critic of art before Ruskin'.
31. 6.364.

CHAPTER 12 Love and Disaster

 1. 18.343.
 2. 20.138.
 3. Ibid.
 4. 20.137.
 5. 20.136.
 6. 20.138.
 7. Jones, p. 307.
 8. 7.208–9.
 9. 18.343.
10. *Table Talk* constitutes 'by any standards a remarkable achievement', says Duncan Wu, 'and must rank as a classic of non-fiction prose'. Duncan Wu,

'Introductory Note', *The Selected Writings of William Hazlitt*, ed. D. Wu, London, 1998, p. x.

11. 12.196.
12. 12.208.
13. 9.112.
14. R. W. Armour, *Barry Cornwall*, Boston, 1935, p. 54.
15. *Macready's Reminiscences*, ed. F. Pollock, 2 vols., London, 1875, 1:213.
16. 8.373.
17. 8.310–11.
18. 16.45.
19. Quoted in Maclean, p. 420.
20. Sarah Stoddart Hazlitt, *Journals*, p. 247.
21. 9.109.
22. 9.108.
23. Robinson, *Diary*, 27 December 1820.
24. 8.91.
25. 9.99.
26. 8.99; 9.244.
27. Howe, pp. 288–94; Wardle, pp. 288–90.
28. 19.264.
29. Some biographers think that he was not present, for there is correspondence from him at Winterslow dated 22 July. In this case he must therefore have heard a detailed description or seen a good contemporary print. But he could easily have seen the coronation on the 19th and reached Winterslow the next day or either of the following two days, and thus have been able to date a letter as he did.
30. 19.264.
31. 17.81.
32. 17.82–3.
33. 17.76.
34. S. C. Wilcox, *Hazlitt in the Workshop: The Manuscript of 'The Fight'*, Johns Hopkins University Press, 1943, pp. 17–18.
35. 8.237.
36. Full text in Jones, *Review of English Studies*, n.s. 17 (1966), pp. 162–70; compare 9.113.
37. 9.106.
38. From the text of the manuscript at SUNY, Buffalo.
39. 9.99.
40. 9.109.
41. 9.118.
42. 12.24.
43. Quoted in Howe, p. 314.
44. Quoted in Jones, p. 325.
45. W. H. Bonner (ed.), *The Journals of Sarah and William Hazlitt*, University of Buffalo Studies, Vol. 24, No. 3, February 1959, pp. 195–6.

46. Quoted in Jones, p. 329.
47. 9.142–3.
48. 9.143.
49. 9.144–5.
50. 9.145–6.
51. 9.146–7.
52. 9.132–3.
53. Bonner, p. 247.
54. 9.156.
55. 9.159.
56. Haydon, 3:375–6.
57. Cornwall, *Recollections*, pp. 81–2.
58. *Letters of Mary W. Shelley*, 1:307.
59. Haydon, 2:382.
60. Bonner, p. 272.
61. Ibid., p. 275.
62. Ibid., p. 276.
63. Ibid., p. 277.

CHAPTER THIRTEEN The Traveller

1. What distinguishes a good writer is that his or her endeavours of creation and justification carry some element of the universal, which speaks to the same or similar concerns in those who read. Literature is a dialogue of voices and answering sensibilities, completing a circle. Some literary theorists think that each act of reading creates a different work out of the given text, but this view overlooks the obvious but profound fact that, in the way just premised, literature conveys aspects of universality. If proof were needed of this assertion, here it is: authors generally write to be understood; readers share a common world and a common human experience. On that fact is based the very possibility of communication.
2. Cornwall, *Recollections*, p. 86.
3. William Jerdan, writing in *The Literary Gazette*, 19 October 1822, quoted in Wardle, p. 352.
4. E. J. Lovel, *His Very Self and Voice*, New York, 1954, pp. 327, 451.
5. Leigh Hunt, *Lord Byron and some of his Contemporaries*, London, 1828, p. 63.
6. 10.18.
7. 17.398.
8. 17.1116.
9. 9.9.
10. Both Stanley Jones and, following him, Duncan Wu point out that the *Literary Register* virtually pirates the whole text of the *Liber Amoris* in this way; see Wu (ed.), *The Selected Writings of William Hazlitt*, 7:xv.
11. The text of this letter first appeared in full in *John Bull*, 22 June 1823, and

ironically is our source for the letter. Jones reprinted it in *Review of English Studies*, n.s. 17 (1966).

12. Robinson, 1:296.
13. De Quincey, *Collected Writings*, 3:79.
14. Mary Russell Mitford, *Letters*, Second Series, ed. H. Chorley (London, 1872), 1:126.
15. 9.188, 207.
16. *The Hazlitts*, pp. 473–4.
17. I imagine that discussions with Sarah Stoddart in Winterslow, and with old Mrs Hazlitt and Peggy in Devon, had brought this solution to the fore. All three women would have strongly recommended this recourse, and he would have seen the sense of it.
18. *Letters of Mary Shelley*, 1:255–7.
19. Stoddard, p. 213. Jones suggests that this lady was Isabella Bridgwater, shortly to figure largely in Hazlitt's life.
20. Patmore, 3:65–6.
21. 20:133–4.
22. Everything now known about Isabella Shaw Bridgwater is the result of Stanley Jones's brilliant detective work; see Jones, pp. 351 et seq.
23. Ibid., p. 361.
24. Landseer, 1:159.
25. Ibid., 1:166–7.
26. Ibid., 1:197.
27. W. C. Hazlitt, *Memoirs*, 2:107.
28. 10.91.
29. 10.97.
30. 10.106–7.
31. 10.108.
32. 10.122–4; Hazlitt represents the interchange in dialogue form, between an Englishman and a Frenchman meeting at the gallery and discussing the paintings informally.
33. 10.173.
34. 10.118–19.
35. Jones, p. 368.
36. W. C. Hazlitt, *Lamb and Hazlitt*, pp. 55–6.
37. 12.310–11.
38. Quoted in Wu (ed.), *Selected Writings of William Hazlitt*, 7:xxviii.
39. 20.393. I have altered the twelfth line to make it scan, substituting 'all' for 'the livelong' – a liberty taken with this harmless piece of doggerel in the interests of flow, which I'm sure Hazlitt would not mind.
40. Wu, 7:xxx.
41. 10.190–91.
42. 10.186–7.
43. 10.220–22.
44. 10.226.

45. 10.268.
46. 10.267.
47. 10.287.
48. 17.161–2.
49. Thomas Medwin, 'Hazlitt in Switzerland: A Conversation', *Fraser's Magazine* 19 (1839), p. 278, quoted in Wardle, p. 418.
50. 10.302.
51. 10.302.
52. Haydon, 3:70.

CHAPTER FOURTEEN Napoleon and Twilight

1. Duncan Wu follows W. C. Hazlitt's suggestion that — — is William Godwin. This is completely unlikely, given the long family friendship, Hazlitt's many obligations to Godwin for help early in his career, and his repeated published respect for Godwin's work, as witness especially the tone and content of his 'Spirit of the Age' on Godwin. Howe is surely closer to the mark in identifying the culprit as the Royal Academician George Dawe, who climbed to the peak of his profession on no talent. Just possibly it is Thomas De Quincey, for whom Hazlitt's respect was not great.
2. Hazlitt is here remembering a line in the manuscript version of Coleridge's 'Ancient Mariner' which does not appear in the published version, and which Hazlitt saw in 1798, twenty-eight years before. The line reads 'Her flesh makes the still air cold.'
3. Howe, p. 350.
4. 20.151.
5. Jones, p. 373.
6. 17.219.
7. 17.219–20.
8. Leigh Hunt, *Correspondence*, 1:251–2.
9. Wardle, p. 437.
10. See above.
11. 17.236.
12. 17.242.
13. 13.ix–x.
14. Robert E. Robinson in *William Hazlitt's 'Life of Napoleon Buonaparte'*, Paris, 1959, shows that about a third of the book is taken from printed sources, and a quarter consists of his own commentary, opinions, personality sketches and analysis.
15. 17.307–8.
16. 17.274.
17. 17.320.
18. There is some controversy over whether he did indeed go to Paris again at this time. The fact that he wrote of life in a cheap Parisian *pension*, which he had never before claimed to experience, suggests that he did.
19. Ibid., p. 466.

20. Ibid., p. 380.
21. 19.334 n.
22. 17.371.

CHAPTER FIFTEEN The Opinion of Death
1. Howe, p. 386.
2. 17.377–8.
3. 17.191.

APPENDIX ONE
1. This account of the Hazlitts in America is based on Margaret Hazlitt's *Journal*, edited by Ernest J. Moyne.
2. MH *Journal*, p. 118.
3. MH *Journal*, p. 56.
4. See William senior's essay 'An account of the State of Rational Religion in America', reprinted as an appendix to MH's *Journal*.
5. Charlestown, South Carolina, is now known as Charleston.
6. MH *Journal*, p. 65.
7. MH *Journal*, p. 148.
8. MH *Journal*, pp. 86–8.
9. MH *Journal*, p. 98.

APPENDIX THREE
1. The edition of the *Essay* used here is the first volume of P. P. Howe's 21-volume *Complete Works of William Hazlitt*, London, 1930–34, called the Centenary Edition because it began to appear on the centenary of Hazlitt's death. References are to volume and page in the standard way.
2. See for example J. L. Mackie, *Inventing Right and Wrong*, London, 1977, passim, for a statement and defence of the doctrine of enlightened self-interest.
3. 1.49.
4. 1.1–49 passim, esp. 1–2, 48–9.
5. See Butler, *The Sermons in the Rolls Chapel*, passim; Butler was an influence on Hazlitt in this respect.
6. See P. F. Strawson, *Individuals*, ch. 3 passim, and A. C. Grayling, *The Refutation of Scepticism*, London, 1985, p. 96.

# BIBLIOGRAPHY

WORKS OF HAZLITT

*Complete Works of William Hazlitt*, ed. P. P. Howe, 21 vols. (London: J. M. Dent and Sons 1928–32).

*The Selected Writings of William Hazlitt*, ed. Duncan Wu, 9 vols. (London: Pickering and Chatto 1998).


SELECTED SECONDARY REFERENCES

Albrecht, W. P., *Hazlitt and the Creative Imagination* (Lawrence, Kansas: University of Kansas Press 1965).

Baker, Herschel, *William Hazlitt* (Cambridge, Mass.: Harvard University Press 1962).

Barrell, John, *The Political Theory of Painting from Reynolds to Hazlitt* (New Haven: Yale University Press 1986).

Birrell, A., *William Hazlitt* (London: Macmillan Press 1902).

Bloom, Harold (ed.), *Modern Critical Views: William Hazlitt* (New York: Chelsea House Publishers 1986).

Bromwich, David, *Hazlitt: The Mind of a Critic* (Oxford: Oxford University Press 1983).

Butler, Marilyn, 'Satire and the Images of the Self in the Romantic Period: The Long Tradition of Hazlitt's *Liber Amoris*, in Rawson (ed.), *English Satire*, pp. 209–225.

Byatt, A. S., *Wordsworth and Coleridge in their Time* (London 1970).

Cameron, K. N. (ed.), *Shelley and his Circle*, 6 vols. (Cambridge, Mass.: Harvard University Press 1961–70).

Coleridge, S. T. *The Literary Remains*, ed. H. N. Coleridge (London: William Pickering 1836–9).

   *Collected Letters*, ed. E. L. Griggs, 4 vols. (Oxford: Oxford University Press 1956–9).

Cowden, Clarke C. and M., *Recollections of Writers* (London 1878).

De Quincey, Thomas, *Recollections of the Lake Poets (1834–40)*, ed. D. Wright (Harmondsworth: Penguin Books 1970).

Eagleton, Terry, 'William Hazlitt: An Empiricist Radical', *New Blackfriars*, March 1973, pp. 108–17.

Foot, Michael, *Debts of Honour* (London: Davis Poynter, 1980).

Gill, S., *Wordsworth and the Victorians* (Oxford: Oxford University Press 1998).

Hayden, J. O., *The Romantic Reviewers 1802–1824* (London: Routledge and Kegan Paul 1969).

Haydon, Benjamin Robert, *Autobiography and Journals*, ed. M. Elwin (London: Macdonald 1950).

Haydon, Benjamin Robert, *Diary of Benjamin Robert Haydon*, ed. W. B. Pope (Cambridge, Mass.: Harvard University Press 1960–63).

Hazlitt, Margaret, *Journal*, ed. E. J. Moyne (Lawrence, Kansas: University of Kansas Press 1967).

Hazlitt, William senior, *Sermons for the Use of Families*, 2 vols. (London: J. Johnson 1808).

Hazlitt, W. C., *Memoirs of William Hazlitt*, 2 vols. (London: Richard Bentley 1867).
  *Four Generations of a Literary Family*, 2 vols. (London: George Redway 1897).
  *Lamb and Hazlitt* (London: Elkin Matthews 1900).
  *The Hazlitts: An Account of their Origin and Descent* (Edinburgh: Ballantyne, Hanson and Co. 1911).
  *The Letters of William Hazlitt*, eds H. M. Sikes, W. H. Bairne, G. Lahey (London 1979).

Hazlitt William and Sarah (Stoddart), *The Journals of Sarah and William Hazlitt*, ed. W. H. J. Bonner (Buffalo: Buffalo University Press 1959).

Holcroft, Thomas, 'Hazlitt's Death-Bed', *Monthly Magazine and British Register*, March 1833, pp. 257–8.

Holmes, R., *Coleridge: Early Visions* (Harmondsworth: Penguin Press 1989).

Houck, J. A., *William Hazlitt: A Reference Guide* (Boston, Mass.: G. K. Hall and Co. 1977).

Howe, P. P., *The Life of William Hazlitt* (Harmondsworth: Penguin Books 1949).

Hunt, Leigh, *Autobiography*, ed. J. E. Morpurgo (London: Cresset Press 1949).

Johns, J., *The Season of Autumn, As Connected with Human Feelings and Changes, A Sermon Occasioned by the Death of William Hazlitt* (London: Exeter 1830).

Johnson, K. R., *The Hidden Wordsworth* (New York: W. W. Norton and Co. 1998).

Jones, Stanley, *William Hazlitt: A Life – From Winterslow to Frith Street* (Oxford: Oxford University Press 1989).

Keats, John, *Letters of John Keats*, ed. H. E. Rollins, 2 vols. (Cambridge, Mass.: Harvard University Press 1958).

Keynes, G., *Bibliography of William Hazlitt* (London: Nonesuch Press 1931).

Kinnaird, J., *William Hazlitt, Critic of Power* (New York: Columbia University Press 1978).

Knowles, R. S., *The Life of James Sheridan Knowles* (London 1872).

Landseer, Thomas, *Life and Letters of William Bewick*, 2 vols. (London 1871).

L'Estrange, A. G., *Life of Mary Russell Mitford*, 3 vols. (London 1870).

Lindop, G., *The Opium-Eater: A Life of Thomas De Quincey* (London: Weidenfeld and Nicolson 1993).

Marshall, W. H., *Byron, Shelley, Hunt and the Liberal* (Philadelphia: University of Pennsylvania Press 1960).

McLachlan, H. *The Unitarian Movement in the Religious Life of England* (London: Allen and Unwin 1934).

Maclean, Catherine MacDonald, *Born Under Saturn: A Biography of William Hazlitt* (London: Collins 1943).

Motion, Andrew, *Keats* (London: Faber and Faber 1997).

Park, Roy, *Hazlitt and the Spirit of the Age* (Oxford: Oxford University Press 1971).

Patmore, P. G., *My Friends and Acquaintances*, 3 vols. (London: Saunders and Otley 1854).

Paulin, Tom, *The Day-Star of Liberty: Hazlitt's Radical Style* (London: Faber and Faber 1998).

Pearson, H., *The Fool of Love* (London: Hamish Hamilton 1934).

Prance, C., *Companion to Charles Lamb: A Guide to People and Places 1760–1847* (London: Mansell Publishing 1983).

Procter, B. W. (Barry Cornwall), *An Autobiographical Fragment* (London 1877).

Robinson, Henry Crabb, *Diary, Reminiscences and Correspondence of Henry Crabb Robinson*, ed. Thomas Sadler, 3 vols. (Boston 1898).

   *Henry Crabb Robinson on Books and their Writers*, ed. E. J. Morley, 3 vols. (London: J. M. Dent and Sons 1938).

Roe, Nicholas, *Wordsworth and Coleridge: The Radical Years* (Oxford: Oxford University Press 1988).

St. Clair, W., *The Godwins and the Shelleys* (London: Faber and Faber 1989).

Saintsbury, George, *A Short History of English Literature* (London: Macmillan and Co. 1912).

Schneider, Elisabeth, *The Aesthetics of William Hazlitt* (Philadelphia: University of Pennsylvania Press 1952).

Southey, Charles, *Life and Correspondence of Robert Southey*, 6 vols. (London: Longman Brown 1849–50).

Stephenson, H. W., *William Hazlitt and Hackney College* (London: Lindsey Press 1930).

Stevenson, Robert Louis, *Letters*, ed. B. B. Booth and E. Mehew (New Haven: Yale University Press).

Stoddard, R. H., *Life, Letters and Table Talk of Benjamin Robert Haydon* (New York 1876).

Talfourd, T. N., *Final Memorials of Charles Lamb* (London 1848).

Thompson, E. P., *The Making of the English Working Class* (London: Victor Gollancz 1963).

Wardle, R. M., *Hazlitt* (Lincoln, Nebraska: University of Nebraska Press 1971).

Watson, J. S., *The Reign of George the Third* (Oxford: Oxford University Press 1960).

# INDEX

Adams, Daniel, 37
Addison, Joseph, 27, 212, 213, 359–60
Alexander I, Tsar, 186–7, 252
Alps, 316
Alsager, Thomas, 224
America, 24; Hazlitt family emigrates to, 8, 9–10, 350–8
American War of Independence, 7–8, 35
Amyot, Thomas, 135
Anne, Queen of England, 10
*The Anti-Jacobin Review and Magazine*, 93, 135, 248
Aquinas, Thomas, 106
Arnold, Matthew, 360
*Atlas*, 337, 338
Austen, Jane, 4, 11, 167, 231–2
Ayrton, William, 102, 103–4, 105, 106

Baldwin, Robert, 266
Bandon, 8
Barbauld, Mrs, 26, 179
Barnes, Thomas, 177, 181, 218
Barry, James, 199
Bastille, fall of (1789), 15–17, 30
Baugh, Sally, 136
Beaumont, Sir George, 82, 83–4, 139, 157
Beckford, William, 78
*The Beggar's Opera*, 166, 174, 180
Belloc, Hilaire, 361
Belsham, Dr, 33, 41
Bentham, Jeremy, 157, 158, 187, 225, 252, 267, 304
Berkeley, George, 44, 55–6, 93, 106, 148
Bessborough, Lady, 253
Bewick, William, 158–9, 196, 197–8, 219, 225, 226–7, 242, 306–7
Birrell, Augustine, 361
Black, John, 156
Blackwood, William, 230, 238, 240, 297
*Blackwood's Magazine*, 135, 225, 230–1, 238–42, 258, 265–6, 285, 294, 297,

299–300, 302–3, 313, 322, 335–6, 342
Blücher, Marshal, 169, 193
Blunden, Edmund, 178, 191
Boccaccio, 105, 121
Booth, Mr, 19
Boston, 10, 13, 354, 355–6
Boswell, James, 104, 106, 119
'Boswell Redivivus', 329, 330–2
Bourbon dynasty, 4, 169–72, 201, 340, 345–6
Bourgoing, Baron de, 126
Bradley, A. C., 220, 250
Bridgwater, Isabella (WH's second wife): marries WH, 305–6; financial security, 305, 327; Continental tour, 307, 308, 316–22; Down Street home, 307, 327, 328; leaves WH, 332–3
*British Critic*, 93, 110, 135, 213, 233
British Institution, 206–7
Bromwich, David, 250
Browne, Sir Thomas, 104
Bunyan, John, 106
Buonaparte, Lucien, 77, 79, 189
Burdett, Sir Francis, 153, 191
Burke, Edmund, 109, 110, 155; *Reflections on the French Revolution*, 17, 34, 46, 47; WH's opinion of, 17–18, 111, 212–13, 326; on New College, Hackney, 41; influence on WH, 45–6; Coleridge on, 52–3, 56, 61; influence on Mackintosh, 68
Burney, Fanny, 58, 102, 188, 229
Burney, Captain James, 102, 105, 145
Burney, Martin, 102, 129, 132, 229, 339
Burns, Robert, 280
Burrell, 147
Bury St Edmunds, 67–8
Butler, Bishop, 55, 106, 148, 149
Byron, Lord, 133, 177, 205–6, 231, 232, 242, 256, 275, 295, 296, 297, 318, 321, 322, 330–1

Cadell, Thomas, 297
Calvinism, 9, 18
Campbell, Thomas, 331, 332
Cardus, Neville, 361
Carlisle, Sir Anthony, 219
Caroline of Brunswick, Princess, 253–5, 268
Carracci, Annibale, 63
Carracci, Lodovico, 63
Castlereagh, Lord, 153, 154, 170, 175, 246, 256–7, 325
Cato Street Conspiracy (1820), 256–7
Cavanagh, John, 243
Cervantes, Miguel de, 28, 48, 236
*Champion*, 169, 171, 176, 177–8, 189–90, 191, 202, 222, 248–9
'Character of Cobbett', 112
*Characteristics: In the Manner of Rochefoucauld's Maxims*, 300–1, 303
*Characters of Shakespeare's Plays*, 217–18, 219–22, 233, 234
Chateaubriand, René de, 135, 194
Chatham, William Pitt, 1st Earl of, 47–8, 109, 110–11
Chaucer, Geoffrey, 45, 55, 105, 155, 213, 226
Chester, John, 60, 62
*Christian Monitor*, 160
Chubb, Thomas, 26
Church of England, 5, 6, 21, 23, 125, 248
Clairmont, Claire, 133
Clarke, Charles Cowden, 326, 334, 337
Clarkson, Thomas, 68, 140, 143
Claude Lorrain, 64, 127, 128, 132, 141, 309
Cobbett, William, 112, 138, 139, 172, 254
Cockburn, Lord, 188
Colbourn, 270, 276, 277, 278, 326
Coleridge, Hartley, 82, 90
Coleridge, Samuel Taylor, 1, 38, 67, 80; on WH, 2–3, 44, 85–6; *Lyrical Ballads*, 4, 49, 58–9, 61; and the French Revolution, 16; Schiller's influence, 40; friendship and influence on WH, 48, 50–62, 84, 89–90, 102; friendship with Wordsworth, 49; as Unitarian preacher, 49–51, 55; WH's

friendship cools, 55, 139–40; friendship with Lamb, 81; attempts to help WH, 82, 83–4, 85–6; WH's portrait of, 82–3; and WH's Keswick incident, 89–90, 219; lectures, 143, 144, 227–8; quarrels with Wordsworth, 151–2; *Remorse*, 160–1; WH attacks, 201–2, 204–5, 207–9, 210, 215–16, 222; WH's disappointment with, 346
Collier, John Dyer, 152
Collier, John Payne, 144, 151
Collins, William, 45, 46
Combe, George, 276–7
Combination Acts (1799–1800), 38
Condorcet, Marquis de, 45
Constable, Archibald, 195, 199, 209, 211, 219, 238, 240, 327–8
Constable, David, 336
'The Conversation of Authors', 215
*Conversations of James Northcote RA*, 65, 324–6, 329, 339, 340
Cooke, John, 27
Cornwall, Barry *see* Procter, Bryan
Corrie, John, 32–3
Cosway, Richard, 79
Cottle, Joseph, 58
*The Courier*, 140, 161–2
Covent Garden Theatre, London, 108, 164, 165, 192, 258–9, 273
Cowper, William, 61
*Critical Review*, 93, 110, 131, 211
Croker, John Wilson, 326, 327
Cromwell, Oliver, 106
Cruikshank, George, 11, 244
Cumberland, Richard, 134, 135

De Quincey, Thomas, 1–2, 88, 161, 300, 303, 360
Descartes, René, 106
Desmoulins, Camille, 15
Dickin, George, 17
Dissenters: William Hazlitt senior and, 5–6, 225, 352; and the French Revolution, 17, 36; New College, Hackney, 31–2; marriage laws, 125; Rev. Johns' sermon on WH's death, 347–8
Donne, John, 105
*Dramatic Literature in the Age of Elizabeth*, 44

Drury Lane Theatre, London, 108–9, 160, 164, 165, 167, 168, 205, 268
Dryden, John, 45, 84, 106
Duns Scotus, 106
Duppa, Richard, 79, 83, 90

Eclectic Review, 94, 213
Edinburgh, 275, 276, 277–80, 285
Edinburgh Magazine, 222, 233, 240–1, 242, 259
Edinburgh Review, 131, 133, 137 0, 152, 173, 181, 187–9, 191, 195, 199, 200, 202, 208, 209, 218, 220, 222, 225, 232, 237, 259, 262, 275, 302–3, 305, 313–14, 338–9, 341
Edwards, Jonathan, 106
Edwards, Dr William, 312
Ellenborough, Lord, 154, 161, 244–5
The Eloquence of the British Senate, 27, 102, 109, 110–12, 152, 153
Emmet, Catherine, 206
Encyclopaedia Britannica, 195, 199, 215, 217
Enfield, 26
Enghien, Duc d', 194, 195
Enlightenment, 5, 6, 23, 35, 349
Erskine, Thomas, 187
Essay on the Principles of Human Action, 45, 92–4, 173, 273, 362–5
European Magazine, 313
Examiner, 149–50, 176, 178–9, 181, 184, 189, 190, 191, 192, 200–3, 208, 209, 210, 212, 215, 216, 218, 222, 237, 247, 297–8, 313, 333, 337
Eyre, Lord Chief Justice, 37

'A Farewell to Essay-Writing', 336
Fawcett, Rev. Joseph, 47–8, 96, 100
Fawkes, Guy, 107, 269, 270
Fielding, Henry, 28, 61, 88, 106
'The Fight', 270–2, 273
Finnerty, Peter, 153–4
Flaxman, John, 175, 178–9
Florence, 317–19
Fonblanque, Albany, 297–8, 313
Fox, Charles James, 77–8, 101, 102, 109, 110–11, 205
France: WH visits, 73–80, 308–12, 337; Napoleonic wars, 95, 101, 102, 186–

7, 191, 193–4, 200–1, 245; Bourbon restoration, 169–72; Revolution of the Three Days, 340
Franklin, Benjamin, 7, 351
Free Thoughts on Public Affairs, 101–2
Freebairn, Robert, 73
French Revolution, 35, 170, 213; importance to WH, 4, 17–18, 38, 39, 167, 185–6, 216–17, 345–6; effects in England, 6, 36–40; fall of the Bastille, 13 18, 30, Dr Priestley's house burnt down, 23, 24–6, 31; Reign of Terror, 36, 69; English opinions of, 68–9; Wordsworth and, 182, 185–6
Fuseli, Henry, 65, 134

Garrick, David, 40, 106
Gentleman's Magazine, 209, 313
George III, King of England, 252, 253, 256
George IV, King of England (Prince Regent), 149, 154, 169, 171, 187, 191, 201, 205, 253–5, 268–9
Germany, 62
Gifford, William, 212, 235, 243–4, 248, 305
Godwin, Mary Jane, 133
Godwin, William, 47–8, 53, 82, 328; friendship with Hazlitt family, 6–7; Enquiry Concerning Political Justice, 34–5, 36; Caleb Williams, 61; WH's opinion of, 35; Treason Trials, 37, 38; friendship with WH, 68; and publication of WH's work, 92, 95–6; Political Justice, 114; commissions WH to write 'Grammar', 126, 129, 130–1; and the Life of Holcroft, 134, 151; campaign for Bourbon restoration, 169
Goethe, Johann Wolfgang von, 48, 298
Goldsmith, Oliver, 45, 106
Gray, Thomas, 61
Greenwich Hospital, 11
Grenville, Lord, 101
Greville, Fulke, 104, 105
'gusto', 21, 178, 198

Hackney see New College, Hackney

Halevy, Eli, 36

Hardy, Thomas, 36, 37, 39

Hartley, David, 24, 33, 43, 44, 68, 92, 106, 148

Haydon, Benjamin Robert, 177, 183, 189–90, 206; on WH's *Old Woman*, 66–7, 157; friendship with WH, 157, 158, 196, 210–11, 322–3; *Christ's Entry into Jerusalem*, 157, 217, 257; at William the younger's christening, 159–60; *Judgment of Solomon*, 187; breakfast for Wordsworth, 192–3; introduces WH to Keats, 209–10; WH's influence, 214; and WH's rift with Wordsworth, 217; buys WH's Louvre copies, 248; and WH's obsession with Sarah Walker, 289, 293–4, 301; and WH's second marriage, 307, 328

Hazlitt, Grace (WH's mother), 301; marriage, 6–7; in America, 9, 350–1, 353, 354, 358; returns to England, 10, 358; and WH's childhood, 19; friendship with Sarah Stoddart, 125; and WH's second wife, 307; and WH's death, 342

Hazlitt, John (WH's brother): in America, 9, 350–1, 353; WH visits in London, 11, 33; artistic ability, 12, 19, 67, 68; WH's letters to, 14–15; teaches WH to paint, 64; alcoholism, 301

Hazlitt, John (WH's son), 195–6, 203, 209, 236

Hazlitt, Margaret (Peggy, WH's sister), 125, 301; in America, 9, 10, 350–8; in Wem, 12–13; on WH, 14, 29, 127; and the French Revolution, 17; WH teaches French to, 18; and the death of WH's son, 129; inheritance from Catherine Emmet, 206; WH gives money to, 243; and her father's death, 259–60; and WH's death, 342

Hazlitt, Mary (WH's sister-in-law), 33

Hazlitt, William senior (WH's father): Unitarianism, 5–6, 7; marriage, 6–7; and the American War of Independence, 7–8; in America, 8, 350–8; in Ireland, 8; moves to Wem, 12–14; income, 12, 187; ambitions for WH, 19, 20, 41–2; sermons, 22; library at Wem, 26; and New College, Hackney, 31, 34; meets Coleridge, 52–3; WH paints portrait of, 70–1, 95; publishes sermons, 116; in old age, 225, 243, 255; death, 259–60

Hazlitt, William: character, 1–4, 85–6; autobiographical writings, 3–4, 272–3; birth, 4; in America, 9–10, 350–8; boyhood in Wem, 12–15, 18, 26–30; early education, 12, 14–15; influence of French Revolution, 4, 17–18, 38, 39, 167, 185–6, 216–17, 345–6; in Liverpool, 18, 20–2, 28; on slavery, 20; at New College, Hackney, 22–3, 31–4, 41, 42–3; first published letter, 23, 24–6; early reading, 26–8; teenage crisis, 28–30, 34; sexuality, 29–30, 86–8; lack of faith, 40–1; love of the theatre, 40; 'metaphysical discovery', 43–4, 56, 88, 89, 91–2; literary knowledge, 45–7, 48; Coleridge's friendship and influence, 48, 50–62, 84, 89–90, 102; discovers art, 62, 63–8; appearance, 67, 76, 196–7, 277, 290, 291, 306, 318, 321, 322; shyness, 67, 86; financial problems, 69–70, 71–2, 120, 139, 150–1, 152, 232, 243, 247–8, 252, 296; career as an artist, 70–1, 72–8, 90–1; visits France, 73–80; copies paintings in the Louvre, 75–8, 79–80, 329–30; self-portrait, 76; friendship with Charles Lamb, 80, 81–2, 303–4; portrait painting, 82–3, 95, 116; attitudes to women, 86–8, 97–8; Keswick incident, 89–90, 183, 193, 204–5, 207, 209, 219, 238; hostility to Wordsworth, 93, 124, 151; meets and courts Sarah Stoddart, 97, 98–9, 116–18; homes, 109, 118, 125, 126–7; marriage to Sarah, 118–25; venereal disease, 119–20; in Winterslow, 126–8, 132–3; landscape paintings, 127; births of children, 128, 143, 195–6; son dies, 129–30; infatuation with Sally Baugh, 136; philosophy lectures, 136, 143, 144, 145, 146–50, 199–200, 257; portraits of, 139, 140–3, 145, 150–1; friendship with Coleridge

Hazlitt, William—*cont'd*

cools, 139–40; friendship with Lamb, 144; house in Westminster, 157–60, 225; portraits of, 157, 217, 306–7; theatre criticism, 160–1, 163–9, 174, 179–80, 218, 222–3, 257, 337, 338; opposition to Bourbon restoration, 169–72; breach with Charles Lamb, 172; meets Leigh Hunt, 177; as an art critic, 178–9, 187, 189; failed infatuations, 180–1, rift with Wordsworth, 181–6, 192, 201–3, 208, 217; income, 187, 243; Scott attacks, 189–90; support for Napoleon, 189, 190–2, 193–5, 245; hears news from Waterloo, 193–4, 196; plays rackets, 197–8; attacks apostate poets, 201–5, 207–8, 210, 215–16, 217; death of his son John, 203, 209; breach with Crabb Robinson, 208, 209, 210; Tory press attacks, 212–14, 223, 230–1, 233, 234–5, 238–42, 243–4, 248; ill-health, 215, 327, 334, 339, 340–1; defends French Revolution, 216–17; lectures on the English poets, 223, 224–31, 232, 233, 235; lectures on English literature, 235–6; marital problems, 236–7; nostalgia, 236; lectures on 'English Comic Writers', 240, 242–3, 244; lectures on Elizabethan drama, 246–7, 249, 251; evicted from York Street, 252, 267; in love with Sarah Walker, 261–5, 269, 272–6, 280–94, 301; divorces Sarah Stoddart, 269, 273, 275, 276, 277–80, 284, 285–6, 287, 294, 319; attends boxing match, 270–2; lectures in Glasgow, 279–80; looks for a wife, 301–2, 305; poetry anthology, 302; breach with Southey, 304; second marriage, 305–7, 328; Continental tour, 307, 308–12, 316–22; Down Street home, 307, 327, 328; travel articles, 307, 308, 316; poetry, 314–15; moves to Paris, 329–30, 337; Isabella leaves, 332–3, 337–8, 340–1; arrested for debt, 339; in love again, 339; death, 4, 341, 347–8; funeral and tombstone, 342, 342–4, 344–5; *see also individual books, paintings and*

magazines

Hazlitt, William (WH's son, died in infancy), 128, 129–30

Hazlitt, William the younger (WH's son), 236, 247, 281; birth, 143; christening, 159–60; childhood, 196; WH gives money to, 243; education, 276, 301, 307; and his parents' divorce, 278–9; and WH's second wife, 307; difficult relations with WH, 332–3; marriage, 330, 341; wants to become a singer, 339; and WH's death, 340–1; publishes WH's lectures, 149

Hazlitt, William Carew (WH's grandson), 143, 344–5

Helvetius, 45, 92, 148

Henderson, Alexander, 239, 286

Hessey, James, 270, 341

Hobbes, Thomas, 44, 106, 145, 146, 148

Hogarth, William, 236

Holbach, Baron d', 43, 45

Holbein, Hans, 196

Holcroft, Thomas, 35, 38–9, 53–4, 73, 110, 130, 133, 134, 151, 209

Hone, William, 207, 244–5, 248

Hook, Theodore, 299

House of Commons *see* Parliament

Howe, P. P., 29

Howel, Mr, 140

Hume, David, 44, 55, 93, 106, 147, 152, 360, 364

Hume, Joseph, 110, 118, 120–1

Hunt, Henry Leigh, 326, 333, 337

Hunt, John: libel trial and imprisonment, 149, 154, 161; *Examiner*, 176, 249; *Yellow Dwarf*, 225; and WH's financial problems, 247; buys the *Old Woman*, 248; friendship with WH, 255–6; *The Liberal*, 295; publishes *Liber Amoris*, 297, 298; and WH's second wife, 307

Hunt, Leigh, 163, 181, 202, 239, 293, 327; libel trial and imprisonment, 149, 154, 161, 176–7; abilities, 149, 501 *Examiner*, 150, 176–7, 189; meets WH, 177; release from prison, 190; and WH's rift with Wordsworth, 192; friendship with WH, 196, 255–6, 328; *The Story of Rimini*, 200; WH attacks

Hunt, Leigh – *cont'd*
Gifford, 235, 243–4; hurt by comments in *Table Talk*, 266–7; and *The Liberal*, 295, 296; in Italy, 318; upset by 'Boswell Redivivus' article, 330–1; and WH's death, 342; essays, 360
Hunt and Clarke, 326, 333, 334, 339
Hunter, Rev. Joseph, 28–9, 86

Inchbald, Elizabeth, 35, 72, 232
Ireland, 8
Italy, 308, 316–20, 332

'Jacobin novelists', 35–6
*Jacob's Ladder*, 127, 136
Jeffrey, Francis, 199, 200, 215, 218, 238, 269, 275; engages WH to write for the *Edinburgh Review*, 173, 187–8; on Wordsworth, 181; reviews *Characters of Shakespeare's Plays*, 219, 222; *Blackwood's* criticizes, 231, 302–3; financial help to WH, 232, 247, 294, 341; WH's opinion of, 305; reviews *The Spirit of the Age*, 313–15, 322
*John Bull*, 298–9, 313
Johns, Rev. John, 347–8
Johnson, Joseph, 36, 92, 95–6, 100–1, 109, 116, 219
Johnson, Dr Samuel, 27, 46, 61, 104, 106, 214, 220, 227, 228, 293, 360
Jones, Stanley, 306
Jonson, Ben, 235–6, 247
Junius, 45, 46, 61, 83–4, 106

Kant, Immanuel, 148
Kean, Edmund, 165, 167–8, 176, 179, 252
Keats, John, 219, 226, 243, 308; WH's influence, 1, 4, 214–15; Haydon paints, 157, 257; friendship with WH, 209–10, 259; *Endymion*, 222, 231, 238–9; *Blackwood's* attacks, 238–9, 258; *Lamia*, 259; death, 265
Kemble, John, 165, 168–9
Kingston, Isaac, 20
Kippis, Rev. Dr Andrew, 7, 12, 22, 41–2
Knowles, Charlotte, 67
Knowles, James Sheridan, 67, 280, 306, 307; *Virginius*, 258–9

La Rochefoucauld, Duc de, 295, 300–1
Lake District, 82, 89–90, 182, 183
Lamb, Charles, 1, 66, 246–7; on WH, 3, 98; friendship with WH, 80, 81–2, 144, 303–4, 328; appearance, 81; essays, 81–2, 360; letters, 95, 96–7, 101, 108, 125, 134; plays, 100, 101, 108–9; *Tales from Shakespeare*, 100; literary salon, 102–8, 173, 196; and WH's marriage, 118–19, 120, 125; on the death of WH's son, 129; admires the *Grammar*, 131–2; visits WH in Winterslow, 132–3, 137; and WH's philosophy lectures, 147, 150; helps WH find work, 152–3; breach with WH, 172; and WH's rift with Wordsworth, 192; loyalty to WH, 210; reads WH's biography of Napoleon, 335; and William the younger, 339; and WH's death, 341, 342
Lamb, John, 196, 208
Lamb, Mary, 80; insanity, 81, 116, 129, 132, 137, 139; as matchmaker, 96, 97, 98–9, 100, 116–18; *Tales from Shakespeare*, 100; literary salon, 102, 105–6, 173, 196; and WH's marriage, 122–4, 128; visits WH in Winterslow, 132–3, 137; and WH's obsession with Sarah Walker, 290; friendship with WH, 328
Lana, 78
Landor, Walter Savage, 318–19
Launay, Marquis de, 16
Lavoisier, Antoine, 23
Lawrence, Sir Thomas, 162, 175
*Lectures on the English Poets*, 233–4, 243
'Legitimacy' campaign, 169–72, 177, 190, 195, 217, 218–19
Leibnitz, Gottfried Wilhelm, 106
Leigh, Augusta, 205–6
Leonardo da Vinci, 79, 107, 320
'The Letter-Bell', 345–6
*Letter to Samuel Whitbread*, 115
'Letter to William Gifford Esq.', 243–4
Lewis, 'Monk', 59, 231
Lewis family, 12
*Liber Amoris*, 30, 117, 274–5, 276, 288–9, 293–4, 297–300, 301, 302–3, 304, 305, 312–13, 326

*The Liberal*, 295, 296, 297, 302, 313, 318

*Life of Holcroft*, 133, 134, 151, 209

*Life of Napoleon Bonaparte*, 194, 329, 333, 334–6, 337

*Literary Examiner*, 303

*Literary Gazette*, 213, 298

*Literary Journal*, 233–4

*Literary Register*, 298

*Literary Remains of William Hazlitt*, 149

Liverpool, 14, 18, 20–2, 28, 70, 72–3, 80, 169

Liverpool, Lord, 170, 246, 256

Llangollen, Vale of, 57

Locke, John, 44, 103–4, 106, 147, 148

Lockhart, John Gibson, 230, 238, 240–1, 265–6, 297

Lofft, Capel, 68

Loftus, Tom, 109–10

London Corresponding Society, 36

*London Magazine*, 44, 149, 176, 249, 257, 259, 265–6, 268, 269–70, 276, 295, 301, 303, 304

*The London Review*, 134, 135

*The London Weekly Review*, 333, 335

Longman, 209

Longman, Hurst, Rees and Orme, 114

Lonsdale, Earl of, 237

Louis XVI, King of France, 15, 16, 34

Louis XVIII, King of France, 171, 194, 217

Louvre, Paris, 73, 75–8, 79–80, 187, 208, 248, 276, 309–11, 329

Lovelace, 74

MacCarthy, Desmond, 361

Mackintosh, Sir James, 34, 52–3, 68–9, 94, 96, 191, 312

Mackintosh, Lady, 173

Macready, William, 259

Maidstone, 7, 8

Malthus, Thomas, 35, 98, 112–16, 137–8, 200–1, 303, 322, 361

Manchester, 70, 71–2

Manning, Thomas, 97, 123, 131

Medwin, Thomas, 321–2

Mérimée, J. F. L., 73, 76

Methodism, 36

Michelangelo, 318

Milbanke, Annabella, 205–6

Mill, James, 158

Mill, John Stuart, 35, 158

Milton, John, 27, 46, 61, 104, 143, 144, 157–8, 185, 192, 196, 212, 214, 215, 226, 228, 252, 280

Mirabeau, Comte de, 30, 36

Mitford, Mary Russell, 174, 175, 183, 228–9, 233, 290, 293, 300, 302, 322–3, 339

Molière, 311

Montagu, Basil, 152, 197, 208, 219, 229, 339, 340

*Monthly Magazine*, 172, 211, 234, 248, 326–7, 335, 336

*Monthly Review*, 93, 111, 116, 222, 249, 326

Montpelier Cricket Club, 10–11

Moore, Thomas, 177, 202

*Morning Chronicle*, 37, 131, 152–6, 160–4, 167, 169, 173–6, 189, 191, 222, 242, 256–7, 307, 308, 315, 316

*Morning Post*, 49, 102

Motion, Andrew, 214, 238

Mudford, William, 161, 163–4

Mudge, Rev. Zachariah, 332, 340

Murray, John, 111, 202, 238, 240, 241

Murray, Lindley, 130–1

'My First Acquaintance with Poets', 296, 360

Napier, Macvey, 199, 200, 215, 338, 339

Napoleon I, Emperor, 4, 73, 208; rise to power, 69; Battle of Austerlitz, 71, 95, 101; and the Louvre, 73, 308, 309; WH's support for, 74, 77, 189–92, 245; Hundred Days, 107; invades Russia, 154, 317; WH owns statuette of, 159, 264, 281, 282, 283, 288; 'Legitimacy' campaign, 169, 171; Frankfurt Proposals, 170; abdication and exile, 171–2, 174; escape from Elba, 189, 190; English supporters, 190–1; defeat at Waterloo, 193–4, 196, 201; WH's biography of, 194, 321, 323, 329, 333, 334–6, 337; death, 167

Napoleonic wars, 95, 101, 102, 186–7, 191, 193–4, 200–1, 245
Necker, Jacques, 15
Nelson, Lord, 69, 95, 96
Nether Stowey, 54, 58–62
Netherlands, 322
*New and Improved Grammar of the English Tongue*, 24, 126, 127, 129, 130–2
New College, Hackney, 12, 22, 24, 29, 31–4, 41, 42–3
*New European Magazine*, 300
*New Monthly Magazine*, 211–12, 241, 270, 272, 295, 302, 304, 312, 328–33, 335, 337, 340
Newton, Sir Isaac, 103–4
Northcote, James, 65, 73, 157, 210, 241, 324–6, 328–9, 331–2, 337, 338, 340
*Notes of a journey through France and Italy*, 308–9, 326–7

*Old Woman*, 65–7, 74, 157, 159, 248
Ollier and Hunt, 219
'On Familiar Style', 215
'On Living To One's Self', 264
'On My First Acquaintance with Poets', 48
'On the Fear of Death', 260
'On the Spirit of Monarchy', 296
'On the Want of Money', 72, 122
*One Hundred Fables*, 338
Opie, John, 65, 73, 77, 134
Orleans Gallery, 63
Ostell, Thomas, 109, 110
Owen, Robert, 200
Oxford, 137

Paine, Thomas, 31, 34, 37, 47, 55, 112, 187
Paley, Dr, 56–7
Paris, 4, 15–16, 73, 74–80, 87, 187, 308, 309–12, 329–30, 337
Parliament, 102, 114–15, 152, 153–6, 245–6, 253–4
Parr, Dr Samuel, 191
Pater, Walter, 250
Patmore, Peter George, 258, 276, 302; on WH's attitude to women, 87, 136, 180, 261; on *Othello*, 179–80; on

WH's appearance, 224–5, 306; and WH's Surrey Institution lectures, 224–5, 226, 230, 238; Scott's duel with Lockhart, 265–6; at boxing match with WH, 270, 272; and WH's obsession with Sarah Walker, 272, 274, 275, 277, 284–5, 286–7; at Fonthill Abbey, 302; *Rejected Articles*, 328
Paulin, Tom, 26
Pellegrini, Domenico, 79
Peninsular War, 126, 139, 154
Perry, James, 37, 152–3, 156, 161, 162–3, 164, 173–6, 191
Peterloo massacre (1819), 38, 246, 256
Philadelphia, 351–2, 354
Phillips, Ned, 129, 132
Phillips, Sir Richard, 172
*Philomathic Journal*, 316
Philosophical Society, 143
Piombo, Sebastiano del, 63–4
Pitt, William the Younger, 36–7, 69, 101–2, 109, 325–6
*The Plain Speaker*, 258, 326–7, 345
*Political Essays*, 244, 245, 248–9, 255
*Political Register*, 138–9
Pope, Alexander, 45, 61, 84, 106, 214, 220, 228
Price, Dr Richard, 6, 7, 8, 12, 17, 30, 32, 148
Priestley, Joseph, 353, 355; and the French Revolution, 6, 17, 30; friendship with William Hazlitt senior, 7; house burnt down, 22, 23–6, 31; achievements, 23–4; funeral oration for Dr Price, 30; WH studies with, 33; WH lectures on, 148
*Principles of Human Action*, 68–9
Procter, Bryan (Barry Cornwall), 246–7, 258–9, 262–3, 266, 281, 289, 341
'A Project for a New Theory of Civil and Criminal Legislation', 26, 28

*The Quarterly Review*, 135, 212, 213–14, 215, 218, 222, 233, 234–5, 243–4, 248, 304
Quintilian, 33

Radcliffe, Mrs, 232
Railton, Joseph, 73, 78, 98
Ralph, Rev. John, 22–3

Raphael, 63, 76, 78, 79, 91, 136, 142, 151, 178, 199, 265, 306–7, 309, 318

Rees, Dr Abraham, 12, 33

Rembrandt Harmensz van Rijn, 64, 65–7, 70, 137, 157, 199, 309, 322

*A Reply to the Essay on Population*, 114–16, 137–8

Revolutionary Society, 17

Reynell, Catherine, 338, 341

Reynolds, John Hamilton, 1, 214

Reynolds, Sir Joshua, 12, 65, 71, 78, 141

Richardson, Samuel, 61, 74, 106

Rickman, John, 79, 102, 161

Ritchie, William, 276, 277, 278, 313

Robespierre, Maximilien Marie Isidore de, 36

Robinson, Anthony, 67–8

Robinson, Henry Crabb, 161; on WH at New College, Hackney, 40–1; friend-ship with WH, 67, 145; WH's Keswick incident, 89; meets Charles and Mary Lamb, 107–8; becomes lawyer, 133–4; and *The London Review*, 134; diaries, 134, 139, 140; attends WH's lectures, 144, 146–8, 149, 150, 226, 227–8, 242, 249; and Wordsworth's quarrel with Coleridge, 151–2; helps WH find work, 152; on WH's success, 156, 162; and WH's support for Napoleon, 172, 189, 190–1; and WH's resignation from the *Morning Chronicle*, 173–4; reads WH's work aloud, 178–9; and WH's rift with Wordsworth, 183–4, 185; on WH's appearance, 196–7; breach with WH, 208, 209, 210; *Quarterly Review* attacks WH, 213–14; *The Times* employs WH, 218; enjoys Jane Austen's novels, 231–2; on *Table Talk*, 264; friendship with WH restored, 265; and WH's obsession with Sarah Walker, 290; on *Liber Amoris*, 300; ignores WH, 304

Robinson, Thomas, 139, 142–3, 150–1

Rome, 319

Roscoe, William, 84, 191, 260

*The Round Table*, 209, 211–14, 257–8, 326

'Round Table' essays, 189, 195, 199, 200, 202, 204, 218

Rousseau, Jean Jacques, 45, 46–7, 48, 57, 180–1, 194, 202, 213, 236, 272, 276, 298, 308, 314, 320–1, 322

Rowlandson, Thomas, 11

Royal Academy, 70, 71, 157, 175, 219

Royal Academy School, 65

Rubens, Peter Paul, 64, 75, 76, 78, 79, 142, 309, 318

Russell, John, 212, 213, 222, 234–5

Russell Institution, 143, 146

Sade, Marquis de, 16

Saint-Pierre, Bernardin de, 57–8, 84–5

Saintsbury, George, 250, 361

Salisbury, 128, 130, 150

Scarlett, James, 94

Scheele, Carl Wilhelm, 23

Schiller, Johann Christoph Friedrich von, 40

Schlegel, August Wilhelm, 199, 200, 220

'The Scotch Character', 296, 297

*Scots Magazine*, 211

*Scotsman*, 276, 313

Scott, John, 191, 222; turns down WH's philosophical essays, 149; and the 'Legitimacy' campaign, 169, 171; employs WH on the *Champion*, 176, 177–8; hears of WH's Keswick inci-dent, 183, 184, 189–90, 193; attacks WH, 190; meets Wordsworth, 193; Wordsworth maligns WH, 202–3; and the *London Magazine*, 249, 257; duel with Lockhart, 265–6

Scott, Sir Walter, 79, 194, 231, 307, 322, 325, 327, 334

Ségur, Louis Phillippe, Comte de, 16

*Select British Poets*, 307–8

Shakespeare, William, 46, 78, 104, 165, 178, 185, 214; WH's love of, 27; Col-eridge on, 61, 143, 144, 161; *Hamlet*, 161, 221–2; *The Merchant of Venice*, 167; WH as drama critic, 167–8; Kemble and, 168–9; *Othello*, 179–80, 181; WH writes *Characters of Shake-speare's Plays*, 217–18, 219–22, 233, 234; *Romeo and Juliet*, 220–1, 273, 299, 320; WH lectures on, 226, 227, 228, 280, 348

Sharpe, Richard, 122

Shelburne, Earl of, 8, 23

Shelley, Mary, 133, 211, 231, 289–90, 291, 301–2, 305, 306, 328, 330–1

Shelley, Percy Bysshe, 133, 153, 211, 238–9, 258, 266–7, 294, 295, 318, 330–1

Shepherd, Rev. Samuel, 72, 73

Sheridan, Richard Brinsley, 165, 205

Shrewsbury, 50, 54–5

Shrewsbury *Chronicle*, 23, 24–6

Siddons, Mrs, 40, 47, 71, 165, 169, 257

Sidmouth, Lord, 246

Simpkin and Marshall, 300

Sismondi, Jean Charles de, 188–9, 262

Six Acts (1819), 38

*Sketches of the Principal Picture-Galleries of England*, 64, 295–6, 301, 302, 306

Smetham, James, 2

Smith, Adam, 6, 155

Smith, Sydney, 188

Smith, William, 218

Society of Friends of the Constitution, 36

Solanges, Comte de, 16

Sophocles, 33

Southey, Robert, 38, 90, 169; and the French Revolution, 17; on the New College, 41; friendship with WH, 68; on WH's portraits, 83; becomes Poet Laureate, 163, 203; breach with WH, 201–2, 203–4, 215–16, 304, 346; *Wat Tyler*, 215–16, 218, 245; WH lectures on, 229

'Speenhamland' system, 113, 114

Spenser, Edmund, 45, 105, 226, 250

Spinoza, Baruch, 106

*The Spirit of the Age*, 35, 244, 258, 270, 304–5, 312–15, 316, 322, 326, 341, 345, 349

Stafford, Marquis of, 64

Steele, Richard, 27, 212, 359–60

Stendhal, 4, 187, 262, 312

Stephen, Leslie, 360

Stephens, Miss (actress), 166–7, 174, 196

Stevenson, Robert Louis, 3, 360–1

Stodart, Richard, 233, 249

Stoddart, John, 139, 265; childhood, 97; at Mackintosh's lectures, 68, 96; as matchmaker, 100; relations with his sister, 117; and WH's marriage, 118, 121, 123, 125; rift with WH, 121–2; and WH's philosophy lectures, 143, 146; opposition to Napoleon, 169–71, 191; WH attacks, 207; sacked from *The Times*, 218

Stoddart, Sarah, visits the Lambs, 96; character, 97; search for a husband, 97, 98–9, 100; WH meets and courts, 97, 98–9, 116–18; financial position, 98, 117, 139, 150, 243; marriage to WH, 118–25; pregnancies and miscarriages, 120, 126, 136, 137, 139, 152, 195–6; children, 128, 143, 195–6; son dies, 129–30; moves to London, 150–1; William the younger's christening, 159–60; marital problems, 236; on Sarah Walker, 263; WH divorces, 269, 273, 275, 276, 277–80, 284, 285–6, 287, 294, 319; and WH's second wife, 307; European tour, 311–12; and WH's death, 342, 344

Strachey, Lytton, 361

Strawson, 363, 364

Stringer, Daniel, 72

Surrey Institution, 224–7, 235, 240, 242–3, 246–7, 249, 280, 344

Swift, Jonathan, 27, 88, 228, 359–60

Switzerland, 308, 320–2, 333

'Table Talk', 257–8, 260, 272–3, 275, 276, 302, 304

*Table Talk*, 264, 266–7, 270, 273, 276, 294, 312

Talfourd, Thomas Noon, 194, 196, 197, 242, 264, 296, 339

Taylor, Jeremy, 61

Taylor, John, 229–30, 233

Taylor and Hessey, 222, 229–30, 233, 234, 240, 242, 269–70, 295, 296, 300, 308

Test Acts, 19, 26

Thackeray, William Makepeace, 193

Thelwall, John, 36, 37, 39

Thistlewood, Arthur, 256

Thompson, E. P., 36, 114

Thomson, James, 61, 228, 280
*The Times*, 68, 133, 152, 156, 169, 170–1, 177, 191, 207–8, 210, 218, 219, 222–3, 240, 246, 254, 342, 344
Tipper, Mr, 135
Titian, 63, 64, 65, 73, 75, 76, 78, 79, 83, 91, 105, 137, 141, 151, 199, 309, 318, 320, 328–9
Tomkins, John, 269, 276, 285, 286, 288–9, 291, 292, 294, 344
Tomlinson, Mrs (housekeeper), 138, 160
Tooke, John Horne, 36, 37, 39, 148, 244
Tories, 163, 200, 201, 205; Tory press attacks WH, 212–14, 223, 230–1, 233, 234–5, 238–42, 243–4, 248
Tracey, Mrs, 14, 18, 20, 22
Treason Trials (1794), 36–9, 187
Trinitarianism, 55
Tucker, Abraham, *The Light of Nature*, 82, 91, 95–6, 101, 103, 109, 110

Unitarianism, 5–6, 7, 9, 24, 49–51, 55, 353–4, 364
Urceus, Anthony Codrus, 181

Van Dyke, Anthony, 64, 76, 78, 128, 196, 309
Van Goyen, Jan, 64
Vanbrugh, John, 63
Venice, 319–20
Veronese, Paolo, 78
'Vetus' (Edward Sterling), 170, 171, 176
Vevey, 320–1
*A View of the English Stage*, 233
Viny, Mr, 7
Virgil, 61
Voltaire, 182, 227, 228

Wainewright, Thomas, 266
Wakefield, Gilbert, 41
Walker, Micaiah, 260–1
Walker, Sarah, 261–5, 269, 271–7, 279, 280–94, 296, 298–9, 301, 308, 344–5
Walpole, Sir Robert, 27, 109
Walter, John II, 170, 218, 246
Walworth, 10–11

Waterloo, battle of (1815), 191, 193–4, 196
Wedgwood, Thomas, 85–6
Wedgwood family, 49–50, 54
*Weekly Political Register*, 112–13
Wellesley, Marquis, 154, 162
Wellington, Duke of, 154, 192, 193, 325
Wells, Charles, 343–4
Wem, 12–15, 18, 30, 44, 70, 90
West, Benjamin, 63, 170
Westmoreland by-election (1818), 237
Whigs, 101, 205
Whitbread, Samuel, 114
Whitman, Captain Abiah, 9
Wilkie, David, 187, 217
Wilson, John, 182, 183, 184–5, 238, 240–1
Windham, William, 135
Winterslow, 117, 122, 123, 126–8, 132–3, 137, 139, 150, 159, 235–6, 246–7, 258, 259, 264, 295, 335–6
Wisbech, 6
Wollstonecraft, Mary, 35, 52, 53, 65, 126, 134
Woolf, Virginia, 3
Wordsworth, Christopher, 93
Wordsworth, Dorothy, 58, 88, 139, 182
Wordsworth, William, 38, 47, 53, 67; *Lyrical Ballads*, 4, 49, 58–9, 61; and the French Revolution, 16, 182, 185–6; friendship with Coleridge, 49; meets WH, 59–60; in France, 74; WH's portrait of, 82–3; WH stays with, 85, 89–90; *Excursion*, 85, 179, 181–5; WH's Keswick incident, 89–90, 183, 193, 209; rift with WH, 93, 124, 151, 181–6, 192, 201–3, 208, 217, 346; *The White Doe of Rylestone*, 124, 192; quarrels with Coleridge, 151–2; government sinecure, 163; *Poems*, 192; Westmoreland by-election, 237; *Blackwood's* attacks, 238, 240; WH's description of, 319

*Yellow Dwarf*, 225, 232
York, Duke of, 252–3